T0327676

Corporate and Project
Finance Modeling

Corporate and Project Finance Modeling

Theory and Practice

EDWARD BODMER

WILEY

Published by John Wiley & Sons, Inc., Hoboken, New Jersey.

Published simultaneously in Canada.

Library of Congress Cataloging-in-Publication Data:

Bodmer, E. (Edward)
   Corporate and project finance modeling/Edward Bodmer.
     pages cm
    ISBN 978-1-118-85436-5 (cloth); ISBN 978-1-118-85446-4 (ePDF);
ISBN 978-1-118-85445-7 (ePub); ISBN 978-1-118-95739-4 (oBook)
  1. Valuation—Mathematical models. 2. Finance—Mathematical models. 3. Financial risk—Mathematical models. I. Title.
  HG4028.V3B52 2014
  658.1501'1–dc23

                                             2014016731

Printed in the United States of America

10 9 8 7 6 5 4 3 2 1

Contents

Preface

Corporate and Project Finance Modeling: Theory and Practice is intended to be a comprehensive guidebook for anyone who is interested in creating and/or interpreting and/or understanding financial models. Through compiling many years of experience in creating, reviewing, and teaching corporate finance, project finance, acquisition, and real estate modeling, I describe in this book how you can master many difficult modeling problems and how you can build highly structured models from the ground up. Flexible, efficient, and stable model structures are explained along with describing unique solutions that address complex issues. In explaining model design as well as detailed programming techniques, *Corporate and Project Finance Modeling* can help you to become a much better modeler, whether you are just beginning or are very experienced and want to take your skills to a really high level. By covering how to build, analyze, and present results from a variety of alternative financial models, the book will provide an understanding of why particular modeling features are generally included in one kind of model but not in others. It is hoped that you will be able to find creative ways to borrow subtle concepts from issues addressed in different modeling applications and apply them to your own models.

Corporate and Project Finance Modeling explains how you can build flexible, transparent, and accurate financial analyses, but it does not simply document techniques that are commonly applied in modern models, which have become ever more elaborate and artistic over the past few years. Instead, the book also introduces unique modeling techniques that address many complex issues that are not typically used by even the most experienced modelers. For example, you can learn how to build user-defined functions to solve circular logic and avoid cumbersome copy and paste macros or how to write a function that derives the ratio of enterprise value to earnings before interest, taxes, depreciation, and amortization (EV/EBITDA) that accounts for asset life, historical growth, taxes, return on investment, and cost of capital. Distinctive modeling techniques introduced in *Corporate and Project Finance Modeling* include accounting for retirements when computing depreciation, automating models to incorporate additional periods of historical data, combining and presenting scenario and sensitivity analysis in a flexible manner, accurately computing net operating loss carryforwards and deferred taxes, adding time series equations and Monte Carlo simulations into financial models without any Microsoft Excel add-ins, normalizing terminal period capital expenditures and deferred taxes, sculpting debt repayments to after-tax cash flow, computing debt service and maintenance reserve accounts, modeling portfolios of assets with different starting and ending periods, and establishing long-term models to prove the treatment of items in the bridge between equity value and enterprise value. Some of the topics address things that you may not even have realized are issues, such as automatically computing the stable level of capital expenditures to depreciation as a function of historical and prospective growth when normalizing cash flow in a corporate model. Many of the unique ways to address risk analysis, circular logic, normalized cash flow, depreciation expense, and modeling multiple assets with different start and end dates are solved by programming user-defined Visual Basic for Applications (VBA) functions.

The goal of *Corporate and Project Finance Modeling* is not only to show you how to solve a modeling problem but also to explain the finance theory underlying why you should construct your models in a particular way. To address modeling issues ranging from the fundamental structure of different types of financial models to the creation of user-defined VBA functions that resolve circular references, each topic is introduced with theoretical discussion clarifying why the issue is relevant from a financial perspective. Theoretical topics that precede explanation of step-by-step modeling mechanics cover different corporate structures; valuation in the context of project finance, corporate finance, and acquisition finance; risk allocation resulting from cash flow waterfalls; credit analysis in corporate and project finance; debt structuring in the context of risk analysis; determination of items that should be in the bridge between enterprise value and equity value; and many other subjects. The modeling subjects are also described in the context of patterns of valuation mistakes and whether a particular aspect of constructing model assumptions could have avoided some of the common and recurring financial blunders. After the theoretical discussion of each modeling concept, modeling problems are explained on a step-by-step basis with many diagrams and screen shots from actual models.

The website, www.wiley.com/go/internationalvaluation, accompanies *Corporate and Project Finance Modeling* and includes exercises, model examples, video explanations, and case studies and is integral to the book. This website contains hundreds of customized exercises; many template project finance, corporate finance, and acquisition models; and a number of featured completed models of business enterprises in a wide variety of different industries. In addition, you can download special utilities to read PDF files into Excel, to make automated waterfall charts, to automatically color cells linked to different sheets, to create a table of contents with hyperlinks, and many other things.

Through using information on the website, there are various ways you can read the book and work with the exercises, models, and videos on the website. One way is to read *Corporate and Project Finance Modeling* from cover to cover without touching an Excel workbook. This would be like reading a cookbook without ever trying out the recipes. Alternatively, if you are relatively new to modeling and you want to become a top-notch modeler, you could work through accompanying models on the website as you read each chapter. A third way to use the book if you already have a lot of experience in modeling is to treat it as a reference manual where you can selectively look up new ways to tackle difficult modeling issues.

In working through the theory and practice of financial modeling, the book is divided into four parts. Part I explains the structure of alternative types of financial models and how to build a financial model from A to Z. Part II describes how to add risk analysis to your financial model. Part III addresses complex issues in corporate models related to computing normalized cash flow, deriving implicit valuation multiples, and evaluating the bridge between enterprise value and equity value. Part IV introduces unique approaches to solving complex problems in project finance and corporate models arising from circular logic related to cash flow sweeps, project funding prior to operation, debt sculpting, and reserve accounts.

The first part of the book describes how to build different types of financial models that can ultimately be effective in performing risk analysis, structuring transactions, and assessing value from a debt and equity perspective. Philosophical differences between a project finance investment with definite begin and end dates relative to a corporation with an indefinite life are discussed from the perspective of designing the architecture of a financial model. These model structures are then used to guide an explanation of how an efficient model should be put together, beginning with a discussion of programming practices that should be avoided. Explanations of how to construct audit checks that quickly identify errors in a model are introduced before working through the logical flow of a model. In describing the modeling process on a step-by-step basis, the manner in which assumptions should be laid out in a model, along with the economic theory underlying the construction of different assumptions is explained first. Next, techniques to creatively build time lines that solve the pesky problems of adding new historical periods in corporate models, evaluating construction delays in project finance models, and simulating alternative transaction dates in acquisition models are described. Once time lines are established, the central structuring idea of beginning with pretax cash flow, moving to after-tax cash flow, and then incorporating financing is covered. In computing taxes and depreciation, techniques that create user-defined functions that dynamically solve for historical growth rates and asset retirements are explained. Adding debt financing to alternative types of models is discussed in the context of simulating cash flow distributions to alternative investors and efficiently modeling cash flow waterfalls.

The second part of *Corporate and Project Finance Modeling* explains how you can use the financial models you build to analyze risks of the investment. The theory of risk analysis is introduced by discussing different possible ways to evaluate risk ranging from a qualitative risk matrix to stochastic time series equations. Next, a host of risk analysis techniques that can be used in different financial models, including sensitivity analysis, break-even analysis, scenario analysis, and Monte Carlo simulation are addressed. Each technique is explained on a step-by-step basis that includes how to make effective presentations using dynamic graphs, drop-down boxes, data tables, and selected macros. A form of scenario analysis that sets up a cockpit master scenario page to drive the model and at the same time allows management to play around with a model using sensitivity tools is described in detail. After discussing scenario analysis, techniques are presented to quickly build tornado diagrams and spider graphs into the financial models. Next, Monte Carlo simulation is explained. Using a bit of VBA programming, you will see how sophisticated Monte Carlo simulation can easily be added to just about any financial model without any add-in programs. In describing how to incorporate stochastic approaches to modeling, *Corporate and Project Finance Modeling* explains how you can use various tools to realistically measure risk rather than just presenting elegant distribution charts. In building simulation models, you will understand the importance of estimating mean reversion, correlation among variables, and boundary conditions for time series equations.

The third part of *Corporate and Project Finance Modeling* addresses challenging issues in corporate models associated with computing terminal value, normalizing cash flow, interpreting and deriving valuation multiples, and computing the bridge between enterprise value and equity value. This part of the book begins by discussing how you can often verify the reasonableness of your assumptions by making an effective presentation of the historical and prospective return on invested capital. Advanced corporate modeling issues are introduced by working through how to decipher which balance sheet items should be classified as financing related and which items should be classified as EBITDA related. To resolve thorny issues of how to treat alternative items in valuation analysis, the efficacy of building a theoretical model that simulates accounting and cash flow elements over a long-term period is demonstrated. The theoretical modeling approach is used to derive simple formulas for applying the half-year convention with varying costs of capital in discounted cash flow models and to explain how valuation errors occur from things like incorrectly assuming that accumulated deferred tax should be treated like debt. A central idea in this part of the book is showing you how to develop unique solutions to the challenging problem of computing normalized EBITDA, capital expenditures, and deferred taxes through writing user-defined VBA functions. After demonstrating how you can master calculation of normalized cash flow techniques, the value driver formula $(1 - g/\text{ROIC})/(\text{WACC} - g)$ is shown to be highly flawed for purposes of computing terminal value. As the value driver formula should not be used in valuations, *Corporate and Project Finance Modeling* shows you how to construct a more accurate user-defined function to compute the EV/EBITDA and price/earnings ratios automatically in the context of changing growth rates, costs of capital, returns, and other factors.

The final part of *Corporate and Project Finance Modeling* explains how to solve complex financial modeling issues using methods that are not traditionally applied in elaborate models built by experienced modelers. The user-defined functions that are developed to work out difficult financial modeling problems do not require you to have a lot of programming knowledge or to write lengthy VBA code. Much of the last part of the book deals with resolving circular logic that arises in corporate models, acquisition models, and especially in project finance models. A central theme of this part of the book is that all circularity references can be resolved without copy and paste macros that arguably ruin a model. After discussing the philosophy of circular reference logic, a simple problem that occurs in acquisition models for cash sweeps is used to introduce the issue. Five different techniques for addressing the circular reference problem, including the clumsy copy and paste macro approach, are discussed, and a method of isolating equations in a user-defined function is suggested as a much better solution. A user-defined function with isolated equations is used to resolve the famous circular problem of interest expense and interest income. Difficult modeling issues in project finance models are covered, including: (1) funding, capitalized interest, and fees; (2) debt repayments and sculpting with taxes; (3) debt service reserve accounts; (4) maintenance reserve accounts; (5) cash sweeps and dividend lockup covenants; (6) debt refinancing and valuation of projects in different stages; and (7) incorporating portfolios of assets in real estate models.

Acknowledgments

I owe a great debt to my many students, from Moscow to Munich, to Singapore, to Bangkok, to Lagos, to Copenhagen, to Lima, to Pretoria, to Paris, to Prague, to Zurich, and so many other cities, who have inspired me to write this book and given me so many ideas, suggestions, modeling techniques, and practical insight.

Financial Modeling Structure and Design

Structure and Mechanics of Developing Financial Models for Corporate Finance and Project Finance Analysis

CHAPTER 1

Financial Modeling and Valuation Nightmares

Problems That Financial Models Cannot Solve

An inevitable step in just about any financial analysis these days is making some kind of explicit or implicit projection of cash flow and/or earnings and/or financial ratios that measure profitability, credit quality, or other key performance indicators. Since valuation of debt or equity is all about making forecasts, you could go to a fortune-teller or read the astrology section of your newspaper to make a prediction about the future. These days, however, forecasts used in valuation are more often founded on fancy financial models built using elaborate spreadsheets. After the East Asian crisis of 1997, the bursting of the dot-com bubble in 2000, the global financial crisis of 2008, the European debt crisis in 2010, and innumerable other less famous valuation disasters or missed investment opportunities where debt and equity valuation failures had relied on sophisticated financial models, it could be argued that going to astrologers and fortune-tellers would have been a better strategy.

Notwithstanding serious questions about the general efficacy of making financial projections and the dangerous ways in which people make forecasts, the fact is that financial models are becoming more and more complex and they are also being used more than ever before in all types of investment analysis. Seemingly sophisticated financial models using elaborate programming functions can appear impressive and even artistic. But these beautiful models are also often almost impossible to use in assessing risk and value. Given the prominence of modeling in financial analysis, the first part of this book describes how to build flexible, accurate, structured, and transparent financial models that can be used to assess various different valuation problems.

When studying many valuation mistakes made in the past decades, it becomes clear very quickly that the most important pitfall in modeling is the development of economic assumptions for prices, volumes, capital expenditures, and operating expenses that are put into the models. The problems did not happen because of making a spreadsheet that did not follow some bureaucratic best practice defined by some IT staff. If you take a step back and think about all sorts of past financial failures ranging from the global financial crisis to bankruptcies of small business enterprises to industry-specific failures such as solar panel manufacturers, there are a few patterns of mistakes that are repeated and that seem obvious after the fact. Before delving into sophisticated mathematical equations, spreadsheet techniques, and model structure issues that deal with methods to resolve difficult project and corporate finance modeling challenges, you should think about why the outcomes of financial analysis using financial models sometimes fail so miserably. You can then leave these ideas somewhere in the back of your brain while you create the ornate models that follow all of the rules about flexibility, accuracy, structuring, and transparency.

Some recurring valuation mistakes related to financial modeling that continue to be made despite more and more sophistication in financial analysis include the following nine errors:

1. Making assumptions in financial models that business entities earning a rate of return substantially higher than their cost of capital and growing quickly can continue this financial performance for a long time even when they do not have some kind of sustained competitive advantage.

Earning a higher return than the cost of capital and growing quickly seems to put a company in the famous powerhouse square shown on management consultant PowerPoint slides, which is supposedly the best place to be for valuation. But when returns and growth are high, valuations are also high. More important, other companies from all over the world will attempt to enter the industry no matter how unique managers of the company claim to be. New capital expenditures from other companies entering the market then lead to industrywide overcapacity, followed by reduced prices and sudden dramatic declines in returns. If demand growth is slower than expected, which happens more often than not, the overcapacity and depressed prices can last for many years and the company suddenly finds itself in the worst box on those management consulting slides. Examples of high growth and returns leading to industry expansion followed by surplus capacity and price crashes include the famous telecom industry meltdown in the late 1990s, in which more than 50 percent of loans defaulted; the merchant electric power crash of 2000–2001 in the United Kingdom, where virtually every electricity plant without a fixed price contract defaulted on its debt; the real estate industry during many periods, most notably before the U.S. crash of 2008; very high returns earned by solar manufacturing companies, followed by massive new entry and dramatic price declines after Chinese manufacturers entered the industry; high returns earned by bulk cargo vessels before 2008, followed by overcapacity and depressed prices that have continued long after commodity prices and other industries recovered; and depressed occupancy rates and room rates for hotels in Iquitos, Peru, following a period of overbuilding that was initiated when the region received UNESCO heritage site status.

2. Entering projected prices in financial models that remain above the long-run cost of production even when capacity is increasing in an industry.

You can define a bubble as a situation in which prices are above long-run marginal cost and/or asset values are not consistent with levels that provide investors with a reasonable return on their investment. Assuming that prices can be sustained above marginal cost is an error that has happened before the U.S. real estate crash, when people believed they could profit by buying and selling (or flipping) a product. It occurred during the famous tulip bubble in Holland in the seventeenth century, and it may be happening in U.S. natural gas prices above the marginal cost of producing shale gas. The assumption that prices could remain above marginal cost was behind the valuation mistakes just discussed in comparing returns to the cost of capital, ranging from the telecom industry crash to overproduction of container ships.

3. Using information in financial models that relies on so-called independent experts, whether these people or institutions are credit rating agencies, large and reputable corporations, consulting companies that create very fancy models, experts speaking on CNBC or Bloomberg, famous finance professors, or former politicians.

Many valuation nightmares have demonstrated after the fact that it is more important to put your feet on the ground by visiting countries, meeting with real consumers, trying out products and services, and having a thorough independent understanding of the business idea than to trust on so-called experts when developing financial projections. Reliance on entities like rating agencies not only was a cause of the global financial crisis of 2008, but has also occurred with traffic studies made for project financings such as the Eurotunnel; toll roads and toll bridges all over the world; theme parks; and the Iridium disaster, in which Motorola promoted its satellite phones; and countless other cases. The famous Panama Canal catastrophe in which French investors lost so much money in the nineteenth century resulted from trusting the opinion of a famous engineer who had visited Panama only once. Relying on the reputations of companies that were thought to be the most innovative in their industry—such as Enron, WorldCom, and Lehman Brothers—without thinking through the fundamental competitive advantages and product quality has turned out to be very dangerous.

4. Trusting financial model results where increasing returns are projected by management, but not recognizing that the projected returns come about only because the company is taking on increased risks.

Companies with declining returns or lower margins than their peers often desperately try to increase or maintain equity returns. But these companies (or individuals) can generally meet their return objectives only by incurring increased risks and then trying to hide those risks using the latest business jargon and/or creative accounting. When taking on new ventures or deploying capital that involves taking greater risk, it is tempting for management to directly or indirectly cover up the risks through not fully disclosing things or worse, by using very sophisticated and confusing financial terms along with financial models that are impossible to understand. Examples of valuation errors caused by presenting confusing information include Constellation Energy in 2006–2008, Enron's impossible to understand financial statements, and innumerable financial institutions that made risky loans or engaged in risky trading behavior to boost their returns before the financial crisis of 2008.

5. Ignoring shifts in the cost structure and demand changes that can quickly render existing assets obsolete when developing risk analysis using financial models.

Sudden shifts in demand and/or price is a particular problem in modeling oligopolistic industries where seemingly stable returns and cash flows can suddenly change on the whim of competitor actions and/or changes in consumer taste and/or global events. Think about the sequence of Hewlett-Packard (HP), Nokia, Research in Motion (RIM, now BlackBerry), and Apple. A few years ago Nokia was all the rage with investors and the company was assumed to have unique products that would yield a sustainable competitive advantage and strong returns over an indefinite period. Then Nokia lost its luster and Research in Motion was the poster child for investors. A couple of years later RIM lost its popularity and Apple became the most valuable company in the world as it somehow made people even more addicted to their cell phones. In the case of automobile companies and airlines, sudden changes in industry demand could not be absorbed by companies with cost structures that contained high proportions of fixed cost from labor contracts, such as General Motors and United Airlines. Commodity industries may be very volatile and not offer extraordinary returns, but at least you can apply basic economic principles when thinking about prices, volumes, industry capacity, and market demand. Oligopolistic industries can be more challenging to evaluate in financial models because seemingly stable cash flows are subject to sudden changes that can occur that result in returns falling to levels below those of companies in competitive industries.

6. Putting faith in fancy, complicated, and innovative new financial paradigms when creating financial models.

At the turn of the twenty-first century the so-called new economy was supposed to replace traditional financial analysis that relied on cash flow and rate of return relative to cost of capital. New economy principles could explain why dot-com companies did not need cash flow or profit to generate value; real option models were used to justify new electricity peaking power plants that did not make economic sense using traditional discounted cash flow analysis; collateralized debt obligations supposedly could somehow reduce risk by putting together a bunch of shady loans that had been granted to people who could not repay them. When such new models cannot be explained in simple terms and when the seemingly sophisticated financial models cannot explain why one can somehow earn high returns without having a sustained competitive advantage, they almost always turn out to be rubbish. It is much better to study fixed and variable costs together when evaluating different possibilities of demand growth.

7. Having confidence in contracts that may be well drafted by sophisticated lawyers but that do not make economic sense, and incorporating those contracts into financial models.

Financial contracts that have turned out to be unsustainable included subprime loans issued before the financial crisis of 2008; electricity purchase contracts called power purchase agreements in Senegal, India, Indonesia, the United States, the Philippines, and many other places; construction contracts for large, complex projects such as the Eurotunnel and Euro Disney that chronically underestimated the actual cost; oil projects where ownership structures resulted in extreme economic profit for private investors; and financial subsidies from governments in Spain and the Czech Republic that led to very high returns for project developers. In each of these cases, financial projections made by analysts assumed contracts that would remain in place even though the contracts allocated risks in crazy ways and led to prices and returns that were far away from returns that could be realized on other projects with comparable risk. When contracts lead to returns that seem too good to be true, they probably are.

8. Inputting symmetrical upside case and downside assumptions into models when developing risk analysis without adequately considering differences in upward limits and downward exposures that create skewed returns.

Not properly accounting for deviations between upside and downside variation led to the California crisis in electricity prices in 2000–2001; it also leads to underestimating exposure to risk of nationalization when oil prices are low, and to retiring large plants when prices are low and have much more potential movement to the upside than to the downside.

9. Ignoring long-term trends in historic data and not understanding the value of long-term historic returns when evaluating financial projections.

In making financial forecasts you should carefully study the past and test your projections in light of any historic data that you can get your hands on. If results of your model do not make sense in the context of history, then something is probably wrong with the assumptions in your model. Similarly, investments for which you have good quality historic data are better than investments that rely on some kind of business plan or consulting study, all else being equal. Valuation mistakes that arise from not looking at history are illustrated by the stock price of General Electric in 2007–2009. In 2007 GE's stock price reached a high of $42 while in March 2009 the stock price fell to a level of $5. The valuation mistake in this case did not concern making a bad investment that went down, but rather failing to capitalize on an investment opportunity. To justify a stock price of $5 you would have had to make a series of pretty unrealistic assumptions about GE's rate of return in light of a long series of historic data. The return would have to reach levels far below those ever experienced in history and it would have to stay at those low levels for a very long time. With hindsight, it is clear that not accounting for historical data when investing in GE and realizing upside was a big mistake.

CHAPTER 2

Becoming a Black Belt Modeler

The four parts of this book explain how to: (1) build and interpret corporate finance, project finance, and acquisition financial models; (2) perform risk analysis using all different kinds of financial models; (3) analyze multiples, terminal values, the bridge between equity value and enterprise value, and normalized cash flow in deriving value from corporate models; and (4) use mathematical programming techniques to resolve circular logic problems related to financing, sculpting, and credit enhancements in corporate and project finance models. While the mechanical descriptions along with practical exercises of these subjects will make your life easier, explaining on a step-by-step basis how to construct the best financial models in the world has little direct effect on the recurring human mistakes discussed in Chapter 1. Because of the importance of recurring valuation mistakes that are a backdrop to the description of modeling techniques, introduction to various subjects in the four parts of the book will periodically return to these chronic errors.

In describing model structure, risk analysis, corporate valuation, and circular logic, this book discusses different model types, including corporate finance models, project finance models, and acquisition models. You may wonder whether the subject is too broad for a single book and if some of the intricate issues that arise in different modeling contexts can be adequately all addressed in one place. The philosophy of dealing with a variety of different types of model types and valuation analyses is that you can discover creative modeling techniques by contrasting different kinds of models. You can also understand why certain model structures are used in particular analyses and others are used in different models through contrasting the different genres of financial models. This will reinforce your ability to set up analyses that address financial structuring, credit analysis, valuation, and risk analysis in your models. Further, while one can make generalizations about the different modeling categories, many actual transactions and investment analyses have overlapping aspects of project finance, corporate finance, and acquisition finance. An investment may be initially structured using project finance concepts; it may then gain characteristics of a corporate finance analysis as it develops a history and expands into other activities. After the corporation has existed for a few years, it may consider acquiring new companies or be the target of an acquisition, requiring acquisition analysis.

As much of this book is designed to be a practical reference guide on how to structure and build models, there are a number of ways to read the book. One way is to read through different chapters without touching a spreadsheet. This may not be very exciting and would be something akin to reading a cookbook without trying out the recipes. A second way to read the book is to work through one of the many accompanying models while you tackle the various issues. More than 200 customized exercises with instructions along with project finance, corporate model, and acquisition model templates are included on the associated website, www.wiley.com/go/internationalvaluation. There are also many carefully designed featured example models that may be the most helpful tools for learning how to become a truly top-notch modeler. These exercises and template models, and the completed model examples on the website, are an integral part of this book. A third way to use this book if you already have experience in modeling is to treat it as a reference manual. You can selectively look up difficult modeling issues, such as constructing a debt service reserve account in a project finance model without any circularity, or writing a function to deal with retirements of assets and accelerated depreciation in a corporate model.

Probably the only real way to learn financial modeling is by working late at night under a tight deadline with the time pressure of a transaction. Actual financial modeling is not a linear process, but instead involves gathering potential information that may or may not be useful, focusing on data that is relevant, and coming up with ways to best represent the revenues and cash flow of a business given available information, which is sometimes very limited. The process of developing the top-line revenue from volume sold and capacity is, and certainly should generally be, the most important part of the model that requires a lot of time and creative thinking. Notwithstanding this nonlinearity of the real-world modeling process, outlining the structure of models and presenting real-world examples in this part of the book can provide a head start for those who have not built models and will eventually have to learn how to do so the hard way.

The principal objective of this first part of the book is to provide you with practical instructions on how to build a well-structured financial model that clearly delineates inputs, effectively presents key value drivers, uses separate modules to organize various components in a logical manner, accurately computes cash flow that is available to different debt and equity investors, and presents results of the analysis that effectively represents risks of the investment. A bit of theoretical discussion of how different types of models can be used to establish value and measure risk is offered for many of the modeling subjects, but the main objective is simply to provide details on how to build better models. In discussing the process for building an efficient financial model, the book covers the following subjects, which correspond to the general structure of a financial model:

- Model objectives and the general notion of keeping models simple
- Structure and layout of alternative types of models
- Avoiding bad spreadsheet programming practices without becoming too bureaucratic
- Sensibly thinking about model inputs and structuring the assumptions in an effective manner
- Organizing and programming time lines in different models
- Projecting revenues, expenses, and capital expenditures to establish pre-tax cash flow in a working analysis
- Developing after-tax free cash flow through computing depreciation expense and working capital
- Programming the debt schedule and modeling cash flow waterfalls that establish the priority of payments to different capital providers
- Creating the financial statements and projected tax payments that include expiring net operating losses
- Performing different types of risk analysis ranging from sensitivity graphs to Monte Carlo simulation
- Including stable ratios and implied multiples in corporate models to accurately measure terminal value, normalized cash flow, and implied valuation multiples
- Programming difficult project finance issues associated with sculpting, debt service reserve accounts, funding, and refinancing

Some of the subjects discussed in the first part of the book such as organizing time periods of the model, using techniques to verify the accuracy of mechanical calculations, and computing tax depreciation are not very glamorous compared to topics such as Monte Carlo simulation, normalized cash flow in terminal value calculations, and sizing debt in project finance. While these topics may not have dramatic effects on valuation, use of good modeling practice can improve the efficiency of the process and allow you to spend more time on the important issue of risk analysis and assumption development. There are many practitioners who have created models the wrong way for a long time who can attest that a few simple ideas regarding structuring and programming models can dramatically improve the operation of a model and ultimately improve valuation analysis.

CHAPTER 3

General Model Objectives of Structuring Transactions, Risk Analysis, and Valuation

Financial models have three general objectives that should be understood before you start writing any spreadsheet formulas or combing the Internet to support your assumptions. These are: (1) coming up with the expected value of an investment, (2) assessing the risk of the investment, and (3) developing the financial structure of a transaction given its risk. Effective assessment of risk is the centerpiece of valuation, and it is also the most fundamental reason any financial model is created. If you believe that all risks in an investment can somehow be avoided, meaning that you do not need a financial model, you will probably make bad decisions and engage in dangerous activities. Taking measured risk is a fundamental fact of life and an inherent part of just about any economic analysis. The most general objective of any financial model is that it can, one hopes, help with your judgment in accepting risk.

Given the importance of risk analysis in valuation, one of the central objectives in building a model of future cash flows is to assess risk in a transaction, whether the transaction is purchasing a stock, borrowing money, investing in an airport, acquiring a company, or signing a contract. Using a financial model to accept prudent risk can involve evaluating the reasonableness of a host of financial ratios ranging from price/earnings ratios when valuing a stock to the senior loan life coverage ratio in a project financing. Depending on the valuation approach, analysis using a financial model may address risk to equity holders, risk to senior debt providers, or risk to other parties such as contract counterparties. Another general objective of building a financial model corresponds to the inference of risk from debt capacity and structuring of transactions. Structuring a transaction using a financial model as a tool may mean sculpting debt repayments in a project financing transaction, sizing the senior debt in a leveraged buyout, or developing the share exchange ratios in a merger.

Once you have attempted to measure risk with your financial model you can then see what kinds of financing structure make sense for a particular transaction given these risks. Creating a transaction structure with different debt and equity characteristics that makes sense in light of your risk analysis introduces you to one of the most difficult balancing acts in finance. That is, to assess the rate of return you would like to earn in order to accept a certain level of risk. Construction of a well-structured financial model along with assessment of real-world prevailing transaction parameters like debt tenors and target returns can allow you to do things like derive the implied value or cost of capital without using the capital asset pricing model that has so many well-documented problems. Creating flexible financial models also lets you judge the value of different transactions through using a set of observed financial statistics such as enterprise value/earnings before interest, taxes, depreciation, and amortization valuation ratios.

After the financial crisis of 2008 that arose in large part from very poor risk analysis and financial modeling of subprime loans made to U.S. homeowners, some have suggested that risk analysis of complicated investments is simply too difficult and opaque for average investors to understand. When packaging subprime and other loans into the famous collateralized debt obligations (CDOs), investment bankers had supposedly created dangerous, overly complex products that could not be modeled or analyzed. To model risks of these structured investments that split up operating cash flows to different investors, financial models had to be created that would measure not only operating cash flow, but also who gets the cash flow in what order for alternative states of the world. Methods used to model the risks of these CDOs were famous for relying on complex statistics like coplets, which were all but impossible to interpret. The outputs of fancy statistical analysis were sold as really representing economic behavior, and sophisticated models that measured value at risk and the probability of default gave people a false sense of comfort that they could take risks that in hindsight turned out to be ridiculously underestimated.

By working through the financial modeling mechanics in this part of the book, you should see that valuation errors made because models or other analyses are incomprehensible is no excuse at all for poor risk assessment. Building a financial analysis where you can see which investor receives cash flow in what order and then performing risk analysis even for a toxic collateralized debt obligation is not difficult. Decision making can be improved if you are careful with the structure of the model, if you make the model flexible enough to handle alternative scenarios, if you make the model easy to understand, and if you make a series of tests to assure the model is accurate. A central idea of this first part of the book is that financial modeling is not very complex or mysterious even though financial modelers sometimes seem to be involved in a conspiracy that makes their analysis all but impossible to understand. It is hoped that the modeling discussion follows Warren Buffett's comment: "Business schools reward difficult, complex behavior more than simple behavior, but simple behavior is more effective."

In order to guide the discussion of different modeling issues associated with valuation, risk analysis, and debt structuring, financial models can be broadly categorized into three different types: deterministic models, stochastic models, and back-of-the-envelope models. Deterministic models are addressed in this first part of the book while the second part of the book moves to stochastic models. Back-of-the-envelope models that should be used to test the other models are too often overlooked when you get lost in a myriad of detailed assumptions and complex mathematical formulas. Back-of-the-envelope models are indirectly covered in the remainder of the book in the context of effectively displaying summary statistics.

1. **Deterministic models.** Deterministic models are the kind of model most of us are familiar with and involve detailed projections of revenues, cash flow, and profit from a series of economic and financial assumptions. Even with all of the methods presented in the following chapters to make the models transparent and logically structured, these deterministic models can become large and difficult to understand unless you spend a whole lot of time in front of your computer. Risk analysis in deterministic models is generally performed using judgmental assessments about how selected variables can change relative to base case assumptions.

2. **Stochastic models.** Stochastic models begin as deterministic models but are modified to include probability distributions around key variables. The probability distributions depend on seemingly sophisticated mathematical analysis of economic variables and their correlation with one another. After the stochastic equations are added to a financial model, you can compute probability distributions associated with key valuation measures such as rate of return or probability of default, which allow you to answer questions like what is the probability of receiving a return of below 3%. These models are essentially trying to transform a business into a mathematical equation with a probability distribution. Whether a business can really be represented by mathematical equations is one of the most controversial issues in finance.

3. **Back-of-the-envelope models.** Simple back-of-the-envelope models can be more important than the other two model types in assessing the value of an investment. These models or analyses may involve developing some kind of metric such as the rate of return on invested capital to check whether the complex model results are reasonable, or they may

involve simple benchmark checks of the valuation. Back-of-the-envelope checks in valuing a hotel could involve calculating the value per room and ensuring it is reasonable relative to the costs of other similar hotels. Alternatively, you may compute the pretax internal rate of return and compare it to the interest rate. If a big fancy deterministic or stochastic model comes up with a really high return derived from very detailed daily room rate, occupancy measures, and fixed and variable operations costs, then you probably need to step back and ask why other investors would not enter the market. Coming up with effective ways to step back and make a simple analysis that checks a model can require more creativity and be more difficult than the other deterministic and stochastic models. An important check is often to evaluate the prefinancing rate of return and question whether the model results in an outcome that is too good to be true.

Large deterministic and stochastic models generally receive the most attention when making valuations and people develop strong attachments to their fancy models. In the past decade simple back-of-the-envelope models seem to be less and less part of the process. Most of the writing in this part and the next part of the book explains many aspects of deterministic and stochastic models in a lot of detail. This does not in any way mean that back-of-the-envelope models should be considered less essential in the valuation process. In fact, developing simple models—and *simple* is in no way synonymous with *easy*—may at the end of the day be more important than any of the other analyses. Proving a valuation concept with a relatively simple analysis should take place at both the beginning and the end of the analysis.

CHAPTER 4

The Structure of Alternative Financial Models

In developing a deterministic financial model it is essential to think about the architecture of a spreadsheet before you begin to enter data, write any spreadsheet formulas, or make any valuations. This notion of coming up with the model structure applies to virtually any analysis in finance, economics, or, for that matter, science and engineering. It involves carefully organizing the model inputs, understanding mathematical calculations that derive key outputs, and effectively presenting outputs. The general design of a financial model involves deciding how to organize the inputs from various information sources in a structured manner, how to formulate the mechanical calculations in a transparent way that is easy to audit and understand, and finally how to present the outputs for purposes of risk assessment and valuation. Other than these basic elements of structuring the inputs, calculations, and outputs of a model, subjects that should be considered in laying out the architecture of a model include programming of time lines, considering methods for verifying model accuracy, and the setting up of alternative scenarios for risk analysis. Much of the process of developing an effective model is understanding the starting point of the model, putting things in a sensible order, and letting the model flow in a natural manner from the inputs to the outputs.

One of the most influential and lasting ideas in finance arose from the work of Franco Modigliani and Merton Miller in 1958, who suggested that the focus of valuation should be on aggregate free cash flow rather than the way the cash flow is split up between alternative investors. If you still believe in the theory developed by Modigliani and Miller that debt and other forms of financing do not make any difference in the way real-world investments are made, or that debt does not influence valuation, then you could end all of your financial models after computing earnings before interest, taxes, depreciation, and amortization (EBITDA), capital expenditures, working capital changes, and taxes on operating earnings. EBITDA, capital expenditures, and working capital changes are the components of the typical definition of free cash flow. There is no need to worry much about the financial structure of a model and create an income statement or compute earnings per share (EPS), equity cash flow, debt service coverage, or a balance sheet. The idea coming from Miller and Modigliani that is essential in any financial model is that you should begin with EBITDA and then evaluate what is needed to generate EBITDA before paying money to investors. Capital expenditures are necessary to generate EBITDA and working capital changes adjust the EBITDA to reflect essential cash flow. Taxes should also be paid before any money is paid to investors.

Although calculating prices, demand, operating cost structure, and the amount paid for new capital equipment to generate EBITDA—the drivers of unleveraged free cash flow—is surely the most important aspect of any model, almost all of the valuation techniques discussed later on in this book require analysis of financing items as well as free cash flow. When financing is explicitly considered, financial models may concentrate on earnings after interest and/or debt and equity cash flows and/or financial ratios such as debt/EBITDA that include balance sheet items. As valuation of debt and equity does depend on financing, much of the discussion of financial models in this chapter considers the financial structure of a company or project financed investment and the distribution of free cash flow to debt investors and equity investors. Notwithstanding the importance of debt analysis to many valuation problems, the structure of virtually any financial model should conform to the ideas of Merton Miller in that your thinking must begin with what the company really does and the free cash flow available to investors. The financing section of a model is then just about separating that cash flow into various different buckets.

The layout and ordering of financing calculations and inputs in a deterministic financial model depend to a large extent on the type of investment being assessed. Most financial models can be classified into six general categories—corporate models, project finance models, acquisition models, merger integration, and financial institution and real estate models. Because of different data sources and alternative valuation techniques, the layout is somewhat different for each of these model types. The valuation techniques, data sources, and outputs of the different model types can be summarized as follows:

- **Corporate model.** The distinguishing feature of this first and most common model type is that a corporation has a history and it is assumed to last indefinitely (although virtually all companies will end up either in bankruptcy or eventually be purchased). This means that valuation of a corporation can only be a snapshot in time that begins with some historical analysis and ends with some kind of terminal value assumption.

The terminal value calculation is necessary because it is not reasonable to make detailed forecasts of cash flow items for the indefinite life of the corporation, which would require forecasts for 30 to 500 years into the future. An important objective in corporate models is often the projection of earnings per share since this is the number that drives valuation by investment analysts. Return on investment and return on equity are also critical outputs of a model that measure the performance of the management of a corporation.

- **Project finance model.** The second type of model, for a project finance transaction, differs from a standard corporate model because the investment is characterized by alternative time phases that have different risks; by the fact that no history on cash flows exists for the investment (no matter how many times a similar new combined cycle plant is built, you don't know how it will work until you switch it on); by the defined lifetime of a project; and by the isolation and quantification of detailed and particular risks. Rather than spending time on studying history as in corporate finance, project finance analysis involves evaluating consulting studies and engineering reports such as traffic studies, price forecasts, and marketing analyses. The project finance models focus on cash flows accruing to equity holders and lenders rather than earnings or balance sheet items, and projections in a project finance model generally cover the entire defined lifetime of the project. Rather than evaluating return on investment, the key outputs of a project finance model are generally the internal rate of return (IRR) that accrues to equity holders or is computed on the basis of free cash flow (project IRR).

- **Acquisition model.** The third type of model, an acquisition or leveraged buyout (LBO) model, measures the returns earned by different types of investors in a transaction. This type of model is built from the amount of consideration paid for the equity of the acquired company, the holding period of the investment, and the assumed exit price, as well as the manner in which the acquisition is financed. To compute equity returns, acquisition models measure the way in which alternative financing sources are repaid, and ultimately compute the IRR earned by equity investors as in project finance models. The information base of evaluating an acquisition is the historical financial statements of a company as in corporate finance models along with management strategy after the transaction.

- **Merger model.** An integrated consolidation model computes earnings per share and credit quality measures both on a stand-alone basis and on a consolidated basis before and after two companies merge. This type of financial model considers the specific financing and accounting of the transaction as well as cost savings or synergies generated by the transaction. An application of such an integrated merger model is to evaluate how much can be paid for a company along with how the transaction will be financed so that earnings dilution will be avoided and bond ratings can be maintained.

- **Financial institution model.** The financial model of a bank, insurance company, or other financial institution cannot begin with pretax cash flow and EBITDA, as with all of the other models. Instead, the model begins with items like loan balances and deposit amounts. Each balance sheet account is used to compute profit loss items such as interest income, fees, or interest expense. Cash flow depends on the increase in loans and deposits where the remaining net cash flow after loan increases and provision of new deposits goes either to temporary securities or other liabilities. A financial institution model should include a target equity-to-asset ratio that is used to compute net new equity issues. When valuing the financial institution, equity cash flow is the basis of the analysis and terminal value is generally computed from a derived market-to-book ratio or a price/earnings (P/E) ratio.
- **Real estate model.** A real estate model is a cousin of project finance models but also has some elements similar to corporate finance analysis and poses some unique modeling challenges. Rather than concentrating on a single investment, a group of multiple investments in a portfolio are often combined together in real estate analysis. A mixed development model may include various alternative residential properties with different construction start and finish dates as well as alternative office, commercial, and shopping mall properties. Real estate models must be able to evaluate cash flows that are produced at different time periods without a clearly defined construction and operation period. Further, the models must be able to quantify the effects of different holding period strategies analogous to terminal valuation analysis in corporate models as well as alternative tax treatments.

The six different model types have many principles and programming techniques in common. They each should have structured time lines, need to be segregated into modules beginning with layout of operating and financing assumptions, require audit and verification procedures, have a starting point, must not contain bad programming practices, and should be structured so as to facilitate effective risk analysis. Except for the financial institution model, all of the financial models should begin by evaluating pretax cash flow from revenues, operating expenses, and capital expenditures and then work through free cash flow after depreciation tax shields and working capital investment. After free cash flow is derived, the financing for all of the model types is computed in a separate module and in any financial model, the balance sheets should compile closing balances from previously defined accounts in various sections of the model. However, each model structure contains unique complexities in terms of incorporating history, computing financing, and constructing valuation. Differences between the structures of alternative model types are discussed next.

Structure of a Corporate Model: Incorporating History and Deriving Forecasts from Historical Analysis

Among other things, forecasts derived from corporate models are used to compute free cash flow and earnings for making valuations and they are the basis for assessing the credit quality of a company in the context of providing loans. Valuation analysis may use discounted free cash flow, it may apply the earnings per share results to P/E ratios, or it could be derived from equity cash flow. Loans may be assessed by gauging the ability to repay debt service from cash flow or, more important, through evaluating the capability of the corporation to repay the loans by making new loans, given a set of credit quality indicators such as ratios of debt to equity and debt to cash flow and/or interest coverage.

The structure of a corporate model is directly tied to the idea that a company has a history and an indefinite future. This contrasts directly with a project finance investment that generally has no historical record and will end once the asset is no longer useful. Whereas a project finance analysis is analogous to a person's life or to a relationship—both of which have a definite beginning and end—a corporation is more analogous to a family, a country, or a city that may have seen better times in the past or may have bright future prospects. For example, Detroit may be having difficult times, but a city of this size and importance will probably not disappear from the map. A corporation—like a city, family, or country—may have ups and downs, but it does not have a certain end date.

The indefinite life of a corporation means that a financial model can only take a snapshot of the company that covers a portion of its history and also that the forecast must stop at some point—the terminal period—while the company is still generating earnings and cash flows. It is usually impracticable to include all periods of history in the corporate financial model, and it would be silly to try to make a forecast that extends infinitely. While incorporating all of the historical financial statements is not realistic most of the time, including enough history in a model so that you can make judgments about its exposures to economic downturns and potential volatility in its cash flow is an essential part of making a corporate model. When Winston Churchill said, "The farther backward you can look, the farther forward you can see," he surely was not talking about the architecture of a corporate financial model, but the quote is relevant to the design of a model. Perhaps the most prominent feature that differentiates corporate models from project finance models is incorporation of historical data, allowing analysis of all sorts of financial information with projected results alongside historical data.

Designing a corporate model should follow a logical and natural progression beginning with history, moving to assumptions, computing operating cash flows, and then adding debt financing to split up cash flow. When setting up a corporate model, the structure should allow users of the model to make judgments easily with respect to whether assumptions are reasonable in the context of historical performance. As part of this historical evaluation of assumptions, it is a good idea to present historical together with projected financial ratios such as return on invested capital, EBITDA margin, and credit ratios in order to tell a story about what has happened to the company in the past and what you expect to happen in the future. By presenting historical and projected financial ratios such as return on investment adjacent to the key assumptions, you and others can quickly see if you made some nonsensical assumptions and your model will be less of a mystery. In addition to recounting a tale about what happened in the past, financial statement analysis of history in a corporate model provides a basis for comparing projections with actual results that can be used as a simple check on the reasonableness of a forecast. If the return on investment has consistently hovered between 8 percent and 10 percent and your forecast produces a return of 20 percent, you had better have a very good and simple explanation about what kind of special thing the company is going to do to earn this higher return. Finally, the most important forecast period in a corporate model is the terminal period after which it is assumed the corporation will somehow reach a period of stability and tranquillity.

To illustrate how corporate finance analysis is centered on analysis of history and should include a narrative about the company, the excerpt shown in Figure 4.1 from the summary page of a corporate model shows how graphs of historical data are connected to assumptions and how the valuation is most effective when it is judged in light of historical and projected financial ratios. The first graph in Figure 4.1 allows you to look at a series of operating assumptions where the past data is shown alongside the projected amounts. The second graph in Figure 4.1 shows the history and forecast for one of the key financial ratios, in this case the return on invested capital. The drop-down boxes allow you to see a wide range of assumptions while the graph on the bottom of the page shows the historical and projected return on invested capital. In a corporate model these kinds of graphs can be shown together with some of the key operating assumptions and a summary of valuation and credit quality indicators.

In a corporate model two very simple ideas can dramatically improve the structure of the model. The first is understanding that the starting point for all

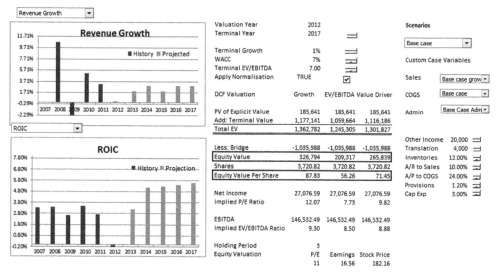

FIGURE 4.1 Illustration of Summary Analysis for a Corporate Model

of the fixed asset accounts, debt balances, working capital items, deferred tax accounts, accumulated depreciation balances, surplus cash accounts, and other items come straight from historical balance sheets. The second is setting up separate accounts for all of these items where historical closing balances come from the historical balance sheet and projected amounts are often directly or indirectly derived from capital expenditure, revenue, and expense forecasts. After painting a picture of the company with historical financial statement analysis, the structuring of forecasts in a corporate model involves defining how you can incorporate history as well as prospective industry structure and economic assumptions to assess the value of a business. The mechanical process uses historical balance sheet items and connects interest expense and interest income in the income statement to the balance sheet debt through evaluating the cash flow. The architecture of a corporate model is illustrated in Figure 4.2.

Figure 4.2 is intended to illustrate some of the important points in structuring a corporate model. You generally begin with an analysis of history and using the historical balance sheets to set up accounts. The working analysis that develops pretax cash flow, the fixed asset balance that derives depreciation expense and enables calculation of after-tax free cash flow, and the debt schedule are all essential intermediate steps that should be completed before even thinking about constructing any financial statements. Determining revenues, operating expenses, and capital expenditures is just about always the most important part of the analysis.

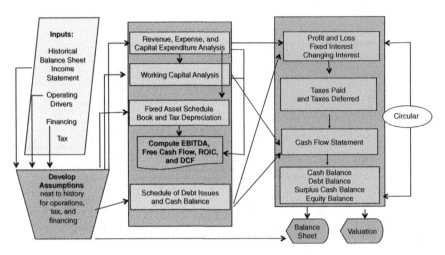

FIGURE 4.2 Structure of a Standard Corporate Model

When making forecasts of revenues, expenses, and capital expenditures, it is generally a good idea to graph history and projections of key variables that drive these three things, such as prices, market share, industry demand growth, capacity utilization, the structure of fixed and variable costs, and capital expenditures per unit.

Once the operating analysis, depreciation, and debt analysis are complete, financial statements can be constructed. Most of the components of financial statements, such as revenues, depreciation, and interest expenses, have already been recorded in separately structured sections. You still need to compute taxes and allocate the remaining cash flow to different financial securities. This last part of the analysis that puts together financial statements should be straightforward once you have a good model structure. In making the model, you should allow your users to input alternative terminal valuation periods as you do not really know when a company will reach the mythical stable equilibrium.

Two of the computational challenges in a corporate model are (1) to determine how surplus or deficit cash should be deployed, and (2) how to develop projections of depreciation and deferred taxes that account for the retirements of different asset classes. Figure 4.2 illustrates how the cash flow calculation can be made by connecting the profit and loss statement with the interest expense and interest income. As interest depends on cash flow and cash flow depends on interest, a famous circular logic problem arises. The arrow on the right-hand side of Figure 4.2 is meant to show that interest expense on new debt calculated from the model is not known until the debt balance is computed from the cash flow, and interest income is not known until the amount of surplus cash is derived. Unlike project finance models where any extra cash flow is distributed, in a corporate model dividends are typically determined from an algorithm such as a payout ratio and are not the end result of the cash flow process.

The final parts of Figure 4.2 show that in structuring a corporate model the balance sheet should be an output of the model rather than part of the mechanical calculations. To construct a projected balance sheet, the common equity balance should be calculated from historical balance sheet data along with projections of net income and dividends as with the other balance sheet accounts (a similar account can be computed for minority interest). With all of the accounts completed, including the equity balance, the balance sheet can then be tabulated by simply gathering together the closing balances of all of the accounts that have already been computed elsewhere in the model. Then you can experience the joy of having your balance sheet in balance for every single period of the model. Much of the remainder of this part of the text is structured to work through each part of the model shown in Figure 4.2. There are separate chapters devoted to discussing economic, financial, and modeling issues associated with the input section, the operating section that derives pretax cash flow, the debt schedule, the profit and loss statement, and the cash flow statement.

Some of the more difficult computational challenges in corporate models are:

- Development of effective assumptions that reflect prospective industry supply and demand (potential surplus capacity) and conversion of capacity, demand, and market share parameters into forecasts of revenues, expenses, and capital expenditures.
- Flexible incorporation of new historical financial data to accept updated financial statements when future financial data become available.
- Modeling projected depreciation expenses that accurately reflects asset retirements, deferred taxes, and net operating losses.
- Computing stable ratios of depreciation to net plant property and equipment (referred to as plant), capital expenditure to depreciation, deferred tax to capital expenditure, and enterprise value (EV) to EBITDA in computing terminal value.
- Including target capital structures in the models rather than simply assuming net cash flow builds up cash balances or accumulates debt.
- Dealing with unfunded pensions, derivative assets and liabilities, stock options, intangible assets, and other items that affect the difference between enterprise value and equity value.

Use of the INDEX Function in Corporate Models

In describing various modeling issues, conceptual issues associated with financial and economic modeling are introduced and then practical spreadsheet techniques that demonstrate how to implement the ideas are presented. To introduce analytical methods, the INDEX and the MATCH functions, which are central to many corporate finance modeling techniques, are introduced in this section. The names of spreadsheet functions are capitalized to clarify the data that you type directly into your model from theoretical equations. For a corporate model, one of the most useful spreadsheet functions is the INDEX function. Among other things, the INDEX function allows development of scenario analysis, can be used to create graphs of all of the assumptions with drop-down boxes, and permits you to make flexible valuation analysis with different valuation start dates and terminal dates.

The INDEX function does nothing other than find the value of a cell in a given area after defining a row, a column, or both a row and a column (it could be called the "find" function or the "search in area" function, but the FIND function is used in working with strings). One way to use the INDEX function is to select all of the cells in an entire sheet and then provide the row and column number to find a value in the sheet. Alternatively, select an entire column (or row) of data and provide the single row (or column) number to find a value. Other examples of using the INDEX function in a corporate model include:

Value = INDEX(Defined Area, Input Row of Area, Input Column of Area)
Value = INDEX(Entire Sheet, Input Row of Sheet, Input Column of Sheet)
Value = INDEX(Defined Column, Row of Column Area)
Value = INDEX(Entire Column, Row in Sheet)
Value = INDEX(Defined Row Area, Column of Row Area)
Value = INDEX(Entire Row of Sheet, Column in Sheet)

The way different ratios, assumptions, or historical items are selected in Figure 4.1 for making graphs of financial ratios and assumptions is to find the row or the column for the item using the MATCH function. This function is the brother of the INDEX function. Suppose the word "revenue" is in the fourth row of the sheet, as shown in the following example. The MATCH function can give you the number 4 if you enter this formula:

Row of Sheet = MATCH("Revenue", Entire Row of Titles, 0)

The MATCH function can also be used to give you the column number if you are looking across a row, and it is not necessary to use the MATCH function with an entire row or an entire column. The zero at the end of the preceding formula is used as an option that specifies that the exact value must be found (this is discussed in more detail later). Once the row is defined from the MATCH function, the INDEX function can use this number to find a value. This is done by copying the INDEX function and fixing the row number (using the F4 shortcut key to fix the row number in different columns). Examples of using the MATCH and INDEX together are:

Value = INDEX(Defined Area, MATCH(Value, Column), MATCH(Value, Row))

Value = INDEX(Entire Sheet, MATCH(Value, Row of Sheet), MATCH (Value, Column of Sheet))

Value = INDEX(Defined Column, MATCH(Value, Row of Sheet))

Value = INDEX(Entire Column, MATCH(Value, Entire Row in Sheet)

Value = INDEX(Defined Row Area, MATCH(Value, Column of Row Area))

Value = INDEX(Entire Row of Sheet, MATCH(Value, Entire Column in Sheet))

When explaining analysis techniques an excerpt from a spreadsheet is often presented to illustrate how the process works. Figure 4.3 includes part of a spreadsheet to show how the MATCH and INDEX functions can be used together. In Figure 4.3 the data validation feature in Microsoft Excel is used to pick alternative variables in a sheet. Once the data item is selected, the MATCH function is used to find the row number from entering the target item and looking in the entire column. After the INDEX function that chooses alternative value is defined, you can create a graph by shading the values computed from

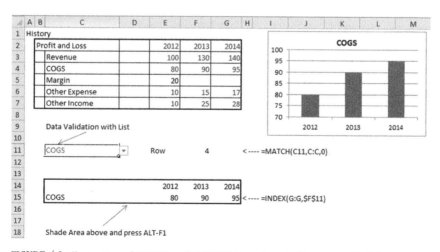

FIGURE 4.3 Illustration of INDEX and MATCH Functions in Corporate Models

the INDEX function and then pressing the ALT and F1 shortcut keys. As you become a spreadsheet wizard, you should show your prowess by stating in an arrogant manner how you use the MATCH and INDEX functions to differentiate you from unsophisticated users who use functions like VLOOKUP.

Easing the Pain of Acquiring PDF Data

In a corporate model, gathering historical data continues to be one of the biggest real world challenges even with all of the data you can get from the Internet. When making forecasts in the 1980s, you had to ring up the company on the phone and beg for somebody to send you an annual report. After that, you had to type in all of the data manually. Life is better now, but certainly not perfect. You can directly download data from free websites or you can pay a lot of money to a service for the data, but you still often need to use some data from the annual report of a company that is not in a nicely structured spreadsheet but instead is very often part of a PDF file. Copying data from a PDF file into Excel

	2012	2011	2010	2009	2008					
(in thousands except per share data)										
Statement of Operation: Data:										
Natural gas, NGLs and oil sales	$					1,351,694 $	1,173,266 $	823,290 $	751,749 $	994,769
Total revenues and other income		1,457,704	1,230,642	961,397	831,095	1,108,038				
Total costs and expenses	1,432,648	1,152,379	821,789	746,322	597,765					
Income from continuing operations	13,002	42,706	88,698	38,980	329,093					
Discontinu operations (net of tax)	-	15,320	-327,954	-92,850	21,947					
Net income (loss)	13,002	58,026	-239,256	-53,870	351,040					
Income from continuing operations per share:										
Basic $		0.08 $		0.26 $		0.56 $		0.25 $		2.18
Diluted	0.08	0.26	0.55	0.24	2.11					
Net income (loss)										
Basic	0.08	0.36	-1.53	-0.35	2.32					
Diluted	0.08	0.36	-1.52	-0.34	2.25					
Costs per mcfe: (a)										
Direct operating expense $			0.42 $		0.6 $		0.69 $		0.85 $	1.06
Production and ad valorem tax expense		0.24	0.15	0.19	0.22	0.46				
General and administra expense		0.63	0.8	1.01	1	0.87				
Interest expense	0.61	0.66	0.65	0.65	0.6					
Depletion, depreciati and amortizati expense		1.62	1.8	1.98	2.32	1.98				
$ 3.52 $			4.01 $		4.52 $		5.04 $		4.97	
Average Daily Production:										
Natural gas (mcf)		591,679	397,825	290,815	248,138	224,477				
NGLs (bbls)	19,036	14,664	9,864	4,343	2,820					
Oil (bbls)	7,790	5,369	5,300	6,912	8,322					
Total mcfe (b)	752,637	518,019	381,800	315,668	291,326					
Balance Sheets Data:										
Current assets (c) $			327,614 $		315,263 $		1,113,570 $		182,810 $	406,557
Current liabilities (d)		455,143	511,932	443,690	321,634	355,760				
Natural gas and oil properties net					6,096,184	5,157,566	4,084,013	3,551,635	3,466,028	
Total assets	6,728,735	5,845,470	5,511,714	5,403,415	5,554,125					
Bank debt	739,000	187,000	274,000	324,000	693,000					
Subordinat notes	2,139,185	1,787,967	1,686,536	1,383,833	1,097,562					
Stockholde equity (e)	2,357,392	2,392,420	2,223,761	2,378,589	2,451,342					
Weighted average diluted shares outstandin	160,307	159,441	158,428	158,778	155,943					
Cash dividends declared per common share	0.16	0.16	0.16	0.16	0.16					
Statement of Cash Flows Data:										
Net cash provided from operating activities $			647,099 $		631,637 $		513,322 $		591,675 $	824,767
Net cash used in investing activities	########	-547,981	-798,858	-473,807	########					
Net cash provided from (used in) financing activities	881,619	-86,412	287,617	-117,854	903,745					
Proved Reserves Data (f) (at end of period):										
Natural gas (Bcf)	4,793	4,010	3,567	2,615	2,214					
NGLs (Mmbbls)	240	142	123	52	24					
Oil (Mmbbls)	45	31	23	34	49					
Total proved reserves (Bcfe)	6,506	5,054	4,442	3,129	2,654					

FIGURE 4.4 Copied Data from PDF before Reformatting Data

or first copying the data into a Microsoft Word file and then into Excel generally results in a mess where words are in not in nicely structured columns and numbers are not in the column consistent with the time period (sometimes the items are not in different cells, which means you should use the text to columns feature in the data tab). After copying data and using the text to column feature, the data may look something like the format in Figure 4.4.

To format the data from the PDF file, you can create a macro to move numbers into a consistent column and then use a function to sum the text into a single cell. These functions are included in the file called PDF_to_Excel.xlsm at www.wiley.com/go/internationalvaluation. Once you run the macro, the format is cleaned up, as shown in Figure 4.5.

(in thousands, except per share data)	2012	2011	2010	2009	2008
Statements of Operations Data:					
Natural gas, NGLs and oil sales	1,351,694.00	1,173,266.00	823,290.00	751,749.00	994,769.00
Total revenues and other income	1,457,704.00	1,230,642.00	961,397.00	831,095.00	1,108,038.00
Total costs and expenses	1,432,648.00	1,152,379.00	821,789.00	746,322.00	597,765.00
Income from continuing operations	13,002.00	42,706.00	88,698.00	38,980.00	329,093.00
Discontinued operations (net of tax)		15,320.00	-327,954.00	-92,850.00	21,947.00
Net income (loss)	13,002.00	58,026.00	-239,256.00	-53,870.00	351,040.00
Income from continuing operations per share:					
Basic	0.08	0.26	0.56	0.25	2.18
Diluted	0.08	0.26	0.55	0.24	2.11
Net income (loss)					
Basic	0.08	0.36	-1.53	-0.35	2.32
Diluted	0.08	0.36	-1.52	-0.34	2.25
Costs per mcfe: (a)					
Direct operating expense	0.42	0.60	0.69	0.85	1.06
Production and ad valorem tax expense	0.24	0.15	0.19	0.22	0.46
General and administrative expense	0.63	0.80	1.01	1.00	0.87
Interest expense	0.61	0.66	0.65	0.65	0.60
Depletion, depreciation and amortization expense	1.62	1.80	1.98	2.32	1.98
	3.52	4.01	4.52	5.04	4.97
Average Daily Production:					
Natural gas (mcf)	591,679.00	397,825.00	290,815.00	248,138.00	224,477.00
NGLs (bbls)	19,036.00	14,664.00	9,864.00	4,343.00	2,820.00
Oil (bbls)	7,790.00	5,369.00	5,300.00	6,912.00	8,322.00
Total mcfe (b)	752,637.00	518,019.00	381,800.00	315,668.00	291,326.00
Balance Sheets Data:					
Current assets (c)	327,614.00	315,263.00	1,113,570.00	182,810.00	406,557.00
Current liabilities (d)	455,143.00	511,932.00	443,690.00	321,634.00	355,760.00
Natural gas and oil properties, net	6,096,184.00	5,157,566.00	4,084,013.00	3,551,635.00	3,466,028.00
Total assets	6,728,735.00	5,845,470.00	5,511,714.00	5,403,411.00	5,554,125.00
Bank debt	739,000.00	187,000.00	274,000.00	324,000.00	693,000.00
Subordinated notes	2,139,185.00	1,787,967.00	1,686,536.00	1,383,833.00	1,097,562.00
Stockholders' equity (e)	2,357,392.00	2,392,420.00	2,223,761.00	2,378,589.00	2,451,342.00
Weighted average diluted shares outstanding	160,307.00	159,441.00	158,428.00	158,778.00	155,943.00
Cash dividends declared per common share	0.16	0.16	0.16	0.16	0.16
Statements of Cash Flows Data:					
Net cash provided from operating activities	647,099.00	631,637.00	513,322.00	591,675.00	824,767.00
Net cash used in investing activities	-1,528,558.00	-547,981.00	-798,858.00	-473,807.00	-1,731,777.00
Net cash provided from (used in) financing activities	881,619.00	-86,412.00	287,617.00	-117,854.00	903,745.00
Proved Reserves Data (f) (at end of period):					
Natural gas (Bcf)	4,793.00	4,010.00	3,567.00	2,615.00	2,214.00
NGLs (Mmbbls)	240.00	142.00	123.00	52.00	24.00
Oil (Mmbbls)	45.00	31.00	23.00	34.00	49.00
Total proved reserves (Bcfe)	6,506.00	5,054.00	4,442.00	3,129.00	2,654.00

FIGURE 4.5 After Running Macro to Reformat Data

Writing the macro and the function to reformat PDF data requires a few lines of code in a macro along with two fundamental concepts. The first is a

FOR and NEXT loop, and the second is the CELLS command. In the next few chapters these concepts are described in detail.

Structure of a Project Finance Model That Accounts for Different Risks in Different Phases over the Life of a Project

Whereas you can think of corporate finance analysis and corporate models as being akin to computing the value of a family, a city, or a country, you can think of project finance models as representing the value of one person from the time that person is conceived until he or she dies. Unlike in corporate finance analysis, there is no history in project finance analysis because the model starts before the person (or project) is born. Instead, the project finance models evaluate risks and returns for different phases in the defined lifetime of a project. As with any investment, when the risk changes, the value also changes and a financial model must be able to represent these different risks. The source of information for project finance analysis is some kind of contract, consulting report, or engineering analysis made before the project is conceived rather than the historical financial statements. If you were evaluating the life of a person rather than the value of a family or a city, you may account for changing risks over the course of a life. The risks may be higher during the teenage years, and the value of remaining cash flows declines with age. Of course, this example is meant to be taken with a grain of salt and to highlight the issue of changing risk in different phases of a project's financial investment, which is much less of an issue in corporate finance. Not all teenagers have high-risk behavior and not all elderly people become worthless. Since there is no historical balance sheet for a project finance entity known as a special purpose vehicle (SPV), the launching point for a model is construction of a sources and uses of funds analysis during the construction phase of a project. Key financial outputs from a project finance model come directly from the cash flow statement rather than the profit and loss statement.

The single statistic that has the most importance for project owners is the equity internal rate of return (IRR) that measures the growth rate in cash flows after money has been paid to lenders (debt service). The equity IRR is often strongly influenced by the amount of debt financing, the method and timing of the debt repayment, and the tenor of the debt. The realized equity IRR also depends on whether and when the project is sold before it ends, as well as whether and when the debt is refinanced. As the financing structure has a large effect on the economics of projects, evaluating a project from the perspective of lenders is an essential part of the modeling process and structure. From the lender perspective, the buffer of cash flow relative to debt service (what percentage is the cash flow above the debt service) that is measured by the debt service coverage ratio (DSCR) is very often a key component of the model. The fact that IRR is a primary output of the model does not mean it is an ideal statistic for analysis of value. The IRR has a number of problems, including the following four: (1) it assumes reinvestment occurs at the same rate as the IRR itself. This can be inappropriate if the IRR is very high or very low; (2) the IRR does not account for the probability of realizing success in the development or exploration stage of the project; (3) the IRR does not value the true risk premium earned from cash flows that are realized in distant future years; and (4) if the IRR is compared to a cost of capital that includes a country risk premium, it will often undervalue the investment.

An example of outputs from a project finance model is shown in Figure 4.6, which includes a representation of the project during the construction phase (before the person is born) as shown by the sources and uses of funds analysis. After the commercial operation, the picture of the project can be summarized by the cash flow relative to the debt service that is shown on the graph that compares cash flow available to pay debt service with the level of debt service. The two pictures of the project demonstrate the fundamental separation between the preoperation phase and the postoperation phase.

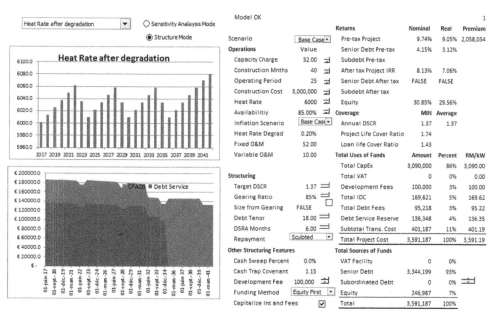

FIGURE 4.6 Illustration of Summary Analysis for a Project Finance Model

Project finance models typically have two distinct objectives. The first is to structure the debt and equity that will be issued in the transaction, including the size of the debt, the tenor of the debt, and the manner in which debt will be repaid. The second is to assess specific risks in different time periods of the project life after the defined financial structure is given. Project finance models should be also be able to assess the effects of different types of refinancing and compute the value of the project over time as the risks change (as the value of your life dramatically changes when you enter into different phases such as graduating from college or getting married).

The general structure of a project finance model is laid out on Figure 4.7. One of the essential elements of a project finance model is that different calculations are made for distinct phases of the project—the development phase, the construction phase, the operation phase, the debt repayment phase, and possibly a refinancing phase. The sources and uses of funds statement is computed during the development and the construction phase but not after the project begins operation. While the things that go into the sources and uses of funds are not complicated to think about—what one spends money on and how one raises the money—this statement provides a good summary picture of what the project is about. From a mechanical perspective, the sources and uses of funds statement replaces the balance sheet as the starting point for the model. This notion is illustrated in Figure 4.7, where arrows from the sources and uses of funds statement launch the fixed assets schedule and the debt schedule. The working module that computes revenues and expenses is similar to the corporate model, as is the fixed asset schedule and the debt schedule. A component of calculating the debt schedule is establishing the interest during construction that is capitalized to the cost of the plant.

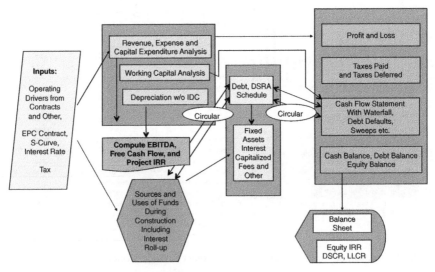

FIGURE 4.7 Structure of a Project Finance Model

A project finance model can involve complex programming issues including:

- Setting up time periods
- Working out a funding cascade during the construction phase for senior debt, subordinated debt, and equity during construction

- Modeling the debt service reserve account (DSRA) and the maintenance reserve account
- Developing a cash flow waterfall that works through cash flow priorities after operation begins
- Sculpting debt repayments to meet a debt service coverage constraint
- Modeling depreciation that depends on calendar years
- Refinancing debt and incorporating cash sweep covenants.

The difficult challenge in creating a project finance model is to address these issues without making the model hopelessly complex and cumbersome with many macros to deal with circular references and with long and complicated formulas. Part IV of the book addresses programming issues to resolve these issues in as painless a manner as possible.

Since a project is generally a one-off investment where debt and equity investors focus on cash flow rather than accounting earnings, the structure for computing cash flow is also different in a project finance model than in a corporate model. For a project finance model, the final part of the cash flow waterfall is the dividends paid to the owners of the SPV (sponsors), meaning that dividends are not defined from a dividend payout ratio, dividends per share, or some other algorithm, but rather are the residual cash flow not paid or reserved elsewhere. Effective modeling of cash flows in a project finance model involves integration of the debt schedule with the cash flow waterfall in the cash flow analysis as well as launching the model from a sources and uses of funds analysis. Finally, as with the corporate model, the balance sheet is part of the output rather than a mechanical calculation. All of the accounts such as plant balance, debt service reserves, senior debt balance, subordinated debt balance, and common equity balance are already defined elsewhere in the model and the balance sheet simply tabulates these accounts. A number of project finance models for different industries are found at www.wiley.com/go/internationalvaluation.

Reconciliation of Internal Rate of Return in Project Finance with Return on Investment in Corporate Finance

The return on historic investment is an important number in corporate finance. However, it is all but irrelevant in project finance. On the other hand, the project IRR is computed in project finance but not used in corporate models. While the metrics seem completely different, over the lifetime of a project, the return on investment weighted by investment level and the cost of money is the same as the internal rate of return (IRR). The equivalence of the IRR and the return on investment (ROI) is illustrated along with a few more Excel techniques in Figure 4.8. A very simple project finance model with no taxes, no debt, and a one-year construction period is shown at the top of the figure. Earnings are computed after depreciation expense on the construction expenditure.

	A	B	C	D	E	F	G	H	I	J	K	L	M	N
22														
23					IRR and ROI Reconciliation									
24														
25			0	1	2	3	4	5	6	7				
26		Construction Phase	TRUE	FALSE	FALSE	FALSE	FALSE	FALSE	FALSE	FALSE				
27		Operation Phase	FALSE	TRUE	TRUE	TRUE	TRUE	TRUE	TRUE	TRUE				
28														
29		EBITDA		70.00	77.00	84.70	93.17	102.49	112.74	124.01				
30		Construction Cost	400											
31		Depreciation		57.14	57.14	57.14	57.14	57.14	57.14	57.14				
32		Earnings		12.86	19.86	27.56	36.03	45.34	55.59	66.87	<---- =J29-J31			
33														
34		Net Plant	400.00	342.86	285.71	228.57	171.43	114.29	57.14	0.00	<---- =I34-J31			
35		Equity	400.00	342.86	285.71	228.57	171.43	114.29	57.14	0.00	<---- =J34			
36														
37		Return on Investment		3.2%	5.8%	9.6%	15.8%	26.5%	48.6%	117.0%	<---- =J32/I35			
38														
39		Cash Flow	-400.00	70.00	77.00	84.70	93.17	102.49	112.74	124.01				
40		IRR	13.042%		<---- =IRR(C39:J39)									
41														
42		Reconciliation demonstrating that IRR is a time, investment and cost of capital weighted average												
43														
44		*Investment Weighting*		25.0%	21.4%	17.9%	14.3%	10.7%	7.1%	3.6%	<---- =I34/SUM(34:34)			
45		Discount Factor		88.5%	78.3%	69.2%	61.2%	54.2%	47.9%	42.4%	<---- =1/(1+$C$40)^J25			
46		*Discount Factor Weighting*		20.0%	17.7%	15.7%	13.9%	12.3%	10.9%	9.6%	<---- =J45/SUM(45:45)			
47		Investment x Discount Factor		5.01%	3.80%	2.80%	1.98%	1.31%	0.78%	0.34%	<---- =PRODUCT(J46,J44)			
48		*Combined Weighting*		31.3%	23.7%	17.5%	12.4%	8.2%	4.8%	2.1%	<---- =J47/SUM(47:47)			
49														
50		Weighted ROI	13.042%		<---- =SUMPRODUCT(48:48,37:37)									

FIGURE 4.8 Reconciliation of Return on Investment and Internal Rate of Return

Because the net investment declines over time, the return on investment increases from 3.2 percent to 117 percent over the lifetime of the project. The IRR on the investment lies somewhere between the low value and the high value of the return on investment. Figure 4.8 demonstrates that the IRR can be computed by typing the IRR function and then clicking on the entire row as long as no numbers other than the cash flow are in the row. Instead of clicking on an entire row, you can press SHIFT and then the SPACEBAR key.

In reconciling the IRR and the ROI, you can compute a series of weighting factors. Then you can apply these weighting factors to the period by period ROI using the SUMPRODUCT function and compute the weighted average. In computing weighting factors, the notion of using the SUM function and an entire row is illustrated on Figure 4.8. The SUMPRODUCT function and the SUM functions illustrated in Figure 4.8 use the entire row number rather than entering both a row and a column number. When entering SUM(34:34), you can simply click on the entire row 34 and save a few seconds' time. The last equation on the diagram shows that you can also click on multiple rows when making calculations with the SUMPRODUCT function. Once the ROI is weighted by both the level of investment in the denominator of the ROI formula and the cost of money as defined by the IRR result, the weighted average ROI is exactly the same as the IRR.

Structure of an Acquisition Model: Alternative Transaction Prices and Financing Terms

If a project finance model is analogous to simulating your life and a corporate finance model is like representing your family, an acquisition model could be thought of as modeling a dramatic change in the structure of a family— perhaps migrating to a different country, changing religion, or borrowing a lot of money for education. To make a model of the future prospects of the family after such an event, you could start with the history of the family as with the corporate model. But then you probably want to adjust the model to reflect the new structure that arises because of the dramatic new event. Making an acquisition model involves both incorporating history as in the corporate model and also starting the new restructured company with a different financial structure as in the project finance model.

Acquisition models may be developed to determine how much to pay for a target company and how much of the purchase price can be financed with different types of financing, including amortizing debt, debt with a bullet maturity, and debt with capitalizing interest (this is sometimes known as "ABC"). Key assumptions in an acquisition model include how much the operating cash flow can grow after new owners take over and a new strategy is developed along with how much the company can be sold for after the holding period. Financial ratios used in assessing an acquisition are often related to the EBITDA. These include the EV (net debt plus equity value) to the EBITDA, the senior debt level to the EBITDA, and the total debt level to the EBITDA. As with a project finance model, an acquisition model can be used to determine whether a financial structure is applied that makes sense as well as risk assessment.

Figure 4.9 illustrates the summary output from an acquisition model that tries to paint a picture of the transaction as well as the net value of the acquisition. Information on the left in the Sources and Uses section shows returns that result from different providers of capital. The graph on the upper right-hand side of Figure 4.9 demonstrates the IRR generated in different periods with different assumed exit values.

The architecture of an acquisition model is illustrated in Figure 4.10. This diagram demonstrates that modeling an acquisition transaction involves combining some aspects of corporate models with other features of project finance models. As with a corporate model, the history of the company is a starting point for painting a picture of the company. However, like in a project finance model, equations in an acquisition model should begin with a sources and uses of funds analysis that shows how much cash is used for the

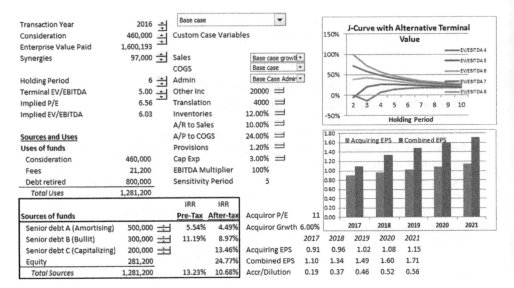

FIGURE 4.9 Illustration of Summary Output from an Acquisition Model

transaction and where the cash comes from. After the sources and uses of funds map is established, a goodwill analysis should be made that allows construction of a pro forma balance sheet. Once a balance sheet exists you have the starting point for a corporate model. When modeling cash flow after the transaction date, analyzing the cash flow priorities—determining who gets

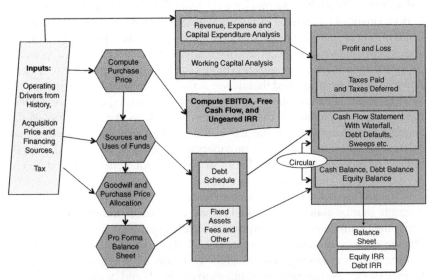

FIGURE 4.10 Structure of an Acquisition Model

the cash first and who gets it last—is central to the process. You should see that some things are like project finance and some are like corporate finance. If you are evaluating acquisitions it is good to have some knowledge of both corporate finance models and project finance models.

The design aspects of an acquisition model involving computation of a pro forma balance sheet through mapping the sources and uses of funds along with a goodwill analysis that incorporates the accounting aspects of the transaction is shown in the second column of Figure 4.10. Once the pro forma balance sheet is created, the modeling process contains similarities to both a corporate model and a project finance model. As with a corporate model that works through different balance sheet asset and liability accounts, an acquisition model does the same thing but the first year closing balance comes from the pro forma balance sheet. As with a project finance model, defining phases in an acquisition model is an essential part of the process—the transaction period should be flexible and should be distinguished from the holding period and the terminal period. The right-hand side of Figure 4.10 shows that the cash flow modeling process is analogous to the methods described for a project finance model where a waterfall progression measures the priority of cash flows to the various sources of funds and ultimately the equity holders.

Some of the challenges in creating models that measure the value of an acquisition or a leveraged buyout are:

- Creating a cash flow waterfall with alternative amortizing, bullet, and capitalizing debt, as well as cash requirements and revolving debt facilities
- Allowing the model to begin at different dates and transferring data from a stand-alone corporate model to an acquisition model
- Developing alternative structuring assumptions and a pro forma balance sheet
- Structuring the cash flow analysis to determine the points at which alternative financing instruments yield returns below the risk-free rate
- Simulating alternative purchase prices to yield required returns with different holding periods, exit multiples, and holding periods
- Modeling income taxes and alternative tax treatments (tax free exchanges or asset purchases) of transactions
- Simulating the structure of equity cash flows to alternative investors from earn-out provisions and equity kickers

Structure of an Integrated Merger Model: Forecasting Earnings per Share

The objective of a merger integration model is to evaluate how much to pay as equity consideration for a company and how to structure the financing of a merger transaction. This kind of model is like a royal marriage in the sixteenth century where the merger of two families was supposed to make the combined new royal family more powerful than the sum of the individual families through putting two countries together. You could also make an analogy to the European Union where synergies are supposed to improve an integrated system. An integrated merger model typically compares earnings per share and credit statistics in the scenario where a merger takes place to a different scenario without a merger. The prospective earnings of the merged company depend on how much is paid for the acquisition and how many synergies are generated from changing management as well as the financing of the transaction. When measuring the costs and benefits of a merger using an integrated model, the information base is the historical operations, projected cost savings, and/or revenue increases for both the target company and the acquiring company, as well as the transaction terms.

Figure 4.11 demonstrates that an integrated model structure mixes elements of an acquisition model and a standard corporate model. As with acquisition models, the starting point of a merger integration model is a sources and uses of funds analysis of the transaction and the pro forma balance sheet after goodwill and other adjustments. A difference between the acquisition model and the integrated model is that the pro forma balance sheet begins with existing balance sheets of both the target company and the acquiring company. For an integration model, the transaction assumptions incorporated in the sources and uses of funds analysis may include a share exchange, multiple debt issues, and new equity offerings.

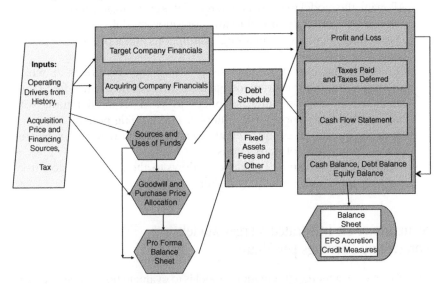

FIGURE 4.11 Structure of an Integrated Consolidation Model

TABLE 4.1 Contrast of Structures in Alternative Models

	Project Finance	Corporate Model	LBO Model	M&A Integration Model
Information base	Contracts and analysis of traffic; commodity prices; and other value drivers	Historical financial statements; analysis of industry demand and supply	Historical financial statements; analysis of value drivers; transaction terms	Historical financial statements; analysis of value drivers; transaction terms
Model starting point	Sources and uses of funds analysis	Historical balance sheet	Sources and uses of funds and pro forma balance sheet	Sources and uses of funds and pro forma balance sheet
Cash flow process	Cash flow waterfall that ultimately measures dividends paid to equity	Net cash flow after dividends that results in changes in short-term debt or surplus cash	Cash flow waterfall that ends in dividends paid to equity	Cash flow changes that result in changes in short-term debt or surplus cash
Debt analysis	New debt issues from transaction	New and existing debt issues	New debt issues from transaction	Existing, retired, and new debt issues
Model termination	End of project life	Arbitrary terminal period	Transaction holding period	EPS analysis period
Model complexities	Net operating loss [NOL]; cash traps and sweeps; construction period cascade; circularity; debt service reserves; debt sculpting	NOL; target capital structures; circularity; depreciation vintage; normalized cash flow in terminal period	NOL; cash sweeps; interest capitalization on subordinated debt; debt service reserves; terminal period	Pro forma balance sheet; minority interest changes; new debt issues
Model output	Equity IRR; project IRR; DSCR	Discounted cash flow valuation; EPS projection; implied P/E; credit quality	Equity and debt IRRs; debt/EBITDA	Project EPS and other ratios on stand-alone versus combined basis

Once the starting balance sheet is established through the pro forma analysis, the remaining calculations and the cash flow process are similar to the corporate model where computation of net cash flow leads to the accumulation of a net cash balance and the net cash balance is separated between short-term debt and surplus cash. In an integrated model the debt schedule includes debt issues retired in the transaction as well as new debt financing to pay for the merger, along with the associated fees and breakage costs. Shares issued in the transaction could come from a new share offering or from the shares issued to target company shareholders as part of a share exchange. Figure 4.11 shows that instead of computing a working analysis to derive revenues, expenses, and capital expenditures, these numbers come from individual stand-alone corporate models for the target company and the acquiring company. The most difficult item to forecast in this type of model is often the synergies that arise from changes in management strategy that come about from the transaction. In practice, these synergy projections must be made with only public information and little time when using a model to construct an offer for a company.

A comparison of the elements that are included in the layouts of different types of financial models is shown in Table 4.1. Subsequent chapters discuss computational issues in creating each of the major model components. In addition to the general descriptions of how equations should be created, there are discussions of some practical programming tips to make the process more efficient for those who are involved in construction of models on a regular basis.

CHAPTER 5

Avoiding Bad Programming Practices and Creating Effective Auditing Processes

For purposes of valuation and investment analysis, financial models do not have to be overly complex with 30 different sheets and tedious detail for items that are relatively insignificant. The reaction of most people to receiving an immense model with a lot of sheets and excruciating detail of operating expenses is to put the model in a folder and not to perform risk analysis. Even if valuation models are relatively simple, creating a model that is flexible enough to handle different risks, that accurately measures profit and cash flow, that presents the key value drivers together with important outputs in an easily understandable and transparent manner, and that does not crash Microsoft Excel because of circular references often requires a disciplined approach to programming. A well-structured transparent model can avoid the ghastly feeling—after completing a model—of being asked by your boss to open and revise a model that you have not looked at for a couple of weeks. This horrible feeling often comes from knowing that you will have to review a long and complex formula with multiple nested IF statements that have become all but impossible to interpret.

To address issues of transferring models among staff, some companies mandate the use of a set of best practices for analysts who program models. While these practices may help in making models transparent and effective for summarizing valuation, you may become obsessed with the programming practices and lose sight of the ultimate objective of a model. For example, in order to keep formulas the same across every single column including the very first column in a sheet in an acquisition model, complicated IF statements may be developed that are very difficult to interpret. With almost every task in a spreadsheet model, there are many different ways to accomplish your objective. Some people like range names, whereas others hate them; some like drop-down boxes, whereas others don't; some use SUMPRODUCT and some accomplish the same thing with SUMIF and yet others like using the regular old SUM function with a formula inside and pressing SHIFT, CNTL, ENTER. It is good to keep an open mind about different programming issues and generally it is also best to try to be as lazy as possible with spreadsheet functions. You should also not become too bureaucratic about best practice rules, especially when they do not make a lot of sense.

Instead of suggesting there is such a thing as a best practice, it is easier to make a list that explains why some bad practices should be avoided and write down good practices that shouldn't be overlooked. Through avoiding some of the bad practices listed here and following the good practices, a model should be easier to interpret and modify:

- There should be no inputs in any part of the model other than in the input page(s). One of the worst and most obvious problems is to include inputs as part of a formula (e.g., A11*5); these partial inputs are difficult to find, and they make the models inflexible.
- Avoid long and overly complex formulas. Keep formulas in the model as simple as possible, and clearly delineate how each formula is derived from the inputs (this is often a problem with long IF statements). Long formulas can almost always be avoided by splitting up equations into multiple different rows and by using TRUE/FALSE switches. Never use nested IF statements. This does not mean that you should follow the silly rule of thumb that formulas not be longer than your thumb (unless you have a very long thumb). But it is safe to say that overly complicated formulas are the worst practice of all.
- Avoid inconsistency. Make sure that spreadsheet columns are consistent throughout the model and that the formulas for each column are identical (with the exception of the very first period in corporate models and acquisition models).
- Include the units (such as tons of gold or thousands of euros) for each column of the inputs and on the working sheet.
- Carefully specify the time period of the model using codes that define alternative phases of the analysis. Put the time line at the top of each sheet. Use the LOOKUP or MATCH and INDEX functions rather than the VLOOKUP or HLOOKUP function to associate inputs with the time period, so users can add rows or columns to the model without worrying about getting different results.
- Divide the model into separate modules. Begin with input modules and make the inputs a separate color (the word "module" simply refers to a separate part of the model—it could be a separate spreadsheet page or

simply a segment of one sheet). When entering inputs in one or more modules, operating inputs should be separated from financial inputs.

- Work through every single balance sheet item. For each asset and liability show the opening balance, additions and subtractions from the account, and the closing balance for the account. This analysis should be made for every single title in the balance sheet, ranging from cash accounts to common equity.
- Limit or avoid the use of macros and iterations to resolve circular references. Circular references are not present in the real world, and fixing circularity makes many risk analysis programming techniques difficult.
- Use the balance sheet and other tests as auditing tools, and include a separate integrity page of the model to present verification checks. There should be a cell in the verification page that points to the location of the model errors so you do not have to look around the model to find problems. Include a dashboard at the top of each page of the model to monitor the integrity and show key outputs of the model.
- Ensure that no formulas in the output part of a model affect anything in any other section of the model. This means that you should be able to delete the output section without causing any reference errors in the mechanical calculation parts of the model.
- Use MIN and MAX instead of IF statements in cash flow analysis. When working through a cash flow waterfall, test various balances such as the debt balance, the net asset balance, the reserve balance, and other items relative to the opening balance using the MIN function instead of IF statements. The MIN function together with the opening balance puts a cap on things that can lead to negative balances. For example, the scheduled debt repayment can be capped at the opening balance— you do not want to pay more than the existing balance back to the bank.

These principles seem obvious when written down in a book. However, in the midst of creating a model to meet a tight deadline, it is very easy to ignore them, as they seem to slow you down. Examples of bad practices include entering input data in the fifth sheet of a model, including complicated revenue and expense calculations with long IF statements directly in the income statement, forcing the balance sheet to balance using some kind of a cash balancing item, computing interest expense without separately listing debt issues, and not being consistent with time periods.

The single worst practice that is often made by otherwise very good modelers is to make formulas that are far too long. An example of a formula from an actual model (for evaluating projected prices of a wind farm) that is not transparent and is almost impossible to verify is shown here:

```
=IF(AB5<14,IF(AB2=6,AA39*(1+inflation),AA39),IF
(AB5=14,'OperatingInputs'!$E$103/'OperatingInputs'!$E$104,IF
(LEN(AB5)=2,AA39,AA39*(1+inflation))))
```

This formula contains a number of bad practices. One problem is that fixed numbers are included in the formula (i.e., the number 14 and the number 6). The larger problem is that the formula is far too complex to easily verify and audit. This formula could be vastly improved if one would split it up into a number of separate rows where one could show the inflation rate, the logical tests, and the alternative results of different conditions. If you are asked to review somebody else's model, it is a good idea to split up formulas like this one. This particular formula was split into about 15 rows, and once the more transparent separate rows were presented, several obvious errors in the formula became apparent.

How to Make Financial Models More Efficient and Accurate

The paragraphs that follow highlight a few programming techniques that implement some of the concepts listed earlier and offer tips to prevent your model from becoming a hopeless mess. If you are more interested in general modeling concepts rather than the implementation details or if you want to be able to read models but not to program them, you should skip the detailed discussion of practical programming and begin reading the next chapter on time periods and valuation.

Creating Shortcut Keys and Setting Up the Model Area So You Can Build Your Model Quickly

This seems like a trivial little detail, but in structuring a model you can make it much easier to read—the transparency objective—by doing a few things before you start typing a single number in the spreadsheet. Models generally are presented in a similar manner to financial statements from annual reports where time (years, quarters, or months) is shown across columns and items such as revenues are listed on different rows. In setting up the columns, it is nice to include some thin columns at the beginning of the sheet so that you can press the CNTL, UP and the CNTL, DOWN keys and move from section to section. The time line section will often be the first section, followed by the assumptions section, the operations section, and the depreciation section. By putting headings in the first column (e.g., the words "time line," "assumptions," "operations," etc.), you can quickly move from section to section. It is also essential to leave a few blank columns between the titles and the model equations. In these special columns after the row names but to the left of the equations, you can display the units, show what inputs are used to drive the equations, and incorporate verification checks of various items. This little idea of including a few extra columns is indispensable in making the process transparent where a reader can, it is hoped, visualize how the equations are working. The idea of using special columns between the row titles and the equations is illustrated in the model excerpt shown in Figure 5.1.

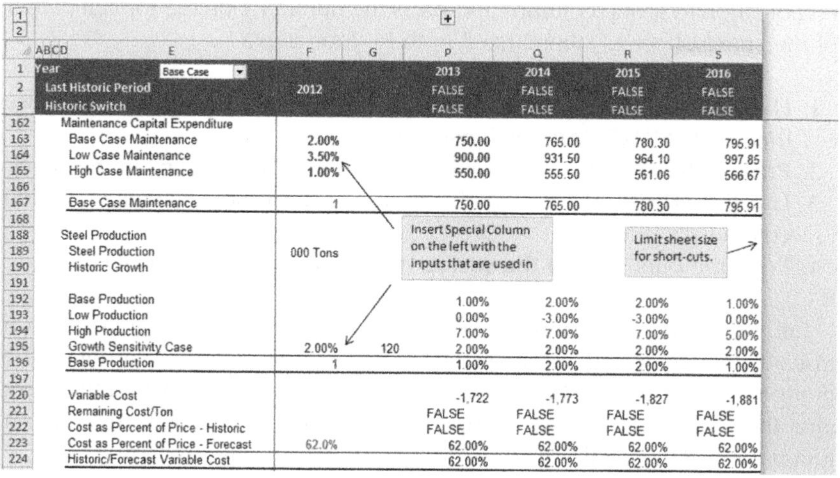

FIGURE 5.1 Setting Up the Structure of a Transparent Model

Using shortcut keys rather than using the mouse will enable you to work faster and more easily develop and modify the model. (In some financial modeling courses imposed on young bankers, the mouse is removed from computers so students learn how to navigate around spreadsheets much more quickly, lest they waste a minute in creating collateralized debt securities out of subprime loans.) Arguing that shortcut keys should be applied instead of dragging your finger across an iPhone may seem a bit odd when you first use them instead of the mouse. But if you practice, they really can make your work on the model easier. Shortcut keys that are very useful for formatting are SHIFT, CNTL, 1 for decimals; SHIFT, CNTL, 3 for dates; SHIFT, CNTL, 4 for currency; and SHIFT, CNTL, 5 for percentages. One of the most helpful shortcuts is the combination of the following two keystrokes, which allows you to very quickly copy and paste rows in a financial model:

1. Press SHIFT, CNTL, → (right arrow) at the same time to mark a row
2. Press CNTL, R to copy the formula or data to the right

This involves two steps rather than pressing CNTL, C and highlighting an area and then pressing CNTL, V. It also works with CNTL, down arrow and CNTL, D. The problem with this shortcut is that it copies the contents of the first cell to each column of the sheet, all the way to the right end of the sheet. To limit the copying of columns to the maximum rows of your sheet (the maximum number of periods that you may forecast), you can hide the columns to which you do not want the item to be copied. To hide columns to the right of the model periods, you can group all of the columns to the right of the last column in your program. To use this method, use the SHIFT, ALT, → combination to group columns and press the number 1 on the top left corner of the spreadsheet as summarized in these four steps:

1. Highlight the entire column of the first column to be hidden (you can use the CNTL, SPACEBAR combination).
2. Press SHIFT, CNTL, → to highlight the remaining columns in the sheet.
3. Use the SHIFT, ALT, → combination to group the remaining selected columns.
4. Press the number 1 in the square box at the top left of the sheet.

If you need the columns to the right, you can press the number 2 button instead of the number 1 button on the top left of the spreadsheet. Results of the grouping approach are shown in Figure 5.1, where the right part of the sheet after the columns have been grouped is tinted gray. After you've done this a few times, setting up the spreadsheet should take a few seconds.

These shortcut combinations are pretty cool, but it is even more useful to make your own shortcuts. When making your own shortcuts, you can simply create a macro around the task you want to repeat. You can, for example, make a CNTL, U and a CNTL, L combination to copy up and to the left as these are not part of a standard workbook. When making a macro to create your own shortcut, you enter a shortcut key as illustrated in the next section, but if you make the macro run with CNTL and lowercase c, then the copy function will no longer work. Instead, you can create the macro with CNTL and capital C so that it works when you press SHIFT, CNTL, C. When creating your own shortcut to do something like formatting cells with two decimal places (unlike the SHIFT, CNTL, 5 combination, which does not include decimals), you can do the following:

Step 1   Go to the cell that you will format with a percent sign and two decimals. You must be on the cell because you should not move the cell as part of the macro process.

Step 2   Record a macro, which is like recording a video on your phone. Do not do anything during the recording process that you do not want to appear in the video (macro). After pressing the record button, define a shortcut key with the SHIFT keyboard key (e.g., press capital D for decimals.) Do not ever move the cursor to another cell after you begin recording the macro, or that will become part of the macro. In this case after you press SHIFT, CNTL, D the cursor will do the same thing that you record.

Step 3 Change the formatting in the cell (you could use the CNTL, 1 shortcut).

Step 4 Stop recording the macro without moving the cursor.

A shortcut that avoids the irritating Excel feature that automatically switches inputs to percentages can be made with the simple macro shown in Figure 5.2.

```
Sub fix_decimal()
    ActiveCell = ActiveCell * 100
    Selection.NumberFormat = "#,##0.00"
End Sub
```

FIGURE 5.2 Function to Fix Problem of Percentage Formatting

Color Conventions and Creating the SHIFT, CNTL, C Macro to Color Inputs

In a well-structured financial model colors should be used as a guide to what is happening in various cells of the model. This means the colors should not be used to make the model into an attractive piece of art; it is better that they provide readers of the model with a quick understanding of where the numbers in a cell come from. One principle is that input cells should be colored differently from other cells, generally through using the fill color and the background color. Some accountants use the RGB rule where cells that come from another sheet are colored red, cells that come from a link in the same sheet are colored green, and cells that are inputs are colored blue. There are a few methods you can use to color inputs automatically. One method is to use the F5 key and then press the Special tab on the bottom left of the menu box that pops up (see Figure 5.3). After the menu appears, select the Constants option that will find all of the inputs except for the text, as shown in Figure 5.4. After finding the inputs, simply select the foreground color you want from the Home tab.

When using the F5 key and the Special button, you can create the process in a macro that allows you to redo the coloring process every time you make a change in your model. To create this macro, you can assign the macro to a CNTL combination and then have your own shortcut key, such as

FIGURE 5.3 Using the F5 Key to Color Input Cells

FIGURE 5.4 Selecting Input Cells with the F5 key

SHIFT, CNTL, C, redo the colors any time you want. Figure 5.5 shows how to begin recording the macro.

A second principle in addition to coloring inputs is that a different font color should be used for cells in which data comes from another sheet. If price data is transferred from the input sheet to the working sheet, that cell should have a color to notify users in what sheet they can quickly find the source of the data. A macro that sets the font color of a cell from the tab color of the sheet is included at www.wiley.com/go/internationalvaluation. Other colors can be

FIGURE 5.5 Recording a Macro for Creating a Shortcut for Coloring Cells

used for cells that have been computed from the Goal Seek feature or the Solver add-in tool and for cells that are computed through the operation of a macro. Finally, cells in which calculations that are not direct links are made from information in the same sheet should not have a font or a fill color.

Figure 5.1 illustrates a few of the setup ideas just discussed. The sheet is set up using the SHIFT, ALT, → method to limit the size of the sheet with the grouping method. When you press 1 at the top left, the columns are hidden, whereas when the number 2 is pressed, the columns are unhidden. Red cells come from the scenario sheet to the left of the sheet presented, which has a red tab color. Cells with a blue font are inputs in the sheet that are colored with the SHIFT, CNTL, C macro. Figure 5.1 illustrates that it is a good idea to make a few small columns on the left of the spreadsheet so that it is clear what rows are subtotals and headings.

When setting up your workbook it is often useful to program a couple of user-defined functions in addition to your customized shortcut keys. Making user-defined functions can open up a whole new set of power in financial models and is discussed at length in solving depreciation problems, computing the EV/EBITDA ratio and dealing with circular references in an efficient manner that avoids the nasty copy and paste macros. Some who are snobbish complain that Excel is a very blunt tool and software programs such as MATLAB are much better. They are in a sense correct that a spreadsheet by definition is somewhat limiting. But you can open up another whole world by adding functions to your workbook that vastly expand its power. Creating your own user-defined functions has some important contrasts to making a macro. In the spreadsheet, your function works like any other function such as the SUM function where you use an equals sign and put cell references or range references inside the parentheses. When creating a function rather than a standard macro, there are a couple of basic concepts that always apply:

1. The name of the function title must be defined as an output variable somewhere in the code.
2. Any value that is used from the spreadsheet must be read into the function; for example, you cannot use something like RANGE("A1") inside the function.

To introduce how functions can help you, a few simple ones are introduced in this chapter. One function that is useful is to show formulas adjacent to the cell where the calculation is made (this function was used in some of the excerpts shown previously). To create such a function you should first go to the Visual Basic screen. To do this you can press ALT and F11. Then you can type in a function as illustrated in Figures 5.6 and 5.7. A simple version of the function named show_form is illustrated in Figure 5.6, and a little fancier version named show_formula is illustrated in Figure 5.7. Note that you must start the code with the name Function rather than SUB.

```
Function show_form(cell)
        show_form = cell.Formula
End Function
```

FIGURE 5.6 Basic Function for Displaying Formulas

```
Function show_formula(cell)
        show_formula = _
            "< ---- Formula for: " & cell.Address & " " & cell.Formula
End Function
```

FIGURE 5.7 Function to Show Display Formulas with Arrow

It is also often useful when setting up a spreadsheet to create a function for showing the sheet name as a formula. This function requires only one line of code, as demonstrated in Figure 5.8.

```
Function sheet_name(cell)
        sheet_name = cell.Parent.Name
End Function
```

FIGURE 5.8 Function for Showing the Sheet Name

After entering this function, you can type = SHEET_NAME(cell) in any cell and refer to the current sheet or another sheet and find the sheet name.

If you have created a whole lot of functions and extra shortcut keys in one sheet and would like to use them in other workbooks, you can go to the Visual Basic for Applications (VBA) menu and export your file, which is like saving a file using any software. Then, in your new workbook, you can import all of the codes by referring to the name of the file that you just exported. The website, www.wiley.com/go/internationalvaluation, has a file named generic .bas that contains many extra shortcut keys and functions.

Creating an Audit Page That Tells You Where Errors Are Located

Part of an efficient model design is creating an auditing method where the program itself reports things that do not work. You can write a message somewhere at the top of each sheet that documents the location of mechanical problems with the model so you do not have to look around the workbook continually to find the source of the problem. On the top of each page you may want to show an overall check on the integrity of the model: Does the balance sheet balance; is the debt balance positive; are the dividends nonnegative; do the sources of cash equal the uses of cash? Sometimes it is useful to also include a series of audit checks as to whether debt is in default as well as mechanical checks.

A good way to set up the integrity check of a model is to use TRUE and FALSE logical variables. Application of TRUE/FALSE switches is helpful in many different parts of the model. Use of TRUE/FALSE variables eliminates the need for painful, nested IF statements that can be very difficult to audit. TRUE/FALSE variables are almost essential in structuring the time line of a model. A TRUE/FALSE switch variable can be created by simply using an equals sign. In the equation = 1 = 1, the result is TRUE. It is often useful to apply the AND function together with a series of logical variables to test if the overall value is TRUE; for example, AND(1 = 1,2 = 2) is TRUE. Further, when IF statements are entered, the TRUE/FALSE switch can be used in the logical section of the function. The following step-by-step process illustrates how to create a verification page with TRUE/FALSE switch variables that will show you where you made an error:

Step 1   After making the balance sheet, subtract the total assets from liabilities on a separate row to compute the difference, which should be 0. Create similar calculations for the debt balance, the sources and uses of funds, and other items. Sometimes creating an equation that tests the model results is not as obvious as it is when you only want to test something in one period of the model or one phase of the analysis. In such situations you can often use the SUMIF function.

Step 2   In a separate row, use a TRUE/FALSE logical variable created by setting one cell equal to another to test whether the difference, after rounding, is equal to 0. In the balance sheet case, the test is whether the difference is 0. The rounding is often necessary because the difference is not precisely equal to 0 if, for example, there is a division by 3 somewhere in the model. For the balance sheet, the formula in each model period is:

$$= \text{ROUND}(\text{difference}, 3) = 0$$

Step 3   Once the TRUE/FALSE result is established for each period, the AND function can be used to test the balance sheet balances in every period of the model. The AND function can be applied to a range of TRUE/FALSE logical variables and placed to the left of all of the year-by-year tests as illustrated in Figure 5.9.

Figure 5.9 illustrates the verification of the balance sheet that then feeds into an aggregate balance sheet test. The row labeled "test" uses a switch and the ROUND function to make sure the balance sheet balances in each period. If all of the other tests like the aggregate balance sheet test are TRUE, then the aggregate test computed with the AND function (shown at the left) is also TRUE.

	E	F	G	I	J	K	L	M
1	ear			2006	2007	2008	2009	2010
2	Last Historic Period	2012	Base Case	FALSE	FALSE	FALSE	FALSE	FALSE
3	Historic Switch			TRUE	TRUE	TRUE	TRUE	TRUE
843	Total assets			8,499.00	18,637.00	19,448.00	16,951.00	17,539.00
844								
845	Historic Assets	Formula for $I$845 =I87------>		8,499.00	18,637.00	19,448.00	16,951.00	17,539.00
846	Difference	Formula for $I$846 =I843-I845------>		-	-	-	-	-
847	Test	Formula for $J$847 =SUMIF(3:3,TRUE,846:846)=0------>		TRUE				
848								
849	EQUITY AND LIABILITIES							
850	Equity attributable to equity holders of the parent entity			4,066.00	5,950.00	4,729.00	5,167.00	5,689.00
851	Non-controlling interests			169.00	406.00	245.00	275.00	247.00
852	Total			4,235.00	6,356.00	4,974.00	5,442.00	5,936.00
853	Non-current liabilities							
854	Long-term loans 21			2,649.00	6,825.00	10,041.00	7,998.00	7,868.00
855	Deferred income tax liabilities 8			277.00	1,690.00	1,329.00	1,231.00	1,072.00
856	Employee benefits 23			117.00	347.00	292.00	307.00	315.00
857	Provisions 25			39.00	132.00	153.00	176.00	279.00
858	Other long-term liabilities 26			47.00	55.00	58.00	68.00	143.00
859	Total Non-Current			3,129.00	9,049.00	11,873.00	9,780.00	9,677.00
860	Current liabilities							
861	Trade and other payables 27			851.00	2,532.00	2,110.00	1,321.00	1,396.00
862	Short-term loans and current portion of long-term			-	-	-	-	-
863	Provisions 25			8.00	55.00	63.00	35.00	54.00
864	Amounts payable under put options			264.00	606.00	428.00	373.00	476.00
865	Liabilities directly associated with disposal			12.00	39.00	-	-	-
866	Total Current Liabilities			1,135.00	3,232.00	2,601.00	1,729.00	1,926.00
867	Total equity and liabilities			8,499.00	18,637.00	19,448.00	16,951.00	17,539.00
868								
869	Difference	Formula for $I$869 =I867-I843------>		-	-	-	-	-
870	Test	Formula for $I$870 =ROUND(I869,2)=0------>		TRUE	TRUE	TRUE	TRUE	TRUE
871	Aggregate Test	Formula for $I$871 =AND(870:870)------>		TRUE				

FIGURE 5.9 Illustration of Balance Sheet Verification

Figure 5.9 also shows how a SUMIF function can be used along with a time period switch to limit the test to the historical period in a model.

Step 4   Link the TRUE/FALSE results from the AND and SUMIF statements and any other test to a separate page of the model that contains all of the other verification checks.

Step 5   Type a title for each individual test and put the linked cell with the value of TRUE or FALSE next to the test title. Identify the sections of the model that have problems using an IF statement that uses the title of the test and the TRUE/FALSE result of the test. The IF statement has the form:

$$= IF(test, \text{""}, title)$$

When making the balance sheet test, the test in the preceding formula would be the aggregate TRUE/FALSE test from the model. The title would be something like "Balance Sheet Test."

Step 6   Once the sections of the model with problems are identified, make an aggregate presentation of all of the problems in the model. This cell that aggregates all of the problems can be placed in each sheet to allow you to find problems without looking around the model each time you make a change. The aggregate presentation of all of the tests has the form:

$$= problem1\&problem2\& \ldots \&problem10$$

In this equation the problem1, problem2 cells come from the IF statement in step 5. The "&" function allows the text to be put together as if you were adding things. For better presentation, it is a good idea to put a space before each title so the problems are delineated. It is surprising that Excel does not have a function that allows you to add all of the text together without all of the irritating & symbols. This is another situation when you can create your own function. This function that adds text together is illustrated in Figure 5.10. In this case the function accepts an array variable and it needs to count the number of elements in the array. A FOR NEXT loop is included in the function to aggregate the text together using the & symbol as if it were done in the spreadsheet. As with the show formula function, the name of the function must be assigned to something in the body of the function. To write your own functions like this, simply go to the VBA editing screen by pressing ALT, F11, and type the following text.

```
Function add_text (series)
        num = series.Count
        For i = 1 To num
                add_text = add_text & " " & series(i)
        Next i
End Function
```

FIGURE 5.10 Function to Combine an Array of Text

An example of a page that shows verification checks using the step-by-step process discussed here is illustrated in Figure 5.11. The end result of this process is a single cell that tells you where you made your errors.

	A B	C	D	E	F	G	H
2			Model Audit Analysis				
3							
4		Item Title from Financial Model	Test from Financial		Display if Error		
5							
6		Development period	TRUE	<---- =Working!L12		<---- =IF(D6,"",C6)	
7		Financial close date	TRUE	<---- =Working!L13		<---- =IF(D7,"",C7)	
8		Construction period	TRUE	<---- =Working!L14		<---- =IF(D8,"",C8)	
9		Commercial Operation Date	TRUE	<---- =Working!L15		<---- =IF(D9,"",C9)	
10		Month before COD	TRUE	<---- =Working!L16		<---- =IF(D10,"",C10)	
11		Operation period	TRUE				
12		Sale date	TRUE				
13		Debt Repayment Period	FALSE		Debt Repayment Period <---- =IF(D13,"",C13)		
14		Debt Retirement Period	TRUE				
15		Re-financing Repayment Period	TRUE				
16							
17		S curve	FALSE		S curve	<---- =IF(D17,"",C17)	
18		Level Repayment	TRUE				
19		Annuity Repayment	TRUE				
20							
21		Permanent Debt	TRUE				
22		Re-Financed Debt	TRUE				
23							
24		Balance Sheet	TRUE				
25							
26			=add_text(F6:F24)---->		Debt Repayment Period & S curve		
27		Aggreagate	FALSE		Problem: Debt Repayment Period & S curve		
28							
29			=AND(D6:D =IF(D27,"Model ok","Problem: " & F26)				

FIGURE 5.11 Illustration of an Audit Page for a Project Finance Model

CHAPTER 6

Developing and Efficiently Organizing Assumptions

In discussing the architecture of various models in Chapter 4 for the corporate model, project finance model, acquisition model, and integrated model, it was evident that each of the financial models have many things in common. All of the models begin with an input section and end with a balance sheet. Each model includes a working section that computes pretax cash flow comprising revenues, expenses, and capital expenditures; each model moves from pretax cash flow to after-tax free cash flow by computing depreciation, taxes, and working capital; each model type has a debt schedule; and each model contains an income statement and a cash flow analysis. These components that are common across the different types of models are described in the next few chapters. This chapter begins the discussion of common model elements by explaining some theory and practical issues associated with model inputs.

Assumptions in Demand-Driven Models versus Supply-Driven Models: The Danger of Overcapacity in an Industry

The most important part of the modeling process is to accurately define and analyze input items that drive the value of an investment and then effectively present how risks associated with these value drivers affect the ultimate investment value. Value drivers can be economic parameters such as industry demand, behavior of competitors, product prices, cost of capital expenditures per unit, and the fixed and variable cost structures. The drivers produce revenues, cash operating expenses, and capital expenditures, which define pretax cash flow and are the starting point of any model. The things that really drive value and should be primary inputs to a model are generally not items such as revenue growth, operating margins, return on investment, or the ratio of capital expenditures to sales, although for very large corporations it may be necessary to use these kinds of gross inputs. The real value drivers that are affected by business strategy and economic conditions are rather quantities of capacity, price per unit, variable operating cost per unit, fixed cost and capital expenditure relative to the amount of new capacity built. The art of modeling involves identifying how changes in the industry structure resulting from capacity additions and demand changes, technology changes, consumer tastes, product life cycles, and other factors affect these primary value drivers. Modeling and valuation mistakes introduced in Chapter 1 were not due to incorrectly structuring a model or having a financial model that was too simple; they were instead generally the result of not using valid economic and financial principles in developing industry demand, supply, and price inputs to the valuation process. These inputs can be studied by reviewing historical data, performing statistical analysis, applying marginal cost concepts, and evaluating changes in the industry structure. When entering value drivers into a model, you should also use judgment as to whether sudden nonlinear changes can occur.

When developing a financial model you can distinguish whether profits and cash flow of a company are primarily driven by demand and market share or, alternatively, if financial results are driven by commodity prices and cost management. The former type of model where demand is the starting point for a model can be referred to as a demand-driven model while the latter in which commodity prices determine revenues can be called a supply-driven model. The starting point for the assumptions should generally be the capacity of the company (reserves of oil, megawatts of electricity, number of planes) in a supply-driven model. The starting assumption is the industry-wide demand in a demand-driven model.

To understand the difference between demand-driven and supply-driven models, consider an upstream oil project for a relatively small producer. The most likely place to begin thinking about the upstream model is with the capacity of oil fields owned by the company in terms of oil and gas reserves. You would probably not begin with an analysis of the worldwide demand for oil as in a demand-driven model because the company operates in a commodity business and it will sell whatever it can produce. Alternatively, for a company operating in a limited market region such as a port or a telecommunications company, the model would begin with demand for the product in the industry followed by an assessment of the industry capacity. With industry-wide demand and supply, an allocation of the industry-wide demand can be made to the particular firm through some kind of market share assessment.

The diagram in Figure 6.1 illustrates construction of value drivers and the modeling process for an electricity generating plant in a supply-driven model.

The drivers for capital expenditures, revenues, and operating expenses all begin with the capacity of the plant. Economic drivers for revenue, operating expenses, and capital expenditures include the cost per unit of building the plant, future trends and volatility in prices, capacity utilization of the plant, and the variable and fixed costs of operating the plant.

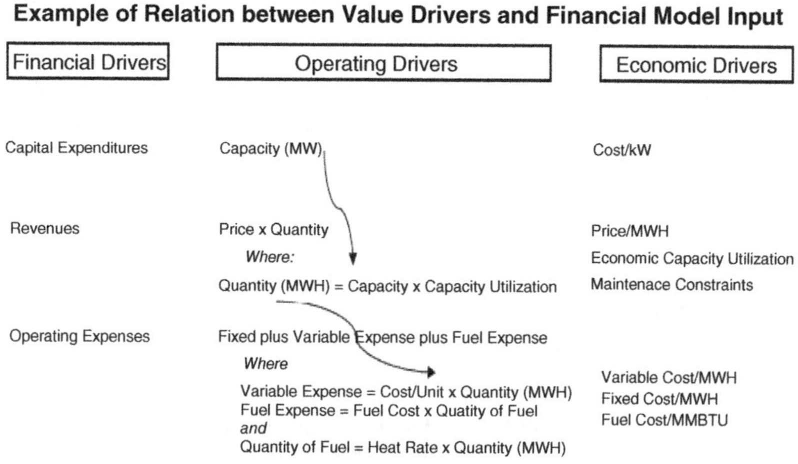

Example of Relation between Value Drivers and Financial Model Input

Financial Drivers	Operating Drivers	Economic Drivers

Capital Expenditures   Capacity (MW)   Cost/kW

Revenues   Price x Quantity   Price/MWH
                             Where: Economic Capacity Utilization
                             Quantity (MWH) = Capacity x Capacity Utilization   Maintenace Constraints

Operating Expenses   Fixed plus Variable Expense plus Fuel Expense
                             Where
                                             Variable Cost/MWH
                             Variable Expense = Cost/Unit x Quantity (MWH)   Fixed Cost/MWH
                             Fuel Expense = Fuel Cost x Quatity of Fuel   Fuel Cost/MMBTU
                             and
                             Quantity of Fuel = Heat Rate x Quantity (MWH)

FIGURE 6.1 Value Drivers for an Electricity Model

The most common form of corporate and acquisition models is the demand-driven model where the starting point should be evaluation of industry supply, demand, and prices. Many valuation mistakes are made when oversupply occurs in an industry because demand does not increase as expected or high returns prompt excessive new supply. The famous top right quadrant of a diagram of return relative to cost of capital versus growth can be an effective way to think about industry demand and supply assumptions in a model. The top right quadrant, called powerhouse companies, includes companies that are both growing fast and earning high returns. This seems like the place that you always want to be. As discussed in Chapter 1, the problem is that it is also the place everybody else wants to be. Unless really strong competitive advantages and barriers to entry exist and companies can make you addicted to their products, other firms from all over the world will want to enter businesses represented by this quadrant. The new entrants will result in industry-wide surplus capacity. When surplus capacity occurs in an industry, prices can dramatically move from levels that support high returns on investment all the way down to the short-run marginal cost of production. With the new entrants coming in and surplus capacity, companies fiercely fight for market share. In thinking about how surplus capacity can arise, the return on investment for firms in an industry along with barriers to entry should be an essential part of the modeling process. If returns are relatively high and entry of new firms is not limited, surplus capacity can come quickly. A recent example of such a phenomenon is the solar power manufacturing industry where high market valuation and strong returns encouraged addition of new capacity. New entrants from all over the world began setting up factories that were fairly easy to build. The new capacity led to dramatic price reductions and declines in market value.

Setting up inputs for a demand-driven model beginning with industry demand and supply is illustrated on the graph in Figure 6.2. In this graph the capacity additions planned by different companies (the shaded areas) are compared to demand (the thick line), demonstrating a looming danger of overcapacity if all of the planned capacity comes on line. When constructing a demand-driven model, illustrating capacity and demand in the entire industry can be very helpful even if inputs for the industry demand and supply cannot be precisely obtained and the capacity additions for other companies has to be subjectively estimated. The idea of understanding projected supply and demand conditions relative to historical levels is an essential conceptual step of the process.

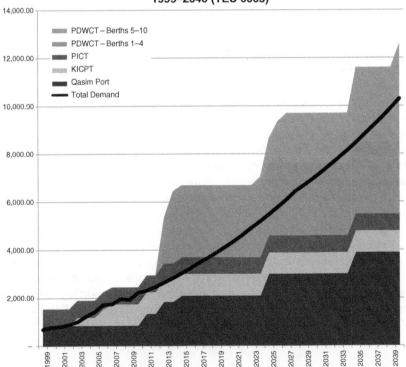

Container Demand and Capacity in Pakistan, 1999–2040 (TEU 000s)

FIGURE 6.2 Illustration of Incorporating Industry Supply and Demand in a Corporate Model

Once the industry supply and demand expectation is established, projections of market share and product prices can be estimated for an individual firm. The next example is intended to prompt you to think about industry demand and supply in setting up assumptions. It is not necessarily a guide as to how a particular model should be set up. The framework for which volume demand and price for a single company could be derived from industry demand and supply estimates is illustrated using a step-by-step process something like the following:

Step 1 Make some kind of projection of industry demand. Possible approaches to calculating prospective demand includes regression analysis, evaluation of historical volatility, exponential smoothing, and judgment.

Step 2 Second, evaluate the industry capacity from the existing supply of individual companies as well as specific knowledge of expected new additions and expected retirements. It is difficult to project surplus capacity without detailed industry knowledge. Companies may not publish capacity expansion plans and it may be very difficult to compile the data, but this assumption may be the most important item in your whole model.

Step 3 Third, calculate the industry-wide surplus capacity. You can then calculate the capacity margin and attribute this industry capacity margin of supply relative to demand for individual companies. You can develop individual company volumes assuming that market share is driven by the capacity of a single company relative to total industry capacity. This calculation is illustrated using the following equation:

Reserve Capacity Percentage = Industry Capacity/Industry Demand
Company Demand = Company Capacity/Reserve Capacity Percentage

Step 4 Derive the assumed price of the product as a function of the reserve capacity percentage. In creating price assumptions, you could relate the price level to the amount of the surplus capacity in an input table. When the surplus capacity is above a certain assumed level you may assume that the price can fall all the way to short-run marginal cost. For other levels of surplus capacity you could input different prices ranging from prices that exceed long-run cost to prices that fall between long-run marginal cost and short-run marginal cost. To implement a process where prices are a function of the relationship between supply and demand and are input in a table you can use a LOOKUP function as shown here. The LOOKUP function is more flexible and stable than either the VLOOKUP or the HLOOKUP functions because it does not require a row or column number.

$$Price = LOOKUP(Reserve\ Capacity,\ Reserve\ Capacity\ Range,\ Price\ Range)$$

Creating a Flexible Input Structure for Model Assumptions

When organizing the inputs of a financial model you should group various relevant input categories together. In general, the order of the inputs should reflect the order of calculations in the model, where timing parameters are entered first, followed by pretax cash flow, after-tax cash flow, and financing. This means inputs should begin with timing parameters, followed by operating inputs, tax and depreciation inputs, financing inputs, and valuation parameters. Inputs can be structured on a period-by-period basis across a spreadsheet page or they can be entered in alternative time increments. The inputs can be in different pages or put in one page while you are developing the model. In a corporate model, the inputs should generally be entered next to historical values and it may be convenient to use conditional formatting to illustrate the history in a different color than the forecast values.

The inputs should be set up in a way that anybody can easily find the assumptions and understand exactly what each input means. If a model has an input labeled "development expense percentage," this may be confusing because one has no idea what the basis is for the percentages. Second, inputs should allow the model to be adjusted and not be restrictive; if there is one inflation rate applicable to all future years, the model has limited flexibility. Third, the inputs should be arranged in a logical manner and grouped together by categories that reflect the structure of subsequent calculations in the model—capital expenditures and revenues first, followed by cash operating costs, working capital, tax and book depreciation, and, finally, financing and valuation parameters. The five general assumption categories should include:

1. Timing assumptions corresponding to the different types of models. In project finance models, the key timing parameters are the financial close date, the commercial date, the debt repayment date, and the decommissioning date. In corporate models, the timing assumptions are the historical period, the explicit period, and the terminal period. For acquisition models the key dates are the acquisition date and the exit period.

2. Capital expenditures enable a company to generate EBITDA and grow. It is essential to include the quantity of incremental production that can be generated from the capital expenditures and associate EBITDA with capital expenditures in as direct a manner as possible. The cost per unit of the capital expenditures and capital expenditures required to maintain the existing plant must also be input. In project finance models, entering an S-curve that is flexible and can accommodate construction delays can be tricky.

3. Revenue assumptions that include the quantity sold and the price, where the price can depend on industry capacity and supply analysis, as described in the earlier discussion of potential surplus capacity. When making long-run assumptions, understanding the long-run marginal cost of production should be considered in the price analysis.

4. Cash operating cost assumptions that are separated between fixed and variable cost so that different sales quantity assumptions can be evaluated and the model can measure risks arising from operating leverage. Understanding what costs are fixed and what costs are variable can be essential in evaluating risk as demonstrated by the bankruptcies of General Motors (GM) and many U.S. airline companies. When GM's demand declined with high oil prices and the cost structure could not react, the EBITDA declined dramatically. To study fixed and variable cost in a corporate model you can make a scatter plot of total costs relative to revenues.

5. Working capital assumptions that can be expressed as days outstanding of accounts receivable and accounts payable and so forth. Alternatively the working capital can be expressed as accounts receivable as a percent of sales and accounts payable as a percent of cost of goods sold (COGS) along with other ratios.

These five assumption categories determine the pretax return on invested capital in a corporate analysis and the pretax internal rate of return (IRR) in a project finance analysis. Two remaining assumption categories are used to derive the after-tax return on invested capital and the project IRR as well as the return after gearing, including the return on equity and the equity IRR. Those categories are:

1. Tax and associated depreciation assumptions, including tax rates, depreciation rates, and inputs associated with the difficult issue of retirements in a corporate model.

2. Financing assumptions that include the amount of debt issued, the manner in which debt will be borrowed and repaid, the interest and fees incurred while debt is outstanding, and credit enhancement features of the debt such as covenants and reserves that are designed to protect lenders.

Alternative Input Structures for Project Finance and Corporate Finance Models

The manner in which inputs are entered into a model corresponds to the structural differences between corporate models and project finance models. Corporate finance models are built from history and virtually every input should be a time series variable. Most of the variables should be entered in a way that enables you to change the inputs from year to year. In a corporate model it is a good idea to display the assumptions adjacent to the history and program the model so the assumptions can either vary by time period or the assumption can be input as a single number that remains constant over the forecast horizon. Figure 6.3 illustrates alternative assumptions for a corporate model using this idea. In Figure 6.3, the first assumption for sales growth includes different sets of time varying inputs that change from year to year. In contrast, the assumptions for working capital apply a single number that is fixed over the forecast period. For sales growth, the different time series are driven by a code number that is shown in red because it comes from another sheet that has a red tab color. The fixed number that drives the projection of accounts receivable is also colored red, but is not a code number. The idea of using a code number to set up assumptions can be implemented with either the INDEX function or the CHOOSE function, as explained in the next section.

In the case of project finance models, the format does not have the same structure where the history is consistently shown next to the forecast. Some inputs may be annual; some may be one-time scalar numbers; some may be switches. An excerpt from project finance model inputs is shown in Figure 6.4.

Setting Up Inputs with Code Numbers and the INDEX Function

To prepare a model for risk analysis, you should set up inputs to the model by entering different possible scenarios in the data input section. For many inputs such as volume growth, prices, interest rates, and other factors different scenarios may have time-changing values over the forecast period, as shown in Figures 6.3 and 6.4. When inputs can take on different values over time like this, your challenge is to enter input data without inordinately cluttering up the model. One reasonable way to enter input data that contains changing values over time and different possible scenarios is to use a code number together with the INDEX or CHOOSE function. The general process of setting up flexible input variables that can change over time at different date increments is summarized as follows:

Timeline	Low case ▼						
		2009	2010	2011	2012	2013	2014
Historic timeline switch	13	TRUE	TRUE	TRUE	TRUE	FALSE	FALSE
Assumptions							
Operating assumtions							
Sales growth							
Historic sales		7.70%	-1.04%	7.75%	9.85%	FALSE	FALSE
Base sales					5.00%	5.00%	5.00%
Low sales					3.00%	3.00%	3.00%
High sales			⊟		8.00%	8.00%	7.50%
Sensitivty case				200	2.00%	2.00%	2.00%
Sales growth code number	2 < ---- ='Master Scenario'!D25						
Actual/forecast sales growth		7.7%	-1.0%	7.8%	9.8%	3.0%	3.0%
COGS margin							
Historic margin		53.45%	52.33%	53.12%	53.10%	FALSE	FALSE
Base margin						53.00%	53.50%
Low margin						54.00%	56.00%
High margin						53.00%	52.50%
Sensitivty case			⊟	530		53.00%	53.00%
COGS margin code	2 < ---- ='Master Scenario'!E25						
Actual/forecasted COGS margin		53.45%	52.33%	53.12%	53.10%	54.00%	56.00%
Working Capital Assumptions							
A/R to Sales Historic		6.87%	6.46%	6.69%	8.41%	FALSE	FALSE
A/R to Sales Projected	10.00% < ---- ='Master Scenario'!F25					10.00%	10.00%
A/R to Sales Actual and Projected		6.87%	6.46%	6.69%	8.41%	10.00%	10.00%
Inventories to CGS Historic		4.39%	4.50%	5.03%	5.63%	FALSE	FALSE
Inventories to CGS Projected						10.00%	10.00%
Inventories to Sales Historic and Projected		4.39%	4.50%	5.03%	5.63%	10.00%	10.00%

ummary / Master Scenario / **Corporate Model** / 🔲

FIGURE 6.3 Illustration of Input Structure for a Corporate Model

Step 1   Enter a scenario code number that will be associated with the input. This scenario number will allow you to change an entire row or column of data in the model by changing the single code number. The reason a whole row or column is changed is because the code number is used by the INDEX or CHOOSE functions to pull one value out of a group of values.

Step 2   Enter data in a series of rows or columns associated with the input that can change over time. When entering the data across time in a project finance model, there should be some time tag such as a year number or a date that can be used to associate the input with the correct column in the financial model. The time variable may reflect the age of the project or a chronological date. The time tag can be allocated to the correct column by using a LOOKUP function as described in Chapter 7.

Step 3   On a blank row below the list of scenarios that include varying time inputs, use either the CHOOSE function or the INDEX function

⊿	ABC	D	E	F	G	H	I	J	K	L	M
1	Assumptions		=sheet_name(F11)---->		Ass Assumptions_sheet						
144	Operating Costs and Inverter Replacement										
145	Inflation Index for Operating Costs						2013	2014	2015	2016	2017
146	Base inflation rate			1			2.00%	1.50%	1.75%	2.00%	1.50%
147	Low inflation rate			2			1.00%	0.75%	1.00%	1.50%	1.50%
148	High inflation rate			3			3.50%	3.50%	3.50%	3.50%	3.50%
149											
150	Low inflation rate			2			1.00%	0.75%	1.00%	1.50%	1.50%
151											
152	Date for Real Operating Expenses	Date	01-nov-13				=INDEX(J146:J148,$F$150)				
153	Operating Expenses										
154	Fixed O&M Expense	USD/MWH	15.00								
155	Other costs	USD 000's	0.00								
156											
157	Inverter Replacement										
158	Cost in Real Currency	USD/kW	517.25								
159	Years to Replacement	Years	25.00								
160	MRA Switch	Switch	FALSE	☐							
161								Capacity (kW)	Inflation Index	Cost USD 000	
				Cost/kW	Period						
162	First Inverter Replacement Date	Date	01-août-39	465.52	73			0	2.19	-	
163	Second Inverter Replacement Date	Date	01-août-64	418.97	123			0	4.59	-	

FIGURE 6.4 Illustration of Input Structure for a Project Finance Model

along with the scenario code number from step 1. You will use numbers created with the INDEX or the CHOOSE functions as the basis of inputs to equations in the model. These two functions simply find a number from a group of numbers according to a given row or column number, which is why the code number is an essential part of the process. Recall that the INDEX function works by highlighting an area or a group of numbers in a row or column followed by a single row or column number that defines which number in the group to select. When using the INDEX function, you should highlight the items for one period and then use the scenario code number as the row or column number. Then you should lock it with the F4 key for the row or column.

Selected Value for Period = INDEX(Column of Data for Scenarios, Scenario Code Number)

Step 4   Once the variable is defined use the LOOKUP function to insert the appropriate variable into the financial model. To apply the LOOKUP function, use the relevant time period indicator in the financial model as the look up index. Then shade the time period in the input data and finally shade the items that will be transferred from the INDEX function.

Value in Model = LOOKUP(Time Line Value, Column or Row of Time Tags in the Input Section, Column or Row of Input Values in the Input Section)

The example in Figure 6.5 illustrates how to set up flexible inputs in a project finance context. The top part of the example shows date inputs that drive the different timing switches. The capacities per turbine are input as fixed amounts that do not change over time. There are typically few inputs that are entered as scalars like this in a corporate model. Items where scenario analysis has multiple different values that can change over time are entered with a code number that defines the scenario in Figure 6.5. Some inputs can be entered on a year-by-year basis even if the model is structured on a monthly or semiannual basis. In Figure 6.5 the timing of the input is flexible and varies according to the date to the left of the input when the financial close and/or the commercial operation date changes. For project finance models, where timing is so essential to the analysis, it is often a good idea to structure many variables according to the time line of the model.

The colors of the inputs shown in Figure 6.5 are made using the SHIFT, CNTL, C homemade shortcut key discussed in Chapter 5, and the selected scenario can be displayed using the conditional formatting feature along with the option that allows you to use a formula for making the formatting. To make conditional formatting, highlight the entire column or row that has been

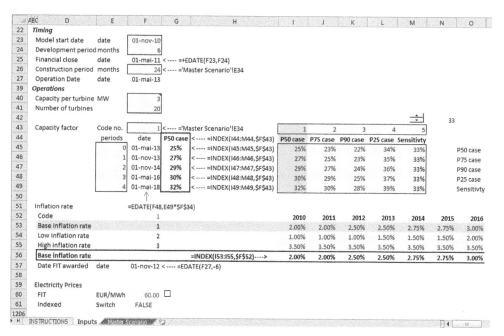

FIGURE 6.5 Illustration of Using INDEX Function and Conditional Formatting in Displaying Inputs

selected with the code number; you can use the general TRUE and FALSE switches introduced in Chapter 5. For creating this highlighting process, you can select the area of the time series inputs that you want to format on a flexible basis depending on the code number that is chosen. Then, under conditional formatting you select the "new rule" and, after that, "use formula to determine which cells to format" option. The formula you enter is the code number (fixed with the F4 key) equal to the individual numbered scenarios (adjusted so that the column is locked but the row is not).

CHAPTER 7

Structuring Time Lines

When filling out applications, applying for a license, and evaluating your performance in various tasks ranging from sporting competitions to employment, one of the first items of information that you are generally asked for is your birth date. The same general notion applies to companies or projects where dates, ages, and life stages go a long way in the programming of a model and in constructing a valuation analysis. This implies that the first thing to program in a well-structured financial model is a carefully designed time line. Presenting the time line in a financial model is like showing the most fundamental facts of a person's life on his or her tombstone, which are the date of birth and the date of death.

Efficiently structuring time periods in a model ensures that you can gauge the effect of valuation issues such as the length of the holding period in an acquisition or real estate project, delays in the construction of a large project or lengthening the concession period in project finance, or evaluating effects of the amount of time before which a stable growth rate is achieved for a corporation. Carefully setting up time periods allows flexible and accurate calculations of items such as interest during construction, terminal value, depreciation and amortization, debt repayments, gain on sale of assets and many other items. An efficient time line also allows you to smoothly move from the historic period to the projected period in a corporate model. Much of the flexibility in all types of financial models directly comes from the careful programming of a time line and the associated TRUE/FALSE switches.

Timing in Corporate Finance Models: Distinguishing the Historical Period, Explicit Period, and Terminal Period

One of the big challenges in a corporate model is to make it flexible enough to accept new data from historical financial statements in the future periods without having to rebuild the entire workbook. This can be accomplished by constructing a historic TRUE/FALSE switch just below the timeline. The timeline of a corporate model should contain a historical period, an explicit forecast period, a valuation date, a terminal period, and sometimes a fade period. For these models, the structure of time periods should begin with the definition of a historical period that is established from the availability of financial statements and allows you to update the model with actual financial data as it becomes available. In corporate valuation and modeling for high growth firms there is a great deal of subjectivity in estimating future growth. You know that high growth rates cannot last indefinitely simply because of the law of large numbers. But claiming that you know exactly when growth will slow down and how much it will slow by is not only arrogant, it is fraudulent. When creating a corporate model, you should therefore construct the time line so as to be able to evaluate different periods after which the explicit high growth forecast period ends.

Corporate models can also be structured to include a fade period in which cash flow growth gradually declines from the rate achieved just before the terminal cash flow period until a stable growth rate is obtained. During the fade period, the growth rate in revenues moves from the relatively high short-term growth rate to a sustainable equilibrium growth rate over the long term, the operating margin may move from the current returns to returns that are reasonable to expect in the long run, and capital expenditures move to levels that are consistent with growth rates and the lifetime of the assets. Figure 7.1 illustrates different time periods in a corporate model and the importance of the assumptions developed for the terminal forecast period.

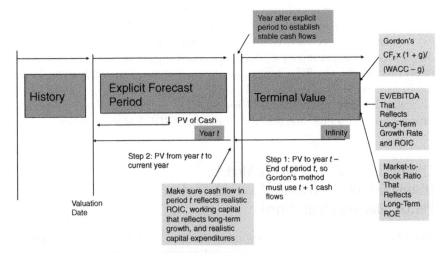

FIGURE 7.1 Terminal Value in Corporate Model

Development to Decommissioning: Phases in the Life of a Project Finance Model

Structuring the dates is critical in project finance models where alternative accounting, financing, and, most important, risk analysis occur for different phases of the project. Stages that occur when making a new investment can include the time period when the project is being developed before construction begins. This development period when risks that the project will not even proceed are high should be evaluated with a staged investment analysis that accounts for probabilities of proceeding to the next step. For this period, the probability of reaching different stages can be used to derive implicit required returns and changing required discount rates for different project stages. Other phases include the period when construction occurs and technical problems may arise, the period of operation of the project when revenues and expenses must be collected, and finally the period in which the project terminates. Many mechanical calculations in a model are different for these different time periods because cash flows into the project before commercial operation while it flows out of the project after the commercial operation. Further, the length of the periods in a model should be flexible to allow for different time periods to be simulated for various phases of a project such as a delay in construction. In modeling the time line of a project's financing you can think of the phases and dates in a project finance model like phases of a relationship. The dating period is the development period that has a high risk of exit; the construction period occurs after a commitment fee (the engagement ring) and risks include the relationship falling apart (technical risks). The marriage date is the commercial operation date when everything completely changes around. After this date you and the project eventually reach the end, or the decommissioning date.

The length of the individual periods represented by columns in a spreadsheet can differ in project finance models depending on the phase of the project. In many project finance models, the construction period is calculated on a monthly basis in order to accurately measure interest during construction since the interest calculation depends on accumulation of debt on a month-by-month basis. When the plant begins operation, the finance page of the model switches to semiannual periods because the debt is repaid on a semiannual basis. In order to construct time periods you can create switches that define each phase of the project as well as the important milestone dates such as the financial close and the commercial operation date when important events such as paying the commitment fee occur. The programming of different phases can become quite complex if the milestone dates do not start at the beginning of a month and if there are different time periods modeled in each phase of a portfolio of projects. This issue is important when there are multiple plants in a project and for real estate investments. An effective technique is to compute the percentages of operation and construction in different periods with a user-defined function instead of switches. This issue is addressed fully in Chapter 47.

A technique you can use to make the modeling relatively simple is to construct a period code that is less than one before operation, accumulates to the number 1 at the commercial operation date, and then becomes positive after commercial operation. Since the period counter is 1 at commercial operation and then grows by 1 for each subsequent period it measures the age of the project. After the model is created where the length of time periods is not annual it is convenient to show numbers on an annual basis and/or a semiannual basis and/or a quarterly basis.

Figure 7.2 illustrates the various stages of a project financing. The challenging finance theory associated with the different stages is how the value of a project changes as the risk of the project moves through the different phases. This issue is discussed in detail in Chapter 45.

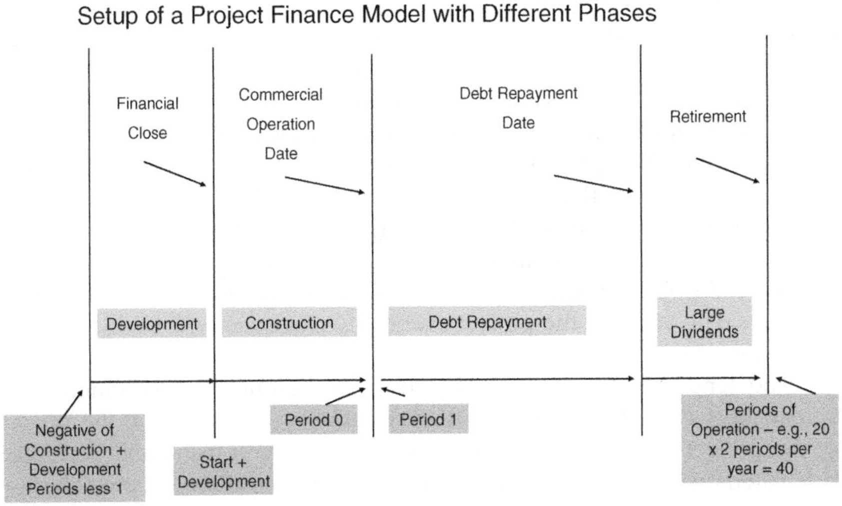

Setup of a Project Finance Model with Different Phases

FIGURE 7.2 Changing Risks in Phases of a Project Finance Model

Timing in Acquisition Models: Separating the Transaction Period, the Holding Period, and the Exit Period

For acquisition models, setting up time lines and time period indicators is just as important as in corporate or project finance models as alternative time periods affect risk and return. For acquisition models different calculations

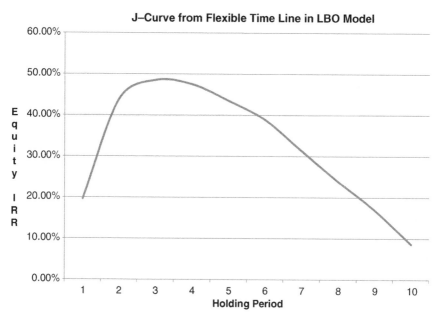

FIGURE 7.3 Effects of Different Holding Periods in Acquisition Models

are made for the acquisition period, the holding period, and the exit period. Through setting up time period switches, a corporate model can be effectively converted into an acquisition model where the transaction can be assumed to occur at different dates. Alternative holding periods can be represented to measure the optimal period to exit the investment. When initially constructing time periods in an acquisition model, a few guidelines can be followed:

- The acquisition period should be a separate period in the model that lasts only one day so that the mechanics of the ongoing calculations are not mixed up with the transaction assumptions.
- The period subsequent to the acquisition period can be a fraction of a year followed by annual periods until the final sale period.
- The exit period can be modeled in a separate column from the holding period in order to isolate assumptions with respect to the sale of the company.
- The MATCH and INDEX functions can be used to transfer different periods of a corporate model into an acquisition model.

Developing periods for an acquisition model in this manner allows you to simulate movements in the transaction date as well as alternative holding periods of the investment. You can then evaluate what happens to the rate of return earned on a transaction when the holding period of the transaction changes and when the exit multiple varies. With the flexible time periods defined, a J-curve illustrating how the rate of return is affected by the length of time between the purchase and the sale can be established. This type of analysis of the effect of different holding periods is illustrated in Figure 7.3. You could also show the graph along with different assumptions for terminal multiples and earnings before interest, taxes, depreciation, and amortization (EBITDA) growth rates. To make the graph you create a data table and vary the holding period while recording the equity internal rate of return. Data tables are explained in Chapter 16.

Structuring a Time Line to Measure History, Explicit Periods, and Terminal Periods in Corporate Models and Risk Phases in Project Finance Models

The remainder of this chapter addresses mechanical issues associated with defining time lines, switch variables, and methods to facilitate different modeling and risk analysis techniques. A few issues that make the time line process more manageable for all project types include:

- Begin the process by defining some kind of age variable (in your personal life, your age tells a lot about you; before you are born, you are assumed to have a negative age).
- Compute the number of months per period that will be in columns of your model from the age variable if the length of a period is input as a different number according to the project phase (such as monthly during construction and semiannual after construction). Use an IF statement with the age variable to define the periods per year (e.g., 12 or 2) in a model.
- Put time lines at the top of each spreadsheet page in which you make forecasts. The time line should generally show the start of the period and the end of the period in each column.
- Explicitly show the start date and the end date of the model, beginning with the first date of history, the date of the financial close, or the date of the transaction, depending on the model type.
- Specify the periodicity of the model in terms of the number of months represented in each column, the number of periods per year represented in a column, and sometimes even the number of days per period (using either a 360-day basis with the DAYS360 function or a 365-day basis by subtracting the end date from the beginning date).

- Add switch variables for the construction phase and the operating phase in a project finance model and for the historical period and explicit period in a corporate model.

Computing Start of Period and End of Period Dates

To set up a model that includes different time increments in alternative columns for different project phases as in some project finance models, it is useful to begin with a period counter that measures how old the project is in each period. Note that this step is not necessary if the timing increments of the model do not change as a function of different time periods. Once you have made such a time period counter and defined the periods included in a column, the dates of the model can be established. These dates can then be used to compute each phase of the project and a host of other essential items. To do this you can use the following step-by-step process:

- First compute the number of periods before commercial operation by adding the number of construction periods to the number of development periods. Use this number to make a period code starting with a negative number for the preoperation periods. If the construction plus development periods are 65, the initial negative number is −64 and the counter adds 1 to that number for each of the construction periods.
- Once the period code is defined with a negative number for periods before you were born (i.e., before the operation date), create a TRUE/FALSE switch that delineates the preoperation period from the operation period. This code defines the time period before which the project is running is created by the following statement:

Pre-Operation Period Code = Period < 1

- Third, use the time period switch from step 2 to define the number of months in each column. The months per period may be 1 during the construction period, meaning the model is computed on a monthly basis, and 6 afterward, implying that operation periods are computed on a semi-annual basis. The 1 and the 6 in the following equation should be defined in the timing input section of the model. Your model's periods could be measured quarterly or annually or use other time periods. It is generally a good idea to also compute the number of months a column takes to accumulate to a year, called the periods per year.

Months per Period in Column =IF(Construction Period, 1, 6)

Number of Period per Year in Column = 12/Months per Period

- Fourth, enter the start date and the end date for each column using the EDATE and the EOMONTH functions as explained in the next paragraph. The ending date should generally be established first and the beginning date is the ending date plus one day. Start with the ending period (the first period is the start date of the model), and increment the date using the EDATE function and the months per period.

Ending Period Date = EDATE(Beginning Period, Months per Period) − 1

Next Beginning Period Date = Ending Period Date + 1

Very First Ending Date in Model = Model Start Date − 1

In general it is not useful to work with days if you want to increment dates. Instead, when increasing a date by one month, the new date cannot be incremented by simply adding a constant number of days to the prior date, because each month does not have the same number of days. Unlike the number of months in a year, which stays constant at 12, this days-per-month problem complicates the analysis of dates. For people working with hourly data, similar problems can arise when there are not 24 hours in a day, because, for example, clocks are changed for daylight savings time. To resolve this problem, instead of working with days to increment dates, you can use the EDATE function or the DATE function to directly increment a date by the number of months instead of by the number of days. When using the EDATE function the number of months is used to increment a date: EDATE (prior date, months as defined by months per period in column). The EOMONTH function takes you to the last date in a month from the defined starting date. EOMONTH(1/1/2016,0) gives you the last day in January. You can also use the DATE function, which uses the YEAR, MONTH, and DAY arguments. To use the DATE function, you should refer to the previous date, and the periods per year should be added to the MONTH argument. Once you have defined the periods per year in a column from the switches that you define, the DATE function would be DATE(YEAR(prior date), MONTH (prior date) + periods per year, DAY(prior date)).

Quarterly models are often used in real estate analysis. When working with dates for a quarterly model there is no analogous function that can easily establish the end of a quarter or the start of the next quarter in a similar manner to the EDATE and the EOMONTH functions. This means that quarterly calculations can sometimes be difficult. In particular, if you have a monthly model and you want to aggregate data across quarters, you need to define the end of the quarter corresponding to each monthly period in the model. To make things easy, you can create a user-defined function. The following function accepts a date and then computes the end of the quarter corresponding to that date. It works by first defining the month of a quarter given the month in the date. Next, the user-defined function uses the EOMONTH function to establish the date associated with the end of the quarter. This function demonstrates how you can access most other spreadsheet functions in a user-defined function or in a macro by using the WORKSHEET.FUNCTION statement.

```
Function EOQtr(date1)
If Month(date1) = 1 Or Month(date1) = 4 Or Month(date1) = 7 Or Month(date1) = 10 Then mnth_eoq = 2
If Month(date1) = 2 Or Month(date1) = 5 Or Month(date1) = 8 Or Month(date1) = 11 Then mnth_eoq = 1
If Month(date1) = 3 Or Month(date1) = 6 Or Month(date1) = 9 Or Month(date1) = 12 Then mnth_eoq = 0
EOQtr = WorksheetFunction.EoMonth(date1, month1)
End Function
```

TRUE and FALSE Switches in Modeling Time Periods

When creating a switch variable that has a value of TRUE or FALSE for a time period phase you can think of a light switch that is either turned on or off. In many places light or power switches have a number 1 representing on and a 0 to indicate off. In a project finance model, the construction phase, operating phase, debt repayment phase, and specific dates should be defined using TRUE/FALSE switch variables that are switched on or off depending on dates defined in the model. In a corporate model similar TRUE/FASLE switch variables should be developed for the historical period, the explicit forecast period and the terminal value period. Use of the logical variables that have a value of TRUE or FALSE was already introduced in Chapter 5 and they are essential in creating the time line section of a model. Using the fact that TRUE is equal to 1 and FALSE is equal to 0 means that you can use these variables to eliminate the need for long IF statements and make the model more transparent.

A switch can be created for defining a time phase by simply using an equal sign (for example, period = test date, period <= 0 or period < decommissioning date). It can also be created using the AND, OR, or NOT functions (for example, AND (period > 0, period <= retirement date) defines a switch for when the plant is operating. When programming the time phase switches, two little structuring hints can be useful. First, the switches always compare a date or a period counter generally at the top of the page that changes for each column to a fixed defined date. Second, it is good to place the starting and ending dates that define a phase in the special left-hand side columns that are between the row title and the model equation. Assuming the time line is in the first row, the switch is evaluated for column G, and the criterion for the terminal year is in cell D10, the formulas for the switches would have the following form:

Terminal Switch: Time Line Year (G1) = Terminal Date ($D$10)

Explicit Switch: AND(Time Line (G1) > Start Criteria ($D$11), Time Line (G1) <= Terminal Date($D$10))

Repayment Switch: AND(Time Line(G1)>COD, Time Line(G1)<Debt Retirement Date)

Note how the fixing of cells works in these formulas. The time line should not have a dollar sign in the column, but the column of cell reference for the criteria should be fixed with the F4 shortcut key. An illustration of setting up time period codes is shown in Figure 7.4. In this example, which shows the time line for selected columns of a project finance model, each formula is very short and simple, conforming to the transparency objective of a model. The inputs that drive the time switches are shown in the special column to the left of the calculations. Different age variables are computed from the switches by, for example, accumulating the TRUE values for the operation phase. The switch variables shown in Figure 7.4 include conditional formatting that allows you to immediately see when it is turned on. This can be done by shading the area and using the conditional formatting feature that allows you to color variables depending on text that contains a certain letter. Since FALSE does not contain the letter T and TRUE does not contain the letter F you can use these letters to create your format.

	From	To	No	Check							
Age in years					-2	-2	-2	-1	0	1	5
Period counter					-24	-23	-22	-1	0	1	9
Pre-COD Switch					TRUE	TRUE	TRUE	TRUE	TRUE	FALSE	FALSE
Months in period					1	1	1	1	1	6	6
Periods per year					12	12	12	12	12	2	2
Start of period					4/1/11	5/1/11	6/1/11	3/1/13	4/1/13	5/1/13	5/1/17
End of period					4/30/11	5/31/11	6/30/11	3/31/13	4/30/13	10/31/13	10/31/17
Year	From	To	No	Check	2011	2011	2011	2013	2013	2013	2017
Development period	11/1/10	5/1/11	6	TRUE	TRUE	FALSE	FALSE	FALSE	FALSE	FALSE	FALSE
Financial close date	5/1/11	5/1/11	1	TRUE	FALSE	TRUE	FALSE	FALSE	FALSE	FALSE	FALSE
Construction period	5/1/11	5/1/13	24	TRUE	FALSE	TRUE	TRUE	TRUE	TRUE	FALSE	FALSE
Commercial Operation Date	5/1/13	5/1/13	1	TRUE	FALSE	FALSE	FALSE	FALSE	FALSE	TRUE	FALSE
Month before COD	4/1/13	5/1/13	1	TRUE	FALSE	FALSE	FALSE	FALSE	FALSE	TRUE	FALSE
Operation period	5/1/13	5/1/33	10	FALSE	FALSE	FALSE	FALSE	FALSE	FALSE	TRUE	TRUE
Debt Repayment Period	5/1/13	5/1/26	10	FALSE	FALSE	FALSE	FALSE	FALSE	FALSE	TRUE	TRUE
Debt Retirement Period	5/1/26	4/1/13	0	FALSE	FALSE	FALSE	FALSE	FALSE	FALSE	FALSE	FALSE
Re-financing Date	5/1/17	5/1/17	0		FALSE	FALSE	FALSE	FALSE	FALSE	FALSE	FALSE
Re-financing Repay Per	11/1/17	11/1/30	1	FALSE	FALSE	FALSE	FALSE	FALSE	FALSE	FALSE	FALSE

FIGURE 7.4 Illustration of Time Switches in Project Finance Model

Some examples of using switch variables after they have been defined in the model include:

Construction Expenditures = Total Cost/Construction Period × Construction Period Switch

Debt Balance = IF(Historical Period Switch, Actual Amount, Opening Balance – Repayments)

Terminal Proceeds = Terminal EV/EBITDA Ratio × EBITDA × Terminal Switch

Interest during Construction = Interest Accrued × Construction Switch

Stable Capital Expenditures = Capital Expenditures/Depreciation × Depreciation × Stable Period Switch

After you are finished defining the time line you can create an annual page that computes all of the variables on an annual or quarterly or semiannual basis. This process involves using the SUMIF and/or SUMIFS functions along with clicking on entire rows of the spreadsheet page with detailed analysis (something like the page shown in Figure 7.4). Conversion from periodic data to more aggregated date is accomplished by using the SUMIF function as illustrated here for establishing annual data and compiling quarterly data from the end of quater (EOqtr) user-defined function discussed earlier.

Annual Data Amount = SUMIF(Year Row in Periodic Model, Year in Annual Model Page, Data Item in Periodic Model)

Quarterly Data Amount = SUMIF(End of Quarter Row Constructed from EOqtr Function, Quarter Established from the EOMONTH Function in on a Quarterly Page, Item in Periodic Model)

The way in which this process can be made transparent and performed efficiently is described in Chapter 15 in the context of making annual graphs.

Computing the Age of a Project in Years on a Monthly, Quarterly, or Semiannual Basis

When developing a model where time increments are not computed on an annual basis (e.g., a monthly model or a quarterly model), it is sometimes useful to express the age of a project or the age of an acquisition in years. Many inputs such as the credit spread, the operation and maintenance expense, the tax depreciation rate, production changes, the extraordinary maintenance, and other variables depend on the age of a project rather than the calendar year, and these variables are often input to the model on an annual rather than a periodic basis. Computing the age of a project in years can be a little tricky in cases where the number of periods is not constant over time. There may be a detailed monthly analysis that is deemed necessary for the initial few years of a project's life, after which a quarterly model could be used.

To calculate the age of a project in years and to make many other analyses with dates, you can use a two-step process. The first step is computing a variable that counts the number of periods (months, quarters, semiannual periods) in the year and then repeats for subsequent years. In a monthly model, you would count from 1 to 12, and in a quarterly model you would count from 1 to 4 for each year in the model. The second step after counting the periods in the year is to compute an age variable in years that increases once a new year has been reached. Increments in the age occur when the counter variable has a value of 1, as if your birthday is on the first day of January. A step-by-step process is illustrated next that addresses these issues and applies to many modeling applications, for example, when you are working with hourly data or when you want to summarize detailed historic statistics on an aggregated basis:

Step 1   Compute a period counter variable. In a project finance model without changing periods per year, this could be calculated using an IF statement where the counting restarts after the maximum number of periods is reached. For example, when the counter reaches 12, reset the counter to 1:

IF(Prior Period Counter = Maximum Periods, Reset to 1, Increment Counter by 1)

Step 2   Increment the age variable when the counter defined previously is equal to 1. This is like having a birthday on one day (or month, or quarter) and increasing your age in years on your birthday.

IF(Counter Variable = 1, Increase Age, Don't Increase Age)

Difficulties in this process involve making sure that the counter begins with a value of 1 at the start of commercial operation and that the counter variable appropriately restarts when the periods of the model change. This can be done by only starting the process in the operation period.

The Magic of a HISTORIC Switch in a Corporate Model

A HISTORIC switch may be the most essential concept in efficiently designing a corporate model. The most painful part of a corporate model is generally acquiring historical data (sometimes from copying PDF files) and finding the data for plant balances, maintenance capital expenditures, production levels, and so forth. The last thing you want to do is to have to repeat this process over and over again each period when new data become available. Application of a historical switch can be established by using a simple logical variable just below the time period as follows:

HISTORIC Switch : (Year <= Last Historical Year)

In this equation the last historical year is a defined input in the model. Placing a historical switch at the top of the page just below the years of the model allows you to do the following:

■ You can change the last historical year or quarter of data and seamlessly add another period of historic data without having to change any of the formulas, without having to add columns, and without having to change the valuation formulas in the model. You simply have to change the input variable that defines the last historic period of the model.

■ When entering a formula for assumptions, like the ratio of accounts receivable (A/R) to revenues, you can make a formula that uses the HISTORIC switch as follows:

Historical A/R to Revenues = IF(HISTORIC Switch, A/R Level/Revenues)

This formula produces a value of FALSE for periods after the historical period and the calculation will automatically update when new data is entered as subsequent data becomes available. It is often useful to leave out the FALSE condition in an IF statement and allow the model to present FALSE when something does not satisfy the logical test of an IF statement. In using the preceding equation, the FALSE result shows up in the projected years.

■ You can model miscellaneous items such as other income as the last historical level or as a fixed level of zero by using another IF function as follows:

Historical/Projected Other Income = IF(HISTORIC Switch, Historical Level, Prior Level)

or

Historical/Projected Other Income = IF(HISTORIC Switch, Historical Level, AVERAGEIF(HISTORIC Switch, TRUE, Historical Amount)

or

Historical/Projected Other Income = IF(HISTORIC Switch, Historical Level, Fixed Input Amount)

If a fixed input amount is used corresponding to the third equation, the fixed level should be shown in the special column to the left of the historical data after the row titles.

- You can enter assumptions that have varying time series amounts for different years by using the INDEX function together with the HISTORIC switch. This formula may apply to items such as revenue growth, cost of goods sold as a percent of revenues, and capital expenditures to sales. The historical switch also facilitates the presentation of assumptions next to the historical level. The way you implement this is to use a scenario code that only applies after the historical period. In this case the formula is a bit long but very useful:

Historical/Projected Price = IF(HISTORIC Switch, Historical Level,
INDEX(Scenario Column, Code))

- For some assets and liabilities that are held constant after the historical period, the HISTORIC switch can be used together with an IF statement to hold the values at the value of the last historical balance sheet. This type of process applies to items like goodwill, the level of other assets, and unfunded pension liabilities. In this case for balance sheet items the following formula can be applied:

Historical Projected Balance = IF(HISTORIC Switch, Historical, Prior Level)

Using selected columns of a model, Figure 7.5 illustrates the various different ways the HISTORIC switch can be used in developing assumptions and how it can present the historic data next to the forecast assumptions. The simple incorporation of a time switch allows the presentation of assumptions to be more transparent. In addition, the time switch makes the model flexible with respect to the addition of new time periods when more data become available. The formulas shown in column G illustrate how the historical switch in row 3 is used to develop different types of assumptions.

The historical switch is also helpful in making a series of calculations after the inputs are developed in the working section of a model. The switch can be used to compute revenues, operating expenses as well as depreciation expense, and items associated with debt issues. In developing formulas where growth rate assumptions are made, the growth rate assumption can be entered first and then the amount can be derived with the historical switch as follows:

Projected Amount = IF(HISTORIC Switch, Actual, Prior Year Amount
× (1 + Growth Rate))

AECD	E		F	G	I	J	P	Q
1	Year				2006	2007	2013	2014
2	Last Historic Period	Base Case ▾	2012		FALSE	FALSE	FALSE	FALSE
3	Historic Switch			=M1<=$F$2---->	TRUE	TRUE	FALSE	FALSE
177	**Revenue Assumptions**							
178	Steel Price							
179	Steel Revenues		USD Mil		8,014	11,908	0	0
180	Historic Price		USD/Ton	=IF(I3,I7/I9*1000)---->	554.33	780.24	FALSE	FALSE
181								
182	Base Price Case						950.00	940.00
183	Low Price Case						900.00	800.00
184	High Price Case						1,050.00	1,100.00
185	Price Sensitivity Case			=IF(I3,I180,INDEX(I182:I185,$F$186))			1,060.00	1,060.00
186	Base Price Case		1		554.33	780.24	950.00	940.00
187								
251	Variable G&A Expenses				194	370		
252	Historic Variable Cost as Pct of Revenues				2.34%	2.88%		
253	Projected Variable SG&A Expense Percent		3.25%				3.25%	3.25%
254	SG&A Variable Cost - Historic and Projected			=IF(I3,I252,I253)---->	2.34%	2.88%	3.25%	3.25%
255								
367	Assumptions for Income Items Not in EBITDA							
368	Other Income Statement Items			=IF(I3,I21+I22,AVERAGEIF(3:3,TRUE,369:369))				
369	Loss on Disposal/Impariment of Assets				41.00	33.00	290.29	290.29
371	Other Gains/Losses				(49.00)	(63.00)	-	-
372				=IF(I3,I30+I31+I32+I33,$F$371)				
373	Income from Associated Investments							
374	Historic Income				40.00	88.00	-	-
375	Historic Balance Sheet Associated Investments				1,494.00	592.00	-	-
376	Average Balance of Associated Investments				1,494.00	1,043.00	280.50	-
1560				=AVERAGE(H375:I375)				
1561								

FIGURE 7.5 Illustration of Uses of the HISTORIC Switch in a Corporate Finance Model

When working through model equations, it is useful to test whether all accounts have been included in the balance sheet and whether the historical amounts computed correspond to the historical amounts reported in the financial statements. If the EBITDA is computed as revenues less operating expenses other than depreciation, the difference between the computed level and the actual historical reported level can also be tested. If you want to include tests of equations only in the historical period, the difference can be summed over the historical period using the HISTORIC switch together with the SUMIF function as follows:

Sum of Differences versus History = SUMIF(HISTORIC Switch, TRUE, Computed Difference)

Once the sum of the difference is computed, a variable can be created by testing whether the sum is equal to 0 and then including this variable in the audit page of the model:

Test of History : Sum of Difference using SUMIF with Historic Switch = 0

One of the most important ways the historic switch is used in a corporate model is in writing equations for various accounts such as the plant balance, the cash balance, the debt balance, and the equity balance. Here the HISTORIC switch can be used to move seamlessly from reported historical levels to projected levels without having different equations across the columns and without making the formulas too long. When you compute these balance sheet items, the closing balance should come directly from the balance sheet in historical years; for projected years, the closing balance is the opening balance plus changes that are projected for the current period. Using the historical switch in this manner is illustrated with the following formula:

Closing Balance = IF(HISTORIC Switch, Historical Amount;
Opening Balance + Change)

Transferring Data from a Corporate Model to an Acquisition Model Using MATCH and INDEX Functions

One of the most useful programming techniques that can be applied in many circumstances is combining the MATCH and INDEX function as introduced in Chapter 4. An example of this technique is to create flexible timing for an acquisition model derived from a completed stand-alone corporate model. To demonstrate this process, take the example that a stand-alone corporate model is computed with annual or quarterly data. After you have made your corporate model with a completed balance sheet you would like to transfer selected data such as prospective EBITDA into a new sheet that corresponds to an assumed transaction date for an acquisition (that may be in the middle of the period). To do this, you can use the following approach:

- Assuming the corporate model is computed on an annual basis and the acquisition model will be computed on a quarterly or a monthly basis, the YEAR function can be used to define the yearly data to be transferred.
- After the year number is established in the stand-alone corporate model, use the MATCH function to find a row or column number that can associate dates in the acquisition model page with the corporate model. The best way to use the MATCH function is not to worry about highlighting partial columns and fixing ranges, but to just click on the entire row. This finds the column number associated with the year from the corporate model:

Column Number = MATCH(Year in Acquisition Model, Entire Row of
Years in Corporate Model)

- Once the column number is established from the MATCH function, you can use the INDEX function to find a variable given a row or column number or both. Assume the revenues are being transferred from the corporate model to the acquisition model. The INDEX function can be used as follows:

Revenue = INDEX(Entire Annual Revenues Row in Corporate Model, Column Number from Above from Match)

Figure 7.6 illustrates how data can be extracted from a corporate model and converted into an acquisition model that begins at an assumed transaction date. Results of the MATCH function are highlighted with a border while the input data that comes from the corporate model using the INDEX function is colored red.

	D	E	F	G	J	K
1	**Dates**					
2	Start Date	Downside Case ▼	05/01/12	01/01/13	01/01/16	01/01/17
3	End Date	05/01/12	12/31/12	12/31/13	12/31/16	05/01/17
4	Year	=YEAR(F3)---->	2012	2013	2016	2017
5	Column from MATCH	→	17	18	21	22
6		=MATCH(F4,'Financial Model Assumptions'!2:2)				
7	Holding Period Switch		TRUE	TRUE	TRUE	TRUE
8	Terminal Period Switch		FALSE	FALSE	FALSE	TRUE
9		=AND(F3='Transaction Assumptions'!$F$7,F7)				
10	Fraction of Year	=YEARFRAC(F2,F3+1)	67%	100%	100%	34%
11						
12	**Operating Section**					
13	Annual	=INDEX('Corp Model'!292:292,I5)*I7				
14	Revenues		1,298.71	1,243.05	2,094.44	2,326.23
15	Expenses		1,315.67	1,260.93	2,041.99	2,275.42
16	Capital Exp		72.72	73.45	104.77	106.87
17		=INDEX('Corp Model'!294:294,I5)*I7				
18	Synergies		80.00	80.00	80.00	80.00
19	EBITDA		63.05	62.12	132.45	130.81
20						
21	Periodic					
22	Revenues	=F14*F10---->	865.81	1,243.05	2,094.44	781.87
23	Expenses		877.11	1,260.93	2,041.99	764.79
24	Capital Expenditures		48.48	73.45	104.77	35.92
25	Synergies		53.33	80.00	80.00	26.89
26						
27	Terminal Proceeds					
28	Exit EV/EBITDA		12.00	12.00	12.00	12.00
29	Exit Proceeds		-	-	-	1,569.71

FIGURE 7.6 Illustration of Extracting Data from a Corporate Model into an Acquisition Model Using MATCH and INDEX

Projecting Revenues, Expenses, and Capital Expenditures to Derive Pretax Cash Flow

When constructing the section of a model that forecasts essential pretax free cash flow items other than working capital changes—revenues, operating expenditures, and capital expenditures—making clear presentations using short formulas that are easy to follow should guide the modeling process. If possible, the working analysis that computes these items should begin with production capacity and quantity demand where the amount of new capacity is connected to the demand and production through making capital expenditures. A mistake sometimes made in some corporate models is to assume that historical capital expenditures that occurred during periods of surplus capacity continue after the capacity becomes constrained even though revenues continue to grow. In project finance models a challenge in computing the capital expenditure component of pretax cash flow is making the model flexible enough to simulate delays in construction and at the same time reflect the different patterns of construction expenditures that may occur over time.

Transparent Calculations of Pretax Cash Flow

To document how formulas for capacity levels, prices, capacity expansion, and revenues are computed, you should try to make the equations as transparent as possible. For a project finance model you generally show the capacity, the production and the prices that drive revenues, expenses, and capital expenditures as illustrated in Figure 8.1. If you set up the calculations in a logical order, they should be clear and easy to understand for people who are reading the model and who have no idea about how to type a single

Start of period					09/01/12	10/01/12	04/01/13	05/01/13	11/01/13	05/01/14
End of period					09/30/12	10/31/12	04/30/13	10/31/13	04/30/14	10/31/14
Year					2012	2012	2013	2013	2014	2014
EBITDA and Capital Expenditures to Compute Pre-tax Flow										
Total Capacity	MW	Input MW	120		0.00	0.00	0.00	120.00	120.00	120.00
Capacity factor	%	Lookup			FALSE	FALSE	FALSE	25%	27%	27%
Availability										
Days in the period	days				30	31	30	184	181	184
Hours in period	hours				720	744	720	4416	4344	4416
Real FIT	EUR/MWh	Base FIT	60		60	60	60	60	60	60
Annual Inflation rate					2.50%	2.50%	2.50%	2.50%	2.75%	2.75%
Periodic Inflation rate					0.21%	0.21%	0.21%	1.24%	1.37%	1.37%
Inflation Index	Start Inflation	01-nov-12			1.000	1.000	1.012	1.025	1.039	1.053
Nominal FIT	EUR/MWh				60.00	60.00	60.75	61.50	62.34	63.19
Revenues	**000 EUR'**				**0.00**	**0.00**	**0.00**	**14509.96**	**15625.77**	**16101.70**
O&M costs	EUR/MWh	Cost/MWH	20		20	20	20	20	20	20
Inflation index					104%	104%	105%	107%	108%	110%
Nominal O&M /MWh					20.78	20.82	21.08	21.34	21.64	21.93
Total O&M	* 000 EUR				0.00	0.00	0.00	2,827.75	3,045.20	3,137.95
Other costs	*000 EUR	EUR/year	4,000		0.00	0.00	0.00	0.00	0.00	0.00
Operating Expenses					**0.00**	**0.00**	**0.00**	**2827.75**	**3045.20**	**3137.95**
Total Costs	* 000 EUR/MW	Cost/kW	1,800		108,000	108,000	108,000	108,000	108,000	108,000
Construction Period	Month				17	18	24	24	24	24
Weibull	Percent	Alpha	1.72		0	0	0	FALSE	FALSE	FALSE
S curve	%	Cstr Mnth	24		3.19%	2.78%	0.99%	0.00%	0.00%	0.00%
Capital Expenses	*** 000 EUR/MW**				**3,449.83**	**2,997.67**	**1,065.07**	**0.00**	**0.00**	**0.00**

FIGURE 8.1 Illustration of Working Analysis to Compute Pretax Cash Flow in a Project Finance Model

formula in a spreadsheet. A fundamental point in project finance models is that calculations should be documented clearly, showing the units in a column to the right of the name of the item being calculated. Further, where factors used to derive the calculation come from an input item in the assumptions section, each of the driver inputs should be shown in another column to the left of the calculations. This is why it is essential when you are setting up a sheet to leave blank columns between the titles of the rows and the calculations. In Figure 8.1, inputs that drive the calculations are shown in red, implying that they came from the input sheet that has a red tab color. Each row includes units, which goes a long way in explaining how the calculations are made.

Capital expenditures in a project finance model or a real estate model are often computed through multiplying the total construction cost by an S-curve. The S-curve is a series of percentages that add up to 1.0 across columns of the sheet that are multiplied by the total construction cost in deriving period by period capital expenditures. When making the project finance model flexible in terms of capital expenditures you can convert the S-curve into a formula that is easily changed when, for example, a different construction period is assumed and/or a different spending pattern is assumed. To accomplish this, you can fit different types of distributions to represent the S-curve. In Figure 8.1 the S-curve is derived from a Weibull distribution that accepts inputs for deviation, midlevel, and the skewness parameters.

In the case of corporate finance models, the documentation of formulas is different than project finance models because of the structure of the inputs that are derived from historical analysis. For corporate finance it is often not possible to display the input assumption in a column to the left of the calculations. Instead, the rows of historic and projected data from the assumption section can be repeated just above the working calculations to make the analysis transparent for a reader of the model. Figure 8.2 illustrates this notion by illustrating a portion of the pretax cash flow analysis for a corporate model. This model is launched from the capacity balance calculation that is in turn driven by industry demand calculations. Once the amount of new capacity is known, computation of capital expenditures comes from the amount of new capacity added along with the assumed cost of new capacity. The capacity calculations are also used directly or indirectly in computing revenues as you cannot sell a product if you do not have enough capacity to produce it. Figure 8.2 also illustrates the issue of separating fixed and variable costs in an

Year Base Case	2006	2007	2011	2012	2013	2016	2017
Last Historic Period	FALSE	FALSE	FALSE	TRUE	FALSE	FALSE	FALSE
Historic Switch	TRUE	TRUE	TRUE	TRUE	FALSE	FALSE	FALSE
Analysis of EBITDA and Capital Expenditures							
Capital Expenditure Analysis							
Capacity Balance							
Opening Capacity	-	14,746.14	16,620.82	16,787.02	16,954.89	18,574.89	19,114.89
Add: New Investment Cap Exp	-	-	-	-	540.00	540.00	540.00
Closing Balance	14,746.14	15,567.24	16,787.02	16,954.89	17,494.89	19,114.89	19,654.89
Capacity per USD Spent	-	-	-	-	1.80	1.80	1.80
Increase in Capacity	-	-	-	-	540.00	540.00	540.00
Maintenance Capital Expenditures	300.00	350.00	500.00	657.00	750.00	795.91	811.82
Investment Expenditure	351.00	394.00	781.00	604.00	300.00	300.00	300.00
Total Expenditure	651.00	744.00	1,281.00	1,261.00	1,050.00	1,095.91	1,111.82
Revenue Analysis							
Steel Price (Assumptions)	554.33	780.24	1,053.31	997.05	950.00	960.00	988.80
Steel Production Growth Rate	0.00%	5.57%	3.63%	-6.45%	1.00%	1.00%	1.00%
Steel Production b/4 Cap Constrain	14,457.00	15,262.00	15,232.00	14,250.00	14,392.50	15,123.70	15,274.93
Steel Production w/ Cap Constraint	14,457.00	15,262.00	15,232.00	14,250.00	14,392.50	15,123.70	15,274.93
Utilisation Percent	98.04%	98.04%	90.74%	84.05%	82.27%	79.12%	77.72%
Steel Revenues	8,014.00	11,908.00	16,044.00	14,208.00	13,672.88	14,518.75	15,103.85
Other Revenues Growth	0.00%	242.09%	-19.64%	45.51%	10.00%	10.00%	10.00%
Other Revenues	278.00	951.00	356.00	518.00	391.60	626.78	473.84
Total Revenues	8,292.00	12,859.00	16,400.00	14,726.00	14,064.48	15,145.53	15,577.69
Growth Rate in Revenues		55.08%	22.44%	-10.21%	-4.49%	3.34%	2.85%
Operating Expense Analysis							
Cost of Revenue							
Growth in Fixed Cost	0.00%	3.00%	3.00%	3.00%	3.00%	3.00%	3.00%
Fixed Cost	1,400.00	1,442.00	1,622.98	1,671.67	1,671.67	1,773.48	1,773.48
Variable Cost/Price	43.17%	48.58%	60.44%	62.40%	62.00%	62.00%	62.00%
Variable Cost per Unit	239.33	379.05	636.62	622.20	589.00	595.20	613.06
Total Cost	4,860.00	7,227.00	11,320.00	10,538.00	10,148.86	10,775.10	11,137.87

FIGURE 8.2 Illustration of Working Analysis to Compute EBITDA and Capital Expenditures in a Corporate Finance Model

analysis. After revenues are computed, the cash operating expense excluding depreciation and amortization are presented. Even if the company does not specify which expenses are fixed and variable, you can perform some statistical analysis to dissect the expenses once you have accumulated the historical data.

Many items in the working analysis section are modeled using the time period switches discussed in the previous chapter. In a project finance model the capacity of a project begins during the operating period defined with a timing switch. For a corporate model, the gross margin is computed using actual data with the historical switch when it is TRUE and then changes to the forecast assumptions when the historical period is FALSE.

Inflation and Growth Rates in Calculations of Pretax Cash Flow

Pretax cash flow items such as prices, variable operating cost per unit, and the cost of new capital expenditures per unit of new capacity added are influenced by the inflation rate. Other inputs such as demand may include assumptions with respect to real growth. In computing formulas for inflation rates or growth rates associated with these items, various problems can arise when time period lengths change in a model such as changing from monthly to semiannual periods and when the starting point for inflation indexes are not clearly laid out in the input section. Inflation should generally be included in the corporate and project finance models rather than making the analysis in real terms, as it is more difficult to convert depreciation and taxes into real terms than it is to add inflation and use the nominal cost of capital when making valuations.

Interest rates, growth rates, and inflation rates are generally input into a model in the assumption module as annual percentage rates. But when modeling inflation rates using periods that do not constitute annual periods, it is not accurate to simply compute the fraction of the year and multiply this fraction by the annual percentage. Dividing the annual inflation rate or growth rate by the periods in a year per column will result in overstatement of interest or inflation. This occurs because amounts that are adjusted by inflation or growth will be compounded in a model. Say the annual inflation rate is very high, such as 120 percent per annum. If the real expenditure for the year before the year's inflation is 100, then the level with inflation should be 220 after inflation is included. If you divide the 120 by 12 and use a periodic rate of 10 percent per month, then by the end of the year the inflation index compounds to 3.38 [$(1+10\%)^{12}$], resulting in a value of 338. This is different from the amount that you wanted, 220. To resolve this problem of overcompounding, the periodic rate can be established using the following formulas:

$$\text{End-of-Period Expenditure} = \text{Beginning of Period} \times$$
$$(1 + \text{Periodic Rate})\,\hat{}\,\text{Periods}$$

and

$$\text{End-of-Period Expenditure} = \text{Beginning of Period} \times (1 + \text{Annual Rate})$$

or

$$(1 + \text{Periodic Rate})\,\hat{}\,\text{Periods} = (1 + \text{Annual Rate})$$

$$(1 + \text{Periodic Rate}) = (1 + \text{Annual Rate})\,\hat{}\,(1/\text{Periods})$$

$$\text{Periodic Rate} = (1 + \text{Annual Rate})\,\hat{}\,(1/\text{Periods}) - 1$$

To apply this periodic inflation or growth rate formula in your model, you can use the fraction of a full year that the model period represents. This is illustrated in the following formula:

$$\text{Periodic Rate} = (1 + \text{Annual Rate})\,\hat{}\,(\text{Months per Period}/12) - 1$$

In modeling items that are subject to inflation you should be careful about specifying the inflation start date and making inflation indices consistent with the assumed real level of costs, prices, or capital expenditures that are part of the input section. If inflation assumptions are made, the fundamental data for prices, operating expenses, and capital expenditures per unit are input in real terms at some given date. To start the inflation index at the appropriate date, you can create a switch that is only TRUE after the inflation begins. Then when you compute the inflation index as (1 + periodic inflation rate) you can turn on the inflation rate only after the inflation start using the formula (1 + periodic inflation rate × inflation switch). This will keep the inflation index at 1 until the beginning of the inflation period. Figure 8.3 illustrates components of a

	A B C	D	L	M	AJ	AK	AL	AS	AT
4		Months in period		1	1	1	1	6	6
5		Periods per year		12	12	12	12	2	2
6		Start of period			09/01/12	10/01/12	11/01/12	11/01/13	05/01/14
7		End of period		10/31/10	09/30/12	10/31/12	11/30/12	04/30/14	10/31/14
8		Year			2012	2012	2012	2014	2014
206		Real FIT			60	60	60	60	60
207		Annual Inflation rate	=LOOKUP(O8,$I$53:$Q$53,$I$57:$Q$57)---->		2.50%	2.50%	2.50%	2.75%	2.75%
208		Periodic Inflation rate	=(1+O207)^(1/O5)-1---->		0.21%	0.21%	0.21%	1.37%	1.37%
209		Inflation Index	=M209*(1+N208*(N6>=$H$209))---->	1	1.000	1.000	1.002	1.039	1.053
210		Nominal FIT	=P206*P209---->		60.00	60.00	60.12	62.34	63.19

FIGURE 8.3 Illustration of Periodic Inflation Calculations in Project Finance Model

working analysis with varying inflation rates, adjustments to convert periodic rates from annual rates, and a start date for inflation that is not the same as the start date of the model.

Valuation Analysis from Prefinancing, Pretax Cash Flow

Once you have calculated revenues, expenses, and capital expenditures, you can compute a few important financial ratios that test whether your results are reasonable before proceeding to the next step of the model. In a project finance model you could calculate the pretax project internal rate of return (IRR) from EBITDA minus capital expenditures. For corporate models you can compute the level of EBITDA relative to gross assets that generate EBITDA. If the pretax IRR in a project finance model (that can be computed on both a real basis and a nominal basis) is lower than the interest rate, then you do not have to go any further with all of the tax and financing aspects of the model.

A basic proposition of finance is that the return should be greater than the cost of capital. If the project has a lower return than the interest rate it is probably realizing a return below the cost of capital and it will not be feasible. By contrast, if the pretax project IRR yields a very high number, you should step back and ask yourself what makes your project so special and why this high IRR will not prompt companies all over the world to try to copy your project. If other companies invest in similar hotels, electricity plants, or manufacturing plants because of the high IRRs, more capacity will be built. Then there will be a whole lot of pressure on prices, margins, and fixed price contracts. Like so many things in life, when the pretax IRR seems too good to be true, it probably is.

In a corporate model, computing the level of EBITDA to assets accomplishes a task similar to evaluating the pretax project IRR. You may label this is the pretax return on investment (although the return should be computed after depreciation.) The net assets can be computed from the accumulated capital expenditures and working capital. Once the ratio of EBITDA to net assets is computed, the important next step is to compare projected levels to the historical ratio. This notion of comparing history with projection is discussed in detail in Chapter 24 using the return on invested capital. If the rate of return on assets skyrockets compared to the history, you need to ask what has changed about the company that allows it to earn such high returns. What you probably need to do when the ratio changes like this is go back and revisit your revenue, expense, and capital expenditure assumptions.

CHAPTER 9

Moving from Pretax Cash Flow to After-Tax Free Cash Flow

You may reject the theory proposed by Miller and Modigliani or you may be a true believer in free cash flow and the irrelevance of the financial structure when assessing investment value. No matter what your opinion of the theory itself, the general approach of separating calculations between operations and financing that these two professors developed is central to the structure of any financial model. The structure of a model (with the exception of financial institution models) becomes much more logical and rigorous when free cash flow is calculated first and only afterward are the debt and equity split in the cash flows included. Once free cash flow is computed from EBITDA less capital expenditures, working capital changes, operating taxes, changes in deferred taxes, and changes in warranty and other provisions, a host of valuations and financial statistics can also be calculated.

In a project finance model the project internal rate of return (project IRR) (but not the equity IRR) can be computed from free cash flow and the value of the project assets at different sale dates. In a corporate finance model the return on invested capital (but not the return on equity) can be derived and the discounted cash flow value can be established with the after-tax free cash flow. Given the usefulness of starting with after-tax operating cash flow and then later splitting that cash flow into debt and equity cash flow, this chapter addresses working capital, depreciation, and deferred tax items that are necessary to move from pretax cash flow to after-tax free cash flow calculation.

Working Capital Analysis

Once revenues, expenses, and capital expenditures have been established, the primary remaining items to compute free cash flow are the working capital changes and taxes. Working capital changes can be thought of as adjusting the EBITDA to reflect the true cash flow collected by the company. Working capital is often computed directly from revenues and operating expenses through inputting the ratio of accounts receivable to revenues, inventories to cost of goods sold, and so forth. For purposes of constructing a model, working capital includes trade working capital and does not include cash, short-term securities, short-term debt, or current maturities of long-term debt. If the days sales outstanding are 30, meaning that you have to wait a month to get paid after you sell an item, then the one month of revenues that is not collected represents about 8.33 percent of total annual revenues. The working capital section must be developed after revenues and expenses have been computed, because the 8.33 percent is multiplied by the level of sales.

The working capital section first derives the level of different working capital items, which will appear on the projected balance sheet. After computing the total level of current assets and the total level of current liabilities, working capital is expressed as the difference between the two amounts. Finally, once the level of working capital is computed, the change in working capital is calculated as the current period working capital less the prior period working capital. Financial institution models such as models of a retail bank follow a similar approach where loan balances, deposit balances, and reserve balances are the starting point of the model. Only after the balances have been established are the cash flow implications derived from the difference in the balances between one period and the next.

One complexity in computing working capital may involve deriving the level of inventories and accounts receivable during periods of declining demand, like the fall in sales that occurred after the financial crisis of 2008. In a detailed model, production can be computed separately from unit sales, implying that inventories grow with production and are used up as sales are made. Here an opening and closing balance of inventories can be established where additions to inventories are a function of production while deductions from inventories can be modeled as a function of demand. If there is a sudden reduction in demand without a similar reduction in production, the inventory balances will shoot up. When sales of a retailing business decline and inventories remain in the stores, the ratio of inventories to sales and cost of goods sold will rise.

Problems in Computing Depreciation Expense in Corporate Models Involving Asset Retirements

In corporate finance models, project finance models, and acquisition models, a well-structured analysis should calculate free cash flow before incorporating financing of assets. It bears restating that there must be a clear distinction between financing and operating analysis in all model types. Previous discussion covered the modeling of revenues, expenses, and capital expenditures as well as working capital changes that are all components of the free cash flow calculation. The remaining item necessary to compute free cash flow is the level of operating tax, defined as the incremental statutory tax rate multiplied by the earnings before interest and taxes (EBIT) and changes in deferred tax. EBIT multiplied by the tax rate is a hypothetical amount of tax that would be paid if the company were financed entirely with equity and had no interest expense, interest income, or income from other activities not related to operations. In order to calculate EBIT and derive operating taxes, a projection of depreciation and amortization expense is necessary. As such, calculating the property plant and equipment assets along with depreciation is the next logical part of the structure of financial models.

Accurately representing depreciation expense in a model is important for many reasons. Tax depreciation influences income tax payments; depreciation expense affects taxes used in computing free cash flow; depreciation expense is used in terminal value calculations where the ratio of capital expenditure to depreciation expense may be applied to derive normalized cash flow; depreciation expense affects earnings and return on equity; and the net plant depreciation rate is a component of deriving stable enterprise value/earnings before interest, taxes, depreciation, and amortization (EV/EBITDA) ratios. Unfortunately, the calculation of depreciation in a corporate model can be one of the trickiest aspects of the whole process. Much of the discussion in Part 3 of the book dealing with stable ratios in a discounted cash flow analysis and computing the implied EV/EBITDA ratio builds from ideas presented in this chapter.

A few difficult programming issues arise when modeling depreciation expense in the different types of models. The biggest problem is in corporate models related to incorporating the effects of asset retirements that come about because of historical capital expenditures that were made before the start of the forecast period. The projected retirements must look backward to the time at which the capital expenditures were made. Another problem that comes about in corporate models is when the depreciation rate is not computed on a straight-line basis. With accelerated depreciation, the age of each tranche of capital expenditure must be remembered so that one can look up the appropriate depreciation rate that depends on the age. For project finance models, the retirement problem for existing assets does not exist because there is no history. However, other programming problems arise because the depreciation expense may be a function of the calendar year rather than the annual age of the project. Depending on the tax treatment of a transaction, distinguishing tax depreciation and book depreciation can be difficult in acquisition models.

Many of these difficult modeling issues associated with depreciation can be resolved with a few user-defined functions. User-defined functions that are discussed next include:

- A function to compute vintage depreciation expense from accelerated depreciation rates, given capital expenditures and depreciation rate
- A function to derive the depreciation rate on net plant given different assumptions about asset life and projected growth rates
- A function that evaluates implied retirements on existing assets derived from historical growth rates
- A function that finds implied historical growth rates computed from accumulated depreciation to gross plant as well as asset life

Portfolios of Assets with a Vintage Process

Corporate models should include effects of differences between tax depreciation and book depreciation because tax depreciation rather than book depreciation affects real taxes paid and ultimate cash flow. If EBIT multiplied by the tax rate is computed using book depreciation in the free cash flow calculation, then there should be a separate adjustment for changes in deferred taxes derived from calculation of tax depreciation. The better calculation of free cash flow to the firm (FCFF) is:

$$\text{FCFF} = \text{EBITDA} - \text{WC Change} - \text{Capital Expenditure} -$$
$$\text{EBIT} \times \text{Tax Rate} + \text{Change in Deferred Tax}$$

Calculation of tax depreciation can be complex when the depreciation rate is not constant for each year if accelerated depreciation rates are part of the tax code. To model tax depreciation expense with accelerated rates and continuing capital expenditures, a matrix with a diagonal pattern is often presented in corporate and project finance models. The matrix comes about because the depreciation expense for an asset depends on its age. If you compute future depreciation you need to remember both the age and the capital expenditure for the calculation. These fancy-looking matrices are sometimes also shown for straight-line depreciation, which is not necessary because the depreciation rate does not depend on the age of the asset (perhaps modelers want to show how sophisticated they can be). Figure 9.1 illustrates calculation of accelerated depreciation using such a vintage matrix.

To make one of these sophisticated-looking matrices, the biggest trick is to compute the age of separate assets that are completed at different times. In the example shown in Figure 9.1, the age of the asset vintage that goes into service in 2015 is one year old in 2015, while the age of the asset class that went into service in 2014 is two years old in 2016, and so forth. A rectangle can be created that shows the date the asset is born on the left and the date of the model at the top that allows the age at each vintage to be computed. Once the age of each vintage of plant for each asset class is established, the LOOKUP function can then be

	G	H	I	J	K	L	M	N	O	P	Q	R	S	T
12														
13		Model Year		2014	2015	2016	2017	2018	2019	2020	2021	2022	2023	2024
14		Capital Expenditure		200.00	218.00	237.62	259.01	282.32	307.72	335.42	365.61	398.51	434.38	473.47
15														
16			0	1	2	3	4	5	6	7	8			
17		Dep Rate		14.29%	14.29%	14.29%	14.29%	14.29%	14.29%	14.29%		100%		
18											=VDB(1,0,7,O16,P16,$S$17)			
19			=TRANSPOSE(J14:T14)											
20									=LOOKUP(J$13-$H22+1,$I$16:$Q$16,$I$17:$Q$17)*$I22					
21		Yr Born	Expenditure											
22		2014	200.00	28.57	28.57	28.57	28.57	28.57	28.57	28.57	-	-	-	-
23		2015	218.00	-	31.14	31.14	31.14	31.14	31.14	31.14	31.14	-	-	-
24		2016	237.62	#N/A	-	33.95	33.95	33.95	33.95	33.95	33.95	33.95	-	-
25		2017	259.01	#N/A	#N/A	-	37.00	37.00	37.00	37.00	37.00	37.00	37.00	-
26		2018	282.32	#N/A	#N/A	#N/A	-	40.33	40.33	40.33	40.33	40.33	40.33	40.33
27		2019	307.72	#N/A	#N/A	#N/A	#N/A	-	43.96	43.96	43.96	43.96	43.96	43.96
28		2020	335.42	#N/A	#N/A	#N/A	#N/A	#N/A	-	47.92	47.92	47.92	47.92	47.92
29		2021	365.61	#N/A	#N/A	#N/A	#N/A	#N/A	#N/A	-	52.23	52.23	52.23	52.23
30		2022	398.51	#N/A	#N/A	#N/A	#N/A	#N/A	#N/A	#N/A	-	56.93	56.93	56.93
31		2023	434.38	#N/A	#N/A	#N/A	#N/A	#N/A	#N/A	#N/A	#N/A	-	62.05	62.05
32		2024	473.47	#N/A	#N/A	#N/A	#N/A	#N/A	#N/A	#N/A	#N/A	#N/A	-	67.64
33														
34		Total		28.57	59.71	93.66	130.66	170.99	214.95	262.87	286.53	312.32	340.42	371.06
35														
36								=SUMIF(J22:J32,"<>#N/A",J22:J32)							
37														
38		Depreciation Function		28.57	59.71	93.66	130.66	170.99	214.95	262.87	286.53	312.32	340.42	371.06
39														
40							=depreciation(J14:T14,J17:P17)							

FIGURE 9.1 Illustration of Vintage Process to Compute Depreciation Expense

used with the age as the lookup index to find the appropriate depreciation rate. To make the vintage depreciation expense calculations from the age of plant, the following steps can be applied in a spreadsheet that contains the year of the model and the projected capital expenditure:

Step 1   Enter the depreciation rate as a function of the age of the plant in a table.

Step 2   Set up a rectangle with the year that the asset was born as a vertical column to the left and model years at the top. To transfer the year numbers from the top row to a column use the TRANSPOSE function (not the copy and paste special as transpose.) To implement the TRANSPOSE function, first highlight the target area (i.e. the column of years the asset is born), then type the function name =TRANSPOSE, and finally press SHIFT, CNTL, ENTER instead of simply pressing the enter key. The result, called an array variable, will include brackets around the result.

Step 3   Compute the age of the plant by subtracting the model year at the
              top of the rectangle from the year the asset was born at the left of
              the rectangle. Make the calculation using relative references such
              as B$6 – $D10 and allow the age to be negative in years before the
              asset was created. Create relative references by pressing the F4
              key multiple times.

Step 4   Use the LOOKUP function to relate the depreciation rate to the
              age of the plant by using the age that you just computed as the
              lookup index and then separately shading the age in the depre-
              ciation table followed by the depreciation rate.

Step 5   Place the projected capital expenditures in a column next to the
              year born by using the TRANSPOSE function again. To do this,
              shade the column next to the year and enter the TRANSPOSE
              function. Then highlight the projected capital expenditures and
              press the SHIFT, CNTL, and ENTER keys.

Step 6   Multiply the depreciation rate by the cost of the asset being
              depreciated that is now in the column next to the year created
              column. Put the IFERROR function around the calculation to
              avoid problems created by N/A.

Step 7   Sum the depreciation for each modeled year column from the
              different vintages to account for the fact that the older plant has
              lower depreciation rates and will retire.

Step 8   Repeat the process for assets with different vintages and for both
              book and tax depreciation.

Instead of this rather long and laborious process, you can create your own
function with a few lines of code that accepts capital expenditures and depreciation rates and then produces the projected depreciation expense. You do
not show the fancy diagonal matrix, but the modeling is much faster. Once
you have created the function one time it can be used in all of your files. The
nature of this function is like the TRANSPOSE function in that the output—
period-by-period depreciation expense—does not go into one cell, but rather
into an array of cells. This means that you must press SHIFT, CNTL, ENTER when
you are finished entering the function. To create a function that produces a row
or column of depreciation expense from an array of capital expenditures and
an array of depreciation rates, you need to know a couple of tricks in computing
an array function. The five elements in generating an array function are:

1. Define the function as a VARIANT in the title of the function.
2. Compute the length of the array (the number of years of capital expenditure) being read into the function for capital expenditures by using the
   COUNT extension.
3. Create an array variable to store period-by-period depreciation expense
   using the REDIM statement to define the size of the depreciation output
   array.

4. Assign the array variable defined with the REDIM statement to the name of the function (rather than a single value).
5. Put the Option Base 1 at the top of the program.

Once you know how to do these things, you can create many sophisticated functions that can make your models efficient and you can make the spreadsheet a powerful tool. The code that produces total depreciation from computing vintages uses two FOR NEXT loops to create an age matrix and then sums the depreciation rate for different vintages across vintage; it is shown in Figure 9.2. As with the step-by-step process for computing a matrix, you first compute the age of the assets class. This is done by making a FOR NEXT loop that goes around both the model year and the year born as was the case when

```
' When the output is an array define as Variant


Function depreciation(capital_expenditure, depreciation_rate) As Variant

asset_life = depreciation_rate.Count ' Find Life from the dep rate array
cap_exp_periods = capital_expenditure.Count

ReDim Depreciation_Expense(cap_exp_periods) As Single

For model_year = 1 To cap_exp_periods   ' loop around each period

    For vintage = 1 To cap_exp_periods  ' make a second loop asset by asset

        age = model_year - vintage + 1   ' calculate the age of each exp

        If (age > 0 And age <= asset_life) Then        ' Only when alive
            Depreciation_Expense(model_year) = _
                capital_expenditure(vintage) * _
                depreciation_rate(age) + Depreciation_Expense(model_year)
        End If

    Next vintage
Next model_year

depreciation = Depreciation_Expense

End Function
```

FIGURE 9.2 Function for Depreciation Expense

you created the age variable from two sets of years. The single calculation in the function that makes it efficient is computing the depreciation for each square by multiplying the capital expenditure that is a function of the year born (vintage in Figure 9.2) with the depreciation rate that is a function of the age and summing the amount across model years. The good thing about functions like this is that after you create them one time you will not have to program them again because you can import them into a new file or even create an add-in.

The function that produces an array in the preceding case allows you to create the function in a single row and not in a column. If you would like to output a column containing the period-by-period depreciation as well as a row, the output variable can be defined as a two-dimensioned array. An additional loop can then be created that defines the second part of the array as using the same value as the first, illustrated as follows:

```
ReDim Depreciation_Expense (cap_exp_periods, cap_exp_periods)
As Single
For i = 1 To cap_exp_periods
    For j = 1 To cap_exp_periods
        Depreciation_Expense (i, j) = dep (i)
    Next j
Next i
depreciation = Depreciation_Expense
```

To implement a user-defined function, it is helpful to define inputs to the function with descriptive variable names. If you do this, you can then use the f_x button next to the data entry box. In this way you can clearly see the variables required by your function, as illustrated in Figure 9.3.

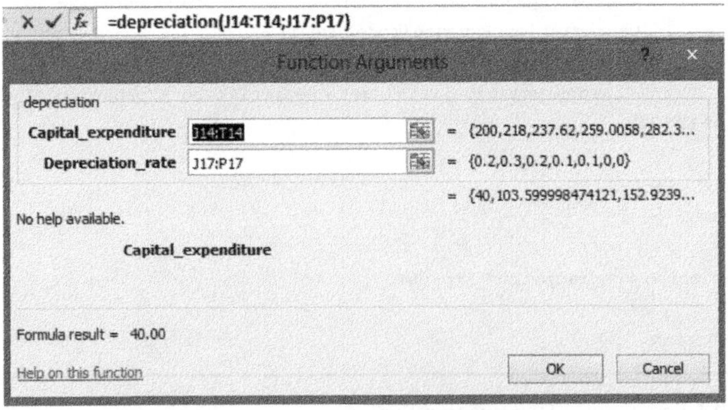

FIGURE 9.3 Illustration of Implementing Function with f_x

The depreciation expense function can be used in project finance models as well as in corporate models. This is particularly helpful where the timing of future capital expenditures for something like new turbines or new inverters in a solar panel project may change depending on input assumptions. In this case, you simply select the entire series of future capital expenditures for the generator or inverter, all of which can be 0 except for the one year the capital expenditure is made, and input them into your depreciation function. As with the function used in the corporate model, you press SHIFT, CNTL, ENTER when you are finished and the entire depreciation expense array is computed.

Accounting for Asset Retirements in Corporate Models

Addressing the problem of asset retirements in corporate models is difficult because information on the plant retirements associated with previously built plants is difficult to obtain. In the previous section, the age of the asset had to be retained when computing accelerated depreciation. A not-so-different problem exists for computing book depreciation in corporate models. Retirement associated with an existing plant depends on previous capital expenditures that occurred a long time ago, write-offs, asset sales, and revaluations for many historical years. As this information on prospective asset retirements is virtually impossible to obtain, modelers have developed various methods to address the problem. Most of the time analysts firmly believe in their own approach and have elegant arguments to support their position. But they cannot really prove their method is accurate. In this section different methods for simulating depreciation and incorporating retirements are addressed and a method to test the efficacy of the different approaches is introduced.

To measure the benefits and problems of alternative depreciation modeling methods it is useful to develop a long-term hypothetical model that computes the theoretically correct level of depreciation expense. This theoretical model can be used as a reference point in evaluating different methods and it illustrates the importance of many capital asset and depreciation issues. When developing such a theoretical model of the true depreciation expense, you should keep in mind the most fundamental aspect of corporate models. This is the fact that corporations have a history and an indefinite life, and the model cannot cover all of the historical and projected periods in the life span of a corporation. Although a real model cannot account for all of these periods, a theoretical model that covers the start-up of the firm, a historical period, a modeled period, and a long-term stable period can be used to prove which of the alternative modeling methods is most accurate in modeling capital assets, retirements, depreciation expense, and net plant depreciation rates. The theoretical model that includes different growth rates for each period can produce the true depreciation expense, the true asset retirements, and the true cash flow for alternative start dates given assumptions with respect to the life of assets and various growth rates. Once this theoretical base is established, alternative methods can be tested against the true value. You can then evaluate what kinds of growth rate assumptions produce really big errors and whether it is reasonable to adopt a particular approach to modeling depreciation expense.

In developing a theoretical base for evaluating different depreciation methods, you can input different growth rates for different periods (the historical period, the modeled period, and the long-term period). The growth rates are used to compute the balance of plant that is required to support the EBITDA. If there is a higher growth rate in EBITDA, a higher growth rate in plant is necessary. The required plant balance to support EBITDA is applied to derive the implied level of capital expenditures. Calculation of the capital expenditures required to support the EBITDA is a bit tricky because the change in plant must compensate for the retirements of plant as well as new growth. The capital expenditures are given by the formula:

$$\text{Change in Plant} = \text{Plant}_1 - \text{Plant}_0 = \text{Capital Expenditures} - \text{Retirements}$$

$$\text{Capital Expenditures} = \text{Plant}_1 - \text{Plant}_0 + \text{Retirements}$$

Retirements that must be replaced to support EBITDA can be determined by going back and remembering the amount of money spent on capital expenditures in earlier periods. If the plant life is five years, then retirements should be the amount of capital expenditures that occurred five years ago. When simulating retirements that in part drive future capital expenditures through evaluating the lag in capital expenditures, one problem is that retirements cannot be computed until a full life cycle of plant has been completed. The first part of a formula for retirements should therefore be an IF statement involving whether the year of the model is greater than the life of the plant—before the first life cycle of plant there are no retirements related to the capital expenditures. After the period of the model is greater than the lifetime of the assets, the retirements can be computed. At this point retirements should look backward from the current year and move backward by the length of the life of the plant. Looking backward can be accomplished using the OFFSET function that begins with a reference cell and moves up or down and backward or forward as shown:

$$\text{Retirements} = \text{IF(Year} >= \text{Asset Life, OFFSET(Capital Expenditure Cell,0,-Asset Life))}$$

The final problem with simulating retirements is that the retirements associated with the initial gross plant must be simulated without a historical record for the capital expenditures that were made to accumulate to those expenditures. To measure these retirements that come from the start-up phase, you can assume that the historical gross plant property and equipment was accumulated through making a series of capital expenditures at a constant growth rate. This can be done by deriving the base level of capital expenditures that were made a lifetime before the current level of property plant and equipment. When the prospective retirements sum to plant balance, the prospective retirements will correctly account for all of the gross plant balance. If you know or make an assumption regarding the earlier growth rate in assets and capital expenditures over the plant life, you could compute this base amount of retirements by making a little model and then using a Goal Seek. Say the plant balance is 1,000, the growth is 10 percent, and the plant life is 10. You could then use the Goal Seek tool to find how much the expenditure made 10 years ago that, when grown by 10 percent, will sum to 1,000. This Goal Seek that finds the base level of capital expenditure ensures that the sum of retirements equals the gross plant property and equipment balance. While this Goal Seek process works, it would be very tedious to put into all of your models. A better way to deal with the problem is to create a flexible function that does the same thing as the Goal Seek.

One trick to making a function that does the same thing as a Goal Seek on a dynamic basis is to use FOR NEXT loops with STEP counters that have smaller and smaller increments. You can then go around the loop with smaller and small increments until the Goal Seek criteria are met. Once you have exceeded the Goal Seek criteria, you go back and reduce the STEP increment in the FOR NEXT loop. You do this until the increment is very small and the Goal Seek value is found. The process of making a Goal Seek that is flexible and changes when you change inputs is illustrated using a flow chart in Figure 9.4.

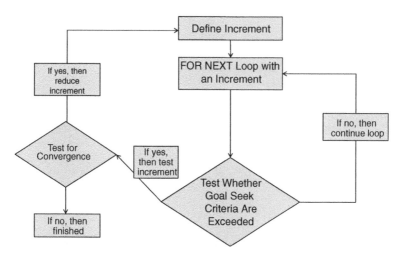

FIGURE 9.4 Diagram of Process to Compute Goal Seek Using a Function

A function to create a flexible Goal Seek formula is shown in Figure 9.5. All of the inputs and formulas for computing the Goal Seek must be contained in the function (you cannot refer to a range name in the spreadsheet). This means that you generally cannot create such a function to

```
'
' This function finds the cap exp that were made at beg of the life
' It is the automation of a goal seek function
'


Function find_base (growth, life)              ' Backs into the pct start

min_base = 0                                   ' Set initial low value
max_base = 1                                   ' set the cap for testing

new_increment:

    increment = (max_base - min_base) / 10     'Re-compute Increment

    For Base = min_base To max_base Step increment ' loop around small inc

        plant = Base              ' Try different values for base
        total_plant = plant       ' This is the integral. You are aiming for 1

        For i = 1 To life - 1
            plant = plant * (1 + growth)  ' Incr the plant by the grwth rate
            total_plant = total_plant + plant ' Add the plant together
        Next i

        If total_plant > 1 Then   ' When too high go back; if not, continue
            min_base = Base - increment     ' Find a smaller starting point
            max_base = Base + increment
            GoTo new_increment
        End If

        If Abs (total_plant - 1) < 0.0000000001 Then  ' Test for convergence
            find_base = Base
            Exit Function
        End If

    Next Base                                          ' Loop over base

End Function
```

FIGURE 9.5 Function for Computing Base Retirements Using Goal Seek Process

replicate a Goal Seek inside a big financial model to do something like find the price to meet a target IRR. The function that finds a base capital expenditure level as a percent of the gross plant must be between 0 and 1. The function works by first assuming the initial base expenditure percentage is 0. Then the initial base is increased in the FOR NEXT loop using the initial step increment and the total plant is computed that should sum to 1.0. After an initial base is found whereby the sum exceeds 1.0, you stop the loop and the increment is recomputed that is just below and just above the base value from the last iteration. Then, the FOR NEXT loop is re-computed using the smaller increments. The process continues until the increment is very small. Once you are finished with making the function you can find the base retirement level that occurred a lifetime ago. All you have to do is to put in assumptions for the lifetime of plant and the growth rate into the function. After you have the base level of retirement, then subsequent retirements are the base retirement multiplied by 1 plus the growth rate.

Once you have derived the retirements associated with historical capital expenditures, you can complete a theoretical model that lasts for hundreds of years with changing growth rates. The model needs to look backward continually to find capital expenditures from the prior life cycles that affect the current levels of capital expenditures.

Alternative Methods for Deriving Retirements Associated with Existing Assets in Corporate Models

For a single asset with no terminal value, straight-line depreciation is the gross amount spent on an asset divided by the plant life. Given this fact, one approach to computing depreciation expense in a corporate model is to keep track of the balance of the gross property plant and equipment (i.e., without deductions for accumulated depreciation). This is tabulated from a balance table beginning with existing plant and adding prospective capital expenditures. As explained in Chapter 7 in the context of timing phase switches, the gross plant balance can be set to actual gross plant during the historical period. It can then be computed as the opening balance plus the capital expenditures in the projection period. Gross plant balance can subsequently be multiplied by the depreciation rate to establish projected depreciation.

The problem with this gross plant method of computing depreciation is that it does not account for any prospective retirements associated with existing plant. By ignoring retirements that reduce gross plant, the method overstates depreciation expense. This implies taxes will be underestimated, income will be too low and a host of other errors will arise. Errors are worse when the asset life is short and when the projected growth rate is relatively slow. If the asset life is short, there would be a lot of retirements on exiting plant but these are ignored. When the growth rate is slow, the retirements should in theory approach 100 percent of depreciation and this is ignored in the calculation.

Figure 9.6 uses the theoretical model that computes true depreciation to evaluate the gross plant method. Comparing the theoretical model with the gross plant method demonstrates that when the growth rate is 5 percent and the asset life is 5 years, the overstatement of depreciation approaches 100 percent after just a few years. If the growth rate is constant, the ratios of accumulated depreciation to net plant, depreciation to net plant, and capital expenditures to depreciation remain stable.

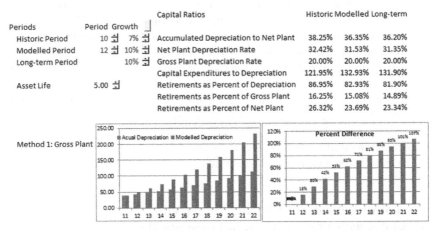

			Capital Ratios	Historic	Modelled	Long-term
Periods	Period	Growth				
Historic Period	10	7%	Accumulated Depreciation to Net Plant	38.25%	36.35%	36.20%
Modelled Period	12	10%	Net Plant Depreciation Rate	32.42%	31.53%	31.35%
Long-term Period		10%	Gross Plant Depreciation Rate	20.00%	20.00%	20.00%
			Capital Expenditures to Depreciation	121.95%	132.93%	131.90%
Asset Life	5.00		Retirements as Percent of Depreciation	86.95%	82.93%	81.90%
			Retirements as Percent of Gross Plant	16.25%	15.08%	14.89%
			Retirements as Percent of Net Plant	26.32%	23.69%	23.34%

FIGURE 9.6 Illustration of Errors in Model from Not Accounting for Retirements on Existing Assets

A second approach sometimes used in modeling depreciation is to separate the depreciation on existing assets from the depreciation on new assets. The depreciation on new assets can be computed using the vintage method described earlier. This accounts for retirements on the new assets. Depreciation on existing assets can either be computed by simply continuing the existing level of depreciation or, better, assuming a decline to account for retirements. If the existing level of depreciation expense does not include any accounting for prospective retirements and the lifetime of new assets is fairly long, the method is not very different from the simple gross plant method discussed previously. In this case where there are no retirements of new assets or existing assets, the depreciation expense can be overstated by a wide margin.

If retirements associated with existing assets are accounted for, some kind of retirement statistic must be entered and then the accumulated retirements should be calculated. Once the accumulated retirements are tabulated, the adjustment to existing depreciation can be computed as the accumulated

Timing

Period	Growth	1	15	16	17	18	19	20
Historic Period	7%	TRUE	TRUE	TRUE	FALSE	FALSE	FALSE	FALSE
Modelled Period	10%	FALSE	FALSE	FALSE	TRUE	TRUE	TRUE	TRUE
Long-term Period	10%	FALSE	FALSE	FALSE	FALSE	FALSE	FALSE	FALSE
Test		TRUE	TRUE	TRUE	TRUE	TRUE	TRUE	TRUE

Simulated Depreciation Method TWO - Existing Depreicaiton Flat and New Depreciation

Existing Depreciation	0.00	0.00	24.60	24.60	24.60	24.60	24.60
Retirements to Deprecaiation	0.00	0.00	0.67	0.67	0.67	0.67	0.67
Retirements	0.00	0.00	16.50	16.50	16.50	16.50	16.50
Accumulated Retirements	FALSE	FALSE	FALSE	16.50	33.01	49.51	66.01
Depreciation on Retirements	0.00	0.00	0.00	0.00	1.38	2.75	4.13
New Plant Balance							
Opening Balance	0.00	0.00	0.00	0.00	46.02	96.16	150.77
Add: Captial Expenditures	FALSE	FALSE	FALSE	46.02	50.13	54.62	59.51
Less: Retirements	FALSE	FALSE	FALSE	FALSE	FALSE	FALSE	FALSE
Closing Balance	0.00	0.00	0.00	46.02	96.16	150.77	210.28
Deprecaiton Rate	0.08	0.08	0.08	0.08	0.08	0.08	0.08
New Depreciaiton Expense	0.00	0.00	0.00	0.00	3.84	8.01	12.56
Total Modelled Deprecation	0.00	0.00	24.60	24.60	27.06	29.86	33.04
Model vs Actual							
Acual Depreciation	#N/A	#N/A	#N/A	24.60	27.06	29.77	32.74
Modelled Depreciation	#N/A	#N/A	#N/A	24.60	27.06	29.86	33.04

FIGURE 9.7 Illustration of Method for Computing Retirements from Separating Existing Plant from New Plant and Estimating Retirements on Existing Plant

retirements multiplied by a depreciation rate. When using this method, a MIN test should be included so that the depreciation reduction on the retirements does not exceed the existing depreciation expense. The approach of separating existing and future assets to model depreciation expense relative to the true depreciation is illustrated in Figure 9.7. When these adjustments are made for retirements, the depreciation expense is more accurate. There are two problems with this method: (1) it is a bit tedious to implement because of accumulating retirements and adjusting the retirements only after the historical period, and (2) one needs information on historical growth and the retirements as a percentage of depreciation expense, which is difficult to obtain.

To approximate retirements associated with exiting plant, some modelers project depreciation on existing assets using the net property plant and equipment balance multiplied by the net plant depreciation rate. They then separately compute the depreciation on new assets from depreciation on existing plant as discussed earlier. Because the balance of net plant declines each period with depreciation expense, the depreciation expense on the net plant balance also declines. This suggests that some level of retirement of assets for existing assets is implicitly reflected in the forecast. If this net plant method is applied, you must make sure that the net plant balance on existing plant does not become negative. Although this approach of splitting up depreciation does indirectly account for retirements, it is not an accurate reflection of retirements unless the rate of retirement for existing assets relative to net plant happens to be same as the net plant depreciation rate in each period.

By reducing depreciation expense according to the declining balance of net plant, the approach assumes that if the net plant depreciation rate is 15 percent, then the implicit retirement rate percentage of existing net property plant and equipment is also 15 percent. Unless the growth rate for the historical period is zero, there is no basis for making this assumption. Another problem with this approach is the assumption that the net plant depreciation remains constant over the lifetime of existing assets. If the true retirements are less than capital expenditures, then the depreciation rate on net plant will increase as the net plant balance declines. To see this, think of a single asset with constant depreciation expense. Over the lifetime of a single asset, the ratio of depreciation expense to net plant—the gross plant less the accumulated depreciation expense—increases as depreciation remains constant but net plant reduces. In the last year of the life of an asset the net plant depreciation reaches 100 percent. For a corporation with many assets, multiplying net plant by a constant depreciation rate can also result in similarly biased results when existing assets are split from future capital expenditures. In the last year before all of the existing assets are

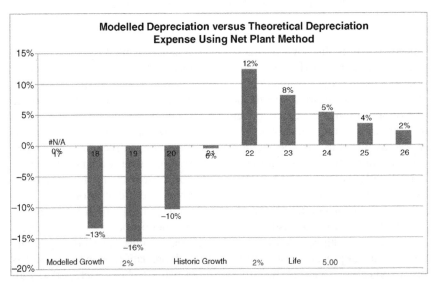

FIGURE 9.8a Percent Error from Using Net Plant Method: Five-Year Plant Life and 2 Percent Historical Growth Rate

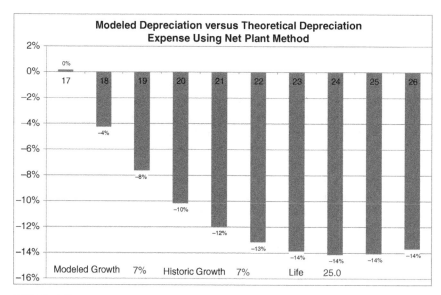

FIGURE 9.8b Percent Error from Using Net Plant Method: 25-Year Plant Life and 7 Percent Historical Growth Rate

retired, the depreciation rate on net plant should be 100 percent just like in the single asset case.

The pattern of errors from applying the net plant method is illustrated in Figures 9.8a and 9.8b for cases with different growth rates and different plant lives. Through simulating the theoretical depreciation and the computed depreciation from the net plant method, Figure 9.8a demonstrates that the net plant method understates depreciation in early years, but overstates depreciation in later years with a short life of 5 years and a low growth rate of 2 percent. Figure 9.8b shows that depreciation is consistently understated using the net plant method when the asset life is long (25 years) and the growth rate is relatively high (7 percent). Where depreciation is understated, the cash flow is understated and the income is overstated. If you are using the formula NOPAT × $(1 - g/\text{ROIC})/(\text{WACC} - g)$ to compute value, then the understatement in depreciation expense results in an overstatement of terminal value. Finally, note that the error in computing depreciation is less using the net plant method than the error from completely ignoring retirements.

The third method of computing depreciation is to directly model the retirements of existing plant using the historical growth rate in capital expenditures and to separately model the new assets using a vintage approach. Application of this method can be accomplished with two user-defined functions. The first finds the historic level of growth and the second finds the base level of capital expenditures. With the two functions and information regularly reported on the financial statements, you quickly make the more accurate depreciation calculation. To make this calculation of depreciation on existing assets from the theoretical retirements, you can follow this step-by-step process:

Step 1   Compute the ratio of the accumulated depreciation to plant from notes in the historical financial statements.

Step 2   Compute the *implied historical growth* from the accumulated depreciation to net plant by making a user-defined function using the Goal Seek approach. This function is similar to the function discussed earlier to find the base level of retirements in Figure 9.5. It is a function that does the same thing as a Goal Seek on a dynamic basis. You start with a loop with a high level of growth as the increment of a FOR NEXT Loop from 100 percent down growth to 0 percent growth and set the "step by" increment in the FOR NEXT LOOP to 1 percent. With each growth rate you compute the ratio of accumulated depreciation to plant through simulating the depreciation over the plant life. Once the target ratio of accumulated depreciation to net plant has been found, you make a smaller increment than 1 percent and repeat the FOR NEXT loop with smaller step increments. You repeat the FOR NEXT process with smaller step increments until you find the growth rate that makes the computed ratio of accumulated depreciation to plant to be just equal to your target level.

Step 3   Compute the *base retirements* as a percentage of gross plant by using the base retirement function defined previously and demonstrated in Figure 9.5. Recall that this function accepts the growth rate and the plant life, both of which have now been determined.

Step 4   Compute retirements of the existing plant over the projected period using the base retirements and the historic growth rate. This can be accomplished by making a switch for the first modeled period to start the calculation with the base retirements. In this first period, the retirements are the opening plant balance multiplied by the base retirements established from the function. For subsequent periods, the retirements are the prior value of retirements multiplied by the growth rate computed in step 2. The formula for retirements that can be inserted in one row is:

Existing Retirements = IF(First Modeled Period,
Opening Gross Plant × Base, Prior Value × (1 + Growth))

Step 5   Compute the opening balance of plant, the depreciation on existing plant, and the depreciation on new plant through multiplying gross plant deprecation rates by gross plant balances.

An example of this process for computing the depreciation is demonstrated in Figure 9.9. Note that the theoretical depreciation and the actual depreciation shown at the bottom of the table converge to be the same.

	D	E	F	G		V	W	X	Y	Z	AA
1	Timing										
2	Period	No TRUE	Growth		0	15	16	17	18	19	20
4	Modelled Period	17	10%			FALSE	FALSE	TRUE	TRUE	TRUE	TRUE
5	Long-term Period	267	10%			FALSE	FALSE	FALSE	FALSE	FALSE	FALSE
6	Last Historic Period					FALSE	TRUE	FALSE	FALSE	FALSE	FALSE
131	Depreciation Method FOUR using Functions										
132	Parameters										
133	Life	12.00									
134	Accumulated Depreciation	39.18%									
135	Implied Historic Growth	7.01%	<---- =find_growth(E134,E133)								
136	Base Retirements	5.59%	<---- =find_base(E135,E133)								
137	Existing Deprecation										
138	Opening Balance	=G140---->				257.85	275.90	295.22	278.72	261.07	242.18
139	Less: Retirements	=MIN(IF(H7,H138*$E$136,G139*(1+$E$135)),H138)				0.00	0.00	16.50	17.65	18.89	20.21
140	Closing Balance	=IF(H3,H36,H138-H139)---->				275.90	295.22	278.72	261.07	242.18	221.96
141	Deprecation on Existing Plant	=H138*(1/$E$133)*H4---->				0.00	0.00	24.60	23.23	21.76	20.18
142	New Depreciation										
143	Opening Balance	=G146---->				0.00	0.00	0.00	46.02	96.16	150.77
144	Add: New Captial Expenditures	=IF(H4,H24)---->				FALSE	FALSE	46.02	50.13	54.62	59.51
145	Less: Retirements on New Plant	=IF(H2>=$E$133,OFFSET(H144,0,-$E$133))---->				FALSE	FALSE	FALSE	FALSE	FALSE	FALSE
146	Closing Balance	=H143+H144-H145---->				0.00	0.00	46.02	96.16	150.77	210.28
147	Depreciation on New Plant	=H143*(1/$E$133)---->				0.00	0.00	0.00	3.84	8.01	12.56
148	Total Modelled Depreciation	=H147+H141---->				0.00	0.00	24.60	27.06	29.77	32.75
149											
150	Theoretical Depreciation					21.49	22.99	24.60	27.06	29.77	32.74

FIGURE 9.9 Illustration of Accounting for Retirements with Base Historical Retirements and Implied Historical Growth Rate

If the historical growth rate is not constant, computing the implied growth rate from the accumulated depreciation ratio may not be precise and, assuming the retirements follow a constant growth rate, will not be perfect. However, an experiment with random growth demonstrates that the error is very small.

Depreciation Issues in Project Finance Models

In a project finance model depreciation should be computed through establishing a gross plant balance account that increases with the construction costs over the construction period. To begin the depreciation at commencement of operation, the tax depreciation rate (which may vary with the age of the project) is multiplied by the balance of the plant as well as the operating switch. As with the nonproject finance models, the accumulated depreciation should be computed after the depreciation expense row.

Computing depreciation can be complicated in a project finance model because of the manner in which tax depreciation is driven by the calendar year rather than the date at which the project begins operation. In some countries if the operation date is December 27, the depreciation is the same as if the operation date had been January 5 of the same year, meaning it is much better to put the plant in service at the end of the calendar year. To resolve this problem, the number of calendar months in the year should be computed and the calendar year must be computed. The following are five tasks you can do to accomplish this:

1. Compute a switch for a new calendar year by making a test switch that evaluates when the month of the start date is greater than the month of the end date. To do this you can use the MONTH function and include a row specifying the month of the model.
2. Use the same switch to make a counter for the calendar year through accumulating the switch.
3. Make an adjustment for the first operating year for which the counter should begin (you also have to make an adjustment so that you do not double-count the first year).
4. Use the COUNTIF function for both the range and the criteria as the annual year to find the number of periods per year.
5. The depreciation rate for the period is 1/life divided by the periods per year.

Modeling the Change in Deferred Taxes in Corporate Models

Measuring free cash flow is one of the primary objectives of any financial model. When evaluating real cash flow received by debt and equity investors, the taxes actually paid must be computed rather than the taxes recorded on the profit-and-loss statement. The taxes paid can be approximated by adding the change in deferred tax to taxes booked, as illustrated by the next formula. This implies that you need to compute deferred taxes in a model. Deferred taxes associated with tax loss carryforwards are discussed in Chapter 12 and deferred taxes associated with financing items such as fair valuation of derivatives are discussed in Chapter 26. This section explains how to deal with the issue of deferred taxes other than by simply pretending that deferred taxes do not exist or that the change in deferred tax will always be 0 (which seems to be a common practice).

Taxes Paid versus Taxes Booked: Change in Deferred Tax Liability

The approach for computing changes in deferred tax related to capital expenditures and depreciation is similar in logic to calculation of depreciation expenses. As with depreciation expense, it is convenient to separate the change in deferred tax between amounts associated with existing assets from amounts associated with new assets. For the new assets, tax depreciation can be computed once you know the tax depreciation life and the tax depreciation method. The vintage approach discussed earlier incorporating accelerated depreciation methods for tax depreciation is often more relevant for that purpose than for book depreciation. Once the tax depreciation is computed, the change in deferred tax liability associated with new assets is simply the tax depreciation less the book depreciation multiplied by the tax rate:

$$\text{Change in Deferred Tax Liability}$$
$$= (\text{Tax Depreciation} - \text{Book Depreciation}) \times \text{Tax Rate}$$

As with book depreciation expense, finding the change in deferred tax associated with existing assets is more difficult than computing deferred taxes associated with new assets. Just as the gross plant balance from the last historical year had to somehow be spread across future years, the prospective reversal of deferred tax changes from accumulated deferred tax associated with accelerated depreciation on existing assets can also be determined. In the case of deferred tax associated with existing assets, the manner in which the liability will reverse that represents a change in deferred tax depends on how the deferred tax originally arose. You could use something like the find_base function illustrated in Figure 9.5 previously, you could simply spread the deferred taxes over the remaining life on a straight-line basis, or you could come up with a more refined approach.

Adjusting the Tax Basis in an Acquisition

For tax purposes, an acquisition can be treated as a purchase of assets or a purchase of shares of stock. This tax treatment must be distinguished from the book accounting for an acquisition that results in revaluation of assets and reestablishing the equity. Assume the acquisition is classified as a purchase of assets rather than the purchase of stock for tax purposes. Then the acquisition price should be higher, as the asset base will be higher and the value of depreciation deductions increases. In evaluating an acquisition, comparative price/earnings or EV/EBITDA multiples should account for the difference in value for purchase of stock versus purchase of assets, just as the multiples should account for the difference in tax rates for different countries. For an asset purchase, the accumulated deferred tax should be set to 0 at the date of the acquisition.

If the acquisition is a tax-free stock transaction, no write-up for tax purposes occurs. Here the seller does not pay tax on the gain realized from selling assets, and the buyer can often use the existing net operating loss. For an asset purchase relative to a stock purchase, the tax depreciation deductions take place over an extended period while the taxable gain must be paid immediately by the seller. Therefore, from the perspectives of both the acquiring company and the target company on a combined basis, a stock transaction generally has a positive tax outcome (lower taxes) because the gain on the sale is taxable as current income while the write-up is deducted on a prospective basis. In terms of present value, if the transaction is classified as an asset purchase, the government treasury wins and the combined shareholders of the two companies lose. In situations with net operating loss, the situation is even worse, as the value of the net operating loss carryforward is lost with an asset purchase.

To establish the tax and book depreciation expense in alternative transaction structures, the following steps can facilitate the development of a model:

Step 1   The existing deferred taxes can be used to derive the existing difference between the tax and book base through dividing the accumulated deferred tax related to depreciation by the income tax rate.

$$\text{Existing Basis Difference} = \text{Accumulated Deferred Tax/Income Tax Rate}$$

Step 2   In a stock transaction, the valuation of the assets increases for books, but the tax basis does not change. The difference in the basis increases the balance of accumulated deferred tax as demonstrated in the following formula:

$$\text{Accumulated Deferred Tax after Transaction} = (\text{New Book Basis} - \text{Existing Basis}) \times \text{Income Tax Rate}$$

Step 3   When computing the goodwill for developing the pro forma balance sheet, the increase in assets as well as the increase of accumulated deferred tax must be accounted for. In addition to other goodwill adjustments, the goodwill formula should include:

$$\text{Goodwill} = \text{Goodwill} - \text{Increase in Asset Valuation} + \text{Increase in Accumulated Deferred Tax Liability}$$

Adding Debt to a Corporate or Project Finance Model by Programming Cash Flow Waterfalls

O nce after-tax free cash flow has been established you can think of the remaining calculations in the model as allocating the cash flow among different investors into alternative buckets. If debt is part of a project finance or acquisition transaction or it is on the balance sheet of a corporation, then some of the free cash flow is distributed to the lenders and some of the cash flow is left over for equity investors. There may be multiple debt tranches and it is possible that further allocations of cash flow must be made among various different debt and equity investors. While much of the time spent in financial modeling must involve analyzing the economics of free cash flow drivers, it is also often essential to accurately reflect the financial structure of the company and the allocation of the free cash flow. This chapter addresses various modeling issues that arise when incorporating debt into a corporate finance, project finance, acquisition, or merger model.

Evaluating risks faced by lenders is vital for a host of financial and economic issues. This implies that reflecting the specific features of debt can be a crucial part of the modeling process. Debt features that need to be addressed in all sorts of financial models include: (1) the size of debt, (2) the manner in which debt is borrowed, (3) the repayment structure and tenor of the debt, (4) interest rates and fees paid on the debt while it is outstanding, and (5) credit enhancements designed to protect lenders, including covenants, cash flow sweeps, and required debt service reserves. The amount of debt issued in leveraged buyouts and project finance transactions (the first item) is a key driver of equity returns and also a big determinant of whether the investment even takes place. The way in which debt is borrowed or drawn (the second item) can have a big effect on the equity internal rate of return (IRR) in project finance. The structure of debt repayments and new debt issues (the third item) is related to the size of the debt and can be the item that consumes the most time in working with lenders in project finance and acquisition finance. The base interest rate and the credit spreads (the fourth item) relative to the project IRR is the whole reason that debt increases returns to equity holders. Depending on the transaction, the covenants and cash sweeps (the fifth item) may be a function of financial ratios, such as the debt service coverage or the ratio of debt to earnings before interest, taxes, depreciation, and amortization (EBITDA) and be a big driver of equity returns and lender risk. Debt structuring is also crucial in many corporate models and merger integration models as the amount of debt issued in a merger can highly influence the accretion or dilution in earnings per share and assessment of credit ratings. In these corporate models evaluating whether debt can be refinanced and how lenders assess the risk of the company is often one of the primary reasons for creating the model.

The amount of debt that can be issued and maintained on the balance sheet for either a project financed investment or for a corporation follows the general idea of using the risk analysis process made by lenders to back into the value of an investment. Rather than coming up with risk through trying to directly measure cost of capital using the failed capital asset pricing model or other tools, the implicit cost of capital can be inferred from the debt level and other loan terms. If, for example, investors typically require a return on equity of about 20 percent when investing in a leveraged buyout, the minimum overall project rate of return, which is the same thing as the weighted average cost of capital, can be backed out with a Goal Seek process once the debt financing terms are known.

Adding the Debt Schedule to a Financial Model

The fundamental process of adding debt to any financial model is to define a debt schedule that reports the balance of debt outstanding and derives the interest expense from the balance of the debt. Presentation of debt amounts should be structured by explicitly including separate rows for the opening balance, the new borrowings, the debt repayments, and the closing balance. Debt balance schedules should be separately entered for each existing and prospective debt facility that will be present during the forecast horizon. It is best if the debt schedule also compiles information on the debt commitment, the method of borrowing, the terms of repayment, the details of interest and fees, and the convents and reserves. For corporate models, the debt schedule may include all of the debt issues that are outstanding as of the last balance sheet date plus any defined new issues that may occur over the forecast period. In the case of project finance models, loans reported on the debt schedule include all of the different tranches of debt that are issued to finance construction as well as facilities for letters of credit, potential for defaults, and reserve accounts that you can think of as negative debt. Acquisition models generally include debt issues that are used in financing the acquisition as well as debt that was issued prior to the acquisition and that will be assumed by the new owners.

In modeling any account that has an opening and closing balance, it is the closing balance that must start the process. The starting point for the debt schedule that establishes the closing debt balance differs depending on the type of model. For corporate models, the closing balance of each debt balance is launched from the financial inputs that should list the amount outstanding in the last historical period balance sheet year for each debt issue. The sum of these individual issues should correspond to the total amount of long-term debt on the balance sheet (including current maturities classified as short-term debt). If the sum of the closing balance of all of the debt issues does not equal the total amount on the balance sheet, the prospective balance sheet will not balance. It is therefore good to include a verification check to ensure that the total debt level on the balance sheet equals the sum of the individual debt issues. Once the opening and closing balances are established, the interest cost (whether capitalized or expensed) can be computed.

For models that include capitalized interest during the construction period or a cash flow sweep, it is convenient and sometimes essential to assume that repayments and/or borrowings occur at the end of the period, meaning the opening balance is the basis for computing accrued interest. Circular reference issues that arise when the average debt balance rather than the opening balance is used as the basis for computing interest are addressed in detail in Chapters 37 through 41. If the repayment and borrowing occurs at the end of the period (say the payments to construction workers are made at the end of the month) then there is no accrued interest on borrowings related to the expenditures. In a corporate model if revenues are collected at the end of the period there is no interest benefit from cash flow received during the period in terms of paying off debt. Where all operating cash flow occurs at the end of the period, the accrued interest is computed on the debt that was outstanding before the new debt was issued or repaid in the current period. This implies that the basis of interest expense should be the opening balance and you can relax about some of the circular reference issues. For monthly or even quarterly models, this idea of assuming that cash flow occurs at the end of the period may be reasonable. For annual models, assuming that all revenues are received on December 31 and assuming that all expenses are paid on December 31 and assuming all capital expenditures are made on December 31 is not acceptable.

The process of adding a debt schedule to a financial model can be summarized as follows:

- Set up the debt schedule with separate lines for:
  - The opening balance
  - Additions from new issues
  - Subtractions from debt repayments
  - The closing balance
- The total closing debt balance in historical years should be derived from the balance sheet.
- The opening balance is always equal to the closing balance in the prior period.
- Put the periodic interest rate in a row below the closing balance.
- Compute the accrued interest and separate the interest between capitalized interest and expensed interest for project finance models through multiplying the accrued interest by the construction switch or the operating switch.
- Include separate lines for the commitment fee and the up-front fee.
- For more complex debt repayment schedules such as sculpted debt include the repayment calculations in rows below the closing balance.

Modeling Scheduled Debt Repayments

The manner in which debt is repaid depends on the nature of the debt issue and the type of the financial model. Repayments may range from complex debt sculpting in project finance models to relatively simple bullet payments in corporate models. For some models, computing the debt repayment is the most complex element of the modeling process that results in seemingly hopeless circularity. Given the importance and the difficulty of computing debt repayments in project finance models, much of the discussion in Part 4 addresses mechanical aspects of debt repayment and associated circularity in detail. In corporate models where loans may be repaid on a single bullet payment date, a simple test can be created from the debt repayment year to ensure that repayment occurs on only a single date. This involves the following:

- Add the usual row for the repayment of the debt after the opening balance.
- Enter a formula that compares the model year with the repayment year to create a logical variable (year = repayment year) within the repayment row that can be multiplied by the opening balance of the debt.

The manner of debt repayment in a project finance model or a leveraged finance model is often designed to correspond to the expected cash flows generated by the investment. Repayments can be input into a model with percentages that are applied to the aggregate amount of debt issued rather than the closing or opening balance. This means it is sometimes a good idea to show the total accumulated amount of the debt issued as a separate line item above the debt balance. Unlike the closing debt balance this amount does not decline over time. The amount of accumulated debt shown above the opening balance can then be multiplied by the repayment percentage to establish the periodic repayments. The balance for the repayment can also be computed as the accumulated debt draws and be put in one of the special columns to the right of the titles and to the left of the calculations.

Because of early debt repayments that can occur if covenants or cash sweeps are triggered, you should make sure that the amounts in the repayment line of a debt schedule do not exceed the opening balance of debt outstanding. To program this, the MIN function can be used. The MIN function compares the opening balance of the debt with the otherwise scheduled debt repayments.

Repayment =MIN(Scheduled Repayment, Opening Balance)

An important audit test in a model is that the debt balance must be 0 after the repayment period. Furthermore, one of the crucial time switches in any project finance model is a debt repayment phase TRUE/FALSE switch. Using this time switch for debt repayment you can design the test with the SUMIF function and one of the two following formulas:

SUMIF(Repayment Switch Row, FALSE, Opening Debt Balance) = 0

SUMIF(Beginning of Period Row, ">=Last Repayment Date", Closing Debt Balance) = 0

Connecting Debt to Cash Flow in Corporate Models

When working with corporate models it is useful to set up a cash account along with some kind of new debt account as the last part of the debt schedule. These accounts connect the balance sheet with the cash flow analysis and are an essential part of the corporate model. There are many different ways to set up the surplus cash and new debt accounts. One relatively simple approach is to make a net cash account that nets short-term debt from surplus cash. This net cash account is a lot like other debt accounts with a couple of important exceptions. The account includes opening and closing balances but the starting point of the account is the cash minus the short-term debt on the historical balance sheets and not a simple reference to debt balances. Second, unlike other accounts, the net cash less debt amount is incremented with items from the net cash flow analysis at the very end of the cash flow statement. This means that formulas for this account cannot be completed until the cash flow statement is finished.

The net cash account contains many features of cash flow waterfall modeling that will apply to more complex analyses in project finance, acquisition finance, and in more detailed corporate models. Four themes with respect to the net cash balance as well as all sorts of debt analysis are: (1) at some point in any financial model there must be some indirect or direct connection between the cash flow analysis and the debt balances, (2) the debt balances collect information from the cash flow statement and not the other way around, (3) in structuring financial aspects of a model it is useful to construct the titles for debt balances and cash flow items before you fill in the model with formulas, and (4) calculations for cash flow allocation generally have different formulas if the cash flow is negative or if the cash flow is positive.

To illustrate how the net cash account works using these four notions, assume there is a negative net cash balance in the last historical year because there is more short-term debt than surplus cash on the balance sheet. If the net cash flow from the cash flow analysis after everything is accounted for is positive by more than the opening negative net cash balance, then the cash can be used to pay off the short-term debt and also build up surplus balances. By contrast, if the net cash account is negative after accounting for new cash flow, then the negative amount can be labeled as debt. This means the net cash account should be split between cash and debt after it has been constructed. To separate the account between cash when it is positive and debt when it is negative you can use the MAX function. The idea of doing one thing if cash is negative and another if cash is positive is common to many different aspects of debt modeling. Use of the MAX function to split up the cash account involves two alternative formulas:

$$\text{Surplus Cash} = \text{MAX(Cash Net of Debt Balance,0)}$$

$$\text{Short-Term Debt Balance} = \text{MAX(}-\text{Cash Net of Debt Balance,0)}$$

The first equation simply takes a number and makes sure it is not negative. The second equation takes a negative number, switches it around to a positive number, and then does the same test on the now positive number. These two equations amount to doing one thing if the net cash balance is positive (putting cash on the balance sheet) and another if the net cash balance is negative (putting debt on the balance sheet). To implement the net cash concept you should:

- Enter an account for surplus cash net of short-term debt with an opening balance and a closing balance. During the historical period, the closing balance comes from the balance sheet, while during the projected period the closing balance is the opening balance plus the net changes in cash that are linked to the last line of the cash flow analysis.
- Net changes in cash come directly from the cash flow statement that has not been developed yet. This implies that the account cannot be completed until the cash flow statement has been made. You can leave the cash flow changes on the net cash schedule empty until the cash flow statement has been completed or you can enter all of the row titles down through the end of the cash flow statement and then find the correct row.
- When linking the changes in net cash to the cash flow statement do not make any calculations other than to link the amount.
- After you have computed the closing balance of the net cash balance, which can either be positive or negative, use the MAX function to put the net cash into a positive surplus cash account if it is positive or a debt account if it is negative. As the net cash account can only be positive, negative, or 0 for a single period, both the surplus cash account and the short-term debt account cannot have positive balances.
- Compute the interest income on the cash balance and the interest expense on short-term debt from the opening balance of the accounts (the prior year's closing balance) to avoid circularity.

As suggested by the last item in the list, a problem of circularity can arise in modeling net cash balances because interest expense drives cash flow, but the debt balance or the interest expense is affected by cash flow itself. The most common circularity problem in corporate models comes from the assumption that operating cash flows and therefore interest expenses occur in the middle of the year. As with most circular references, the problem comes about because of an artifact of the financial model—in the real world you do not first compute interest expense and then recompute it because the debt is increased by the interest expense itself. Solutions to the famous circular reference problem for corporate models using a relatively simple user function and more complex modeling processes that include minimum balances are discussed in Chapter 38.

With a Structured Process, You Can Model Any Cash Flow Waterfall

Any time debt is issued to finance capital expenditures and other cash outflows, a loan agreement can define various restrictions on uses of cash to pay dividends, subordinated debt service, discretionary expenditures, and other items. These credit enhancements require you to construct a cash flow waterfall when modeling debt facilities. A cash flow waterfall simulates the manner in which a loan agreement establishes priorities in the use of cash flow. Cash flow waterfalls can be thought of as analogous to multiple hydroelectric plants in a cascade on a river. For such a cascade, water can be held in reservoirs and not be allowed to flow downstream by closing various taps. Only if the reservoirs are full can the water be allowed to flow downstream. If reservoirs are not full there may be requirements to fill them up before any water can be used by subsequent hydroelectric plants in the cascade.

In the hydroelectric plant analogy, water that is allowed to drip down at the very end of the cascade represents the dividend paid to equity investors. Restrictions on cash flow defined by a loan agreement may include a cash flow sweep, a cash trap covenant, and a debt service reserve account. A cash flow sweep of 100 percent does not allow any dividends to be paid until all of the debt is paid off. This is like a big reservoir where all the debt must be paid before any cash can flow down to subordinated claims. A debt service reserve account forces the company to maintain a minimum cash balance. The debt service reserve (reservoir) has to be filled up before cash can be released to other sources. A cash trap dividend covenant means that cash is not allowed to flow to other sources unless a financial ratio like the debt service coverage ratio or debt-to-EBITDA ratio is above the covenant level defined in the loan agreement. Dividends are only allowed when the financial ratios are above the covenant level, at which time cash can be released from the reserves. A cash flow waterfall that defines priorities in uses of cash is illustrated in Figure 10.1. For project finance models and acquisition models, simulating the mechanics of cash flow waterfalls that include cash flow sweeps, new borrowings, and repayment of revolving credit facilities, cash trap covenants, top-ups and withdrawals from debt service reserve accounts (DSRAs), debt defaults and repayment of defaults, as well as interest and repayment of subordinated debt seem intimidating, much less able to be analyzed in a clear and concise manner.

When setting up a cash flow waterfall you can apply a few techniques and make the seemingly complex waterfall process relatively easy to program. Procedures that facilitate the waterfall modeling include the following four: (1) setting up the row names for debt schedule items without any formulas because inflows and outflows from the debt balance are not known until the cash flow statement is complete, (2) structuring the cash flow statement with a lot of subtotals so that MIN and MAX functions can be used, (3) separately modeling dispositions and accumulations of cash flow when subtotal accounts are positive or negative using the MAX function, and (4) ensuring that you have not exceeded defined limits of debt or reserve balances by using the MIN function. These techniques are analogous to the discussion of the net

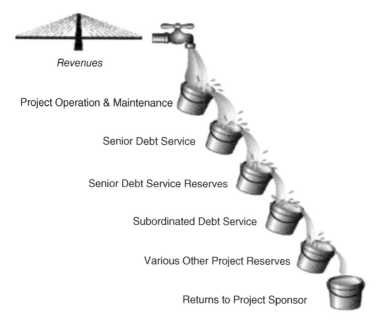

Revenues

Project Operation & Maintenance

Senior Debt Service

Senior Debt Service Reserves

Subordinated Debt Service

Various Other Project Reserves

Returns to Project Sponsor

FIGURE 10.1 Example of Project Flow of Funds

cash account with added details. Construction of a waterfall using a five-step process includes:

1. Type in account titles for the debt schedule and reserve balance schedule. Along with opening and closing balances the titles may include prepayments from sweeps, uses of revolving credit, repayments of revolving credit, and availability of revolving credit. Reserve balances could include titles for required balances, uses of the reserve, and top-ups of reserve. A balance for defaulted debt can be added that contains movements from defaults and repayments of default.

   ▪ For each item like cash flow sweeps, defaulted debt, and repayment of defaulted debt that comes from the cash flow statement, leave the amount in the debt schedule blank and just enter the title. Calculations of these amounts are made in the cash flow statement and not in the debt schedule. Links to the cash flow analysis should occur at the end of the process, meaning that all of the formulas to determine how much will be removed or placed in a debt or cash account or a debt balance are performed in the cash flow analysis. An example of debt schedule accounts without formulas for an acquisition model is shown in Figure 10.2.

Financing- Debt schedule					Capitalizing Debt		
					opening balance		
Existing Debt					add: capitalizing interest		
Opening Balance					less: cashflow sweep		
less: repayment	7.0	28			closing balance		40.00
Closing Balance			20.00				
Existing Debt Test					Revolving debt		
					Total debt commitment		
Periodic rate					less: amount borrowed		
Interest expense					remaining amount to borrow		
Amortising debt					Periodic Commitment Fee	2%	0.50%
opening balance							
less: repayment	5.0	20			opening balance		
closing balance			140.00		add: drawings		
Amortising Debt Test					less: repayments		
					closing balance		
Bullet Debt							
opening balance					Defaulted debt		
less: scheduled repayment					opening balance		
less: cashflow sweep					add: defaults		
closing balance			130.00		less: repayments of default		
					closing balance		
Capitalizing Debt							
opening balance							
add: capitalizing interest					Total Interest Expense		
less: cashflow sweep					Repayment		
closing balance			40.00		Total Senior Debt Opening Balance		-
					Total Senior Debt Closing Balance		290.00
					Average Interest Rate		

FIGURE 10.2 Illustration of Titles for Debt Facilities Used for Modeling a Cash Flow Waterfall

- For accounts such as letters of credit and debt service accounts, you will need to know how much is available to meet cash flow needs or how much more cash is needed to meet required balances defined by the loan agreement. To do this you can set up account titles that track the remaining amount of available usage or the remaining required funding that is in the account. For a letter of credit, the remaining amount that is available for use is the total commitment less the amount that has already been borrowed. The amount already borrowed is in turn the opening balance. For a debt service reserve account, the amount that must be funded is the total required funding often defined by prospective debt service less the amount that is already in the account. Accumulated amounts already in the accounts are defined by the opening balances of the accounts. Setting up a letter of credit that can be used to fund deficit cash flow is illustrated as follows, where the borrowings and the repayments come from the cash flow analysis:

Total Debt Commitment
Less: Amount Already Borrowed (Opening Balance of Loan)
Remaining Amount to Borrow
Opening Balance of Loan
Add: Amount Borrowed (Linked from Cash Flow Statement)

Less: Amount Repaid (Linked from Cash Flow Statement)
Closing Balance

2. Set up the cash flow account titles and the priorities of the cash flow waterfall in the model without entering any formulas. It is a lot easier to fill in the formulas after the structure of the cash flow statement has been built. Make the cash flow statement with various titles before filling in the income statement even though the income statement will be between the debt schedule and the cash flow statement.

- In setting up titles include many subtotals. Subtotal accounts should be made after virtually every element, including before and after borrowing from and paying back the working capital facility, before and after debt service reserve flows, before and after debt defaults and repayment of defaults, before the cash flow sweep, and before the cash trapped by the covenant.

- The order of priority in terms of which investor receives cash flows should be the same as the ordering of items in a cash flow analysis. An example of setting up the cash flow analysis with subtotals with a debt service reserve account, a letter of credit, and defaults and a cash flow sweep is illustrated as follows:

Operating Cash Flow
Less: Interest Expense on Senior Debt
Less: Repayments of Scheduled Debt
Subtotal 1: Cash Flow after Scheduled Debt Repayment
Add: Withdrawals from DSRA if Cash Flow Is Negative
Less: Top-ups of DSRA if Cash Flow Is Positive
Subtotal 2: Cash Flow after DSRA
Add: Uses of Letter of Credit if Cash Flow Is Negative
Less: Repayment of Letter of Credit if Cash Flow Is Positive
Subtotal 3: Cash Flow after Letter of Credit
Add: Defaults on Debt if Cash Flow Is Negative
Less: Repayments of Defaulted Debt if Cash Flow Is Positive
Subtotal 4: Cash Flow after Default
Less: Cash Flow Sweep if Cash Flow Is Positive
Subtotal 5: Cash Flow after Sweep
Less: Cash Flow Trap if Covenant Fails
Add: Cash Released from Lock-up Account if Covenant Passes

3. Enter formulas for each step of the cash flow waterfall that depends on whether the cash flow subtotal is positive or negative using various combinations of the MAX and MIN functions. As you get the hang of using the MIN and MAX functions you will forget about any possibility of using IF statements. The MAX and MIN functions make the cash flow formulas more transparent and less subject to error.

- Use the MAX(Subtotal Cash Flow,0) function to test for positive numbers, and use the MAX(−Subtotal Cash Flow,0) to test for negative numbers. If the cash flow after senior debt service is negative then you may have to draw from the revolving credit account. This means you would use MAX(−Subtotal Cash Flow,0). If cash flow is positive you should use available cash to repay balances and apply the MAX(Subtotal Cash Flow,0) function.

4. In determining how much cash is available to repay debt or how much cash must be used to pay back various items, use the MIN function. This tests the cash flow level against the opening balance to see if any more can be borrowed or to see if there are limits on repayment.

   - Many calculations in the cash flow waterfall will include both a MIN and a MAX function. For example, when modeling the amount of cash flow that is borrowed from the letter of credit account, the formula should look something like:

   MIN(Balance of Available to Borrow, MAX(−Subtotal Cash Flow,0))

   - If the cash flow subtotal is positive in the previous formula, then the second component of the formula is zero. This means the minimum of zero or the balance available to borrow will also be zero.

   - When the cash flow is positive, cash flow can be used to repay amounts in the working capital facility, as shown in the following formula. If the opening balance is zero, meaning that the debt is paid off, then the formula will result in zero, as it will if the cash flow is negative:

   MIN(Opening Balance of Revolving Debt, MAX(Cash Flow Subtotal,0))

5. Link accounts in the cash flow waterfall to the debt schedule. This implies that all computational formulas with MIN and MAX are in the cash flow portion of the model. The debt schedule additions and subtractions should only include links without any math.

   - In linking debt schedule accounts, the formulas should all be simple links. The evaluations computed with MAX and MIN formulas need to assess cash flow availability that is part of the waterfall. The rule is to keep the formulas in the debt schedule extremely simple. Figure 10.3 illustrates how the cash flow waterfall is a collection of MIN and MAX functions and subtotals.

Defaults on Debt and Measuring the Debt Internal Rate of Return

In using a model to assess an investment financed with debt you may want to determine the point at which a loss occurs for lenders. The loss on debt is

A B C	D	E	F	G	H	I	AA	AB	AD
1	**Timings**								
2	Date			10/01/15	01/01/16	04/01/16	10/01/20	01/01/21	07/01/21
3	Cash flow date			10/01/15	11/16/15	02/15/16	08/16/20	11/16/20	05/16/21
4	Holding period				TRUE	TRUE	TRUE	TRUE	TRUE
5	Exit period				FALSE	FALSE	FALSE	FALSE	FALSE
201	Operating cash flow				18.47	15.01	25.99	26.38	27.45
202	Less: CAPEX				7.56	7.62	6.38	6.46	6.62
203	Add: exit proceeds				-	-	-	-	-
204	Add: Notes Receivable				2.93	2.93	2.93	2.93	2.93
205	Less: Pensions				-	-	-	-	-
206	Less: Commitment Fee				0.22	0.22	0.22	0.22	0.22
207	**Cashflow before financing**	=H201-H202+H203+H204-H205-H206			13.62	10.09	22.31	22.62	23.53
208	less: senior repayments				7.71	7.71	7.71	0.71	0.71
209	less: senior interest				2.61	2.51	0.15	0.04	0.02
210	**Cashflow after sr debt service**	=H207-H208-H209---->			3.29 -	0.13	14.44	21.87	22.80
211	add: draws on revolver	=MIN(MAX(-H210,0),H147)---->			-	0.13	-	-	-
212	less: repayments of revolver	=MIN(MAX(H210,0),H151)---->			-	-	-	-	-
213	**Cashflow after revolver**	=H210+H211-H212---->			3.29	-	14.44	21.87	22.80
214	less: repayment of default	=MIN(MAX(H213,0),H164)---->			-	-	-	-	-
215	**Cashflow after repay of default**	=H213-H214---->			3.29	-	14.44	21.87	22.80
216	less: cashflow sweeps	=MIN(MAX(H215,0),H118-H119)----;			3.29	-	14.44	1.58	-
217	**Cashflow after sweep**	=H215-H216---->			-	-	-	20.29	22.80
218	add: default on senior debt	=MAX(-H217,0)---->			-	-	-	-	-
219	cashflow after senior debt	=H217+H218---->			-	-	-	20.29	22.80
220	less: repayments of the sub-debt	=MIN(MAX(H219,0),H131+H132)----;			-	-	-	20.29	19.95
221	**Cashflow to equity**	=H219-H220---->			-	-	-	-	2.85

FIGURE 10.3 Illustration of Formulas in Cash Flow Waterfall with MIN and MAX Functions

defined to be the point at which attempts to restructure the debt do not allow earlier defaults to be repaid, meaning that at the end of the life debt is still outstanding. Modeling the point at which cash flow is low enough to make a loss arise can be useful in credit analysis. If you know the probability of realizing the loss, you also know the probability of default multiplied by the loss given default associated with the debt. Once you have measured the probability of default and the loss given default you can then evaluate the credit spread on a loan that compensates lenders for taking default risk.

If debt cannot be repaid by the end of the life of a project and a loss on the loan arises, then the IRR realized by lenders is less than the promised interest rate. The IRR earned on debt can be computed in a similar manner to any other IRR where cash outflows are compared to cash inflows. In measuring the debt IRR, the cash flow dispersed to lenders is the cash outflow and the debt service received by lenders along with fees is the inflow. If there is a loss on the debt, the cash inflow realized is less than the scheduled debt service. The highest the debt IRR can be is the promised interest rate plus the fees received by lenders. But in the downside the loss is not limited.

The process of incorporating defaults into a financial model and measuring the potential loss on debt involves linking the cash flow statement with the debt schedule. This can be done using the cash flow waterfall concepts discussed earlier. The amount of the default is computed in the cash flow analysis using a subtotal account and the MAX function. The amount of default that can be repaid is computed by comparing the opening balance in the default account with the cash flow after other obligations, so long as the cash flow is positive. Because a positive test is made and the amount of the repayment is limited by the opening balance, you can use the MAX and MIN functions together. The following step-by-step process works through how to compute the defaults:

Step 1   Set up a balance for the defaulted debt in the debt schedule with line items, including the opening balance of defaulted debt, the additions from defaults, the repayments from positive cash flow, and the ending balance of defaulted debt.

Step 2   Compute the subtotal of the cash flow account after the scheduled debt is paid and after all possible other contingent accounts have been used up, including the debt service reserve accounts, letters of credit, and working capital facilities. Evaluate the defaults in two rows below this subtotal. When the amount in the subtotal is negative a default occurs. If the amount is positive you may have to repay the default if there is any opening balance in the defaulted debt. The amount of the default that occurs when cash flow is negative is limited to the amount of debt service that was assumed to be paid earlier in the cash flow waterfall and can be computed using the formula MAX(−Subtotal Cash Flow,0) along with a MIN function that limits the default to the debt service. The following formula can be used to make this calculation:

$$\text{Default} = \text{MIN}(\text{Debt Service}, \text{MAX}(-\text{Subtotal Cash Flow}, 0))$$

Step 3   Below the debt defaulted row in the cash flow statement, set up a line for the repayment of default. The repayment of default is a function of the subtotal cash flow and the opening balance for the debt default. Repayment of cash flow occurs only when the cash flow is positive, meaning a MAX(Subtotal Cash Flow,0) function should be used. The repayment of default cannot be more than the total amount of the default, which means it should be capped by the opening balance of the defaulted debt. This means the defaulted debt repaid is the minimum of the positive cash flow or the opening balance of the defaulted debt as shown in the following formula.

$$\text{Repayments of Default} = \text{MIN}(\text{Opening Balance of Defaulted Debt}, \text{MAX}(\text{Subtotal Cash Flow}, 0))$$

Step 4   Link the defaults in debt and the repayment of defaulted debt to the defaulted debt in the debt schedule. As with other items in the cash flow waterfall such as the debt service reserve account and letters of credit, calculations of cash flow movements should be made in the cash flow statement where they can be directly linked to subtotals. For the debt schedule the only formula should be a link.

Step 5   Compute the cash inflow realized by lenders for the purpose of computing the debt IRR and the debt net present value of the debt through deducting defaults and adding repayment of defaults to the scheduled debt service. The debt cash flow can be computed using the following formula:

$$\text{Debt Cash Flow} = \text{Interest Paid} + \text{Repayments} - \text{Defaults} + \text{Repayment of Default} - \text{Cash Debt Invested}$$

Assessing Risk and Return Characteristics of Subordinated Debt

The most basic issue in finance is assessing risks of receiving cash flow relative to returns from an investment. The issue of risk and return is highlighted in analysis of subordinated debt. Here, the higher credit spread on subordinated debt relative to senior debt can be evaluated relative to the higher risk of subordinated debt not realizing the interest rate as compared to senior debt. To consider the value of subordinated debt, a financial model should be able to determine the point at which the loss occurs so as to measure the risk and return characteristics of the subordinated debt. In modeling subordinated debt for a project finance transaction or for an acquisition model, the first step is to include the debt in the sources and uses of funds analysis that builds up the amount of the debt. This is explained in detail in Chapter 40. When developing a subordinated debt schedule for this risk analysis, it is possible that interest accruals are capitalized and added to the balance of the debt rather than currently paid. If interest is capitalized in this manner, then in the final period when the subordinated debt matures, the amount of the debt repayment is the sum of the opening debt balance and the interest capitalized for the final year.

Once the structure and row titles of the subordinated debt balance is established, the cash flow statement analysis should reflect the lower priority of the subordinated debt relative to senior debt service. If debt with a differing priority is included in the cash flow statement, then a cash flow waterfall should be modeled that presents the specific priority of each debt provision, including the interest, repayment of debt service, covenants, and cash sweeps

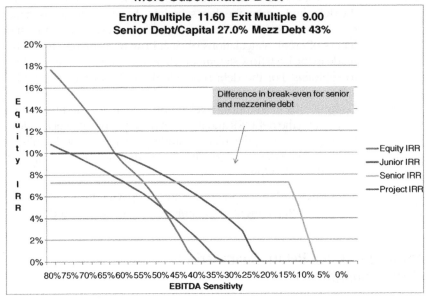

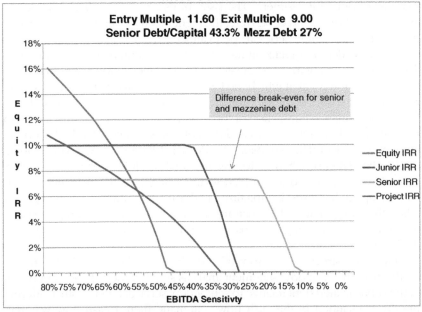

FIGURE 10.4 Internal Rate of Return on Senior versus Subordinated Debt with Different Capital Structures

that could all be part of a loan agreement for subordinated debt as well as a senior debt agreement. When structuring a cash flow analysis with alternative priorities, the ordering of titles in the cash flow analysis must conform to the priority of cash flow claims in the different loan documents. If there is a cash flow sweep for senior debt and subordinated debt interest paid rather than capitalized, then the senior debt sweep must occur after the junior debt interest payments and not before. Otherwise the subordinated interest line in the cash flow analysis would never receive any money.

To illustrate how a financial model can be used to assess the risk of senior debt relative to subordinated debt a sensitivity analysis on operating cash flow or EBITDA can be performed for the senior IRR, subordinated IRR, equity IRR, and the overall project IRR. The difference in EBITDA level at which the senior IRR and the junior IRR cross can be a measure of the risk. If there is a big difference in the points at which the EBITDA leads to declines in the IRR, then there is a large difference in risk for the senior relative to the subordinated loan. If the difference is small, then there is not much of a difference in EBTIDA that will cause the loss on debt and in theory the credit spread should not be very different. Figure 10.4 illustrates this idea where difference in EBITDA is shown on the *x*-axis and the different IRR levels are shown on the *y*-axis. The graph in Figure 10.4 is made using a data table that is explained in detail in Chapter 15. The case with more subordinated debt has more risk, as demonstrated by the break-even points.

CHAPTER 11

Alternative Calculations
of Equity Distributions

The final aspect of allocating free cash flow in a financial model relates to the manner in which dividends are paid to equity holders and new equity issues or buybacks are added to a model. Some shareholder agreements may distribute dividends using complex formulas rather than simply allocating common dividends in a proportionate manner to all shareholders. These agreements define the manner in which some investors receive a priority on the cash flow after debt service relative to others, which is analogous to the way in which loan agreements define priorities on free cash flow. Shareholder distribution structures can involve a technique known as a flip where one group of priority or senior shareholders is allocated the majority of dividends until a given internal rate of return (IRR) criterion is met. After achieving the IRR target, the dividend distribution scheme changes and the second investor receives a majority of the dividends. Other dividend structures known as ratchets can allocate a portion of cash flow in excess of a target to management or to developers. In these structures management may receive 10 percent of the excess cash flow after a target IRR of 20 percent is obtained. In acquisition transactions, earn-out provisions can be established whereby a portion of the purchase price is allocated to existing owners, but they are allowed to share in upside profits only after a defined target is obtained.

Addressing the equity cash flow in a model may also involve simulating a target capital structure rather than allowing surplus cash or short-term debt to build up on the balance sheet. If a target capital structure is used as an input assumption then the model needs to allow for the possibility of new equity issues or share buybacks in the cash flow analysis. The manner in which target capital structures can be reflected in corporate models is addressed along with different possible dividend distributions in this chapter. Techniques for incorporating target capital structures in a corporate model are the same as provisions for simulating capital adequacy ratios for a financial institution, which is an essential part of the analysis in modeling banks and other financial firms. The target debt-to-capital calculations can be made on the basis of the book value of debt and equity or the simulated market value.

Modeling Dividend Distributions

Cash flow sharing that is defined in shareholder agreements has analogies to the cash flow waterfall applied for debt modeling discussed in Chapter 10. When modeling a cash flow waterfall applied to equity distributions, the formula for dividend payments must be understood and reflected in the cash flow analysis so as to compute returns to different groups of shareholders. If dividends are not distributed in a proportional manner to all shareholders, there must be some kind of trigger mechanism that defines the distribution among different investors. In some cases, selected investors can receive an implicit priority on cash flow through either a shareholder loan or the right to a higher proportion of dividends relative to their investment in early cash flow periods. As these investors have lower risk they should also in theory have a lower expected return.

As with the cash flow waterfall for computing debt balances and reserve accounts, cash flow should be distributed among investors who have the different priority claims according to the definitions of relevant financing agreements. Complexity in modeling the cash flow distributions can arise if the criterion for defining when senior equity receives cash flow depends on an IRR limit, as previously described. One technique is to compute a rolling IRR that gradually increases as the project matures. You could then change the dividend formula after the target IRR has been achieved. However, because you have to allocate cash among equity investors for the period in which the target IRR is obtained, this method may not produce completely accurate results. In this period when the target IRR for investors with the higher priority on cash flow has just been achieved, some of the cash flow must be allocated to the highest priority investor, and some is allocated to a second investor who receives residual cash flow. To resolve this issue of cash flow distributions in the flip period, a more accurate technique than computing a rolling IRR is to set up a yield tracking account. Similar techniques to the yield tracking accounts can be applied to alternative equity distribution structures including earn-outs, management incentives, and equity kickers.

The yield tracking account has many analogies to a debt balance account. As with loans, an opening balance and a closing balance are reported on a schedule. Like debt issues that contain cash flow sweeps, the amount that is paid to each equity investor as a dividend depends on the cash flow analysis. Furthermore, in a similar manner that capitalized interest increases the debt balance of subordinated debt, the tracking account balance increases by the target IRR before the flip occurs. Finally, when writing equations associated with the tracking account in the cash flow statement, the MIN function is used. The process of setting up a yield tracking account includes the following six steps:

First, assumptions are input for both the amount of the funding that will be made by alternative equity investor groups and the manner in which the dividends are paid before and after the defined flip IRR criteria. The manner in which you can enter these inputs in the financial analysis section of a model is illustrated in Figure 11.1.

Partnership Inputs				Annual	Periodic
Classes of Equity Contribution	Capital	Pre-Flip	Post-Flip	Flip Rate	Flip Rate
Class A	60%	80%	25%	9.00%	2.18%
Class B	40%	20%	75%		

Sources and Uses of Funds		
Uses of Funds	Amount	Percent
Capital Expenditures	1,100,000	139%
Less: Grant	306,900	39%
Net Uses of Funds	793,100	100%
Sources of Funds		
Class A Stock	475,860	60%
Class B Stock	317,240	40%
Total Sources of Funds	793,100	100%
Sources and Uses Test	TRUE	

FIGURE 11.1 Illustration of Alternative Equity Funding in Project Finance Model

Second, set up an equity tracking account in a module somewhere above the cash flow analysis. This account has a repayment row that represents dividends paid to the senior equity tranche and it reaches a level of zero once the flip IRR target is achieved. The yield tracking account keeps track of the amount of money that is due to the senior equity after reflecting the earnings that must be realized for the yield or IRR to be met. To demonstrate how the account works, pretend the flip criterion IRR is zero. Here the dividends would stop after the opening balance of the tracking account falls to zero as dividends are paid, and the tracking account is like a debt balance account where all of the repayments (dividends) come from a cash flow sweep. With a positive IRR flip criterion, the cost of funding should be added to the opening balance like the opening balance of capitalized interest is added to payment-in-kind debt. After adding the yield to the balance of the account, the total amount of dividend payments to the senior equity results in the target IRR when the account balance reaches a zero balance. The tracking account is similar to the other balance accounts except that the opening balance is increased by yield that must be earned. This is illustrated in the layout of the yield tracking account. As with a debt schedule where you do not fill in amounts for the cash flow sweep until the cash flow statement is complete, do not fill in the formula for the dividends until the cash flow statement has been laid out.

Opening Balance
Add: Earnings on Investment (Opening Balance × Required Yield)
Subtotal: Balance after Yield
Less: Dividends Distributed to Senior Partner
Closing Balance

Third, when modeling the sources and uses of funds for a project financed investment or an acquisition, incorporate the different equity contributions through multiplying the total amount of equity issued by the input funding percentages. Assuming you know the total required equity funding amount, this process multiplies that total funding by the given percentages from the inputs as illustrated in Figure 11.1. Further detailed discussion of modeling a sources and uses of funds analysis is included in Chapter 40.

Fourth, add a subtotal in the cash flow waterfall measuring the cash available to equity. You can use this subtotal line to evaluate how much cash flow should be paid to shareholders with the higher dividend priority. The amount that is received by the senior equity cash claim can be computed from the minimum of the (1) cash flow subtotal multiplied by the pre-flip input dividend percentage or (2) the subtotal balance of the tracking account, as demonstrated here:

Senior Equity Dividend before Flip = MIN(Opening Balance of Tracking Account after Yield, Subtotal Cash Flow) × Percent Distribution Percentage to Senior Priority Equity before Flip

Fifth, compute the junior equity claim cash flows before the flip has occurred as the using a similar formula, except the cash flow is computed with the junior dividend percentage instead of the senior percentage:

Junior Equity Dividend before Flip = MIN(Opening Balance of Tracking Account after Yield, Subtotal Cash Flow) × Percent Distribution Percentage to Junior Equity before Flip

Sixth, after the tracking account has been extinguished, meaning the target IRR has been reached, apply the alternative post-flip dividend percentages that are defined by the flip. This can be computed by creating another subtotal account and using this new subtotal as the basis for the second dividend formula. The set up of a cash flow waterfall that includes the alternative dividend calculation could have the following titles:

Total Cash Flow to Investors after Debt
Subtotal 1: Cash Flow to Senior Investors before Yield Constraint
Less: Cash Flow to Senior Investors before Yield Constraint Using Pre-flip
    Distribution Percent and MIN Function
Less: Cash Flow to Junior Investors before Yield Constraint Using Pre-flip
    Distribution Percent and MIN Function
Subtotal 2: Cash Flow after Yield Constraint
Less: Cash Flow to Senior Investors after Yield Constraint Using Post-flip
    Distribution Percent
Subtotal 3: Cash Flow after Yield Constraint and Senior Dividend
Cash Flow to Junior Investors

An example of applying a flip structure with a cash flow waterfall applied to tax equity is illustrated in Figure 11.2.

	ABC	D	F	H	I	J	K	N	O	P
1	Timing		Base	▼						
2	Time Period				-1	0	1	2	5	6	7
4	Repayment Period					FALSE	TRUE	TRUE	TRUE	TRUE	TRUE
144	**Tax Equity Schedule**										
145	Opening Balance			=H150---->	-	11,747.5	9,587.6	1,259.2	-	-
146	Add: Time Value of Money		7.50%	=I145*$F$146---->	-	881.1	719.1	94.4	-	-
147	Subtotal			=SUM(I145:I146)-	-	12,628.5	10,306.7	1,353.6	-	-
148	Add: Drawdowns			11,747.45	-	-	-	-	-	-
149	Less: Dividends Received			-	3,040.9	4,526.9	1,353.6	-	-
150	Closing Balance			11,747.45	9,587.6	5,779.8	-	-	-
151										
175	**Cash Flow Waterfall**										
176	EBITDA				-	1,010.6	1,026.8	1,087.7	1,108.5	1,129.6
177	Less: Taxes				-	(2,030.3)	(3,500.1)	(903.9)	(240.7)	421.8
178	Cash CFADS				-	3,040.9	4,526.9	1,991.6	1,349.1	707.7
179	Less: Debt Repayment			-	-	-	-	-	-	-
180	Less: Interest			-	-	-	-	-	-	-
181	Cash After Debt Service			=J178-J179-J180---->	3,040.9	4,526.9	1,991.6	1,349.1	707.7
182	Less: Tax Equity Div Pre-Flip		100%		3,040.9	4,526.9	1,353.6	-	-
183				=MAX(MIN(J181,J147),0)*$F$182 ↗						
184	Less: Class 2 Equity Pre-Flip		0%	-	-	-	-	-	-
185				=MIN(MAX(J181,0)*$F$184,J147) ↗						
186	Cash Flow After Flip Period			=J181-J182-J184---->	-	-	638.0	1,349.1	707.7
187	Senior Equity Post Flip		1%	=J186*$F$187---->	-	-	6.4	13.5	7.1
188	Dividends to Class 2 Equity			=J186-J187---->	-	-	631.6	1,335.7	700.7

FIGURE 11.2 Illustration Process for Equity Distributions in Project Finance Model with Flip Structure

Computing a Target Capital Structure through Simulating New Equity Issues and Buybacks

Equity cash flow accruing to investors may include share buybacks or new equity issues as well as dividends. Share buybacks go into the pocket of existing shareholders while new issues dilute the interests of current shareholders and influence value when using equity cash flow as the basis for valuation. Including equity issues in a model may be necessary if you would like the balance sheet to reflect a target capital structure where debt and equity proportions remain at some predetermined level. This contrasts with accumulating cash on the balance sheet in the case of negative cash flow or allowing debt to continually rise if cash flow is negative. One way to incorporate a given target capital structure is to use the SOLVER tool. You can think of using the SOLVER when you need to run the goal seek multiple different times. In using the SOLVER you derive the amount of new equity issues or buybacks in each period so that the capital structure resulting from the model equals the capital structure that you enter as an input. If you are working on a financial institution model, implementing a target capital adequacy ratio can be an essential part of the process. You can also solve the problem by working through some algebra or by creating a user-defined function.

When simulating a target capital structure you will need to add inputs for the target capital structure and you will need space somewhere in the model for the new equity issues that will be established from using the SOLVER. New equity issues should be included in a separate row and they must be on the same page as the cash flow statement in the model because the SOLVER only works if all calculations are made on one spreadsheet page. Making the calculation for the target capital structure only works if you already have constructed a balance sheet and you can compute the projected debt to capital ratio or the debt to equity ratio. Once you have completed the SOLVER, you can attach it to a macro so that you can rerun it any time you make a change in model assumptions.

To incorporate a target capital structure in your model you can use the following steps:

1. Input the year-by-year target debt to capital ratio or the equity to asset ratio or the capital adequacy ratio at the bottom of the assumption module that contains other financing inputs.
2. Just below the balance sheet add a row for the computed debt to capital ratio or the other ratio that you are using to design your target capital structure. Also enter a row title for the target ratio that you put into your assumptions module as well as the period-by-period difference between the target and actual.

3. Enter a row at the top of the cash flow analysis or above the debt schedule named equity issues and share buybacks. This row will be the place where the outputs of the SOLVER will be placed. You should then insert a similar row near the bottom of the cash flow statement and link it to the row that will contain results of the SOLVER analysis. Revise the subtotal at the bottom of the cash flow statement so that net cash balances are incremented to include the new equity issues.

4. Include the new equity issues in your calculation of the equity balance that now should begin with the opening equity balance taken from the balance sheet in historical periods. The equity balance is then incremented by both retained earnings as well as the net new equity issues in the projection period.

5. Add-in the SOLVER feature to your spreadsheet and create a routine that sets the difference between the target and the actual debt to capital ratio to zero by changing the new equity issues. If you were making this calculation for only one period, you could easily use the Goal Seek feature to do this. Since you are in a sense rerunning the Goal Seek every period

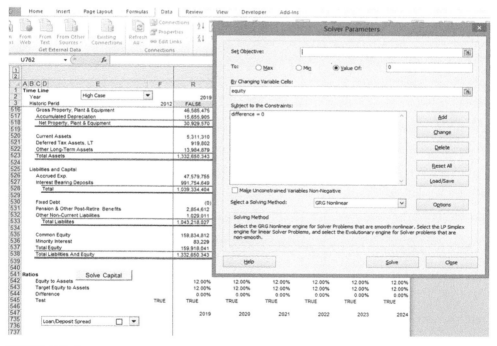

FIGURE 11.3 Illustration Using the Solver to Compute New Equity Issues in a Financial Institution Model

you can accomplish the same result with the SOLVER feature. To use the SOLVER, you enter a range of set cells as the row of the equity issues. You can then add a constraint that the row containing the differences between the modeled target debt to capital ratio and the input debt to capital ratio is zero.

6. You can add a macro to the SOLVER that enables the process to be easily repeated. Adding a macro is explained in Chapter 37.

Use of the SOLVER feature to derive a target capital structure is illustrated in Figure 11.3. In this case equity issues are defined by a range name and the difference between the modeled and ratio and the input ratio is also defined as a range name.

CHAPTER 12

Putting Together Financial Statements and Calculating Income Taxes

O nce the module that computes revenues, expenses, and working capital is established along with the depreciation schedule to derive after-tax cash flow and the debt schedule to calculate interest expense, the profit and loss statement, the cash flow statement and the balance sheet can be put together. In a corporate model, the profit and loss statement produces essential results for valuation analysis, as the net income defines the earnings per share and the return on equity. For a project finance model, earnings are not so important in presentation of the results, but calculation of the profit and loss statement is required to develop the line item for taxes paid that is used in the cash flow waterfall.

An effective way to structure the profit and loss statement is to compute earnings before interest, taxes, depreciation, and amortization (EBITDA) after revenues are subtracted from cash operating expenses and then subtract various letters like DA to end up with E (earnings). The EBITDA can be computed from the revenues and cash operating expenses that were developed in the pretax analysis. Depreciation and amortization (DA) can then be subtracted to derive EBIT. If you have set up your model with different modules, this is easy because the depreciation expense is already defined as a component of computing free cash flow. After computing EBIT, interest expense is subtracted and interest income is added, resulting in EBT. As with depreciation expense, the interest expense and interest income are taken from a module that you have already computed, this time from the debt schedule. With EBT tabulated, book taxes—the single calculation in the profit and loss statement that is not a subtotal—are computed through multiplying the EBT by the tax rate. This is the only item in the profit and loss statement, except for minority interest, that is not derived from somewhere else in the analysis.

Finally, you can subtract income claimed by minority shareholders to arrive at earnings that are realized by common shareholders.

The one calculation in the profit and loss statement that can involve some detailed analysis is the calculation of cash taxes. The tax analysis may sometimes seem complicated, but as with so many other issues, it is not too painful if the model is efficiently structured. The computation of taxes can have an important effect on capital-intensive projects such as renewable energy projects where rapid tax depreciation may be allowed, but the taxable income is not sufficient to use all of the tax deductions that include high levels of interest expense at the beginning of the modeling period. To address issues such as tax depreciation and other tax/book timing differences you can add a separate tax schedule after the profit and loss statement. This module evaluates taxes paid that can be derived from a net operating loss (NOL) carryforward analysis as well as the timing and permanent differences in pre-tax income for books and for tax returns. Errors in the calculation of taxes paid and/or simplistic accounting for taxes can cause large overstatement or understatement of cash flow and end up in distorted valuation.

Computation of Taxes Paid and Taxes Deferred

A modeling technique you can use to compute taxes is to first calculate taxes recorded on the books in the income statement and then subsequently calculate the cash taxes actually paid in a separate section. One of the items that can seem difficult to incorporate in the model are net operating loss carryforwards. After the income statement is completed, the EBT that was computed in the income statement can be used as the first step for computing the cash taxes that are paid on tax returns. If the company is generating a loss, book taxes can be negative but actual taxes paid must be positive or zero.

In making a tax analysis and starting with the book EBT, the first step is to make adjustments that convert the EBT that comes from book accounting policies into the earnings before taxes for purposes of computing real taxes paid. Taxes paid use expenses that are allowed to be recorded on the tax return that may be different from book taxes. These adjustments to arrive at taxable income on a tax return may involve adding back book depreciation and then deducting tax depreciation, adding back intangible amortization or making adjustments for other items such as the recording income on the change in derivative value.

Once the adjustments for book versus tax expenses and income are made, a new EBT line for purposes of computing cash taxes should be created. This line item representing EBT on the tax return drives the analysis of net operating loss carryforwards. Analysis of net operating loss carryforward involves determining the balance of the net operating loss and making various adjustments that increase or decrease the carryforward balance. The carryforward generated and the net operating loss used can be evaluated using very similar concepts to the cash flow waterfall with the MIN and MAX functions discussed in Chapters 10 and 11. When you have finished calculating taxes paid, you can also calculate the change in deferred taxes and the balance of accumulated deferred tax.

To compute taxes paid and a net operating loss carryforward, you can use the following step-by-step process in the module that is placed below the income statement. The process described here assumes that book taxes have been computed on the income statement through multiplying EBT by the statutory tax rate. The net operating loss balance is computed on the basis of taxable income rather than taxes paid.

Step 1   Begin by creating a row that repeats the EBT from the income statement.

Step 2   Adjust the book EBT for depreciation and other items that cause cash taxes to differ from the taxes accounted for on the book profit and loss statement. Use the adjustments to derive a line item named EBT for taxes.

Step 3   Set up an account that maintains the NOL balance, including the opening balance, additions that accrue to the account from creating the NOL when taxable income is negative, and reductions in the NOL when the carryforwards from earlier years are used to reduce taxes that would otherwise be paid if there is positive taxable income.

Step 4   Compute the amounts deposited into the NOL balance account when EBT for the tax return is negative through converting the negative amounts into positive numbers. As with the cash flow waterfall, you can use the MAX function to convert negative numbers into positive numbers and then to cap the converted number to zero.

$$\text{Additions to NOL} = \text{MAX}(-\text{EBT}, 0)$$

Step 5   Calculate the amounts removed from the operating loss balance and used to offset taxable income through determining the minimum of either the opening balance or the taxable income in a similar manner to the tests that were made in evaluating the cash flow waterfall with the MIN function. As the net operating loss balance can only be used when taxable income is positive, a MAX function is also necessary. Thus, the use of net operating loss carryforwards applies to both the MIN and the MAX functions—

the MIN function limits the use to the taxable income or the opening NOL balance.

$$\text{Applications of NOL to Reduce Taxable Income}$$
$$= \text{MAX(MIN(Opening Balance, EBT for Tax Return), 0)}$$

Step 6   Compute the adjusted taxable income after accounting for inflows and outflows from the net operating loss carryforward balance. Taxable income is increased by the additions to the NOL to assure that it cannot be negative. Taxable income is reduced by applications or subtractions to the NOL balance.

$$\text{EBT after NOL} = \text{EBT for Tax} + \text{Additions to NOL}$$
$$-\text{Application of NOL to Taxable Income}$$

Step 7   Multiply the adjusted taxable income by the statutory tax rate to determine the cash taxes per the tax return.

Step 8   Subtract the book taxes from the cash taxes to compute the change in accumulated deferred tax liability. When the book taxes are greater than taxes paid, the liability increases, and when book taxes are less than taxes paid, the liability declines.

Step 9   Accumulate the deferred taxes through adding the changes in deferred taxes computed in Step 8 to the prior year's balance. If the balance of accumulated deferred taxes is positive, put the balance on the liabilities side of the balance sheet; if they are negative, change the sign and put the account on the assets side of the balance sheet.

This step-by-step process to compute taxes paid is illustrated in Figure 12.1.

If the tax law includes provisions whereby the NOL can expire after a certain period of time, then the calculations of the NOL balance become a lot more painful. The problem with an expiring NOL is that one needs to look backward to find when the NOL was previously lost and, more important, the expired NOL must be adjusted so as not to include NOL balances that have already been applied to taxable income. To compute this more complex NOL calculation that includes potential for expirations, a three-step process can be applied beginning with calculation of the amount of NOL that would have expired had no NOL been used up. The NOL that was generated in prior periods, however, does not necessarily represent the amount that will expire because some of the NOL may have already been used up from positive EBT in the intervening periods. In the extreme it is possible that all of the NOL was already used before the expiration date, meaning there is no expired NOL.

	C	D	E	F	G	H	I	J	K	L	M	N	O
1	Tax Rate		27.50%										
2			1	2	3	4	5	6	7				
3	Book Income Statement												
4	EBT - Book		(500.0)	(300.0)	100.0	200.0	300.0	400.0	500.0				
5	Tax Expense		(137.5)	(82.5)	27.5	55.0	82.5	110.0	137.5		<---- =K4*Tax_Rate		
6	Net Income		(362.5)	(217.5)	72.5	145.0	217.5	290.0	362.5				
7													
8	Tax Calculation												
9	EBT - Book		(500.0)	(300.0)	100.0	200.0	300.0	400.0	500.0				
10	Less: Added Dep for Tax		100.0	100.0	100.0	(100.0)	(100.0)	(100.0)	-				
11	EBT - Tax		(600.0)	(400.0)	-	300.0	400.0	500.0	500.0				
12													
13	NOL Balance												
14	Opening Balance		-	600.0	1,000.0	1,000.0	700.0	300.0	-				
15	Add: Tax Losses		600.0	400.0	-	-	-	-	-		<---- =MAX(-K11,0)		
16	Less: Used NOL		-	-	-	300.0	400.0	300.0	-		<---- =MAX(0,MIN(K14,K11),0)		
17	Closing Balance		600.0	1,000.0	1,000.0	700.0	300.0	-	-				
18													
19	Adjusted EBT		-	-	-	-	-	200.0	500.0		<---- =K11+K15-K16		
20	Taxes Paid		-	-	-	-	-	55.0	137.5		<---- =K19*Tax_Rate		
21													
22	Deferred Tax Change		(137.5)	(82.5)	27.5	55.0	82.5	55.0	-		<---- =K5-K20		
23	Accumulated Deferred Tax		(137.5)	(220.0)	(192.5)	(137.5)	(55.0)	-	-		<---- =J23+K22		
24													

FIGURE 12.1 Illustration of Basic Net Operating Loss Process in Financial Models

Because of this, the second step of the process is to accumulate the amount of the NOL that has been already applied to reduce taxes in previous periods. The third step is to compare the amount of the NOL that would expire had there been no previous use of the NOL with this accumulated amount of expired NOL that was computed in the second step. The adjustment to the expired NOL is the amount of the accumulated unused NOL.

The unadjusted expiry of the NOL from step 1 can be computed with the OFFSET function where the line item for the NOL created is used as the reference cell. This is illustrated in Figure 12.2. The OFFSET function is used to look backward to the date when the NOL was generated from the standard NOL table. Next, a balance is accumulated that adjusts for the NOL that has been previously used. This accumulated amount of NOL previously used adds the NOL that has been applied in reducing taxable income to the opening balance. The amount of used NOL that has been reduced from current or previous usage is computed using the MIN function where the test is the amount that would have expired without any previous usage relative to the opening balance of the accumulated prior usage. The MIN function is used because the expired NOL cannot be more than the amount generated in the earlier period and it cannot be more than the accumulated NOL used up. Finally, the NOL expired is computed as the amount of the NOL that would have expired without accounting for prior reductions from the accumulated prior usage. This is the line titled "Expired NOL: Adjusted less Reduction" shown on Figure 12.2.

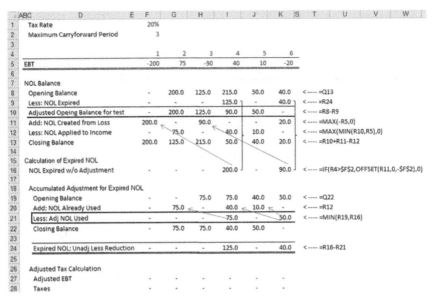

ABC D	E	F	G	H	I	J	K	S T U V W
1	Tax Rate		20%					
2	Maximum Carryforward Period		3					
3								
4			1	2	3	4	5	6
5	EBT		-200	75	-90	40	10	-20
6								
7	NOL Balance							
8	Opening Balance		-	200.0	125.0	215.0	50.0	40.0	<---- =Q13
9	Less: NOL Expired		-	-	-	125.0	-	40.0	<---- =R24
10	Adjusted Opeing Balance for test		-	200.0	125.0	90.0	50.0	-	<---- =R8-R9
11	Add: NOL Created from Loss		200.0	-	90.0	-	-	20.0	<---- =MAX(-R5,0)
12	Less: NOL Applied to Income		-	75.0	-	40.0	10.0	-	<---- =MAX(MIN(R10,R5),0)
13	Closing Balance		200.0	125.0	215.0	50.0	40.0	20.0	<---- =R10+R11-R12
14								
15	Calculation of Expired NOL							
16	NOL Expired w/o Adjustment		-	-	-	200.0	-	90.0	<---- =IF(R4>$F$2,OFFSET(R11,0,-$F$2),0)
17								
18	Accumulated Adjustment for Expired NOL							
19	Opening Balance		-	-	75.0	75.0	40.0	50.0	<---- =Q22
20	Add: NOL Already Used		-	75.0	-	40.0	10.0	-	<---- =R12
21	Less: Adj NOL Used		-	-	-	75.0	-	50.0	<---- =MIN(R19,R16)
22	Closing Balance		-	75.0	75.0	40.0	50.0	-	
23								
24	Expired NOL: Unadj Less Reduction		-	-	-	125.0	-	40.0	<---- =R16-R21
25								
26	Adjusted Tax Calculation							
27	Adjusted EBT		-	-	-	-	-	-	
28	Taxes		-	-	-	-	-	-	

FIGURE 12.2 Illustration of Complex Net Operating Loss Calculations with Expired NOL

Cash Flow Statement and Balance Sheet

The structure of all types of financial models includes a cash flow statement and a balance sheet as the final part of the model calculations before risk analysis and valuation. Detailed issues associated with the cash flow statement were discussed earlier in the context of the cash flow waterfall, and the cash flow statement should have a similar presentation to the cash flow waterfall. With the exception of cash flow waterfall issues, programming the cash flow statement and the balance sheet should only involve linking to other calculations that have already been made.

Because of issues associated with making a cash flow waterfall, it is better to construct a cash flow statement in a direct manner with revenues, expenses, and EBITDA rather than using an indirect method that begins with net income. If net income is the starting point of cash flow, then interest expense and interest income are already included in net income. But to compute a cash flow waterfall, the senior interest may have to be separated from subordinated interest expense, and interest income generally is available for cash flow. Other than the MIN and MAX statements that are used to define the cash flow priorities discussed in Chapter 10 and Chapter 11, every item on the cash flow statement either is a subtotal calculation or comes directly from the debt schedule, the income statement, the working capital module, or another module. The end of the cash flow statement differs depending on the type of model. For corporate models and integrated models, dividends are included in the financing section of the model. In these situations the end of the cash flow statement is surplus or deficit cash flow that feeds into the short-term debt and the surplus cash. In project finance models and acquisition models, changes in cash are included as required reserve accounts such as the debt service reserve account. For these model types the last line is the dividend distribution.

Start of period	03/01/13	04/01/13	05/01/13	11/01/13
End of period	03/31/13	04/30/13	10/31/13	04/30/14
Year	2013	2013	2013	2014
Balance Sheet				
Equty Balance				
Opening Balance	51,879.22	52,648.47	57,257.15	46,643.11
Add: Funding	769.25	4,608.69	0.00	0.00
Add: Income	0.00	0.00	-8,653.14	-8,148.09
Less: Dividends	0.00	0.00	1,960.90	2,465.96
Closing Balance	52,648.47	57,257.15	46,643.11	36,029.07
Assets				
DSRA Balance	0.00	3,936.08	3,880.20	3,824.33
Lockup Balance	0.00	0.00	0.00	0.00
Net Plant Base	112,334.93	113,400.00	100,800.00	88,200.00
Net Plant IDC	2,834.79	3,047.99	2,709.32	2,370.66
Unamortised Fees	1,438.91	1,439.67	1,336.83	1,234.00
Total	116,608.63	121,823.73	108,726.36	95,628.99
Liabilities and Capital				
Construction Debt	63,960.16	0.00	0.00	0.00
Permanent Debt	0.00	64,566.58	62,083.25	59,599.92
Re-financed Debt	0.00	0.00	0.00	0.00
Defaulted Debt	0.00	0.00	0.00	0.00
Equity	52,648.47	57,257.15	46,643.11	36,029.07
Total	116,608.63	121,823.73	108,726.36	95,628.99
Difference	0.00	0.00	0.00	0.00
Test	TRUE	TRUE	TRUE	TRUE

FIGURE 12.3 Illustration of Balance Sheet in Project Finance Model

The last part of constructing a model is the balance sheet. For people who have done a lot of modeling, seeing their balance sheet balance can be one of the best feelings in the world. To the contrary, not being able to find where the balance sheet has gone wrong can be very frustrating. For the balance sheet to be an effective auditing tool, each item in the balance sheet should already be computed in the model. The balance sheet should have no calculations other than links, meaning you should simply find and collect all of the closing balances and connect them to an integrated balance sheet. The balance of accounts receivable, cash, plant, and debt should already exist in various other modules. For other assets on the balance sheet that are not modeled in detail such as investments and operating reserve accounts, balances should also be established. Separate accounts should be created for the book balance of assets and the tax balance of assets if there is a difference in depreciation methods or in the basis for depreciation.

An essential part of putting an integrated balance sheet together is making an equity balance account. This account is like any other balance and includes the additions to an opening balance for net income and reductions for dividends. Since net income is the last line of the profit and loss statement and dividends are at or near the end of the cash flow statement, the account cannot be computed until the other statements are complete. The equity account and a balance sheet are illustrated in Figure 12.3. A similar presentation should be made for minority interest that also derives items from the income statement and the cash flow statement. Figure 12.3 illustrates this process of putting together all of the closing balances and seeing if the balance sheet balances with a TRUE/FALSE test at the end.

PART II

Analyzing Risks with Financial Models

Sensitivity Analysis, Scenario Analysis, Break-Even Analysis, Time Series, and Monte Carlo Simulation

CHAPTER 13

Risk Assessment

The Centerpiece of All Valuation, Contracting, and Credit Issues in Finance

One of the tasks required to manage any business is the honest and somewhat boring job of accounting for its historical financial results by keeping track of profit and asset value. A perhaps less noble and much more challenging task faced by all but the very simplest of business endeavors as well as by those who make investments is to make implicit or explicit forecasts of future cash flow. The problem with making such a forecast is that it by definition encompasses an unknown and uncertain future. With the possible exception of forecasting nominal cash flow earned on German government bonds, all cash flow forecasts from all financial models will turn out to be wrong.

Financial modeling techniques described in the first part of the book addressed issues involving how to construct a financial model but did not consider how to quantify potential uncertainty in assumptions for key variables that drive projected revenues, operating expenses, and capital expenditures. This part of the book moves to the more difficult and interesting question of how to assess the uncertainty associated with economic variables such as price, industry demand, expense structure, cost of new production capacity, and interest rates. The amount by which implicit or explicit forecasts of these items could differ from realized results forms the framework for thinking about risk. This framework contrasts with attempting to measure risk with elaborate statistics advocated by academics such as beta and value at risk (VaR). Assessing the risk associated with potential variation in future cash flows is at the heart of just about every issue in finance and is essential in many other professions. When Winston Churchill said that "true genius resides in the capacity for evaluation of uncertain, hazardous, and conflicting information," he was probably not talking about adding risk analysis to financial models, but he could have been.

The process of evaluating uncertainty that comes from how much cash flow forecasts will differ from expected levels may involve estimation of how much estimated growth rates will be wrong, what will be the possible change in interest rates, how much actual product prices and costs will be different from predicted prices and costs, what will be the change in public attitudes to various products, or what sudden changes in political events could occur. This somewhat ambiguous concept of risk that is defined as the potential variation in outputs of a financial model from base case amounts is not consistent with suggestions that risk can be captured in a single number defined from statistical analysis that is the subject of much finance literature.

Attempting to measure risk is by no means a new subject in finance, and over the past 50 years Nobel Prizes have been awarded to economists who have developed various supposedly revolutionary mathematical or statistical approaches to measuring risk ranging from beta, to probability of default, to VaR. Notwithstanding the elegant formulas and complex statistics that attempt to put a specific number on risk, application of new and seemingly promising innovative mathematical methods to risk assessment have turned out to be frustrating in practice. As more and more complex mathematical risk assessment tools are developed, the conflict as to whether risk should be evaluated using statistical analysis or if it should be measured by more traditional business judgment has become an issue that provokes a lively debate in finance. After the global financial crisis of 2008 when many were burned by relying on statistics like VaR, bankers, stock analysts, financial managers, and consultants often would rather perform a relatively simple scenario analysis instead of attempting to represent a company as a complex mathematical equation that incorporates a probability distribution.

In describing the mechanics of measuring risk, this part of the book begins by reviewing risk assessment techniques that rely on business savvy and economic judgment—qualitative risk matrices, sensitivity analysis, break-even analysis, scenario analysis, and tornado diagrams. This fundamental risk analysis is explained in Chapters 14 to 18 using step-by-step explanations of how to add various features to a financial model. After addressing risk assessments that require judgment with respect to what can happen to a particular variable or sets of variables, Chapters 19 through 22 describe how to create stochastic time series models that measure risk on a mathematical basis. The discussion of mathematical risk analysis demonstrates how you can use a combination of mathematics and judgment to create probability distributions of various outputs in your financial model. To develop mathematical models and probability distributions, a tool kit of statistical parameters is introduced that includes volatility (the dispersion in prices), mean reversion (the speed at which prices come back to long-run average levels), correlations among variables (such as the correlation between natural gas and oil prices), lower and upper price boundaries on movements in a parameter, sudden jumps, long-run trends, and long-run equilibrium prices.

Six Alternative Ways to Assess the Risk of a Company, a Project, or a Contract

These days, corporations hire people with finance, mathematics, physics, or economics degrees and give them a title of risk manager. Presumably, in one way or another, risk managers are supposed to evaluate how various decisions affect risk and value of equity and debt investors or other stakeholders. The somewhat mysterious job title of risk manager seems to encompass everything from a junior analyst computing historical financial ratios for periodic credit reviews to a person with a PhD in physics who develops VaR statistics derived from complex mathematical equations. In practice, quantification of risk can encompass a whole lot of different analyses, ranging from simply graphing an economic driver of your model and observing how that variable affects cash flows and value, to computing the probability distribution of cash flows using time series equations and Monte Carlo simulations.

The different sorts of risk analysis can be classified according to their mathematical and programming complexity. At one end of the risk assessment scale is a purely qualitative list of risks that may include some kind of estimate of their relative importance as well as their possible mitigation. Other approaches along the mathematical complexity spectrum move from sensitivity analysis to break-even analysis to scenario analysis to tornado diagrams and finally to Monte Carlo simulations. Table 13.1 lists six different approaches to risk analysis along with a brief description of what sort of analysis is involved in each technique.

Table 13.1 puts judgmental approaches to risk assessment in the left columns and moves to the more mathematical methods in the columns listed at the right. A lot of the discussion in this part of the book addresses Monte Carlo simulation, the rightmost column of the table. This approach seems to measure risks in a financial model without having to apply much judgment. Instead, the variation in parameters comes from supposedly objective statistical analysis. The lack of business judgment required when implementing this approach does not imply that Monte Carlo models produce a better assessment of risk than does careful business judgment. Very intelligent people who have made a large personal investment in the study of complex mathematical approaches to risk assessment do have a natural desire to apply their knowledge in practice. However, none of the valuation mistakes discussed at the beginning of the book would have been rectified through more use of elaborate statistical analysis, simulation, and time series models. Indeed, some business valuation mistakes have been aggravated by inappropriately

TABLE 13.1 Alternative Methods for Risk Analysis

Risk Matrix	Sensitivity Analysis	Break-Even Analysis	Scenario Analysis	Tornado Diagram	Monte Carlo Simulation
List economic and financial factors that can influence the financial performance of an investment, and determine whether the risks are mitigated through contract provisions and/or hedging. For variables that are not mitigated, use adjacent risk analysis techniques.	Choose an important economic variable for which the risk is not mitigated, and make a graph of how the variable affects the outputs of financial variables related to valuation such as NPV and internal rate of return.	Make a table that computes outputs of financial variables alongside an economic variable, and determine when the financial variable becomes unacceptable. Once the break-even level is established, evaluate the likelihood of the economic variable realizing the break-even level.	Evaluate a series of different output variables given a set of different input variables. The series of variables often includes a downside case that evaluated if different levels of debt can be serviced. If the downside case cannot support the level of debt, then alternative debt structures can be developed.	Tornado diagrams evaluate which variables have the most significant effect on the financial output of a model and which variables have a relatively insignificant impact. This tool can be used for due diligence analysis, or to demonstrate the relative upside potential and downside risk.	Simulation produces a distribution of returns and can predict the likelihood of a valuation variable such as IRR or DSCR falling within a certain range. The simulation depends on time series equations that are derived from parameters such as volatility, mean reversion, correlation, and price boundaries.

applying historical data to complex financial models without using enough judgment as to how distributions of cash flow can change in the future.

A valuation nightmare that illustrates conflicts between different ways to assess risk is found in the case of Long-Term Capital Management (LTCM) and its demise in the late 1990s. LTCM was a hedge fund created in part by Nobel laureates Myron Scholes and Robert Merton that, when it failed, almost brought the entire financial system to its knees and required federal government intervention—although the problems seem like very small change compared to Lehman Brothers, Merrill Lynch, American International Group, and other problem institutions of 2008. LTCM is interesting to study from a risk management perspective because it was created to make money by developing sophisticated mathematical models that evaluated statistical relationships and supposedly carefully managed many risks. Risks were measured through complex mathematical techniques, so at the heart of the LTCM case is the question of whether mathematical models and statistics can replace business judgment when gauging risk.

In making investments on the basis of statistical analysis and mathematical models, the LTCM case contained an explosive mixture of the valuation errors discussed in Chapter 1. Some of the errors included:

- Assumptions that historical statistical relationships can be used to predict the future and be reestablished after a period of time. LTCM failed when many economic variables did not act as they had in the past and sudden nonlinear shocks occurred without historical precedent.
- Lack of transparency in presenting financial information (that's management speak). Both investors and lending banks (the largest Wall Street banks) were not allowed to see how trades were made and what models were used. It was impossible for outsiders to measure risk with sensitivity analysis or break-even analysis.
- Belief that staff employed by the fund was smart enough to continually beat the market and earn returns well above the cost of capital in extremely competitive financial markets. This notion that the fund could continually earn returns that were seemingly above the cost of capital (the powerhouse square) ultimately caused the fund to take on higher and higher risks when returns began to fall (return envy). The changing risk structure of the company was not apparent to outside investors because of the secrecy rules.
- Investment strategies that were derived from highly complex mathematical models that supposedly discovered new ways to make money without being fully vetted. If LTCM could really make money by studying mathematical relationships (anathema to believers in efficient markets such as Scholes and Merton themselves), then others would be able to copy the formulas. After a business is copied, the potential to earn profits

above the cost of capital goes away (new business entry when returns are high).

■ Faith in the reputation of other people—Merton, Scholes, and a famous bond trader named John Meriwether—without independently assessing whether the fundamental business concepts were viable. This is similar to many other cases in which the name of a bond rating agency, the reputation of a large corporation, or trust in a famous person ends badly.

■ Investments that were made without verifying the underlying economics with simple back-of-the-envelope checks and putting your feet on the ground. The fund invested in Russian bonds by studying mathematical relationships rather than by visiting the country and seeing that military officers and secretaries were not being paid. Similar problems occurred before the 2008 financial crisis when financial modelers refused to get out of the tour bus to look at real estate facilities they were modeling.

The LTCM case raises a fundamental question of whether risk analysis can really be reduced to a series of mathematical equations. LTCM's dramatic demise demonstrated that complex quantitative techniques for risk measurement cannot be used without any supplemental business judgment. This tension between relying on mathematical equations on the one hand versus using judgment on the other that was raised in the LTCM case provides a backdrop in considering how best to assess the six different approaches to risk assessment introduced in Table 13.1.

Using Direct Risk Assessment to Measure Cash Flow and Financial Ratios

None of the methods shown in Table 13.1 mentions the single parameter that finance theory implies is the only thing you need to measure the relative risk of a stock, namely the beta parameter. Finance courses and textbooks implicitly or explicitly suggest that one has to go further than measuring beta from stock prices, which then translates into the weighted cost of capital, when measuring risk. This risk-adjusted discount rate along with expected cash flows can measure value; no scenario analysis, no Monte Carlo simulation, no other direct measurement of risk is necessary. As beta supposedly contains all relevant information about risk, none of the techniques in the table should be necessary, because risk is measured in the discounting process. Risk analysis methods discussed in Chapter 14 through Chapter 22 are premised on the alternative notion that risks cannot magically be stuffed into one cost of capital number.

To contrast risk analysis using beta and weighted cost of capital with other approaches, consider the following two different hypothetical presentations made by well-dressed investment bankers who are pitching an acquisition proposal.

Investment Banker Number 1: Valuation from Financial Theory and Risk Measurement with Beta

In pitching his proposal, the first adviser values the target company by carefully applying techniques taught in business school, including computation of free cash flow, measurement of the weighted average cost of capital (WACC), and use of stable terminal growth rates after an explicit forecast period. He makes elegant calculations of the cost of equity capital from statistical analysis of historical stock prices through computing the unlevered beta with mean reversion on daily stock prices, and applies market weights to the capital structure through relevering the beta. This method results in valuation of the target company on a stand-alone basis that is adjusted for the value of synergies generated from the merger. The first investment banker even makes a fancy waterfall graph that shows the different components of value as illustrated in Figure 13.1. You can make this graph yourself in minutes by using a template file included at www.wiley.com/go/internationalvaluation.

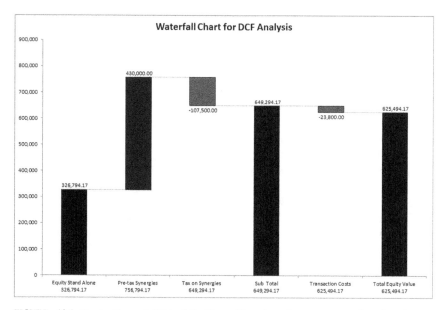

FIGURE 13.1 Illustration of Waterfall Chart Showing Components of Value in an Acquisition

In coming up with the valuation, many people looking at the discounted cash flow (DCF) analysis will immediately recognize that two of the most subjective assumptions in the valuation—the weighted average cost of capital derived from beta and the growth rate—can lead to a very wide variation in value, as illustrated in Table 13.2. Table 13.2 is a typical presentation of value made by investment banks that often produce a large difference in value resulting from different discount rates and growth rates. Note that in Table 13.2 the top right-hand entry has a value of 5.75 while the bottom left-hand entry has a value of 16.61.

TABLE 13.2 Range in Implied EV/EBITDA from Applying the Discounted Cash Flow Model

		Weighted Average Cost of Capital			
		7%	8%	9%	10%
	0%	8.34	7.26	6.42	5.75
Terminal	1%	9.38	8.00	6.97	6.17
Growth	2%	10.82	8.99	7.68	6.70
Rate	3%	12.99	10.37	8.62	7.37
	4%	16.61	12.44	9.94	8.27

Adviser Number 2: Accretion and Dilution from Financial Models

The second adviser uses an integrated financial model (see the discussion on the structure in Chapter 4) to assess risk and value of the merger rather than applying discounted cash flow analysis. He creates two corporate models: one for the acquiring company without a merger, and another for the combined acquiring company and the target company using the integrated merger model. Then, after synergies are included in the analysis, he makes a presentation of whether earnings per share are higher in the combined case (accretion) then the stand-alone case or whether earnings per share decline (dilution). He also makes an assessment of whether the company can maintain its investment-grade bond rating given the proposed financing applied in the merger. This integrated analysis accounts for the actual proposed financing of the transaction, the effect of the transaction on interest costs and earnings, the estimated synergies, the accounting for goodwill, and the fees paid for advisory services. This second investment banker defines the maximum value that can be paid for the target company as the purchase price level that avoids dilution in earnings per share.

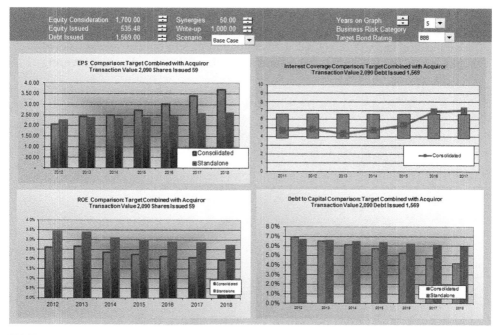

FIGURE 13.2 Illustration of Summary Outputs from an Integrated Merger Model

An example of the type of analysis that comes from his integrated model is shown in Figure 13.2. In the presentation made by this second investment banker, there is no WACC to be computed from beta and no terminal value or growth rate to be estimated. Further, the investment banker can apply similar assumptions for the acquiring company and the target company to eliminate bias.

Knowing that valuations using the DCF technique can be so easily manipulated by making small changes in the beta-driven WACC or the terminal growth rate—two variables that are very difficult if not impossible to measure—the company considering the merger most likely would pay more attention to the technique presented by the second adviser. Then, rather than pretending that the risk of making the acquisition can really all be incorporated in the WACC, the decision maker could ask for a series of different scenarios and break-even analyses that test how sensitive the accretion or dilution estimates are to key variables that drive the forecasts. This type of risk analysis may evaluate the break-even point for the growth rate before which the merger becomes dilutive. Through applying break-even analysis, sensitivity analysis, or scenario analysis to the integrated financial model, the financial officer is directly assessing risk rather than assuming it can be stuffed into the beta parameter. In a similar vein, decision makers assessing the risk of a project-financed investment or a leveraged acquisition can use direct risk analysis techniques to directly assess risks of the equity IRR falling below a certain level and/or the cash flow not covering debt service.

CHAPTER 14

Defining, Describing, and Assessing Risk in a Risk Allocation Matrix

The first step in assessing risk is often to categorize, describe, and put some kind of subjective probability weight on different risks in a structured manner rather than diving into any quantitative analysis. At this stage of the analysis, a financial model is not part of the process. The idea of categorizing risks by writing them down in a table should force you to think about, discuss, and understand a variety of different risks; how the risks may be mitigated by contracts; the likelihood of the risks occurring; the magnitude of the problem if the risks arise and how those risks could potentially affect investment returns. Qualitative analysis may involve preparing a memo on key risk issues, categorizing various risks into a matrix that describes the risks, or some other similar approach. This first step of risk analysis highlights the problem with lack of transparency when a company uses fancy financial language that may be a method of hiding real problems. Without information being presented in a transparent manner and without access to data that allows assessment of value drivers, analysts cannot even identify the risks.

In creating a structured list of potential risks, the matrix can become rather boring and mechanical where construction delay risks are mitigated by liquidated damages, interest rate changes are mitigated by interest rate swaps, operation and maintenance (O&M) expenses are mitigated by a fixed-price O&M contract, and so forth. But this mechanical process often misses the point. You should instead use the risk identification and analysis exercise to think carefully about small risks that can explode, whether the cost structure of the investment makes sense, and whether mitigation measures are really effective. When categorizing risks, describing risks, and then mitigating risks, you should also implicitly or explicitly put some kind of weighting on the likelihood of the risks becoming a problem and the magnitude of difficulties if the risk is realized.

Once the risks are defined and described in a risk allocation matrix, you should consider whether some of the risks can be mitigated. Mitigation techniques generally boil down to one of three techniques: (1) insurance, (2) contracts, and (3) hedges. Mitigation of risks using one of these three methods involves some kind of explicit or implicit cost to investors for transferring the risk. One of the objectives in financial models may be to consider trade-offs between the benefits and the costs of mitigating different risks. To demonstrate how risk matrices could be useful in evaluating the costs and benefits of mitigation strategies, you could imagine applying the process in your personal life every day when you wake up in the morning. Alternatively you could make a qualitative risk assessment in the context of evaluating the health care of a relative who has recently fallen down. Health professionals sometimes tend to concentrate primarily on attempting to minimize a risk without evaluating the cost of the risk mitigation in terms of lifestyle and monetary cost. In the extreme, you may eliminate the risk of someone falling down by not allowing a person to leave the bedroom. The real task should be to assess whether the benefits of this mitigation strategy to reduce the probability of a fall is worth the cost of the loss of freedom from being locked in a room. When developing a financial model, the real task is often to gauge whether measured risks that cannot be mitigated are acceptable.

Say all risks in an investment could somehow be perfectly mitigated (if you could do this for your life, it would be unbearably boring). In this case the investment would be risk free, and valuation could be established through simply discounting cash flows at the risk-free interest rate. For virtually any investment, some risks will not be mitigated by insurance, contracts, or hedging. Further, even if the risks could seemingly be mitigated by contracts, those contracts could be broken, resulting in a different type of risk.

For risks that cannot be completely mitigated, financial models can be used to assess whether the unmitigated risk is acceptable. The relationship between a financial model and a risk allocation matrix is the column of the matrix that lists unmitigated risk. These risks in the last column should be evaluated with the financial model. When using a financial model to evaluate whether the risks are worth taking, you can apply one or more of the other risk assessment techniques like break-even analysis, scenario analysis, and Monte Carlo analysis. The risk analysis techniques evaluate the magnitude of the risk and determine whether the risk is acceptable for lenders and/or equity investors. Consider an extreme case where all of the risks are mitigated except for changes in the interest rate. Once the risk matrix demonstrates that other risks are mitigated, you can use the financial model to do things like determine how high interest rates would have to move before the investment cannot pay back its debt or how high interest rates would have to rise before returns to equity holders fall below the risk-free rate.

Table 14.1 illustrates the types of items that could be included in a risk matrix. Examples of items to include are the likelihood and the impact of a risk.

TABLE 14.1 Illustration of Risk Allocation Matrix

Risk Category	Description	Probability/ Likelihood	Impact	Mitigation	Analysis of Unmitigated Risk	Example
Development Phase						
Permits				Spend Less Earlier		Collapse of Geothermal Development Wells
Resource Study				Increased Study		Problems with Wake Effect of Off-Shore Wind
Construction Phase						
Construction Overrun						
Material Prices				Contracts/Hedges	Break-Even Effect on IRR/Debt	Petrochemical Plants with Increasing Steel Prices in 2006
Labor Costs				LSTK Contracts	Cost of Comparable Projects	Eurotunnel with Costs Increasing from 4 Billion GBP to 11 Billion
Exchange Rates				Hedges	Break-Even/Scenario/ Monte Carlo	Petrozuata Appreciation of Peso Cost USD 450 Million
Force Majure				Insurance	Difficult to Put in Model	Fukushima Needed to Protect Against Act of God
Seemingly Minor Items					Include in Model	Problems with Transport of Wind Towers

(continued)

TABLE 14.1 (*continued*)

Risk Category	Description	Probability/Likelihood	Impact	Mitigation	Analysis of Unmitigated Risk	Example
Construction Delay Primary Project				Contracts-Liquidated Damage	Break-Even Effect on IRR/Debt	1970's Nuclear Plant Cost from Delay Where Interest Cost was Half of Plant Cost
Associated Projects				Contracts	Break-Even Effect on IRR/Debt	Reduced Availability of Nigerian Plants from Gas Supply
Technical Failure Resource Quantity				Resource Studies/Tests	Analyze Reserve Report	Fradulent Study by U.S. Consultant in Phillipines
Plant Efficiency				Contracts-Liquidated Damage	Analyze Independent Engineering	Availability of Combined Cycle Plant in Saudi Arabia
Operation Phase Price				Contracts/Hedges/Options	Break-Even/Scenario/Monte Carlo	Telecom Price Collapse after Increase in Merchant Capacity
Volumes				Contracts	Break-Even/Torndao Diagram	Chronic Overestimation of Traffic on Toll Roads
Cost Structure				Contracts/Hedges	Break-Even/Torndao Diagram	Failed Attempts of MCV Cogeneration to Hedge Gas Prices to Coal Prices

Risk	Mitigation	Analysis	Example
Royalties	Contracts/Political Insurance	Break-Even/Scenario/Monte Carlo	Assumption of Petrozuata That Could Earn High Returns and Not Pay Royalties
Political			
Contract Abrogation	Political Insurance	Price Analysis/Off-Taker Credit	Enron Attempts to Charge High Prices in Dabhol Contract
Nationalization	Political Insurance	Option Price Analysis	Venezuela Nationalization of Marriott Hotel after Conference Cancellation
Currency Convertibility	Political Insurance/Local Banks		Problems in Conveting Zimbabwe Dollars for Mines during High Inflation Period
Political Instability	Political Insurance		Change in Law for Illinois Biomass Plants
Financial			
Interest Rate Changes	Hedges/Options	Break-Even/Scenario/Monte Carlo	Change in Interest Rates for Subprime Loans
Inflation Rate Changes	Contracts	Break-Even Effect on IRR/Debt	Inflation and Exchange Rate Made Indonesia PPA Contracts Unsustainable
Refinancing Risk	Hedges/Options	Break-Even/Scenario/Monte Carlo	Built-In Refinancing Risk in Subprime Loans

The matrix should specify a low-probability risk with high consequences and a relatively high-probability risk with relatively low consequences. It should also include the technique for mitigation of the risk using contracts, problems with the risk mitigation such as a counterparty default on contracts, the relative importance of residual risks not mitigated, and the risk analysis used to evaluate the residual risks. The column on the right of Table 14.1 lists selected cases in which unmitigated risks caused problems with the performance of investments.

CHAPTER 15

Presentation of Risk Analysis through Adding Sensitivity Analysis to Financial Models

R isk analysis is often a lot about effective presentation. One of the simplest and most effective ways to analyze risk is through changing one of the inputs to the financial model and gauging the effect on key output variables such as the value of the company, the internal rate of return, or the debt service coverage ratio (DSCR). If management can visualize how a key variable such as energy production affects cash flow and at the same time can see statistics such as the DSCR, there may be little else managers really need to do in analyzing risk. Allowing people to play around with variables and to understand what happens to cash flow, earnings, or debt balances may be one of the most important things you can do with a financial model and a lot of it is about presentation. This sensitivity analysis process involves making an effective display, often with a graph, to illustrate what happens to some measure of value when the level of a key value driver changes.

High-powered analysts who compute statistics such as value at risk (VaR), probability of default, and complex option price premiums for credit default swaps may scoff at sensitivity analysis as being overly simplistic. But consider a variable that is very difficult to predict such as the level of traffic that will occur between England and France in the famous Eurotunnel project, electricity demand growth in the Philippines, the level of U.S. housing prices before 2007, or electricity prices after a change in the structure of the UK market—all of which caused valuation nightmares. Given the difficulty in forecasting these variables, an effective picture of what happens to the value of the investment when the variable changes may be the best thing that you can realistically do. Think about assessing the value of collateral debt obligations that accumulated subprime mortgages. It surely would have been very useful to employ your financial model and paint a picture of what would happen to the value of the investments under alternative housing demand-and-supply assumptions. For example, if the supply of housing increased by 20 percent in a region, what would happen to the value of the debt? Or consider the case of Constellation Energy Corporation after the 2008 financial crisis. Management of the company presented VaR statistics and maintained that the purpose of its trading activities was primarily to hedge other parts of the business. This risk analysis, which included all sorts of VaR statistics, frustrated some investors and provided little useful information. In hindsight, a much more helpful presentation would have been a simple graph with a sensitivity analysis illustrating what happens to Constellation's cash flow and earnings when the prices of oil and natural gas change. This chapter addresses presentation issues for risk analysis.

Figure 15.1 illustrates sensitivity analysis in the case of evaluating the acquisition of an upstream oil company. This model evaluates acquisition of the company that was funded by senior debt, subordinated debt, preferred stock, and common equity. The graph in Figure 15.1 is taken from a cash flow waterfall that is accumulated on an annual basis. A series of controls to manage sensitivity analysis allow you to examine how projected cash flow is distributed in the context of different financing structures and different operating assumptions. Through pushing the oil price up or down with the spinner

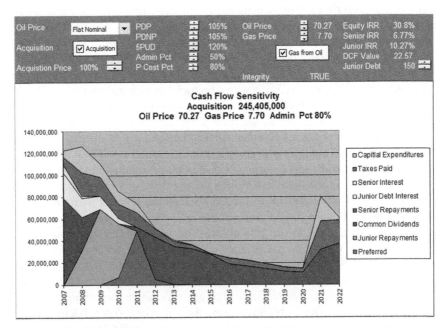

FIGURE 15.1 Sensitivity Analysis in the Case of Evaluating Acquisition of an Upstream Oil Company

button shown in Figure 15.1, you can see how the length of time for the repayment of a loan changes, what happens to the rate of return earned on different securities, and the point at which the given rate of return cannot be achieved. For a senior debt, subordinated debt, or equity investor, you could imagine decision makers spending their time pushing the spinner button up or down to vary the oil price. Rather than wasting a lot of time on forecasting oil prices, the investor could begin with the desired return and back into what long-term level of oil price is required to attain the desired cash flow and the target rate of return. The picture shown in Figure 15.1 is intended to demonstrate that sensitivity analysis mostly involves presentation and creatively summarizing key input drivers along with different measures of value.

Setting Up Data for Making Graphs by Converting Periodic Data into Annual, Semiannual, or Quarterly Data

To make an effective presentation of sensitivity analysis, it is generally better to graph data on an annual basis rather than showing detailed monthly or quarterly data, which may be the basis of your financial model. This can be particularly useful in graphing components of a cash flow waterfall that shows where cash comes from and where it goes. If a model is developed on a periodic basis using monthly, quarterly, or semiannual time increments, you can quickly create a summary of annual cash flows or income statement items that can be used for presentation of a sensitivity analysis. In a similar way, you could also make a quarterly analysis out of monthly data. You can also present balance sheet accounts that do not accumulate over the year, such as the closing balance of plant or debt on an annual basis.

Annualizing periodic data can be accomplished by first defining the year or quarter value below the date in the sheet or sheets of the model that are modeled on a detailed monthly, quarterly, or semiannual basis. You can then use the SUMIF function or the SUMIFS function to accumulate the periodic cash flows within the year and present these variables in an annual sensitivity graph. To demonstrate the process of creating annual (or quarterly) numbers from periodic data, the following steps walk through a technique that allows you to very quickly convert periodic cash statements to annual statements.

Step 1   Compute a time variable such as a year and switch indicator for the end of the fiscal year in a detailed section of the model.

The SUMIF or the AVERAGEIF functions are very useful in many parts of financial models and can compute a series of aggregated values or aggregated averages across a larger series of rows or columns. A straightforward example is a case where there are data for 12 months of a year that should be summed in a sheet that simulates many years of monthly data. To find the annual sum across many years of monthly data, first establish the year number in the sheet with detailed time increments (using the YEAR function) or a quarter end date (with the EOqtr user-defined function discussed in Chapter 6). This year or quarter variable is the basis for the summations. The year or quarter end is called the range in the SUMIF or the SUMIFS functions.

In creating a quarter by quarter variable, you can also make a quarterly counter from a month indicator. To do this, use the ROUNDUP function on the month number divided by 3. The formula for a quarter number and adding time periods for use in the SUMIF is illustrated in Figure 15.2.

$$Quarter = ROUNDUP(Month/3, 0)$$

	A B C	D	F	G	N	O	P	X	Y
1	Age in years				-1	-1	-1	1	2
2	Period counter				-8	-7	-6	2	3
3	Pre-COD Switch				TRUE	TRUE	TRUE	FALSE	FALSE
4	Months in period				1	1	1	6	6
5	Periods per year				12	12	12	2	2
6	Start of period	=M7+1---->			01-nov-13	01-déc-13	01-janv-14	01-févr-15	01-août-15
7	End of period	=EDATE(N6,N4)-1---->			30-nov-13	31-déc-13	31-janv-14	31-juil-15	31-janv-16
8	Month	=MONTH(N7)---->			11	12	1	7	1
9	Quarter	=ROUNDUP(N8/3,0)---->			4	4	1	3	1
10	Year	=YEAR(N7)---->			2013	2013	2014	2015	2016
11	End of Quarter	=EOQTR(N7)---->			31-déc-13	31-déc-13	31-mars-14	30-sept-15	31-mars-16
12	Quarter and Year	=N10&":"&N9---->			2013:4	2013:4	2014:1	2015:3	2016:1

FIGURE 15.2 Illustration of Preparing Periodic Model for Summary Quarterly Model

If you are summing balance sheet accounts or items such as accumulated production capacity, you can add an identifier for the end of the period that will be summed. One way to do this is to make a switch variable that will be true at the end of the year (e.g., month = 12). In a project finance model, it is convenient to use the month after the commercial operation date. If the month of the period after the commercial operation date of a model is equal to the fiscal month (e.g., June), then the fiscal month switch is TRUE.

Period Switch: Month(Ending Date) = Fiscal Month

Step 2   To make an annual or quarterly summary that can be used for sensitivity graphs, you generally add a new sheet that will contain aggregated data. In this new sheet begin with a simple year or quarter counter by starting with the first year or quarter that you want to present and then increment the year by one. To create a quarterly counter, select an end of quarter date to begin the process and use the EOMONTH function and with 3 as the increment.

Step 3   Copy selected account titles of cash flow, balance sheet, and other items that you would like to present on an annual basis into the annual sheet. This sheet will be the basis for presenting data with graphs in the risk analysis.

Step 4   Apply the SUMIF function or the SUMIFS function for cash flow items, profit and loss items, or operating items. The SUMIF function accepts three variables—a range, a criterion, and a sum range. The first argument for the SUMIF function is the range from the model with detailed time periods (the year number or end of quarter) that you are summarizing into aggregate periods. The range is often the year from the model that is computed on a monthly, quarterly, or semiannual basis as illustrated in Figure 15.2 and explained in step 1. If a monthly model is used, then there are 12 columns that have the same year number. The second argument required in the SUMIF function is a single criterion that will be used to summarize the data. This is the counter variable from the annual sheet or the quarterly sheet that was described in step 2. The third argument is the sum range or the average range. This range variable comes from the detailed sheet that contains the monthly data.

The most effective way to apply the SUMIF function for making graphs and creating sensitivity analysis is through clicking on the entire row (or column) for the year range and the sum range in the page with the detailed periodic data (the first and third arguments). If you are pressing the F4 key to make fixed references when using the SUMIF function, you are wasting a lot of time. The idea of clicking on an entire row (which can be done by pressing the SHIFT and SPACEBAR keys for rows and the CNTL and SPACEBAR keys for columns) makes the process far easier and avoids the need for fiddling around with creating fixed references for columns.

To aggregate data by time period, first click on the entire row of years (or quarter and year) in the detailed sheet with periodic data and press the F4 shortcut key to fix the first argument in the SUMIF function. This establishes the test for which columns will be summed. Next, refer to the year entered in the annual sheet in step 2 and use a relative reference to lock in the row number but not the column name (press the F4 key twice). Finally, refer to the range to be summed by clicking on the entire row in the detailed sheet without locking in the row number or the column number using the F4 key. The SUMIF function using this idea is illustrated in the two formulas in Figure 15.3. The sheet with the detailed periodic data is named "Working," and row 10 of that sheet includes the year associated with each monthly period. The key to making this process easy is to use the entire rows in the detailed sheet, as demonstrated in Figure 15.3.

A B	C	D	F	G	H	I	J
2							
3	Year		2015	2016	2017	2018	2019
4							
5	Generation	=SUMIF(Working!$10:$10,Annual!E$3,Working!59:59)*E29---->	1,004,913	1,001,903	998,902	995,910	992,926
6	Nominal FIT	=AVERAGEIF(Working!$10:$10,Annual!E$3,Working!77:77)*E29---->	136.19	137.17	138.20	139.14	140.07
7	Nominal Merchant Price	=AVERAGEIF(Working!$10:$10,Annual!E$3,Working!82:82)*E29---->	50.54	49.04	50.76	50.02	51.52
8	Revenues	=SUMIF(Working!$10:$10,Annual!E$3,Working!85:85)*E29---->	136.82	137.40	138.01	138.54	139.05
9	EBITDA	=SUMIF(Working!$10:$10,E$3,Working!102:102)*E29---->	129.23	129.71	130.20	130.61	131.01
10	NOL Created	=SUMIF(Working!$10:$10,E$3,Working!435:435)---->	134.81	60.82	13.95	0.00	0.00
11	NOL Used	=SUMIF(Working!$10:$10,E$3,Working!436:436)---->	0.00	0.00	-3.47	-18.58	-34.05

FIGURE 15.3 Illustration of Using SUMIF and AVERAGEIF to Compute Annual Data for Purposes of Sensitivity Graphs

Annualized Amount = SUMIF(Row of Years in Monthly Sheet, Year Counter in Annual Sheet, Row of Data)

Annualized Amount = SUMIF(Working!$10:$10,Annual:C$5, Working!20:20)

Step 5 Sometimes you would like to present items such as debt or production capacity on the annual sheet when graphing sensitivity analyses. The problem with these balance sheet accounts is that they do not accumulate across months or quarters and you cannot use the SUMIF approach described in step 1 to step 4. To set up accumulated accounts for sensitivity graphs, one method is to use a TRUE/FALSE switch in the detailed monthly sheet to separate dates that will be used to accumulate single values over the year. As there is only one TRUE switch for a year in the periodic sheet, the sum will be taken only from the column in the detailed sheet at the end of the fiscal year period. Then you can use the SUMIFS function to include the year end TRUE switches as a criteria as the SUMIFS function allows you to enter multiple criteria. You enter one criterion for the year number and another for the switch that defines the end of the year. In the following example, row number 21 is summed in the detailed model and row number 13 includes a switch variable that is true only for the last period in each year (e.g., December in a monthly model):

Annualized Amount = SUMIFS(Sum Range in Detail, Range for Testing Period, Criteria 1, Range for Testing Period 2, Criteria 2, . . .)

or

Annualized Amount = SUMIFS(Detail!21:21,Detail!$12:$12, Annual:C$5,Detail$13:$13,TRUE)

Step 6   A problem with the preceding process is that when you want to pull a variable from the detailed spreadsheet for making a sensitivity analysis you have to adjust the SUMIF formula manually. The equation must refer to a particular row in the detailed sheet. This means that you have to manually change the last argument of the SUMIF formula. You cannot simply copy the SUMIF formula for each line item in the annual or quarterly sheet and then somehow refer to a row and have the formula automatically adjust. Instead of retyping the last part of the SUMIF formula you can use a fancier method that allows you simply to put a row number from the detailed model into the annual sheet. Then you can copy the SUMIF or the SUMIFS function to as many rows as you want and you do not have to change the formula. This approach uses the INDIRECT function.

The INDIRECT function accepts a range name like D10 and gives you the value associated with this range. You may wonder why you do not just enter =D10 instead of the function =INDIRECT("D10"). But the INDIRECT function can be surprisingly useful and is probably worth learning. This is especially true if you create a macro that automatically reads data from the Internet as described in Chapter 36. The advantage of using the INDIRECT function is that if you are going to collect data from D10, D15, D32, and so on, then you can make a flexible variable with the & sign. With this function you do not have to manually change the cell references in the spreadsheet formula.

To create a flexible process where you do not need to manually change the row number in the SUMIF or SUMIFS formulas, you can use the INDIRECT function to refer to the row number in the detailed sheet that contains the data you want to collect. This can be accomplished by using the ROW function as well as a sheet name. The spreadsheet name can be created by making a simple user-defined function. Using the INDIRECT function you can then make a range name that is used as the last argument in the SUMIF function rather than manually changing the row number for each accumulated item. The trick to using the

INDIRECT function is to make a range name that includes the sheet name of the sheet that contains the detailed financial data. To create a range name, you can use the & operator and enter an exclamation point, as explained in the next section.

Using the INDIRECT Function to Automate Conversion to Time Period Data

The following process shows how you can use the INDIRECT function to automatically adjust the SUMIF function without having to retype details for the last argument for the function.

Step 1   Use the ROW function to enter the selected row number in the annual sheet. You can refer to any column for the row in the detailed periodic model that you would like to summarize in the annual sheet. For example:

Row number = ROW(detail!:A20)

Step 2   Unlike when using the ROW and COLUMN functions, there is no simple function to find the sheet name. To resolve this you can create your own function. In creating this function that can find the sheet name of the detailed sheet, you can use the code shown here. You just need to remember a rather obtuse extension called .Parent.Name:

```
Function sheet_name(cell_reference)
        sheet_name = cell_reference.Parent.Name
End Function
```

Step 3   Use the sheet name and the row number found from previous steps to create a cell reference for the INDIRECT function. Do this by combining the row, column, and sheet name cells into one range name. To make a range name from the sheet name and the row number, you need to add quotation marks and codes that are used in a range name, as illustrated:

Range Name = """ & Sheet Name "!" &
Row Number & ":" & Row Number

If you have a lot of instances that require making a range name, you could create a function that accepts the sheet name and the row number and puts in all of the tedious quotation marks.

Step 4   Once the range name is defined, the INDIRECT function can be
used as an argument in the SUMIF function or the SUMIFS
function. To apply the SUMIF function using the previous example, the following formula would be entered:

SUMIF(Range of Years in Detail Sheet, Year Criteria in
Annual Sheet, INDIRECT(Range Name)

Use of the INDIRECT function in creating a quarterly summary report is illustrated in Figure 15.4. It may seem somewhat
tedious from the preceding description, but when you have
created one SUMIF function with the INDIRECT function, you
can copy it as much as you like. Now you do not have to manually
change the row numbers in the detailed sheet.

	D	E	F	G	H	I	L	Q	W
1									
2	Quarter					31-mars-13	31-déc-13	31-mars-15	30-sept-16
3	Year					2013	2013	2015	2016
24			=SUMIF('Mixed Use Model'!$5:$5,'Mixed Use Quarterly'!I$2,INDIRECT('Mixed Use Quarterly'!$G30))						
25									
26	=ROW('Mixed Use Model'!E180)		=""&F30&""!""&E30&":"&E30						
27									
28			=sheet_name('Mixed Use Model'!E180)						
29	Construction Expenditures								
30	Land	180	Mixed Use Model	'Mixed Use Model'!180:180		225,555	230,611	-	-
31	Infrastructure	181	Mixed Use Model	'Mixed Use Model'!181:181		-	45,000	-	-
32	Residential 1	182	Mixed Use Model	'Mixed Use Model'!182:182		-	-	-	-
33	Residential 2	183	Mixed Use Model	'Mixed Use Model'!183:183		-	-	-	-
34	Residential 3	184	Mixed Use Model	'Mixed Use Model'!184:184		-	-	1,650,000	-
35	Retail	185	Mixed Use Model	'Mixed Use Model'!185:185		-	-	-	2,796,955
36	Office	186	Mixed Use Model	'Mixed Use Model'!186:186		-	-	-	3,167,187
37	Shopping Centre	187	Mixed Use Model	'Mixed Use Model'!187:187		-	-	-	864,916
38	Total	188	Mixed Use Model	'Mixed Use Model'!188:188		225,555	275,611	1,650,000	6,829,058

FIGURE 15.4 Illustration of Using the INDIRECT Function in Creating a Quarterly
Summary Report

Making Flexible Graphs for Sensitivity Analysis

In creating a financial model you can easily generate thousands of graphs for
sensitivity analysis by selecting different variables and pressing the F11 key.
Some models have 20 to 30 graphs while others have none at all. Rather than
presenting information that has marginal use for valuation, the art in making
an effective sensitivity analysis presentation is often to select data that shows
risks and values in a summary page. For a project finance model, one of the
essential graphs should be of the cash flow available for debt service relative
to the debt service over the operating life of the project, which can be taken

directly from the cash flow waterfall. This graph not only demonstrates the cash flow buffer for cash relative to debt service payments, but also illustrates the equity returns that are driven by the various structuring aspects of the debt, including the DSCR, the debt tenor, the type of funding, the debt service reserve account, and so forth. In the case of a corporate model, presenting historical and projected return on invested capital effectively summarizes many of the important assumptions and results of the analysis. Both the graph of the cash flow and debt service in a project finance model and the graph of return on investment in a corporate model can be obtained from the accumulated annual analysis. The graphs should be flexible with respect to different key dates used in the model such as the terminal date in a corporate model or the construction period and the operating life in a project finance model. It is more important to make these focused graphs flexible and effective than to present a hundred graphs that do not have much meaning in terms of risk and value.

Figure 15.5 is a presentation of cash flow and debt service that paints a picture of what is happening in the operating phase of a project finance model. Using graphs like this you can create a spinner button to see how much selected variables such as the electricity production of the plant can fall in order for cash flows in a downside case to cover debt service. If cash flows cannot cover debt service in a downside case, then bankers may suggest that the amount of the debt should be reduced or the terms of the debt structure should change. In order to help you quickly and effectively graph important cash flow and valuation statistics in the context of economic and financial structuring variables, the remainder of this chapter walks through how to make the data ready for graphing, how to create graphs that correspond to timing variables in your financial model, how to put flexible titles on your graphs, and how to add spinner buttons to graphs when making sensitivity analysis.

Step 1: Using F11 or ALT, F1 to Make a Quick Graph

To make a graph that summarizes risk, select a variable from the financial model and put the data in a separate section of the annual or quarterly sheet in the model. If you structure the rows and columns in this part of the model with the title for the output variable in the cell that is immediately to the left of the data and then add the x-axis for the graph (e.g., the year) just above the row of data, then you can press the F11 key and very quickly make a graph of the data. The F11 key should quickly become one of your favorite shortcut keys. You can also use the ALT and F1 keys to place the graph in the same spreadsheet. The general approach of structuring the data for a graph is shown in Figure 15.6.

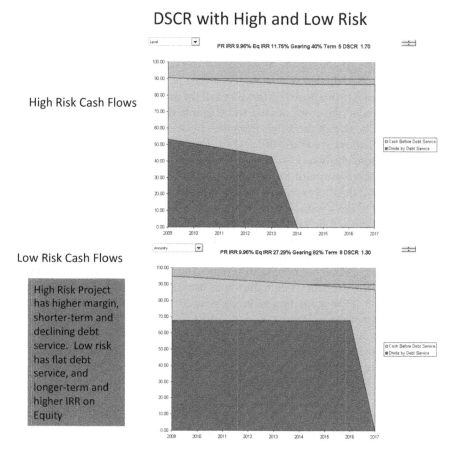

FIGURE 15.5 Debt Capacity from Cash Flows with Different Volatilities

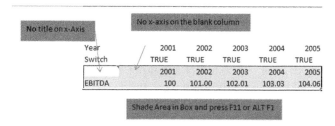

FIGURE 15.6 Setting Up Data to Graph Using the F11 Key or the ALT and F1 Keys

While the F11 key is a very nice and simple method, there are a few points that can make the process of creating a graph much more flexible and effective:

- Create a variable for the *x*-axis above the data if the data is arranged in rows (and to the left of the data if the data is arranged in columns). If you want years to be shown on the *x*-axis of the graph, then add a row with the years above the rows of data to be graphed.
- Delete the title of the *x*-axis from the cell above the row that you want to graph. This means that if the years are going to appear on the *x*-axis, then make sure the word "year" is not to the left of the data. The way the spreadsheet program knows that it is supposed to put the item on the *x*-axis is if the there is no title for the row (or column). This idea of leaving the title of the *x*-axis blank is an important point that can make all sorts of presentations much easier. It is also essential when you want to make *x-y* charts quickly that can evaluate the fixed versus variable cost to evaluate risks associated with operating leverage.
- If there are blank columns between the data that are to be graphed and the titles of the data, then begin the *x*-axis data only in the column that is to be graphed. If the graph begins in the year 2014, which is in column G, and the titles are in column D (i.e., E and F are blank), then enter the year above column G and leave the year title for other columns (E and F) blank.
- Shade the area of the data, including the *x*-axis and the blank cell that is to the left of the data for the *x*-axis. After the data are highlighted, press the F11 key (or the ALT and F1 keys).

An example of setting up data to graph it effectively using the F11 key or the ALT and F1 keys is illustrated in Figure 15.6.

Step 2: Illustrating the Effect of Selected Variables with Spinner Buttons and Drop-Down Forms

The idea of presenting sensitivity analysis is to show how an input variable affects the output variables that are chosen for presentation with something like a spinner button or a drop-down box. A spinner button or one of the other forms such as a drop-down box or a scroll bar can be effective because you can keep your assumption variables in the input sheet, but you can also manipulate those input variables from other places in a workbook such as on the summary page or on the top of an output graph. The input for operating expenses should still be on the input page, but if you use a spinner button, you can change the value of the operating expenses from either the summary page or a graph or both, while keeping the input where it is supposed to be. The disadvantage of using spinner buttons is that you can forget what the values were for the original data that you input in the base case. Resolving this problem and having the ability to quickly return to base case values is discussed in Chapter 17. To make a graph with a spinner button that can be used to adjust the input variables, first choose one or more input variables that have an important effect on the rate of return, value, or credit quality. In Figure 15.1 a spinner button was attached to the oil price input. Unfortunately, there are a few quirks that complicate this process, particularly when the graph is on a different page from the input data. A process for making the use of forms such as the spinner button more effective includes the following:

- In order to create a form such as a spinner button, use the View, Toolbars, Forms menu in Excel 2003. In Excel 2007 or later you must include the Developer tab on your ribbon, which can be a little tricky to find from the FILE ribbon. Once the forms are shown on the menu or the Developer ribbon is on the screen, you can use the Insert Controls tab from the Developer menu (make sure to use the Form Controls and not the ActiveX Controls) and insert a spinner button, drop-down box, or slider bar on the sheet. Click on one of the forms (at the top part) and then paint the form in the spreadsheet. Figure 15.7 illustrates how to find Form Controls.

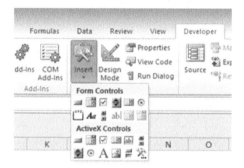

FIGURE 15.7 How to Find Form Controls

- Once you have painted the form on the sheet, click on the form with your mouse and then press the right mouse button (right click). After that, select the Format Controls option to attach the control to the input cell with the cell link and define minimum and maximum values. The nice thing about a form like a spinner button is that you can copy it anywhere else in the workbook and still maintain the input number in an appropriate place.
- The problem with using the cell link is that the spinner button or the drop-down box form attaches only to a cell in the particular sheet where the form is placed. If you put the spinner button in Sheet 1, then a particular cell attached in the cell link such as E1 will be changed in Sheet 1 when

you change the spinner button. But if you copy the spinner form to Sheet 2, the spinner button will change to E1 in Sheet 2 rather than the number that you wanted to be changed in Sheet 1. This all but defeats the benefit of using forms like the spinner button because the point of a spinner button is to be able to change data in the input sheet without moving inputs to another sheet such as a summary sheet. It also means that you cannot copy the form to a graph if the graph is in a separate stand-alone sheet.

■ The solution to this problem of copying or moving the spinner button and other Form Controls to different sheets is to include the name of the sheet (e.g., input sheet) in the cell link value of the spinner button. This can be accomplished with a technique some call the windshield wiper method. To use the windshield wiper approach, first click on any sheet that is different from the sheet that contains the input value that you are adjusting (other than a chart sheet). Then move the cursor right back to the current sheet so that the sheet name is included in the cell link. Including the sheet name in the cell link is illustrated in Figure 15.8. Once you have created a form and attached it to an input cell in this manner you can copy the form to other sheets as much as you want and place the spinner button or other form directly at the top of the graph.

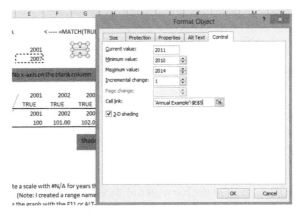

FIGURE 15.8 Illustration of the Windshield Wiper Method in Creating Spinner Buttons and Drop-Down Forms

Step 3: Adding Titles to a Graph with Summary Statistics

It is often useful to display a title on the graph that contains both text and numerical statistics that represent important valuation outputs. Maybe you would like to have the title of the graph show the internal rate of return for the project, the minimum debt service coverage ratio, or the net present value of cash flows. You may want to show one or more of the key input variables that are being changed with the Form Controls, such as the oil price that was illustrated in the Figure 15.1. Using the process to copy a spinner button to a graph described in step 2, you can add a title (or a text box or a custom data label) from a set of spreadsheet cells using the following process:

- When combining text and numbers on a graph, you must first enter all of the information that will be included in the title into a single row (or column) somewhere in your workbook. You can change the format of the numbers and make the title as long as you would like. But the title of the graph cannot come from two or more different rows (or two different columns). Say you want to show the discounted cash flow value—the output—and the weighted average cost of capital (WACC)—the input— on the graph. You could then enter the following information on different cells of a single row:

  Enterprise Value: 4,556 Euros Using WACC of 6.4%

- Once the information that will become the graph title has been entered in the single row or column, select the existing title on the graph (if there is no existing title, then you must create one). When selecting the title, make sure that you do not double-click on the title. With the title selected, press the equals sign on the keyboard and then shade the single row or column of the title where you entered the data. This process of making a flexible title is illustrated on Figure 15.9. After shading the area where you typed in the single row representing the title, press the ENTER key and the title should appear on the graph.

- If you would like the title on the graph to have multiple rows as in the oil price example in Figure 15.1, you cannot press the ENTER key on the graph title to make a new line. Instead, you can create a new line character in the single row graph title. To insert a new line character, press the ALT and ENTER keys together at various cutoff points in the single row that you constructed for the graph title.

Optional Step 4: Making Dynamic Graphs with the OFFSET Function or the #N/A Symbol

Sometimes you would like to make a flexible graph in which the length of the data on the *x*-axis of the graph can vary. In a project finance model, the length of the concession agreement may vary, in a corporate model the explicit period may change, and in an acquisition model the length of the holding period may vary. There are two ways to make a dynamic graph where the *x*-axis changes as a function of the model timing inputs and where periods that

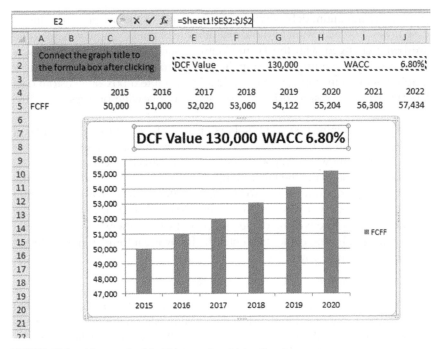

FIGURE 15.9 Adding a Flexible Title to a Sensitivity Graph

you do not want to present on the graph can be excluded. One relatively easy way is to make the x-axis have a #N/A symbol for periods that you do not want to be graphed. A second technique is to construct a graph using a dynamic range name created from the OFFSET function.

To apply the #N/A technique, you must replace the x-axis with #N/A for all of the periods that you do not want on the graph. When the scale of the graph is a date (not a year), you must also replace the data itself that you want to graph with the #N/A symbol. You could make a #N/A symbol somewhere in the sheet and then create a range name so you do not have to type #N/A multiple times (being lazy with spreadsheet formulas is a good thing). This can be accomplished by using the MATCH function with both TRUE and FALSE – MATCH(TRUE,FALSE)=#N/A. To use the #N/A approach in making a graph with a flexible time line you should select the x-axis and change the scale to a DATE AXIS. This will exclude all of the columns that have the #N/A from the graph. Setting up the x-scale of a graph with the #N/A method is illustrated in Figure 15.10. In using the #N/A technique, there is a quirk whereby you must make the data itself have values of #N/A if the graph is not annual. If the graph is from an annual summary sheet, you do not need to make this adjustment.

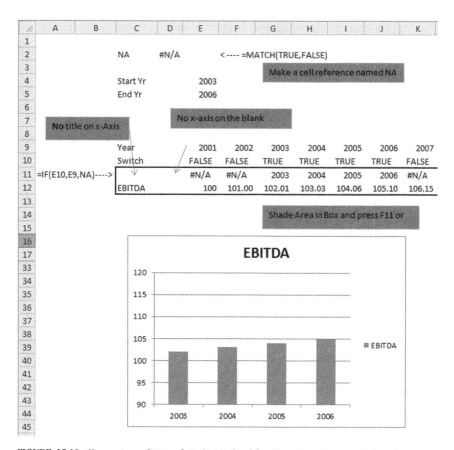

FIGURE 15.10 Illustration of Use of #N/A Method for Creating a Dynamic Graph

A second technique that you can use to make dynamic graphs is to create a flexible range name with the OFFSET function. You can then use the flexible range name as the source of data in the graph. This method is more flexible than the #N/A method. Further, if you are creating a lot of statistical analysis, it does not slow down your calculations the way that the #N/A method sometimes does. To create such a dynamic range name and a flexible graph, the first step is to understand the OFFSET function, which has the following form:

=OFFSET(Reference Cell, Rows Down, Columns Across, Length, Width)

The first three arguments in the OFFSET function are required arguments and the last two are optional. But the last two are essential in creating a flexible range name. The first argument in the OFFSET function is the cell reference that will be used as a starting point. The second argument is the number of rows to go down from this starting cell reference. The third is the number of columns to move to the right of the cell reference. The function OFFSET (A1,1,1) would result in cell B2; it would start with A1 and then go down by one row and to the right one column. The number of rows and columns can be negative, implying you can go up rather than down and you can go to the left rather than to the right.

The important part of the OFFSET function in creating dynamic range names is not the two arguments just discussed that allow you to move around, but rather the final two arguments relating to the height and the width. These arguments are generally used in the context of another function or as an array function. An example of how the height and width arguments can be used is shown in the following two examples of making an operation on a flexible range, which varies according to some other variable in the spreadsheet:

$$=SUM(OFFSET(A1,2,3,2,5))$$

$$=NPV(10\%,OFFSET(Cash\ Flow\ Reference,0,Last\ Historic$$
$$Period+1,1,Explicit\ Period)$$

The SUM function begins with the cell A1 and then moves down two rows to row 3 and moves across three columns to the right to column D. This implies that the starting point for the sum calculation is D3. The NPV function begins with the first column, which is a historical period, and then moves across to the end of the historical data. Once the starting cell is established, the sum in the first statement covers two rows and five columns because of the last two arguments of the function. This means the area from D3 to H5 is summed with a length of 2 from 3 to 5 and a width of 5 from column D to H. In the second statement, the NPV is computed for a single row that extends for the explicit period. If the explicit period is changed, the NPV adapts to the new period.

Once you understand the general way that the OFFSET function works, you can create a dynamic range name. Then you can create a chart with a dynamic range using the following steps:

Step 1   Create a range name that will use the OFFSET function as an equation that defines the length and the width of the range. To make a new range name, you can press the CNTL and F3 keys (shortcut keys associated with range names use the F3 key).

Step 2   After defining the name of the range, select the range name and enter the OFFSET function in the "refers to" part of the range name menu with the equal sign. You can use an equation with a function in a range name instead of simply referring to a cell or a range of cells. If you want to make a range called flex_name that begins at D5 and has a width of 8, the OFFSET function in the range name would not move away from D5 as the starting point. It would have a height of 1 and a width of 8, as demonstrated in Figure 15.11. The parameters for the OFFSET function—the row start, column start, the height, and the width—should generally be entered as cells in the spreadsheet as shown Figure 15.11:

$$=OFFSET(D5,0,0,1,8)$$

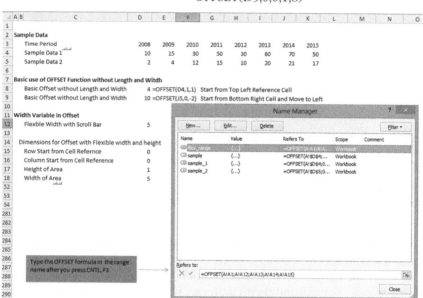

FIGURE 15.11 Use of the OFFSET Function to Create Dynamic Range Names

Step 3   Make a graph that will soon be changed to include the flexible range name instead of a normal fixed area. To make the graph, you can use the F11 shortcut as described earlier.

Step 4   After making the graph, select the data series option from the graph drop-down menu. When editing the data series, modify the range and replace the current range reference with the range name that you created. But when modifying the range, do not change the sheet name. This means that you should only replace the range after the exclamation point in the current range and keep the name of the sheet preceding the explanation point. For example, if the range is sheet1!A1:A5, the A1:A5 will be replaced by the defined range name. Do not change the sheet name to the left, as illustrated in Figure 15.12.

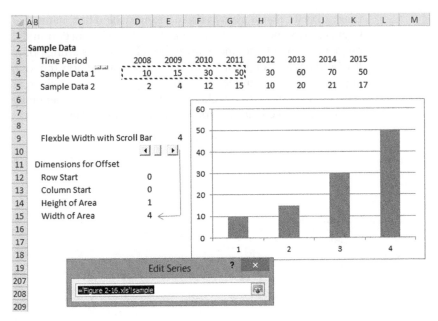

FIGURE 15.12 Illustration of Using a Flexible Range Name in a Graph by Changing the Range Name Only after the Exclamation Point

Before moving to the next part of risk analysis, it should be reiterated that adding a whole lot of spinner buttons to inputs in a financial model can be a bad idea. The danger is that you mess around with a lot of different variables using spinner buttons and then you forget what the base case values were. Say there is a spinner button for oil price variables, quantity variables, margin variables, and other items. A solution to this problem is described in Chapter 17, where the spinner buttons are combined with scenario analysis and where a special custom scenario is created that allows you to use spinner buttons. Later, after using the spinner buttons, you can reset values in them. If this technique is used, you can switch back to the base case or the downside case after playing around with the different variables.

CHAPTER 16

Using Financial Models to Establish Break-Even Points for Key Input Variables with Data Tables

The value of a corporation comes from differentiation in cost structure, technological innovation, location, marketing strategy, and various other aspects of business strategy. In the long run, relative value does not generally arise because a company is better than its competitors in forecasting commodity prices, gross domestic product growth, trends in interest rates, or other economic variables. These variables to be sure do have important if not dramatic effects on value. But anybody who claims to differentiate their business by making superior forecasts of variables such as the oil price is arguably committing fraud. Instead of wasting time on consulting studies or marketing reports that attempt to forecast variables such as GDP growth or interest rates, you can use your financial models to compute break-even values for the economic variables that are difficult to forecast. Break-even analysis is similar to making a graph with a drop-down box discussed in Chapter 15. The subtle but important difference between methods introduced in this chapter and those discussed in Chapter 15 is that with break-even analysis you can quantify risk as a single number that represents the cushion or the distance from current levels that various different value drivers can move up or down before something really bad happens. Once you have this cushion defined you can use your judgment to assess whether the buffer is sufficiently big to accept the risk.

One of the supposed advantages of fancy statistical measures such as value at risk, the probability of default, or beta is that these numbers seemingly place all of the risk of an investment into a single number. With risk put into a single statistic or letter grade such as AAA, analysts can supposedly compare the levels of risk of different investments without doing a lot of work. By expressing risk as the break-even point, a similar kind of thing is accomplished, but in a more intuitive way.

A famous valuation debacle was the case of the Eurotunnel, in which dramatic errors from forecasting the volume of traffic created massive losses on debt and equity capital. If you were an investor in one of the many tranches of junior debt and you wanted to evaluate the risk that your debt service would not be paid, you could construct a financial model of the project, then you could keep pushing the traffic volume down (with a spinner box if you like) until it reaches the level at which your debt cannot be repaid and you lose money. Once you have computed this break-even traffic level, you could then think hard about the chances that the actual traffic level will be below this break-even traffic level. If you believe the chance of reaching the break-even level is very low, you can then be confident that your debt will be repaid. On the other hand, if the cushion between your base case traffic level and the break-even level is thin, then the likelihood of default on your debt may be quite high. The break-even traffic level has implicitly defined the risk of the project.

Similar break-even statistics could be developed for commodity prices, demand growth, cost structure, and other items. The break-even statistics can be computed for different classes of investors—equity, senior debt, subordinated debt, and preferred stock. For each investor group you could find out how low a variable can go before the IRR reaches the risk-free rate. When the IRR is equal to the risk-free rate you might have just as well invested in a safe bond. Here the break-even value shows the risk you are taking relative to a risk-free investment, meaning you can directly gauge risk and return. An example of break-even analysis from a project finance analysis is illustrated in Figure 16.1, where the break-even that would produce a debt service coverage ratio (DSCR) of at least 1.0 is compared to the historic level of the oil price. As the break-even price for the project is consistently below historical levels in the graph, you could be reasonably confident that falling prices would not cause a big problem with the project.

Figure 16.2 illustrates break-even analysis using the oil transaction introduced in Figure 15.1 for senior debt, subordinated debt, and equity. The three lines on the graph show the rate of return earned on senior debt, subordinated debt, and equity, while the x-axis lists a range in potential oil prices. The level at which the variables fall below the risk-free interest rate can be defined as the break-even point since a basic alternative to investing in any security is the purchase of a risk-free bond. Different levels of break-even oil prices at which the senior debt, subordinated debt, and the equity yield a return below the risk-free rate are shown in the title of the graph. The graph title is created using the method described in Chapter 15, involving placing the items that you want in the title on one row somewhere in the spreadsheet. For example: When making a risk assessment with the information in Figure 16.2, say the current

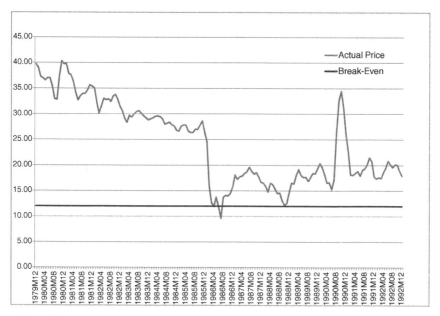

FIGURE 16.1 Break-Even Level of Oil Prices from a Financial Model Compared to Historical Oil Prices

oil price is $82 per barrel. The cushion for the equity break-even is quite thin, while the cushion for the senior debt is much greater because prices can fall all the way down to $43 per barrel before the internal rate of return (IRR) on senior debt falls below the risk-free rate.

The break-even analysis can be used in structuring a transaction as well as in making risk assessment from a given capital structure. If the transaction was financed with different levels of debt or equity, the break-even values would change. Were more senior debt and less equity issued, the break-even cushion would be thinner for the senior debt. Making a break-even presentation like the one shown in Figure 16.2 may not define the exact required return necessary to compensate for taking risk, but it does display risks relative to returns for alternative funding groups and it does allow you to make a judgment concerning whether the expected return on the security compensates for its risk.

While the general intuition behind a break-even analysis is straightforward, there are a few issues in computing and presenting break-even analysis that can be tricky. The first issue is establishing an effective criterion for purposes of deriving the break-even point. Choosing the criterion at which the break-even is assumed to occur—when the DSCR equals 1.0 or the IRR equals the risk-free rate interest rate—seems pretty obvious. However, the break-even criteria can require judgment and understanding of the principles

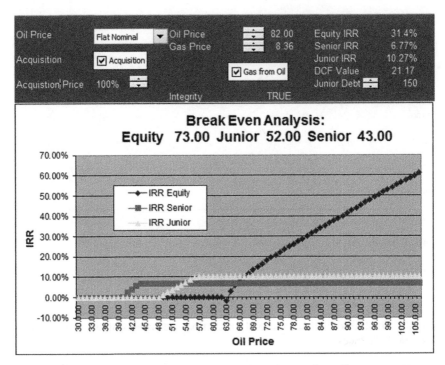

FIGURE 16.2 Illustration of Break-Even Analysis for Oil Prices for Different Securities

underlying financial ratios. A second issue in working with break-even analysis involves developing mechanical techniques to automatically compute the break-even level whenever a structural variable changes in your financial model. When you vary the level of senior and/or subordinated debt or the interest rate or the purchase price in a transaction, the break-even points change. In presenting the break-even analysis on a summary page of your model you may want to display new different break-even points automatically when something else in your model changes. The mechanical discussion of creating break-even analysis with data tables later in the chapter demonstrates a technique you can use to automatically compute changing the break-even points.

Establishing Break-Even Criteria When Analyzing Financial Models

The process of establishing a criterion for determining the break-even point is not as simple as it seems at first blush. To understand the problem, consider the perspective of senior lenders in a project finance transaction and assume that the most important risk variable is the projected growth rate in some variable. Pretend the break-even analysis involves finding the lowest growth rate before something bad happens to the loans. For a project finance analysis, one approach is to measure how low the growth rate can fall before the minimum debt service coverage ratio becomes 1.0. The break-even amount is the level at which cash flow just covers debt service on a year-by-year basis. This occurs because the debt service coverage ratio is defined as cash flow available for debt service (CFADS) divided by debt service. The 1.0 criterion measures the level at which cash flow is insufficient to meet the required loan payment, which seems to be a natural basis upon which to compute the break-even point. If the DSCR falls below 1.0 and there are no reserve accounts, then there is a default whereby lenders will not be paid.

The minimum debt service coverage, however, does not necessarily represent the actual loss on debt that the bank would incur. Even if the DSCR is below 1.0, the project company may still be able to ultimately repay its debt after missing a single debt service payment, as there could be enough cash flow to restructure the debt from available cash flow after the scheduled tenor of the debt. An alternative break-even analysis therefore could involve computing how low the growth rate can go until debt cannot be repaid at the very end of a project. A third way to look at the issue could be to evaluate how low the variable such as the growth rate can fall until the IRR on debt falls below the risk-free rate. This approach uses the notion that an investor has an option to invest in either a risk-free security or risky investments and the break-even should show what risks are taken to achieve a higher return than the risk-free rate.

These three different criteria—the DSCR, the debt outstanding at the end of the project, or the point at which the IRR falls below the risk-free rate—can lead to substantially different break-even points. Similar issues arise with respect to break-even points for equity investors, for acquiring companies in merger analysis, for government agencies, and for other decision makers. Figure 16.3, showing cash flow available for debt service and debt service in a hypothetical project finance transaction, illustrates the difference between evaluating break-even points using a debt service coverage ratio criterion and break-even points derived from a criterion that accounts for the total cash flow over the lifetime of a project. In a project financing much of the analysis from a debt perspective is about buffers or cushions in cash flow relative to debt service. A primary buffer is the area between the cash flow and the debt service over the debt tenor that defines the debt service coverage ratio (DSCR). The second buffer is the area of surplus cash flow after the debt has been repaid, which can be called the tail. If the break-even point is derived from the DSCR, then the risk buffer from the tail is ignored. To account for the value of

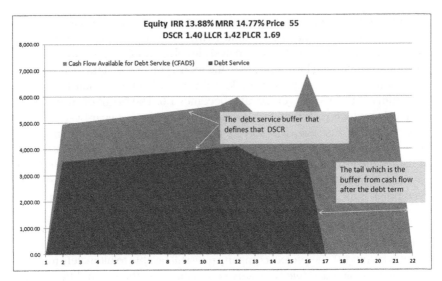

FIGURE 16.3 Illustration of Cash Flow Relative to Debt Service with Tail Measured by PLCR

the tail, the project life coverage ratio (PLCR) can be used as the basis for computing the break-even point instead. This ratio is similar to the DSCR but defined in terms present value. This time the present value of the cash flow over the life of the project using the interest rate on debt is divided by the present value of the debt service. When the PLCR reaches a level of 1.0, the cash flow is just barely sufficient to pay off debt by the very end of the project even if the DSCR is below 1.0. As the present value of debt service equals the value of the loan, the DSCR and the PLCR can be defined as follows:

$$DSCR = Cash\ Flow\ Available\ for\ Debt\ Service/Debt\ Service$$

$$PLCR = NPV(Interest\ Rate\ on\ Loan, CFADS)/Loan$$

A third ratio can be computed that evaluates the ability of cash flow to service the loan over the term of the debt, called the loan life coverage ratio (LLCR). This ratio ignores the value of the tail but evaluates the safety buffer of the cash flow to debt service over the entire period of the loan. When the LLCR is 1.0, cash flow is just enough to pay off debt at the end of the debt tenor even if the DSCR is below 1.0 for individual periods. To compute this ratio, the formula is the same as for the PLCR, except that the present value of cash flow is limited to the life of the loan rather than the life of the project. The following formula can be accomplished by pressing SHIFT, CNTL, ENTER rather than only ENTER. Whenever you would like to put a formula inside the parenthesis of a function, you just have to make it an array variable by pressing the SHIFT, CNTL, ENTER sequence.

$$LLCR = NPV(Rate, CFADS \times Loan\ Phase\ Switch)/Loan$$

Figures 16.4a, 16.4b, and 16.4c demonstrate the difference in computing break-even points using three different financial ratio criteria. In Figure 16.4a, there is no tail and the debt service buffer (the DSCR) remains constant over the life of the project, which is called sculpting. Here the DSCR, PLCR, and LLCR all result in the same break-even value. In this first case, the DSCR can be used to derive the approximate break-even point. If the DSCR is 1.6 then cash flow can decline by about 37 percent (60 divided by 160) and debt service can still be met.

In Figure 16.4b, the debt service buffer is sculpted to the cash flow, but there is a tail that offers additional protection to lenders. In this second case, the LLCR equals the DSCR but the PLCR is greater than either the DSCR or the LLCR because of the risk buffer from the tail. If the break-even is defined on the basis of the amount that cash flow can decline and still pay off the loan, the cash flow can decline by a larger amount in Figure 16.4a than in Figure 16.4b.

The third graph, in Figure 16.4c, assumes the debt service is not tailored to the cash flow and the buffer increases over the term of the loan. Here, the minimum DSCR in the first year is less than the DSCR in later years. If you use the minimum DSCR of 1.0—the point at which a default occurs—to gauge the break-even point, the analysis will be different from when you use the LLCR or the PLCR as the break-even criterion. Where the DSCR is used as the break-even point there is a single year default, but the loan may eventually be restructured and repaid. If the LLCR of 1.0 is used as the criterion in the break-even analysis, the break-even point is defined as the point where one or more single-year defaults may occur, but the loan is repaid by its scheduled repayment date. If you would like to find out how low a variable can go before an ultimate loss occurs on the loan, the PLCR of 1.0 can be used as the break-even criterion.

Establishing break-even criteria from a lender perspective in corporate finance can be more challenging than in project finance because there is no defined life and because the real source of repayment for corporate loans is refinancing of the loan. In corporate finance, the break-even analysis must evaluate how bad things can get before refinancing becomes impossible. To do this, some financial ratio such as the debt-to-EBITDA ratio can be measured and then judgment must be used in determining how high the debt-to-EBITDA ratio can get before refinancing will not be possible and the company will not be able to continue financing capital expansion. Say

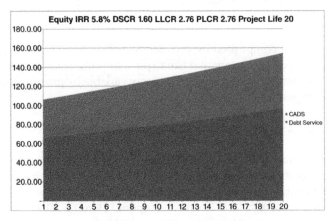

FIGURE 16.4a Alternative Break-Even Criteria from Applying DSCR, LLCR, and PLCR—I

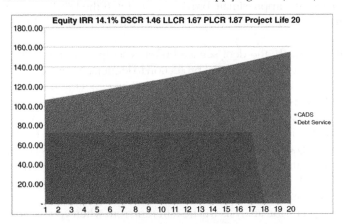

FIGURE 16.4b Alternative Break-Even Criteria from Applying DSCR, LLCR, and PLCR—II

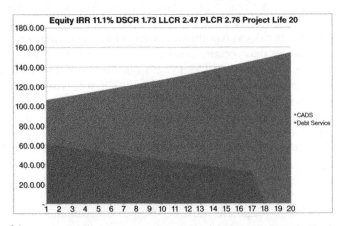

FIGURE 16.4c Alternative Break-Even Criteria from Applying DSCR, LLCR, and PLCR—III

the highest the debt-to-EBITDA criterion can get for a BB-rated company with similar business risk characteristics is six times. The break-even analysis may then involve pushing down a variable until the ratio reaches this level that implies new financing will become impossible.

Mechanics of Using Data Tables to Compute Break-Even Points Automatically

Once you have come up with financial criteria that will be used to derive the level at which break-even occurs, the mechanics of computing and presenting the break-even statistics can be developed by applying a few different spreadsheet techniques. One technique is to use a spinner button and a graph to push down a variable until something like the PLCR reaches a level of 1.0. Here, implementing break-even analysis can be simply thought of as a subset of sensitivity graphs discussed in Chapter 15. Say that you were assessing the risk of subordinated debt for the transaction shown in Figure 15.1. You could then push down the oil price with the spinner button shown on the graph until the IRR on the subordinated debt falls below the risk-free interest rate. Another method of computing the break-even point is to use the Goal Seek tool to derive the required level of the input variable that just meets the break-even point.

A third approach described in the following paragraphs is to use the data table tool and list increments of the break-even variable such as the oil price next to values produced for the financial criteria variables. For the case shown in Figure 15.1, the oil price would be part of a table along with the debt and/or equity IRR. By placing multiple financial ratios next to a list of different values for the key variable in question you could compute break-even points for different investments using alternative financial criterion such as the DSCR and the PLCR. With the data table tool you can then present the break-even points in a summary output section of your model without rerunning the Goal Seek process each time something else changes in the model. Data tables that can be used to perform break-even analysis are often a favorite tool of bankers but be aware that they can also mess up your spreadsheets and make Excel operate very slowly. The step-by-step instructions that follow explain how to compute break-even values using data tables and also show you how to avoid some of the bad aspects of data tables using a bit of Visual Basic for Applications (VBA) code.

Step 1: Creating a Data Table

The first step in the process of automatically presenting break-even points in the summary section of your model is to use the data table tool to create a one-way data table. For a one-way data table, the sensitivity values are increments of the break-even variable and are listed in a column or a row. The data table produces a set of values for the output criteria such as the DSCR, LLCR, or PLCR next to each of the increments. The data table tool accessed from the what-if button in the Data tab is both one of the best and one of the worst features of Excel. The good aspect of data tables is that you can quickly create scenarios and produce different break-even values for varying transaction structures. The bad aspects include: (1) the data tables must be in the same sheet as the input variable used (i.e. the break-even variable); (2) data tables can seriously slow down the spreadsheet (unless the automatic except data tables option is used in the Formula tab); (3) data tables cannot be used together with the Goal Seek or copy and paste macros; (4) data tables cannot be used easily to make a graph; and (5) the data tables are recomputed when you save the file even if you use automatic except data tables as the calculation option, meaning that after you press CNTL, S, the program will be very slow. To fix these problems, an alternative to data tables that uses VBA code is explained at the end of the chapter.

In understanding how to effectively use data tables, you should first know the difference between setting up one-way data tables and two-way data tables. The objective of data tables is to perform a sensitivity analysis where an output variable (such as DSCR, debt/EBITDA, or IRR) is presented next to a range of input variables. The differences between a two-way table and a one-way table are:

- A two-way data table can evaluate only one output variable but allows you to enter two sensitivity input variables to be used in presenting the sensitivity analysis of the single output variable.
- A one-way data table allows only one sensitivity input variable to be used in the sensitivity analysis, but it can display the sensitivity analysis of this single variable for as many output variables as you want.

Creating a two-way table is a little more intuitive than creating a one-way data table and is explained first. Two-way data tables can be developed by applying the following three steps:

Step 1   Type in ranges for two different input variables somewhere in the same spreadsheet where you entered the inputs. You must enter the variables in a particular structured format where one of the sensitivity variables is typed in a row and the other is typed in a column. When you begin, there must be an empty cell in the top left corner between typing in the range of one input variable and the second input variable. The cell between the input variables will contain an equation that is linked to an equation in the model that depends on the values of the row range and the column range. The top left cell is highlighted in Figure 16.5. If you do not type the sensitivities in like this and if you do not link the top left cell, the data table will not work.

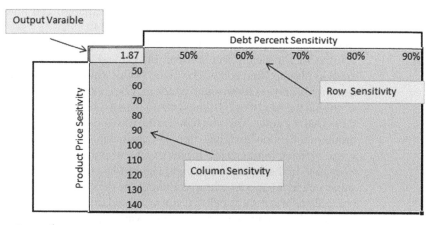

FIGURE 16.5 Illustration of the Setup of a Two-Way Data Table

After typing in the ranges of input variables, link an output variable in the cell that you initially left blank (the cell in the upper left-hand corner) between the row and the column cell. You can call this variable in the upper left-hand corner the output variable. In Figure 16.5, the row sensitivity is the percent debt commitment, the column sensitivity is the product price, and the output variable in the top left cell is the PLCR that is computed in the model. So far, the input ranges you put in the row and the column sensitivities have absolutely no effect whatsoever on any output of the model including the PLCR.

Step 2 When you have finished carefully typing the structure of the sensitivity variable as illustrated in Figure 16.5 with the output variable at the top left, you can fill in the sensitivity analysis. In Figure 16.5, the data table is completed through changing the debt percent in the model from 50 percent to 90 percent and changing the product price input in the model assumptions from 50 to 140. These sensitivity variables that are typed in the row and column ranges are not connected to anything in the financial model and do not yet have any effect on the output variable. To implement the data table and connect the row and column sensitivity ranges to the output variable, the spreadsheet program must know how to make the sensitivity variables listed to the left and above the data table run the model. This is done by first selecting the area of the table that includes the output variable beginning in the top left corner, the numbers in the sensitivity row and column ranges, and the results area. The selection must not include the titles to the left of the column sensitivity or on top of the row sensitivity. In Figure 16.5 begin by selecting the top left (output variable) cell and shade up to the 90 percent and down to the 140.

Step 3   After selecting the area of the data table including the row and column sensitivities, select the data ribbon and then the what-if analysis ribbon. Then you will be asked to type in something called a row input and a column input, which may be confusing when you do this for the first 10 or 100 times you try. This is where you connect the sensitivity ranges that you typed in the row and the column with inputs in the model that drive the output variable. You must find a single variable in the model inputs that corresponds to the sensitivity row. In the example shown in Figure 16.5 you should find a single cell in the model where you input the debt percent. This is one cell and it is not any cell that you just typed from the data table structure. Next, you must find the single variable that corresponds to the sensitivity column. This is the price input variable in Figure 16.5, which is entered in the assumptions section, far away from the data table. This business of finding single row and column inputs may seem somewhat confusing at first. But you will get used to the idea after trying it a few times if you remember that the data you entered in the rows and columns have no connection at all to the model. The process of entering row input and column input is illustrated in Figure 16.6. Note that the row and column inputs ask for a one single input cell and not a range of cells.

In developing a break-even analysis, the two-way data table shown in Figure 16.6 is not very useful. A data table where you display a number of outputs along with a single input variable is much more useful. This is called a one-way data table. A one-way table concentrates on one input rather than two input variables. With two dimensions inside a spreadsheet you are limited to either putting in two input variables and creating a sensitivity analysis for one output variable or entering a single input sensitivity with multiple output variables. For break-even analysis where you may want to evaluate the break-even points for multiple funding sources and/or multiple financial ratios like the DSCR, LLCR, and PLCR, you often will want the tables structured as a one-way data table.

When structuring a one-way table you must arrange the output variables and the single input variable in a different way than in the two-way table. With a one-way table, the sensitivity data is entered in a single column (or row) and you leave the rectangular corner cell above the sensitivity column and to the left of the output variables blank (see Figure 16.7). The one or many output

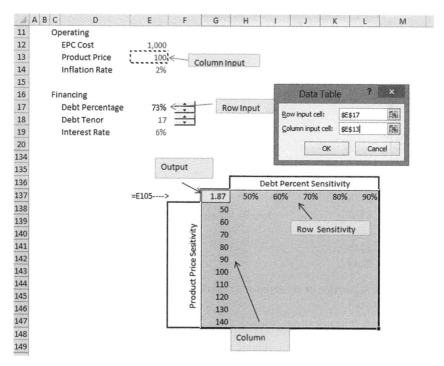

FIGURE 16.6 Illustration of the Process of Entering a Row Input Cell and a Column Input Cell in a Data Table

variables can then be entered through linking the cells to the right and above the single column that contains the sensitivity range. As with the two-way table, there is no flexibility at all in structuring the table. If you set it up wrong, it won't work. Figure 16.7 shows that when you are finished setting up the table, there should be a blank cell above the sensitivity variables and to the left of the output variables. The process would also work if you entered the sensitivity range as a row and you put the links to the output variables below and to the right of the sensitivity row.

When you have finished carefully setting up the one-way data table as illustrated in Figure 16.7 you should then select the area of the data table. As with the two-way table, start shading by including the top left corner blank cell illustrated in Figure 16.7. Again, you must not include the titles of the row and the column in the selection. After shading the area, go to the data tab and the what-if ribbon and again enter a row and a column input cell. The nonintuitive aspect of a one-way data table is that you should leave the row input completely blank because the items across the rows are outputs, not inputs. For the column input cell you need to find an input assumption in the financial model in a similar manner as you did with the two-way data table. After

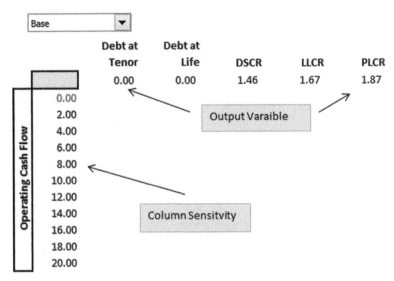

FIGURE 16.7 Illustration of the Setup of a One-Way Data Table

entering the data table, it should have a structure something like that shown in Figure 16.8. You can use a similar process if you want the row to be the sensitivity variable. In this case enter the output variables on a column instead of a row and the sensitivity variables in a row instead of a column. If you make a one-way table like this you must enter a connection to the variables in the sensitivity row for the row input and nothing at all in the column input. Entering nothing whatsoever in the row input cell is another thing that may take some practice and make you frustrated.

Data tables can make the spreadsheets run slowly and the file can seem to take forever to save. This can be such a bad problem that some companies do not accept spreadsheets that contain data tables. There are a couple of things you can do to make this problem a little more bearable. First, you can change the calculation option in the workbook to automatic except data tables, which can be found in the Formula tab. Then when you want to run a data table you can press the SHIFT and F9 keys (F9 recalculates all sheets in all open workbooks whereas the SHIFT, F9 combination recalculates only the current sheet). To make the spreadsheet run faster after you press CNTL, S for saving, you can include the following command in the AUTO_OPEN macro, which runs when you open the spreadsheet. To implement this macro, you must change the calculation setting to manual and then you can reset the setting at the end of the code that saves the file.

Application.CalculateBeforeSave = False

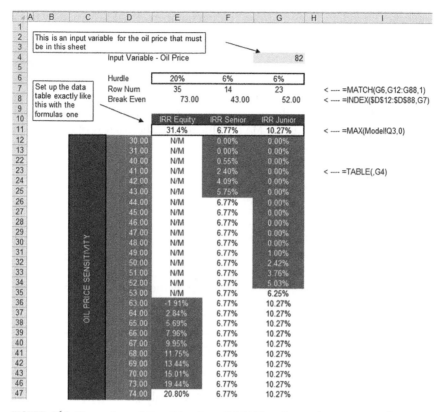

FIGURE 16.8 Illustration of One-Way Data Table Together with MATCH and INDEX Using Conditional Formatting

Step 2: Using MATCH and INDEX Functions to Find Break-Even Points

After creating a one-way data table you can pull out the value that represents the break-even point, which is what you want for the risk analysis. Say that you have created a data table that lists the input sensitivity variable such as capacity factor of a wind farm next to the output variable(s) such as DSCR, LLCR, and PLCR. If the break-even is defined by you to occur when the values reach a level of 1.0, you can return to the two functions that are like good friends and useful in so many different instances, the MATCH function and the INDEX function. The MATCH function finds the break-even value and then the INDEX function displays the break-even value for each financial statistic criterion. Recall that the MATCH function produces a row number or column number once you enter a criterion. The INDEX function picks out an item from a given area after providing a row and/or a column number—INDEX(Area, Row from MATCH, and Column from MATCH).

To use the MATCH and INDEX functions in finding a break-even point, first enter the MATCH function to find the row number of the table that corresponds to the break-even criterion (in the following example, the assumed criterion for the risk-free rate is 6 percent). The MATCH function would then be written in the equation that follows for a table with different IRRs. An example of using the MATCH function in the context of break-even analysis is shown in Figure 16.8. That figure also uses conditional formatting to show values below the break-even.

Row of Break-Even =MATCH(Break-Even Criterion (6%), Column of Numbers in Data Table)

Once the row number has been found by using the MATCH function, the INDEX function can be applied to find the break-even value of the input variable that is associated with the row number that has been identified. To do this you first highlight the input sensitivity value of the data table. In Figure 16.8, for example, this is the oil price. Then enter the break-even row from the MATCH function as follows:

Break-Even Value = INDEX(Sensitivity Row Range, Break-Even Row from MATCH)

Step 3: Attaching Spinner Buttons for Sensitivity Analysis

After you have created the one-way data table with the sensitivity variables on the left-hand side and the output variables inside the table, the break-even value resulting from the INDEX function can be presented in the summary sheet or the dashboard of your model. Using the INDEX and MATCH to find the break-even value means that if you change a structuring variable such as the level of debt in the transaction, you can then immediately see what happens to a variety of different break-even values for DSCR, IRR, and other financial ratios. To make the break-even value flexible, the formulas must be set to automatic or a simple macro should be recorded from pressing the SHIFT and F9 keys. You can then attach this recalculate macro to your spinner buttons and drop-down boxes.

Say you want to recompute the break-even analysis with different debt to capital ratios. You can make a spinner button for the debt-to-capital ratio and copy it to above the data table (after you have used the windshield wiper method discussed in Chapter 15). You can then attach the recalculation macro to the spinner button, meaning that every time you change the debt to capital ratio, the whole data table will recalculate.

Creating Data Tables Using VBA Instead of the Data Table Tool

Data tables can surely be useful tools in break-even analysis, sensitivity analysis, and many other applications. However, despite the benefits of the data table tool, they may present a number of difficulties, including: (1) the data table cannot be presented in a sheet other than where the inputs are used in the data table; (2) a data table cannot be used together with Goal Seek or macros in the model; (3) a data table is awkward for making graphs because you cannot make the upper left-hand cell blank, which is so important for making a graph with the F11 key; and (4) a data table cannot be used from another table where the inputs to a second data table come from the first data table. To resolve these issues, a macro can be created in lieu of the data table. The key to creating a data table with VBA is to use a FOR NEXT loop together with the CELLS statement. If you get used to writing code with FOR NEXT loops, a whole world of possibilities will open. The FOR NEXT loop goes around different rows or columns and then uses the CELLS statement to define an input according to a cell reference, or alternatively assigns a cell defined by a row and a column in a sheet. To see how to combine a FOR NEXT loop with the CELLS function, a simple one-way data table is demonstrated with only one output variable. After that, additional complexities are added to the VBA process through creating a one-way table with multiple output variables and finally a two-way data table.

To create a one-way data table, first make a FOR NEXT loop. This loop repeats calculations over the number of rows in the data table. Once you go around the rows, you can then use the CELLS statement in VBA to redefine an input cell in the spreadsheet from the row and the column number that you input. Finally, you can use the CELLS statement to define the output. The following two statements drive the process:

$$\text{Input} = \text{Cells(Row Number, Column Number)}$$

$$\text{Cells(Row Number, Column Number)} = \text{Output}$$

By cycling around the rows and entering different values into an input cell (such as the price of the product) you can first assign the input variable over and over again to the sensitivity column of a data table. Each time you change the input variable you can then assign an output cell to a series of different rows defined in the FOR NEXT loop. You must assign the input variable before extracting the output variable because of the logic of a data table. For a one-way table with only one output variable, the FOR NEXT loop could have the following form where the input variable row could have any valid range name. After the FOR NEXT loop goes around rows in the spreadsheet, the first command shown in the following VBA code assigns the input variable such as the product price to the series of numbers defined in the sensitivity range. In the next line, the output cell is recomputed for each of the values for the input. The VBA code represents just what a data table does. It goes around a row or a column, changes the input variable (the row or column input), and then compiles the output variable in a data table.

```
For row = 1 to number of rows
   Range(financial model input) = CELLS(row, column number of sensitivity
   variable)
   CELLS(row, column number of break-even output) = Range(financial model output)
Next row
```

To make a one-way data table with more than one output variable, you can just add one or more output variables and define more column numbers where the other output variables will be placed. In this case you would have to add lines after the definition of output cells in the VBA code in the previous example.

If you want to make a two-way table, the trick is to use two FOR NEXT loops. The first one loops around rows as before; the second FOR NEXT loop works through the columns. The number of rows is the length of the column sensitivity, and the number of columns is the length of the row sensitivity, meaning that you do not have to input these values into the macro. The following code demonstrates the technique of using two FOR NEXT loops to construct a two-way data table. One input variable (the column input) should be changed as you go around the rows. The second input variable (the row input) should be changed as part of the column loop. Finally, the output variable is assigned inside both the row and column loop. You can then add range names to make the two-way table flexible.

```
For row = 1 to number of rows
   Range(column input) = cells(row, column of sensitivity variable)
   For column = 1 to number of columns
         Range(row input) = cells(column, row of sensitivity variable)
         Cells(row, column) = range(output)
   Next column
Next row
```

To make any of the data tables more flexible, you should use named ranges for the column number of the sensitivity variable, the column number of the output variable, the number of rows, and the range name for the input and output variables. There should be no code that refers to cell references such as A1. In this way you can put the data table wherever you want in the sheet by changing the row or the column start and you need only enter the range names for the input and output variables in your sheet rather than putting the range names in the VBA code. You could even make multiple data tables by using the INDEX function that picks out different row and column numbers from a series of possibilities. Further, when you create a flexible table like this you can copy the code into other sheets and replicate the process. This can be accomplished by using the ROW and COLUMN functions as illustrated:

```
Row Start = ROW (First Row of Sensitivity)
Row End = ROW (Last Row of Sensitivity)
Column number of sensitivity variable = COLUMN (One of the Sensitivity
    Variables)
Column of sensitivity variable output = COLUMN (Column Where You
    Want Output)
```

Figure 16.9 illustrates how you can create a series of range names for a flexible data table using VBA through typing the name in an adjacent column and then shading the value as well as the name. After typing the names into adjacent rows or columns, the SHIFT, CNTL, F3 shortcut can be an effective technique to use in creating the names because it forces you to document the names in your spreadsheet.

	O	P	Q	R	S	T	U	V	W	X	Y	Z
1												
2		Routine for Allowing Multiple VBA table with Range Names										
3												
4		Table Number		1		Rows, Columns and Range Names for Data Table						
5												
6	=INDEX(U6:V6,$R$4)---->			22	Row Start		22	34	49	68	<---- =ROW(D68)	
7	=INDEX(U6:V6,$R$4)---->			28	Row End		28	40	58	77	<---- =ROW(D77)	
8	=INDEX(U6:V6,$R$4)---->			5	Column Start		4	5	5	5	<---- =COLUMN(E68)	
9	=INDEX(U6:V6,$R$4)---->			25	Column End		25	12	9	10	<---- =COLUMN(J72)	
10			EV_EBITDA	Output Variable		EV_EBITDA	EV_EBITDA	Eq_IRR	Ung_IRR			
11			Targ_IRR	Row Input		Targ_IRR	Ung_IRR	Exit_Mult	Exit_Mult			
12			Debt_EBITDA	Col Input		Debt_EBITDA	Debt_EBITDA	Holding_Per	Holding_Per			
13												

FIGURE 16.9 Illustration of Creating Range Names for Use in Data Tables

The code illustrated in Figure 16.10 demonstrates how a flexible data table can be made whereby you can create multiple data tables using range names together with the INDEX function. To make the VBA data tables flexible, everything in the macro shown in Figure 16.10—the row and column numbers and even the range names for the output variables and the column and row input variables—comes from a named range. This ensures that when you add or delete rows or columns, the code still works. It also means that you can create multiple data tables with the same VBA code. Further, the initial value for the input variable is retained at the beginning of the program, and it is restored at the end of the program. In Figure 16.10 the status bar is adjusted to display the row that is being computed. To make the data table, instead of pressing the F9 key, you must press a button that runs the macro. It is a little more work when you first do it, but it removes all of the irritations and problems with the data tables.

```
Sub data_table()
'
' First, Define Variables from range names
'
output = Range("Output_Variable")
row_input = Range("Row_Input")
col_input = Range("Col_Input")

row_start = Range("Row_Start")
row_end = Range("Row_End")
column_start = Range("Column_Start")
column_end = Range("Column_End")

initial_row_input = Range(row_input)    ' keep initial value of row input
initial_col_input = Range(col_input)    ' keep initial value of col input

'
' Loop around and first change inputs, then get the outputs
'
For Row = row_start To row_end

    Range(col_input) = Cells(Row, column_start - 1)

    For Col = column_start To column_end

        Range(row_input) = Cells(row_start - 1, Col)

        Cells(Row, Col) = Range(output)                    ' define the output cell

    Next Col
Next Row

Range(row_input) = initial_row_input   ' reset to initial value
Range(col_input) = initial_col_input   ' reset to initial value

End Sub
```

FIGURE 16.10 VBA Code for Creating Flexible Two-Way Data Tables

Summary of Break-Even Analysis

Although the break-even analysis presents risk as a single number, there are a few problems with the break-even risk analysis technique. First, the break-even analysis does not measure what happens when a cohesive set of variables can move together, for example, when quantity declines and price declines at the same time because of increased capacity and competition. In an extended recession, sales, prices, and fixed costs may all decline together. All of the perfect storms that seem to occur much more than would be expected if variables would really move independently demonstrate this point. Second, the analysis depends on a single value of the break-even variable; the oil price, for example, is assumed to stay at the constant level over the term of the modeling period. This means that use of a break-even analysis is difficult to accomplish when a variable is volatile and the price can have sharp upward and downward moves as well as mean reversion. Analysis of multiple variables is addressed by a scenario analysis in the next chapter. Changes in variables that may be volatile from period to period are discussed in Chapters 19 through 22, which walk through a Monte Carlo simulation on a step-by-step basis.

CHAPTER 17

Constructing Flexible Scenario Analysis for Risk Assessment

An alternative to using beta, value at risk, or other statistics to measure the risk of a corporation or a project is to ask bankers how much money they will lend to a company. The debt capacity of a project, an acquisition, or a corporation can be one of the best ways—much better than the Capital Asset Pricing Model—to derive the implicit equity risk. This is because banks in theory should be willing to lend relatively more money to a company that has less volatile cash flow and is not taking dangerous risks. These are exactly the same kind of risks that equity investors should be worried about. The extensive due diligence made by lenders in assessing downsides has so much importance in finance because a banker should in theory have no direct vested personal or psychological interest in completing the project. By putting his stamp of approval on a project and by directly investing money in the project or corporation, the risk analysis made by the banker provides crucial risk information to decision makers. Similarly, the investment will probably not be made if bankers do not approve a loan for the project. If the banker concludes that the project is too risky, an equity investor has a very strong signal that something is fundamentally wrong with the investment and he should probably stay away from the investment. So much for Modigliani and Miller.

In evaluating how much debt can be supported by an investment there is no single statistical formula that can give you a simple answer. No one really knows exactly how banks and other lenders make decisions when they discuss loans in the credit committee. However, one often-mentioned reasonable theory is that bankers come up with a carefully considered downside case and then make sure there is some remaining buffer of cash flow relative to debt obligations in this downside scenario. When bankers do not make reasoned decisions, overinvestment can arise and economic crises can occur. This is why scenario analysis is so crucial.

To illustrate the general idea of using a downside case to derive debt capacity and infer equity risk, consider the example of a wind farm in Germany that receives a fixed feed-in tariff from the state and can hedge operations and maintenance risk using contracts with equipment suppliers. With energy prices and expenses fixed, the primary remaining risk is the possibility of electricity output from wind being lower than expected. This production risk is addressed by consultants who make detailed probabilistic forecasts of how turbines will work in different wind conditions. They come up with a host of statistical parameters that measure relationships between different wind speeds and a variety of technical parameters associated with the wind turbines. In determining how much debt a wind project like this can support, a one-year P90 production level for wind speed computed by the consultant could be used as a downside case, meaning that in any one year there is a 90 percent chance that the wind will be higher than the P90 level. To compute the debt capacity of the project, the bank may add a 15 percent buffer on top of the downside case cash flow (implying a debt service coverage ratio of about 1.18). The example demonstrates how assumptions made in the downside scenario drive the debt sizing and hence the investment decision. The size of the debt and the viability of the investment depend not on the base case, which may be a P50 case, but rather on the P90 downside case assumptions. The equity investment decision in turn is driven by the ability to raise debt in the transaction.

The big difference between scenario analysis compared to the sensitivity and break-even techniques discussed in Chapters 15 and 16 is that for a scenario analysis, multiple different input variables are changed at the same time rather than only focusing on a single variable. In developing a scenario analysis, you must come up with a comprehensive outlook with respect to a number of economic variables rather than simply seeing how much one variable can change before something bad happens. If a company can easily survive a downside case and it can repay debt out of cash flow or easily refinance debt maturities without cutting dividends and without changing capital expenditure policy, then the credit rating should be well above investment grade. If the company cannot survive the downside case—perhaps meaning it cannot repay or refinance maturing debt without big cuts in discretionary capital expenditures, dividends, and other items—then the credit rating could be below investment grade (BBB– in the Standard & Poor's scale). In a project finance context, the downside case can be used to establish covenants, debt service reserves, and other elements of a transaction, as shown in Table 17.1.

When developing a scenario analysis to make a valuation for a corporate model, a base case, downside case, and upside case could be created with different terminal valuation techniques. The result of this scenario analysis will demonstrate the range in valuation of equity. A well-structured scenario analysis should be able to present the variation in any output variable in

TABLE 17.1 Potential Uses of Different Scenarios in a Financial Model

Scenario	Use in Project Finance Model
Base case	Establish the schedule for repayment of debt.
Downside case	Establish the level of debt service reserve.
	Set the covenant levels.
	Develop repayment flexibility.
Upside case	Establish cash sweep mechanics.
	Develop the prepayment structure.

the financial model such as the DSCR, loan life coverage ratio (LLCR), project life coverage ratio (PLCR), or internal rate of return (IRR) in the context of different financial structuring assumptions. For a project finance model, downside scenarios may be presented with different assumptions for the debt commitment, debt tenor, and other debt structuring variables, meaning that after you change a debt structuring variable, you can immediately see statistics like the DSCR, LLCR, and PLCR in the downside case scenario. A simple version of this analysis would be to put a spinner button on the top of a data table and see how much debt can be put in a downside case scenario before the LLCR falls to 1.0. If the LLCR is below 1.0, you can just reduce the amount of the debt with the spinner button.

The most important issue in developing scenario analysis is determining assumptions for the levels of different variables in the alternative cases. It is difficult enough to come up with base case assumptions that are intended to give the expected or most likely outcome (generally not the budgeted case presented by company management, which often contains an optimism bias related to completion of projects and implementation of business strategy). In creating a downside case, you must not only derive reasonable values for the variables, but you should also have some sense of what the downside case is supposed to represent. Banks sometimes define the downside case as a 20 percent probability case, which demonstrates that the downside case is not simply imagining some very negative outcomes for each of the variables. However, when a guideline such as 20 percent is given, nobody has any idea whether the comprehensive set of variables representing a downside scenario really has a 20 percent chance of occurring. It is very easy to come up with an extremely pessimistic set of variables with a very low probability; it is much more difficult to develop a set of consistent variables that are quite negative and guide the acceptance of taking a prudent amount of risk.

In the wind project example discussed earlier, the downside case is relatively easy to develop if you believe consultant forecasts of wind production, because the risks of different wind conditions and technical functioning of a turbine can be observed from objective past data. As the structure of wind variation should not deviate much from historical data (there can be variation from year to year), future possibilities for wind speeds can be taken from a probability distribution. In contrast, construction of a downside case for subprime mortgages would have been much more difficult to establish. To come up with a subprime downside scenario, you would have to project future housing prices, future income levels, the relationship between housing foreclosure and income, and many other economic variables. Unlike projection of the wind speed in the case of the German wind turbines, historical observations of past data proved to not be very useful in forecasting what could happen to the value of homes underlying subprime mortgages. The difficulty in coming up with the sort of judgmental analysis required for scenario analysis is one motivation for developing mathematical representations of variables (Chapters 19 to 22) that supposedly measure the probability of the scenarios.

An example of potential variation in variables from the base case to the downside case is illustrated in Table 17.2, which deals with technical parameters associated with electricity generating plants. Table 17.2 replicates ranges in values that the Fitch Ratings agency uses for base case and downside scenarios. Other reports can be found that describe the downside criteria used in other industries.

TABLE 17.2 Indicative Rating Case Stress Levels for Thermal Projects

	Change from Base Case (%)		
Project Stress	Coal Plants	Combined Cycle	Peaking Plant
Heat rate	+1 to +5	+1 to +5	+1 to +5
Availability	−1 to −10	−1 to −10	−1 to −10
Operation and maintenance costs	+5 to +15	+5 to +15	+5 to +15

Source: Fitch Ratings.

Mechanics of Scenario Analysis

The remainder of this chapter describes the mechanics of adding a scenario analysis to a financial model whereby different assumed cases can be quickly added to any model. The manner in which scenario analysis can be tested and presented along with alternative transaction structuring variables is also discussed. Programming a scenario analysis in a spreadsheet is certainly not as important as coming up with the appropriate values to use in the different cases—particularly in the downside case. But creating a well-structured and effectively presented scenario analysis can allow you to spend more time on the important issue of debating what assumptions should be included in the downside case. The type of scenario analysis explained in the following paragraphs describes a technique where you can adjust structural variables such as the size of debt and you can view what happens in alternative base, low, and high cases. The approach adds a master scenario page to a model in which a host of different variables are chosen including variables that have changing values over time. The scenario analysis technique also allows you to use spinner buttons and drop-down box features in the context of a master scenario page without losing track of the values that were established in the base case.

A well-designed scenario analysis in a financial model should allow you to:

- Add multiple different scenario cases and evaluate as many different output variables as you would like.
- Change transaction structuring variables such as debt size and evaluate what happens to outputs across multiple scenarios such as what happens to the PLCR in the worst case.
- Easily insert a separate master scenario page that can be adjusted to change input variables, output variables, and scenario cases.
- Include variables in the scenario analysis that are structured with changing values over time such as varying inflation rates, growth rates, interest rates, and commodity prices.
- Insert a special custom scenario case that uses spinner buttons and drop-down boxes for sensitivity analysis and at the same time resets those variables to the base case and other cases any time you would like.
- Extend the scenario analysis into a tornado diagram and a spider diagram, which are described in Chapter 18 and Chapter 19.

All of the mechanical items listed can be accomplished by using the INDEX function together with the Data Table tool or, alternatively, a small Visual Basic for Applications (VBA) program to replace the Data Table tool, as described in Chapter 16. You could also try to use the scenario manager tool to construct scenario analyses, allowing you to change a number of different variables and create a report containing multiple output variables. However, the scenario manager is not very flexible. Problems with the scenario manager tool include: (1) new scenario pages must be created each time a change in the structure of the transaction, and you must rerun the scenario manager each time a new scenario is evaluated; (2) the titles of the input variables and output variables must be manually entered; (3) the input variables must be input into a data form rather than on a spreadsheet; (4) the scenario manager is difficult to manage when input variables are located on different pages; and (5) you cannot make drop-down boxes to manage and present the scenarios. Given these problems, the alternative of using the

INDEX function combined with a one-way Data Table is described next on a step-by-step basis. Once you have inserted a master scenario page a few times, you will see that it is easier than the scenario manager and much more flexible.

To explain the mechanics of developing a scenario analysis that uses a combination of the INDEX function and the Data Table feature, a basic example is presented first. This example uses variables that do not vary over time; it does not include the flexibility to add spinner buttons to a special custom case; it is not extended to include tornado diagrams or spider graphs; and it does not incorporate any VBA code. After the fundamental approach is established, subsequent discussion explains how to incorporate other items that are slightly more complex. These additional items include incorporating time series variables and inserting a custom case with spinner buttons. At the end of the chapter a somewhat more elegant technique that links variables with range names and applies VBA instead of Data Tables is described. Chapter 18 extends the scenario analysis through describing how to modify it to add tornado charts and spider diagrams.

Step 1: Setting Up a Master Scenario Page
with a Scenario Number

To create a scenario analysis, the initial step is to add a new page to your model and name it something like "master scenario page." The first thing you can put on the page is a scenario code number. You normally enter this number somewhere at the top of the page. A fundamental concept behind creating any scenario analysis is that various scenarios should be associated with some type of code number. The single scenario number at the top of the page defines which scenario will be implemented in your financial model. The scenario number will also be the row or column number for implementing the INDEX function and it will be the cell link for the drop-down or combo box that allows different scenarios to be operated from alternative places in the model. In addition, the scenario number becomes the column input or row input cell for the data table. The scenario analysis process works by using the code number to identify variables that will be used in running the model, and it defines the scenario variables that will be used as inputs to run the model. If scenario number 1 is used, then input data for the scenario on the first row of the table are applied. This is illustrated in Figure 17.1, where the scenario number is placed at the top of the page and, because number 1 is entered for the scenario number, the first row of data is also presented at the bottom of the table. The notion of using a scenario number is similar to the manner in which time series variables with a changing structure over time were discussed in Chapter 6.

Step 2: Entering Data for Different Input Variables in the Master Scenario Page

The most time consuming part of making a scenario analysis is entering data for different base, downside, and high cases in the master scenario page. Because key input parameters that drive the model come from this exercise of typing alternative variables into the scenario table, some people call the master scenario page the cockpit of the model. This somewhat gimmicky term highlights the fact that the scenario page becomes the place from which you can drive the model as if you are the pilot of a rocket ship. Putting data in the master scenario page means that data entry for the base case, the downside case, the upside case, and a set of different sensitivity scenarios now does not come only from the input sheet. You can put the data for different cases in separate rows, with values for different assumptions (e.g., price, demand, and cost structure) in separate columns. An example of entering scenario inputs is shown in Figure 17.1, which illustrates a completed master scenario page. There is no limit to the number of scenario cases that can be added in this process. The example shown in Figure 17.1 includes a number of sensitivity scenarios in which only one variable differs from the base case value that is discussed further in Chapter 18. It also includes a custom scenario row at the bottom.

Scenario Number		1									
	Construction Period	Useful Life of Plant	PPA Life	Average Plant Production MW per Hour	Average Hours of Production per Day	Availability Factor	General U.S.Inflation Rate Code	General Mexican Inflation Rate Code	Change USD/Mexican Exchange Rate	Base Construction Cost of Equipment
Developer Case	15	40	20	35	24	86.50%	1	1	1	44,400,000
Base Case	15	40	20	35	22	86.50%	1	1	1	44,400,000
Low Case	20	30	20	33	20	86.50%	2	2	2	50,000,000
High Case	15	40	20	35	24	86.50%	3	3	3	40,000,000
1 Construction Period	20	40	20	35	24	86.50%	1	1	1	44,400,000
2 Useful Life of Plant	15	30	20	35	24	86.50%	1	1	1	44,400,000
3 Average Plant Production per Hour	15	40	20	35	24	86.50%	1	1	1	44,400,000
4 Average Hours of Production per Day	15	40	20	33	24	86.50%	1	1	1	44,400,000
5 Availability Factor	15	40	20	35	20	86.50%	1	1	1	44,400,000
6 General U.S.Inflation Rate Code	15	40	20	35	24	83.00%	1	1	1	44,400,000
7 General Mexican Inflation Rate Code	15	40	20	35	24	86.50%	2	1	1	44,400,000
8 Real Change USD/Mexican Exchange	15	40	20	35	24	86.50%	1	1	1	44,400,000
9 Base Construction Cost of Equipment	15	40	20	35	24	86.50%	1	1	2	50,000,000
10 Contingency	15	40	20	35	24	86.50%	1	1	1	44,400,000
18 Consumables per kWh	15	40	20	35	24	86.50%	1	1	1	44,400,000
Custom Case	15	25	20	35	24	86.50%	USD Inflatio ▼	Mexico Inflation ▼	1	44,400,000
Developer Case	15	40	20	35	24	87%	1.00	1.00	1.00	44,400,000

FIGURE 17.1 Illustration of Entering Input Data into the Master Scenario Page with INDEX Function at the Bottom of the Table

Step 3: Using the INDEX Function to Find Input Data Associated with a Scenario Number

The central idea behind the INDEX and Data Table approach for making a scenario analysis is to use the defined scenario number to drive changes in a comprehensive set of inputs for running the model. Say the data for different cases (base case, downside case, and so forth) are entered across a column with different scenarios listed in rows as shown in Figure 17.1. Then the array argument in the INDEX function uses one single column across the rows that you have input. The row number used in the INDEX function is the scenario number and it is the same for each column. The result of the INDEX function is the shaded row at the bottom of the table in Figure 17.1. These values are the same as the first row of the table because 1 is used as the scenario number. They are the values that will now be used in driving the financial model. If you want, you could call the data in the row created with the INDEX function the driver row for the model. In making the INDEX function, the scenario number should be fixed with the F4 key so you can copy the same formula across different columns.

Model Driver = INDEX(Shaded Area of Rows in a Single Column,
Scenario Number Fixed with the F4 Shortcut)

Step 4: Adding a Drop-Down Box to Run Scenarios from Different Places in the Workbook

To present results of your different scenarios in graphs or on the summary page or in the guts of the financial model, it is often convenient to include a drop-down box that lists the alternative scenarios (the base case, low case, and so forth). Adding a drop-down box is similar to the process of adding a spinner button described in Chapter 16 for making flexible sensitivity graphs. In the case of the drop-down box, you select the Developer ribbon go to the Insert icon in the middle of the page, and paint a combo box somewhere on the scenario spreadsheet page. To create a drop-down list that contains the scenario names, right-click on the combo box, and then select the Form Controls option, as was the case for the spinner button. The combo box requires an input range, which is the list of items that will appear in the drop-down box. For a drop-down box associated with a scenario analysis, the drop-down list should be the names of the various scenarios such as the base case and downside case. The input range can only contain a series of row titles in one column of data and it does not work with titles that are listed across rows.

As was the case with the spinner button, the windshield-wiper method of clicking on another sheet with the mouse and then moving back to the scenario sheet should be used to ensure that the sheet name is included in the input range that lists the different scenario cases. After selecting the input range, a cell link must be entered into the format control. The cell link simply reports the result of the drop-down selection as a number. It puts the number for the row of the selected name from the drop-down list in a spreadsheet cell. In the case of our scenario analysis, the cell link will be the same number as the scenario number. Because INDEX function is used to drive the selection of the scenario, the scenario number or the cell link now also corresponds to the scenario list. The same windshield-wiper method should be used with the cell link, which is attached to the scenario number so that the cell link includes the sheet name. Figure 17.2 illustrates the process of entering the input range and the cell link on the left-hand side of the diagram. Results of applying the drop-down box to the scenario list are shown on the right-hand side of Figure 17.2. Almost every time you make a drop-down box you will probably use the INDEX function. You will use the INDEX function because once you input the cell link that is a counter for the input range of rows, you can use this number to find elements associated with the input data. The process is just the way the INDEX function works through defining a continuous array and finding an associated cell. Note also that the cell link is simply an input, as was the cell link in the spinner button. This means that by using a drop-down box you can still directly input the master scenario number manually in the cell (which also changes the selection of the combo box). Alternatively, you can select an item in the combo box, which changes the scenario number and is the cell link for the drop-down box.

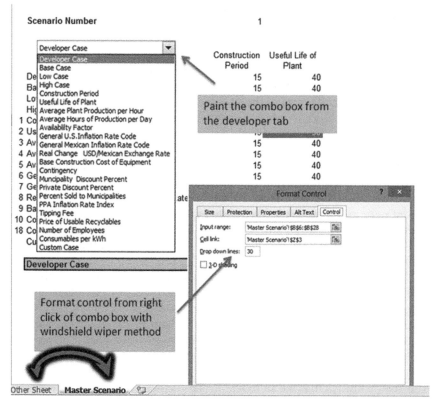

FIGURE 17.2 Application of the Windshield-Wiper Method to a Drop-Down Box

Step 5: Linking Financial Model Inputs to Scenario Page

The only tricky and somewhat awkward aspect of the scenario approach using INDEX and Data Table is that financial model assumptions that were directly input to the model must now be linked to the driver row in the master scenario page. This is the row defined by the INDEX function. Say that one of the assumptions on the master scenario page is for the price of the product, and that many alternative prices are input for the different downside, upside, recession, and other scenario cases in your cockpit page. Through using the INDEX function described earlier to establish the driver row, a single one of the price inputs (depending on the scenario number selected) is listed at the bottom of the scenario page. The single price input that comes from the INDEX line (or the line to the right of the inputs if scenarios are set up with columns instead of rows) must now drive the model instead of the input that was originally entered. To ensure the model is driven by the line on the master scenario page, the input part of the financial model should be linked to the cell defined by the INDEX or model driver line of the master scenario page. To emphasize, the model inputs come from the value driver and not the other way around. Do not link the value driver line to the model inputs. After linking the model inputs to the master scenario page, you can change the scenario number either manually or by using the drop-down box, and then all of the assumptions in the model input page that are linked to the master scenario will change. If you do not like this idea of adjusting model inputs, see the VBA code discussion at the end of the chapter for an alternative apporach.

To make the process of linking model inputs to the master scenario page less tedious, you can display both the model input sheet and the master scenario sheet on the same screen. After presenting two sheets on one screen you can go to the model inputs section, enter an equals sign, and then link your assumptions from the model input pages to the INDEX line of the scenario sheet. To be able to edit two different sheets of the same workbook on the same page, go to the View menu and first press New Window. This opens two versions of the same workbook. Next, press the Arrange All option and select the "Windows of active workbook." Also, check the box for the vertical option, as shown in Figure 17.3.

After you have two views of the same workbook open you can use the CNTL, PAGEUP or CNTL, PAGEDN shortcut keys so that one sheet shows inputs to the financial model and the second shows the master scenario page. Then you can work your way down the financial model inputs and link various inputs to the INDEX or the driver line of the master scenario page. The process is illustrated in Figures 17.3 and 17.4 where the arrows indicate that the links are made and the flow is from the master scenario page to the financial model. The rule is always that the numbers in the financial model come from the scenario page and not the other way around. It is data from the master

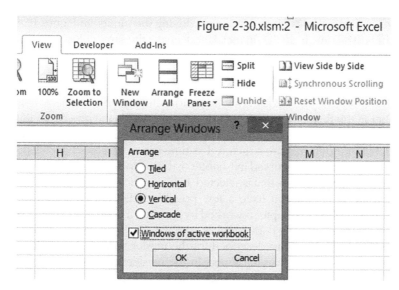

FIGURE 17.3 Illustration of the Process to Create Two Views of a Workbook on One Page

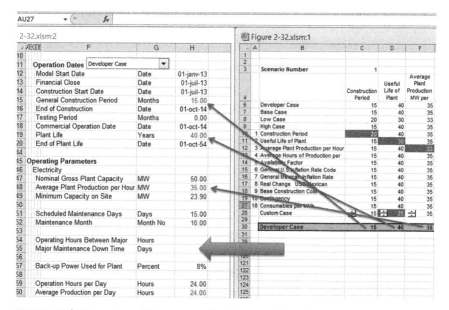

FIGURE 17.4 Illustration of the Process of Linking Numbers from the INDEX line of the Master Scenario Page to the Input Section of the Model

scenario page or the cockpit that is now driving the model. In Figure 17.4 the numbers that come from the financial model have the same color as the master scenario page.

For some inputs such as the tax rate, a gross margin percentage that is assumed to be constant over the forecast horizon, or a single ratio of accounts receivable to sales that does not change for future years, there is one input number in the financial model. For this type of variable the process of linking from the INDEX row to the input value in the assumption page is straightforward. Other inputs that are structured as time series variables have changing values over time. As discussed in Chapter 6, these inputs use code numbers to define the time series row that is selected. If the inflation rate changes from one year to the next and you have a few possible inflation rate scenarios, the method described in Chapter 6 worked by entering a code number and using the INDEX function. The code number combined with the INDEX function is much like the method just described for the master scenario page. To select different series of time-varying inputs in the master scenario page, you can enter different code numbers in the scenario table. Figure 17.1 contains inputs for general U.S. inflation and general Mexican inflation. In the input section of the model, the time series variables for this data were entered with a code number. When implementing a master scenario, link the code number input in the assumption sheet to the INDEX line in the master scenario page in the same way you would for any other variables. Do not link a code number to the master scenario code, ever. Linking the code number from the master scenario sheet to the input sheet is illustrated in Figure 17.5 where the number 1.00 in the box in the center of the financial input page comes from the INDEX line of the master scenario page.

If you use the method discussed in this step of the process to link variables, one minor problem is that financial model inputs come from the master scenario page. This means that inputs contain formulas that are now linked to the master scenario page instead of being pure numbers without formulas. You may not like this part of the technique because the input page is no longer pure in the sense that you can type hard inputs on that page. You would mess up the model if you typed an input number over the formula that is now linked to the master scenario page. Some people would rather keep the assumptions in the model as hard inputs and make the scenario analysis independent of the master scenario page. To do this you can use the VBA approach described in the last part of this chapter.

Step 6: Linking a Set of Outputs alongside the Scenario Inputs in the Master Scenario Page

Once the INDEX function has been used to drive financial model inputs from the master scenario page you can create a table that presents selected

⚐ ÆCCE	F	G	H	I	J
82 General Inflation and Exchange Rate Assumptions					
83					
84 Exchange Rates used in Construction Assumptions					
85 Base Date for Currency			01-janv-13	07-janv-13	
86					
87 Pesos/Dollar			13.10	12.74	
88 Pesos/ Euro			17.04	16.8	
89 Dólar/Euro			1.30	1.32	
90					Comes from the master scenario page
91 General Inflation Rates					
92 Inflation Rate Code Number from Cockpit			1.00		
93					
94			2013	2014	2015
95 Mexico Inflation - Base Case	Annual Pct		3.80%	3.91%	3.65%
96 Mexico Inflation - Low Case	Annual Pct		1.00%	1.00%	1.00%
97 Mexico Inflation - High Case	Annual Pct		4.00%	4.00%	4.00%
98					
99 Mexico Inflation - Base Case	Annual Pct		3.80%	3.91%	3.65%
100					
1010 Uses the INDEX		=INDEX(H95:H97,$H$92)			
1011 function with the					
1012 scenario number					
1013					

FIGURE 17.5 Illustration of Linking Code Numbers for Time Series Variables from the Master Scenario Table to the Input Page

outputs from the model next to the various scenarios. An easy way to do this is to make a one-way data table to the right of the scenario inputs. Recall that in creating a data table the format of the inputs is crucial. You can construct a data table that displays outputs like the DSCR, LLCR, and PLCR next to the base case, downside, and other scenarios by entering the code number of the scenario in a single column between the inputs and the outputs. You must first gather the outputs from the model and place them into the master scenario page. This involves linking the output variables to the master scenario page. Note that the direction of the link is now the opposite of the links for the inputs. Here the formula remains in the financial model and it will be put into the master scenario sheet. Because of restrictions in the way a one-way data table must be formatted, the links to these variables from the model calculation sheet should be placed one row above and one row to the right of the scenario numbers. For such a one-way data table to work, the column sensitivity range is the list of the scenario numbers, meaning that you must enter a counter for the various scenarios one column to the left and one row below the output variables. The format and result of the data table process is illustrated in Figure 17.6.

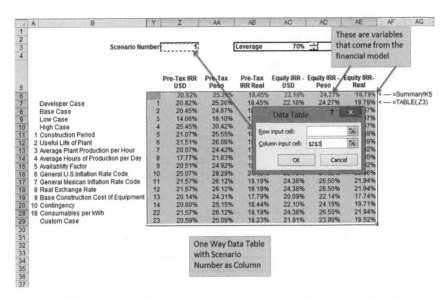

FIGURE 17.6 Illustration of Creating a Data Table with Code Numbers in a Scenario Analysis

Step 7: Creating a One-Way Table That Lists the Results of Multiple Scenarios

The final step of creating a scenario analysis is using the Data Table tool to list the results of each scenario on the master scenario page. This involves the same techniques as described previously for the break-even analysis where the one-way data table was introduced. When the scenarios are carefully set up in the manner described in step 6 with a counter to the left, the outputs one row above, and a blank cell in the upper left corner, you can create the data table. This is accomplished by selecting the area beginning with the sequential list of scenario numbers and then using the Data, What-If Analysis, and Data Table tools. After the data table is highlighted and the data table feature is selected, the column input of the data table is assigned to the single scenario number, which cycles through each scenario and lists the output variables for the scenarios.

Once you have created the one-way data table, alternative transaction structuring variables can be added to the analysis. In this way you can see the scenario case results with different transaction structures such as different levels of debt. The table in Figure 17.6 includes a spinner button next to the debt leverage that allows you to see what happens to the IRR in different scenarios when the leverage changes. If the leverage is increased or decreased by moving the spinner button around, all of the results for the different scenarios change along with the change in leverage (you could attach a simple calculation macro to the spinner button as explained in Chapter 16). In this way you can test things such as how much debt a project can support before the DSCR, LLCR, or the PLCR falls to a level of 1.0 in the downside case or the stress case.

Using VBA Code to Create a Scenario Analysis

There are two potential problems with the INDEX and Data Table scenario process just discussed that some people may not like. The first problem involves the fact that the workbook becomes slow and clumsy (even if the calculation option specifying recalculation without data tables is selected from the Formula ribbon) because data tables are used for the spreadsheet calculations. The second is that the financial model variables are linked to the master scenario page, meaning that the assumption section of the financial model no longer contains fixed data that can be adjusted manually. Instead, if you want to change data you must go back to the master scenario page. Both of these problems can be solved by working through similar steps as described earlier, but with a little VBA code. If you add a macro to the analysis you will have to press a button each time you want to run a new scenario, which is not a big deal. The first part of a macro to create scenario analysis assigns data to inputs in the financial model, eliminating the need to link variables. The second part of the macro replaces the data table with a FOR NEXT loop and the CELLS statement as explained at the end of Chapter 16.

Creating a Macro That Assigns Variables from the INDEX Line of the Scenario Page to the Financial Model Inputs

If you want to develop VBA code that links the financial model inputs to the master scenario page you can assign variables in the financial model input page to the INDEX row of the master scenario cockpit. When you assign a number with a macro rather than linking the value with a formula, the process is similar to copying and pasting with fixed values. This means that there is no formula in the input page even though the values that are changed still come from the master scenario page. Programming this can be a little tedious, as you must make a formula that corresponds to each input. You also should enter a range name for each of the variables that will be possibly adjusted from the master scenario page. The following code illustrates how to assign a variable that has an assigned range name (actual range names would be much shorter with no spaces):

```
Range("Financial Modeling Inputs") = Range("Index Formula for Item
in Index Function on Scenario Page")
```

This code will replace the various financial model inputs, but it will leave the cells with input data as fixed values rather than formulas that are linked with an equals sign to the master scenario page. As with the other VBA code discussed previously, it is essential to name the ranges when creating a macro. In this situation each input in the financial model that will be assigned a variable from the master scenario page should be assigned a range name (it is good to use the SHIFT, CNTL, F3 shortcut to do this). For the INDEX range that will be used to transfer the variables to the financial model input page, a range name can be assigned to the whole row (you can also construct a range name that covers multiple cells with the SHIFT, CNTL, F3 sequence). Once the range name is assigned, the CELLS statement can be used to find the column of that range name that will be used as the basis of assigning the variables. To illustrate the approach of assigning variables from a range name that contains multiple cells using VBA code, assume the price variable is being defined to come from the master scenario page. In the financial model, the range name is assumed to be named PRICE, and the row computed with the INDEX function in the master scenario page is named SCENARIO. Also assume that on the master scenario page the price variable defined by the various scenarios is the third variable from the left. Using the CELLS method, the VBA code would have the following form:

```
Range ("PRICE") = Range ("SCENARIO") .Cells (3,1)
```

If you want to link the input using this macro method, this kind of code would have to be added for each variable that is changed by the master scenario page. The macro can be assigned to the drop-down box that lists the scenarios so that whenever you chose a new scenario, the data that have assigned range names will be revised. If the macro is attached to the drop-down box, whenever you run the drop-down box the macro will assign new data to the variables to the financial model. In the macro you should add routines that allow you to return to the place where you began, and put back the inputs that were originally in the assumptions page. You can do this with the Activesheet.Name statement and the Activecell.Address statement as shown in the next section.

The second kind of VBA code that can be used in developing scenario analysis is a macro that creates the data table. The method of using FOR NEXT loops along with the CELLS statement that was described Chapter 16 in the context of creating break-even analysis. Exactly the same code could be used for the scenario analysis can be applied. Using VBA code to create data tables for a scenario analysis is illustrated in Figure 16.10.

Getting the Best of Both Worlds: Creating a Special Custom Scenario That Allows Use of Spinner Buttons and Drop-Down Boxes

In Chapter 15, the idea of creating a flexible graph with spinner buttons and drop-down boxes was described in detail. The attraction of this method for risk analysis is that you can allow management to play around with key variables and visualize what happens to things like cash flow, earnings, or debt balances. If all of the key input variables come from a structured master scenario or, if you like, cockpit page, there are no spinner buttons and the idea of playing around with a variable seems to be no longer an option. Recall that a problem with allowing management to play around with a model is that they can ruin your inputs and you may not be able to remember what values you had input for the base case. This section describes a technique by which you can still use spinner buttons and drop-down boxes for risk analysis presentation. But then when you are finished playing around, you can also quickly reset all of the inputs to one of the cases in the master scenario page.

One way to create a combined scenario and sensitivity analysis is to insert an extra scenario case in a line below all the rest of the scenario cases on the master scenario page. In this special scenario case you can attach spinner buttons or combo boxes to all the data in the scenario so that the variables can be adjusted in a similar manner as in the sensitivity analysis discussion. In the master scenario page illustrated on Figure 17.1, the last row named the custom case is an example of this idea. If you look back at Figure 17.1, each input on that last row that is not a time series variable is assigned a spinner button. The variables that change over time such as the inflation rate and are entered with a code number have an associated combo box. By attaching spinner buttons and drop-down boxes to inputs in such a custom scenario, you can change individual variables in the summary page of a model as long as the scenario case number is set to the number for the special custom case.

There are two challenges when creating this type of special custom case. The first problem is that you would probably like to reset the custom case to the base case, low case, or high case after playing around with the spinner buttons and combo boxes. This is because you will soon forget values for the base case and it is a pain to push the spinner buttons around until you get back to the original values. The second problem is that when attaching the spinner buttons to values in the custom scenario, many of the inputs are expressed as percentages or as very large numbers. Spinner buttons, however, accept only whole numbers between 0 and 30,000. This means that spinner buttons do not work for percentage inputs, for large numbers without adjustments, or for inputs that you would like to present with decimal numbers such as 5.26. To fix this problem you can make a spinner button with the CELL LINK attached to an intermediate number instead of the input that the spinner button represents. Then you can make the input a formula that adjusts the intermediate number created with the CELL LINK. To better understand this, say you want to enter a percentage input that moves between 1 percent and 100 percent. You can then create an intermediate cell that moves from 1 to 100 that is attached to the CELL LINK. After that, you can divide the intermediate number created with the CELL LINK by 100 and use the spinner button. This means that whenever you want to present a number that is not a whole number using the spinner button, you must develop a two-step process. The first part of the process is to set the CELL LINK to an indirect cell and the second part is to divide or multiply that intermediate CELL LINK number by some constant such as 100 or 0.10.

In the context of a custom scenario case you can address the problems of attaching spinner button when the data are not simple whole numbers and also address the business of resetting data by adding a few rows below the line that was created with the INDEX function. Using a little VBA code you can automatically reset the scenario to the base case or another case by making a copy and paste macro that puts the base case or other cases back into the custom case.

The new added rows include space for adjustments to address problems with the spinner buttons. One of the lines contains intermediate cells that can be transferred through multiplying or dividing data, which can then establish the custom case. The added rows also allow you to reset the custom case to the base case, high case, or low case. The last additional row below the INDEX model driver row contains the data that can be referred to in the spinner button row. This row can be attached to the CELL LINK as it contains numbers like 10 instead of 10 percent or 100 instead of 100,000. The numbers used that adjust the CELL LINK values back to input values can be called multipliers. With the 10 percent and the 100,000 input value examples, the first multiplier could be 100 and the second multiplier could be 0.01. These multipliers that are entered to a row below the INDEX row have two functions. The first objective is to multiply the unadjusted data that is copied from the base case so that it can be used in CELL LINK of the spinner button. The second function is to readjust the intermediate spinner button values so that they can be expressed in the correct units in the financial model. Using this idea of multipliers, the following step-by-step process explains the technique that you can use to reset the custom case to the base case, low case, or high case scenarios and also make the custom case operate with spinner buttons.

Step 1   Begin the process by recording a macro. With the macro recording, copy the base case row, the low case, or any other case to a row a few lines below the INDEX function line. This line is named the Copied row in Figure 17.7. The Copied row cannot be used with

A	B	C	D	E	F	G	H	I
15								
16						Maintenance	Cost of Revenue	
17			Scenario	Production	Steel Price	Expenditures	Fixed Growth	Variable
19	1	1	Base Case	1	1	1	4.00%	62.00%
20	2	2	Low Case	2	2	2	6.00%	64.00%
21	3	3	High Case	3	3	3	3.00%	61.00%
52		34	Custom Case [Base Price ▼]	1 [Base Produ ▼]	1 [Base Case ▼]	1	▲▼ 4.00%	▲▼ 62.00%
53								
54			Base Case	1	1	1	4.00%	62.00%
55								
56								
57			Copied	1	1	1	4.00%	62.00%
58			Multiplier	1	1	1	1000	1000
59			Adjusted	1	1	1	40	620
60			Spinner	1	1	1	40	620
61								
62			=E60/E58				=H57*H58	=I60/I58

FIGURE 17.7 Illustration of Inserting Rows below the Scenario Table to Create a Flexible Custom Case Scenario

spinner buttons if any of the variables are expressed as percentages or may have values larger than 30,000 or have values that can change in manner other than whole numbers. After copying the scenario row to the raw data line, stop recording the macro.

Step 2   Input the various multipliers in a row below the raw data row copied from step 1. This data that you enter is not directly affected by a macro. If the scenario data are code numbers that adjust time series inputs or the data are already whole numbers between 10 and 30,000 that can be expressed without fractions, then the multiplier can be 1.0. For other data that contain percentages, where a fraction is desired, or where the number is larger than 30,000, a multiplier should be entered that is either a multiple or a fraction of 10. An illustration of this process is shown in Figure 17.7 were the multipliers are 1.0 for time series variables with code numbers, but are 1,000 when the input data is expressed as a percentage.

Step 3   Create a third row that you can name the Adjusted row. In this row multiply or divide the row copied from the base case or another case by the multipliers in a third row. This row will have values that can be adjusted with either spinner buttons or combo boxes. In the example shown in Figure 17.7, the row is named Adjusted and it is the Copied row divided by the Multiplier row. The formula in this row should be left alone, meaning that it should not be attached to a spinner button or a drop-down box. You will need formulas in this row to remain intact when you redo the process later on. If you are using the spinner button to push a value up or down, you want to adjust a fixed value and not a formula.

Step 4   Start recording a second macro that copies the Adjusted row (the Copied row divided by the multiplier) and paste it as values into yet another fourth and final row. Then stop recording the macro. This fourth row has fixed values rather than formulas. It is the row named Spinner in Figure 17.7. It is the row that is used as the intermediate CELL LINK by all of the spinner buttons and the combo boxes for defining the custom case. You need to copy and paste the cells as values to this new row because the spinner button will fix values and you will want to redo the process later on. If you do not create this intermediate step by copying and pasting with values, you can perform the process after copying the base case only a single time. After that, you could not reset the custom case scenario. Say you would like to change the base case or run the custom case from the low case. This process allows you to retain the flexibility whereby the raw Copied data is adjusted with a formula without fixing the data. Once you have copied and pasted the final Adjusted row to the Spinner row, stop recording the macro. For cosmetic purposes, after you have recorded the macro, add a line in the VBA code to turn off the marking for the copied row using the statement:

```
Application.CutCopyMode = FALSE
```

Step 5   To create the spinner buttons for each data item in the custom case, refer to the Spinner row in step 4 when you are connecting each CELL LINK. This value in the Spinner row should be a whole number that can be adjusted by the spinner button. The Spinner row is the last row shown on Figure 17.7.

Step 6   When you have computed the last row containing the intermediate data that is adjusted by the multiplier, you can establish the custom scenario row that will be used in the model when the master scenario code is set to the custom case number. The custom case scenario uses the Spinner line that you created containing fixed adjusted values and then readjusts this line using the multiplier factors. For example, if the base case input is an interest rate of 5.2 percent, then the value expressed as a decimal is copied to the raw data row, resulting in the number 0.052 using the first macro. Next, the raw data row named Copied is multiplied by 1,000, yielding a value of 52. This value of 52 is in turn copied to the fixed Spinner row. The value of 52 is attached to the spinner button as the CELL LINK using the windshield-wiper method of clicking on another sheet and returning to the master scenario sheet. Finally, the number in the custom row of the scenario table and used to transfer data to the model is divided by 1,000, and that number is ultimately used in the financial model.

This all sounds a bit dense but remember it is really accomplished by two copy and paste macros. When you are finished with the process, management can select the custom scenario with the drop-down box and then play around with the interest rate as much as they want. But when they have finished playing around you can reset the custom case scenario back to the base case by pressing a button attached to the copy and paste macros.

Step 7   The final step of the process to create a custom scenario case is to put the two macros that you created from the preceding steps together. As with any macro you should create range names for anything that is copied and pasted. This macro should be attached to the drop-down box so that the basis for the custom case can be the base case, the low case, or any other case.

To program a macro that copies different cases depending on the scenario chosen you can use the SELECT CASE statement in VBA followed by the END SELECT statement. This method will allow you to copy different cases to the copied data row depending on which scenario is selected. If you are attaching the macro to the drop-down scenario box, then when you use the SELECT CASE statement, you can apply a different copy and paste routine depending on the scenario selected. To use the SELECT CASE method, put the variable that will change next to SELECT CASE. In this case a reference to the master scenario number is entered after the SELECT CASE statement using the RANGE statement as shown next. The variable is the range name for our famous scenario code number. If the scenario number is assigned a range name (as it should be) the VBA code would be:

```
SELECT CASE RANGE("Scenario Number")
```

Below this statement you would enter CASE 1:, CASE 2:, and so forth depending on how many cases can be copied to the raw data Copied line and used in the custom case. Here, the numbers 1, 2, and 3 refer to the scenario code number. Underneath CASE 1: you then put the copy and paste statement

```
Sub custom()
'
' custom Macro
'
    Application.ScreenUpdating = False            ' Turn off screen updating for copy

    If Range("scenario") > 4 Then Exit Sub        ' Only copy the first three scenarios

    current_cell = ActiveCell.Address             ' Remember cell for re-set
    current_sheet = ActiveSheet.Name              ' Remember sheet for re-set

    scenario_sheet = Range("scenario_sheet")      ' Get scenario sheet name
    Sheets(scenario_sheet).Select

    Select Case Range("scenario")                 ' Select different cases for copying
        Case 1: Range("base_case").Select
        Case 2: Range("low_case").Select
        Case 3: Range("high_case").Select
    End Select

    Selection.Copy
    Range("copied").Select                        ' Copy to first row
    Selection.PasteSpecial Paste:=xlPasteValues, Operation:=xlNone, SkipBlanks _
        :=False, Transpose:=False

    Range("adjusted").Select         ' Select line after the multiplier formulas
    Selection.Copy
    Range("spinner").Select          ' Copy to fixed spinner box line as fixed

    Selection.PasteSpecial Paste:=xlPasteValues, Operation:=xlNone, SkipBlanks _
        :=False, Transpose:=False
    Application.CutCopyMode = False

    Sheets(current_sheet).Select                  ' Re-set the sheet and the cell
    Range(current_cell).Activate
End Sub
```

FIGURE 17.8 Illustration of Macro to Create Custom Scenario from Copying and Pasting Alternative Cases

that copies the base case to the raw data line below the INDEX function as illustrated:

```
CASE 1:
Copy base case to raw data row
CASE 2:
Copy low case to raw data row
```

Once you are finished with the copy and paste functions as part of the SELECT CASE process, you must write the END SELECT statement. Then, below the END SELECT statement, move the copy and paste code that copies the Adjusted row to the Spinner row. This part of the macro copies the Adjusted line computed from the raw data multiplied or divided by the multiplier to the fixed Spinner row. The second part of the macro is necessary because this last fixed line is used by the spinner button. Finally, if you do not want the copy and paste functions to apply to selections from the drop-down box other than the first three cases (base case, the low case, and the high case), you can use the following code:

```
Case > 3
    Exit Sub
```

A completed macro to accomplish this custom case process with range names is shown in Figure 17.8. This macro includes the ability to remember the sheet location and the cell location where you were when you began running the macro and it will take you back to the same starting point.

CHAPTER 18

Generating Tornado Diagrams, Spider Charts, and Waterfall Graphs

When constructing a scenario analysis using the procedure discussed in Chapter 17, there is often a very large difference between an output for the base case and the downside case as a whole lot of inputs are changed at the same time. The base case may have something like a 12 percent internal rate of return (IRR) whereas the downside case could have a −20 percent IRR. To make sense of a scenario analysis such as this, it is useful to understand which of the input variables are most instrumental and which are least instrumental in causing the IRRs to change. An analysis that isolates on the effect of individual variables is useful for a few reasons. First, it can allow you to better understand which particular variable is the one that really matters in driving changes in the output. Second, it is a very effective way for you to find errors in your model. Third, it is a good way to impress people with fancy graphs that demonstrate your prowess in spreadsheet programming.

When isolating the effect of individual assumptions on the difference between scenario outcomes, the general approach described in this chapter is to create a number of different sensitivity cases that adjust the base case by one single variable at a time. Once you have created these multiple sensitivity cases you can present the analysis in various different forms. One technique is to make a tornado diagram, which involves making a bar chart that illustrates differences in a model output between low case and base case inputs as well as differences between high case and base case inputs. Bars on the chart can be arranged from the input variable that has the highest effect to the input variable that has the lowest effect on the selected output parameter. A second presentation technique for displaying the sensitivity analysis is creating a spider diagram. This type of graph shows increments for all of the selected input variables on the x-axis and presents the resulting output on a series of line graphs. A third style of presentation involves displaying how the low case or the high case is built up from the base case value. This is often referred to as a waterfall graph.

This chapter begins by discussing why you may want to present a tornado diagram or a spider diagram in risk analysis. It then explains how to make the tornado and spider graphs through extending the scenario analysis discussed in Chapter 17. The next few paragraphs describe two different ways to create a tornado diagram. A subsequent section of the chapter discusses how to make spider diagrams. The final part of the chapter explains how to present sensitivity analysis in a waterfall chart.

Tornado Diagrams That Display Which Variables Have the Largest Effect on Value and Which Variables Have the Least Effect on an Output Variable

The scenario analysis described in Chapter 17 did not show which of the input variables are most important and which are insignificant in influencing an output variable of your model. You can perform this kind of risk analysis by making a tornado diagram. A tornado diagram gets its name because it is supposed to look like the whirlwind created by a tornado, which is normally larger on the top and smaller on the bottom. In this vein, input variables that have the highest effect on a selected output variable are shown as horizontal bars at the top of the graph and variables that have a smaller impact are shown at the bottom. Through presenting sensitivity analysis in this manner a tornado diagram can be used as a tool to determine which variables are most important in a sensitivity analysis and should thus be the focus of more study and due diligence. In addition, a tornado presentation can be used to illustrate whether an investment has more upside risk or more downside exposure. If the tornado is bending toward the upside case or the downside case, as tornadoes sometimes do, then there is more upside potential or downside risk in your investment. Third, a tornado diagram can be used as an auditing tool to test the mechanics of a financial model. If the variables that have the highest effect on the output metric are not intuitive or they have not effect at all, you should then go back to the financial model and carefully examine the formulas related to the nonintuitive variable.

Figure 18.1 illustrates how a tornado diagram can be used in risk analysis. Data is entered for a number of inputs for the base case, downside case, and upside case scenarios in the same format as the scenario analysis discussed in Chapter 17. While the structure is the same as the scenario analysis, the downside and upside cases do not necessarily have to represent a consistent single integrated scenario. In the case of a tornado diagram, every variable is entered as a low or a high value and one variable does not mitigate the effect of another. If sales decrease, then operating costs may also decrease in a scenario analysis, but this would not be part of a tornado analysis. Figure 18.1 illustrates the format of a tornado diagram. Data shown on the left of the *y*-scale are the low case, base case, and high case inputs. Which of these to use depends on your judgment. Given the inputs for the three cases, each bar on the diagram shows how the variation in the downside case input relative to the base case input or the upside input relative to the base case input affects the output variable.

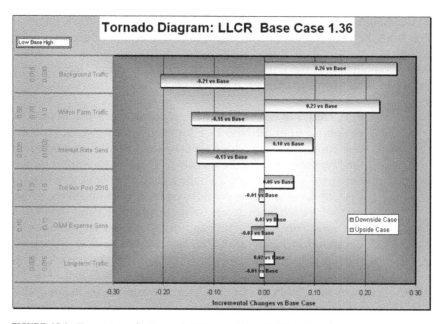

FIGURE 18.1 Illustration of a Tornado Diagram for a Toll Road Project

The tornado diagram illustrated in Figure 18.1 shows which variables have the largest effect on the loan life coverage ratio (LLCR) for a toll road project financing. It demonstrates that the variable that has the highest effect on the LLCR is the background traffic. For the downside case assumption, this variable causes the LLCR to fall by 0.21, when all other variables are set to the base case. The top bar also shows that if the background traffic increases by 3 percent per year the LLCR increases by 0.26 relative to the base case. Other bars on the chart representing variables such as the operation and maintenance expense and the long-term traffic projections have a smaller effect on the LLCR. If the LLCR is an important statistic for lenders, you would not have to worry quite as much about getting these other variables right in your model as long as the judgmental downside and upside assumptions are reasonable.

Creating a Tornado Diagram by Extending Scenario Analysis

You do not need some kind of fancy add-in to create a tornado diagram. Instead, you can make the diagram that illustrates the sensitivity of each variable straight from extending the scenario analysis described in Chapter 17. To construct a tornado diagram similar to the one displayed in Figure 18.1 you should add two new scenario rows for each input variable. Then you can use the Data Table tool to summarize all of the scenarios at the same time. Once a data table is constructed with all of the additional scenario rows, information from the resulting data table output can be used to build a graph like Figure 18.1. As with the scenario analysis, the entire process is accomplished with a combination of the Data Table and the INDEX function. Detailed steps to construct the Tornado diagram that displays sensitivity analysis include:

Step 1   First, add a whole lot of new scenario rows that represent deviations from the base case for each separate input variable. The good news about this is that you do not have to spend much time typing in data for the scenarios. This is because data for the new rows come straight from the base case, low case, and high case inputs. The new scenarios you enter will contain base case values for each input except for the single input value defined as the sensitivity case. This set up of sensitivity scenarios is illustrated in Figure 18.2. The first sensitivity case represents the low case for sales growth. This sensitivity scenario uses base case inputs for all values except for the sales growth. For the sales growth input, the low case is assumed. By creating this new scenario you will be able to see how much the sales growth assumption affects the value of the company in isolation, because all of the other inputs are still set to the base case.

To make these scenarios where a single value is altered from the base case you should first insert a lot of rows to allow space for the scenarios. You can then use the TRANSPOSE function to make scenario titles for each of the new sensitivity rows. Say that you already have the base low and high case scenarios in a table on the master scenario page. First, count on your fingers how many input variables you have. Then in the column that contains the scenario titles select the number of rows that you just counted. Next, make a title for each of the new sensitivity scenarios by highlighting the variable titles and using the TRANSPOSE function. If one of the variables represents prices, another represents quantities, and a third represents interest rates, then these variable names are presented as sensitivity scenarios below the low case as shown in Figure 18.2.

	D Scenario	E Production	F Steel Price	G Maint Exp	H Fixed Growth	I Variable
17						
19	Base Case	1	1	1	4.00%	62.00%
20	Low Case	2	2	2	6.00%	64.00%
21	High Case	3	3	3	3.00%	61.00%
22	=TRANSPOSE(AN17:BB17)&" Low Case"			1	4.00%	62.00%
23	Steel Price Low Case	1	2	1	4.00%	62.00%
24	Maint Exp Low Case	1	1	2	4.00%	62.00%
25	Fixed Growth Low Case	1	1	1	6.00%	62.00%
26	Variable Low Case	1	1	1	4.00%	64.00%
37	Production High Case	3	1	1	4.00%	62.00%
38	Steel Price High Case	1	3	1	4.00%	62.00%
39	Maint Exp High Case	1	1	3	4.00%	62.00%
40	Fixed Growth High Case	1	1	1	3.00%	62.00%
41	Variable High Case	1	1	1	4.00%	61.00%
53						
54	Base Case	1	1	1	4.00%	62.00%
55						
106						
107	=TRANSPOSE(AN17:BB17)&" High Case"				=H$19	=I21
108					base	high
109						

FIGURE 18.2 Illustration of Scenario Table with Sensitivity Analysis for Each Variable

To use the TRANSPOSE function, you need to press SHIFT, CNTL, ENTER rather than just the ENTER key as TRANSPOSE is an array function. Say there are six variables in the scenario analysis as shown in Figure 18.2. You then can insert 12 new rows that will have a low case and a high case next to the name for each variable. In each scenario, the values all are the base case inputs except for one variable that has the low case or high case title. The sensitivity row titles can say something like "Base Case Except Sales Growth Low Case."

To make these titles you can either add the text to the TRANSPOSE function with the & symbol or you can simply refer to the low case and high case title. If you are creating your own text, next to each sensitivity row you can use the TRANSPOSE function as follows:

- Select six rows.
- Enter "Base Case Except" & TRANSPOSE("Variable Row Titles") & "Low Case."
- Press the SHIFT, CNTL, ENTER combination.

If you just want to use the low case or high case title that you already have entered, you can use the TRANSPOSE function together with another cell reference as follows:

- Select six rows.
- Enter TRANSPOSE("Variable Row Titles") & Cell Reference for low case (e.g. C7).
- Press the SHIFT, CNTL, ENTER combination.

Once you have made the sensitivity titles like these for the low case, you can shade the next six rows and make similar titles for the high case.

Step 2   After making row titles for the different sensitivity scenario cases, copy all of the values in every single scenario to the base case. You can quickly copy all of the values from the base case to other rows by linking one of the variables with the equals sign and then pressing the F4 key twice so that the row number will be fixed and the column number will be flexible. When you have linked the base case value for one cell, copy the same link to the entire block of remaining rows and remaining columns using SHIFT, CNTL, → and SHIFT, CNTL, Down Arrow. Alternatively, you can hold the SHIFT key and go to the bottom right column and then click. After the entire block is shaded then press CNTL, R and CNTL, D to copy the base case value to each cell.

Step 3   Once you have the block of new rows for the sensitivity cases all assigned to the base case, work through each row and change the value of the variable that is listed in the sensitivity case to the low case. If the first row is a sensitivity case for sales growth, then you should link the cell in the column for the sales growth to the low case value instead of the base case. This means that the sales low case sensitivity row will have the base case value for every input except for the sales growth. After you have finished the same process for each sensitivity case row, there should be a diagonal pattern. All variables should have the same base case value except one single input that is different in one row below and one cell to the right of the previous changed cell. Creating these multiple scenarios allows you to isolate the effect of the downside value or the upside value for each data item.

If you want to illustrate which values in a scenario are altered from the base case, you can use the conditional formatting tool. As with previous examples of conditional formatting you can work with the option to enter a formula. To apply this approach of formatting depending on the equality of two values, begin by highlighting the area that you want to format. Next, enter the current cell in the conditional formatting slot without any fixed references (i.e., without the dollar signs) by pressing the F4 key a few times. Then, test whether the variable is equal to the low case or the high case. When testing the value relative to the low or high case, use the fixed reference on the row number for the low or high case so the conditional formatting will work across all of the scenarios. Coloring cells that are equal to the low case or high case using this technique is illustrated in Figure 18.3.

Step 4   After adjusting the selected values of individual variables in the downside case, follow the same process for the upside case, meaning that you first transpose the titles. As was the case for the downside scenario, link the base case values to the whole block

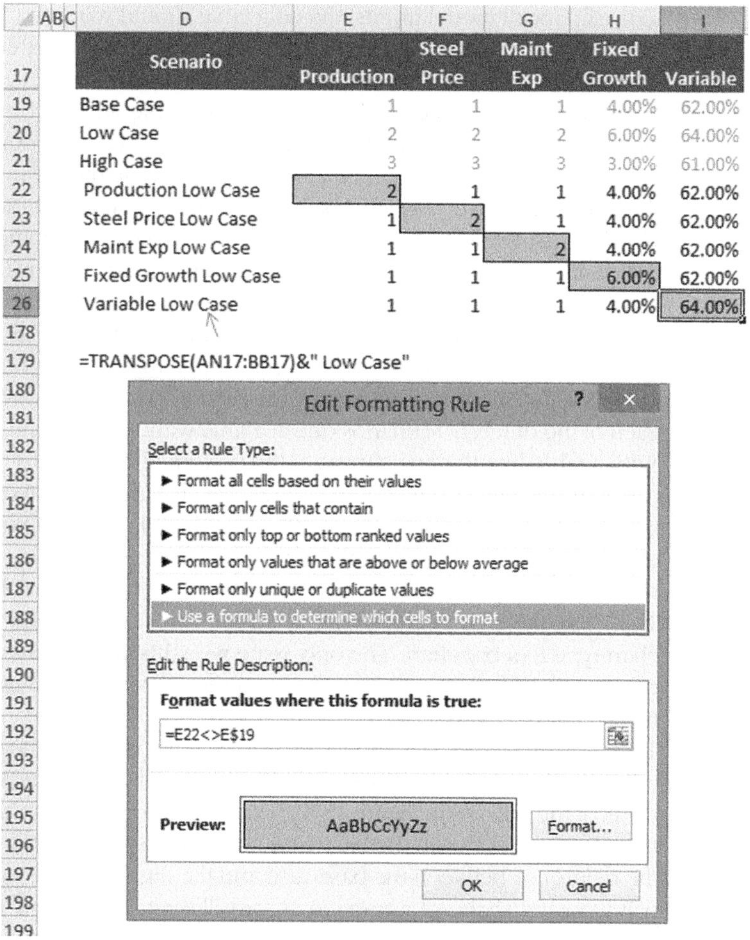

	Scenario	Production	Steel Price	Maint Exp	Fixed Growth	Variable
17						
19	Base Case	1	1	1	4.00%	62.00%
20	Low Case	2	2	2	6.00%	64.00%
21	High Case	3	3	3	3.00%	61.00%
22	Production Low Case	2	1	1	4.00%	62.00%
23	Steel Price Low Case	1	2	1	4.00%	62.00%
24	Maint Exp Low Case	1	1	2	4.00%	62.00%
25	Fixed Growth Low Case	1	1	1	6.00%	62.00%
26	Variable Low Case	1	1	1	4.00%	64.00%

| 178 | |
| 179 | =TRANSPOSE(AN17:BB17)&" Low Case" |

Edit Formatting Rule   ?   ✕

Select a Rule Type:

► Format all cells based on their values
► Format only cells that contain
► Format only top or bottom ranked values
► Format only values that are above or below average
► Format only unique or duplicate values
► Use a formula to determine which cells to format

Edit the Rule Description:

Format values where this formula is true:

=E22<>E$19

Preview: AaBbCcYyZz   Format...

OK   Cancel

FIGURE 18.3 Use of Conditional Formatting with the Formula Option to Color Cells That Are Not the Same as the Base Case

of inputs and then change the input value to the upside case for only the sensitivity variable in question.

Step 5   When data for the low case and the high case sensitivities are entered as new sensitivity rows, adjust the INDEX function and the Data Table to include the additional cases. To revise the INDEX function, include the added rows as part of the array in INDEX function. You must also add the new sensitivity case numbers in the column to the right of the data table as was shown in Figure 18.2. The data table is developed as usual by shading the extended scenarios and attaching the column input to the scenario number. Since numbers from the INDEX row are already attached to the financial model inputs, the data table should work just fine.

Step 6   With the extended data table created you can evaluate the effect of each input variable on the output variable in isolation. To make this comparison, add some rows below the data table where you will subtract values in the data table for each sensitivity case from the base case value in the table. In subtracting, compute the change of the sensitivity case from the base case. First create a list of the variables using the TRANSPOSE function. Next to the list compute the upside case value minus the base case value for each sensitivity row. In a second column make a similar calculation for the downside sensitivity. This process is illustrated in Figure 18.4. Calculations for these incremental differences can be made by fixing the base case cell in the data table with the F4 key and then subtracting each of the different scenarios one at a time without fixing the cell.

Step 7   With a table like the one shown at the bottom of Figure 18.4, you can make a graph that demonstrates which variables have the largest effect on the output variable and which have the smallest effect on the variable. Simply highlight the table including the titles and the blank cell at the top left as shown in Figure 18.4. Then use the F11 key to create a graph. After that, change the chart type to a bar chart. The only issue with this graph is that it is not yet sorted for presentation. An example of the unsorted graph is illustrated in Figure 18.5.

Step 8   The remaining task in creating a tornado diagram is sorting the data (although you may be satisfied with the unsorted graph that is the result of the process in Figure 18.5). If you sort the absolute value of the difference between the base case and low case combined with the difference between the base case and the high case, the graph will have the shape of a tornado as was illustrated in Figure 18.1. Unfortunately, use of the sort tool is not very helpful in this instance for a variety of reasons. First, you probably do not want to change the order of all the variables in the scenario table. Second, if you

	C	D	E	F	G	H	I	J	K
1	Scenario number	1							
2	Synergy Sensitivity		100%						
3	Premium		20%						
4		Sales Growth	COGS margin	Sales to A/R	Inv to CGS	Cap Exp to Sale	AP to Exp	Sc Num	Equity IRR
5									18.44%
6	Base case	1	1	8.40%	5.60%	1	5.60%	1	18.44%
7	Low case	2	2	10.00%	10.00%	2	3.00%	2	16.15%
8	High case	3	3	7.00%	5.00%	3	7.00%	3	25.83%
9	Sales Growth Low Case	2	1	8.40%	5.60%	1	5.60%	4	12.28%
10	COGS margin Low Case	1	2	8.40%	5.60%	1	5.60%	5	15.15%
11	Sales to A/R Low Case	1	1	10.00%	5.60%	1	5.60%	6	18.23%
12	Inv to CGS Low Case	1	1	8.40%	10.00%	1	5.60%	7	18.14%
13	Cap Exp to Sale Low Case	1	1	8.40%	5.60%	2	5.60%	8	18.30%
14	AP to Exp Low Case	1	1	8.40%	5.60%	1	3.00%	9	18.15%
15	Sales Growth High Case	3	1	8.40%	5.60%	1	5.60%	10	21.74%
16	COGS margin High Case	1	3	8.40%	5.60%	1	5.60%	11	20.90%
17	Sales to A/R High Case	1	1	7.00%	5.60%	1	5.60%	12	18.62%
18	Inv to CGS High Case	1	1	8.40%	5.00%	1	5.60%	13	18.48%
19	Cap Exp to Sale High Case	1	1	8.40%	5.60%	3	5.60%	14	19.81%
20	AP to Exp High Case	1	1	8.40%	5.60%	1	7.00%	15	18.60%
21	Custom Case	1	1	8.40%	5.60%	1	5.60%	16	18.44%
23	Base case	1	1	8.40%	5.60%	1	5.60%		
33			Low v Base	High v Base					
34		Sales Growth	-6.16%	3.30% <---- =K15-$K$6					
35		COGS margin	-3.29%	2.46% <---- =K16-$K$6					
36		Sales to A/R	-0.21%	0.18% <---- =K17-$K$6					
37		Inv to CGS	-0.30%	0.04% <---- =K18-$K$6					
38		Cap Exp to Sale	-0.14%	1.37% <---- =K19-$K$6					
39		AP to Exp	-0.29%	0.16% <---- =K20-$K$6					

FIGURE 18.4 Creating a Table Showing the Incremental Downside Sensitivity Cases and the Upside Sensitivity Cases Relative to the Base Case

have used the Data Table function, you cannot sort items in the data table. Third, when you rerun the analysis by changing something in your model, you do not want to redo the sort.

Instead of using the sort tool you can use a combination of the SMALL function, the MATCH function, and the INDEX function. If you use the SMALL function along with the MATCH and the INDEX functions, the original values that you sort will be left alone and you can perform the sort process somewhere else in the spreadsheet. The general approach is to begin by using the SMALL function to sort the variables, where you list the array of items to sort and a counter variable. Then you must create a special variable representing a sort key that will be used for tabulating the whole set of variables in a sorted order. This can be

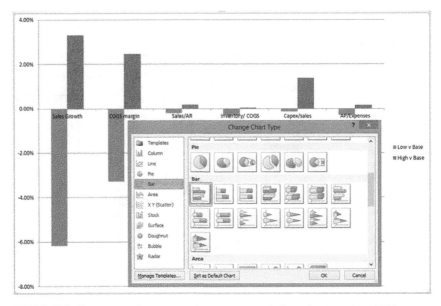

FIGURE 18.5 Illustration of Creating a Sensitivity Graph from the Sensitivity Table

accomplished with the MATCH function. Once the sort key is created from the MATCH function, you can use the INDEX function to present selected variables in sorted order and make your graph. Details of this process include the following five actions:

1. First compute the absolute value of the differences between the low case and the base case combined with the difference between the high case and the base case. Then make a new column or row next to the sum of the absolute values. To use the SMALL function to sort these absolute values you need a counter variable, as the SMALL function gives you the first smallest value, the second smallest value, and so forth. To do this, enter the SMALL as illustrated:

SMALL(Row or Column to Sort, Counter)

2. After you have used the SMALL function to sort the absolute values, you have the sorted values but you have lost the variable names and other information associated with each of the values. To retrieve the names associated with each of the values and to retrieve the base relative to low and the base relative to high values, you can make a counter or index variable. You can use this variable to associate the

titles and the other values with the sorted items. The most important step in doing this is to use the MATCH function to produce a counter variable that finds the original row or column number of the sorted variables. This can be called the sort key. The sort key that has the original row or column number for the sorted data is essential because it is the basis for the INDEX function that will produce the original names and data to make the graph. When computing the sort key, use the MATCH function to create an exact match. For this, you must enter a 0 as the match type, as illustrated in the following equation:

MATCH(Sorted Single Value, Row of Unsorted Values, 0)

3. Sometimes, two or more of the sorted variables have the same value. In this situation you can add the RAND( )*.000001 to the variable to be sorted (before it is sorted), which in our case is the absolute value of the differences. This assures there is a unique value for each sorted item.

4. To make a graph you will need the title of each sensitivity variable, as the *x*-axis and the low versus the base as well as the high versus the base data items. In setting up the data for making a graph, use the INDEX function along with the sort key that you just created from the MATCH function. When using the INDEX function for the *x*-axis, enter the original unsorted titles (fixed with the F4 key) in the INDEX function and use the sort key as the column number as illustrated:

INDEX(Original Series of Titles – Fixed, Sort Key)

An illustration of this optional sorting process is included in Figure 18.6.

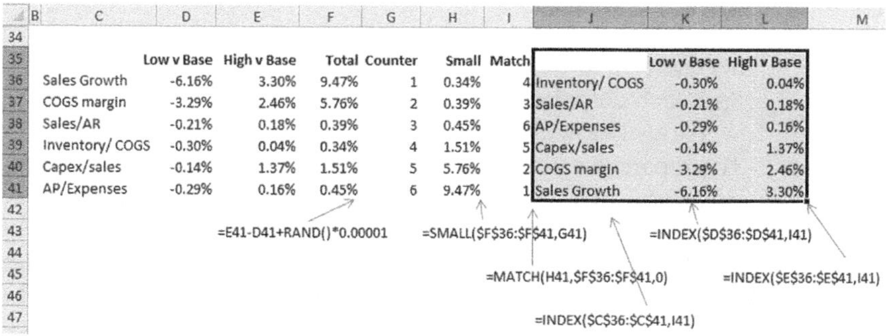

		Low v Base	High v Base	Total	Counter	Small	Match		Low v Base	High v Base
36	Sales Growth	-6.16%	3.30%	9.47%	1	0.34%	4	Inventory/ COGS	-0.30%	0.04%
37	COGS margin	-3.29%	2.46%	5.76%	2	0.39%	3	Sales/AR	-0.21%	0.18%
38	Sales/AR	-0.21%	0.18%	0.39%	3	0.45%	6	AP/Expenses	-0.29%	0.16%
39	Inventory/ COGS	-0.30%	0.04%	0.34%	4	1.51%	5	Capex/sales	-0.14%	1.37%
40	Capex/sales	-0.14%	1.37%	1.51%	5	5.76%	2	COGS margin	-3.29%	2.46%
41	AP/Expenses	-0.29%	0.16%	0.45%	6	9.47%	1	Sales Growth	-6.16%	3.30%

=E41-D41+RAND()*0.00001   =SMALL($F$36:$F$41,G41)   =INDEX($D$36:$D$41,I41)

=MATCH(H41,$F$36:$F$41,0)   =INDEX($E$36:$E$41,I41)

=INDEX($C$36:$C$41,I41)

FIGURE 18.6 Illustration of Sorting Data Using the SMALL Function with MATCH and INDEX

5. Graph the sorted variables using the F11 function, and change the chart type to a stacked bar chart. As usual, make sure that there is no caption next to the titles in the upper left-hand cell so Excel will know that this is the *x*-axis.

Creating a Tornado Diagram Using a Two-Way Data Table

A tornado diagram can also be constructed using a two-way data table together with a TRUE/FALSE test variable and a row number code. This method changes each variable one at a time and also changes the scenario number for the base case, low case, or high case. For each change in the variable and the scenario, the result is reported in a two-way data table. When implementing this second method you do not have to make a lot of sensitivity rows as with the TRANSPOSE process shown previously. However, there are a couple of drawbacks to this method. First, you need to add extra steps if you want the flexibility to present both the sensitivity analysis and the scenario analysis. Second, adding a separate custom scenario is difficult. Creating a two-way table to make a tornado diagram is similar to the method that is described later on to create spider diagrams. As with the row-by-row method of creating tornado diagrams discussed in the previous section, the general process involves isolating the effect of one variable while all of the other variables are held at the base case value. When using the two-way data table approach, you can think of cycling around each input variable one at a time and finding the output variable and also cycling around the base case, low case, and high case scenarios. If you were writing a program, there would be two FOR NEXT loops.

To create a tornado using this two-way data table process, you can take the following steps:

Step 1   Set up a scenario analysis using the normal INDEX and Data Table approach described in Chapter 17, but do not add all of the extra scenarios below the low case.

Step 2   To prepare the analysis for a two-way data table rather than a one-way table, add a code number for the variable number in addition to the scenario code number at the top of the sheet. The variable number could be entered near the scenario number that was the first thing entered in the master scenario page at the top. Next, add a number associated with each variable in an analogous manner to the way you entered the scenario number to the left of the data table. Entering the variable number above each variable name and putting the single variable number code at the top of the sheet are illustrated in Figure 18.7.

Step 3   Underneath the normal INDEX row for the basic scenario analysis, add a new row that includes a TRUE/FALSE test. This switch variable tests whether the variable number in the column of the table is the same as the variable code number that you input at the top of the page. If there are six variables, there should be a list of numbers from 1 to 6 above the variables. The switch variable evaluates whether the code number at the top of the table equals the number associated with the variable. If the row code number is 2, then the row below the INDEX function will be FALSE in every column except for the second column. Because of the way the numbers are set up there is always only one value that is TRUE for the list of variables. The formula for the test variable should use the F4 key for the variable code number and compare this to each formula as illustrated:

$$=\text{Variable Number Input at the Top} = \text{Number Associated with Each Variable}$$

Step 4   Add another row below the TRUE/FALSE switch variable that uses an IF function to establish the model driver. This row assures that only one variable at a time will be changed in your financial model. If the test variable is TRUE, then use the value from the INDEX function discussed in step 2 to run the model. If the variable is FALSE, then you simply use the base case value. Using this approach, every variable remains at the base case value except the variable that equals the variable code number that you input. This is the trick that allows the two-way table to present

	D	E	F	G	H	I	J	K	L	M
1										
2	Variable Number	2								
3	Scenario Number	2								
4										
5	Variable Number ---->	1	2	3	4	5	6	7		
6		Investment	Price	Quantity	Cost	Inflation	Terminal	Life		
7	Base Case	100%	100%	100%	100%	100%	100%	100%		
8	Low Case	140%	80%	90%	120%	140%	70%	80%		
9	High Case	95%	120%	115%	90%	90%	140%	120%		
10										
11	Low Case	140%	80%	90%	120%	140%	70%	80%	< ---- =INDEX(K7:K9,$E$3)	
12	Var Code	1	2	3	4	5	6	7		
13	Test	FALSE	TRUE	FALSE	FALSE	FALSE	FALSE	FALSE	< ---- =K12=$E$2	
14	Input to Model	100%	80%	100%	100%	100%	100%	100%	< ---- =IF(K13,K11,K7)	
15										

FIGURE 18.7 Formulas for the Switch Variable and the IF Test to Set Up a Two-Way Data Table for a Tornado Diagram

how each variable affects the output value in isolation from the others. The IF test has the following form:

IF(TRUE/FALSE Test, INDEX from Normal Scenario in Step 3, Base Case from Scenario Table)

Figure 18.7 shows formulas for the switch variable that contains either TRUE or FALSE as well as the variable created with the IF test that will drive the model.

Step 5   After entering scenario inputs, the variable code number, the test TRUE/FALSE switch variable, and the IF test as shown in Figure 18.7, you should link the input variables in the financial model row with the last row that contains the IF test instead of linking them to the INDEX function row. This means when you change the variable code number and put the scenario number to the low case, only the low case is implemented for the single variable number in the financial model. When you have finished linking variables in the input section to the last row shown in Figure 18.7, you are ready to set up a two-way data table where one of the sensitivity variables is the variable number and a second variable represents the scenario number for the base case, low case, and high case. The general structure of this two-way data table is illustrated in Figure 18.8.

Step 6   In Figure 18.8, the first row represents the base case, the second is the low case, and the third is the high case. Each column contains the value of the selected output variable whereby the input variable is changed in isolation and every other variable remains set to the base case value. Once the table is set up, run either a two-way table or, if you want to be a little fancier, write some VBA code that does the same thing. The row input for the two-way data table is the variable code number and the column input is the scenario number.

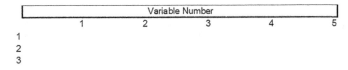

FIGURE 18.8 Setup of Two-Way Data Table for Tornado Diagram

Step 7   When the two-way data table has been calculated, the base case output is repeated for each variable and there is no difference in the output variable across the row. The downside and the high case contain the sensitivity effect of the single value. After the table is computed, the base case relative to the low case and the base case relative to the high case can be established. This is done by subtracting the low case row from the base case row and by subtracting the high case row from the base case row. The subtraction of the alternative cases from the base case are the bars that can then be presented in the tornado diagram. All that is left to do is to sort and present the data. An illustration of this process is shown in Figure 18.9. In this example the variable with the largest effect is variable number 6 and the second largest is variable number 2. Variable number 4 comes in last place. To find the ordering of the variables, look in the row named "Absolute Difference," which adds the absolute value of the low case relative to the base case and the high case relative to the base case.

	D	E	F	G	H	I	J	K	L
1									
2	Variable Number	1							
3	Scenario Number	1							
4									
18	Two Way Data Table								
19		Investment	Price	Quantity	Cost	Inflation	Terminal	Life	
20	$1,228.45	1	2	3	4	5	6	7	
21	1	1,228.45	1,228.45	1,228.45	1,228.45	1,228.45	1,228.45	1,228.45	< --- =TABLE(E2,E3)
22	2	864.81	1,003.75	1,116.10	1,220.96	1,369.05	913.00	1,255.02	
23	3	1,273.90	1,453.15	1,396.97	1,232.19	1,196.29	1,649.04	1,235.13	
24									
25	Low vs Base	-363.64	-224.70	-112.35	-7.49	140.61	-315.44	26.57	< --- =K22-K21
26	High vs Base	45.45	224.70	168.53	3.75	-32.16	420.59	6.68	< --- =K23-K21
27									
28	Absolute Difference	409.09	449.40	280.88	11.24	172.77	736.04	33.25	< --- =ABS(K25)+ABS(K26)
29									
30	Small	11.24	33.25	172.77	280.88	409.09	449.40	736.04	< --- =SMALL($E$28:$K$28,K20)
31	Match	4	7	5	3	1	2	6	< --- =MATCH(K30,$E$28:$K$28,0)
32									
33	Area for Making Graph								
34		Cost	Life	Inflation	Quantity	Investment	Price	Terminal	< --- =INDEX($E$19:$K$19,K31)
35	Low vs Base	-7.49	26.57	140.61	-112.35	-363.64	-224.70	-315.44	< --- =INDEX($E$25:$K$25,K31)
36	High vs Base	3.75	6.68	-32.16	168.53	45.45	224.70	420.59	< --- =INDEX($E$26:$K$26,K31)
37									

FIGURE 18.9 Creating Tornado Analysis from Two-Way Data Table

Step 8   To sort the data from highest to lowest when making a tornado graph, use the same process described in step 8 in the previous step-by-step description of extending the scenario analysis. This involves first computing the sum of the absolute values of the differences and then using the SMALL, MATCH, and INDEX functions as shown in Figure 18.9.

Step 9   A drawback of this approach is that if you connect the financial model inputs to the row with the IF statement that isolates on one variable, you can no longer use the same data for making a standard scenario analysis. To rectify this you can add an option variable that switches between the scenario analysis and the sensitivity analysis. In allowing this flexibility you can add a form control that permits selection of either a scenario analysis or a tornado diagram. If the scenario analysis is chosen, the link to the financial model will come from the INDEX row. If the tornado diagram is selected, the link will come from the IF statement. Instead of using a spinner button or a drop-down box you can use multiple option buttons this time. To apply option buttons, insert a button from the developer tab and then right click on the button as usual and select a cell link. Whereas drop-down boxes work together with the INDEX function, the option buttons work well with the CHOOSE function.

Step 10   In order to make the model operate with either the scenario analysis or a tornado diagram, you can enter yet another row below the IF statement row. This row selects whether the INDEX function row is used to drive the financial model inputs as was discussed in Chapter 17, or the IF statement that sets all variables to the base case except for the single variable in question is the model driver. To tell the model whether to apply the INDEX row or the IF row you can use the CHOOSE function together with the cell link from the option button. The new row will be set to either the INDEX value for the scenario option, or the IF function for the tornado option. An illustration of this part of setting up a tornado diagram was presented in Figure 18.8. The last line in the table shown in Figure 18.8 is used as the basis for the link that drives inputs of the financial model.

Spider Diagrams That Illustrate How Each Range in Input Variables Affects an Output Variable

In evaluating how different input variables affect an output variable, some people like to see a graph where the percentage variation of different input variables is shown on the x-axis and the output variable changes are presented on the y-axis. As the graph can be presented for many variables, you compare the slope of different variables to see how sensitive the output variable reacts to changes in the various input variables. This diagram with multiple line graphs is called a spider diagram. If the output variable is the IRR, then the price input variable should have an upward-sloping line because price increases raise the IRR. On the other hand, the cost variable should have a downward slope. Variables that have a steeper slope have more of an effect on the output variable, whereas variables that do not have much of an effect should have a relatively flat line.

While this kind of diagram may have some minor cosmetic interest, the big problem is that each variable may not have the same level of potential variation. Some variables may have a range of only 5 percent whereas others may have a range of 200 percent, but a typical spider diagram uses the same percentage changes for each of the input variables.

Figure 18.10 illustrates the format of a spider diagram where various input variables that affect the net present value of an investment are shown together with the associated effect on the output variable. Instead of showing simple percentages on the *x*-axis, the *x*-axis range in Figure 18.10 displays potential values labeled from very low to very high. In this diagram a judgment is made as to the range that a potential variable can change by in terms of percentages. This amount by which a variable can potentially change is similar to the idea of volatility discussed later. Indeed, thinking about percentage ranges in the input variables is a transition between purely judgmental low case and high case inputs to the discussion of stochastic risk analysis methods. In Figure 18.10, the amount spent on the capital investment has the largest negative effect on the value, as very low values lead to a high net present value while the terminal value has the opposite effect. The real question in this analysis is to determine how large the possible percentage variation (or volatility) is for each of the variables.

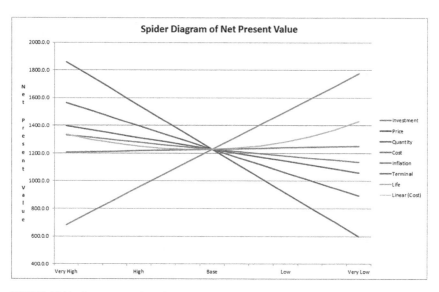

FIGURE 18.10 Illustration of Spider Diagram That Shows How Net Present Value Reacts to Changes in Different Variables

How to Create a Spider Diagram Using a Two-Way Data Table

The mechanics of creating a spider diagram are similar to the construction of a tornado diagram using a two-way data table. The graph in Figure 18.10 is created by highlighting results produced by the two-way data table and pressing the F11 key. The two-way data table is generated by allowing your financial model to accept percentage factors for various different input variables, adding a row code number associated with the different input variables to a scenario-type table, linking the percentage factors in the financial model to the row of sensitivity factors created with an INDEX function, creating a two-way data table with a variable row code number and a scenario code number, and, finally, producing the two-way data table that can be graphed. The process for creating the spider diagram using this process includes the following steps:

Step 1   Insert a new sheet in your model (press the SHIFT and F11 keys). Set up a table with input data much like the list of scenarios in the master scenario page discussed earlier, with the input variable names on different columns. This time enter percentages in each row rather than naming the scenarios the base case, downside case, and upside case. The first row may contain 10 percent across the whole row, the second row could contain 20 percent across all of the columns, and so forth. Include enough rows so that the percentages eventually increase to well above 100 percent. Somewhere near the middle of the table a row with 100 percent across all of the columns should be included. This 100 percent row is like the base case scenario for a tornado diagram. These percentage changes will drive the output variable changes in the spider diagram. You can think of each of the percentage change rows as a different scenario in a scenario table.

Step 2   Revise the financial model so that sensitivity factors can be accepted as inputs. This means that a factor like 80 percent should be added to each important input in a model. A good way to do this is to put the percentages in a column to the left of the calculations and multiply the existing formula by the percentage factor.

Step 3   Create a scenario code number and a variable code number in the same way that you entered the variable code and the scenario code number for the analysis of a tornado diagram using a two-way data table. As with the two-way table for the tornado diagram, enter a line below the last row of the table using the INDEX function and the scenario number. Then add another row that includes a TRUE/FALSE test derived from the variable number. Finally, add an IF statement that applies either the number in the INDEX row or 100 percent base case, depending on the TRUE/FALSE switch variable. An example of the setup for a spider diagram is shown in Figure 18.11.

Step 4   Link the row created with the IF test to the percentage factors in the financial model. As in all of the scenario analysis, the direction

	A	B	C	D	E	F	G	H	I	J	
1	Scenario No		8								
2	Variable No		3								
3						Variable Number					
4				1	2	3	4	5	6	7	
5				**Moisture Content**	**Heat Content**	**Heat Rate Sensivity**	**Construction Cost/Ton/D**	**Capacity Factor**	**Tipping Fee**	**O&M Cost**	
6			1	70.00%	50.00%	50.00%	50.00%	50.00%	50.00%	50.00%	
7			2	75.00%	60.00%	60.00%	60.00%	60.00%	60.00%	60.00%	
8			3	80.00%	70.00%	70.00%	70.00%	70.00%	70.00%	70.00%	
9			4	85.00%	80.00%	80.00%	80.00%	80.00%	80.00%	80.00%	
10	Scenario Num		5	95.00%	90.00%	90.00%	90.00%	90.00%	90.00%	90.00%	
11			6	100.00%	100.00%	100.00%	100.00%	100.00%	100.00%	100.00%	
12			7	105.00%	110.00%	110.00%	110.00%	110.00%	110.00%	110.00%	
13			8	110.00%	120.00%	120.00%	120.00%	120.00%	120.00%	120.00%	
14			9	115.00%	130.00%	130.00%	130.00%	130.00%	130.00%	130.00%	
15			10	120.00%	140.00%	140.00%	140.00%	140.00%	140.00%	140.00%	
16			11	125.00%	150.00%	150.00%	150.00%	150.00%	150.00%	150.00%	
17											
18	Index Function		8	110%	120%	120%	120%	120%	120%	120%	<---- =INDEX(J6:J16,$C$1)
19	Test on Variable Number			FALSE	FALSE	TRUE	FALSE	FALSE	FALSE	FALSE	<---- =J4=$C$2
20	Sensitivity Applied in Model			100.00%	100.00%	120.00%	100.00%	100.00%	100.00%	100.00%	<---- =IF(J19,J18,J11)
21											
22	Two Way Data Table										
23				Moisture Content	Heat Content	Heat Rate Sensivity	Construction Cost/Ton/D	Capacity Factor	Tipping Fee	O&M Cost	
24			0.92	1	2	3	4	5	6	7	
25		Very Low	1	0.76	0.76	0.38	0.47	1.36	0.82	0.63	<---- =TABLE(C2,C1)
26		75.00%	2	0.76	0.76	0.46	0.52	1.16	0.81	0.65	
27		80.00%	3	0.76	0.76	0.53	0.58	1.02	0.80	0.68	
28		85.00%	4	0.76	0.76	0.61	0.64	0.91	0.79	0.71	
29		95.00%	5	0.76	0.76	0.69	0.70	0.83	0.77	0.74	
30		Base	6	0.76	0.76	0.76	0.76	0.76	0.76	0.76	
31		105.00%	7	0.76	0.76	0.84	0.82	0.71	0.75	0.79	
32		110.00%	8	0.76	0.76	0.92	0.88	0.66	0.74	0.82	
33		115.00%	9	0.76	0.76	0.99	0.94	0.63	0.73	0.85	
34		120.00%	10	0.76	0.76	1.07	1.00	0.59	0.72	0.87	
35		Very High	11	0.76	0.76	1.15	1.06	0.56	0.71	0.90	

FIGURE 18.11 Illustration of the Setup of Spider Diagram Analysis with a Two-Way Data Table

of the link is from the scenario or spider table toward the financial model input, meaning that the financial model has an equals sign that links to the spider diagram page.

Step 5 Create a two-way data table by entering the variable numbers on different columns and the scenario numbers associated with different percentages across the rows as illustrated in Figure 18.8. Then pick one of the output variables from the financial model such as the IRR, and place it in the upper left-hand corner cell of the table. Now you can create the two-way data table. As with the tornado analysis discussed previously, the row input cell for the data table is the variable code number and the column input cell is the scenario code number. Once you have made the data table, add titles above the first row for the names of the variables, and add the percentage inputs to the left of the columns. In Figure 18.11, the titles for the rows are the variable names and the titles for the columns are the percentage changes.

Step 6 Use the data table combined with F11 or ALT, F1 to create the line graphs. To adjust the data table and make a graph, you can group (temporarily hide) the scenario numbers and the variable numbers that are the basis for the row and column inputs of the data table. This can be done by clicking on the single row and the single column and then using the SHIFT, ALT, → shortcut. This step is unfortunately necessary to avoid the upper left corner number messing up the graph as illustrated on Figure 18.11. If you create a data table with a macro, you do not need the number in the top left corner and this step is not required.

Step 7   Adjust the input percentage ranges to reflect different potential variations in the variables. For all variables, the 100 percent line will remain the same, but commencing from the 100 percent line there could be movements up or down by different percentages. For example, the price may vary by 20 percent to the upside and 10 percent to the downside. The cost of goods sold (COGS) percentage on the other hand may vary by only 5 percent to both the upside and the downside for each increment. If there are five rows to the upside and five rows to the downside, the percent change in each price increment is 20 percent divided by 5 (= 4 percent) while the percent change in the downside case is 10 percent divided by 5 (= 2 percent). In the case of the COGS percent, the upside and the downside percentages are increased and decreased by 5 percent divided by 5 (= 1 percent).

If the percentages are not constant, you cannot use them as data labels for the x-axis of a spider diagram. Instead, when making titles, you can use labels such as the high case, the very high case, and the high range case. Everything else is similar to the process described previously where all variables increase or decrease by the same percentage. The process of adjusting ranges in this manner illustrates that variables do not have the same volatility, that there are lower or upper boundaries on variables, and that the upside may not be the inverse of the downside case.

Presenting Sensitivity Analysis with a Waterfall Chart

A third way to present sensitivity analysis in addition to the tornado chart or the spider diagram is to create a waterfall graph. This way of presenting sensitivity can show how different variables fall down from the base case to the low case or build up from the base case to the high case. An example of using a waterfall chart to demonstrate sensitivity analysis is shown in Figure 18.12 in the context of an electricity generating plant. The graph visually demonstrates which of the different variables is most instrumental in moving from the base case to the low case.

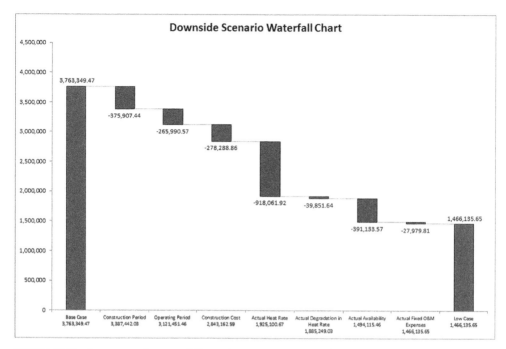

FIGURE 18.12 Illustration of a Waterfall Graph to Demonstrate Downside Sensitivities

Making this graph with connector lines, data labels, hidden bars, different colors, and negative values can be time consuming and bothersome. Because of this, a template is provided at www.wiley.com/go/internationalvaluation. All you have to do is to open a file and you can put the graph in any model. The template will allow you to change anything in the file and the waterfall graph will also change. You don't have to import any macros or apply some kind of add-in. Once the graph is made, if you change inputs, the graph will also change.

To set up data for a waterfall chart the process is similar to the first method for making a tornado diagram, where separate sensitivity rows were added to the master scenario page. The difference in this case is that instead of changing only one variable at a time, you keep accumulating the variable changes as shown in Figure 18.13. To do this you can put row numbers above the variable names and column numbers next to the variable names. Then you can write an IF statement and use the low case whenever the row number is greater than the column number. Otherwise you use the base case row. For the final step of the process you can make a data table as usual and compute the increments from one case to the next. The manner in which increments are computed from the data table and set up for the waterfall chart template is shown in Figure 18.14.

	D	E	F	G	H	I	J	P	Q
1	Scenario Number		1	Base Case		▼			
2									
3		1	2	3	4	5	6		
4		Construction Period	Operating Period	Construction Cost	Realised Capacity	Actual Heat Rate	Actual Degradation in Heat Rate		Cumulative Pre-tax IRR
5									9.74%
6	Base Case	40	25	3,000,000	1,000	6,000	0.20%	1	9.74%
7	Low Case	60	23	3,300,000	980	6,100	0.25%	2	5.85%
8	High Case	35	30	2,850,000	1,100	5,900	0.18%	3	12.64%
9								4	
34	Base Case	40	25	3,000,000	1,000	6,000	0.20%	29	9.74%
35	Construction Period	60	25	3,000,000	1,000	6,000	0.20%	30	8.91%
36	Operating Period	60	23	3,000,000	1,000	6,000	0.20%	31	8.68%
37	Construction Cost	60	23	3,300,000	1,000	6,000	0.20%	32	7.76%
38	Realised Capacity	60	23	3,300,000	980	6,000	0.20%	33	7.76%
39	Actual Heat Rate	60	23	3,300,000	980	6,100	0.20%	34	6.74%
40	Actual Degradation in Heat Rate	60	23	3,300,000	980	6,100	0.25%	35	6.65%
41	Inflation	60	23	3,300,000	980	6,100	0.25%	36	6.71%
42	Actual Availability	60	23	3,300,000	980	6,100	0.25%	37	6.71%
43	Actual Fuel Price per kJ	60	23	3,300,000	980	6,100	0.25%	38	5.92%
44	Actual Fixed O&M Expenses	60	23	3,300,000	980	6,100	0.25%	39	5.85%
45	Actual Variable O&M Expenses	60	23	3,300,000	980	6,100	0.25%	40	5.85%
46									↑
55		=IF($C45<E$3,E$34,E$7)							=TABLE(,F1)

FIGURE 18.13 Adding Cumulative Sensitivity Rows for a Waterfall Graph

Waterfall Chart Data	Increment	Value
Base Case	2,058,054.26	2,058,054.26
Construction Period	-254,245.84	1,803,808.43
Operating Period	-193,676.54	1,610,131.90
Construction Cost	-278,288.86	1,331,843.05
Actual Heat Rate	-459,030.97	872,812.09
Actual Degradation in Heat Rate	-39,208.87	833,603.22
Actual Availability	-302,764.15	530,839.07
Actual Fixed O&M Expenses	-27,979.81	502,859.26
Low Case		

Shade title for the waterfall graph and one colum to the right.
After opening waterfall template, then run macro to make the chart with SHIFT, CNLT, V

FIGURE 18.14 Computing Increments from the Data Table to Create a Waterfall Graph

Adding Probabilistic Risk Analysis and Time Series Equations to Financial Models

The remainder of the risk analysis addressed in this chapter and in Chapters 20 through 22 addresses application of mathematics and probability analysis to risk assessment in financial models. One of the differences in using statistical analysis to gauge risk as compared to the methods discussed in Chapters 13 to 18 is that the mathematics and probability analysis does not depend as much as the prior methods do on the subjective opinions of people with respect to the assumption of how high or how low some variable may move in the future. Another difference is that a range of output values for single periods and variations in the output variable across multiple periods is produced from inputs that are expressed in terms of volatility and other mathematical parameters. With these ranges of output values, you can generate probability distributions for any output variable computed in your financial model.

One way to think about stochastic risk analysis is that ranges in variables for sensitivity analysis, break-even analysis, and scenario analysis come from statistical parameters rather than judgmental assessments of potential ranges. Inputs to scenario and sensitivity analysis that drive the analysis for techniques described in Chapters 15 to 18 can be biased upward by managers having a favorable attitude toward an investment concept. The judgment can also be biased downward if managers disagree with a business idea or if, as happened in the dark days of the financial crisis of October and November 2008, bankers had such a pessimistic outlook on the future that they would not make loans to corporations like Siemens. Such biases can theoretically be avoided by using cold, hard statistics such as volatility parameters that can be computed from historical data or derived from forward-looking market expectations through analyzing traded securities.

Using fancier language, the process of developing statistical analysis to measure risk can be termed applying a stochastic diffusion process to prediction of economic variables. Because probability distributions are output from the diffusion process, applying probabilistic analysis in financial models allows you to answer questions that cannot be seemingly resolved with sensitivity analysis, break-even analysis, or scenario analysis. Examples of some financial questions that can be answered include: What is the probability of the internal rate of return (IRR) to equity and the IRR to different debt tranches being below the risk-free rate? What is the required credit spread on alternative types of debt securities? What is the probability of achieving different levels of earnings per share (EPS)? What is the chance of financial ratios such as the interest coverage ratio falling to levels below those of investment grade companies?

Some people reading the preceding paragraphs may already be red in the face with disgust from a listing of these supposed benefits of mathematical risk analysis. Skeptics of this kind of stochastic risk analysis scoff at the idea that judgment can somehow be taken out of the risk analysis process. These doubters may emphasize that the pretention that you can transform a business into a mathematical equation with a probability distribution is pure fantasy. Five of the problems in attempting to apply probabilistic risk analysis in financial models are:

Problem 1 Historical data used in establishing probability distributions is often a poor predictor of the future dispersion in economic variables, especially where the variables are driven in part by human behavior. Economic variables like price and demand growth are distinguished from physical variables such as wind speeds, reserves of oil underneath the ground, or hydroelectric power conditions that do not depend on the whims of human beings. Prices and volumes can experience sudden jumps or falls not seen in historical statistics when industry market structure changes. The changes are often not close to being linear when surplus capacity increases above a certain level and prices collapse to short-run marginal cost.

Problem 2 Parameters required for implementing probability analysis in financial models—especially mean reversion, correlation, price trends, boundary levels, and jumps—are often very difficult if not impossible to estimate on an objective basis from historical data or from implied market expectations. However, in many situations the mean reversion parameter and the other factors that cannot be reasonably estimated have a more important effect on the outcome of the risk analysis than the volatility estimate. If models require parameters that cannot be computed, they are not really very useful.

Problem 3 If prices or other variables follow cyclical patterns that contain mean reversion, then an estimate of the long-run equilibrium value must be included in the analysis. If this long-run value also is stochastic, the whole process seems to boil down to a whole lot of random numbers.

Problem 4 The implicit or explicit assumption that rates of changes in variables come from a normal distribution is very often not valid. This renders the whole process biased if not useless, especially when analyses focus on the tail end of distributions in estimating credit losses. Attempting to incorporate distributions other than the normal distribution into a financial model requires added parameters for potential jumps, skewness, or changing volatility that can be almost impossible to estimate.

Problem 5 Even with efficient software and fast computers, the process of implementing Monte Carlo simulation into large financial models can be time-consuming and tedious.

Given the problematic issues that arise when attempting to convert a business into a stochastic mathematical equation, you may wonder why so much discussion is devoted to the subject of stochastic modeling in this part of the book. The answer is that the objective of discussing mathematical approaches to risk analysis is not necessarily to advocate the approach or to suggest that you should go out and immediately apply time series and Monte Carlo simulation to your financial models. Five reasons for understanding stochastic risk analysis techniques besides making a Monte Carlo simulation in your financial model are: (1) making sure that you will not be intimidated or overly impressed when presentations are made using Monte Carlo simulation from financial models, (2) explaining the flaws as well as the benefits of the stochastic modeling techniques, (3) discussing how the mathematical techniques can be combined with business judgment to make the process applicable in some practical situations, (4) using the stochastic representations of economic variables as a framework to think about how differences in the risk structure of input variables affect value, and (5) using the statistical analysis associated with Monte Carlo simulation to understand various problems in finance and economics that do not directly use Monte Carlo simulation but do involve analogous statistical analysis. Examples of issues that involve statistical analysis associated with financial models that do not necessarily involve Monte Carlo simulation can be found in renewable energy analysis as well as in oil and gas production. For renewable energy financial models, electricity production is often represented by probabilities associated with wind speeds, solar irradiation, and hydroelectricity production. Similar probability distributions can be applied in financial models for oil and gas reserves and traffic studies.

The fourth point in the last paragraph involving how key variables can move is worthy of a bit more elaboration. To implement a time series equation for a variable, you must come up with statistical parameters that represent long-term trends, variations around the trends, eventual reversion to long-run levels, lower and upper boundary values, possible sudden moves, and the relationship between the variable in question and other variables. Computing these parameters and, more important, thinking carefully about what economic factors influence them forces you to consider how key input variables can potentially move in the future whether or not you ever make a Monte Carlo simulation. When coming up with parameters in time series equations you should understand the underlying economic supply and demand factors that drive parameters such as volatility and mean reversion, so that you can better deal with the real sources of risk in an investment. If you think about the statistical parameters when you establish the downside case and upside case assumptions for scenario analysis you should think about such questions as: What is the lower limit? How much can the variable move in a year? Will the variable move back to a long-term equilibrium level? What is that equilibrium level? Can a perfect storm cause a dramatic change in the variable? How does the variable move when other variables change?

Definition of Some Terms for Adding Stochastic Analysis to Your Financial Models

Much of the challenge in applying a Monte Carlo simulation to financial models is understanding the terminology. A few terms that are used in creating probabilistic analysis include "time series equations," "volatility," "normal distributions," "mean reversion," "long-term equilibrium," and "Monte Carlo simulation." The manner in which probability analysis is applied in financial models can be achieved through expressing various operating assumptions in terms of time series equations. Time series equations are mathematical formulas that describe an economic variable in terms of its potential dispersion as well as the expected level of the variable. Say the formula for product price in a financial model is $P_t = P_{t-1} \times 1.1$. This simply means that the current year's price is last year's price increasing at a rate of 10 percent. An equation such as this is a deterministic equation. If the equation were changed to a time series equation, then the next year price would be modeled with a possible dispersion around the expected price. Say the price may increase by 20 percent, 10 percent, 0 percent, or by some other amounts. The expected value is still a 10 percent increase, but the time series equation includes probabilities of different values within the range. The manner in which the price can vary around the expected increase of 10 percent can be expressed by a volatility parameter. If the volatility is close to 0, there is little chance of the price moving by much more or much less than 10 percent. If the volatility parameter is high, the price can move by a wider amount.

Using time series equations rather than deterministic equations in a financial model allows you to project ranges in values rather than focusing on only one case scenario at a time. This also means that all of the outputs of the model such as the IRR, the debt service coverage ratio (DSCR), the amount of debt that is repaid, and any other output variable from the model can be expressed as a probability distribution with ranges that result from the input time series equations. Among other things, including time series equations with volatility parameters drives the probability of default in credit analysis, the time series equations determine the value of real options, time series equations are used to measure the effect of hedging risks through long-term contracts, and the time series equations with volatility are central in computing value at risk. Volatility, which is generally expressed as a percentage, can be defined as the standard deviation of the rate of change in a variable. The rate of return upon which the standard deviation is computed can be the rate of change in stock prices, the rate of change in oil prices, the rate of change in demand, the rate of change in cost, or any other assumption in a financial model.

If you could somehow know that the percent change in a variable comes from a normal distribution, volatility as measured with standard deviation can be used to measure the probability that future values will be above or below a certain level. To see how volatility is related to standard deviation it is necessary to remember a little bit of statistics that most of us forget. In a normal distribution the probability of being within one standard deviation above and below the mean is 68.27 percent. The probability of being two standard deviations above and below the mean is 95.4 percent. If the mean is 4 and the standard deviation is 3, then there is a 68.27 percent chance that the observed value will be between 7 (4 + 3) and 1 (4 − 3).

The normal distribution is so convenient in working with volatility because any probability can be obtained if you know only the mean and the standard deviation. Since volatility is generally defined as the standard deviation of the annual percent change in a variable, if you know the volatility, the probability of achieving a value for the next year can be estimated. Say the volatility of oil prices is 20 percent per year, which is the approximate actual volatility from historical levels before 2007. Also say the average oil price in January is $54 per barrel, which was the actual oil price at the beginning of 2007. Then there is a 68 percent chance that the oil price will fall between $43.20 and $64.80 by the end of the year (an increase and decrease of 20 percent). Similarly, there is a 95 percent chance that the oil price will be between $32.40 and $75.60, which represent two standard deviations above and below the mean or a 40 percent increase and a 40 percent decrease. These approximate values for 2007 oil prices are driven by the assumption of a normal distribution. By the way, the price at the end of 2007 was $96 per barrel, well outside of the 95 percent range. Either the change in price for 2007 was a very low probability event, or oil price changes do not really come from a normal distribution.

Using Probability Distributions with Spreadsheet Functions Rather Than Equations with Greek Letters

To understand time series equations you can work through the mechanics of a couple of spreadsheet functions that derive the probabilities of normal distributions. In evaluating normal distributions there are two functions that are particularly useful in determining whether the rate of change in variables really comes from a normal distribution. The first function, NORMDIST, uses the mean, the standard deviation, and an observed value from the distribution as inputs and then returns the probability of achieving a particular value. If the mean rate of change is 2 percent, the standard deviation is 15 percent, and you would like to know the probability of realizing a rate of change of less than 20 percent, you can use the cumulative option in the NORMDIST function as follows:

$$\text{Cumulative Probability} = \text{NORMDIST}(x = 20\%, \text{Mean of } 2\%,$$
$$\text{Standard Deviation of } 15\%, 1)$$

In this equation, the switch of 1 at the end of the formula means that the probability output is a cumulative distribution, and the $x = 20\%$ means that the probability output is less than or equal to 20 percent (NORMDIST (20%,2%,15%,1)). The probability of achieving a growth rate of 20 percent or less is 88.5 percent (the mean of 2 percent is much lower than 20 percent). If a distance of one standard deviation above the mean or 17 percent is used (2 percent plus 15 percent) in the NORMDIST function (NORMDIST (17%,2%,15%,1)), then the probability of being below this number is 84.13 percent. If the observation is one standard deviation below the mean or −13 percent (2 percent minus 15 percent), then the probability from the NORMDIST is 15.87 percent (NORMDIST(−13%,2%,15%,1)). The difference between these values found with the NORMDIST function (84.13 percent minus 15.87 percent) gives you the famous 68 percent chance of being within one standard deviation above or below the mean.

You can also use the NORMDIST function to compute the probability of falling into various increments on a noncumulative basis. In the preceding example you may want to find the probability of achieving 20 percent rather than the probability of the result being less than or equal to 20 percent. This can be accomplished by using the same NORMDIST function with a switch of FALSE or 0, rather than TRUE or 1. The problem with this formula when computing a noncumulative or incremental number is that you have not told Excel the width of the range to use in computing the probability. The probability of achieving a particular number in a very small range between .19999999 and .20000001 would be very low. In contrast, the probability of achieving a number between 0 and 1.2 would be large. To resolve the problem when using the NORMDIST function to find incremental probabilities, you can simply multiply the NORMDIST formula by the increment desired and you will get the probability. In the example using a mean of 2 percent and a standard deviation of 15 percent, if you wanted the probability within 1 percent of the 20 percent number (i.e., between 19 percent and 20 percent), you would multiply the outcome of the NORMDIST function by 1 percent. This would yield a probability value of 1.29 percent. The 1 percent multiplied by the NORMDIST function represents the difference between 19 percent and 20 percent. To demonstrate how this works say you are working with wind speed data and there is a mean wind speed of 7 meters per second along with a standard deviation of 0.5 meters per second. Say also that you want to find the probability of achieving 8 meters per second. You would use the NORMDIST function for a range of 1.0 to get the value between 7.5 and 8.5. This time you do not multiply the result by 1 percent but by 1.0 as the increment between 7.5 and 8.5 is 1.0. You can verify the noncumulative method for creating increments of a variable and then inserting the probability into an adjacent column. As this whole noncumulative business of using the NORMDIST is a bit confusing, when you use the NORMDIST function it is a good idea to put all of the incremental probabilities in a table and then sum the probabilities to make sure they add up to 1.0.

A second function that is useful when working through mechanical issues associated with stochastic modeling is a function in which you input a probability and you then reverse the process to find the number in the normal distribution associated with this probability. Using the previous example, suppose you would like to find the percent change that has a 99 percent probability, meaning that there is a 99 percent chance that the actual value will be below the computed value (on a cumulative basis). This is the essential concept of value at risk. In the example using a 2 percent mean and 15 percent standard deviation, you can use the inverse of the normal distribution called the NORMINV function to find a particular value. The arguments for the NORMINV function are the probability, the mean, and the standard deviation (without a cumulative or noncumulative switch). To find the percent change for which you can be sure that 99 percent of the time we will be below the number, you would enter NORMINV(99%,2%,15%). The result of this formula is 37 percent. This value can be called the P1 case as there is a 99 percent chance of it being below the number. Using the oil price example from 2007 discussed earlier, if the volatility is 20 percent and we want to be 99 percent sure that the price will be below a computed value, we would find that the implied percent change in price is 47 percent. This implies a 2007 year-end price of $79.19 per barrel and means that if the price was $54 at the beginning of the year, you could be 99 percent sure that the price would be below $79.19 at the end of the year. Recall that the actual price was $96. With a beginning price for the year of $54, a volatility of 20 percent, and an ending price of $96, you can use the NORMDIST function to show that the probability of achieving that value or more is 99.996 percent.

To see how the NORMINV function can be used in financial models, consider the example of wind power where estimates are made for electricity production with a short-term P90 case and a long-term P90 case. These statistics measure the production or the capacity factor at which one can be 90 percent sure that the production will be exceeded. If the P50 case has a 25 percent capacity factor, the P90 case would have a lower value of something like 18 percent. The short-term P90 case includes variation in power that occurs from changes in wind from year to year, whereas the long-term P90 case averages out short-term fluctuations.

The long-term P90 case includes factors such as badly estimating the effects of wind speeds at different heights (wind shear) and the effects of one wind turbine on other turbines (the wake effect). If the wind shear, the wake effect, or a host of other variables are wrong, they will be wrong for the entire life of the project. For the long-term P90 value, there is no cyclical effect of high wind speeds in one year offsetting low wind speeds in another year. As the short-term P90 covers both the cyclical effects of wind speed changes and the estimation problems discussed earlier, there is a bigger dispersion in the short-term measure than the long-term measure. For example, if the P50 case capacity factor is 25 percent, the short-term P90 case may have a lower capacity factor value of 15 percent and the long-term P90 case may have a value of 18 percent.

Using the data for short-term and long-term P90 values, the standard deviation associated with long-term changes and the standard deviation associated with both long-term and short-term changes can be derived using the Goal Seek tool along with the NORMINV function. As the P90 case has a 10 percent change of occurring, the NORMINV formula can be used with a simple Goal Seek function to derive the standard deviation in capacity factor that will result in the P90 value. Once you have the standard deviation, you can convert this to a volatility statistic and apply it in the Monte Carlo analysis discussed in the next three chapters.

Any point on a normal distribution curve can be expressed in terms of the mean and standard deviation. This implies that you can subtract the mean from each value of a distribution and divide the result by the standard deviation to come up with a standard normal value. The standard normal value gives you the number of standard deviations away from the mean for any value of the distribution. In the earlier example where the mean was 2 percent and the standard deviation was 15 percent, the standard normal value of 20 percent is (20% − 2%)/15%, or 1.2. This means that the 20 percent value is 1.2 standard deviations from the mean. The probability of this value can be found with the NORMSDIST function where the S is included for the standard normal distribution. A graph of the standard normal distribution is shown in Figure 19.1 (as usual the graph is created by pressing the F11 key). To make this graph, simply enter in a spreadsheet the standard normal values beginning with −4 and increasing to +4 (the chance of a normal distribution falling outside of four standard deviations is tiny). Once this series of numbers from −4 to +4 is entered in a column, use the NORMSDIST function in the adjacent cell and make the graph.

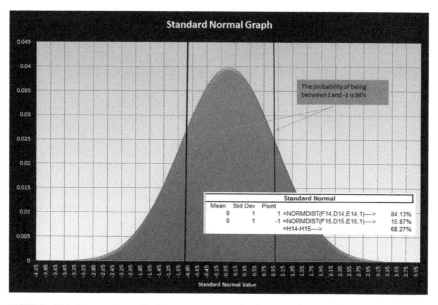

FIGURE 19.1 Illustration of Creating a Standard Normal Distribution Using the NORMDIST or NORMSDIST Function

In addition to the NORMSINV function that accepts the number of standard deviations and produces a probability, a reverse function, the NORMSINV is available. To use this function you enter the probability and the standard normal value or the number of standard deviations away from the mean is generated. The NORMSINV function is convenient to use together with the RAND() function. This is because the RAND() function gives a probability of falling between 0 and 1 and the NORMSINV function can translate the RAND() function into the distance that a random number falls away from the average. Time series equations discussed in Chapter 20 through 22 use this idea: Accept a random number and find how many standard deviations from the mean are produced. If this number of standard deviations from the mean is multiplied by the standard deviation or the volatility, you can find the percentage change in a value associated with a random number.

Taking the Mystery out of Applying Time Series Analysis and Monte Carlo Simulation in Financial Models

S ome who have studied hard in university or who work with stochastic models and computer programs such as At Risk or Crystal Ball may develop a little arrogance about the superiority of stochastic models. For these people, deterministic models are looked down upon as being intellectually inferior. One of the ideas of this and the next couple of chapters is to show how you can make elegant analysis with stochastic models so you don't have to feel inferior. You will be able to present statistics such as probability of loss, earnings at risk, and many pictures of the distribution of financial ratios that would not be possible with deterministic models. But even if graphs are beautiful and the equations are complicated, the attitude that creating a time series equation and running a simulation somehow produce better risk analysis is naive and dangerous. Attempting to remove judgment from predicting how economic variables will move is simply impossible in modeling most businesses. Analysis of underlying economic and business factors that drive key assumptions in a model cannot be avoided.

Before discussing some of the nuances of time series models, a step-by-step example of how you can easily create risk measures with Monte Carlo simulation is presented in this chapter. The idea of this is to remove any anxiety you may have about applying Monte Carlo simulation and time series analysis to financial models. But the fact that the mechanics of applying Monte Carlo simulation are not complicated does not mean that you should go out and add Monte Carlo simulation to all of your financial models. Instead, the mechanics of Monte Carlo simulation are explained so as to ensure that you

are not intimidated by the stochastic modeling process. It is also presented to
warn of the dangers that can occur from simplistically applying statistical
concepts to risk analysis.

The step-by-step discussion that follows shows how you can integrate
seemingly sophisticated risk statistics into financial models. The analysis
involves computing the probability of earning returns that are more than
the risk-free rate and the required credit spread (CS) for alternative types of
debt using different volatility parameters and different transaction structures.
The only requirements for making this analysis are an equation that includes
volatility, knowledge of how to construct a time series equation, and a blank
spreadsheet. There are no special add-ins or Visual Basic for Applications
(VBA) programs. The analysis uses a simple investment of 1,000 with operating cash flow of 150 and a 10-year life. Without financing and without
volatility, the modified internal rate if return (MIRR) is 5.57 percent assuming
a risk-free reinvestment rate of 3 percent. This return is shown in the line titled
"Project MIRR" of Figure 20.3 that is illustrated later in the chapter.

To add stochastic risk analysis to the investment, assume that the cash flows
have a volatility of 20 percent. By including only this volatility parameter in the
analysis you can convert the 150 of cash flow into a time series equation. Then,
using Monte Carlo simulation, you can answer questions like what the probability is that the equity internal rate of return (IRR) will be below zero. Figure 20.1

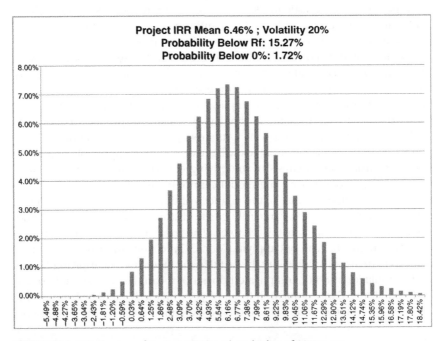

FIGURE 20.1 Distribution of Project MIRR with Volatility of 20 Percent

illustrates the distribution of IRRs that results when the volatility of cash flows is included in the analysis and there is no debt in the financial model. The graph demonstrates that it is possible to earn as much as 18 percent and that the probability of earning a return less than or equal to 0 is 1.7 percent. Without debt, the IRR distribution is not skewed.

To make the example a bit more interesting, the investment of 1,000 is assumed to be financed with 600 of senior debt and 100 of subordinated debt. Also, the volatility is assumed to increase from 20 percent to 30 percent. This financial structure changes the equity IRR but leaves the project IRR at 5.57 percent. Without volatility the base case equity IRR increases to 12.47 percent as shown in Figure 20.3. But this statistic does not tell us about the risk to either lenders or equity investors when debt is included in the financing structure. Through making the Monte Carlo simulation you can see that the probability of realizing a return below 0 increases to 13 percent for equity investors. This is illustrated in Figure 20.2. But there is also a chance of earning as much as 55 percent rather than being limited to 18 percent upside. Further, through adding the Monte Carlo simulation to the financial model, the risk incurred by senior and subordinated debt holders can be measured. The senior debt needs a credit spread of 0.09 percent while the subordinated debt needs a credit spread of 6.21 percent to make the debt have returns that are equivalent with

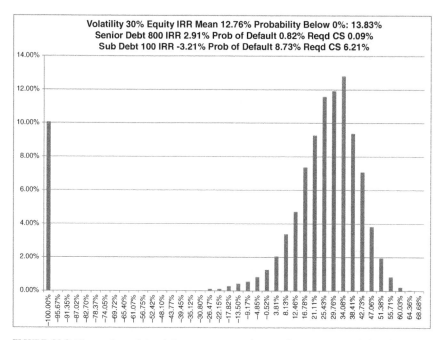

FIGURE 20.2 Illustration of Applying a Monte Carlo Simulation to a Model with Senior and Subordinated Debt

returns on risk-free debt. Figure 20.2 shows that distributions of returns to equity holders with debt financing no longer have a normal distribution even though volatility in the time series equation is assumed to be normally distributed. The large bar on the left of the graph shows the probability that the equity holders will lose their entire investment. Since the equity holders cannot lose more than their investment, the distribution of equity IRR is highly skewed, meaning that there is a limited downside and a wide variation of upside returns.

Results of the analysis change with different volatility parameters. If the volatility of cash flows is 20 percent instead of 30 percent, then the upside and the downside for equity holders decrease. The probability of a return below 0 decreases to about 4.7 percent, but the relative chances of earning a very high return also decrease.

Step-by-Step Procedure to Incorporate a Monte Carlo Simulation into Your Models

The remainder of this chapter describes how to add distribution graphs and analysis of alternative loan structures such as those shown in Figures 20.1 and 20.2 to any financial model. The first step is reformulating a few of the equations of the financial model so as to compute output variables that can be measured with probability distributions. Next, time series equations that contain a volatility parameter are attached to the cash flow. Finally, the possible variability in selected output variables is evaluated through using random number variables combined with a probability distribution and Monte Carlo simulation.

To perform the Monte Carlo analysis, the discussion begins with instructions on how to build a one-column financial model that evaluates IRRs and the defaults on senior and subordinated debt. Next, the theory and mechanics of putting a simple time series equation into the one-column financial model is explained. The final section describes techniques for computing risk statistics through making many different scenarios by drawing random numbers and applying them to the time series equation. The one-column model is created so that Monte Carlo simulation can be illustrated without a macro. After the simulation is established without a macro through copying and pasting the one-column model, the last part of the chapter explains how the simulation can be performed with a short VBA program.

Step 1: Building a Flexible Deterministic Financial Model That Accepts Wide Variation in Cash Flow

The first and perhaps the most difficult step in the exercise of incorporating Monte Carlo analysis in a model is not the time series equation or compiling the simulations. It is instead creating a financial model that computes the default on different types of debt as well as the rate of return earned by equity using a modified IRR calculation. The general method of creating a model to compute defaults using subtotals and the MIN function was described in Chapter 10 in the context of cash flow waterfalls. Here, the waterfall concepts are converted to a one-column model.

The one-column model uses the following five-step process and is illustrated in Figure 20.3:

1. Compute the future value (FV) of cash flows with no financing, showing the year-by-year cash flow in a single column. To do this, make a column for a FV factor with an index calculation using an assumed risk-free rate. The FV factor is a compound index of the risk-free rate beginning with 1.0. The FV of the cash flows can be computed through using the SUMPRODUCT function and multiplying the cash flow by each FV factor. These calculations could be computed using present value rather than FV. The only reason for computing FV is computation of the IRR, discussed next.
2. Compute the FV of the senior debt and the subordinated debt obligations. The FV of debt is the amount of debt issued multiplied by the FV factor for final period.
3. Compute the FV of the operating cash flows accruing to senior and subordinated debt assuming a cash sweep structure is applied. If the value of the future operating cash flows is less than the FV of the senior debt, then there is a default on the senior debt. This means that the value of the senior debt is the minimum of the nominal value of future debt or the FV of the cash flow. The debt default only occurs when the cash flow minus the nominal debt is negative. This means the value to the senior debt can be computed with a MIN function comparing the nominal FV to the FV of the operating cash flow.

FV Realized by Senior Debt = MIN(Nominal FV of Debt, FV of Operating Cash Flow)

4. Compute the value of the cash flow available to subordinated debt. After calculating the FV of senior debt using the MIN function, include a subtotal computing the value of the total cash flow less the value of the senior debt. Then use the MIN function with this subtotal to compute the value available to the subordinated debt as shown below.

Subtotal Value to Subordinated Debt = FV of Operating Cash Flow− Senior Debt Value Realized

Value Realized by Subordinated Debt = MIN(Nominal FV of Subordinated Debt, Subtotal to Subordinated Debt)

5. Determine the cash flow to equity as the FV of operating cash flow with no financing less the FV of senior and subordinated debt. The modified internal rate of return on equity can then be computed as the compound growth rate in equity cash flow. This is the growth implied by the FV of equity cash flow relative to the equity investment. To make this IRR or growth rate calculation, divide the FV by the original equity issued and raise the product to 1.0 divided by the number of years. The only reason for using FV rather than present value in the preceding analysis is so that the IRR can be computed as a growth rate in cash flow. The FV is computed using a predetermined reinvestment of rate, which in this case is the risk-free rate. This means the IRR is the modified IRR rather than the typical IRR computed with the IRR function. In the typical IRR function, the re-investment rate is the same as the IRR itself, which is why the IRR function requires a guess. You could make a user-defined function to replicate computation of the IRR using this approach and iterating around the process with new estimates of the reinvestment rate.

$$\text{FV of Equity} = \text{FV of Operating Cash Flow} - \text{FV of}$$
$$\text{Senior Debt Paid} - \text{FV of Subordinated Debt Paid}$$

$$\text{Equity IRR} = (\text{FV of Equity}/\text{Equity Issued})$$
$$\wedge(1/\text{Years of Analysis}) - 1$$

The IRR is computed in a similar manner for project cash flow, senior debt cash flow, and subordinated debt cash flow.

An example of such a one-column model is shown in Figure 20.3. The project IRR and the equity IRR shown in Figure 20.3 are the 5.57 percent and 12.47 percent numbers referred to earlier. As the reinvestment rate is the risk-free rate, when the IRR is equal to the risk-free rate, no risk premium has been earned. You could make a more elaborate model and display separate rows for interest expense on senior debt and subordinated debt as well as the debt levels and the amount of defaulted debt. The reason for making a one-column model is so that it can be copied across multiple columns creating many different scenarios. This idea of copying the model allows you to make a Monte Carlo simulation without any VBA code.

Step 2: Creating Time Series Equations for Key Assumptions in a Financial Model

To incorporate stochastic analysis in the financial model, the operating cash flow can be modeled as a time series equation that includes random variation.

	A	B	C	D	E	F	G	H	I	J
1		Interest Rate (Rf)	3%							
2		Investment	1,000.00	FV (Zero Coupon)						
3		Senior Debt	600.00	806.35			<---- =$C$3*$D$10			
4		Sub Debt	200.00	268.78			<---- =$D$10*$C$4			
5		Equity	200.00							
6		Operating Cash Flow	150.00							
7		Investment Life	10			=(1+Cost_of_Capital)^(Investment_Life-C10)				
8		Volatility	0%							
9					FV Factor	Cash Flow				
10				0	1.34	-1,000.00				
11				1	1.30	150.00				
12				2	1.27	150.00				
13				3	1.23	150.00				
14				4	1.19	150.00				
15				5	1.16	150.00				
16				6	1.13	150.00				
17				7	1.09	150.00				
18				8	1.06	150.00				
19				9	1.03	150.00				
20				10	1.00	150.00				
21										
22		FV of Operating Cash Flow			1,719.58		<---- =SUMPRODUCT(E11:E20,$D$11:$D$20)			
23		Debt Paid (Zero Coupon)			806.35		<---- =MIN(E22,$D$3)			
24		Value to Sub Debt			913.23		<---- =E22-E23			
25		Sub Debt Paid (Zero Coupon)			268.78		<---- =MIN(E24,$D$4)			
26		Value to Equity			644.45		<---- =E24-E25			
27										
28		Project MIRR			5.57%		<---- =(E22/Investment)^(1/Investment_Life)-1			
29		Senior MIRR			3.00%		<---- =IF($C$3,(E23/$C$3)^(1/Investment_Life)-1)			
30		Sub MIRR			3.00%		<---- =IF($C$4,(E25/$C$4)^(1/Investment_Life)-1)			
31		Equity MIRR			12.41%		<---- =(E26/$C$5)^(1/Investment_Life)-1			

FIGURE 20.3 Illustration of a One-Column Financial Model for Generating Monte Carlo Simulations

The simplest form of a time series equation is driven by only the volatility parameter. When creating random variations, you can assume the cash flow follows a random walk process that is a function of volatility and no other parameters. For a random walk, the variable can move up or down from one period to the next with equal probability. One can think of this process by imagining a drunken man starting to walk along a line. After each step, the man may stumble in one direction or another with equal probability. After he takes the first stumble, the process begins again from the point of the last stumble. From that point, the man can stumble again in each direction with equal probability. The prior stumble has no effect on the direction of subsequent stumbles. Depending on the how many steps the man takes, he may wander in quite large lateral directions from the initial starting point. The range in size of each lateral stumble can be thought of as volatility.

The random walk model could be modeled with the following equation of the current price purely a function of last period's price and random movement, ε:

$$P_t = P_{t-1} + \varepsilon$$

The ε term in this equation is a random term that can move up or down with equal probability. Furthermore, movements of ε in one period are independent of movements in other periods. To make this formula work in a spreadsheet, this ε term can be replaced by the volatility percentage combined with a random number draw:

$$P_t = P_{t-1} + \text{Random Number} \times \text{Volatility Percentage} \times P_{t-1}$$

When applying the equation, the random number should have an expected value of 0, meaning that when a lot of random numbers are drawn, the average of the random numbers should be zero. In the time series equation, the current period price is a function of the prior period price, the random variable, and volatility. Volatility influences the price because it magnifies the effect of the random shock represented by the random number. To see how the equation works say the volatility parameter is 20 percent and the random number happens to be 1.0, then the price would increase by 20 percent above the earlier price. Should the random number be −1, then the price would decrease by 20 percent. If the volatility parameter were 0 in the last part of the equation, there would be no movement in prices no matter what the random number is. If the random number would happen to be 0, then the price would not move no matter what the volatility parameter is.

To implement the preceding time series equation into a financial model assume that the volatility is the standard deviation of the percent change in the cash flow variable. Assume also that the cash flow percentage changes come from a normal distribution. By assuming a normal distribution, the number of possible deviations from 0 should range from a maximum of +4 to a minimum of −4, reflecting the potential number of standard deviations away from the average. If the volatility or the standard deviation is 20 percent, then the most extreme cases are where the price moves by four times the standard deviation of 20 percent (i.e., 80 percent) in a single year.

To create this time series equation with such a normal distribution, the functions RAND() and NORMSINV can be used together. The NORMSINV function accepts a probability number from 0 to 1.0 and produces the standard normal value that is the number discussed previously, which can vary from about −4 to +4. This number represents the possible number of deviations from the mean. Since the RAND() function generates a number between 0 and 1.0 this function can be used to derive a random draw from a normal distribution.

$$\text{Cash Flow}_t = \text{Cash Flow}_{t-1} + \text{Volatility Parameter}$$
$$\times (\text{NORMSINV(RAND())}) \times \text{Cash Flow}_{t-1}$$

If cash flow is derived from a continuous distribution, the equation takes the form:

$$\text{Cash Flow}_t = \text{Cash Flow}_{t-1} \times \text{EXP} - .5 \times \text{Volatility} \wedge 2$$
$$+ \text{Volatility Parameter} \times (\text{NORMSINV(RAND())})$$

When this equation is plugged into your spreadsheet, if the random number is 0.5, then the result of the NORMSINV is 0 and the whole latter term drops out. Only in very extreme probability cases when RAND() is very close to 0 or when RAND() is very close to 1.0 does the NORMSINV produce values anywhere near +4 to −4. Due to the characteristics of a normal distribution discussed in Chapter 19, there is a 68 percent chance that the NORMSINV (RAND()) factor will produce a value between +1 and −1. This means there is a 68 percent chance the next year price will be between 1.0 plus the volatility percentage and 1.0 minus the volatility percentage.

To implement this time series formula in the one-column financial model, simply change the formula in the second year of the model (i.e., the second 150 in the model shown in Figure 20.3). Instead of making the second year cash flow equal to the first cash flow, add a term that allows the cash flow to vary as a function of the random draw. For example, if the first year cash flow is in cell C5, the formula for the next period cash flow in C6 is C5 × (1 + Volatility × NORMSINV(RAND())). Once this formula is entered for the second year cash flow, copy the same formula to all of the remaining rows. This means a new random number will be drawn for each year after the first year. It also implies that the next value is a function of the prior value like the drunken man taking lateral steps.

Step 3: Adding Monte Carlo Analysis without VBA Code

Once a time series equation is defined using the method described in step 2, the financial model can be used to create probability distributions of model outputs through using Monte Carlo simulation. Monte Carlo simulation was supposedly originally used in development of the atomic bomb in the 1940s (although, without computers back then, somebody would have had to spend a lot of time typing random numbers on sheets of paper). The general idea of Monte Carlo simulation is to construct a large number of possible scenarios from using multiple random numbers in the time series model. In the alternative scenarios, the movements in a variable are driven by the volatility parameter that represents the standard deviation of percent changes in the variable.

Using the time series equation in the one-column financial model, the Monte Carlo simulation can be created by copying the same one column over and over again thereby creating many different scenarios with different random numbers. In Excel 2007 and later versions, there are more than 16,000 columns that can be used for the multiple simulations. This means that using SHIFT, CNTL, → combined with the CNTL, R technique to copy the model across the columns of the page results in more than 16,000 different scenarios. As each scenario has nine different random numbers, the spreadsheet becomes very slow. The first six cash flow scenarios from this copying process with the 30 percent volatility scenario are shown in Figure 20.4. Note how some scenarios result in a cash flow near 0 whereas others result in very high cash flows. In general, the variance in prices for different scenarios increases as time passes, which is expected for a random walk process.

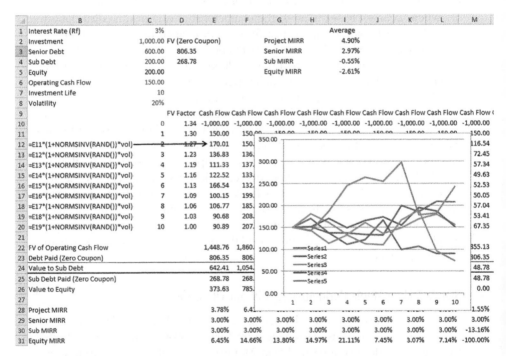

FIGURE 20.4 Paths for Six Scenarios

Step 4: Presenting Results of Simulations in a Frequency Chart

With the results of multiple scenarios created by copying the single-column model over and over again, the IRR and the default statistics can be summarized. Some of the scenarios result in a relatively high IRR and some a low IRR; some result in no default and some result in a large default. With all of the scenarios computed, the average level of default across scenarios can be divided by the level of the debt to compute the required credit spread on senior debt and subordinated debt. Using output variables from the multiple different scenarios, the frequency graphs displayed in Figures 20.1 and 20.2 can be calculated using the FREQUENCY function as follows:

- Compute the maximum and minimum values across all scenarios for the variable that you would like to present in the frequency graph. Alternatively, you can calculate the mean plus and minus 3 or 4 standard deviations. Say you are making a frequency distribution for the IRR. You would first compute the standard deviation across all of the Monte Carlo scenarios made from copying the model across columns with the STDEV function. Then you could multiply the standard deviation value by +4 and −4 and add the product to the average. This process of computing maximum and minimum values is demonstrated in Figure 20.5.
- With the maximum and minimum values established, you can create a data list of bins then that will accumulate the number of scenarios into various increments and list the increments in a row or a column. The formula for the increment is the maximum minus the minimum divided by the number of increments minus 1. You need to enter the number of increments desired. If the minimum from step 1 is −200 and the maximum is 1,000, then you could make increments beginning with −200 and increasing by 50 until 1,000 is reached. This formula that contains 25 bins is also shown in Figure 20.5.

	N	O	P	Q	R
10		Min DSCR	LLCR	PLCR	
11					
12	Average	0.87	1.96	2.73 < ----	=AVERAGE(D:D)
13	Std Dev	0.54	1.09	2.18 < ----	=STDEV(D:D)
14	Count Below 1.0	5,949	1,196	642 < ----	=COUNTIF(D:D,"<1")
15	Total Count	10,000	10,000	10,000 < ----	=COUNT(D:D)
16	Percent Below 1.0	59.49%	11.96%	6.42% < ----	=O14/O15
17					
18					
19	Deviations	3	3	2	
20	Min	-0.74	-1.31	-1.64 < ----	=O12-O13*O19
21	Max	2.49	5.23	7.09 < ----	=O12+O13*O19
22	Range	3.22	6.54	8.73 < ----	=O21-O20
23	Bins	15.00	15.00	15.00	
24	Increment	0.23	0.47	0.62 < ----	=O22/(O23-1)
25					

FIGURE 20.5 Calculating Bins and Increments for Computation of Frequency Distributions

- Select a group of cells across rows in the column next to the increments and enter the FREQUENCY function. This is an array function, which first accepts the entire range of values from the simulation and then accepts the bins you created in the last step. When you are finished entering these arguments into the function, press the SHIFT, CNTL, ENTER sequence as you did for the TRANSPOSE function. The SHIFT, CNTL, ENTER function is used because results of the function go into a range of cells rather than a single cell.
- Once the bins are entered and the numbers from the FREQUENCY function are created, you can use the F11 key to make a graph. You can also compute associated probabilities through dividing the frequency by the sum of all of the observations. If there are no other numbers in the row or the column of the frequency data, you can use the SUM function for the entire row or column as illustrated:

$$\text{Probability} = \text{C10/SUM(C:C)}$$

The process of using the FREQUENCY function to create probability distributions is illustrated in Figure 20.5 and Figure 20.6. Figure 20.5 shows

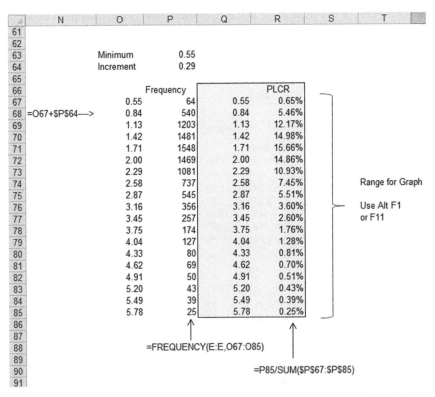

FIGURE 20.6 Computing Frequency Distribution from a Monte Carlo Simulation

how to compute the minimum value and the increment used to establish the 15 bins of the distribution. Figure 20.6 illustrates how to use the FREQUENCY array function to make the graph.

Step 5: Creating Monte Carlo Scenarios with Simple VBA Code

Instead of using the SHIFT, CNTL, → shortcut and copying the model over and over again to added colums, with CNTL, R you can create many different scenarios by writing a little macro that repeats the random draw process and outputs selected variables. Two of the advantages of using such a macro are that (1) you can keep the output from the simulation in a separate sheet and (2) you do not have to make a one-column model so that you can copy it. To create this macro, you can combine the FOR NEXT loop with the CELLS statement in a similar manner as discussed in Chapter 16 in the context of creating a data table with VBA. The FOR NEXT and the CELLS statements are such good friends because the FOR NEXT can loop around rows or columns and the CELLS can read or write to the area covered by the FOR NEXT loop.

The code shown next can perform the Monte Carlo simulation and place outputs in a sheet named output_sheet beginning in column 5 for the first variable to be output. In this program, the number of simulations are entered from the INPUTBOX tool, and two different outputs from the financial model are collected, the Project IRR and the Senior Default. The STATUSBAR command in the FOR NEXT loop allows you to see which iteration number is being computed at the bottom of the spreadsheet. It should be reset to FALSE after the loop. The CELLS statements allow you to put results of the multiple random draws in a separate sheet.

```
num_of_simulations = INPUTBOX(" Enter Number of Simulations")
FOR Row = 10 to num_of_simulations
    Sheets("output_sheet").CELLS(Row, 5) = Range("Project_IRR")
    Sheets("output_sheet").CELLS(Row, 6) = Range("Senior_default")
    Further rows for recording other variables . . .
Application.StatusBar = " Iteration Number " & Row
NEXT Row
Application.StatusBar = FALSE
```

Constructing Probability Distributions with Trends, Mean Reversion, Price Boundaries, and Correlations among Variables

This chapter turns to more complex aspects of time series models that include parameters for time trends, mean reversion, lower and upper boundaries, jump processes, and correlations. The time series equation introduced in Chapter 20 that only has a volatility parameter would not generally be appropriate for use in financial models. That equation assumed a normal distribution of random numbers, no mean reversion, no upper or lower price boundaries, and no interdependence between different variables. Actual time series equations for financial models should be more complex because representation of real variables generally include added parameters (trends, boundaries, jumps, and so forth), because of transformation to logarithms, and because the random draws may be filtered through a probability distribution other than the normal distribution. A more representative time series equation (without jumps, price boundaries, or correlations, and not in logs) could be written as:

$$\text{Price}_t = \text{Price}_{t-1} \times \text{Trend Factor} + (\text{Average Price Adjusted for Trend} - \text{Price}_{t-1})$$
$$\times \text{Mean Reversion Factor} + \text{Volatility Parameter} \times \text{Inverse Normal}$$
$$\text{Distribution (Random Draw)} \times \text{Price}_{t-1} + \text{Adjustment for Correlation}$$

While this equation is more complex than the basic equation that only had volatility, no matter how the time series equation is specified and no matter what probability distribution is used, the process always boils down to the idea of drawing a random number, adjusting it for volatility, and making the next period price a function of the prior period price. For purposes of the discussion in this chapter, parameters such as volatility, mean reversion factors, correlations, and other factors are assumed to be given in advance. The important question of how to find these parameters is discussed in Chapter 22.

Figure 21.1 shows the summary page of a project finance model with Monte Carlo simulation added for two different variables. When you press the F9 button in this model, a new scenario is computed from new random variables. The new scenario results in different cash flow and credit statistics such as the debt service coverage ratio (DSCR), loan life coverage ratio (LLCR), and project life coverage ratio (PLCR). Instead of pressing the F9 button for one scenario, you can run thousands of simulations and compute distributions for any of the output variables. The remainder of this chapter explains how you can add this sort of process with more complex time series equations to any of your models.

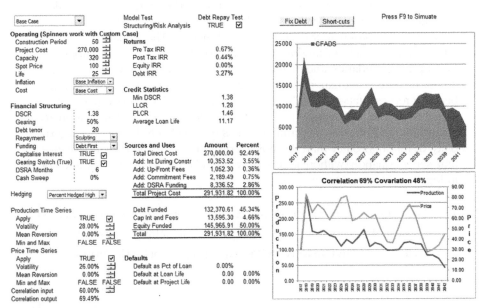

FIGURE 21.1 Illustration of Summary Page from a Project Finance Model with Time Series Equations Included

Starting Point for Developing Time Series Equations—Brownian Motion and Normal Distributions

The most common set of time series models applied to financial instruments such as stocks, options, and other derivatives are random walk models built on the assumptions that rates of change follow a normal distribution and that changes in price are independent of past prices. In the Black-Scholes option pricing model, for example, an underlying assumption is that prices follow a normal distribution and historical price changes have nothing to do with prospective price changes. A fundamental mathematical property of these models is that prices are nonstationary, meaning that they have no memory and they can wander all about without coming back to some average level.

Efficient markets theory in finance is consistent with the notion that stock prices follow a random walk process where price changes should be independent from earlier price changes. The general idea is that any change in stock prices arises from new information—the change from new information does not have a memory of earlier information that has already been incorporated into the price. If new information is normally distributed and if prior information has already been included in prices of a security, the price process follows a random walk process where past prices—P_{t-2}, P_{t-3}, and so forth—have no forecasting value. If past prices are irrelevant, then there is no mean reversion in prices; prices are only correlated with other prices that also have random walks; and, in terms of the rate of return, there is no upper or lower boundary. While this theory may or may not apply to stock prices, it clearly does not apply to many variables that are entered into financial models and that drive risk assessment. In the case of electricity prices, a change of one direction in the price of electricity often means that subsequent prices will at some point in the future change in the opposite direction. Here, past electricity prices are clearly very relevant in predicting future price changes, implying that electricity prices do not follow a random walk.

The equation used to represent time series distributions for financial securities is similar to the equation used in Chapter 20 where random draws are extracted from a normal distribution. However, an assumption is made that the rate of change in prices follows a continual change process rather than changes happening in discrete increments at the end of a period. With continual growth, the price in the next period is not defined as this period's price multiplied by 1.0 plus the volatility as in the previous equation, but rather this period's price change is the exponent of volatility, as shown:

Discrete: $P_t = P_{t-1} \times (1 + P_{t-1} \times \text{Volatility Percent} \times \text{Standard Normal Draw})$

Continuous: $P_t = P_{t-1} \times (\text{EXP}(-\text{Volatility Percent} \wedge 2 \times .5$
$\times \text{Standard Normal Draw}))$

Use of the continuous distribution prevents the possibility of a negative price (the EXP function cannot result in a negative value even when the volatility is negative) and involves mathematical equations that are a bit more complicated. If the time increments are continuous rather than discrete, the random walk becomes Brownian motion. In Brownian motion the ϵ term is a draw from a normal distribution with a variance that increases on a linear basis over time. If the variance is expressed on an annual basis, the variance for two years is twice the variance for one year. If the standard deviation or volatility is used rather than the variance, the increase for two years is multiplied by the square root of 2.

Figure 21.2 illustrates how you can add volatility into your model using the idea that the standard deviation should be adjusted by the square root of the time period in a year. The top part of Figure 21.2 demonstrates how to convert annual volatility into periodic volatility when your model is not an annual model. The lower part of Figure 21.2 demonstrates equations for applying the volatility, random variable, and normal distribution into your model. The base value before the time series is shown followed by the volatility and the random factor. Then the adjusted parameter is shown along with switch variables that allow you to turn the random process on and off.

AEC	D	E	F	G	H	BH	BI	BJ	BK	BL
1 Start Date						01-sept-17	01-oct-17	01-nov-17	01-déc-17	01-janv-18
2 End Date						30-sept-17	31-oct-17	30-nov-17	31-déc-17	31-janv-18
3 Year		Model Test	Model OK			2017	2017	2017	2017	2018
4 *Timing Analysis and Project Phases*										
7 Operations Switch						300 TRUE	TRUE	TRUE	TRUE	TRUE
8 Debt Repayment Switch						240 TRUE	TRUE	TRUE	TRUE	TRUE
52										
53 *Volatility Parameters*										
63 Production Volatility										
64 Apply Volatility		TRUE	☑							
65 Annual		28.00%								
66 Periodic		8.08%								
67										
68 Minimum		FALSE								
69 Maximum		FALSE								
70 Mean Reversion		0.00%								
71 Correlation		60.00%	⊟							
146 **Operating Analysis**										
147										
148 *Revenues*										
149 Production without Volatility	Capacity	320.00		=$F$149*BH7---->		320.00	320.00	320.00	320.00	320.00
150 Periodic Volatility	Volatility	8.08%		=$F$150*BH7---->		8.08%	8.08%	8.08%	8.08%	8.08%
151 Random Factor	Apply	TRUE		=NORMSINV(RAND())*BH150*$F$151-		-0.49%	-1.54%	-2.29%	-5.20%	0.18%
152										
153		Mean Rev		=IF(BH10,BH149,BG154+BG154*BH151+(BH149-BG154)*$E$154)*BH7						
154 Production Before Min/Max	0.00%	Min	Max	➘		320.00	315.07	307.87	291.85	292.38
155 Production with Min/Max		FALSE	FALSE	=MAX($F$155,MIN(BH154,$G$155))---		320.00	315.07	307.87	291.85	292.38
156										
157 Real Price without Volatility	Price	100		=$F$157*BH7---->		100.00	100.00	100.00	100.00	100.00
158 Periodic Volatility	Volatility	7.51%		=$F$158*BH7---->		7.51%	7.51%	7.51%	7.51%	7.51%
159 Random Factor	Apply	TRUE		=NORMSINV(RAND())*BH158*$F$159-		6.65%	1.82%	8.32%	0.32%	-5.07%
160 Adjusted Random Factor	Correlation	60.00%		➙		5.03%	0.54%	5.28%	-2.87%	-3.95%
161				=BH151*$F$160+BH159*(1-$F$160*2)^0.5						
162 Real Price before Min/Max	Man Rev	0.00%		➙		100.00	100.54	105.85	102.81	98.75
163				=IF(BH10,BH157,BG162+BG162*BH160+$F$162*(BH157-BG162))						

FIGURE 21.2 Illustration of Applying Volatility in a Financial Model

Testing the Assumption That Input Variables Are Normally Distributed

One of the fundamental assumptions in a model with Brownian motion is the underlying assumption of a normal distribution and independence of price changes between periods. If you want to test whether rates of change in a variable have followed a normal distribution in the past, you can use the NORMDIST function that is explained in Chapter 20. In order to compare the historical distribution of a variable to a normal distribution, you can use the following process:

Step 1	Compute historical percent changes in the time series from period to period and then calculate the mean and the standard deviation of those percent changes. Establishing the mean and the standard deviation is almost always the starting point for analysis of a normal distribution.
Step 2	Create a list of bins to use for a frequency distribution that are listed on a column starting with a low number and gradually increasing. You can begin with something like the mean minus the standard deviation times 4, which would be a very extreme low value for the normal distribution. Then you can enter the number of increments that you would like to present on your graph, perhaps something like 20. The increment for the graph and the counter for the bins would then be the standard deviation multiplied by 8 and divided by 20. You could start with the minimum definition and increase the counter by the increment.
Step 3	Count the number of observations that fit into the various bins by using the FREQUENCY function. To use the FREQUENCY function, highlight the area next to the bins, type = FREQUENCY and press the SHIFT, CNTL, ENTER series of keys. Then you can compute the probability associated with each number in the bin through dividing the frequency calculation by the total number of observations. This column of data is the actual distribution.
Step 4	Establish the probability distribution that would exist if it came from a normal distribution. The probability can be derived by using the NORMDIST function. You can compute this with the mean and standard deviation that you have already established. In making the calculation you should use the switch for a noncumulative distribution as the last argument. To make a normal distribution from the mean and standard deviation of the time series on a noncumulative basis, you need to multiply the result of the NORMDIST function by an increment as explained in Chapter 20. For this analysis, the

increment is the same as the increment used to compute the bins in step 2.

Step 5   Use the F11 key to make a graph. Shade the frequency distribution column together with the distribution that would exist from the standard deviation and the mean using the normal distribution.

Figure 21.3 demonstrates how you can compute the range for the bins and the increments for distributions with different characteristics. The column on the left is the data that is used to make the graphs and can be taken from alternative data series. It uses a similar approach to the selection of a scenario, where a code number is entered; a drop-down box is created from using the code number as a CELL LINK, and the INDEX function is used to select from the various options.

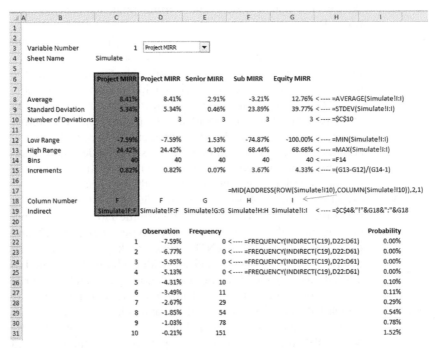

FIGURE 21.3 Setting Up Bins and Increments for Evaluating Normal Distributions with the FREQUENCY and the NORMDIST Functions

Once you work through the process for creating bins and increments a few times, it will go quickly and you can test all kinds of different time series for normality. Say you want to test whether the distribution of wind over a year comes from a normal distribution. You would first compute the mean and the standard deviation of wind speeds across many years. Next you can then simulate the series as a normal distribution by using the NORMDIST function. To illustrate how you can test for normality, the results for daily changes in the value of the Standard & Poor's (S&P) 500 index are shown in Figure 21.4, where percent changes are computed from LN(price/prior price). These data can be easily accessed from the Yahoo! Finance website at finance .yahoo.com. You can make a process to automatically read the data from the Internet by finding the URL, then using the F3 function from a browser to copy the data to your spreadsheet and making a macro with the WORKBOOKS.OPEN statement. This process of automatically reading data from the Internet is explained in detail in Chapters 32 and 36. Without making any highly sophisticated econometric analysis, the question of whether stock prices follow a normal distribution can be evaluated. Figure 21.4 illustrates that daily stock price changes have not been normal. The little bar on the right is of particular concern because it demonstrates that extreme downside possibilities are much more than would be predicted from a normal distribution.

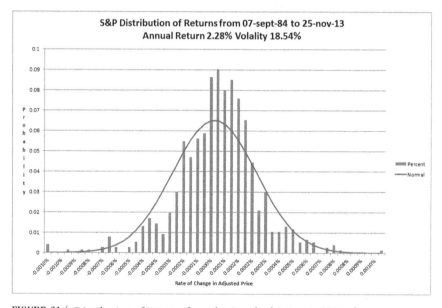

FIGURE 21.4 Distribution of Returns from the Standard & Poor's 500 Index

Given that changes in stock prices do not follow a normal distribution, you could attempt to fit another kind of distribution to the data such as a Weibull distribution. But that also would be difficult and dangerous. The danger comes from the very small chance that the percent change in price has been as much as six times away from the mean. Since 1950, there have been 17 days that percent changes have been in the negative six standard deviations bucket. In a normal distribution, the chance of reaching minus six standard deviations away from the mean is one day in 4.02 million years. This can be computed using the NORMSDIST function, plugging in –6 to find the probability, which yields 9.86588E-10. If this number is multiplied by 10 billion, it implies that 9.8 days out of 10 billion years would be six standard deviations away from the mean. To arrive at the 402 million years, you multiply the probability by 252 trading days per year and then compute 1 divided by the result.

Normality tests can be made for any time series where you can acquire sufficient data. You can go to the World Bank website and pick up data for all sorts of commodity prices and compare the distributions of percent changes to a normal distribution. Then you can make a macro with the WORKBOOKS .OPEN statement to automate the process as described in Chapter 36. Figure 21.5 shows the distribution of the monthly rate of change in real oil prices compared to a normal distribution. As with the S&P 500 stock prices, there are a number of observations that exceed four standard deviations, which would be almost impossible if monthly oil price changes were really normally distributed.

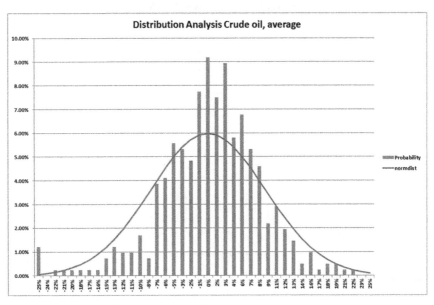

FIGURE 21.5 Distribution of the Monthly Rate of Change in Real Oil Prices Compared to a Normal Distribution

Price Boundaries and Short-Run Marginal Cost

For the time series equation introduced in Chapter 20, the price can suddenly or gradually fall to low levels or reach very high levels. Because of the mathematical formulation of the time series equations, after the price reaches a low level, the volatility is applied to the new low price level and prices tend to remain at low levels. The opposite can occur with high prices, where the volatility parameter is magnified after high prices are reached. This mathematical effect does not necessarily represent how the input variables in your financial models really work. If prices of commodities or other products would really reach the extreme values in actual markets, the prices would prompt responses by consumers or suppliers that would effectively put upper and lower limits on the prices. In the case of low prices, limits occur because producers will cease production when prices fall to short-run marginal cost. In the case of high prices, upper limits come from consumers who reduce demand. If prices fall below short-run marginal costs, companies will eventually choose not to produce. The reduced supply increases price and limits the decline in price to short-run marginal cost. This implies that prices in time series models should have a lower boundary defined by short-run marginal cost. Upper price boundaries can also be appropriate in time series models, because if prices reach high levels, demand may be curtailed by influences such as substitute products.

Boundary conditions can be incorporated into time series models through placing limits on the lower or upper possible prices. The model equations can include a conditional formula using an IF function so that when prices drift above the upper boundary or below the lower boundary the price is set to the boundary level. As with the other components of a time series equation, these boundaries themselves could be stochastic random variables with volatility and mean reversion. Implementing lower and upper boundaries can be accomplished through using a MIN and a MAX function instead of the IF function, as shown in Figure 21.6. The excerpt shown in Figure 21.6 illustrates that the production before applying the MAX and MIN is above the maximum constraint in the two periods. When you want to turn the constraints off, you can enter FALSE as values for the minimum and maximum inputs. If you enter zero, the MIN and MAX combination will not work, because the maximum limit of zero will always be in force.

Adjusted Value =MAX(Min, MIN(Unconstrained Value, Max))

ABC	D	E	F	G	I	BI	BJ	BK	BL
1	Start Date					01-oct-17	01-nov-17	01-déc-17	01-janv-18
2	End Date					31-oct-17	30-nov-17	31-déc-17	31-janv-18
151	**Operating Analysis**								
152									
153	*Revenues*								
154	Production without Volatilty	Capacity	320.00	=Capacity*J7---->		320.00	320.00	320.00	320.00
155	Periodic Volatilty	Volatilty 1	8.08%	=Volatilty_1*J7----		8.08%	8.08%	8.08%	8.08%
156	Random Factor	Apply 1	TRUE			-20.11%	16.88%	-3.08%	-6.15%
157				=NORMSINV(RAND())*BI155*Apply_1					
158		Mean Rev 1	30.00%						
159				=IF(J10,J154,I160+I160*J156+(J154-I160)*Mean_Rev_1)*J7					
160	Production Before Min/Max	Min	Max	---->		255.64	318.11	308.87	293.22
161	Production with Min/Max	250.00	300.00	---->		255.64	300.00	300.00	293.22
162				=MAX(Min,MIN(BI160,Max))					
163	Real Price without Volatility	Price	100	=Price*J7---->		100.00	100.00	100.00	100.00
164	Periodic Volatility	Volatilty 2	7.51%	=Volatilty_2*J7----		7.51%	7.51%	7.51%	7.51%
165	Random Factor	Apply 2	TRUE			-1.04%	-3.34%	8.05%	12.79%
166				=NORMSINV(RAND())*J164*Apply_2					
167									
168	Adjusted Random Factor	Correlation	50.00%	---->		-10.96%	5.55%	5.43%	8.00%
169				=BI156*Correlation+BI165*(1-Correlation^2)^0.5					
170									
171	Real Price before Min/Max	Mean Rev 2	30.00%	---->		89.04	97.27	103.37	110.63
172				=IF(BI10,BI163,BH171+BH171*BI168+Mean_Rev_2*(BI163-BH171))					

FIGURE 21.6 Implementing Lower and Upper Boundaries by Using a MIN Function and a MAX Function

Mean Reversion and Long-Run Equilibrium Analysis

When an economic variable exhibits cyclical behavior or reverts to some kind of average level such as long-run marginal cost, the variable can be modeled as a mean-reverting process rather than as a random walk process. For time series equations with mean reversion, variables still have random shocks driven by volatility, but after a random shock causes the process to move away from mean levels, prices in subsequent periods tend to move back to a defined equilibrium level. The speed at which prices revert to the long-run equilibrium after a random shock can be expressed in terms of an annual percentage. If the long-term equilibrium or average price is 100 and a shock causes prices to move to 150, then a mean reversion parameter of 40 percent would mean that the next year's price tends to move down by $50 \times 40\% = 20$. The equation for a mean-reverting process that includes a mean reversion factor begins with the mean price and subtracts the prior period price. When you enter this kind of formula in a spreadsheet make sure the mean price is always first, ahead of the last period price, as the formula produces crazy results if the mean price and the last period price are reversed:

$$P_t = P_{t-1} + \text{Mean Reversion Factor} \times (P_m - P_{t-1}) + \varepsilon$$

For a time series equation with mean reversion, the mean price term P_m should in theory approximate the long-run cost of production, and the ε term incorporates volatility and draws from a normal distribution, as was the case for random walk processes using the NORMSINV(RAND()) functions. The mean reversion factor in the equation should generally be between 0 and 1.0, although it in theory could be negative. If the mean reversion parameter is 1.0, then the P_{t-1} terms cancel and the equation becomes $P_t = P_m + \varepsilon$. This equation implies that prior period observations have no influence on the forecast and everything starts again from the average in the next period. When the mean reversion parameter is 1.0, there are still movements away from the mean level due to random shocks, but the process starts over at the mean level in the next period. You could think of variations in wind and solar power due to wind speed or solar irradiation as following a process like this. On the other hand if the mean reversion factor is 0, the equation becomes the same as the random walk. In this case, prior period prices have no forecasting value and the process is nonstationary.

It is sometimes helpful to think of the mean reversion factor in terms of how many years it takes for a market to come back to equilibrium after a random shock. For example, if a market has deficient supply resulting in high prices and it takes three years to construct new manufacturing plants, then the annual mean reversion factor should theoretically be around 33 percent. If the prices are expressed in annual terms, 1.0 divided by the mean reversion factor in the equation can be thought of as roughly the number of years it takes for prices to come back to the equilibrium level. With a mean reversion factor of 0.5, it takes two years on average to revert to the mean.

Variables that are modeled as Brownian motion wander around and gradually move farther and farther away from their initial value. While this behavior may be characteristic of some variables such as the percent change in stock prices, many if not most economic variables move in cycles rather than in random walks. In the case of price variables for a financial model, the cyclical movement back to an average value is due to the simple fact that high prices will prompt increased supply, thereby moderating the price increase. Very low prices in contrast will cause new supply to slow down and demand to increase. For electricity prices, where storage is not generally available, the very high level of mean reversion comes from the fact that demand itself is mean reverting due to the weather and due to the steep slope of the supply curve. Most commodity prices, including oil, gas, real estate, iron, copper, coal, and electricity, should eventually move in the direction of their long-run cost of production rather than continually moving up or down without limits.

The Effect of Mean Reversion Parameters on Risk Distributions from a Financial Model

Adding mean reversion factors to a time series equation can have a large effect on the measures of risk as compared to implementing a time series equation without mean reversion. If a modest annual mean reversion parameter of only 10 percent is assumed, which implicitly assumes that it takes 10 years to reach equilibrium through changes in construction of new plant or demand increases, measures of risk can be reduced a lot compared to a situation with no mean reversion. The fact that a small mean reversion parameter has large effects on the credit statistics and the variation in return on equity demonstrates the care that must be taken when trying to apply Monte Carlo simulation to your models. Creating the pretty graphs is not too difficult, but thinking about how variables can move in the future and incorporating factors such as mean reversion and price boundaries into your time series analysis can be very challenging.

Figures 21.7 and 21.8 show results of a project finance analysis without mean reversion and with 10 percent mean reversion. The probability of default is measured by compiling the number of scenarios that result in defaulted debt remaining at the end of the project life. Without mean reversion, the loss

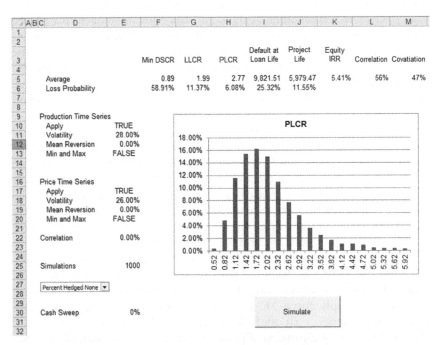

FIGURE 21.7 Illustration of Summary Results of a Project Finance Analysis without Mean Reversion

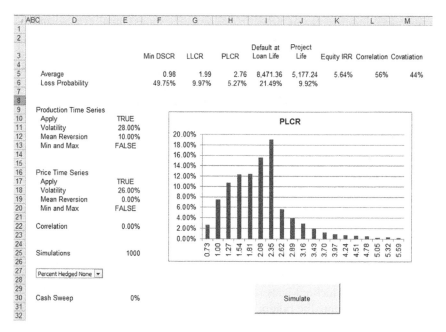

FIGURE 21.8 Illustration of Summary Results of a Project Finance Analysis with 10 Percent Mean Reversion

probability is 11.55 percent. With 10 percent mean reversion, probability of loss falls to 9.92 percent.

The simulation summarized in Figures 21.7 and 21.8 is made by creating the same kind of Visual Basic for Applications (VBA) code discussed at the end of Chapter 20 with a FOR NEXT loop and the CELLS statement. This code can be added to any financial model that includes time series equations with a random variable process. The model can be as large and as complex as you like. It just must have the NORMSINV(RAND()) or a similar process somewhere in the spreadsheet. The simulation is made by pressing the Simulate button shown in the figures and using 1,000 simulations. The excerpts in Figures 21.7 and 21.8 illustrate the manner in which you can summarize results of a simulation and how differences caused by mean reversion affect various outputs of the model.

Modeling Correlations among Variables in Time Series Equations

Up to this point the time series equations have been discussed for one variable without regard to how the movement in that variable is affected by changes in other variables. In most situations, analyzing a time series equation in isolation is inappropriate because key variables are correlated with one another. This means that movement of one variable will affect the way other variables change. In some cases, correlated variables can aggravate the variability in cash flow. When demand falls and overcapacity becomes prevalent, price can also fall dramatically. Prices can quickly move from levels that resulted in profits above the cost of capital all the way down to levels close to short-run marginal cost. This implies that demand and prices in a model may be closely correlated. In other circumstances, the correlation among variables can mitigate risk because, for example, costs may decline at the same time that prices decline. If a time series equation is used in forecasting the price of electricity, changes in the price of natural gas in many markets should move closely together with changes in the price of electricity. This is because of the ability to substitute fuels, because natural gas plants are often marginally running plants that drive the price, and because the price of natural gas influences the type of new plants that are constructed. Because of the movement of natural gas and electricity prices in tandem, the cash flow volatility of gas plants may be less than the cash flow volatility of other technologies.

When simulating the potential distribution of more than one variable, the mechanical process is straightforward if the variables are not correlated with one another. In this case with independent variables, the time series equations for each variable can be modeled as separate equations. As random draws are independent from one another when the RAND() function is applied, the standard normal draws from the NORMSINV(RAND()) are also independent. This means that if you want to create a model with a series of independent variables, the Monte Carlo analyses described earlier can be run separately for each variable. However, if the variables you are simulating are correlated with one another, the single Monte Carlo simulation without accounting for correlation is not correct. Instead, you should model the variables simultaneously using an analytical approach that adjusts time series equations so that the random variation of one variable is dependent on the random variation of another variable.

If you are creating time series equations for variables that are correlated with one another, the correlation coefficient combined with volatility parameters can be used to make a forecast of how variables move in tandem. The procedure for incorporating correlation between variables into a time series model involves changing the way random draws are computed. When constructing a random draw for the second correlated variable, you want it to be, in part, a function of the random draw for the first variable. To make the random draws related, you can use something called Cholesky factors for developing the random draw for the second series. In the case where two variables are correlated with each other and there is no mean reversion or boundaries and the variables come from a normal distribution, the standard normal draw for the correlated second variable is the weighted combination of a new random draw and the random draw for the first variable. The following equations illustrate how Cholesky factors can be applied. In these equations a volatility parameter is multiplied by a factor (z_t) that is driven by a random variable.

$$z_1 = \text{Inverse of Standard Normal}(u_1 \text{ for First Variable}) \text{ or NORMSINV(RAND())}$$

When applying a similar factor to the second correlated variable, the standard normal draw for this variable can be defined as z_2:

$$z_2 = \text{Inverse of Standard Normal}(u_2) \text{ or NORMSINV(RAND())}$$

After the second random draw is made and filtered through the normal distribution, an adjusted random factor is applied to the volatility from the correlation between the variables. The adjusted factor for the second variable is a weighted average of the first two factors according to the following equation:

$$z\,\text{adj}_2 = z_1 \times \text{Correlation}_{1,2} + z_2 \times (1 - \text{Correlation}_{1,2}{}^2)1/2$$

$$z\,\text{adj}_2 = \text{NORMSINV(RAND())} \times \text{Correlation}_{1,2} + \text{NORMSINV(RAND())}$$
$$\times (1 - \text{Correlation}_{1,2}{}^2)1/2$$

The weighting factor for the two different random draws depends on the correlation between the variables. Two extreme cases demonstrate the way correlation is implemented in a financial model using these two equations:

1. If there is no correlation between the two variables, the factor for the second variable should not be influenced by random draws for the first variable. In applying the preceding equation, when the correlation factor is 0, z_1 falls out of the equation for the z_2 adjusted term. The second term of the equation is not affected by the correlation, as 1.0 minus 0 raised to the ½ power is still 1.0. Therefore, with no correlation, the entire weight of the standard normal draw is given to the second random draw as expected; z_2 adjusted $= z_2$.
2. If the variables are perfectly correlated, the entire process should be driven by the random draw for the first variable and there should be no weight given to the second random draw. When the correlation factor is 1.0, the second part of the equation for z_2 adjusted falls out, and z_2 adjusted $= z_1$. This is the expected result because any random shock that affects the first variable should directly affect the second variable.

After entering the equation for the adjusted random factor, the z_2 adjusted variable has characteristics should be present for a standard normal distribution. In particular, it should have a mean of 0 and a standard deviation of 1.0. Figures 21.9 and 21.10 demonstrate how you can verify this using a little VBA code and a simple simulation. The excerpt in Figure 21.9 illustrates that the second variable representing z_2 has a standard deviation of 1.0 and a mean of 0, which is what should happen. The top panel of Figure 21.9 demonstrates how to create the random factors with correlation. Figure 21.10 shows how to write VBA code to make a simulation with correlated variables.

	A	B	C	D	E	F	G	H	I	J	K
1											
2											
3						Simulate			9	10	11
4		Correlation	1						z1	z2	z2 adj
5											
6		z1	0.40201 <---- =NORMSINV(RAND())						-0.2813	-0.4270	-0.9093
7		z2	0.72108 <---- =NORMSINV(RAND())						2.4223	0.5665	0.9634
8									1.3819	0.6509	-0.7592
9		z2 adj	0.40201 <---- =C6*C4+C7*(1-C4^2)^0.5						0.5808	0.8596	0.1652
10									2.9978	0.0735	1.2839
11									2.7040	0.9884	0.3755
12		Average z1	0.0111 <---- =AVERAGE(I6:I1006)						0.1666	0.0581	1.5692
13		Average z2	0.0012 <---- =AVERAGE(J6:J1006)						-1.8907	-1.0673	-0.9786
14		Average z2 Adj	-0.0263 <---- =AVERAGE(K6:K1006)						-0.9300	1.2238	0.6234
15									-0.3534	-0.4501	0.0010
16		Standard Dev z1	0.9954 <---- =STDEV(I6:I1006)						-1.6415	1.1230	-0.3433
17		Standard Dev z2	0.9959 <---- =STDEV(I7:I1007)						1.7555	-0.5835	0.0883
18		Standard Dev z2 Adj	0.9934 <---- =STDEV(I8:I1008)						1.8433	-1.6941	-0.0019
19									-0.0369	-1.3300	-1.4920
20									0.9477	-1.2682	-0.2638
21									-0.7755	0.3005	-0.0901
22									0.3699	-0.1063	1.5357
23									0.9309	-0.7484	2.0005
24									-1.3964	0.1918	-1.1210
25									-2.4227	1.6142	0.3133
26									0.5054	0.2473	-0.4897
27									0.3329	1.4959	-0.6070
28									-0.1905	0.9016	-0.0239
29									2.5892	-0.5345	0.2065

FIGURE 21.9 Results of Monte Carlo Simulation for Correlated Variables

```
Sub simulate ()

For Row = 6 To 1006

    Cells (Row, 9) = Range ("z1_")
    Cells (Row, 10) = Range ("z2_")
    Cells (Row, 11) = Range ("z2_adj")

    Application.StatusBar = " Iteration " & Row - 6

Next Row

End Sub
```

FIGURE 21.10 VBA Code for Creating Monte Carlo Simulation

If three variables are correlated with one another rather than only two, a similar process can be used as in the two-variable case. In this situation the correlation between the third variable and the second can be used in the equation for deriving the adjusted random variable. Further, the equation for the third random draw does not require a memory of the random draw from the first variable even though they are correlated. This is because as the second variable is already affected by the first variable. When the simulation process is finished, the first variable will be correlated with the third variable. Say the price of coal (variable 3) is correlated with the price of natural gas (variable 2), which in turn is correlated with the price of oil (variable 1). If the correlation between the price of gas and the price of coal is defined as $\rho_{2,3}$, the standard normal draw for the third variable, the coal price is:

$$\text{Standard Normal Draw}_3 = \text{Standard Normal Draw}_2 \times \rho_{2,3}$$
$$+ \text{NORSMINV(New Random Draw)} \times (1 - \rho_{2,3}^2)^{1/2}$$

The Difficult Problem of Estimating Volatility, Mean Reversion, Time Trends, Correlations, and Price Boundaries from Historical Data or Market Data

You may have noticed that none of the discussion in Chapters 20 or 21 explained how to compute parameters necessary to run a simulation such as mean reversion, volatility, or any of the other parameters that are input into time series equations. The exercises in Chapter 21 show the importance of volatility, mean reversion, correlation, and other variables in the risk measurement process, but not what those parameters should be. If the construction of time series equations using parameters of volatility, mean reversion, price boundaries, price jumps, and correlations is to be useful in modeling, you must be able to derive the parameters.

This chapter discusses practical and theoretical issues that arise when attempting to use analysis of past data in computing the various parameters required for a time series equation. In discussing how to compute the various parameters, this chapter explains how to test whether the parameters that are input produce consistent and expected output results as well as mechanical computation of statistics from historical data. To illustrate the importance of testing input parameters relative to output results, assume that a volatility of 20 percent is computed from monthly historical data. But also assume that there is a high degree of mean reversion that is modeled as part of the process. Because of the tight mean reversion, the input parameter of 20 percent for volatility computed from historic data will not necessarily be the same as the resulting volatility in simulated cash flows in your financial model when cash flow is computed on an annual basis, which may be much lower than 20 percent. If you compute 20 percent volatility from annual time series data using the standard volatility formula and then put a high mean reversion parameter into your model computed on a monthly basis, the resulting volatility will not correspond to the true underlying volatility. Instead, it will be much lower than 20 percent for long-term periods.

Calculation of Volatility from a Random Walk Process

Volatility is often defined as the standard deviation of annual percent changes in a time series. Since volatility is computed from the percent change rather than from absolute price levels, the unit of measurement for volatility is percentage. Volatility can be 20 percent, but it would not be expressed as $30. Because volatility is stated in terms of an annual percentage rather than a daily or monthly percentage, if the standard deviation is computed from percentage changes in smaller time increments than annual increments, annualization adjustments are required. In the case of Brownian motion, when smaller time periods than annual increments are used in computing volatility, the standard deviation should be multiplied by the square root of the number of time periods in a year. This is because the variance increases directly with time. However, if the time series includes mean reversion or boundaries, this periodic adjustment using the square root of time cannot necessarily be made. This crucial property of price series that do not contain mean reversion can be used to test whether a series has mean reversion or other properties not consistent with Brownian motion.

There are a variety of ways to compute the volatility of a time series that does not have mean reversion, price boundaries, or price jumps. The important thing is that the way you compute volatility must correspond to the time series equation that you input in your model. You could calculate volatility as the standard deviation of historical price changes, you could also measure the standard deviation of historical price divided by the average level, or alternatively you can use regression analysis of the change in price against the prior period price. If traded options exist for the variable in question, you could also compute the volatility parameter that the market believes will occur in the future.

The three-step procedure for calculating volatility of a random walk series without mean reversion using historical data involves first computing the rate of change in prices using the LN function so the changes are assumed to occur on a continual rather than a discrete basis. After deriving continual percent changes, the standard deviation of the series of rates of change is calculated. Finally, an adjustment is made for cases in which the rate of change is calculated for time increments different from the time dimension of measured volatility, which is usually annual. Three formulas corresponding to these three steps show how to compute volatility using both discrete and continual compounding. In the discrete and continual cases, the first step is computing the rate of return over the period for reported prices. In the case of continual compounding, the rate of return is computed using the natural log of the current price divided by the prior period price:

$$\text{Rate of Return}_i = \text{Natural Log}\,(\text{Price}_i/\text{Price}_{i-1})$$

For discrete compounding where the change is assumed to occur at the end of the period, the return is just the growth rate:

$$\text{Rate of Return}_i = (\text{Price}_i/\text{Price}_{i-1}) - 1$$

Once a series of rates of return is established, the standard deviation of the periodic rate of return is measured. If the prices are reported on an annual basis, the standard deviation of annual returns is volatility.

$$\text{Period Volatility} = \text{Standard Deviation}\,(\text{Rate of Return}_i)$$

The third part of the process for computing annual volatility where periodic prices are not measured on an annual basis is converting the periodic volatility into an annual figure. Because of the mathematical properties associated with Brownian motion already discussed, standard deviation of the rate of return increases with longer time periods. Since the variance of Brownian motion increases directly with time, the standard deviation increases with the square root of time. This means the period volatility defined from the standard deviation of the rate of return should be multiplied by the square root of the time increment measured in years (t) to develop the annual volatility. Annual volatility is therefore defined as:

$$\text{Annual Volatility} = \text{Standard Deviation}\,(\text{Rate of Return}_i) \times (t)^{1/2}$$

The three equations can be programmed into a user-defined function that accepts the raw time series data, computes percent changes using the WORK-SHEETFUNCTION.LN statement, and then works through a loop to derive the standard deviation and the adjustment for the number of periods in a year.

Attempting to Measure the Presence of Mean Reversion in Historical Data

The mean reversion parameter that measures how long it takes for a series to come back to average levels is very difficult to extract from historical data. Further, when volatility is computed from historical data using the standard deviation of the rate of change and then applied in a time series equation with mean reversion, the volatility parameter that is input will not necessarily be the same as the resulting volatility of cash flow in your financial model. If the volatility is measured from historic prices that bounce around from 10 to 100 in a short-term period but are measured on a long-term basis, the resulting volatility will be much less than the volatility that should be input on a short-term basis. Unfortunately, methods using simple formulas to derive the volatility and mean reversion from historical data do not work very well.

When making a simple graph of many commodity prices, it is often pretty obvious to see that mean reversion exists. Prices follow cyclical patterns and tend to decline after a large increase. The question is not really whether mean reversion is present, but how to compute the mean reversion parameters. One way that statisticians suggest to test for the presence of, and also to estimate, mean reversion is to make a regression equation of the change in price relative to the last period price. If there is no mean reversion, the coefficient on the change in prices should be close to 0, because the current period change does not depend on historical prices. However, if there is mean reversion, the coefficient should be significantly different from zero since when there is a big change in price in one direction, there should eventually be an opposite change. The suggested regression equation is:

$$\text{Change in Price} = (P_t - P_{t-1}) = \alpha + \beta \times P_{t-1}$$

If the regression equation is estimated using annual data, resulting coefficients can be used to compute both the mean reversion parameter and the volatility parameter. When the data are expressed in monthly, daily, or hourly terms, adjustments must be made to convert the regression estimates to annual parameters. In this regression equation there are some statistical problems with the β parameter, which is biased toward zero. This means that that true mean reversion is difficult to detect and that there may be mean reversion even if the parameter is zero. But if you do use the regression, you can easily compute statistics using the SLOPE, INTERCEPT, and TTEST functions. If the slope is significantly different from 0 as measured by a t-statistic that is above 2.0, the process is clearly mean reverting. When running the regression, there is no need to make fancy adjustments for autocorrelation or other complexities.

Before discussing how to use regression estimates of α, β, and the standard error of the regression to establish the mean reversion and the volatility parameters, expected parameters of the regression equation are described. Consider first the situation where the β coefficient is equal to zero. In this case the change in price has no relationship to the last period price. When the price is very low, changes in price are not more typically positive than negative if the process is mean reverting. For a mean-reverting process, if the price is high, then the change in price would tend to be negative, meaning the slope parameter should be negative. Similarly if the price is low after a decline, some future change in price would tend to be positive. If the change in price is independent of historical prices, the equation meets one of the basic presumptions of Brownian motion process and a random walk. That is, that changes in price are not a function of past prices.

The standard error of the regression is a similar notion to standard deviation. For a regression equation, the standard error is defined as the deviation in the computed predicted relative to actual values. When the β parameter is zero, the standard error of the regression is about the same as the standard deviation of the change in price. With the slope of zero, the prior price changes do not influence the equation and the standard error is the standard deviation of the price change. The standard deviation of the change in price divided by the average price is about the same as the volatility computed from the standard deviation of the price change.

If the β parameter is significantly different from zero, the regression suggests that mean reversion is present in the time series. With mean reversion, the price change depends to a certain extent on the history of prices. Using the regression equation, the mean price is computed as:

$$\text{Mean Price} = -\alpha/\beta$$

The fact that this formula produces the mean price is demonstrated by a little algebra. The formula for the change in price is: $(P_t - P_{t-1}) = \alpha + \beta \times P_{t-1}$. Over the sample period, the expected value of the change in price is zero. Further, the expected value of the last period price—$E(P_{t-1})$—is the average price. Therefore, on an expected value basis, the formula reduces to:

$$0 = \alpha + \beta \times \text{Average Price}$$

This formula can be rearranged to $-\alpha/\beta = \text{Average Price}$. The mean reversion factor can in theory be computed from the β coefficient in the regression equation:

$$\text{Mean Reversion Factor} = -\log(1 + \beta)$$

In this equation if β is 0, the natural log of 1 minus 0 or 1 is also 0, so the mean reversion parameter is 0. If β is -0.63, the mean reversion factor is 1.0. If the β coefficient estimated from the regression equation is -0.395, the mean reversion factor is 0.5, implying that in each period, prices move halfway back to the mean level after a shock.

The third parameter of a time series equation that can be derived from the regression equation is the volatility. Volatility can be defined from the regression equation using the formula:

$$\text{Absolute Volatility} = \text{Standard Error of Regression}$$
$$\times [(\log(1 + \beta)/((1 + \beta)^2 - 1)]^{(1/2)}$$

and

$$\text{Percent Volatility} = \text{Absolute Volatility}/\text{Average Price}$$

The percent volatility is the standard error of the regression divided by the average price, or the standard deviation of the change in price divided by the average price. If β is greater than zero, the term $\log(1 + \beta)$ is less than the term $(1 + \beta)^2$. This means that the greater the β term, the smaller the volatility estimate. Intuitively, this means that if reversion to and back from the mean is causing some of the observed volatility that would exist without mean reversion. This volatility created from mean reversion should be removed from the volatility that occurs exclusive of the mean reversion.

Attempting to Measure the Presence of Mean Reversion by Evaluating Changes in Periodic Volatility

While the use of regression seems like an elegant way to try to find mean reversion, it usually does not work very well. You can test this out by entering a mean reversion parameter and a volatility parameter in a spreadsheet with a time series equation. Then you can run a simulation using the techniques described in Chapter 20 and Chapter 21 to establish a time series of projected values. Finally, you can run a regression on each separate one of the time series equations that comes out of the simulation process and compute the mean reversion as well as the volatility implied from the regression and the formulas discussed in the last section. When you do this, you end up with mean reversion and volatility parameters for all of the time series simulations.

After computing all of the mean reversion parameters from each simulated time series using the SLOPE and INTERCEPT functions, you can compute the average, graph the data and compute other statistics (you have to construct your own function to compute the standard error of the regression in one single cell). If the regression produces similar results in terms of the mean reversion parameters that you input into the time series equation, then the exercise demonstrates that the regression process is valid. If it does not generate mean reversion and volatility parameters that are similar to the numbers that you input, then something is wrong. When performing this exercise, you will find that unless a mean reversion parameter of zero is used, the regression does not work well at all.

Given that the regression does not produce effective estimates of the mean reversion parameter, an alternative way to find the mean reversion parameter is to use the power of your computer and back into the number. This can be done through evaluating how volatility for different time period increments changes in the time series when different mean reversion parameters are used. In the presence of mean reversion, the volatility is not constant when it is measured for different time period increments. If there is mean reversion, the longer the time period increment, the lower the volatility. With a high level of mean reversion, the volatility measured on an annual basis is less than the volatility measured on a monthly basis. However, in the case of a random walk series, the annualized volatility should be about the same when the calculation is made for average values over long time period increments as it is for prices in short periods. You could compute the volatility for daily, average weekly, average monthly, average quarterly, average annual, and five-year average prices. Without mean reversion, the annualized volatility should be similar using all of the time increments. With mean reversion, the volatility gradually declines as the period increment becomes longer.

The alternative method for computing mean reversion is to first compute the volatility for different time periods. You can then input different measures of volatility and mean reversion and run multiple simulations. As explained in Chapter 20 and demonstrated further in Chapter 21, this is not a complicated process and can be accomplished with a few lines of Visual Basic for Applications (VBA) code. Once you have entered the mean reversion and the volatility parameters, you can compare the simulated results with the actual volatility parameters for different time increments to see if you entered a reasonable level of mean reversion and volatility. You would compare the results of the simulations in your model with the changing volatility that is present in the historical data.

To illustrate this alternative process for deriving the mean reversion parameter, assume you have a long historical time series and you compute the average for one-year time increments as well as the moving average for longer periods such as three years or six years. Once these historical calculations have been made, volatility (or the standard deviation of the percent change) in three-year and six-year average prices can be compared to the standard deviation of price changes computed on an annual or monthly basis. Without mean reversion, the standard deviation of percent changes for the longer three-year period should be about six times as great as the monthly standard deviation (the square root of 3×12). If the standard deviation of percent changes for the longer three-year period is smaller than the standard deviation of the monthly percent changes, there is evidence of mean reversion.

Changes in volatility are illustrated in Table 22.1 and Table 22.2 for the cases of natural gas prices and stock prices, respectively. For natural gas prices, the volatility is much higher for shorter periods than for long-term averages. This clearly demonstrates mean reversion in the case of natural gas. For stock prices, changing volatility over different time periods is much less. In the stock price case there is evidence of mean reversion, but the volatility decline using weekly, monthly, annual, or multiannual periods is minor compared to that of natural gas. If you are making a stochastic model with natural gas prices it is far more important to include the mean reversion than in the case of stock prices.

TABLE 22.1 Volatility for Natural Gas Prices for Different Periods

	Monthly	Annual	Three-Year
Standard deviation	14.93%	28.29%	9.25%
Annualized	51.71%	28.29%	5.34%

TABLE 22.2 Volatility for Stock Prices for Different Periods

	Monthly	Annual	Three-Year
Standard deviation	2.08%	12.88%	20.12%
Annualized	15.03%	12.88%	11.62%

To make sure that the results of your model are consistent with historical data, meaning, for example, that you would mimic the natural gas price changes in volatility, you can test different mean reversion factors and run a simulation. If the volatility over long-term periods such as a year relative to a month, or five years relative to one year, is not as much as the change in the historical data, then you can put in a higher mean reversion and a higher volatility and rerun the simulation. This may mean you have to run a lot of simulations with different inputs for mean reversion and volatility, and check whether the output is consistent with the input. It seems painful, but with a little coding you can make it reasonable. You can write some VBA code analogous to the code that replicates the Goal Seek to run multiple batches of the simulations. Each of the simulations would show the historical values for changes in volatility beside the simulated changes in volatility. The following step-by-step process shows how this could be done.

Step 1   Compute the historical volatility using averages for different time period increments in the data. If you have annual data, you can compute volatility for a three-year average and over a one-year period. Alternatively, if you have monthly data, you can compute the volatility on a monthly basis and on an annual basis as shown in Tables 22.1 and 22.2.

Step 2   Create a time series equation and run a simulation with a mean reversion parameter as well as a short-term volatility parameter. If you are making a monthly series, input a monthly volatility parameter and start with zero mean reversion. After running the simulation, compute the volatility for different periods in the simulated data. Then try the process with higher and higher levels of mean reversion and volatility parameters.

Step 3   Inspect the simulated volatility for different time periods in each of the Monte Carlo scenarios. Modify the mean reversion and the short-term volatility parameters until the simulated volatilities resemble the historical volatilities for different time period increments. This can be done by creating a function that changes increments of mean reversion and short-term volatility until resemblance with historical periodic volatility is realized.

Risk Analysis Summary

The risk analysis chapters have walked through a variety of different techniques. The objective in Chapters 13 through 22 is to explain how to use financial models to understand whether accepting a reasonable level of risk is worth the added profit benefits that can be realized from taking the risk. This is the fundamental reason for sensitivity analysis, break-even analysis, scenario analysis, and Monte Carlo simulation. When running simulations to evaluate whether taking a risk and getting paid to take the risk are reasonable, it is the parameters for volatility, mean reversion, correlations, and boundaries that are important. It is hoped that the step-by-step techniques explained in this part of the book will allow you to spend more time on the crucial questions of what range in assumptions or time series parameters you should enter into your financial model.

PART III

Advanced Corporate Modeling: Modeling Terminal Value with Stable Ratios in the Discounted Cash Flow Model, Deriving Implied Multiples, and Computing the Bridge between Equity Value and Enterprise Value

CHAPTER 23

Overview of Issues When Computing Normalized Cash Flow and Terminal Value

W hen thinking about the most important things that affect valuations in corporate analysis, making appropriate assumptions is front and center. As Chapter 1 discusses, classic and recurring valuation problems arise from the following seven causes:

1. Assuming that firms in industries where entry is relatively easy can indefinitely earn a rate of return substantially higher than their cost of capital
2. Ignoring the effects of looming increases in capacity in an industry where planned capacity additions outpace growth in demand
3. Relying on opinions and analysis of big companies, famous consulting firms, well-respected experts, and others who are not putting their own money into the investment
4. Believing in fancy newfangled valuation analysis that supposedly produces value from factors other than earning a return above the cost of capital
5. Trusting optimistic forecasts of companies that are trying to increase or maintain returns in the face of stiff competition and that hide information by using incomprehensible financial jargon
6. Misjudging shifts in cost structures and demand in an oligopolistic industry that can quickly render existing assets obsolete
7. Not appreciating and using historical data when evaluating forecasts

While avoiding these types of pitfalls from making bad assumptions is the central basis for any valuation along with having good business judgment, there are also some mechanical financial modeling issues that can distort measurements of the value of a corporation. These problems are related to calculation of terminal value; use and interpretation of price/earnings (P/E) and enterprise value/earnings before interest, taxes, depreciation, and amortization (EV/EBITDA) multiples; computation of weighted average cost of capital (WACC); and correctly measuring the difference between enterprise value and equity value.

Unlike humans or project financed investments, corporations are assumed to last indefinitely. The indefinite life means that when making a valuation you have two choices. First, you could make a forecast that lasts for centuries. Second, you could stop the forecast at some arbitrary date a few years from now and try to compute the value at that future date. The latter approach of finishing the forecast sometime in the not too distant future means that you have to compute terminal value. Given the indefinite life, calculating terminal value is the only practical way to construct the valuation of a corporation. In virtually any analysis that is derived from an explicit period of earning free cash flow or dividends followed by realizing a lump-sum terminal value, it is the set of explicit or implicit assumptions used to derive the terminal value that usually has the largest influence on value.

Coming up with terminal value in a financial model means that you have to make explicit or implicit assumptions about the three fundamental items that affect the value of just about anything: (1) how the corporation will be able to earn returns in the long run, (2) what will be the risk or cost of capital for the corporation, and (3) how high is the sustainable growth rate that can be realized over an indefinite period in the future. To incorporate these items in the terminal value of a corporate model you need to input the weighted average cost of capital applicable to the terminal cash flow; you must compute the bridge between enterprise value and equity value; you should understand the derivation of P/E and EV/EBITDA multiples; and you need to incorporate stable rates of depreciation, capital expenditures, deferred taxes, and working capital in calculation of normalized cash flow for the terminal period.

Chapters 23 through 36 address terminal value, multiples, and other issues specifically related to corporate valuation. The discussion is not intended to be a typical textbook treatment of discounted cash flow (DCF) analysis that describes how to compute free cash flow, add the terminal value to explicit cash flow, and then discount the cash flow to the present at the WACC. Instead, the focus in this part of the book is on more subtle nuances in the valuation analyses that arise from incorrectly considering stable rates of earnings growth, capital expenditures, deferred taxes, and working capital when evaluating normalized cash flow, earnings multiples, and items that form the bridge between equity value and enterprise value. Further, when evaluating P/E, EV/EBITDA, and market-to-book multiples in a valuation analysis, issues like how to select comparable company samples for applying the P/E and EV/EBITDA ratios are not the primary focus. Instead, financial models discussed in the next chapters are used to demonstrate which factors such as asset life, inflation, growth, risk premium, rate of return, tax policies, and timing factors are the most important drivers of implied multiples. Concepts that establish stable ratios of capital expenditures and deferred taxes also drive the computation of multiples when growth rates, returns, and cost of capital are changing over time.

Many ideas about valuation such as the definitions of the weighted average cost of capital, free cash flow, and net debt are taken for granted by finance professionals, students, and academics without working through the underlying valuation logic. Some calculations commonly applied are too simplistic and others are just plain wrong. For example, a value driver formula that includes returns, growth, and the cost of capital, $(1 - g/\text{ROIC})/(\text{WACC} - g)$, is sometimes used in computing terminal value. But this formula contains a large number of implicit assumptions as well as mechanical errors when it is applied in a model with changing growth rates. Use of this formula results in biased valuations when the typical assumption of a return on invested capital (ROIC) that converges to the cost of capital is assumed. A second example of a commonly applied technique that can be wrong is that when applying the DCF in a model, the terminal value is universally discounted at the same rate as the free cash flow over the explicit period. This assumption is made even though the company is assumed to have stable cash flow after the terminal period and should be less risky because of the less volatile cash flow. A third example of a commonly applied technique is the practice of delevering and then relevering the beta in computing cost of capital. The formula generally used is mathematically incorrect if the cost of debt is different from the risk-free rate. Other examples of practices that are wrong include incorrectly assuming that deferred taxes should be treated like debt, ignoring the value of derivatives on the balance sheet, using inflated country risk premiums taken from the Internet that implicitly assume extremely high probability of expropriation, and making calculations of equity value that subtract the balance sheet value of warranty provisions. The next few chapters explain how you can potentially avoid the many distortions in the terminal value calculations and other aspects of discounted cash flow analysis in your corporate models.

Modeling issues that are addressed in this part of the book relating to terminal value, multiples, and stable ratios include:

- How can you make reasonable explicit or implicit assumptions with respect to the long-term growth, profitability, and risk that are required in terminal value calculations and in the derivation of multiples?
  - For companies that are expected to grow faster than the overall economy over the explicit forecast period and that are earning returns substantially above their cost of capital, one generally should assume that growth and returns stabilize. The problem is that the time frame for

stabilization, the transition speed of the movement to stabilization, and the ultimate level of long-term profitably are virtually impossible to predict. The first step is admitting that this is a fundamental problem with DCF analysis that cannot be resolved by elegant financial theory, fancy financial models, or use of the value driver formula, $(1 - g/\text{ROIC})/(\text{WACC} - g)$.

- How should normalized cash flows in the stable period that is the basis for terminal value be adjusted when alternative assumptions are made for stable growth rates, profitability, and cost of capital over time?
  - All elements of free cash flow in the terminal period including capital expenditures, working capital changes, deferred taxes, and EBITDA should be normalized to be consistent with growth and return assumptions. When EBITDA is assumed to grow at a lower stable level in the future relative to the explicit cash flow forecast period, capital expenditures that support that EBITDA growth should also change and be consistent with the new growth rate. So should working capital investment and deferred taxes. Mechanically, this means the ratio of depreciation to net plant, the ratio of capital expenditures to depreciation, the ratio of deferred taxes to capital expenditures, and the ratio of the movement in working capital to EBITDA can be used to derive stable values when the assumed stable growth rate changes. It is wrong to assume that the terminal growth rate can be applied on a simple basis only to EBITDA in a financial model without also changing a variety of other relationships that drive normalized cash flow.
- How can you compute the ratio of capital expenditure to depreciation for normalized cash flow in a financial model after a change in growth rate, given that it takes at least a full life cycle of a plant before the ratio stabilizes again?
  - If the growth rates in investment changes and capital assets have a life span of more than one year, a new ratio of depreciation to net plant and capital expenditures to depreciation is not achieved immediately. Instead, because future capital investments must replace retiring assets and because depreciation on a new investment continues to affect the net plant balance, the change in these ratios is gradual. The manner in which future capital expenditures are needed to support continuing EBITDA depends on retirements of existing plant that are in turn affected by the historical growth rate of assets. Normalized cash flow in a financial model should account for transition effects that arise over the life cycle of the investment and that depend on historical growth.
- How can you compute implied P/E ratios, EV/EBITDA ratios, and market-to-book ratios so that they are consistent with stable growth rates along with alternative assumptions for the cost of capital and the earned return on invested capital?

- Deriving multiples such as the EV/EBITDA ratio is a reasonable way to avoid many of the errors that regularly occur in computing terminal value. Use of multiples also limits the extreme sensitivity of DCF valuations to variations in the cost of capital. It is possible to develop formulas that derive multiples that account for changes in growth rates, stable ratios of depreciation to capital expenditures, taxes, and other factors. However, the multiples cannot be accurately computed from the value driver formula $TV = NOPLAT \times (1 - g/ROIC)/(WACC - g)$, unless there is no change in the rate of return and/or the growth rate from current levels. Carefully computing implied multiples that do not come from this value driver formula can be used to establish terminal values. These implied multiples need to account for transition periods that work through an entire life cycle of a plant.
- When you make a growth rate assumption, how is valuation affected by the type of growth in EBITDA or capital expenditures that you are implicitly assuming?
  - If the growth rate changes from 15 percent in the explicit period to 3 percent in the terminal period, the decline in growth may be due to: (1) sales declines where the return on invested capital stays constant, (2) declines in the return on investment that cause revenues to fall, or (3) declines in outlays for capital expenditures and working capital investment along with a constant return, which means that the sales decline is not the same as the assumed growth rate decline. More important, you cannot assume that all three occur together or even that two out of the three are present. Depending on which factor drives the growth rate, the terminal value will differ.

CHAPTER 24

Computing the Return on Invested Capital for Historical and Projected Periods in Corporate Models

The value of any investment comes from the ability to earn a return above the cost of capital as well as the growth rate in sales or income applied to the premium return. Given this most basic proposition in finance, the return on investment and the growth rate should be prominently presented and analyzed in a corporate financial model. You could compute hundreds of different ratios from financial statements generated by a model, but the key ratio that ultimately drives the value of a company and also demonstrates the reasonableness of the assumptions you have made in the model is the return on equity and/or the return on invested capital. These rate of return statistics compare to the amount of investment that providers of capital have made in the company to the profit that is generated. The invested capital that is put into a company comes either directly from capital provided or indirectly through shareholders not taking dividends when earnings are created.

To illustrate how returns are important in verifying assumptions, pretend that the return on investment was 10 percent in historical periods, but your forecast assumes the return will increase to 30 percent in the next few years. For the return to increase like this you had better have a very good story using economic fundamentals—competitive position, cost analysis, industry structure, and so forth—and proving that the competitive advantage of the firm will become stronger. You'd better also have a theory about how long the increase can be sustained. You can create a highly sophisticated model with careful development of many detailed assumptions, but if you do not show the return on investment, your model is not really complete, and, worse, it might not make any sense and you don't even realize it.

Working with a Free Cash Flow Perspective, an Equity Cash Flow Perspective, or Both in Computing Financial Ratios

Some people become emotional about whether it is better to focus on the return on equity or the return on invested capital when measuring the performance of a company and whether value should be calculated through discounting equity cash flow at the equity cost of capital or free cash flow at the weighted average cost of capital. The equity versus free cash flow issue comes from a more general debate as to whether it is better to focus on overall assets or on equity investment and return that comes from money taken out of, and put into, the pockets of shareholders. While there is important and subtle reasoning underneath the free cash flow versus equity cash flow argument, when making a financial model it is usually a good idea to include both free cash flow and equity cash flow perspectives as you paint a picture of management performance and value.

Various different measures of profitability, cost of capital, rate of return, value, and other ratios can be computed from either a free cash flow standpoint or an equity cash flow point of view. The ratios computed for the two perspectives are shown in Table 24.1. At this point in the discussion of corporate modeling and valuation no position is taken about which side of the column you should use. Instead, it is more important to keep equity valuation measures consistent with equity returns, equity cash flows, and equity cost of capital, and to do the same for the free cash flow column.

TABLE 24.1 Free Cash Flow versus Equity Cash Flow Perspective in Computing Financial Ratios and Measures of Value

Item	Equity Cash Flow	Free Cash Flow
Cost of capital	Cost of equity (k)	WACC
Value measure	Market capitalization	Enterprise value
Income	Net income	NOPAT [EBIT $\times (1 - t)$]
Profitability	Return on equity	Return on invested capital
Growth	Earnings growth	Asset/EBITDA growth
Earnings valuation	P/E ratio	EV/EBITDA ratio
Market valuation	Market-to-book ratio	EV/invested capital
Rate of return	Equity IRR	Project IRR
Present value	PV of equity cash flow	PV of free cash flow
Value driver formula	$(1 - g/\text{ROE})/(k - g)$	$(1 - g/\text{ROIC})/(\text{WACC} - g)$

If a company does not have associated investments, surplus cash, discontinued operations, unfunded pension liabilities, deferred taxes, provisions for warranties and reclamation cost, fair valuation of derivatives, minority interests, stock options, or other complicated items on its balance sheet, the return on equity can easily be reconciled to the return on invested capital. In this simple case without any complicated balance sheet items, the return on invested capital can be computed in an analogous way to return on equity where debt is included along with equity in the denominator, as illustrated in the following equation. The return on debt to lenders or the all-in cost of debt is the interest expense plus the interest tax shield divided by the net debt. Using a couple of equations, the return on invested capital (ROIC), the return on debt, and the return on equity can be reconciled.

$$\text{EBIT} \times (1 - t) = \text{Net Income} + \text{Net Interest} \times (1 - t)$$

and

$$\text{Return on Equity} = \text{Net Income}/\text{Equity Invested}$$

and

$$\text{Return on Debt} = \text{Net Interest Expense} \times (1 - t)/\text{Net Debt Capital}$$

Combining the two implies

$$\text{Return on Capital (ROIC)} = [\text{Net Income} + \text{Net Interest} \times (1 - t)]/$$
$$(\text{Equity} + \text{Net Debt})$$

This means:

$$\text{ROIC} = \text{EBIT} \times (1 - t)/\text{Capital Invested}$$

Given the frequency of using $\text{EBIT} \times (1 - t)$ in the ROIC formula and in other circumstances, the number is often labeled net operating profit after tax (NOPAT). This means the definition of return on invested capital can be restated as:

$$\text{ROIC} = \text{NOPAT}/\text{Invested Capital}$$

In this formula, invested capital is assumed to be equal to the level of debt plus the level of equity. Because the balance sheet balances, the sum of debt and equity also equals total net assets. Further, as the balance sheet still balances when more complex items are included, the idea that the ROIC can be computed from the asset side or the liability side of a balance sheet remains true. Therefore, the level of invested capital could be replaced by the term net assets that generate EBITDA. The alternative definition of return on invested capital is:

$$\text{ROIC} = \text{NOPAT}/\text{Net Assets That Generate EBITDA}$$

This alternative definition of ROIC using the asset side of the balance sheet can be helpful in corporate models because it can be computed before the financial structure of the model is developed. The calculation requires EBITDA, capital expenditures, working capital, and depreciation to derive NOPAT and net assets. The net assets that generate EBITDA include items such as net working capital and net plant assets, which are part of the free cash flow development of a model that should be developed before the financing section. The notion of computing returns after free cash flow but before financing is similar to computing the project internal rate of return (IRR) for project finance models before working through any of the financing items.

When evaluating your operating assumptions, an argument for focusing on the ROIC rather than the return on equity (ROE) is that the ROE is affected by changes in the capital structure, assumptions with respect to other income, dividend policy, interest rate changes, and other factors not directly related to the fundamental business of the company. Through reviewing the ROIC in a model, you can make sure that your evaluation is not affected by these other items. As explained further in Chapter 25, the more refined definition of invested capital should be carefully defined by evaluating capital that is funding activities that generate EBITDA.

Presenting Return on Invested Capital in Financial Models

A summary page that paints a picture of the key outputs of the model is an essential part of the modeling process (these days people use the term *dashboard*). For a corporate model, the historical and projected ROIC as well as some of key operating assumptions can be presented as part of the summary. In the example shown in Figure 24.1, you can select from a list of different assumptions in the top left-hand side panel, show various financial ratios in the bottom left-hand side panel, and look at the valuations for different scenarios in an area adjacent to the graphs. When creating a page like this that summarizes the model, it is a good practice to allow flexible presentation of a host of different assumptions next to historical levels and observe what happens to the rate of return. By including the drop-down box for scenarios you can review both the returns and the assumptions to see whether various cases are reasonable in light of history.

To create flexible graphs as part of a summary page like that shown in Figure 24.1, the following things can be done:

Step 1   Make a section of the model below your working analysis where you can put all of the assumption titles and their values as well as the financial ratio titles and their values for purposes of making

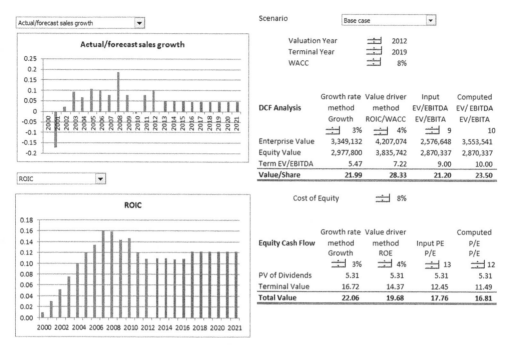

FIGURE 24.1 Illustration of Summary Page for a Corporate Model Displaying Return on Invested Capital, Key Assumptions, and Valuation from Equity and Free Cash Flow Perspective

graphs. To make a combo box that displays outputs or inputs you probably want to exclude blank lines and you want to put some column titles together. You can do this by creating a couple of additional small columns at the left of the sheet. These columns can be grouped and then hidden with SHIFT, ALT, —>. In one of the columns at the left, use the ISBLANK function that evaluates whether a column of the model that is part of the history or projection. If the value of ISBLANK is TRUE, exclude the line from the drop-down box. You can then make a counter variable that increments only when the value of ISBLANK is FALSE. Accumulate a counter variable that is a function of the ISBLANK test in one of the added columns.

Step 2   Insert a drop-down box and use the INDEX function to create a flexible graph. This could be below the assumptions and/or the financial ratios. The code number from the drop-down box will select one of the assumptions and/or one of the financial ratios. The accumulation of assumptions in a section and the addition of a drop-down box are illustrated in Figure 24.2. Chapter 15 includes

Timeline	Base case ▼						
			2000	2001	2004	2013	2014
Historic timeline switch		13	TRUE	TRUE	TRUE	FALSE	FALSE
Assumptions							
Projected Cap Expenditures/Sales			0.00%	4.31%	3.52%	5.00%	5.00%
Actual/forecast sales growth			0.00%	-17.17%	6.77%	5.00%	5.00%
Actual/forecasted COGS margin			57.38%	49.32%	50.24%	53.00%	53.50%
Actual/forecasted SGA			591489	557957	632895	1136746	1186576
A/R to Sales Actual and Projected			7.21%	8.01%	7.59%	8.40%	8.40%
Inventories to Sales Historic and Projected			9.88%	13.89%	4.68%	5.60%	5.60%
A/P to Expenses Actual and Projected			6.76%	7.01%	5.23%	5.60%	5.60%
Other Current Assets			39,332.00	39,006.00	33,916.00	74,733.00	74,733.00
Other Current Liabilities			74,077.00	86,586.00	112,033.00	129,006.00	129,006.00
Actual/Forecasted Deprecation Rate			7.20%	5.81%	6.52%	7.00%	7.00%
Actual/Forecast Income Tax Rate			28.02%	44.53%	38.50%	35.00%	35.00%
Actual/Projected Deferred Tax Change			0.00%	4.88%	-23.10%	5.00%	5.00%
Actual/Projected Interest Income Rate			0.00%	22.26%	12.87%	13.50%	13.50%
Actual/Projected Interest Expense Rate			26.77%	5.97%	3.08%	4.00%	4.00%
Actual/Projected Cash as Percent of Sales			0.75%	0.94%	3.06%	0.80%	0.80%
Actual/Projected Dividend Payout Ratio			0.00%	0.00%	38.27%	70.00%	70.00%
Goodwill and Intangibles			567,449.00	-	58,567.00	269,897.00	269,897.00
Other Assets			143,216.00	147,695.00	34,276.00	432,942.00	432,942.00
Pension Liabilities			22,331.00	25,466.00	22,590.00	159,158.00	159,158.00
Other Liabilities			593,750.00	12,746.00	24,714.00	48,891.00	48,891.00
Other Income	Actual/forecast sales growth ▼		511.00	20,083.00	-	-	-
	2						
			2000	2001	2004	2013	2014
Actual/forecast sales growth			0.0%	-17.2%	6.8%	5.0%	5.0%

		2000	2001	2004	2013	2014
Actual/forecast sales growth	History	0	(0.17)	0.07	FALSE	FALSE
	Projection	FALSE	FALSE	FALSE	0.05	0.05

FIGURE 24.2 Illustration of Creating a List of Assumptions with a Drop-Down Box for Selecting a Particular Assumption

	a detailed step-by-step explanation of making drop-down boxes with the INDEX function.
Step 3	Once you have the selected ratio or assumption from the INDEX function, create two additional rows below the table that split the selected variable between historical and projected levels. Use the HISTORIC period switch to separate the variable into two rows. After the rows are separated as shown at the bottom of Figure 24.2, make a graph using the F11 key. Finally, move the graph of both the assumptions and the financial ratios onto the summary page.
Step 4	Sometimes there is an irritating problem of the minimum y-scale changing or becoming 0 when you change graphs with the drop-down box. To fix this problem you can create a function to round a variable depending on the value of the variable. After making the rounding function, you can compute the minimum value of the row after rounding. Finally, you can create a little macro to adjust the scale on the graph and set the lower scale to the number generated from the minimum function. This macro can be attached to the drop-down box.

The idea behind presenting the return on investment is to allow you to judge whether your assumptions are reasonable. This is analogous to project finance analysis where you can evaluate whether returns are too good to be true by looking at the project IRR. It does not make sense to compute the return on invested capital in project finance, because as a plant depreciates and dividends are paid, the level of invested capital declines, as was demonstrated in Figure 4.8. If the EBITDA is stable or increases over time, the return on investment increases over the life of the project, meaning that assessing the return on invested capital does not tell you much about the investment. This means the project IRR is a good place to stop modeling and take a look at the results in a project finance model rather than the ROIC in a corporate model. If the project IRR is below the interest rate on debt, it is doubtful that the project will proceed. However, if the project IRR is very high, you need to ask why other developers are not racing to create similar projects. If they are coming to the market, you should ask how the IRR can be sustained when supply is increasing. The project IRR therefore provides a sanity check on the model before other complicated details involving debt structuring are programmed. For a corporate model, the analogy is analysis of the return on invested capital, which should also be independent of financing and can be computed before financing elements are added to the model.

If computed correctly, the return on invested capital measures the return on all capital provided from the primary business activities of the company and is not affected by the financing structure. The return on invested capital is not affected by whether a company like Apple has $140 billion of cash on its balance sheet earning about 1 percent or if another company has 90 percent leverage. Financial aspects of a company may change over the forecast horizon, but these financing items do not affect the return on invested capital. This is one of the reasons that the return on invested capital is such a convenient way to check whether you have made reasonable operating assumptions and explain why the value of a company is changing with different operating assumptions. Before proceeding to the next chapter where detailed mechanics of the return on invested capital calculation are discussed, a few of the difficulties with computing the return on invested capital should be noted. If a corporation has had a large impairment of plant, the equity balance and the invested capital balance will suddenly decline, which decreases both equity investment and invested capital. In subsequent years, the return on invested capital will be higher than it would have been if the write-off had not occurred. This is because the denominator of the ratio will be lower in future years. The higher return after the write-off has nothing to do with efficient operations, and the amount of investment made by investors has not gone down. A similar problem occurs after a large impairment to goodwill or a large restructuring charge where the equity is reduced. Over time and adjusted for the time value of money, the low return on investment with the plant write-off is the same as it would have been had no write-off occurred, but return statistics are typically not computed in this manner. Alternatively, after a large acquisition where goodwill and intangible assets increase, the return on invested capital can fall suddenly.

In these situations with write-offs and acquisitions you should be cautious about interpretation of the return on invested capital and potentially make adjustments to the calculation. In particular, when attempting to make comparisons between the return on investment and the cost of capital, the analysis can be distorted if management seems to be efficient simply because returns increase after a large write-off of plant. Sometimes it may be preferable to recompute the invested capital by going back in time and taking away the effect of the write-offs or even attempting to compute the incremental NOPLAT earned from one year to the next divided by the incremental invested capital. Similarly, you could present the ROIC with and without goodwill and intangible assets for purposes of evaluating the fundamental performance of the company. The ROIC without goodwill represents the return on original investment made by investors, while the ROIC with goodwill demonstrates whether a corporate strategy of making acquisitions results in satisfactory returns from the investors who are putting up capital for the acquisitions.

CHAPTER 25

Calculation of Invested Capital

The invested capital calculation used for computing the return on invested capital (ROIC) involves dissecting the balance sheet into different categories. The idea is to identify items that are related to generating earnings before interest, taxes, depreciation, and amortization (EBITDA) such as working capital and net plant and equipment. These items should be distinguished from items that produce income and expenses other than EBITDA such as financial investments in bonds that generate interest income. It may seem mundane and relatively simple to establish asset and liability items that should be included in the invested capital using the guiding principle as to whether the balance sheet items are involved in producing EBITDA. However, when dealing with actual balance sheets, the process can be quite tricky. The next two chapters are devoted to this subject because understanding what assets or liabilities are associated with the operating and EBITDA side of a business rather than the financing part of a company provides the foundation for many valuation and financial modeling subjects. Three specific benefits from carefully segregating the balance sheet include:

1. Once balance sheet items are identified and segregated on the basis of those that lead to the generation of EBITDA for purposes of computing invested capital, the same segregation process can be used to evaluate the difference between equity value and enterprise value. This is an essential step of computing equity value using the discounted cash flow method. While the same segregation is made, in computing the difference between equity value and enterprise value, all of the balance sheet items should be measured at market value rather than book value.
2. In the context of an acquisition, when deriving enterprise value from market capitalization for establishing the transaction EV/EBITDA ratio or for computing the aggregate value, it is also necessary to identify balance sheet categories that bridge the enterprise value with the equity value.

Items that form this bridge (and should be measured at market value) can be identified using the same thought process in segregating the balance sheet and computing invested capital.

3. When computing the weighted average cost of capital (WACC) associated with free cash flow, not only should the weights and percentages used in a table include things like debt and preferred stock, but the capital structure percentages should also in theory be adjusted for items like associated investments, surplus cash and long-term investments, fair value of derivatives, and other items in the bridge between equity value and enterprise value. This means that if you are measuring cost of equity with valuation metrics derived from equity cash flow such as equity beta, more items than just plain debt should be used in deriving the WACC from the equity cost. If equity cost of capital is derived from the market-to-book ratio analysis or from using a growth rate together with the P/E ratio, the same series of adjustments derived from the invested capital analysis should be made in computing WACC.

To illustrate the general process of segregating balance sheet items for purposes of computing invested capital, assume a company has associated investments on the balance sheet and assume that other income from associated investments is not included in EBITDA. Income from associated investments is not included in the numerator of the ROIC calculation because it is not included in EBITDA, EBIT, or net operating profit after tax (NOPAT), which is defined as $EBIT \times (1 - t)$. As income from associated investments is not in the numerator of the calculation, the investment in associated assets should also not be included in the denominator of the ROIC calculation. This means that some of the debt and equity that is tabulated as the invested capital of the company has been implicitly used to finance those investments that do not produce EBITDA. As some of the financing on the balance sheet is attributable to non EBITDA-producing assets, the amount of debt and equity on the balance sheet that can be attributed to financing EBITDA should be reduced. For purposes of invested capital where investments are measured at the historical amount invested, the invested capital should be reduced by the associated investments. If the income from associated investments were included in EBITDA, there would be no adjustment in the invested capital calculation. As the treatment depends on the calculation of EBITDA, this example is presented to demonstrate how generation of EBITDA is the guiding principle in balance sheet segregation.

The example of associated investments can be extended to valuation using the discounted cash flow method. Because free cash flow begins with EBITDA, the present value of free cash flow and therefore also the enterprise value also do not include the income generated from investments in associated companies if income from associated investments is not included in EBITDA.

But income from associated investments does accrue to the equity owners of the company, as these assets have value if they are generating income and they can be sold off. This means that the value of investments in associated companies should be added to the enterprise value. Here, the associated investments are part of the bridge between equity value and enterprise value. The manner in which the associated investments are an adjustment to the invested capital calculation and at the same time an adjustment in the bridge that moves from enterprise value to equity value is the same for many other items on the balance sheet. The general rule is that if an item is removed from invested capital because it is not directly associated with producing EBITDA, this item is probably also a component of the bridge between enterprise value and equity value.

Dissecting the Financial Structure of a Corporation to Understand the Bridge from Enterprise Value to Equity Value

Determining which items should be included and which should not be included in the invested capital calculation can be messy until you strictly follow the principle that items that do not generate ongoing EBITDA should not be included in invested capital. Further, because the level of invested capital comes from items on the balance sheet and because the balance sheet must balance, invested capital can be computed from an indirect financing perspective or a direct EBITDA perspective. The two methods of computing invested capital can be defined as follows:

1. The first perspective is the indirect financing method. This is the method that is most commonly applied in deriving invested capital. The idea is to compute debt and equity capital provided by investors associated with investments that generate EBITDA. When starting from the debt and equity capital perspective, any net asset that provides cash flow that is not part of EBITDA should not be included in invested capital. Similarly, any liability that involves finance costs should be included in invested capital. This perspective is often labeled the financing perspective in the following discussion.

2. The second perspective is directly identifying assets and liabilities that are associated with producing EBITDA. For example, the balance of net plant, the level of accounts receivable (A/R), and the level of accounts payable (A/P) are items that are directly associated with the operations of a company and the EBITDA. This perspective is labeled the net asset–producing EBITDA perspective.

Both the indirect and the direct method should provide the same answer in terms of invested capital, and it is a good idea to make the calculation both ways to be sure you have worked through the entire balance sheet. A method that can be applied is to create a couple of columns next to all of the items on the balance sheet and input a −1,0,1 code number in a column next to each item specifying whether the account is related to EBITDA or to financing. You can then use the SUMPRODUCT with the code number columns and the balance sheet items to aggregate balance sheet items into the invested capital calculation. If the direct method is used, the TRUE or 1 would be placed next to items such as net plant and working capital. For the indirect financing method, you would add another column and add switch inputs next to items such as equity capital and debt capital. After you have computed invested capital using the SUMPRODUCT and the 0/1 inputs and ensured that you end up with the same invested capital number, you have also completed a lot of the process for identifying items that are in the bridge between equity capital and enterprise value. Items other than equity capital that use the financing perspective do not affect enterprise value but are part of the equity value of the company and should be included in the bridge between equity value and enterprise value.

Figure 25.1 illustrates how you can derive invested capital beginning with the liability side of the balance sheet and subtracting net assets that do not produce EBITDA using inputs that are −1, 0, or 1 switches. It also shows how you can use the switch variables to compute the same number starting from the asset side of the balance sheet. The test row below the two calculations shown on Figure 25.1 verifies the equality of both approaches. The inputs −1, 0, or 1 are entered next to each balance sheet item to identify whether it is EBITDA related or financing related. Using this approach, there are two columns, one for the EBITDA-related direct method and one for the financing method. For each balance sheet item that is not a subtotal or a total, you can enter +1 or −1 in one of the two columns. For example, under the financing method, you would enter a +1 for the equity account, as this is added to invested capital, and a −1 for surplus cash. In the EBITDA-related column, you would enter a +1 for plant-related assets and a −1 for accounts payable. Once you have entered the +1 and −1 in columns in this manner, you can use the SUMPRODUCT function to compute the invested capital using both methods for each period of the model, as illustrated in the following formulas:

$$\text{Invested Capital} = \text{SUMPRODUCT (EBITDA} + 1 \text{ or } - 1 \text{ Input,}$$
$$\text{Balance Sheet Item)}$$

$$\text{Invested Capital} = \text{SUMPRODUCT (Financing} + 1 \text{ or } - 1 \text{ Input,}$$
$$\text{Balance Sheet Item)}$$

Timing								
Year	Base case		▼		2007	2012	2013	2014
Historic switch		2012			TRUE	TRUE	FALSE	FALSE
Explicit period		2017			FALSE	FALSE	TRUE	TRUE
Terminal value switch					FALSE	FALSE	FALSE	FALSE
				EBITDA Financing				
Assets	Debt	Net debt	Bridge	Invested capital				
Cash, Loans and Depoists		-1	1	-1	48,608	98,416	58,613	60,371
Accounts Receivable		1		0	253,550	239,998	293,065	301,857
Inventories		1		0	246,783	267,711	321,785	326,005
Other Current Assets		1		0	7,948	0	0	0
Gross PPE		0		0	0	2,985,326	3,041,441	3,098,917
Accumulated Depreciation		0		0	0	1,110,591	1,153,106	1,196,372
Net Plant		1		0	1,402,398	1,874,735	1,888,335	1,902,545
Intangible Assets		1		0	16,476	3,194	1,882	1,109
Investment Property			1	-1	80,253	18,387	18,387	18,387
Deferred Tax Assets		1		0	8,686	20,378	20,378	20,378
Derivative assets			1	-1	5,771	1	1	1
Total assets					2,070,473	2,522,820	2,602,447	2,630,654
TRUE					0	0	2,602,447	2,630,654
Liabilities								
Accounts Payable			-1	0	486,286	672,858	643,571	652,011
Other Current Liabilities			-1	0	5,637	2,462	2,462	2,462
Total debt	TRUE	1	-1	1	836,576	1,094,720	1,186,387	1,175,807
Derivative Liabilities			-1	1	18,550	58,072	58,072	58,072
Unfunded pensions	TRUE	1	-1	1	0	0	0	0
Provisions			-1		35,228	31,459	35,168	36,223
Equity				1	688,196	663,249	676,787	706,079
Total liabilities and equity					2,070,473	2,522,820	2,602,447	2,630,654
					0	0	0	0
Balance Sheet Test				TRUE	TRUE	TRUE	TRUE	TRUE
Invested Capital - Financing					1,408,690	1,699,237	1,844,245	1,861,199
Invested Capital - EBITDA					1,408,690	1,699,237	1,844,245	1,861,199

FIGURE 25.1 Reconciliation of Investment Calculation Using the Direct EBITDA Approach and the Indirect Financing Approach

You can use similar approaches with +1 or −1 in a column to the left of the balance sheet to compute total debt, net debt, total capital, and the book value of items that form the bridge between equity value and enterprise value.

Figure 25.1 is consistent with adjustments that are made in moving between the enterprise value and the equity value when computing the equity value in a discounted cash flow analysis. The exercise of computing invested capital in this manner ensures that you have not left anything out and that you have considered which side of the ledger every item should be on as a function of whether it generates EBITDA. The next paragraphs of this chapter discuss how to classify various items that may appear on the balance sheet of a company.

A similar process to reconciling invested capital can be developed for determining the aggregate enterprise value of a transaction in the context of an acquisition. Once the aggregate value is computed, you can determine the overall project IRR on the transaction before taxes as well as the project IRR after taxes in a similar way to how these statistics are computed in a project finance analysis. In an acquisition analysis, the aggregate value of the transaction should stay the same no matter how the acquisition is financed. As with the case for reconciling the balance sheet, the acquisition can be presented using two different approaches, both of which result in enterprise value. One way to compute the enterprise value is to start with the equity amount paid in the sources and uses of funds and then add debt financing and other items that are assumed in the transaction. Another way to compute aggregate value is to begin with equity consideration and adjust for existing balance sheet items like debt, pensions, and associated investments as shown in Figure 25.2.

Sources and uses of funds	01-oct-15	Entreprise Value Reconciliation	
Uses of funds		**Equity Paid**	
Consideration	473.00	Total Equity Paid	227.38
Debt fees	4.65	Total Debt Retained	330.00
Advisory fees	4.73	Add: Pensions	60.00
Existing debt paydown	100.00	Less: Notes Receivable	-130.00
Dividend payment	40.00	Total	487.38
Interest rate swaps	30.00	**Consideration**	
Total uses of funds	652.38	Consideration	473.00
		Fees	9.38
Sources of funds		Dividends Paid	40.00
Senior amortising debt	140.00	Debt	120.00
Senior bullet debt	130.00	Add: derivative liabilities	30.00
Capitalising dent	40.00	Add: Pensions	60.00
Cash	40.00	Less: Surplus Cash	-40.00
Sale of assets	75.00	Less: associated investments	-75.00
Equity	227.38	Less: notes receivable	-130.00
Total uses of funds	652.38	Total	487.38

FIGURE 25.2 Reconciliation of Enterprise Value in Corporate Acquisition Beginning with Equity Paid and Equity Consideration

Drawing an Imaginary Line underneath EBIT to Understand the Financial Structure of a Corporation

The important and tricky part of computing invested capital is determining whether a balance sheet item is associated with generating ongoing EBITDA. Using EBITDA to guide on which side of the invested capital ledger to place an item is not always clear from the title of an item on the balance sheet or even from a theoretical perspective. Further, it is difficult to come up with a simple checklist that can be used in every case to split up the balance sheet for purposes of computing invested capital or for establishing the bridge between enterprise value and equity value. In deriving invested capital from the perspective of funding, you can begin with equity capital, including minority interest. All of the short-term debt, long-term debt capital leases, and other items that carry an interest charge should be included in the invested capital using the indirect financing perspective as long as the interest expense is not included in EBITDA. Somewhat more complex items involve pension liabilities, long-term notes and accounts receivable, vendor financing, derivatives, stock options, decommissioning provisions, warranty provisions, deferred taxes, and operating cash. If a vendor provides an interest-free loan that at the same time increases operating expenses that are part of EBITDA, then the vendor loan should not be part of invested capital using the indirect financing method. On the other hand, if the vendor loan includes interest and thus does not affect the EBITDA, it should not be included in invested capital.

To illustrate this guiding principle of EBITDA, consider the example of long-term notes receivable and long-term accounts receivable. A company may provide loans to other associated companies or to nonassociated companies that produce some kind of interest income. If the interest income is not included in the EBITDA and free cash flow that establishes enterprise value, then the notes receivable, whether classified as long-term notes or short-term notes, should be part of the bridge between enterprise value and equity value, as they do not generate EBITDA. When the notes are redeemed, cash flow will be realized by investors, and this cash flow from note redemption should not be part of EBITDA or free cash flow. If the notes receivable are made at below-market rates of interest, then the market value of the notes included in the bridge should be lower than the amount that is recorded on the balance sheet because investors will receive as much on the notes as they would on other investments. A long-term account receivable should in theory be similar to a note receivable, and the timing of when the receivable is due is not relevant in the analysis. If the redemption of the account receivable is not already included in free cash flow as an increase from lower working capital, then it should be included in the bridge between equity value and enterprise value. Otherwise redemption of the long-term receivable is included in the free cash flow, and no adjustment to invested capital is necessary.

On the liability side of the balance sheet, the guiding principle of EBITDA is illustrated by the case of unfunded pension obligations that arise when a company does not place sufficient funds in a trust fund to cover liabilities created from its defined benefit plans. These liabilities should be included as comparable to any other kind of debt when segragating the balance sheet. To demonstrate this, consider an example with two companies that have different unfunded pension obligations. The first company has a surplus in its pension trust fund, and the second company has a liability for unfunded pension obligations. For the company with the pension surplus, part of the debt and equity investment in the company made by investors was implicitly used to finance the extra amount in the pension fund over and above defined liabilities. This amount of investment is not needed to fund EBITDA and the amount of cash taken from equity investors will be realized by investors because they have less pension obligations than the trust fund investment. Here, the investment attributed to the surplus pension fund does not generate EBITDA, and it should not be included in the invested capital using the direct method. Where the company has a deficit in the pension plan, the principle is the same. This time not enough debt and equity have been invested to support the EBITDA, meaning that the invested capital must be increased.

Distinguishing between accounts receivable and inventory as well as other related current assets on the one hand and surplus cash on the other hand illustrates a more complex process of segregating balance sheet accounts. If a company stopped operating today, the accounts receivable and inventory would produce cash flow for shareholders just like the surplus cash. However, there are key differences between these current asset items and the surplus cash. First, the implicit finance cost of accounts receivable and inventory is incorporated in EBITDA and enterprise value. If a company demands faster payment to reduce accounts receivable balances, the decrease in these balances will probably force the company to reduce prices or the volumes of sales may be lowered. Alternatively, if a company is more generous with payment terms, revenues and EBITDA should increase. In both of these situations the financing effects of accounts receivable are part of the EBITDA. For the case of inventories, the company may be able to reduce its inventory, but it may have to increase the cost of goods sold expense that reduces EBITDA to offset the inventory reduction, implying that financing effects of the inventories are included in the EBITDA. In contrast to the accounts receivable and inventory items, there should be no relationship between surplus cash and EBITDA, because the income from the surplus cash asset is recorded as interest income. Furthermore, unlike surplus cash, the accounts receivable and inventory items are necessary in order to produce the free cash flow and are therefore incorporated into enterprise value. Third, as long as the firm is in existence and growing, the value of accounts receivable and inventories will never be realized as cash flow to equity investors over and above enterprise value, because previous accounts receivable are replaced with investments in new accounts receivable and old inventories are replaced with new inventories.

Constructing a Long-Term Model to Create Proof of Corporate Finance Concepts

When attempting to segregate various items in determining how a particular item such as deferred reclamation provisions on the liability side of a balance sheet affects value, analysts often make general theoretical arguments that can be disputed by counter opinions. A lot of time is wasted by smart people with quasi-political beliefs about the treatment of items in a valuation analysis. For example, in arguing that accumulated deferred taxes should be included in the calculation of invested capital, an analyst sent an e-mail noting that: "Buffett's Berkshire has over $50b in deferred tax liability, and he brags about it for over 30 years now more as a source of 'asset' financing than a pure liability reality. Hence, I think deferred taxes are a form of financing (and hence included in invested capital)."

Instead of wasting a lot of time going around and around on this type of argument, you can develop a long-term simulation model to prove how the item is treated for purposes of the invested capital calculation. The notion of creating a long-term financial model comes directly from the idea that a corporation is supposed to have an indefinite life. By working through the accounting and the cash flow implications of various issues you can use the long-term analysis to definitively resolve many concerns such as treatment of deferred taxes in enterprise value. The general idea of creating a long-term analysis as described is also applicable to a number of subjects addressed in this part of the book. Later on, questions about whether the value driver formula $(1 - g/\text{ROIC})/(\text{WACC} - g)$ really works and how to compute stable levels of capital expenditures relative to depreciation are addressed using this framework. Developing a long-term analysis to demonstrate the appropriate treatment of an item in valuation can be accomplished using the five steps that follow:

Step 1   Set up assumptions for the long-term analysis, including the growth rate and discount rate. Create rows for cash flow generated to equity holders and model accounting aspects of the issue that establish the balance sheet amount. Use about 300 columns in the spreadsheet, which is enough to represent forever (formulas for net present value [NPV] will not work if you go all the way to the end of a sheet).

Step 2   Input a valuation year after the start of the model so that balance sheet items such as accumulated deferred taxes, accounts payable, and other items are allowed to accumulate in value for a historical period. This also allows the accounting balances to be evaluated for purposes of the simulated valuation.

Step 3   Create a TRUE/FALSE switch beginning in the valuation year (after a few periods that establish balance sheet items) and extending to the end of the model. This represents the posthistorical period for evaluating cash flow in a corporate model. Starting from the valuation year and going all the way to the final year, compute the true value of the cash flows through discounting cash flow over the long-term period.

Step 4   Input an assumed terminal year and create a terminal switch as well as an explicit period switch as you would if you were making any valuation analysis in a corporate model. Use the same growth and cost of capital assumptions to simulate a second discounted cash flow model with a terminal value and a bridge between equity value and enterprise value. This means that you compute the second discounted cash flow to equity using a model with the standard truncated explicit period rather than the indefinite period.

Step 5   Evaluate the difference between the equity value computed in step 2 using the long-term analysis (model 1) and the equity value computed in step 3 (model 2) using the explicit period to verify the valuation treatment of an item in a truncated model.

To illustrate the manner in which such a long-term model can resolve different valuation issues, consider the relatively simple case of accounts payable. One could potentially make the argument that accounts payable are not unlike other debt obligations that come due. If that was the case, accounts payable should be included as part of financing in the indirect method of computing invested capital, just like notes payable and long-term debt. But unlike other forms of debt, the implicit cost of delaying payments from suppliers is part of EBITDA. If a supplier offers very attractive payment terms but at the same time increases the direct cost of supplying materials, this increased cost is included as an operating expense and is implicitly part of EBITDA. The valuation treatment of payables is also affected by the question of whether the level of accounts payable changes over time. In general, the accounts payable are assumed to increase with the growth of the company, implying that the accounts payable provide cash flow and never become a lump-sum liability that must be repaid. If the accounts payable continue to grow and the growth is included in the working capital changes in the free cash flow, then there is no cash flow outflow that must be incurred by equity investors. Instead, they are replaced by new payables, and the implicit financing cost of the new higher level of accounts payable is included in the operating expenses.

The first part of a long-term simulation model demonstrating the appropriate treatment of accounts payable is shown in Figure 25.3. The example assumes a sales growth rate of 5 percent, an operating margin of 30 percent (implying that expenses are 70 percent of sales), a WACC of 10 percent, and an assumption that expenses are paid in 100 days. In modeling the accounts payable, the increase in true cash flow that is paid to suppliers is computed from the cash flow that is avoided in the current period, which is 27.4 percent of the operating expense (100 days/365 days). This true cash flow consists of the revenues less the outflow of cash to suppliers. A portion of the model is illustrated in Figure 25.3 (the actual model extends to year 300).

Assumptions

Sales Growth	5.00%
Operating Margin	30.00%
A/P Days	100
A/P as Percent of Expenses	27.40%
WACC	10.00%
Initial Level of Sales	200.00
Valuation Year	5.00
Explicit Period	4.00
Terminal Period	9.00

True Cash Flow to Equity

Period	Driver	0	1	4	5	6	7	8
Valuation Period		FALSE	FALSE	FALSE	FALSE	TRUE	TRUE	TRUE
Sales	5.00%	200.0	210.0	243.1	255.3	268.0	281.4	295.5
Operating Expenses	70.00%	140.0	147.0	170.2	178.7	187.6	197.0	206.8
Op Exp Paid in current yr	72.60%	101.6	106.7	123.5	129.7	136.2	143.0	150.2
Op Exp Paid from Prior yr	27.40%		38.4	44.4	46.6	49.0	51.4	54.0
Equity Cash Flow			64.9	75.2	78.9	82.9	87.0	91.3
Equity Cash Flow for Valuation			FALSE	FALSE	FALSE	82.85	87.00	91.35
True Value of Company	1,657.07	NPV of Above Line at 10%						

FIGURE 25.3 Excerpt from Theoretical Long-Term Model Demonstrating Value Treatments

To model the value of a corporation assuming that the company is valued in year 5, a number of techniques that were introduced in Part I can be applied as follows:

1. Construct a period counter that extends to 300 years (the entire spreadsheet using 16,000 columns cannot be used with the NPV function and causes the spreadsheet to be slow and large). Use the SHIFT, CNTL, → and SHIFT, ALT, → keys to cut off the sheet after deleting the year number for columns after the year 300.
2. Create a switch variable that is TRUE when the period counter is greater than the valuation year. This is assumed to be year 5 in Figure 25.3.
3. To compute the net present value at year 5 using the NPV function, replace the equity cash flows before the year in question with FALSE using the IF function. If the cash flows before year 5 have a value of zero instead of FALSE, then the present value of the cash flow accrues to the first year in the model instead of the year 5 valuation year. In order to place a FALSE in the cash flow cells rather than a zero for the first five

years, use an IF statement without an argument for the false condition as illustrated:

Cash Flow for Valuation = IF (Valuation Period Switch, Equity Cash Flow)

Value = NPV(Cost of Capital, Cash Flow for Valuation)

4. You can use conditional formatting to make the prevaluation period, the explicit period, and the long-term period different colors. To do this, you can highlight the entire sheet. Then, after selecting conditional formatting, use the option to set the formatting with a formula. Next, find the row with the TRUE/FALSE switches and use the relative reference for the first cell with in the row.

Once the correct value has been established from the long-term model, another model that contains an explicit period and terminal period along with different theories of value using balance sheet items can be developed. In creating this model, you can start with the initial year of the model and see how much the balance sheet item—in this case accounts payable—has built up. Then you can compute the explicit cash flows and the terminal value and simulate the valuation calculation where the accounts payable are treated like debt in the bridge between enterprise value and equity value. To simulate a valuation that begins in year 6 and ends in year 9 you can do the following:

1. Construct switch variables for the valuation year, the explicit period, and the terminal year using the AND function.
2. Compute the accounts payable balance using an opening balance, adding the amounts created from the delaying expenses in the current year, and subtracting amounts paid from liabilities in the prior year as shown in Figure 25.4. You can also compute the EBITDA that is used as the starting point for cash flow (CF) in the DCF model that does not account for the timing of revenues and expenses. This EBITDA represents the entire cash flow if accounts payable are treated as debt rather than a change in working capital. The exercise demonstrates that when you make a proof, you need to work through both the accounting treatment and the true cash flow.
3. Compute the explicit period cash flow using an IF statement as for the long-term model where the explicit cash flow has a value of FALSE in periods before the valuation year and it also has a value of FALSE after the terminal period. By applying the switch, valuation of the explicit cash flow will be as of year 5, and years prior to the valuation year will contain a value of FALSE. After adjusting the explicit cash flow with the switch, compute the value of the explicit period cash flows using the NPV formula.

A B C	D	E	F	G	J	K	L	M	N	O
47 Valuation with Working Capital Treatment			1	2	5	6	7	8	9	10
48 Explicit Period			FALSE	FALSE	FALSE	FALSE	TRUE	TRUE	TRUE	TRUE
49 Terminal Period			FALSE	FALSE	FALSE	FALSE	FALSE	FALSE	FALSE	TRUE
50 Valuation Period			FALSE	FALSE	FALSE	TRUE	FALSE	FALSE	FALSE	FALSE
51										
52 EBITDA			60.00	63.00	72.93	76.58	80.41	84.43	88.65	93.08
53 Working Capital Changes			-38.36	-1.92	-2.22	-2.33	-2.45	-2.57	-2.70	-2.83
54 Free Cash Flow			98.36	64.92	75.15	78.91	82.85	87.00	91.35	95.91
55		NPV								
56 Free Cash Flow in Explicit Period		281.36	FALSE	FALSE	FALSE	FALSE	82.85	87.00	91.35	95.91
57 Terminal Value		1,375.71	FALSE	FALSE	FALSE	FALSE	0.00	0.00	0.00	2,014.18
58 Total Enterpise and Equity Value		1,657.07								
59				=IF(G48,G54)						
60 True Value		1,657.07				=IF(K48,K54*(1+$E$3)/($E$7-$E$3)*K49)				
61										
62 =NPV($E$7,G56:KT56)										
63										

FIGURE 25.4 Illustration of Simulated Valuation Assuming Accounts Payable Are Treated Like Debt

4. Compute the terminal value using the formula $CF \times (1+g)/(WACC - g)$, and multiply the result by the terminal value switch so it is only applied in one year. To ensure that the value will be computed as of the valuation year, also create an IF statement with the explicit year switch. This will insert a zero in the terminal value row for the years after the valuation year and before the terminal period. The formula is demonstrated in the following equation and shown in Figure 25.4. After using the formula to put in FALSE values, compute the present value of the terminal value using the NPV function.

$$\text{Terminal Value} = \text{IF (Explicit Switch, } CF \times (1 + g/(WACC - g)* \text{ Terminal Switch)}$$

5. As accounts payable are assumed to be treated like debt, deduct the balance from the NPV of cash flow. To find the balance of the accounts payable in the valuation year you can use the MATCH and INDEX functions. The MATCH function can be used with the entire row of the period counter to find the column number for the valuation year. Then the INDEX function can be used with the accounts payable balance line as follows:

$$\text{A/P in Valuation Year} = \text{INDEX (A/P Balance Row, MATCH} \text{ (Value Year, Entire Row of Years))}$$

6. Sum the NPV of the explicit cash flows and the NPV of the terminal cash flow to establish the total enterprise value. Then you can subtract the closing balance of the accounts payable to compute the equity value.

Finally, compare this value to the true value of the equity cash flows using the long-term model.

Figure 25.4 demonstrates that if accounts payable were to be treated as debt in the bridge between enterprise value and equity value, the value of the company would be understated relative to the true value. In Figure 25.4, which demonstrates selected columns including the column representing the terminal year, this understatement is 97.90. The understatement comes about because (1) accounts payable are subtracted from the enterprise value even they do not come due, and (2) the EBITDA does not reflect true cash flow in that true cash outflows are reduced because of the continuing delay in payment of bills.

When correcting these two problems and computing the value using the techniques just shown with the explicit period and terminal period cash flow, the value becomes exactly the same as the true long-term amount. This is illustrated in Figure 25.5. In this excerpt, the accounts payable changes are added together with EBITDA to establish free cash flow. Further, the balance of accounts payable is not included in the bridge between equity value and enterprise value.

	A	B	C	D	E	F	G	K	L	M	N	O	P
26	Valuation assuming A/P is Debt					0	1	5	6	7	8	9	10
27		Explicit Period				FALSE	FALSE	FALSE	TRUE	TRUE	TRUE	TRUE	FALSE
28		Terminal Period				FALSE	FALSE	FALSE	FALSE	FALSE	FALSE	TRUE	FALSE
29		Valuation Period				FALSE	FALSE	TRUE	FALSE	FALSE	FALSE	FALSE	FALSE
30													
31		A/P Balance											
32			Opening Balance			0.00	38.36	46.62	48.95	51.40	53.97	56.67	59.50
33			Add: Amounts Generated			38.36	40.27	48.95	51.40	53.97	56.67	59.50	62.48
34			Less: Amounts Re-paid			0.00	38.36	46.62	48.95	51.40	53.97	56.67	59.50
35			Closing Balance			38.36	40.27	48.95	51.40	53.97	56.67	59.50	62.48
36													
37		EBITDA				60.00	63.00	76.58	80.41	84.43	88.65	93.08	97.73
38		EBITDA in Explicit Period		=IF(F27,F37)---->	FALSE	FALSE	FALSE	80.41	84.43	88.65	93.08	FALSE
39		PV of EBITDA		273.05 <---- =NPV(E7,38:38)								
40		Terminal Value				FALSE	FALSE	FALSE	0.00	0.00	0.00	1,954.67	FALSE
41													
42		Enterprise Value		1,608.11 <---- =NPV(E7,40:40)+E39								
43		Less: A/P Classified as Debt		48.95 <---- =SUMIF(29:29,TRUE,35:35)								
44		Net Equity Value		1,559.16								
45													
46		Value Difference		97.90			=IF(N27,N37*(1+$E$3)/($E$7-$E$3)*N28)					

FIGURE 25.5 Valuation Model Where Working Capital Changes Are Added to EBITDA and Accounts Payable Are Not Included in the Bridge between Enterprise Value and Equity Value

This whole process may seem like a lot of work to prove something that you probably already know, but the idea of making the proof is important in many aspects of corporate modeling. It is hoped that the idea of creating a long-term analysis and then establishing balance sheet items from growth rate assumptions can help you resolve the arguments. The same approach can be used to demonstrate that changes in deferred tax related to depreciation should be included in the direct invested capital, that provisions for warranty expense should be treated like accounts payable, and that deferred taxes related to derivative assets should be in the indirect calculation of invested capital, and so forth.

CHAPTER **26**

Complex Items in Balance Sheet Analysis

Deferred Taxes, Operating Cash, and Derivative Assets

Many balance sheet items can be simulated with the type of process described in Chapter 25 used for accounts payable and have an unambiguous classification in terms of invested capital and enterprise value. The answer for other balance sheet items in terms of classification for invested capital analysis in a financial model is sometimes not as clear. Items discussed in this chapter that are more ambiguous than accounts payable for structuring a financial model include accumulated deferred taxes, operating cash, and derivative assets and liabilities. The treatment of these and other items can be resolved only by understanding the accounting as well as ongoing cash flow implications of the items. An issue related to classification of these assets and liabilities discussed in this chapter is how the various classifications affect the weighted average cost of capital (WACC) calculation.

Treatment of Accumulated Deferred Taxes Arising from Depreciation

Accumulated deferred taxes are a common source of error and confusion when segregating balance sheet items between those related to generation of earnings before interest, taxes, depreciation, and amortization (EBITDA) and those related to costs and income that are not part of EBITDA in a corporate model. Accumulated deferred taxes often appear as a liability on the balance sheet representing the accumulated amount of taxes that have not yet been paid relative to the amount of taxes that have been recorded on the profit and loss statement. The accounting notion behind deferred tax is that actual taxes paid to the government have been reduced on a temporary basis and that book taxes should reflect the book income recorded on the income statement. Eventually, the taxes paid will be more than the taxes recorded on the books because the beneficial tax deductions that are temporary in nature will expire. The most typical example is that of book and tax depreciation, where the tax depreciation rate is greater than the book depreciation in the early years of the life of an asset. In computing book income taxes for net operating profit after tax (NOPAT), in calculating book tax on the income statement, and in the calculation of free cash flow, book depreciation and intangible amortization are used rather than tax depreciation. However, actual cash taxes paid by a company determine true cash flow. Value is therefore driven in part by tax depreciation and amortization allowable for tax purposes.

The accounting and cash flow treatment of deferred taxes recognizes that future tax will increase when the accelerated depreciation expense deducted on tax returns becomes less than book depreciation expense. Since these future taxes above recoded taxes will come due, a liability is recorded. The idea of accumulated deferred taxes on the balance sheet reversing is illustrated in Figure 26.1, where an asset has a four-year book life and a two-year tax life. In this example, the accumulated deferred tax liability increases for the first

Assumptions				
Book Life	4			
Tax Life	2			
Tax Rate	40%			
Capital Expenditures	1,000			
Book and Tax Depreciation				
Year	1	2	3	4
Book Depreciation	250	250	250	250
Tax Depreciation	500	500	0	0
Tax - Book Depreciation	250	250	-250	-250
(Tax - Book Depreciation) x Tax Rate	100	100	-100	-100
Accumulated Deferred Taxes				
Opening Balance	0	100	200	100
Add: Deferred Tax Change	100	100	-100	-100
Closing Balance	100	200	100	0

FIGURE 26.1 Simple Example of Deferred Tax from Difference between Book and Tax Life

two years when the tax depreciation expense is greater than book depreciation expense and taxes paid are less than taxes booked. After the tax depreciation expires in the third year, the deferred tax change becomes negative and the accumulated deferred taxes decline. By the end of the life of the asset, the accumulated deferred tax balance falls to zero.

The problem with the simple example shown in Figure 26.1 is that if capital expenditures are continually made, tax depreciation keeps increasing and it remains more than book depreciation on an indefinite basis. Again, the fundamental distinguishing feature of a corporation is that it has an indefinite life and keeps growing. Chapter 31 includes a discussion of how growth affects the amount of deferred taxes on the balance sheet. It is demonstrated in Chapter 31 that after a cycle of plant is complete and retirements of earlier capital expenditures begin, the changes in deferred tax stabilize to a fixed level relative to capital expenditures as long as the growth rate in capital expenditures is constant. As capital expenditures continue to be made for a corporation to support EBITDA growth, the deferred tax liability never comes due and it continues to increase.

If accumulated deferred taxes recorded on the balance sheet cause equity investors to have to incur future cash outflows for tax payments that are not already deducted as part of free cash flow, as in the example shown on Figure 26.1, then the value of the accumulated deferred tax liability should be deducted from enterprise value. This would account for the cash outflows that are not part of EBITDA or the free cash flow calculation. However, when a company is continually making capital expenditures, the negative future cash flows that this liability represents are never incurred. Here, as was the case with accounts payable, a new and larger cash inflow from a new liability continually replaces the earlier liability as the company grows. Further, as is the case with accounts payable, there are no interest expenses below the EBITDA line that are associated with this liability. Thus, when segregating deferred taxes for purposes of computing invested capital and enterprise value, the treatment for deferred taxes associated with capital expenditures such as accelerated depreciation should be treated as a positive part of free cash flow and not included as an obligation of equity holders. Therefore, free cash flow for purposes of defining enterprise value should be computed by adding deferred tax changes using the formula:

$$\text{Free Cash Flow} = \text{EBITDA} - \text{Capital Expenditures} -$$
$$\text{Working Capital Changes} + \text{Deferred Tax Changes}$$

The notion of including deferred tax changes as part of cash flow and not adjusting the bridge between enterprise value and equity value for deferred taxes can be demonstrated using the type of theoretical financial model discussed in Chapter 25 in the context of accounts payable. This idea that deferred taxes are analogous to accounts payable implies that when computing invested capital, accumulated deferred taxes should generally be on the direct EBITDA side of the ledger along with accounts payable, net plant, inventory, and other items that support EBITDA. Accumulated deferred tax should not be on the financing side along with items such debt and surplus cash. Deferred taxes associated with depreciation are a fundamental component of investing in the asset and affect the cash flow arising from the asset. To demonstrate this, assume that two companies are identical in every respect except that one company is able to use accelerated depreciation and the second cannot. The company that can use deferred taxes has a cost advantage vis-à-vis the other company. It should have higher value and a higher return on invested capital (ROIC) by virtue of a lower invested capital balance.

Deferred taxes can arise from many items that are not related to accelerated depreciation. One example is the case of deferred tax assets generated from a tax carryforward where the company's income is negative. This situation is more complex, in part because these deferred taxes do not necessarily arise from EBITDA and free cash flow items. When the carryforward is created in periods of negative income, taxes recorded on the books are negative while the actual taxes paid are zero. In later periods when the income is positive and the carryforward is used up, recorded taxes are positive. But cash flow is now greater than recorded income because of the net operating loss (NOL) that is used. In this case the accumulated deferred tax is an asset on the balance sheet as taxes paid of zero are higher than negative tax recorded on the profit and loss statement. The NOL should result in increased future cash flow just like any other asset such as an account receivable or plant balance. For deferred taxes associated with carryforwards, one can imagine that the company has made an investment in the deferred tax assets and will receive the cash flow and returns on the asset when the carryforward is used. This deferred tax asset related to the carryforward does not generate NOPAT, as the taxes are derived from book income.

The classification of deferred taxes associated with carryforwards for purposes of valuation is more complicated than the case of accumulated deferred taxes that arise from accumulated depreciation. If the cash flow from the explicit period encompasses the full period until the extinguishment of the carryforward, then the free cash flow should include all of the effects of building up and extinguishing the NOL. This case of including the whole period of the NOL in a model implies that no adjustment should be in the terminal value calculation and is similar to the treatment of deferred taxes associated with accelerated depreciation. However, if the explicit period ends when the carryforward is still being used up or being generated, then there is some value of the carryforward that continues after the terminal period. This value cannot be measured by simply assuming that the after-tax cash flow adjusted for the use of the NOL continues and grows using the standard growth formula.

Unless the NOL is completely used up by the end of the explicit period, accumulated deferred taxes associated with an NOL cannot be modeled in the same way as deferred taxes associated with accelerated depreciation where the change in deferred tax is reflected in cash flow and the invested capital from a financing perspective does not include the accumulated deferred tax. However, adding the accumulated deferred tax associated with NOL to the enterprise value is also not precise, as the deferred tax balance is measured in nominal terms without discounting the future value of cash flows. The pure way to measure the cash flow associated with an expiring tax loss carryforward is to directly estimate the cash flows associated with the NOL over the remaining period in which the NOL will be entirely used up (that could be longer than the explicit cash flow period) and then to discount those cash flows at the cost of capital in the free cash flow calculation. If this is impossible, the alternative of adding the accumulated deferred taxes arising from the NOL that is presented in the notes to the balance sheet and then including this amount in the bridge between enterprise value and equity value is most accurate. This means that deferred taxes resulting from NOLs have a different treatment than deferred taxes from accelerated depreciation. The difference in treatment comes about because deferred taxes associated with the NOL do not continue to grow along with the EBITDA and cash flow as do other items. Similar issues arise with deferred taxes related to goodwill that do not continue to grow.

Classification of Operating Cash That Produces Interest Income below the EBITDA Line

In terms of surplus cash and other investments that are not necessary for operating a business, the treatment for the invested capital calculation is clear. However, appropriate classification of operating cash (sometimes measured as 2 percent of revenues as a rule of thumb) needed to operate the business is more complex. In the case of surplus cash, income is recorded as interest income below the EBITDA line, and the surplus cash is not an asset that is necessary to produce EBITDA. When computing amounts of financing required to generate EBITDA, as some of the debt and equity financing has been used to finance surplus cash instead of assets that generate EBITDA, this amount should be deducted from the total invested capital used to finance EBITDA producing assets. Turning to operating cash, you could make the argument that operating cash is like surplus cash because it generates income below the EBITDA line. You could also make the argument that operating cash is like accounts receivable where the investment made is necessary to generate EBITDA. When a company needs more operating cash, it will have to increase invested capital. If operating cash is classified as a financing item like surplus cash, the equity value is increased relative to the enterprise value, whereas if the operating cash is considered as a necessary asset for running the business, then free cash flow is lower and the equity value is reduced as is the case for accounts receivable. Using the 2 percent rule of thumb, this swing could be 4 percent of the equity value of a company.

It is often taken for granted that operating cash should be differentiated from surplus cash. In practice, this issue is not so obvious. The idea behind accounting for operating cash in a similar manner to accounts receivable is that some level of operating cash is necessary to run the business and that EBITDA/free cash flow could not be generated without the operating cash. However, a counterargument can be made that operating cash is a by-product of operating a company, and it provides value to equity through reducing the cost of capital as well as through generating interest income. The issue can be clarified by taking account of the effect of cash on the weighted average cost of capital. The fact that cash normally generates a lower return than is earned on other investments is offset by the effect of the cash on the cost of capital. Once the effect on the cost of capital is included, the treatment of operating cash as part of the bridge between equity value and enterprise value is clarified. If the weighted average cost of capital does not include an adjustment for operating cash, then the valuation is biased. In an example of two companies with the same assets and financing except that one of them requires much more operating cash, the company with the bigger cash balance will have a lower risk and lower weighted average cost of capital. If the weighted cost of capital without the effect of operating cash is applied to free cash flow of both companies, and if operating cash flow is not included in the bridge between enterprise value and equity value, the company with a lot of cash will be undervalued relative to the company with little cash. The best way to account for operating cash is to both change the cost of capital and include it as a bridge between enterprise value and equity value as is the case for surplus cash.

The relationship between measurement of the weighted cost of capital and treatment of operating cash is demonstrated by the process of deleveraging and then releveraging the beta, which is common in analyses made by investment banks. The net debt rather than the gross debt is often used when computing the unleveraged beta and cost of capital, as illustrated in Figure 26.2. Note that this approach produces biased results if the cost of debt does not equal the risk-free rate used in establishing the cost of equity capital. You can demonstrate this bias by backing into the cost of equity from a weighted average cost of capital table where you assume that companies with a different capital structure have the same weighted cost of capital. When you hold the WACC constant and back into the cost of equity and then derive the beta from that cost of equity, the levered beta is not correct unless the interest rate equals the risk-free rate. As the cash lowers the amount of net debt, the

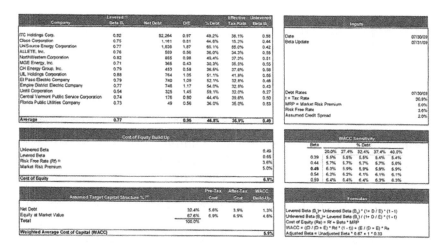

Company	Levered Beta BL	Net Debt	D/E	%Debt	Effective Tax Rate	Unlevered Beta BU
ITC Holdings Corp.	0.92	$2,264	0.97	49.2%	38.1%	0.58
Cleco Corporation	0.75	1,161	0.31	44.6%	15.3%	0.44
UniSource Energy Corporation	0.77	1,836	1.87	65.1%	55.0%	0.42
ALLETE, Inc.	0.76	569	0.56	36.0%	34.3%	0.55
NorthWestern Corporation	0.82	865	0.98	49.4%	37.3%	0.51
MGE Energy, Inc.	0.71	365	0.43	30.3%	36.5%	0.55
CH Energy Group, Inc.	0.79	453	0.58	36.5%	37.6%	0.58
UIL Holdings Corporation	0.88	764	1.05	51.1%	41.8%	0.55
El Paso Electric Company	0.79	740	1.09	52.1%	32.8%	0.48
Empire District Electric Company	0.77	748	1.17	54.0%	32.5%	0.43
Unitil Corporation	0.54	325	1.45	59.1%	32.0%	0.27
Central Vermont Public Service Corporation	0.74	176	0.80	44.4%	39.6%	0.50
Florida Public Utilities Company	0.73	49	0.56	36.0%	35.0%	0.53
Average	**0.77**		**0.95**	**46.8%**	**35.9%**	**0.49**

Inputs

Date	07/30/09
Beta Update	07/31/09
Debt Rates	07/30/09
t = Tax Rate	30.9%
MRP = Market Risk Premium	5.0%
Risk Free Rate	3.6%
Assumed Credit Spread	2.0%

Cost of Equity Build Up

Unlevered Beta	0.49
Levered Beta	0.65
Risk Free Rate (Rf) =	3.6%
Market Risk Premium	5.0%
Cost of Equity	**6.9%**

WACC Sensitivity

Beta	20.0%	27.4%	32.4%	37.4%	40.0%
0.39	5.5%	5.5%	5.5%	5.4%	5.4%
0.44	5.7%	5.7%	5.7%	5.7%	5.6%
0.49	6.0%	5.9%	5.9%	5.9%	5.9%
0.54	6.2%	6.2%	6.1%	6.1%	6.1%
0.59	6.4%	6.4%	6.4%	6.3%	6.3%

Assumed Target Capital Structure %

		Pre-Tax Cost	After-Tax Cost	WACC Build-Up
Net Debt	32.4%	5.6%	3.9%	1.3%
Equity at Market Value	67.6%	6.9%	6.9%	4.6%
Total	100.0%			
Weighted Average Cost of Capital (WACC)				**5.9%**

Formulas

$$\text{Levered Beta }(B_L) = \text{Unlevered Beta }(B_U) * (1 + D/E) * (1 - t)$$
$$\text{Unlevered Beta }(B_U) = \text{Levered Beta }(B_L) / (1 + D/E) * (1 - t)$$
$$\text{Cost of Equity }(Re) = Rf + Beta * MRP$$
$$WACC = (D/(D + E) * Rd * (1 - t)) + (E/(D + E) * Re)$$
$$\text{Adjusted Beta} = \text{Unadjusted Beta} * 0.67 + 1 * 0.33$$

FIGURE 26.2 Illustration of Cost of Capital Calculation with Net Debt Instead of Gross Debt

implicit cost of capital and the unleveraged beta increase. Consider the case of companies like Apple and Microsoft that have a whole lot of cash on their balance sheets. The measured equity beta of each company from stock prices understates the risk associated with free cash flow because equity cash flow includes the low volatility safe cash on the balance sheet. If net debt rather than gross debt is used in adjusting the cost of capital, then the measured cost of capital relative to the observed equity beta increases because of more cash on the balance sheet. The cost of capital adjusted for net debt reflects the volatility associated with the underlying EBITDA excluding the effects of cash balance, which is what it is supposed to do. If the operating cash as well as the surplus cash is used in unleveraging and releveraging beta for computing WACC, then the treatment of operating cash flow as an element of the bridge between equity value and enterprise value is correct.

The idea of adjusting the weighted average cost of capital calculation so as to isolate the risk associated with operating cash flow does not only apply to operating and surplus cash. Say a company has associated investments that are much more risky than the assets that create EBITDA. In this case the cost of capital applied to free cash flow should remove the effects of these risky investments. This is accomplished by removing the associated investments from the asset beta of comparable companies as operating cash was removed from the calculation, and by attributing a cost of capital to the associated investments. Similarly, if a company is financing itself with unfunded pensions instead of debt, the asset beta should be adjusted for this form of financing that is equivalent to debt. You should see a pattern.

Every item that is classified on the financing side of the invested capital ledger should also be part of the process of adjusting the asset beta and be incorporated into the weighted average cost of capital. The process of segregating the balance sheet for purposes of invested capital not only drives the return on investment, but also affects the enterprise value to equity value bridge and the weighted average cost capital.

Treatment of Derivative Assets and Liabilities Depending on How Derivatives Affect EBITDA

The fair value of derivative liabilities and assets recorded on the balance sheet must be classified on either the finance side or the net asset side of the invested capital ledger like any other asset or liability. A few years ago, the value of derivative assets or liabilities such as interest rate, foreign exchange, or commodity swaps, options, and forward contracts were not valued in financial statements before settlement of the contracts. These days, the market value changes of derivatives are put on the balance sheet even though the changes in value did not arise from a cash outflow made by investors. For example, if an interest rate swap used to hedge variable-rate debt has a positive value because short-term interest rates have risen, the value that could be realized from selling the swap in financial markets would be classified as an asset. Similarly, if a commodity price swap has a negative value because oil prices have declined, then a liability is recorded on the balance sheet. Changes in the values of these derivatives may or may not be included on the profit and loss statement, depending on whether the derivatives are classified as hedges. If the derivatives are classified as hedges, the income from the change in value is not included in EBITDA, interest income, or interest expense. Instead, the change in value is put into accumulated other comprehensive income.

To understand how derivatives should be treated in the invested capital calculation and in the bridge between enterprise value and equity value, the first step is to understand the accounting, as was the case for deferred taxes, accounts payable, or any other item. Derivatives that are classified as hedges do not have an effect on income recorded on financial statements until the contract is settled, whereas derivatives under the fair value treatment affect profit any time the value changes. To illustrate the accounting and valuation effects of a derivative, one can consider two cases of interest rate swaps and commodity price swaps. For the first case say a futures contract fixes the price of oil for three years for an upstream exploration company. Assume that the price is fixed at 150 in the commodity price swap while the current price of oil is 100, implying that the swap contract has a positive market value. The second case is an interest rate swap that fixes interest rates at 4 percent for three years.

In this case assume the current market interest rate is 2 percent, implying that the swap has a negative value and is classified as a liability. If hedge accounting is used for the oil futures contract, revenue and EBITDA are not recognized until the oil exploration company settles the contract in three years. For the intervening years, the value appears on the balance sheet as an asset, and the accumulated other comprehensive income is also increased. By the expiration date of the contract when it is settled, the swap has no value and the value shown on the balance sheet must also decline to zero. This happens when income that is recognized from settlement of the contract is offset by reduction in some other income or increase in an expense. If the company uses fair value treatment for the oil price forward contract, the EBITDA is increased when the value of the contract changes, rather than when the contract is settled in three years. With the fair value treatment, accumulated other comprehensive income does not change as the value of the swap changes because income affects the common equity account. The same sort of treatment could occur for the interest rate swap, but there would be a liability instead of an asset and the loss would be below the EBITDA line.

Unlike other balance sheet items, the segregation of derivatives may differ for purposes of computing invested capital and for purposes of evaluating the bridge between enterprise value and equity value. Recall from Chapter 23 that invested capital is supposed to represent the amount of money that investors initially put into the business in order to generate EBITDA. For derivatives that are accounted for either using the hedge treatment or the fair value treatment, the balance sheet value no longer represents investment that has been made by investors. Instead, the balance sheet value includes some components that are measured from market value changes. If the invested capital is to be measured, then the value of the derivatives could be removed from the equity value in the financing side of the ledger. But they also should not be included on the direct EBITDA-related side of the invested capital calculation because they were not investments made to produce EBITDA. Note that using this logic, any impairment or asset write-up should also be adjusted for purposes of computing invested capital because these things also essentially represent changing the balance sheet from an invested capital calculation to a market-based number.

The reason for not including derivatives on the net asset side of the ledger can be demonstrated by thinking of the derivatives as taking a bet. If the company has made a good bet and derivatives, then the ROIC increases and management performance looks good. If the company has made a bad bet, the ROIC declines. But there was no investment associated with making this bet. The denominator of the ROIC should not be affected by changes in the value of the derivative. The implication of all of this is that the equity balance on the balance sheet should in theory be adjusted for the value of the derivative when either the ROE or the ROIC is computed.

Classification of derivatives for purposes of evaluating the bridge between enterprise value and equity value depends on the nature of the derivative and is more straightforward. For purposes of computing the bridge between equity value and enterprise value, the market value of derivatives can be used to compute the difference between the market value and the book value of items on the balance sheet. The general rule for classifying derivatives when computing the bridge between enterprise value and equity value is the same as usual and is driven by whether ultimate cash flows from the derivative are already included in EBITDA. If settlement of the derivative is already reflected in projected EBITDA and free cash flow as part of the forecast, the value of the derivative is already in the enterprise value and including it again in the bridge between equity value and enterprise value would amount to double-counting the item. On the other hand, if the derivative has not been valued as part of EBITDA and free cash flow, it should be part of the bridge. To demonstrate this idea, return to the example of the oil forward contract and the interest rate swap introduced at the beginning of this section. If the 150 oil price from settlement of the forward contract is included in the projection of EBITDA, then the value of the derivative is already in the enterprise value derived from discounting free cash flow value. In the case of the interest rate swap, if the book value of debt is taken from the balance sheet for computing the bridge, the value of the swap can be used to move the debt from book value to market value. For the interest-rate swap, the derivative should be included as part of the value of the debt rather than left out of the analysis. As the WACC should use debt and equity market value, the derivatives that are included in the bridge between equity value and enterprise value should also be included in the WACC table.

When discussing the discounted cash flow model, finance texts often describe the example of land that is held for a future factory as something that should be included in the bridge between enterprise value and equity value. Similarly, a large lawsuit that has a certain probability of resulting in large cash outflows is sometimes discussed. If the land is not currently earning income but it has a market value and could be sold at a substantial sum, the additional amount should be included in the bridge between enterprise value and equity value. You could also even make an adjustment to the weighted average cost of capital calculation for this land. Say a hotel company buys land all over the world that may or may not be used in developing hotels; then the beta associated with the free cash flow should adjust for risks associated with land speculation, implying that the value of the land should be included as an element in the weighted average cost of capital calculation and attributed a high beta. This adjustment to the WACC would probably never really be made, but it illustrates how to think through the problems.

CHAPTER 27

Four General Terminal
Value Methods

The discounted cash flow (DCF) model is the culmination of a series of finance theories encompassing Modigliani and Miller, the capital asset pricing model (CAPM), and the philosophy that companies with an indefinite life eventually reach some kind of stable equilibrium. In theory, a DCF analysis should be made that reflects the fundamental factors that drive the value of a company, including return on capital, cost of capital, and growth rates. The DCF method is the central valuation approach taught by academics, and in its pure form it is not dependent on the opinions of other investment analysts. The primary alternative valuation approach to the DCF model applies multiples such as the price/earnings (P/E) ratio and enterprise value/earnings before interest, taxes, depreciation, and amortization (EV/EBITDA) to current or projected income. Application of multiples is sometimes called relative valuation because, in contrast to the DCF model, these valuations are at least in part dependent on the judgments of others. P/E and EV/EBITDA multiples taken from a comparable sample indirectly depend on the implied returns required in the market as well as expectations of future income growth. When using multiples and relative valuation, you are constrained by the implicit assumptions that players in the market have made about future rates of return, risks, and growth.

In spite of the theoretical advantages of the DCF model in its pure form (i.e., without using multiples in the terminal value), the method is fraught with both practical and theoretical difficulties. Big problems in computing the cost of capital include the accuracy of beta in measuring risk and difficulties in assessing the equity market risk premium. Uncertainties associated with cost of capital problems can translate into such wide ranges of value when applying the discounted cash flow model that the whole process can become all but useless in practical situations. Difficulties in measuring the cost of capital are compounded by required assumptions with respect to the date at which a company will reach some kind of mythical equilibrium and will begin to grow in a slow and smooth manner. Finally, applying growth rates in the terminal value formula of the DCF method without being very careful about adjustments to depreciation expense, working capital (WC) changes, capital expenditures (Capexp), and deferred tax can lead to highly biased valuations.

Perhaps the biggest practical problem with the DCF method in its pure form is that there is such a high dependence on the weighted average cost of capital (WACC) to compute the present value of cash flows. All one has to do is ask somebody who has made a valuation analysis using the discounted cash flow technique to see how much the results can be fudged through tinkering a bit with the terminal growth, the discount rate, or one of the assumptions to see how it is subject to manipulation. An illustration of the classic DCF problem is shown in Figure 27.1, taken from a sell-side stock analyst presentation. In Figure 27.1, the WACC changes only from 5.7 percent to 6.3 percent—a very small variation given all of the well-known problems and uncertainties associated with the capital asset pricing model. Further, the terminal growth rate varies only between 2.5 percent and 3.1 percent, which again is a very small range considering all of the unknowns about the future state of the economy, future inflation, and other company-specific factors. Given this small variation in the cost of capital and the growth rates, the value of the stock varies from a low of 31.98 to a high of 65.43 or a range of more than 100 percent. This wide range in valuation that results from small changes in variables that are very difficult to estimate— WACC and growth—renders the model useless even if the model faithfully applies all of the financial theories.

Exhibit 5: **DCF Valuation: Perpetual Growth**

		Discount Rate						
		5.70%	5.80%	5.90%	6.00%	6.10%	6.20%	6.30%
Terminal Growth Rate	2.50%	48.33	45.18	42.22	39.43	36.80	34.33	31.98
	2.60%	50.72	47.40	44.28	41.36	38.60	36.01	33.56
	2.70%	53.27	49.76	46.48	43.40	40.51	37.79	35.22
	2.80%	55.99	52.28	48.81	45.57	42.53	39.67	36.99
	2.90%	58.91	54.98	51.31	47.89	44.67	41.67	38.84
	3.00%	62.05	57.86	53.97	50.35	46.96	43.79	40.82
	3.10%	65.43	60.97	56.83	52.99	49.40	46.05	42.92

FIGURE 27.1 Example of Extreme Range from Using the DCF Model
Source: Company data, Credit Suisse estimates.

The reason for such wide value differences in the table is almost entirely due to the manner in which terminal value is computed using the formula:

$$\text{Terminal Value} = [\text{Stable Cash Flow} \times (1 + g)/(\text{WACC} - g)]$$
$$/(1 + \text{WACC})^{\text{number of periods}}$$

This formula applies WACC in two places, both in computing the terminal value for the last period and then also for discounting the value back to the present. This sensitivity of the terminal valuation to WACC is the driving force behind analyses that range from creating integrated models with accretion and dilution to using a leveraged buyout model to derive the implicit cost of capital. The alternative methods do not include a direct estimate of WACC and do not contain a terminal value assumption.

To introduce issues in applying the DCF model that arise from measurement of terminal value, four alternative approaches to the terminal value are compared in this chapter. These methods include the stable growth method just discussed; using a predetermined EV/EBITDA multiple applied to EBITDA in the terminal year constituting relative valuation; applying the value driver formula $(1 - g/\text{ROIC})/(\text{WACC} - g)$ to estimates of net operating profit after tax (NOPAT) in the terminal year; or using an implied EV/EBITDA multiple that accounts for return on invested capital (ROIC), WACC, and growth through benchmarking or in a regression analysis. Before describing mechanical modeling details that apply to all of these methods in subsequent chapters, a few of the benefits and the problems associated with each option are discussed here.

Method 1: Stable Growth Using the $(1 + g)/(\text{WACC} - g)$ Formula

Application of a stable growth formula discussed in the introduction to this chapter derives value from a normalized cash flow estimate when computing terminal value. This method assumes a constant growth rate in the normalized cash flow that applies in perpetuity. Advantages of the constant growth method are that it does not depend on the valuation made by others, and that it can be applied with a simple formula. Disadvantages are that it does not account for changes in cash flow that arise from changes in the future rate of return and that it results in a very wide range of results as already demonstrated in Figure 27.1.

Using a little bit of calculus you can prove that the integral of a series that is discounted at a constant cost of capital for an infinite period results in the formula:

$$\text{Value}_0 = \text{Cash Flow}_1/\text{Cost of Capital}$$

Since the growth rate applied to normalized cash flow is the reverse of discounting and since the cash flow in the next period is the current period multiplied by 1 plus the growth rate, the formula is the same as assuming that the cash flow continually grows and the risk associated with the normalized cash flow does not change. Because the WACC is in the denominator of the formula, the terminal value changes by a wide margin when the WACC varies. The formula is also very sensitive to the growth rate, as a high growth rate can make the denominator very small.

The stable growth formula can be translated into the EV/EBITDA ratio. Terminal value computed by the formula is the enterprise value, and free cash flow to the firm (FCFF) is a function of the EBITDA. The following equation demonstrates how you could compute the implied EV/EBITDA ratio from the growth and cost of capital assumptions, and the factors that would lead to a different implied EV/EBITDA ratio. The implication of this equation is that when you put an EV/EBITDA assumption in your model, you are implicitly making an estimate of cost of capital and growth. Similarly, if you input growth and cost of capital into the terminal value calculation, you are making an implicit assumption with respect to the EV/EBITDA ratio.

$$EV = FCFF/(WACC - g) = (EBITDA - Capexp - WC\ Change - Tax)/$$
$$(WACC - g)$$

When applying the growth formula to compute terminal value it is common to assume that growth is limited to the rate of inflation. While questionable logic such as assuming real growth will stop is part of this assumption, and errors in the prediction of growth are pervasive in valuation, the problems in valuation analysis discussed in the next few chapters are not related to underestimating or overestimating growth. Precisely because the exercise of predicting growth is so difficult, it would be presumptuous to assert that valuation analyses were flawed when someone made an optimistic or pessimistic growth rate estimate. One area in which growth rate logic can lead to mechanical distortions is the relationship between nominal growth and cost of capital. Difficulty in predicting growth is a big part of the reason that cash flows themselves are uncertain. Where valuations depend on high growth, there should also be a high cost of capital no matter what the CAPM suggests. When you grow fast there is a bigger chance of falling harder. Given the inherent uncertainty of guessing at what date growth rates will change, investments that do not depend on achieving high growth for a long time period should have less risk than investment strategies that cannot easily adjust to changes in growth.

One of the big challenges in applying the constant growth method is determining the normalized level of all of the cash flow items that should be used when the growth rate changes. A basic and simple idea that surprisingly is not often applied when implementing the DCF model with constant growth is the notion of consistency between EBITDA growth and investment. Capital expenditures and working capital investment that are necessary to support EBITDA should be directly related to the terminal growth assumption. A fundamental notion in any model is that if there is more growth in EBITDA, more capital expenditures and more working capital investment are necessary to generate that higher level of EBITDA. The next few chapters explain how you can develop assumptions for normalized working capital investment, deferred taxes, capital expenditures and other items that are consistent with changing growth rates. Earlier chapters described computation and presentation of the return on invested capital that is so important in judging whether your models are reasonable. The ROIC in the terminal EBITDA is the most important number to evaluate.

To summarize issues in computing terminal value using the constant growth formula, you can evaluate each of the items in the free cash flow formula. In developing a reasonable normalized cash flow calculation, the following analysis techniques can be applied to each of the components of cash flow:

EBITDA: Review ROIC in the terminal year and ensure that forecasts are reasonable in the context of history and the competitive structure of the industry.

Working Capital Investment: Apply the formula, Stable WC Change $= \text{WC/EBITDA} \times \text{EBITDA} \times g/(1+g)$.

Capital Expenditure: Develop a user-defined function that computes a stable value of capital expenditures to depreciation that can be applied to an accurate estimate of depreciation in the terminal period.

Deferred Tax: Develop a user-defined function that computes a stable value of deferred taxes to capital expenditures.

Depreciation Expense: Assume that the growth rate of depreciation is consistent with the growth rate in EBITDA.

Method 2: Value Driver Method—Incorporating the Return Relative to Cost of Capital in Terminal Value

In theory, there are only three things that drive the value of any business enterprise. The first is how much money is earned relative to the amount of investment, measured by the return on invested capital. The second is the risk associated with those earnings as measured by the WACC. The third is the growth rate in the investment, the importance of which depends on your ability to earn a return above the cost of capital. You can account for both growth and return on capital relative to the cost of capital through applying a formula to derive EV from the NOPAT. Recall that NOPAT is $EBIT \times (1 - t)$:

$$\text{Enterprise Value} = \text{NOPAT} \times (1 - \text{Asset Growth}/\text{ROIC})/$$
$$(\text{WACC} - \text{Asset Growth})$$

This formula implies that the value of a company can be computed from the three value drivers—the growth rate, the cost of capital, and the return parameters—along with the current level of after-tax income.

The formula seems to be magic in a few different ways. First, the equation accounts for all of three value drivers instead of only growth and WACC, which was the case with the stable growth rate method. Second, the value driver formula does not include capital expenditures or working capital investment so that you do not seem to have to worry about the stable ratios for these items. Third, if the ROIC is assumed to be equal to WACC, the value is not sensitive to the growth rate, and the problem of wide ranges in value with respect to different growth rate assumptions can be eliminated.

While some analysts argue that this formula is the only way to compute terminal value (TV), there are a number of problems with the method that make applying it not such a good idea. First, although it is easy to plug things into the formula, it is difficult to explain the logic of the different items in a simple way. Second, implicit assumptions about the manner in which a company moves from the current return to the stable rate of return depend on the growth rate. With a faster growth rate there is a faster decline in the rate of return, which is not consistent with economic theory. Third, and most important, the equation is not mechanically correct when the growth rate and/ or the rate of return changes from one level to another. This problem is very serious because evaluating changing growth and return is the whole reason for applying the formula in the first place. These problems with the formula $TV = \text{NOPAT} \times (1 - g/\text{ROIC})/(\text{WACC} - g)$ are so important that they are the entire subject of Chapter 33. Valuation errors from applying the formula can be demonstrated by applying a long-term model for proving what the value should be with different growth and return assumptions using the technique that is introduced in Chapter 25.

Method 3: Use of Multiples from Comparative Analysis

If the ROIC is assumed to be greater than the WACC, the range in value resulting from alternative WACC and growth can be almost as much as the range that results from the first method when the value driver formula

$(1 - g/\text{ROIC})/(\text{WACC} - g)$ is applied. The effect of the WACC in DCF analysis can be reduced if you multiply the terminal EBITDA by an assumed EV/ EBITDA ratio. To see why the range is less sensitive to the WACC, look at the two terminal value formulas. The formula for the stable growth includes WACC in two places:

$$\text{Terminal Value} = [\text{Stable Cash Flow} \times (1 + g)/(\text{WACC} - g)]/$$
$$(1 + \text{WACC})^{\text{number of periods}}$$

By contrast, if a terminal multiple is used from multiplying EV/EBITDA by EBITDA, the WACC is in only one place:

$$\text{Terminal Value} = (\text{EBITDA} \times \text{EV}/\text{EBITDA})/(1 + \text{WACC})^{\text{number of periods}}$$

To implement this method, you could try to estimate the EV/EBITDA by making some kind of comparative company analysis in which the ratios for similar companies are evaluated. Some suggest that if you examine multiples over many years they tend to stabilize. Furthermore, if the multiples are applied, you do not have to worry about the normalized amount of working capital, capital expenditures, or deferred tax in a stable year. Despite these advantages, applying an EV/EBITDA ratio to terminal value has some serious theoretical problems. Two of the problems are: (1) the EV/EBITDA ratio derived from financial market data may have dramatically different implicit growth, return, and cost of capital assumptions relative to the assumptions on terminal growth and cost of capital in your financial model; and (2) the EV/ EBITDA ratio in the initial valuation year when there is expected growth in EBITDA differs from the terminal year when the growth rate declines. This latter problem is illustrated in Figure 27.2, in which the EV/EBITDA at the valuation date is 22.2 while the ratio at the terminal date after the growth slows is 14.8. The example also shows the wide range in valuation from changes in the growth rate and in the discount rate, as the highest multiple is 48.4 and the lowest implied multiple is 14.9.

Method 4: Derived Multiple Formula

A final method for computing the terminal value is to derive a theoretical EV/ EBITDA multiple from explicit assumptions about growth rates, returns, cost of capital, capital expenditures to depreciation, asset lives, working capital, and tax rates. This method still requires measuring the cost of capital, but it allows you to see the implicit assumptions associated with multiples in the market, and the method avoids many of the problems of the other three

Timing Assumptions

Initial Year	2014
Valuation Year	2018
Terminal Year	2025

Operational Assumptions		Valuation Assumptions	
EBITDA	100	WACC	9%
Acc Payable/EBITDA	20%	Terminal EV/EBITDA	10.0x
Explicit Period Growth	10%	WACC / ROIC Spread	3%
Terminal growth	2%	ROIC	12%

Timing

Year			2014	2015	2016	2017	2018	2019	2020	2024	2025
Explicit Period			FALSE	FALSE	FALSE	FALSE	TRUE	TRUE	TRUE	TRUE	TRUE
Terminal Year			FALSE	FALSE	FALSE	FALSE	FALSE	FALSE	FALSE	FALSE	TRUE

Valuation 2 - Valuation with growth rate

			2014	2015	2016	2017	2018	2019	2020	2024	2025
EBITDA		100.0	110.0	121.0	133.1	146.4	161.1	177.2	194.9	285.3	313.8
Explicit CFs		$1,242.88	FALSE	FALSE	FALSE	FALSE	164.0	180.4	198.4	290.5	319.5
Terminal CF(s)		$2,336.83	FALSE	FALSE	FALSE	FALSE	-	-	-	-	4,656.3
Enterprise Value		3,579.71									

Implicit EV/EBITDA - Valuation Date	22.2x
Implicit EV/EBITDA - Terminal Date	14.8x

		Growth				
		0%	1%	2%	3%	4%
WACC	7%	24.9x	27.8x	32.0x	38.1x	48.4x
	8%	21.4x	23.5x	26.3x	30.1x	35.9x
	9%	18.8x	20.3x	22.2x	24.8x	28.4x
	10%	16.7x	17.8x	19.2x	21.0x	23.4x
	11%	14.9x	15.8x	16.9x	18.2x	19.9x

FIGURE 27.2 Illustration of Difference in Terminal EV/EBITDA Relative to Initial EV/EBITDA

methods discussed. Some of the advantages of computing derived multiples and applying these multiples include:

- Deriving a multiple from the three value drivers along with explicit transition periods, tax rates, asset lives, and working capital allows you to compute the EV/EBITDA ratio that is consistent with marginal changes in growth, cost of capital, and rate of return included in the model. It also corrects problems with applying the EV/EBITDA multiple from comparable public company analysis without any adjustment for changes in growth and cost of capital, which is a major problem with method 3.
- Computing the EV/EBITDA multiple with explicit assumptions about historical growth, future growth, tax and book asset lives, and the tax rate eliminates problems associated with the value driver formula that arise because of the difficulty of interpretation of the formula and the logical errors in the formula.
- Through using a formula to derive implicit multiples along with regression analysis, you can benchmark cost of capital and/or growth rate inputs to be consistent with financial markets. You can then adjust these implied numbers to be consistent with stable conditions. This can eliminate the large range in value that occurs with the stable growth method.

Coming up with a model for the EV/EBITDA ratio that can be applied in the terminal value calculation should account for varying transition growth and return periods, stable ratios of capital expenditures to depreciation, stable depreciation rates, and stable levels of deferred taxes relative to net plant. This approach of deriving the implicit EV/EBITDA multiple forces you to consider directly a host of variables that drive the long-term value, including different rates of convergence between return and cost of capital, declines in cost of capital during stable growth periods, changing growth rates, income tax rates, and required asset replacements necessary to support ongoing EBITDA. Advantages of this approach are that it is flexible and it reduces large variation in valuations. Disadvantages of the method are that it requires a number of somewhat complicated calculations and it is not commonly used in valuation.

The remainder of this part of the book addresses theoretical issues associated with measuring stable growth rates and resolving DCF problems using the four alternative approaches. Topics include the theoretical and practical issues associated with applying a terminal growth rate formula to normalized cash flow (Chapters 28 through 31); the value driver formula and general issues related to the convergence of cost of capital and return on capital (Chapter 32); how growth and cost of capital can be translated into a P/E ratio; and how the derived P/E ratio can consider changes in real growth, movements in rates of return, and variation in the cost of capital (Chapters 33 and 34). Chapter 35 works through calculation of the implicit EV/EBITDA ratio given assumptions for growth, asset lives, tax rates, and other factors. This analysis is built upon development of stable ratios for depreciation rates on net plant, capital expenditures to net plant, and deferred tax to net plant.

CHAPTER 28

Terminal Value and Philosophy
Company Growth Rates and Overall Economic Growth

The necessity of computing terminal value in corporate models comes from the idea that corporations, unlike humans, are assumed to last indefinitely. This notion means that long-term forecasts of items such as earnings before interest, taxes, depreciation, and amortization growth, rate of return, and cost of capital cannot be avoided when valuing a company. Winston Churchill's commented: "It is always wise to look ahead, but difficult to look further than you can see" summarizes the fundamental problem when thinking about growth in a financial model. In forecasting cash flow, you cannot really see more than a few years into the future at the absolute furthest, which begs the question of how you can possibly make a reasonable forecast of growth, return on capital, and risk on an infinite basis.

Given this problem, the convention in valuation is to resort to a rather vague philosophical concept rather than to attempt to make a detailed forecast. Since valuation of a corporation requires some explicit or implicit assumption with respect to growth, you can begin by eliminating unreasonable assumptions. It does not make sense to assume that high growth rates can occur for long periods above the overall nominal growth rate in the economy. You can easily demonstrate that if a company grows by 10 percent above the growth rate in the economy, it will, in the not-too-distant future, take over the economy. If you assume that Apple can continue to grow at 40 percent while the overall economy is growing by 3 percent, then in about 30 years there would be nothing other than Apple products in the economy—no food, no clothes, and no cars, just iPhones, iPads, and other Apple products (some may believe this could be possible). This is just due to the law of large numbers.

However, it is just as unreasonable to assume that every company will eventually simply fail and end up in bankruptcy. As products of a company reach the end of their life cycle or become obsolete, management obsessively tries to develop new products and new business lines in an attempt to sustain high growth and profitability. It is not likely that the management of all companies will become so bureaucratic and so inept that they cannot find any investment that earns a return above the cost of capital.

With the two extremes, (1) maintaining growth above the overall economy or (2) simply dying, the philosophy of making a compromise and assuming a stable growth rate seems reasonable in making valuations. While this idea of realizing a stable growth rate sometime in the future can be defended relative to other possible approaches, the date at which the transition from short-term to long-term growth begins and the length of the transition period are still completely arbitrary, as is the assumption for the long-term nominal growth rate of the economy.

To resolve problems with making unreasonably high growth rate assumptions, analysts who perform discounted cash flow (DCF) analysis generally make a pessimistic assumption that growth in cash flow once a terminal period occurs will be limited to the projected rate of inflation. This means that companies will stabilize to a tranquil zero real growth rate in a period of somewhere between 5 and 10 years, perhaps after a smooth transition period until this supposed tranquility is obtained. The typical assumptions derived from the philosophy that a company will stabilize to a zero real growth rate are illustrated in Figure 28.1.

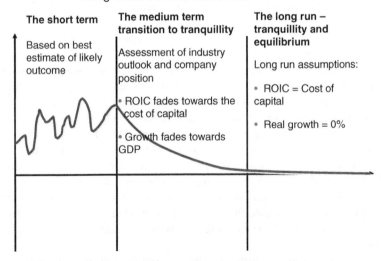

FIGURE 28.1 Typical Assumptions Made in DCF Analysis with Respect to Long-Term Growth and Return Relative to Cost of Capital

Given the well-documented optimism of sell-side stock analysts, it may seem a little surprising that analysts, consultants, investment bankers, and others who perform discounted cash flow analysis generally make assumptions like those shown in Figure 28.1, where growth in cash flow once a terminal period occurs will be limited to the projected rate of inflation. Growth at only the rate of inflation implies that there is no real growth in any company. While the assumption is commonly made, it is difficult to come up with any company—or person, for that matter—that has reached this kind of tranquil nirvana or has managed such a transition to equilibrium. Further, if all companies somehow reach this kind of equilibrium where there is no real growth in cash flow, no companies would contribute to real economic growth, and the world economy would stagnate in a never-ending recession. It could also be argued that all growth in the economy will come from new start-up companies that do not currently exist and that all existing companies will become inefficient slow-growth entities.

When reviewing the growth rate in revenues for individual companies over long time periods you can find downward trends in growth due to the difficulty of achieving a high rate of growth after becoming really big. But you cannot find the sudden changes from high growth to no real growth that are generally assumed in the discounted cash flow model. Over the past decade, the growth rate of Microsoft has declined, but the decline did not happen in five years and the growth rate has not come all the way down to the overall rate of inflation. Similar examples can be found with many companies that have become large and successful. In evaluating these large companies, one should keep in mind the issue of survivorship bias, as it is more difficult to acquire data on smaller companies that have never grown or have failed. If you are valuing ABC Company, there is a chance that it will continue to grow like Samsung, but there is also a probability that it will decline to nothing, as happened to Eastman Kodak. Needless to say, one can get into endless philosophical and economic arguments about growth rates, survivorship bias, and reaching a period of stability. But when applying the DCF model, some explicit or implicit assumption is required, and assuming a high rate of growth over an indefinite period is not reasonable. At the end of the day, there is no single correct answer, and it is not useful to get emotional about the issue. It is better to admit that you simply don't know the length of the period before growth stabilizes and what the stable growth rate will be.

Computing Transition Periods Using Compound Growth Rates and Switch Variables

If you would like to make a model that has a transition period like the line shown in the graph in Figure 28.1, you can use a technique that applies switch variables to a time line along with computing the implied compound annual growth rate (CAGR) during a transition period. To illustrate the mechanics of computing growth during the transition period, pretend that you would like to assume growth of 15 percent for the first five years followed by a transition period of seven years and then a stable growth rate of 3 percent. The following step-by-step process shows how to develop multiperiod growth rates from assumed given short-term growth, a transition period, and then a constant long-term growth rate.

Step 1: Set Up Switches for the Short-Term, Long-Term, and Transition Periods

Begin the process by defining time period inputs for the short-term period and the transition period. The long-term period can then be calculated as the short-term period plus the transition period. If the short-term period is 5 and the transition period is 7, the long-term period is 12. Once the time period and growth rate inputs are defined, enter the period number beginning at the top of the sheet with the number 1 and then add three rows for switch variables. The three switch variables, all of which have values of TRUE or FALSE, are computed using the following:

- For the first switch variable, simply make a comparison of the period number with the definition of the short-term period:

    Short-Term Switch : Period <= Short-Term Period

- For the second switch variable, define the long-term period as: period > long-term period. The long-term period can be calculated as the short-term period plus the transition period:

    Long-Term Switch : Period > Short-Term Period + Transition Period

- The transition period can then be derived as the equivalence of the short-term period and the long-term period. This is because during both the short-term period and the long-term period there is one TRUE and one FALSE value, while in the transition period the two values are FALSE. Because of this, the transition period can be simply defined as:

    Transition Period : Short-Term Period = Long-Term Period

Step 2: Compute Compound Growth Rates for Interpolation in the Transition Period

During the transition period, the different growth, return, cost of capital, and other variables gradually move from the level defined at the end of the short-term period to the long-run stable amounts. To calculate the value on a period-by-period basis in the transition period, a compound growth rate can be used to interpolate the period-by-period values. Once the transition period growth rate is computed, the value during the transition period can be established using the following formula:

$$\text{Value}_t = \text{Value}_{t-1} \times (1 + \text{Transition Period Growth Rate})$$

In deriving the growth rate for the transition period, the compound annual growth rate equation can be established using the long-term assumed value and the short-term assumed value. When applying the formula, the number of periods you should use is the number of transition years plus 1.

$$\text{Transition Period Growth Rate} = (\text{Long-Term Value}/\text{Short-Term Value})^\wedge$$
$$[1/(\text{Transition Years} + 1)] - 1$$

To see why you must add 1 to the transition years in the formula, consider a simple example where the transition period is only one year. With a single period transaction, if the transition factor were computed without adding 1, the growth rate would be the ratio of the long-term value to the short-term value, yielding a simple one-period growth rate. However, because of the single transition period between the short-term and the long-term, this would not be correct. With a transition period of one year, if this growth were multiplied by the short-term value, the transition year would contain the long-term value and not something in between. When the transition factor is computed through adding a year to the transition period, the transition factor correctly measures the CAGR because the transition adds another year to the process. Using the example with a short-term value of 10 and a long-term value of 15 along with a one-year transition period, the transition growth rate would be 22.5 percent and not 50 percent:

$$\text{Transition Growth} = (\text{Long-Term Value}/\text{Short-Term Value})^\wedge$$
$$[1/(\text{Transition Years} + 1)] - 1 = (15/10)^\wedge (1/2) - 1 = 1.225 - 1 = 22.5\%$$

Step 3: Compute Compound Growth Rates for Interpolation in the Transition Period

Given different TRUE and FALSE values for the short-term, long-term, and transition period switches as well as the transition factors and the long- and short-term parameters, the period-by-period values for growth, return, and other factors can be computed using the following formula if the growth rate method for transition is used:

$$\text{Periodic Value} = \text{Short-Term Value} \times \text{Short-Term Switch} + \text{Long-Term Value}$$
$$\times \text{Long-Term Switch} + \text{Last Year Value}$$
$$\times \text{Transition Growth Rate} \times \text{Transition Switch}$$

Figure 28.2 illustrates how the three switches can be used to derive transitional values for inflation and costs of capital. The formulas include range names.

ABC	D	E	F	J	K	L	M	N	O	P	Q	R
4	**Assumptions**											
5	Returns/Inflation and Cost of Capital											
6	Short-term Inflation	1.00%										
7	Long-term Inflation	2.50%										
22	Timing											
23	Short-term	5										
24	Transition	4										
25	Transition Factors											
26	Inflation Transition	1.20	<---- =(Long_term_Inflation/Short_term_Inflation)^(1/(Transition+1))									
27	Risk Premium Transition	0.87	<---- =(Risk_Premium_Long_term/Risk_Premium_Short_term)^(1/(Transition+1))									
28	ROIC v WACC Transition	0.83	<---- =(Return_above_COC_Long_term/Return_above_COC_Short_term)^(1/(Transition+1))									
29	Growth Rate Transition	0.92	<---- =(Growth_Rate_Long_term/Growth_Rate_Short_term)^(1/(Transition+1))									
37	**Model**											
38	Period	0	1	5	6	7	8	9	10	11	12	13
39	Short-term Switch		TRUE	TRUE	FALSE	FALSE	FALSE	FALSE	FALSE	FALSE	FALSE	FALSE
40	Long-term Switch		FALSE	FALSE	FALSE	FALSE	FALSE	FALSE	TRUE	TRUE	TRUE	TRUE
41	Transition Switch		FALSE	FALSE	TRUE	TRUE	TRUE	TRUE	FALSE	FALSE	FALSE	FALSE
42												
43	Inflation Rate		1.00%	1.00%	1.20%	1.44%	1.73%	2.08%	2.50%	2.50%	2.50%	2.50%
44	Real Interest Rate		1.50%	1.50%	1.50%	1.50%	1.50%	1.50%	1.50%	1.50%	1.50%	1.50%
45	Nominal Interest Rate		2.50%	2.50%	2.70%	2.94%	3.23%	3.58%	4.00%	4.00%	4.00%	4.00%
46												
47	Risk Premium		4.00%	4.00%	3.48%	3.03%	2.64%	2.30%	2.00%	2.00%	2.00%	2.00%
48	Total Cost of Capital		6.50%	6.50%	6.18%	5.97%	5.87%	5.88%	6.00%	6.00%	6.00%	6.00%
49												
50	ROIC/WACC		5.00%	5.00%	4.16%	3.47%	2.89%	2.40%	2.00%	2.00%	2.00%	2.00%
51	Total Rate of Return		11.50%	11.50%	10.35%	9.44%	8.76%	8.28%	8.00%	8.00%	8.00%	8.00%
52												
173	=F39*Short_term_Inflation+F40*Long_term_Inflation+F41*E43*Inflation_Transition											

FIGURE 28.2 Illustration of the Use of Switches to Compute Transition Growth Rates

Computing Explicit Period Cash Flow and Terminal Value with Different Starting and Ending Points

Subsequent chapters address conceptual problems associated with computing terminal value using the four different approaches introduced in Chapter 27. Before considering the numerous theoretical issues arising from different growth and rate of return assumptions associated with normalizing cash flow, computing implied multiples, and evaluating the value driver formula for terminal value calculations, a couple of mechanical issues associated with computing the discounted cash flow in an annual model are addressed in the paragraphs that follow. To illustrate timing and discounting issues, assume that the value of a company after reaching the stable period is calculated by the normal stable growth model:

Terminal Value = [Free Cash Flow in Terminal Period

× (1 + Terminal Growth)]/(WACC − Terminal Growth)

This formula was previously introduced in the context of proving valuation concepts related to the bridge between equity value and enterprise value. The reason one plus the growth rate is in the numerator of the formula is due to the mathematics of discounting cash flows whereby an integration from zero to infinity is used. This comes from the mathematical fact that the value of a cash flow in perpetuity is the next period cash flow—not the current period cash flow—divided by the discount rate.

If an annual model is used for valuation and the standard NPV function is applied, then you are implicitly assuming that the cash flows all occur at the end of the year. This means that a company selling food would receive all of its revenues, pay all of its expenses, and incur all of its capital expenditures at midnight on December 31. Making this assumption is of course unrealistic and can result in valuation errors. Not all revenues suddenly occur on the last day of December of each year, and each valuation does not happen on the first day of January of the year. Cash flows actually occur in small increments, day by day or hour by hour. If your model uses annual periods, a reasonable approximation of continual cash flow is to assume that cash flows occur in the middle of the year as long as there is not too much seasonality. However, if the company were to be sold and valued at the end of some defined holding period, as is the assumption for terminal value, this cash flow does occur at a single point in time and not in small separate increments. If more realistic timing assumptions are made in a valuation model rather than end-of-year assumptions, the measured value of the company is increased.

To correctly incorporate timing of cash flows in a model, it can be helpful to draw a time line as shown in Figure 28.3. Laying out a time line seems to suggest that the discount factor should be different for the terminal value and the periodic cash flows because the terminal value comes in one period while the cash flows are modeled in the middle of the year.

You could work through the time line shown in Figure 28.3 and create different discount factors for the explicit cash flows and the terminal cash flow each time that you make a model. Alternatively, you can create a theoretical long-term model where the company is not sold, but it instead lasts for

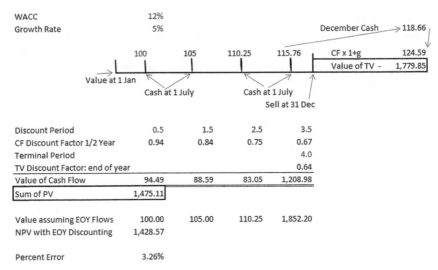

Discount Period	0.5	1.5	2.5	3.5
CF Discount Factor 1/2 Year	0.94	0.84	0.75	0.67
Terminal Period				4.0
TV Discount Factor: end of year				0.64
Value of Cash Flow	94.49	88.59	83.05	1,208.98
Sum of PV	1,475.11			
Value assuming EOY Flows	100.00	105.00	110.25	1,852.20
NPV with EOY Discounting	1,428.57			
Percent Error	3.26%			

FIGURE 28.3 Diagram of Time Line for Half-Year Discounting Convention in DCF Analysis

something like 300 years as introduced in Chapter 25. If the company is not sold and cash flows are always realized in the middle of the year, the value of the company should be the same as if you separately compute the present value of explicit period cash flows and the present value of terminal cash flow. This long-term theoretical exercise demonstrates that all of the business of midyear discounting ends up in a simple formula that can be implemented as follows:

- Compute the value of explicit cash flows and the value of the terminal value as if you were using the end-of-year cash flows, meaning that you can use the regular old NPV function.
- Multiply the final result by $(1 + WACC)^{.5}$ to adjust for the half-year assumption.

To demonstrate that this formula works, you can create a proof in the same manner for proving how items associated with the bridge between enterprise value and equity value should be treated. The value of cash flows in the long-term model establishes the theoretically correct value of the company. This is the same value that should be obtained from the sum of the terminal value and the value of the explicit cash flow. The value of the terminal cash flow as measured by the terminal value is in a sense just a shortcut, as the buyer at the terminal date should pay the theoretical long-term value. When you assume that the explicit cash flows occur at the middle of the period and the terminal value occurs at the end of the period, but the buyer makes a valuation from receipt of cash flow in the middle of the period, the valuation is the same as the simple formula shown earlier. Figure 28.4 illustrates how to prove that you can use end-of-year discounting and then adjust your final answer, multiplying by the factor $(1 + WACC)^{.5}$.

ABC	D	F	G	H	I	J	M	N	O
18	Timing								
19	Year	Periods	2014	2015	2016	2017	2020	2021	2022
20	Date of Cash Flow		01-janv-16	01-janv-16	01-juil-16	01-juil-17	01-juil-20	01-juil-21	01-juil-22
21	Terminal Period		FALSE	FALSE	FALSE	FALSE	FALSE	TRUE	FALSE
22	Explicit Period	6	FALSE	FALSE	TRUE	TRUE	TRUE	TRUE	FALSE
23	Valuation Period	299	FALSE	FALSE	TRUE	TRUE	TRUE	TRUE	TRUE
24	Short-term Growth Period	8	TRUE	TRUE	TRUE	TRUE	TRUE	TRUE	FALSE
25	Long-term Growth Period	293	FALSE	FALSE	FALSE	FALSE	FALSE	FALSE	TRUE
26									
27	Cash Flow and Valuation								
28	WACC	10%							
29	Growth Rate		20.00%	20.00%	20.00%	20.00%	20.00%	20.00%	3.00%
30	Cash Flow	100.0	120.0	144.0	172.8	207.4	358.3	430.0	442.9
31	Cash Flow for Valuation		FALSE	FALSE	172.8	207.4	358.3	430.0	442.9
32	NPV with EOY Assumption	4,755.92	<---- =NPV(F28,G31:KU31)			=IF(J23,J29)			
33	PV Factor	1.00	1.00	1.00	1.10	1.21	1.61	1.77	1.95
34	NPV Check	4,755.92	<---- =SUMPRODUCT(G31:KU31/G33:KU33)						
37	PV Factor with 1/2 Year		1.00	1.00	0.95	0.87	0.65	0.59	0.54
38	Long-term Value with 1/2 Year	4,988.05	<---- =SUMPRODUCT(G31:KU31*G37:KU37)			=1/(1+$F$28)^M36			
39	Cash Flow zeros in first period		0.00	0.00	172.80	207.36	358.32	429.98	442.88
40	Check with XNPV	4,983.90	<---- =XNPV(F28,G39:KU39,G20:KU20)						
41	Apply the Adjustment to EOY	4,988.05	<---- =F34*(1+F28)^E14						
42									
43	Application of TV		=NPV($F$28,G44:KU44)						
44	Expicit Cash Flow Value (EOY)	1,184.56	FALSE	FALSE	172.80	207.36	358.32	429.98	FALSE
45	Terminal Value	3,571.36	FALSE	FALSE	0.00	0.00	0.00	6,326.87	FALSE
46	Enterprise Value (EOY)	4,755.92							
47									
48	Timing Adjustment (1+WACC)^.5	4,988.05	<---- =F46*(1+$F$28)^0.5						

FIGURE 28.4 Illustration of Model That Proves the Half-Year Convention Should Be Made Using the Formula $(1 + WACC)^{.5}$

Computing Value with Changing Weighted Average Cost of Capital and a Midyear Convention

The preceding example works well when the weighted average cost of capital (WACC) is constant in each period, but not if the WACC varies over time. WACC should not in theory change when the capital structure changes but it could change if different inflation rates are input or a sensible assumption is made that the risk is lower when things are assumed to stabilize. When the WACC changes, you cannot use the formula $1/(1+WACC)^{period}$ to discount cash flows in different periods. This formula has no memory of prior cash flows and does not account for changes in WACC that occurred in earlier periods. If there was a high rate of inflation in the past or if the risk has changed, the value of prospective cash flows depends on the prior value that has already been discounted. Instead of using the old-fashioned discount factor, you should create a compound index using the same process as you apply for an inflation index. In this case you can just use the changing WACC rather than the changing inflation rate. Then, when you compute the present value (NPV) of the cash flow, apply the SUMPRODUCT function with a divide sign as illustrated next. Note that the Excel explanation of the SUMPRODUCT formula does not include the operators like multiply and divide even though they are much more effective than the comma operator. Allowing multiplication and division operators makes the SUMPRODUCT a much better tool:

NPV = SUMPRODUCT(Cash Flow Array/Compound WACC Index Array)

Applying a midyear cash flow assumption together with a changing WACC is a little more challenging than if you are using a midyear convention with a constant cost of capital. With changing WACC, the compounding formula should include half of the current-year WACC and half of the prior-year WACC. To implement the half-year convention, in the very first year the prior-year WACC is zero. Further, when applying the half-year WACC you should account for partial-year compounding to be precise. Formulas for computing the compound discount rate include:

Half-Year Discount Rate with Compounding $= (1+WACC)^{\hat{}}.5 - 1$

Compound Factor$_t$ = Compound Factor$_{t-1}$ × (1 + Half-Year Rate$_t$)

$\times$ (1 + Half-Year Rate$_{t-1}$)

When computing the terminal value, the normal formula $CF \times (1+g)/(WACC-g)$ can be used, but it must be discounted to the present using the compound factor just shown. As with the simple case where the WACC does not change, the efficacy of the method can be demonstrated through creating a theoretically true value in a long-term model. An excerpt from this sort of analysis along with a display of the various formulas is shown in Figure 28.5. The bottom part of Figure 28.5 shows that if you apply the SUMPRODUCT formula with the compound discount factor along with the standard terminal value formula, you arrive at the theoretically correct value.

	D	E	G	H	I	J	K	M	O	P
19	Timing									
20	Year	Periods		2014	2015	2016	2017	2019	2021	2022
22	Terminal Period	1		FALSE	FALSE	FALSE	FALSE	FALSE	TRUE	FALSE
23	Explicit Period	8		TRUE	TRUE	TRUE	TRUE	TRUE	TRUE	FALSE
24	Valuation Period	301		TRUE	TRUE	TRUE	TRUE	TRUE	TRUE	TRUE
25	Short-term Growth Period	8		TRUE	TRUE	TRUE	TRUE	TRUE	TRUE	FALSE
26	Long-term Growth Period	293		FALSE	FALSE	FALSE	FALSE	FALSE	FALSE	TRUE
27	Year Counter			1	2	3	4	6	8	9
28	Theoretically True Value									
29	Growth Rate			20.00%	20.00%	20.00%	20.00%	20.00%	20.00%	3.00%
30	WACC			25.00%	25.00%	25.00%	25.00%	12.00%	8.00%	8.00%
31	1/2 Year WACC			11.80%	11.80%	11.80%	11.80%	5.83%	3.92%	3.92%
32				=(1+J30)^0.5-1						
33	Cash Flow		100.00	120.00	144.00	172.80	207.36	298.60	429.98	442.88
34	Incorrect PV Factor	=1/(1+H30)^H27 ----->		0.80	0.64	0.51	0.41	0.51	0.54	0.50
35	Compound PV Factor	=G35*(1+H30) --	1.00	1.25	1.56	1.95	2.44	3.06	3.57	3.86
36	PV of Cash Flow/Varying WACC	3,258.44	<----- =SUMPRODUCT(H33:KV33/H35:KV35)							
37	PV Factor for Middle of Year		1	1.12	1.40	1.75	2.18	2.89	3.44	3.71
38	True Value of Cash Flow	3,418.36	<----- =SUMPRODUCT(H33:KV33/H37:KV37)			=J37*(1+J31)*(1+K31)				
39										
40	Replication of Value with Teminal Value			=SUMPRODUCT(H41:KV41/H37:KV37)						
41	Explict Value	841.42		120.00	144.00	172.80	207.36	298.60	429.98	FALSE
42	Terminal Flows			0.00	0.00	0.00	0.00	0.00	8,857.62	0.00
43				=H41*(1+$E$4)/(H30-$E$4)*H22						
44	Terminal Value Std Formula	2,576.95	<----- =SUMPRODUCT(H42:KV42/H37:KV37)							
45	Enterprise Value	3,418.36	<----- =SUM(E41:E44)							

FIGURE 28.5 Excerpt from Long-Term Analysis with Changing WACC and Midyear Convention

CHAPTER 29

Normalizing Terminal Year Cash Flows for Stable Working Capital Investment

The next few chapters consider various adjustments to normalized cash flow in the terminal period that should be made to accurately measure value when growth rates change from short-term assumptions to long-term steady rates and when rates of return on investment are assumed to stabilize. If you review articles about valuation, you can comb the Internet and find hundreds of references to normalizing cash flow in the terminal period. But it is difficult to find anybody who explains exactly how you should compute this normalized cash flow in practice. Instead, you typically just come accross some general language about cash flow being at a steady level. This chapter introduces the notion of using stable relationships to determine normalized cash flow. The effects of stable relationships that can be used to derive normalized cash flow and that result from changing growth and rate of return come into play in addressing various issues. The stable ratios are used in normalizing cash flow in the terminal period, computing terminal value using the value driver formula $(1 - g/\text{ROIC})/(\text{WACC} - g)$, and deriving implied price/earnings (P/E) and enterprise value/earnings before interest, taxes, depreciation, and amortization (EV/EBITDA) ratios.

To understand both the valuation theory and the modeling mechanics involving changes that move from a growth rate in the explicit period to a stable growth rate, it is convenient to begin the discussion with working capital (WC) and then proceed to capital expenditures, depreciation, and deferred taxes. Working capital investment is simpler to analyze than capital expenditures, depreciation, and deferred taxes because the change in working capital is a function only of current and the last period revenues and expenses. This contrasts with depreciation and capital expenditures, where a change in growth in capital expenditures affects depreciation expense for an entire future life span of plant. Once the modeling of working capital is established, you will have a stepping-stone to understand the more difficult issues associated with depreciation, capital expenditures, and deferred taxes.

Effect of Changes in Growth on Working Capital Investment, Capital Expenditures, Depreciation, and Deferred Taxes

When the growth rate in revenue and expense changes as a result of the philosophy that companies will reach a state of stable equilibrium, analysts sometimes do not assume that other items of cash flow, including working capital movement and capital expenditures, change to support different EBITDA growth rates. In the explicit forecast period, capital expenditures and working capital investment are made to support the EBITDA growth. Over the long term, increased growth in EBITDA can occur only if capital expenditures and working capital investment are made to support that growth. When the growth rate in EBITDA changes, the investment made to maintain the changing growth should also change. An assumption that capital investment and working capital investment remain at levels that were consistent with growth during the explicit period, even though the prospective and stable EBITDA has a different (generally lower) growth rate, creates a number of inconsistencies that can distort valuation.

When you make errors in logic with respect to normalized cash flow in the terminal period, working capital investment and capital expenditures are wrong from the terminal period to infinity. If the revenues grow at a slower rate after the explicit forecast period, then the rate of EBITDA also slows, which means that less working capital investment and lower capital expenditures are required to support the slower EBITDA growth. Further, with lower capital expenditures, there will be less deferred taxes. Accurately modeling the manner in which investment changes when growth rate changes should be an essential part of the modeling and valuation process. In the standard free cash formula defined as EBITDA less working capital changes less capital expenditures less operating tax less change in deferred tax, each of the four items that are subtracted from EBITDA should be normalized to be consistent with the terminal growth rate of EBITDA along with the WACC.

When creating a corporate financial model, the normal assumption is that if revenues and income change, the working capital changes in a direct linear manner as a function of revenues. Most of the time accounts receivable are modeled as a percentage of revenues, and many operating costs are also expressed as a percentage of revenues. This implies that if accounts payable and inventories are related to expenses, they also move in direct proportion to revenues. All of this means that if the growth rate in revenues slows, then the growth of working capital investment will also slow. Errors in modeling normalized working capital changes in the terminal year can occur if in the last year of the explicit forecast period, the revenue growth that drives working capital change does not reflect the new terminal growth rate. But the working capital investment in the future will decline if the terminal growth rate is lower than the growth rate in the explicit period. The decline in revenues from the lower terminal growth rate is reflected in the valuation because the total free cash flow, including working capital investment and everything else, implicitly grows at the terminal growth rate when the formula Terminal Value = Final Year Cash Flow × (1 + Terminal Growth)/(WACC − Terminal Growth) is applied. Nothing in this formula adjusts for the prospective lower investment in working capital associated with the lower growth rate. If the working capital investment is not normalized, a downward bias in valuation arises because the growth rate declines and working capital investment does not move in a commensurate manner. Working capital changes in the terminal year cash flow must be consistent with prospective working capital changes that will occur to support the lower terminal growth rate.

To illustrate the problem of not normalizing terminal cash flow for stable working capital, say that revenue growth is 50 percent in the final explicit forecast year, and assume this results in a revenue level of 150 for cash flow at the end of the year. Also assume that (1) the terminal growth is 3 percent, (2) the company has only revenues and accounts receivable, and (3) the increase in working capital resulting from the revenue increase in the final explicit period with high growth is 50. In this example, the cash flow in the final year subtracts a large number associated with investment in working capital that is derived from the last explicit year's projected 50 percent growth. If the standard perpetuity formula is applied to the last explicit year cash flow, the revenues of 150 less working capital investment of 50 is implicitly assumed to grow at 3 percent. This means the 150 revenues are assumed to grow at 3 percent and also the working capital investment of 50 is assumed to grow at 3 percent. In fact, if revenues grow by only 3 percent, the working capital investment will be much less than 50, meaning the starting base of net cash flow after working capital change that grows at 3 percent should be higher. To solve this problem, you should create a separate calculation for the normalized terminal year cash flow that includes an adjusted amount for the working capital investment.

Developing a Simple Equation for Normalizing Working Capital

A relatively simple formula can be developed to normalize working capital changes in the terminal year. If assumptions for the days accounts receivable, days accounts payable, days of inventory, and the operating margin are constant, then the level of working capital relative to EBITDA will also be constant. With the constant ratio of working capital to EBITDA, the working capital in two different periods can be expressed as:

$$\text{Working Capital}_{t-1} = \text{Working Capital/EBITDA} \times \text{EBITDA}_{t-1}$$

and

$$\text{Working Capital}_t = \text{Working Capital/EBITDA} \times \text{EBITDA}_{t-1} \times (1 + \text{Growth})$$

These two formulas can be combined to derive the amount of working capital changes as a function of growth:

$$\text{Working Capital Change} = \text{Working Capital/EBITDA}$$
$$\times [\text{EBITDA}_{t-1} \times (1 + \text{Growth}) - \text{EBITDA}_{t-1}]$$

or

$$\text{Working Capital Change} = \text{Working Capital/EBITDA} \times \text{EBITDA}_{t-1} \times \text{Growth}$$

Substituting $\text{EBITDA}_t/(1 + \text{Growth})$ for EBITDA_{t-1} gives:

$$\text{Working Capital Change} = \text{Working Capital/EBITDA} \times \text{EBITDA}_t$$
$$\times \text{Growth}/(1 + \text{Growth})$$

This formula for working capital change can be applied in a corporate financial model to normalize working capital for changes in terminal growth.

When implementing this formula in your model, the normalized free cash flow for purposes of computing terminal value is different from the last year explicit period cash flow. The normalized cash flow should include the working capital change from the preceding formula where the growth rate is the terminal growth rather than the last period working capital computed from the explicit period cash flow. However, cash flows during the explicit period remain the same and include the working capital change that is driven by cash flow in the last period that is modeled.

To demonstrate that this formula appropriately normalizes cash flow you can create a long-term proof in a similar manner as was used to verify other issues. In establishing the proof, make one scenario where the model continues for a couple of hundred years and the true theoretical value is derived from the long-term cash flow. In this long-term simulation you should include changing growth rates where the explicit period growth rate is modeled for a few years and then the terminal growth occurs for all of the remaining years.

The changing growth rates drive revenues and EBITDA as well as the level of working capital. Working capital investment is modeled as the change in the working capital balance. Once you have established the long-term model, using the same assumptions, you can simulate an explicit period and a terminal value with no adjustment for normalizing working capital investment. This will show that the valuation is biased. Finally, you can create a third case that normalizes working capital changes in the terminal period using the formula shown earlier. This will demonstrate that the normalized cash flow produces the same value as the first theoretical case that simulated cash flow for hundreds of years after a changed growth rate.

The following few steps demonstrate how to develop a model that contains such as a proof. If you work through this theoretical model you will be able to apply many of the same ideas in the valuation analysis that is part of a standard corporate model.

Step 1   Start by creating a long-term model to compute the theoretical true value after a change in growth rates. Include growth rates that change from a high rate in the explicit period to a low terminal growth rate. You can use a short-term switch and a long-term switch as in many of the other examples. With the switches defined, compute revenues, working capital level, and the change in working capital using the changing growth rates. Calculate free cash flow from revenues less working capital changes and discount free cash flow over the entire period to compute the true value.

Step 2   Use the growth rate and working capital inputs to compute valuation with a terminal period and no stable period adjustment. Add switches for the explicit period and the terminal period, and then compute value from the explicit period cash flow plus the terminal value rather than over the entire long-term period. Calculate the explicit period value using the explicit period switch multiplied by the cash flow established in step 1. Compute the terminal value using the terminal value switch, the perpetuity formula, and the terminal year cash flow. The discounted present value computed from this method produces a lower number than the true theoretical value established from the long period model in step 1.

Step 3   Use the same explicit period and terminal period switches from step 2, but add a calculation for the normalized working capital change in the terminal value cash flow using the formula:

$$\text{Working Capital Change} = \text{Working Capital}/\text{EBITDA} \times \text{EBITDA}$$
$$\times \text{Terminal Growth}/(1 + \text{Terminal Growth})$$

Add a line for the terminal year cash flow by using the EBITDA in the terminal year but replacing the working capital change with the amount computed from the working capital equation to normalize cash flow in the terminal period. Do not change any of the explicit cash flow calculations. When the present value of the terminal value is recomputed and the present value of explicit cash flows are added to the terminal value computed using the normalized cash flow, the total value is the same as the theoretically correct value established in step 1.

Figure 29.1 illustrates results of this step-by-step process. The valuations show that the true value of the corporation is obtained when the normalized adjustment is made and that the valuation is biased if the non-normalized free cash flow from the explicit period is used. In Figure 29.1, the terminal period is shaded using conditional formatting. This formatting is made by using the formula option and putting in the terminal value switch with a relative

Timing										
Period		0	1	2	3	8	9	10	11	12
Explicit Period			TRUE	TRUE	TRUE	TRUE	TRUE	TRUE	FALSE	FALSE
Terminal Period			FALSE	FALSE	FALSE	FALSE	FALSE	TRUE	FALSE	FALSE
Short-term Growth Period			TRUE	TRUE	TRUE	TRUE	TRUE	TRUE	FALSE	FALSE
Long-term Growth Period			FALSE	FALSE	FALSE	FALSE	FALSE	FALSE	TRUE	TRUE
Theoretical Value										
Growth Rate			30%	30%	30%	30%	30%	30%	2%	2%
Revenues		100	130.0	169.0	219.7	815.7	1,060.4	1,378.6	1,406.2	1,434.3
Operating Expense	20%		104.0	135.2	175.8	652.6	848.4	1,102.9	1,124.9	1,147.4
A/R Level	25%	25.00	32.5	42.3	54.9	203.9	265.1	344.6	351.5	358.6
Change in Working Capital			7.50	9.75	12.68	47.06	61.18	79.53	6.89	7.03
Free Cash Flow			18.5	24.1	31.3	116.1	150.9	196.2	274.3	279.8
PV of Free Cash Flow - True 1,721.26										
Valuation using Terminal Value without Stable Period Adjustment										
Explicit Cash Flow	399.14		18.5	24.1	31.3	116.1	150.9	196.2	FALSE	FALSE
Terminal Cash Flow	964.37		0.0	0.0	0.0	0.0	0.0	2,501.3	FALSE	FALSE
EV - No Normalization	**1,363.51**									
Valuation using Terminal Value with Stable Period Adjustment										
WC to EBITDA			1.25	1.25	1.25	1.25	1.25	1.25	1.25	1.25
Terminal Growth	2%		2%	2%	2%	2%	2%	2%	2%	2%
Stable WC Change			0.64	0.83	1.08	4.00	5.20	6.76	6.89	7.03
Stable Cash Flow	10%		25.36	32.97	42.86	159.15	206.89	268.96	274.34	279.83
Terminal Cash Flow	1,322.12		0.00	0.00	0.00	0.00	0.00	3,429.23	0.00	0.00
Explcit Cash Flow	399.14									
Total EV with Adjustment	**1,721.26**									

FIGURE 29.1 Excerpt from Theoretical Model Demonstrating the Importance of Normalizing Working Capital Investment

reference (fixing the row number) after shading the whole area where the calculations are made.

Incorporating Terminal Period Normalized Cash Flow in a Corporate Model

Once the formula for the stable ratio of working capital changes derived from the terminal growth rate, the working capital-to-EBITDA ratio, and EBITDA has been established, the normalized working capital can be incorporated into a corporate model. This can be done in a transparent and flexible manner using the terminal value switch. The normalized cash flow calculation should accept different explicit time period assumptions, with different working capital assumptions, different stable growth rates, and different EBITDA projections. In structuring a corporate model so that it can be changed to allow different timing, normalized cash flow, and terminal growth assumptions, a good presentation is important. A few ideas for computing and presenting normalized cash flow are illustrated in Figure 29.2:

- You can create an input variable that is TRUE or FALSE to apply the normalized or unadjusted cash flows in computing the terminal value.

Timing				2011	2012	2013	2014	2015	2016	2017
Year	Base case ▼									
Historic switch	2012			TRUE	TRUE	FALSE	FALSE	FALSE	FALSE	FALSE
Explicit period	2017			FALSE	FALSE	TRUE	TRUE	TRUE	TRUE	TRUE
Terminal value switch				FALSE	FALSE	FALSE	FALSE	FALSE	FALSE	TRUE
				TRUE	TRUE	TRUE	TRUE	TRUE	TRUE	TRUE
Enterprise Value Module										
EBITDA				143,608.00	77,298.00	146,532.49	196,207.00	200,131.14	206,135.07	212,319.13
Less: capital expenditures				-123,530.00	-67,720.00	-87,919.49	-90,557.08	-92,368.22	-95,139.26	-97,993.44
Less: working capital changes				-66,410.00	140,902.00	-136,428.63	-4,571.81	482.97	738.95	761.11
Add: increases in Provisions				-2,998.00	-1,252.00	3,708.80	1,055.03	724.46	1,108.42	1,141.67
Less: taxes on EBIT				-12,460.40	898.20	-14,180.30	-23,817.38	-24,506.44	-25,325.14	-26,417.95
Add: Changes in Deferred Tax										
Free cash flow				-61,790.40	150,126.20	-88,287.14	78,315.77	84,463.91	87,518.03	89,810.52
Capex/depreciation				1.72	0.91	1.18	1.19	1.20	1.20	1.22
Working Capital to EBITDA				-19%	-217%	-21%	-14%	-14%	-14%	-13%
EBIT				62,302.00	-4,491.00	70,901.48	119,086.88	122,532.21	126,625.72	132,089.76
NOPAT=EBIT(1-t)				49,841.60	-3,592.80	56,721.18	95,269.51	98,025.76	101,300.58	105,671.81
Working Capital				-26,709.00	-167,611.00	-31,182.37	-26,610.55	-27,093.52	-27,832.47	-28,593.58
NPV of explicit cashflow	185,641.13			FALSE	FALSE	-88,287.14	78,315.77	84,463.91	87,518.03	89,810.52
Normalized WC	-13%	-0.13%		0.00	0.00	0.00	0.00	0.00	0.00	38.13
Normalized Cap Exp	40.45%	40.21	3.00%	0.00	0.00	0.00	0.00	0.00	0.00	87,752.13
Normalized taxes	20%			0.00	0.00	0.00	0.00	0.00	0.00	26,449.59
Normalized cash flow				0.00	0.00	0.00	0.00	0.00	0.00	98,079.28
Cash Flow for Terminal Value	TRUE			0.00	0.00	0.00	0.00	0.00	0.00	98,079.28
NPV of terminal value / growth r	1,177,141.0	7%		FALSE	FALSE	0.00	0.00	0.00	0.00	1,651,001.20

FIGURE 29.2 Illustration of Incorporating Normalized Terminal Cash Flow in a Corporate Model

This way you can demonstrate the effects of applying the techniques to normalize cash flow. In Figure 29.2 the terminal value column has a different shading.

- Include rows that show the EBITDA, the working capital, and the ratio of EBITDA to working capital, as well as the terminal growth rate that are drivers for the stable ratio calculation. Alternatively, you can include the drivers such as the ratios of working capital to EBITDA, capital expenditures to depreciation, or deferred tax to capital expenditures in a column to the left. This is illustrated in Figure 29.2.
- Add a separate line for the normalized working capital change that is computed from the formula WC/EBITDA $\times$ EBITDA $\times$ $g/(1 + g)$.
- Include a section in your valuation analysis for displaying normalized cash flow separately from cash flow over the explicit period.

The row in Figure 29.2 titled "Normalized Working Capital" illustrates that you should think about each line item of the free cash flow calculation when normalizing cash flow. The normalized EBITDA should be consistent with a sustainable return on invested capital.

CHAPTER 30

Relationship of Growth, Capital Expenditures, Depreciation, and Return on Investment

If you could come up with formulas for normalized depreciation expense, capital expenditures, and deferred tax in the same sort of way that the stable working capital formula was derived in Chapter 29, computing normalized cash flow would be a straightforward process. You could then make a routine adjustment in the valuation section of your corporate models through adding normalized calculations for working capital, capital expenditures, and deferred taxes in the terminal free cash flow calculation. Similar types of adjustments could be made in using these types of formulas for stable ratios to compute implicit valuation multiples and in evaluating the value driver formula. Unfortunately, while the approach of applying a formula can be used for working capital changes, finding easy formulas to apply for capital expenditures and deferred taxes is more complex. The difficulty arises because of the manner in which changes in growth influence prospective levels of depreciation and because capital expenditures have a lifetime that is more than one year.

Because a simple one-line formula for normalized capital expenditure cannot be developed, the ultimate objective of this chapter is to come up with an easy-to-apply user-defined function for the ratio of capital expenditures to depreciation expense. With such a function that you can pop into any corporate model from information that is readily available from financial reports, the process of making normalized adjustments can be manageable. This function can be programmed to accept the historical growth rate, the weighted average cost of capital (WACC), future growth, and the plant life to compute a ratio of capital to depreciation that is used to compute terminal cash flow. The remainder of this chapter explains how you can create two user-defined functions that will derive the stable level of capital expenditures that accomplish this. These functions, which will be documented in detail next, are:

Historical Growth = Find_Growth(Accumulated Depreciation to
Gross Plant, Plant Life)

Stable Capital Expenditures to Depreciation = Stable_Cap_Exp(Historical
Growth, Future Growth, Plant Life, WACC)

You can use these two functions in the left-hand columns of the valuation section of your financial model to establish the stable level of capital expenditures to depreciation. Then you can include stable ratios for working capital changes as well as stable capital expenditures in deriving normalized terminal cash flow. In Chapter 31, similar adjustments are discussed for computing normalized deferred tax changes. The subject of how to develop functions that compute normalized capital expenditures and depreciation expense does not apply only to stable ratios in the free cash flow analysis. A similar problem requiring these functions arises in computing the implicit enterprise value/earnings before interest, taxes, depreciation, and amortization (EV/EBITDA) ratio given the value drivers and to correct for major flaws in the value driver formula $(1 - g/ROIC)/(WACC - g)$. As with other corporate valuation problems discussed in previous chapters, the user-defined functions are verified by developing a theoretical long-term analysis. The big challenge in this process is to derive the function that correctly accounts for changes in growth between the explicit modeled period and the terminal period.

The Long-Term Stable Ratio of Capital Expenditures to Depreciation and the Ratio of Depreciation Expense to Net Plant

The general question of how to compute capital expenditures in a corporate model is important in valuation, particularly in the terminal period. Some level of capital expenditures is needed to generate the EBITDA in virtually any model. The capital expenditures should be consistent with the assumed long-term stable growth rate in the same way that the working capital investment is necessary to earn income. If capital expenditures in the past few years have been relatively low, perhaps because of surplus capacity, and you assume that the future capital expenditures will be consistent with the recent past, then your valuation will be too high because the EBITDA cannot grow over an indefinite period from this base of low capital expenditures. In contrast, if the capital expenditures are high during the explicit period and they are assumed to continue to grow from the high base, assuming that the EBITDA will decline along with the terminal growth assumption will produce a valuation that is too low. This is because the level of capital expenditures subtracted from free cash flow would support a higher growth rate in EBITDA. The difficult question is if and how this mysterious level of sustainable capital expenditures for purposes of normalizing cash flow can be computed from available financial data.

When deriving a stable level of capital expenditures, it is often convenient to express the capital expenditures as a percentage of depreciation expense. The ratio of capital expenditures to sales or the ratio of capital expenditures to EBITDA could also be computed, but these ratios depend on the return on investment. If the return on investment is higher, for example, then the ratios imply a lower level of capital expenditures relative to EBITDA. To understand the relationship between capital expenditures and depreciation, consider a case where a company does not grow in nominal terms. In this case the depreciation expense just covers the amount of money that is required to replace retiring assets. If the level of periodic capital expenditures is equal to the depreciation expense in this no-growth case and the return on investment remains constant, then the capital expenditures that are equivalent to depreciation will support the continuing nongrowing level of EBITDA. When a company is growing in nominal terms, the capital expenditures should be greater than the depreciation expense. Here, the future capital expenditures include the replacement of assets as well as increases in capital expenditures resulting from the requirement to allow growth in EBITDA. This occurs even if the growth is only related to inflation, because the depreciation expense measures past expenditures, and the new capital expenditures to replace retiring assets are expressed in nominal current currency.

To rectify errors that can arise because of using the final-year capital expenditures that come from the explicit period in a model, analysts sometimes assume that a level of capital expenditures equal to depreciation will sustain the EBITDA growth. This means that in the terminal year you would compute the capital expenditures directly from the depreciation expense. While this may seem to be too simple a rule of thumb, it does have some logic. If there were no growth in EBITDA, which is not so different from a low inflation rate assumption, the plant balance should be sufficient to maintain the EBITDA. This process of setting capital expenditures equal to depreciation demonstrates the importance of making an accurate forecast of depreciation expense that is discussed in Chapter 9.

There are a few problems in simply equating depreciation and capital expenditures for purposes of developing normalized cash flow. First, if inflation and growth have occurred in the past, the depreciation expense may overstate or understate the required replacement capital expenditures. Replacement of assets involve looking backward to prior capital expenditures. Equating capital expenditures with depreciation only works if there has been no growth in the past because the timing of retirements that result from replacing existing capital can affect the future requirements. This means that if low levels of retirements occur in the upcoming years because of high past growth, implying that plant is relatively new, the capital expenditures could be overstated if they are equated to depreciation. Finally, if the nominal growth rate in EBITDA is above zero, the capital expenditures should exceed the depreciation expense.

Developing a formula to compute the sustainable ratio of capital expenditures to depreciation after a full life cycle of plant is analogous to deriving the sustainable payout ratio from the growth rate in earnings [Dividend payout ratio = $(1 - g/ROE)$] or computing the stable ratio of working capital ratio changes [WC Change = WC/EBITDA $\times$ EBITDA $\times g/(1 + g)$] discussed in Chapter 29. The formula for prospective growth in assets can be derived as follows:

$$\text{Growth} = \text{Depreciation Rate on Net Plant}$$
$$\times (\text{Capital Expenditures}/\text{Depreciation} - 1)$$

The retention rate formula is much more useful when it is rearranged as dividend payout ratio = 1 − growth/ROE. Similarly, it is useful to rearrange the capital expenditures growth formula. You can then compute the ratio of capital expenditures to depreciation as a function of the net depreciation rate and the growth rate. Note that the formula does not work with the gross depreciation rate. Unlike the gross depreciation rate which is simply 1 divided by the lifetime of the assets, the net depreciation rate depends on the age of the plant. If there was no issue about earlier capital expenditures resulting in different replacement requirements and if you could easily establish the net plant depreciation rate, then you could stop with this formula for the stable ratio:

$$\text{Capital Expenditures}/\text{Depreciation} = \text{Growth}/\text{Net Depreciation Rate} + 1$$

This formula implies that if the stable growth rate is 0, then the ratio of capital expenditures to depreciation is equal to unity. If the stable growth rate is positive, then the ratio is above 1. As the depreciation rate is lower with a longer plant life, the ratio of capital expenditures to depreciation is greater for long-lived assets than for short-lived assets. Say the lifetime of assets is only one year, implying a depreciation rate of 100 percent. In this case the formula for capital expenditures to depreciation expense becomes 1 plus the growth rate. This result is intuitive because the capital expenditures must cover the retirements from the past year, but they must also increase by the growth rate required to support the additional EBITDA.

One problem with the formula (*g*/net depreciation rate + 1) is that you probably do not know the net depreciation rate. The gross depreciation rate, which is 1 divided by the asset life for straight-line depreciation, cannot be used in the formula. The net depreciation rate is not constant across the life of a plant like the gross depreciation rate. The net depreciation rate becomes larger as a plant ages. This is like comparing the depreciation of an old man to that of a teenager. Because things in your body fall apart as you age, you depreciate. This depreciation can be divided by the state of your body as a healthy young teenager, which is the gross rate. Alternatively, the rate can be computed by the current state of your body, which is the net depreciation rate. As you become old, the net depreciation rate approaches 100 percent because there is not much left of your body. You may depreciate by the same amount, but the net rate is much larger when you get old. The net plant depreciation rate is always greater than or equal to the gross plant depreciation rate because the net plant is defined as the gross amount spent for capital expenditures less the accumulated depreciation. For a portfolio of assets, the net depreciation rate depends on the growth rate, which drives the age of the portfolio, whereas the gross depreciation rate is independent of growth. If the growth rate is very high and assets are relatively new like the young population of a country, the depreciation on net plant approaches the depreciation rate on gross plant, but if the growth rate is low, the depreciation rate on net plant can be much higher than the depreciation rate on gross plant.

To compute the stable rate of capital expenditures to depreciation using different growth rate assumptions, you can create a relatively simple user-defined function that derives the net depreciation rate as a function of growth. The net depreciation rate depends on two things: (1) the life of the plant and (2) the growth rate in capital expenditures. Computing the net depreciation rate as a function of the growth rate and the plant life can be accomplished by making a little model and working through a life cycle of plant where the capital expenditures continue to grow over the lifetime of an investment. Once the life cycle is finished and old assets are replaced by new assets, the retirements of plant offset the new additions. Eventually, the net plant depreciation rate reaches a stable level so long as the growth rate does not change. This stable net plant depreciation rate can be converted to a user-defined function that uses the life of the plant and the growth rate as inputs.

After deriving a function for the net depreciation rate you can compute the ratio of capital expenditures to depreciation. All you have to do is input the growth and the plant life in a function for net depreciation and then use the formula capital expenditures to depreciation = growth/net depreciation rate + 1. Before deriving the user-defined function for establishing the net depreciation rate, a theoretical long-term model is be used to demonstrate the process. To compute the relationship between capital expenditures and depreciation and other problems associated with capital assets, a life cycle model verifies the capital expenditures to depreciation formula and the net plant depreciation function. The model can be extended indefinitely, but it shows that all sorts of ratios stabilize at the end of the life cycle of the plant as long as the growth rate does not change.

To set up a capital asset model, begin with capital expenditures that grow continually and then compute retirements from the lagged level of capital expenditures. Next, simulate future retirements as the time lag in capital expenditures. Retirements cannot be computed until a full life cycle of plant has completed. The first part of a formula for retirements should be an IF statement to test whether the year is greater than the life of the plant because before the first plant life cycle is complete, there are no retirements related to the capital expenditures. But when the year of the model is greater than or equal to the lifetime of the asset, the retirements can begin. After the first life cycle is complete, retirements should look backward from the current year by the length of the life of the plant. Looking backward can be accomplished by using the OFFSET function that begins with a reference cell and moves up or down and backward or forward from that cell. For computing retirements, the OFFSET formula can be used as follows, assuming that the capital expenditures are in the line above the retirements:

Prospective Retirements = IF(Year >= Asset Life, OFFSET(Current Cell, -1,
-Asset Life))

Alternatively, the OFFSET function can start with the capital expenditures row as follows:

Prospective Retirements = IF(Year>= Asset Life, OFFSET(Capital Expenditure,
0, -Asset Life))

Once retirements are established, the gross plant balance can be defined as the opening balance plus new capital expenditures less the retirements. Depreciation expense can then be calculated as the gross plant balance divided by the plant life. As with the gross plant balance, the balance of accumulated depreciation can be computed once the retirements are known. The accumulated depreciation balance is defined as the opening balance of the accumulated depreciation balance plus the depreciation expense and less the retirements. Finally, once the gross plant balance and the accumulated depreciation balances are derived, the net plant balance is the gross investment balance less the accumulated depreciation. These formulas for computing balances of plant and depreciation given the retirements are:

$$\text{Gross Plant}_t = \text{Gross Plant}_{t-1} + \text{Capital Expenditures} - \text{Retirement}$$

$$\text{Depreciation Expense} = \text{Gross Plant}_{t-1}/\text{Plant Life}$$

$$\text{Accumulated Depreciation} = \text{Accumulated Depreciation}_{t-1}$$
$$+ \text{Depreciation Expense} - \text{Retirement}$$

$$\text{Net Plant} = \text{Gross Plant} - \text{Accumulated Depreciation}$$

With the balance of net plant established you can compute the ratio of net plant to depreciation and the ratio of capital expenditures to depreciation. The model excerpt in Figure 30.1 demonstrates that these two ratios stabilize after a life cycle of plant. In addition to the ratio of capital expenditures to depreciation,

	A B	C	D	E	F	G	H	I	J	K
6	Assumptions									
7	Growth			10.00%						
8	Life			5						
9	Net Plant Depreciation Rate			31.35%						
10	Cap Exp/Depreciation			131.90%						
11	Timing Code			1.00		=IF(I13>=$E$8,OFFSET(I17,0,-$E$8))				
12										
13	Period		0	1	2	3	4	5	6	7
14	Capital Expenidture		100.0	110.0	121.0	133.1	146.4	161.1	177.2	194.9
15	Plant Balance									
16	Opening Balance			100.0	210.0	331.0	464.1	610.5	671.6	738.7
17	Add: Cap Exp		100.0	110.0	121.0	133.1	146.4	161.1	177.2	194.9
18	Less: Retirements			FALSE	FALSE	FALSE	FALSE	100.0	110.0	121.0
19	Closing Balance		100.0	210.0	331.0	464.1	610.5	671.6	738.7	812.6
20										
21	Depreciation		0.0	20.0	42.0	66.2	92.8	122.1	134.3	147.7
22										
23	Accumulated Depreciation									
24	Opening Balance			0.0	20.0	62.0	128.2	221.0	243.1	267.4
25	Add: Deprecation Expense			20.0	42.0	66.2	92.8	122.1	134.3	147.7
26	Less: Retirements			FALSE	FALSE	FALSE	FALSE	100.0	110.0	121.0
27	Closing Balance		0.0	20.0	62.0	128.2	221.0	243.1	267.4	294.2
28										
29	Net Plant		100.0	190.0	269.0	335.9	389.5	428.4	471.3	518.4
30										
31	Cap Exp/Depreciation			550.0%	288.1%	201.1%	157.7%	131.9%	131.9%	131.9%
32	Net Plant Depreciation Rate			20.0%	22.1%	24.6%	27.6%	31.3%	31.3%	31.3%
33	Acc Dep/Gross Plant			0%	10%	19%	28%	36%	36%	36%

FIGURE 30.1 Capital Asset Simulation Showing Stable Ratios after Five-Year Period Assuming 10 Percent Growth Rate

other ratios including the ratio of depreciation to net plant, the ratio of capital expenditures to net plant, and the ratio of capital expenditures to EBITDA can be computed. Figure 30.1 illustrates how the ratio of capital expenditures to depreciation, the ratio of net plant to depreciation, and the ratio of accumulated depreciation to gross plant all stabilize to constant ratios after the five-year period that is the defined five-year life. Driven by the assumed 10 percent growth rate, the ratio of capital expenditures to depreciation stabilizes at 132 percent.

Instead of computing the ratios with a model like that shown in Figure 30.1, you can make a function that does all of the calculations and puts the output into one single cell. The function uses plant life and growth as inputs and then works through the lifetime of the investment as with the preceding formulas. The theoretical model shown in Figure 30.1 illustrates that you only have to go through one life cycle to establish the stable percentages. A function for computing the net plant depreciation rate that makes the same calculation is shown in Figure 30.2. This function uses a FOR NEXT loop to cycle around each year of the plant life and computes

```
' Function for computing net depreciation rate

Function net_depreciation_rate(life, growth)

cap_exp = 100
plant_balance = 0

For i = 1 To life + 1

    net_plant = plant_balance - accum_dep      ' Opening Balance

    depreciation_exp = plant_balance / life

    cap_exp = cap_exp * (1 + growth)              ' Cap Exp After Depreciation

    plant_balance = plant_balance + cap_exp  ' Closing Balances
    accum_dep = accum_dep + depreciation_exp

Next i

net_depreciation_rate = depreciation_exp / net_plant

End Function
```

FIGURE 30.2 Function for Computing the Stable Level of Depreciation Expense to Net Plant

capital expenditures, plant balances, depreciation expense, and accumulated depreciation for each year of the plant life. Functions similar to the one shown in Figure 30.2 can be created for the stable ratio of accumulated depreciation to net plant, the stable level of capital expenditures to depreciation, the stable level of retirement to gross plant, and other ratios. These functions could be written by either assuming that the depreciation is computed on the basis of the opening plant balance, the closing balance, or the average plant balance.

After you have written the depreciation function or alternatively copied it from another sheet, you can use the function in a spreadsheet to create a sensitivity analysis. Figure 30.3 demonstrates results of the sensitivity analysis for the plant life and for the growth rate using a data table. Relative to the gross plant depreciation rate, the net plant depreciation rate is highest when the growth rate is slow and when the life of the plant is long. Alternatively, with a long life and a very high rate of growth, the net plant is similar to the gross plant and the net plant depreciation rate is similar to the gross plant depreciation rate.

Life	Gross Plant Depreciation Rate	Net Plant Depreciation Growth Rate										
		-1%	0%	1%	2%	5%	10%	15%	20%	30%	50%	100%
1	100.0%	100.0%	100.0%	100.0%	100.0%	100.0%	100.0%	100.0%	100.0%	100.0%	100.0%	100.0%
2	50.0%	66.8%	66.7%	66.6%	66.4%	66.1%	65.6%	65.2%	64.7%	63.9%	62.5%	60.0%
5	20.0%	33.6%	33.3%	33.1%	32.9%	32.3%	31.3%	30.5%	29.8%	28.5%	26.6%	24.0%
10	10.0%	18.5%	18.2%	17.9%	17.7%	16.9%	15.9%	15.1%	14.4%	13.4%	12.2%	11.1%
15	6.7%	12.8%	12.5%	12.2%	11.9%	11.2%	10.3%	9.6%	9.1%	8.4%	7.7%	7.1%
20	5.0%	9.8%	9.5%	9.2%	9.0%	8.3%	7.4%	6.8%	6.4%	6.0%	5.6%	5.3%
30	3.3%	6.8%	6.5%	6.2%	5.9%	5.3%	4.6%	4.2%	4.0%	3.7%	3.6%	3.4%
50	2.0%	4.3%	3.9%	3.6%	3.4%	2.9%	2.5%	2.3%	2.2%	2.1%	2.1%	2.0%
100	1.0%	2.4%	2.0%	1.7%	1.5%	1.2%	1.1%	1.1%	1.1%	1.0%	1.0%	1.0%

FIGURE 30.3 Sensitivity Analysis of Net Plant Depreciation Rate to Growth and Plant Life

Computing the Ratio of Capital Expenditures to Depreciation When Historical Growth Differs from Prospective Growth

Calculation of the stable ratio of capital expenditures to depreciation and calculation of the stable net plant depreciation rate could be accomplished using the function described in the preceding section if the growth rate in capital expenditures never changed. With a constant growth rate you could put the net plant depreciation rate in a column to the left of the calculations in the same way that working capital changes can be adjusted. Then you could compute normal capital expenditures directly from the depreciation expense. This process of using the net plant depreciation rate function does not work however, if the growth rate changes because future capital expenditures for replacing assets in part depend on the growth rate that occurred in the past. If the past growth rate was relatively slow, implying old plant while the future growth rate is relatively fast, capital expenditures required to replace prior assets may be almost as much as depreciation. In contrast, if past growth was high and the average age of plant is young, replacement capital expenditures will look back to the beginning of the life cycle when expenditures were low and when the company was smaller. To illustrate the problem of changing growth, consider the analogy of a country with changing population rates. If you were simulating the long-term growth in the population of a country and you wanted to know how many births (capital expenditures) it will take to both replace dying people (retirements) as well as to increase the population, you would have to measure how long people live, when they die, the average age of the population, and the rate of births. Say there was a large increase in births after a war, implying a high historical growth rate of the population. Even if attitudes toward family size subsequently change, resulting in a lower birth rate (a lower terminal growth), new births would be necessary to support population growth until the baby boomers die. In the context of financial models, the pattern of past expenditures from historical growth similarly affects future required replacement of assets necessary to maintain a future assumed rate of growth.

When growth rates change, the calculation of the ratio of capital expenditures to depreciation requires inputs for both historical growth and projected growth. Dissecting historical data from financial statements to derive the level of capital expenditures that supports a level of EBITDA where the growth rate changes is challenging because of the issue of past growth introduced in the previous paragraph. The issue of adjusting the ratio of capital expenditures to depreciation for past growth also arises when computing the implied EV/EBITDA ratio where growth rates change. This issue also comes up in evaluating whether the value driver formula $(1 - g/ROIC)/(WACC - g)$ can produce reasonable results. Because the pattern of earlier expenditures affect prospective capital expenditures, you need to know the historical growth rates to make an accurate calculation of normalized capital expenditures.

To derive the historical growth rate from financial statements you can use the ratio of accumulated depreciation to gross plant and the plant life. This process was introduced in Chapter 9 where a user-defined function that performs a dynamic Goal Seek is explained to derive the implied growth using a FOR NEXT loop. The loop includes declining increments in the STEP part of the FOR NEXT process. To find the historical growth rate you can start with a very low growth rate that implies a high ratio of accumulated depreciation to gross plant and then gradually increase growth rates until the target ratio of accumulated depreciation to gross plant has been achieved. Once the target accumulated depreciation ratio that you input has been exceeded, you move to a smaller STEP increment for the growth rate and repeat the process. Each time you exceed the target ratio of accumulated depreciation to gross plant, you can reduce the size of the STEP increment until the growth increment is very small. Results of a function named Growth_Find that derives the implied growth rate from the plant life and the ratio of accumulated depreciation to gross plant is illustrated in Figure 30.4. The bottom of the figure shows how the derived growth from the user-defined function is the same as the growth rate that is input into the model. In this analysis, the plant life cycle and the accumulated depreciation ratio are simulated. The fact that the input growth rate equals the simulated growth rate establishes the accuracy of the process.

	D	E	F	G	H	I	J
14	Periods	Period	Growth				
15	Historic Period	12	9%				
16	Modelled Period	20	9%				
17	Long-term Period		5%				
18							
19	Initial Gross Plant	100.00					
20	Plant Life	15.00					
21	Accumulated Depreciation	42.90					
22	Random Factor	0.00%					
23	Compound Growth	9.00%					
28							
29		Historic	Modelled	Long-term			
30	Accumulated Depreciation to Gross Plant	42.90%	42.90%	47.32%			
31	Net Plant Depreciation Rate	12.73%	12.73%	13.29%			
32	Capital Expenditures to Depreciation	170.72%	170.72%	137.63%			
33	Retirements as Percent of Depreciation	46.87%	46.87%	66.20%			
34	Retirements as Percent of Gross Plant	3.12%	3.12%	4.41%			
35	Retirements as Percent of Net Plant	5.47%	5.47%	8.38%			
36	Gross Plant Depreciation Rate	6.67%	6.67%	6.67%			
37							
38	Implied Growth from User Function	9.00%	9.00%	5.00% <---- =Growth_Find(G30,E20,3)			
39	Input Growth	9.00%	9.00%	5.00%			
40							

FIGURE 30.4 Illustration of Using a Function to Find Implied Historical Growth

In pondering the modeling of depreciation and capital expenditures, you can imagine jumping from one platform to another platform in a warehouse. In the case of working capital, the relationship between working capital investment and growth is immediate and one directly jumps to the second platform. In the case of capital expenditures and deferred taxes, the transition can take a long time and you cannot jump from one platform to another. Instead, the process will take an entire life cycle of plant and the value depends on how one jumps to each intermediate platform. Because the normalized capital expenditures depend on the replacement of capital expenditures that in turn depend on the average age of existing assets, the calculation is more complex. Working with historical growth makes it difficult to create a simple formula for the ratio of capital expenditures to depreciation in the face of changing growth.

When the terminal growth rate declines, the capital expenditures required for increasing the size of the plant to support EBITDA growth decline, but the capital expenditures to replace old plant must still be made. The growth rate over the historical period affects the replacement capital expenditures, meaning that historical growth has an effect on the stable ratio of capital expenditures to depreciation used for computing normalized cash flow. Over the prospective life cycle of a plant, the level of capital expenditures required to replace the existing plant is equal to the current level of gross plant on the balance sheet. This is the level of plant that has not yet been retired or written off. Without any historical growth, the level of replacement capital expenditures would be flat. Alternatively, with a high rate of historical growth, the replacement of the fixed level of plant is pushed into the future, meaning that less replacement capital expenditure occurs early on and more replacement capital expenditure occurs in the later years. Figures 30.5a and 30.5b illustrate

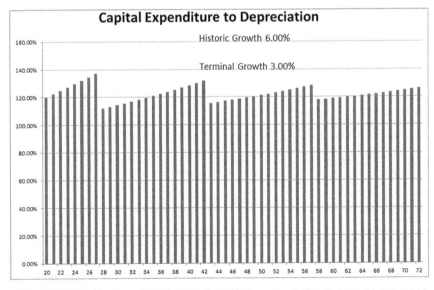

FIGURE 30.5a Ratio of Prospective Capital Expenditures to Depreciation with Historical Growth of 6 Percent and Terminal Growth of 3 Percent

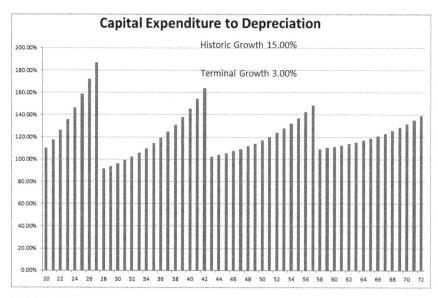

FIGURE 30.5b Ratio of Prospective Capital Expenditures to Depreciation with Historical Growth of 15 Percent and Terminal Growth of 3 Percent

the pattern of capital expenditures after a change in growth rate for two different scenarios. Figure 30.5a shows a case with a relatively slow historical growth rate of 6 percent, a terminal growth rate of 3 percent, and, by implication, plant that is relatively old. In Figure 30.5a, the pattern of historical expenditures is similar to the future expenditures, and the future ratio of capital expenditures to depreciation is relatively flat. Figure 30.5b shows a case with 15 percent historical growth and a 3 percent terminal growth rate. In this case the replacement capital expenditures are delayed and the pattern of future capital expenditures follows a sawtooth pattern. The challenge in computing normalized cash flow is to convert the varying capital expenditures into a normalized stable level.

To create a practical technique that accurately measures normalized future capital expenditures when the prospective growth rate is different than historical growth that be practically used in a financial model, the varying patterns of the ratio of capital expenditures to depreciation shown in the graphs must be reduced to a single number. Because the patterns of capital expenditures differ with time, if you would simply compute the average level of the ratio of capital expenditures to depreciation in the future, you would not account for the time value of money. To find a single number to plug into terminal value calculations, the different values of future expenditures relative to current expenditures must be accounted for using a discount rate. A low discount rate near zero would mean that future expenditures have a similar value to current expenditures, and you could apply the ratio of capital expenditures to depreciation by averaging the ratios illustrated in Figures 30.5a and 30.5b. Here the shape and the time pattern that results from historical growth of capital expenditures would not have much of an effect on the valuation analysis. However, when the discount rate is high, the historical growth can have a more important effect on valuation and you should put more weight on the ratio in the near term than in the long term. The discount rate can be used to compute a weighted average level of capital expenditures to depreciation that is sometimes called a levelized amount.

Computing the Ratio of Capital Expenditures to Depreciation

Creating a function to simulate a single number for the ratio of capital expenditures to depreciation must account for (1) the level of capital expenditures driven by the prospective terminal growth rate, (2) the pattern of expenditures required to replace existing plant, and (3) the valuation effects of the shape of future expenditures driven by the discount rate. A single levelized value of capital expenditures to depreciation can be established by developing a user-defined function that accepts the discount rate and the historical growth rate as well as the future growth rate and the plant life. The notion of computing levelized amounts is used in other applications to summarize the value of a time series with different values. A prominent example is computing the levelized cost of electricity for different types of technologies.

Step 1: Computing the Normalized Depreciation Expense from Changing Growth Rates

To see how to create a function that adjusts for historical growth, consider a simple example of how changing growth affects capital expenditures. Assume that your company makes some kind of product and you need factories to produce your product. The cost of building the factory is 1,000 per unit (pretend that there is no inflation). If you produce a lot more, you must buy new equipment that costs 1,000 per unit, whereas if your company grows at a slower rate, you need less new equipment. As your business grows older, you also must buy new equipment to replace the old equipment that has worn out.

In thinking about how capital expenditures work, begin with the amount of capacity rather than any financial data. If you want to grow revenues by 2 percent per year, then the capacity must also grow by 2 percent per year, as demonstrated by the following simple equation:

$$\text{Capacity}_t = \text{Capacity}_{t-1} \times (1 + \text{Growth Rate})$$

The amount of new capacity you build each period cannot be modeled by the equation $\text{Capacity}_t - \text{Capacity}_{t-1}$ because new capacity must also be purchased to replace old capacity that is retiring. If you know how much capacity must be replaced, then the new capacity can be represented as:

$$\text{New Capacity} = \text{Capacity}_t - \text{Capacity}_{t-1} + \text{Retirements}_t$$

As the cost per unit of capacity remains constant, the balance of capacity grows at the same rate as the EBITDA. While the balance of the gross plant grows at the same rate as the capacity, the capital expenditures and the net plant do not. The net plant depends on depreciation and can grow at different rates. Since the depreciation expense is driven by the gross plant balance multiplied by the constant gross plant depreciation rate and not the net plant balance, the depreciation expense does grow at the same rate as the overall plant balance, which in turn grows at the EBITDA growth rate. All of this leads to the key implication that the depreciation expense grows at the same rate as the overall EBITDA. This applies to historical growth as well as projected growth. If the EBITDA growth was 5 percent in the historical period and the cost per unit of capital expenditures remains constant, the gross plant had to grow at that 5 percent rate to support the growth, meaning that the depreciation would have grown at the same rate.

In the terminal period, the starting base for depreciation is the same as the starting base for EBITDA and the depreciation grows at the same rate as the EBITDA. This implies that if the ratio of capital expenditures to depreciation is used to compute normalized capital expenditures, you can apply it to depreciation expense without making any normalization adjustment to depreciation expense itself. You do not have to worry about normalizing the level of depreciation expense in the way that capital expenditures are adjusted, because depreciation will grow at the same rate as EBITDA if the firm does not have surplus or deficit capacity at the terminal date. The relationship between depreciation expense and growth is illustrated by the following formulas:

$$\text{EBITDA}_t = \text{EBITDA}_{t-1} \times (1 + \text{Growth Rate})$$

$$\text{Plant Balance}_t = \text{Plant Balance}_{t-1} \times (1 + \text{Growth Rate})$$

Because the gross depreciation rate is constant as long as the asset life does not change:

$$\text{Depreciation}_t = \text{Depreciation}_{t-1} \times (1 + \text{Growth Rate})$$

Step 2: Establishing Retirements from Historical Growth in First Pass

In developing a normalized ratio of capital expenditures to depreciation that can be applied to simulate future capital expenditures in a financial model, the effect of historical data that drives replacement capital expenditures should be accounted for. The following equations illustrate how historical retirements affect prospective capital expenditures:

$$\text{Future Capital Expenditures}_t = \text{Plant Balance}_t - \text{Plant Balance}_{t-1}$$
$$+ \text{Retirements}_t$$

where

$$\text{Retirements}_t = \text{Capital Expenditures}_{t-\text{life}}$$

To compute new capital expenditures associated with replacing retirements arising from the prior life cycle of plant, the base level of retirements that occurred at the start of the earlier life cycle should be established. This base level of capital expenditures from the prior life cycle can be computed using a function that automates a Goal Seek to find a starting level of capital expenditures to accumulate to a given level of plant with inputs for the life of the plant and growth rate. Such a function, named find_base, is described in detail in Chapter 9. Once the base level of capital expenditures from the beginning of the prior life cycle is established, the capital expenditures for the remaining prior life cycle are given by a historical growth rate index:

$$\text{Starting Replacement Capital Expenditures}_{\text{Current period-life}} =$$
$$\text{Find\_Base(Historical Growth Rate, Life)}$$

$$\text{Capital Expenditures to Replace Retirement} =$$
$$\text{Replacement Capital Expenditure}_{t-1} \times (1 + \text{Historical Growth})$$

The objective of the process is to derive the ratio of future capital expenditures to depreciation that include capital expenditures for prospective growth as well as for replacement of retirements. With this data on prospective capital expenditures, the present value of the capital expenditure to deprecation ratio can be established in a function. To do this, you can create a function with two different FOR NEXT loops. The first pass works around one life cycle of the plant with a FOR NEXT loop to simulate prospective retirements associated with existing plant. This begins with the find_base function to establish the starting capital expenditures. This first of the process places derived historical capital expenditures into an array variable that can later be used to compute prospective retirements and create a pattern like that shown in Figures 30.5a and 30.5b. The pattern of the retirements that is placed in the array is driven by the historical growth rate that finds the implied starting value of the capital expenditures. If the historical growth rate is higher, meaning the average age of plant is younger, the starting level of retirements is lower because the total level of current gross plant must equal the sum of the historical capital expenditures. Once historical capital expenditures that drive retirements are computed, the second pass and FOR NEXT loop works around the future capital expenditures. This second loop computes the present value of these expenditures over a very long period and accounts for the changing sawtooth pattern of expenditures that can come from a changing growth rate.

Step 3: Computing Present Value of Future Capital Expenditures in Second Pass

Once the retirements from the prior life cycle have been established with the first path around the plant life, the second FOR NEXT loop is added to compute the prospective capital expenditures and the prospective depreciation yielding the future ratio of capital expenditures to depreciation. As this ratio is not constant because of the difference between the historical growth rate and terminal growth rate, you should compute the present value of the capital expenditures to depreciation ratio. The present value calculation results in a single ratio that can be applied in terminal value calculations and normalized cash flow. A present value calculation should be made over a long period of time as the level of capital expenditures follows a cyclical pattern and the shape of the curve influences the normalized level of capital expenditures. The second loop includes calculation of a present value factor and derives a single levelized value for the level of capital expenditures to depreciation. The function that includes both FOR NEXT loops is shown in Figure 30.6. This function has similar functions as other Visual Basic for Applications (VBA) programs described in previous chapters. The first part contains a loop from 1 to the plant life, and the second part has a loop that starts with the plant life plus 1 and continues indefinitely. The function includes provision to compute depreciation expense from the opening balance, the average balance, or the closing balance of plant.

Implementing the Stable Ratio of Capital Expenditures to Depreciation in Valuation Analysis

The function shown in Figure 30.6 accepts historical growth, terminal growth, WACC, and plant life and gives you a single value for the ratio of capital expenditures to depreciation. One of the good things about developing a user-defined function like the one shown in Figure 30.6 is that once you have made the function a single time you can use it in all of your models and you do not have to reprogram it. To reuse the function, you can simply find a model that

```
Function stable_capexp(historic_growth, future_growth, _life, wacc,
  timing_code)
Dim cap_exp(800)

base_retirement = find_base(historic_growth, life)
cap_exp(1) = base_retirement              ' First pass around history

For i = 2 To life                         ' First Pass to find retirements
    cap_exp(i) = cap_exp(i - 1) * (1 + historic_growth)
Next i

Balance = 1                               ' Begin long-term loop
Starting_Balance = 1
pv_factor = (1 + wacc)

For i = life + 1 To 500      ' Second pass using retirements from first round

    Balance = Balance * (1 + future_growth)

    Select Case timing_code
      Case 1: Base = Starting_Balance
      Case 2: Base = (Balance + Starting_Balance) / 2
      Case 3: Base = Balance
    End Select

    Depreciation_Expense = Base / life    ' Depreciation
    retirement = cap_exp(i - life)        ' Retirements from lag

    cap_exp(i) = Starting_Balance * (1 + future_growth) _
               - Starting_Balance + retirement   ' Replace retirements

    Starting_Balance = Balance            ' retain opening balance

    pv_factor = pv_factor * (1 + wacc)        ' PV factor for valuation
    pv_cap_exp = pv_cap_exp + cap_exp(i) / pv_factor
    pv_dep = pv_dep + Depreciation_Expense / pv_factor

Next i
stable_capexp = pv_cap_exp / pv_dep
End Function
```

FIGURE 30.6 Integrated Function for Computing the Normalized Capital Expenditures to Depreciation That Incorporates Historical Growth and Cost of Capital

already has the function and then copy the code into your model. You can also import the module containing the function into your VBA code or, alternatively, you can create an Excel add-in with an .XLA file that you can incorporate into your spreadsheet.

To illustrate the effect of modeling the normalized capital expenditures in the terminal period with different formulas and different growth rates, Figures 30.7a and 30.7b show the effects of four different normalization approaches for capital expenditures. The first method establishes terminal value with a base long-term theoretical analysis as discussed in the context of other issues and does not require a stable ratio or normalized cash flow as the model extends for hundreds of years. In this analysis the company begins in some historical period with stable ratios of capital expenditures to depreciation, accumulated depreciation to gross plant, and other factors driven by historical growth. The company is then assumed to experience a sudden change in the growth rate. After the change in growth rate, the company's EBITDA, plant balances, depreciation expense, and return grow at the lower terminal growth rate. After the change in growth rate, the capital expenditures, net plant, and return on investment do not grow at that constant rate. The value of EBITDA less capital expenditures after

Plant Life   15.00

Historic Growth   6%
Modelled Growth   6%
Terminal Growth   3%

	Cap Exp to Dep Ratio	Value	Percent Difference from True Value
Theoretically Correct Value		302.58	
No Stable Value Adjustment	145.70%	226.44	-25.2%
Simple Stable Value Adjustment	121.99%	291.63	-3.6%
Adjustment with Historic Growth	116.99%	305.38	0.9%

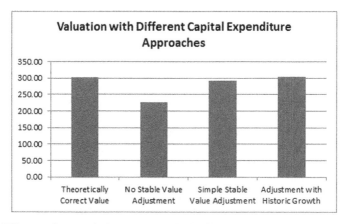

FIGURE 30.7a Simulation of Alternative Methods for Computing Normalized Capital Expenditures with 6 Percent Historical Growth Rate and 3 Percent Terminal Growth

Plant Life   15.00

Historic Growth   15%
Modelled Growth   15%
Terminal Growth   3%

	Cap Exp to Dep Ratio	Value	Percent Difference from True Value
Theoretically Correct Value		2,202.99	
No Stable Value Adjustment	223.07%	304.84	-86.2%
Simple Stable Value Adjustment	121.99%	1,974.02	-10.4%
Adjustment with Historic Growth	108.12%	2,202.99	0.0%

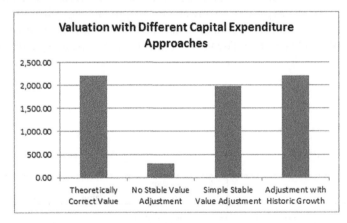

FIGURE 30.7b Simulation of Alternative Methods for Computing Normalized Capital Expenditures with 15 Percent Historical Growth Rate and 3 Percent Terminal Growth

the change in growth rate in this first theoretical long-term model is used as the benchmark for evaluating the effectiveness of other approaches.

Once the true theoretical value of the corporation is established from long-term analysis, three techniques of deriving normalized capital expenditures are compared to the theoretical true value. The first of these does not make use a stable ratio for in normalizing cash flow. Instead it simply applies the last year of capital expenditures from the free cash flow formula in computing the terminal value. The level of capital expenditures does not change when the terminal growth rate changes if this method is applied. Cash flow from the terminal period is converted to value using the standard $(1 + g)/(WACC - g)$ formula.

The next method applies a stable ratio of capital expenditures to depreciation expense, but makes no adjustment for historical growth. This second method uses the user-defined function shown in Figure 30.2 to derive the net plant depreciation rate. The net plant depreciation rate is computed with the terminal growth rate. After the net plant depreciation rate is derived, it is used to compute the stable level of capital expenditures using the formula capital expenditures to depreciation = growth/net plant depreciation rate + 1. This stable value of capital expenditures to depreciation does not account for the effects of historical growth on the ratio. Terminal value is computed through multiplying the depreciation in the terminal period by the stable capital expenditures to depreciation ratio and then applying the factor $(1 + g)/(WACC - g)$ to the normalized cash flow.

The final method uses the function shown in Figure 30.6 to compute the adjusted stable ratio of capital expenditures to depreciation. This method uses the present value of capital expenditures relative to depreciation and it accounts for the historical growth rate that drives the time pattern of prospective asset retirements.

The effects of applying different methods to compute normalized capital expenditures are demonstrated with two different historical and future growth scenarios in Figures 30.7a and 30.7b. Figure 30.7a shows the true value and the three other capital expenditure methods assuming a relatively slow historical growth rate of 6 percent and a terminal growth rate of 3 percent, which is not very different from the historical growth rate. Figure 30.7b demonstrates the valuations using the three alternative capital expenditure methods in a scenario that assumes 15 percent historical growth and 3 percent terminal growth. Figures 30.7a and 30.7b also demonstrate the stable ratio of capital expenditures to depreciation used to normalize capital expenditures in the terminal period.

In the scenario shown in Figure 30.7a that assumes similar historical and terminal growth rates, two of the methods come reasonably close to the theoretical value. But the technique with no adjustment at all to normalize for growth understates value by 25 percent. The method using the function that accounts for historical growth correctly values the corporation because it applies essentially the same formulas as used in the theoretically true model.

Figure 30.7b illustrates that making the adjustment for historical growth is more crucial when the growth rate changes by a large margin from the historical period to the forecast period. Without any adjustment to normalize cash flow, the capital expenditures are far too high, which understates valuation by almost 100 percent. Using the technique that does not consider historical growth but does include future growth understates value by 10 percent. Further sensitivity analysis demonstrates that the effect of the adjustment is more when the asset life is long than when the asset life is short.

CHAPTER 31

Computing Normalized Deferred Tax Changes

Financial analysts are sometimes intimidated by working through issues associated with deferred taxes because of all of the accounting techniques that underlie the calculation. Yet errors and inconsistencies in modeling deferred taxes can result in big valuation biases. Without too much accounting and using concepts introduced in earlier chapters, you can work through the deferred taxes and develop a level of normalized deferred tax changes that is consistent with the terminal growth rate. As explained in Chapter 25 when discussing the bridge between enterprise value and equity value, deferred taxes associated with accelerated depreciation should be directly included in the calculation of free cash flow and should not be part of the bridge between enterprise value and equity value. If increases in deferred tax liability are added to the free cash flow, value is higher as compared to the cash with no deferred taxes. However, if the inappropriate assumption is made that accumulated deferred tax should be treated as a debt like liability, the value is less than it would be if there were no deferred tax. Other deferred tax items that arise from free cash flow items such as warranty provisions should also be part of the free cash flow analysis.

For the case of deferred taxes associated with acceleration of tax depreciation where the tax depreciation rate is greater than the book depreciation rate, taxes paid are less than taxes booked in the early part of a plant's life. Since taxes booked are more than taxes paid, the change in deferred tax liability results in increased free cash flow. This means that instead of the simple free cash flow calculation that includes earnings before interest, taxes, depreciation, and amortization (EBITDA), capital expenditures, and working capital (WC) changes, a more careful calculation of free cash flow should be of the form:

Free Cash Flow = EBITDA – WC Change – Capital Expenditures + Deferred Tax Changes Associated with Accelerated Depreciation + Change in Warranty Provisions Associated with EBITDA + Deferred Tax Changes Associated with Provisions

In computing the deferred taxes during the explicit modeling period, the deferred taxes associated with existing plant should be separated from deferred taxes associated with new plant. This is the same way that depreciation expense should be modeled during the explicit period where existing and new plant are separated. As was the case for retirements associated with existing plant that should be accounted for in computing book depreciation, the challenge for the deferred tax calculation is discerning the amount of deferred taxes associated with existing plant from information in financial statements.

Stable Ratio of Deferred Tax to Capital Expenditure without Change in Growth Rate

Stable ratios that incorporate normalized changes in deferred taxes into a financial model can be computed in a similar manner to the normalized capital expenditures. As with establishing normalized capital expenditures, a stable ratio that reflects historical growth, projected growth, and the lifetime of assets can be established by writing a user-defined function. When deferred tax is a liability on the balance sheet, the future tax depreciation will be less than the book depreciation. The accumulated deferred tax on the balance sheet contains the nominal value, not discounted, of the liability that would be due if there were no more capital expenditures or if the tax depreciation rate suddenly was changed and made equal to the book depreciation rate. But if the company keeps growing as is assumed with a terminal growth rate, the new capital expenditures will continue to generate new deferred taxes. Using the terminal growth rate, a stable rate of new deferred taxes can be computed in a similar manner to the ratio of capital expenditures to depreciation that is the subject of Chapter 30. The stable ratio can be thought of as analogous to the ratio of accounts payable to EBITDA, as accounts payable is also recorded as a liability and is not paid back as long as the company does not cease operations.

To compute the ratio of deferred tax changes to capital expenditures for purposes of computing normalized cash flow, you can create a model with continuing capital expenditure growth analogous to the model used to compute the net plant depreciation rate and the ratio of capital expenditures to depreciation (as shown in Figure 30.6). As with book depreciation and the book plant balance, an investment balance is set up for the tax plant balance and the tax depreciation. The difference between the tax depreciation and the book depreciation multiplied by the tax rate yields the change in deferred tax, which is the amount that is added to free cash flow for valuation.

In developing the stable ratio of deferred tax change to capital expenditures, the amount is influenced both by the prospective terminal growth rate of EBITDA and by the historical growth rate, as is the case for the ratio of capital expenditures to depreciation. The process of computing the ratio of deferred tax changes to capital expenditures can be understood by beginning with a case where the growth rate does not vary between the historical and explicit period relative to the growth rate after the terminal period. Once the stable ratio is calculated in this constant growth case, the effects of changes in growth rate for the historical period and the terminal period can be incorporated. This requires working through the historical life cycle and using a discount rate to establish a levelized stable value for the change in deferred taxes relative to capital expenditures, just as in the case for the ratio of capital expenditures to depreciation.

If the growth rate does not change, calculation of the ratio of stable deferred tax change to capital expenditure can be computed in a similar manner to the net plant depreciation rate explained in Chapter 30 and demonstrated in Figures 30.1 and 30.2. As with the ratio of capital expenditures to depreciation, the ratio of deferred tax change to capital expenditures stabilizes immediately after a single life cycle of a plant has been simulated. This ratio measures the amount that the capital expenditures are implicitly reduced because of advantageous tax depreciation. To compute the stable ratio of deferred taxes to capital expenditures you can make a long-term financial model. Alternatively, you can create a user-defined function that establishes the calculation in a single cell. If you are calculating the stable ratio using a constant growth rate assumption, you need to input both the tax and book depreciation rates as well as the tax rate.

Figure 31.1 illustrates how the ratio of deferred tax to capital expenditures stabilizes at a constant 15.57 percent after a plant life cycle. The ratio in Figure 31.1 is high for the following four reasons: (1) the tax life is short, (2) a double declining balance method for tax depreciation is applied, (3) the income tax rate is high, and (4) the growth rate is high. Because capital expenditures are growing and the tax depreciation rate is not straight-line, the tax depreciation is computed using the depreciation function explained in Chapter 9. The implication of the ratio of deferred tax change to capital expenditures is that the tax depreciation reduces the cost of making the capital

	A B	C	D	E	F	G	H	I	J	K	L	M	N
4	Change in Deferred Tax to Cap Exp		15.57%		<---- =deferred_tax(E7,E8,E9,E10,E15:AH15)							
5													
6	Assumptions					Outputs							
7	Growth			20.00%			Change in Deferred Tax/Cap Exp				15.57%		
8	Book Life			10			Cap Exp/Depreciation				198.8%		
9	Tax Rate			50%									
10	Timing Code			3.00									
11	Tax Life			5									
12	Decline Factor			2.00									
13													
14	Tax Depreciation Year		0	1	2	3	4	5	6	7	8	9	10
15	Depreciation Rate			40.00%	24.00%	14.40%	10.80%	10.80%	FALSE	FALSE	FALSE	FALSE	FALSE
16													
17	Period		1	2	3	4	5	6	7	8	9	10	11
18	Capital Expenidture		100.0	120.0	144.0	172.8	207.4	248.8	298.6	358.3	430.0	516.0	619.2
19	Plant Balance												
20	Opening Balance			100.0	220.0	364.0	536.8	744.2	993.0	1,291.6	1,649.9	2,079.9	2,595.9
21	Add: Capital Expenditure		100.0	120.0	144.0	172.8	207.4	248.8	298.6	358.3	430.0	516.0	619.2
22	Less: Retirements			FALSE	FALSE	FALSE	FALSE	FALSE	FALSE	FALSE	FALSE	FALSE	100.0
23	Closing Balance		100.0	220.0	364.0	536.8	744.2	993.0	1,291.6	1,649.9	2,079.9	2,595.9	3,115.0
24													
25	Book Tax Depreciation		10.0	22.0	36.4	53.7	74.4	99.3	129.2	165.0	208.0	259.6	311.5
26	Tax Depr w/ Function		40.0	72.0	100.8	131.8	168.9	202.7	243.2	291.9	350.3	420.3	504.4
27													
28	Difference		30.0	50.0	64.4	78.1	94.5	103.4	114.1	126.9	142.3	160.7	192.9
29	Change in Deferred Tax		15.0	25.0	32.2	39.0	47.2	51.7	57.0	63.4	71.1	80.4	96.4
30													
31	Deferred Tax/Cap Exp		15.00%	20.83%	22.36%	22.59%	22.79%	20.78%	19.10%	17.71%	16.54%	15.57%	15.57%
32	Cap Exp/Depreciation			5.45	3.96	3.22	2.79	2.51	2.31	2.17	2.07	1.99	1.99

FIGURE 31.1 Computation of the Stable Ratio of Deferred Tax Changes to Capital Expenditures from Simulation Model

expenditures by 15.57 percent relative to a case where the tax depreciation is equal to the book depreciation.

The ratio shown in Figure 31.1 can also be computed through making a user-defined function that works through the life cycle of a plant investment just like the case with the function for computing capital expenditures to depreciation. This function should compute both tax and book depreciation, and you will need to input both the book depreciation life and the tax depreciation rate into the model as shown in Figure 31.2.

Without accounting for the differences between prospective growth and historical growth, the ratio of deferred tax to capital expenditure is a function of the tax rate, the tax life, the type of tax depreciation rate applied (double declining balance, etc.), and the growth rate. Assuming a growth rate of 5 percent, a tax rate of 30 percent, and a book life of 20 years, Figure 31.3 demonstrates the stable ratio that results from different tax lives and different depreciation methods. The table shows that the method of depreciation ranging from triple declining balance to straight-line depreciation does not make much of a difference compared to the tax life when the tax life is relatively short. The ratios in Figure 31.3 illustrate that the ratio of deferred

```
Function deferred_tax (growth, life, tax_rate, _
                    timing_code, tax_depreciation_rate) As Variant

asset_life = tax_depreciation_rate.Count
plant_balance = 0
opening_plant_Balance = 0
Dim capital_exp(100) As Single

For year1 = 1 To life                    ' loop around each period
  If year1 = 1 Then cap_exp = 100
  If year1 > 1 Then cap_exp = cap_exp * (1 + growth)
  capital_exp(year1) = cap_exp
  tax_depreciation_expense = 0
  For vintage = 1 To life          ' make a loop to evaluate asset by asset

    age = year1 - vintage + 1     ' calculate the age of each expenditure

    If (age > 0 And age <= asset_life) Then    ' Only when asset is alive
        tax_depreciation_expense = _
            capital_exp(vintage) * _
            tax_depreciation_rate(age) + tax_depreciation_expense
    End If

  Next vintage        ' Vintage is used for capital expenditure

  opening_plant_Balance = plant_balance
  plant_balance = plant_balance + cap_exp - retirement

  average_plant_balance = (opening_plant_Balance + plant_balance) / 2

  Select Case timing_code
      Case 1: depreciation_base = opening_plant_Balance
      Case 2: deprecaition_base = average_plant_balance
      Case 3: depreciation_base = plant_balance
  End Select
  book_depreciation_expense = depreciation_base / life

  deferred_tax = ((tax_depreciation_expense - book_depreciation_expense) _
              * tax_rate) / cap_exp
Next year1
End Function
```

FIGURE 31.2 Function for Computing Stable Ratio of Deferred Tax Change to Capital Expenditures

Book	20	Growth		5.00%	Tax Rate		30.00%
Stable Ratio of Deferred Tax Increase to Capital Expenditure							
			Declining Balance Factor				
		1.00	1.50	2.00	2.50	3.00	
	1	10.37%	10.37%	10.37%	10.37%	10.37%	
	2	9.66%	10.01%	10.37%	10.37%	10.37%	
	4	8.30%	8.69%	9.16%	9.58%	9.91%	
	6	7.02%	7.48%	8.07%	8.61%	9.04%	
Tax Life	8	5.82%	6.36%	7.06%	7.70%	8.23%	
	10	4.70%	5.29%	6.10%	6.84%	7.47%	
	14	2.64%	3.36%	4.36%	5.27%	6.04%	
	16	1.71%	2.48%	3.56%	4.55%	5.38%	
	18	0.83%	1.64%	2.80%	3.86%	4.75%	
	20	0.00%	0.86%	2.08%	3.20%	4.15%	

FIGURE 31.3 Stable Ratio of Deferred Tax Change Relative to Capital Expenditures That Results from Different Tax Lives and Depreciation Methods

tax change to capital expenditures stabilizes at a relatively low percentage of 3 percent to 10 percent if the tax rate is 30 percent.

Normalized Deferred Tax with Change in Growth Rate

The notion of recording accumulated deferred tax as a liability is that lower amounts of taxes that have been paid in early years because of things like accelerated tax depreciation will reverse one day in the future. When accelerated depreciation is no longer available, you will have to pay more taxes than the amount recorded on the books and the tax cash flow amount implied by the formula EBIT $\times$ (1 − t). If capital expenditures stopped, the deferred taxes would become negative and the liability really would be paid through actual taxes paid that are higher than reported book taxes. The general idea of deferred taxes reversing when capital expenditures decline is similar to this idea that deferred taxes completely reverse when capital expenditures stop. For the extreme example with zero capital expenditures, you should use a negative amount for the normalized level of deferred tax changes. Say the growth rate during the explicit period was 30 percent and then it becomes −5 percent in the terminal period. The capital expenditures have not stopped, but something not so very different has happened. The normalized deferred tax should account for the prospective reversal of deferred tax resulting from deferred taxes created during the high-growth historical period in addition to the new deferred taxes generated from the ongoing EBITDA and capital expenditure growth. To account for this decline in deferred taxes associated with existing depreciation, you need to put the historical growth rate into the analysis just as was the case for deriving normalized capital expenditures. Then you can work through both the historical life cycle and the future life cycle and compute the present value of the prospective deferred tax changes as well as the prospective capital expenditures. Once you have created this function, you can add it to your model and use it in the left-hand columns of the model.

CHAPTER 32

Terminal Value and the Ability of a Company to Earn Returns above the Cost of Capital

The most fundamental objective of any business entity is to create economic profit. Economic profit occurs when the rate of return earned exceeds the opportunity cost of capital that reflects the risk of the business. If a company earns economic profit, new investment and capital expenditures increase the value of the corporation. If the return is below the cost of capital, management should contract the business. Any financial model that computes the value of a firm implicitly measures the ability of a firm to earn an economic profit. For business enterprises operating in a competitive environment, earning an economic profit is certainly not easy, and companies are by no means always able to earn a return above their cost of capital. But if a business cannot earn a return on invested capital that exceeds the weighted average cost of capital (WACC), it should try to exit the business or it may be forced to exit in one way or another. In computing valuation multiples, the next three chapters address different ways to account explicitly for the level of economic profit in the terminal value section of a corporate financial model.

The discussions of stable ratios in Chapters 29, 30, and 31 that address normalized cash flow do not explicitly discuss the return on invested capital. But that does not mean return on invested capital is not an implicit assumption in the valuation analysis made in those chapters. If the growth rate terminal value method is used in valuation, the rate of return earned in the final explicit cash flow period is assumed to approximately continue indefinitely. As emphasized in Chapter 24, one of the best ways to review whether your model makes sense is to make a graph of the return on invested capital and ask difficult questions about whether the projected return is reasonable. By the time that your EBITDA forecast reaches the stable level in the terminal period, the rate of return should be reasonable and reflective of the ability to earn that value in the long run. This is the underlying philosophy of constructing normalized cash flow in a stable period. Just because your model does not have an explicit assumption for the return on invested capital relative to the WACC, it does not mean that you have not implicitly made such an assumption. In making valuations using the value driver formula or the implied valuation multiples, the return assumption is an explicit rather than an implicit assumption.

The Myth of Convergence of Return on Capital to Cost of Capital

The discussion of terminal growth made it seem that if a company can grow, its value will increase. While the growth formula [CF $\times$ (1 + g)/(WACC – g)] does apply two key factors that drive value—the growth rate and the cost of capital—it does not account for the third factor, namely the rate of return on capital. The rate of return on capital earned relative to the cost of capital influences the way growth rate affects value. If a company is earning a return below its cost of capital, then value increases with lower growth or, better yet, a negative growth rate. The implication that higher growth increases value only if the return is above the cost of capital is that the return relative to the cost of capital should explicitly or implicitly be a consideration in computing terminal value. To illustrate this idea, consider a very simple example where a company is created to buy Treasury bills and give the interest and principal payments back to shareholders as dividends. This example is used because the cost of capital is clear. Say that the initial investment made by owners of the company is 100 and the return is 2 percent after the company wastes money on administrative costs. To finance the company, a bank makes loans at an interest rate of 5 percent, which is the same rate that investors could make if they invested in the Treasury bills themselves. The return of 2 percent is below the cost of capital of 5 percent. Anytime this company grows by either reinvesting profits or by acquiring new equity capital, it is making its investors worse off. This case is clear because investors are earning a return below what they could have made by investing in the Treasury bills themselves. The best case for investors is for the company to cease operations and certainly not to grow.

If the earned return is equal to the cost of capital, then the growth rate does not affect the value to investors, as the company is doing nothing either to add or to destroy value. This implies that to resolve problems with wide variation in terminal value driven by growth rates, you could try taking the growth rate out of the process by simply assuming that the future rate of return equals the cost of capital in your model. If the return is equal to the cost of capital, then the value does not change whether the growth rate is 10 percent or −5 percent. All you have to do is to make a seemingly sensible assumption that over the long run, competition will push returns down to the cost of capital as products become more commoditized. An additional justification for this assumption is sometimes that the product life cycle may be coming to an end and competitive advantages may be lost.

While one can make general arguments that competitive advantages will eventually cease and returns will converge to the cost of capital, the idea that rate of return will decline to the cost of capital is more difficult to accept than the idea that companies will stop growing at a faster rate than the economy. If a company cannot earn more than its cost of capital, it should not be in business and it should not make new investments. So then how could you make an assumption that is inconsistent with the fundamental notion about why firms exist? One way to look at the issue is that companies will make more and more efforts to make consumers addicted to their products.

The fact that the market value divided by the book value of most traded companies is substantially above 1.0 provides empirical evidence that the companies do realize a rate of return above their cost of capital. Figure 32.1 demonstrates the market-to-book ratio for a variety of companies and shows that the companies generally have a market-to-book above 1.0. If mature

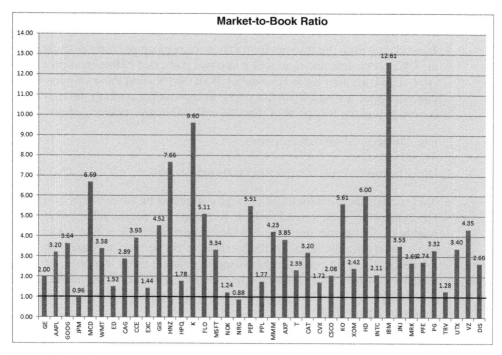

FIGURE 32.1 Market-to-Book Ratio for Variety of Companies

companies are earning their cost of capital, the market-to-book ratios in Figure 32.1 would hover around 1.0. This is because when the return on equity equals the cost of equity, the present value of equity cash flows equals the amount of the original common equity investment. The market-to-book ratio demonstrates whether management has taken the investment of equity investors and done something productive or not. When management does something productive, meaning the returns are above the cost of capital, the market-to-book ratio is above 1.0. If management has wasted shareholder money by making investments that earn returns below the cost of capital, the market-to-book ratio is less than 1.0.

Figure 32.1 is developed by creating Visual Basic for Applications (VBA) code that uses the WORKBOOKS.OPEN statement together with the INDIRECT function. In working with data for corporate models, this statement can allow you to create powerful techniques to read data for multiple companies from the Internet. To apply the WORKBOOKS.OPEN method combined with the INDIRECT function you can use the following steps:

- To read data from the Internet for a variety of companies, go to the Internet and copy the URL for one company into a spreadsheet. An example of the link is:

  http://finance.yahoo.com/q/ks?s=AAPL+Key+Statistics

- To read data from the Internet for a variety of companies, you can copy the URL to two cells and then split it into two parts, one before the ticker symbol and one after the ticker symbol. With the URL split into two parts, you can create a new URL that accepts different ticker symbols through concatenating the two parts of the URL with alternative ticker symbols:

  http://finance.yahoo.com/q/ks?s=
  +Key+Statistics
  http://finance.yahoo.com/q/ks?s=XOM+Key+Statistics

- After creating the combined URL through concatenating the two cells, you can create VBA code to read multiple files and then put the information read from the Internet into different files. When creating this VBA code, begin by storing the name of the workbook, the sheet name, and cell reference. The VBA code can loop around different ticker symbols and read the new information from the Internet for each ticker. After reading the data you can copy and paste it to a new sheet in your current book as shown in Figure 32.2.

- The data that is put into different sheets will have the same format since it is read from different Internet pages. Once you have put the data in separate sheets, you can use the INDIRECT statement to put the data into a

```
Sub get_all()

    For num = 1 To Range("count_no")
        Range("ticker_no") = num
        get_company
    Next num

End Sub


Sub read_company()
    Workbooks.Open (Range("url"))
End Sub

Sub get_company()
    '
current_book = ActiveWorkbook.Name
current_sheet = ActiveSheet.Name

read_company

    temp_book = ActiveWorkbook.Name
    Cells.Select
    Selection.Copy

Windows(current_book).Activate

Sheets.Add After:=Sheets(Sheets.Count)

    Selection.PasteSpecial Paste:=xlPasteValues,_
        Operation:=xlNone, SkipBlanks _
        :=False, Transpose:=False

    On Error Resume Next
    ActiveSheet.Name = Range("ticker")
    Windows(temp_book).Close

End Sub
```

FIGURE 32.2 VBA Code to Read Data from the Internet for Multiple Companies

master sheet that pulls data out from the various individual spreadsheets created from the VBA code. Chapter 15 introduces the INDIRECT function that accepts cell references, including the sheet name. This function can allow you to create an equation that extracts data from different sheets where each sheet has the same structure. Figure 32.3 illustrates how you can use the INDIRECT function with the MATCH function to find row numbers and to select particular data.

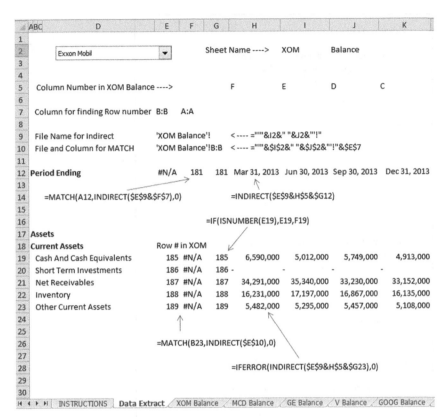

FIGURE 32.3 Use of INDIRECT and MATCH Functions to Extract Data from Individual Spreadsheets

The market-to-book ratio analysis shown in Figure 32.1 demonstrates that returns do not generally converge to the cost of capital for large companies. This is logical. Even in circumstances where companies are mature and have a slow growth rate, it makes little sense to assume that the company will make new investments without expecting some kind of economic profit. On the other hand if a company is currently earning returns far above its cost of capital, it is not reasonable to assume that such profits can last indefinitely. In this situation where returns are very high, companies from all over the world can copy products, management techniques, marketing strategies, and cost structures. As new companies enter the business, companies will not be able to realize extraordinary returns in the long run unless they have some kind of strong competitive advantage.

For mature companies it is more difficult from a theoretical and empirical standpoint to find a consistent trend where the return on capital converges to the cost of capital than to find evidence of declining growth rates. Figure 32.1 shows that it is quite rare to find companies that are just earning their cost of capital as evidenced by a market-to-book ratio of 1.0. As explained in Chapter 24, it is also sometimes tricky to compute the return on capital after the company experiences a large write-off for goodwill or asset impairment as the subsequent investment balance declines and the balance sheet no longer represents invested capital. Some argue that finding evidence of declining returns in statistics like the market-to-book ratio is flawed because of survivorship bias in the statistical analysis of financial data, meaning that companies where returns fall to low levels and/or that go bankrupt and/or that stop producing things do not show up in comparative information. Others argue that when companies become big, they are very careful to make investments only where the return will be above the cost of capital, and you cannot assume that the economic profit will go to 0. As with the survivorship bias argument involving growth rates, this argument is impossible to ever resolve as, by definition, the data to prove the case do not exist if companies do not survive. One is again left with only some general philosophical beliefs.

Despite logical difficulties in making the assumption that returns will suddenly or even gradually converge to the cost of capital, three general points about the relationship between returns and the cost of capital should be kept in mind as you develop valuations from financial models:

1. When a company is earning a very high return on invested capital, it is reasonable to assume that the return will begin to converge toward the cost of capital, although it is not at all reasonable that the return will completely converge to the cost of capital.
2. When constructing a financial model, you should be very suspicious of projected returns that are substantially above the level of historical returns. This implies that computing and presenting returns on equity and returns on invested capital for historical and projected time periods is an essential part of the corporate modeling process.
3. When evaluating returns, it is often better to use the return on invested capital rather than the return on equity. The return on equity can be distorted by changes in the historical or future capital structure of a company. If you do not maintain a constant capital structure in your financial models, the return on equity is less comparable with historic data than return on invested capital.

CHAPTER 33

Errors and Distortions in Applying the Value Driver Formula

A formula referred to in this chapter as the value driver formula explicitly considers both the growth rate and the prospective return in establishing value. This formula, (1 − Growth/Return)/(Cost of Capital − Growth), can seemingly simulate alternative assumptions with respect to convergence in returns and cost of capital over the long term. The formula is popular with some technicians for computing terminal value and with some university professors. As the value driver formula considers all three value drivers—returns, risks, and growth—it seems to solve problems inherent with both the stable growth rate method and the application of valuation multiples. Further, as the formula is applied to operating income rather than cash flow, it seems to avoid the need for evaluating normalized working capital, capital expenditures, and deferred taxes. The biggest difference between the stable growth method discussed in the last couple of chapters and the value driver formula discussed in this chapter is that you can directly make an assumption with respect to the rate of return relative to the cost of capital. The growth rate formula FCFF/(WACC − g) used in Chapters 30, 31, and 32 implicitly assumes that the return on investment that exists in the terminal period will be approximately the same indefinitely. Note that the return in the growth formula does not stay precisely the same as the return in the terminal period because the net plant, which is the basis for investment, does not grow at the same rate as the gross plant, which is the basis for revenue and EBITDA growth.

This chapter presents a critical analysis of the value driver formula and demonstrates that the formula is not the nirvana that can solve all of your valuation problems. To the contrary, the value driver formula contains biases and implicit assumptions that leave it all but useless unless you make irrelevant valuations. The formula does not work when you assume changes in the growth rate between the historical period and the terminal period, which is a fundamental proposition of the discounted cash flow method. It also does not work if you assume returns will gradually converge to the cost of capital, which is the whole idea of applying the formula. Some of the problems with the value driver formula include:

- The implicit manner in which the current realized return converges to the incremental return in the formula is not logical and does not incorporate the replacement of existing assets.
- When the earnings growth rate or the earnings before interest, taxes, depreciation, and amortization (EBITDA) growth rate changes, meaning that the investment required to support the new level of earnings or EBITDA also changes, then the return on investment changes, too. Attempting to make the return on investment a fixed input is not possible when things change. This idea that growth affects return is inconsistent with the basic premise of the value driver formula and implies that the formula produces a biased valuation. Capital expenditures that are made to support EBITDA growth result in earnings that do not grow at the same rate as investment. If growth of EBITDA is input into the value driver formula and investment growth exceeds earnings growth, valuation is overstated.

Before discussing how the value driver produces biased results and renders the formula useless, derivation of the formula is reviewed.

Deriving the Value Driver Formula for the Price/Earnings Ratio and Equity Value

To assess the value driver formula, it is useful to begin by working through derivation of the formula. In deriving the equation you can begin with an equity perspective that establishes the formula for the price/earnings (P/E) ratio using return on equity (ROE), cost of equity, growth in earnings along with the current level of earnings. Once the formula for the P/E is established as $(1 - g/\text{ROE})/(k - g)$, an analogous formula can be developed for the enterprise value/net operating profit after tax (EV/NOPAT) multiple using the return on invested capital (ROIC) and the weighted average cost of capital (WACC). While the formula for enterprise value is more useful in computing terminal value, the formula for equity value that uses ROE, growth, and cost of equity is more convenient in demonstrating the derivation.

To understand the value driver formula, begin with the dividend discount model in which the current price of a stock is determined by the cost of capital and an estimate of the growth rate in equity cash flow. By assuming that marginal investors believe the growth rate in dividends is constant forever, the dividend discount formula can be derived from calculus where an equation is integrated from 0 to infinity. The value of a share is the next period anticipated dividend divided by the difference in the cost of equity and the growth rate in dividends. This comes from the mathematics of the formula (integrating the present value of dividends from zero to infinity) that requires using the next-year cash flow rather than the current-period dividend:

$$P_0 = D_1/(k - g)$$

When combining this dividend discount formula with the sustainable growth rate formula, you can replicate the value driver formula. The sustainable dividend growth formula demonstrates that the dividend growth rate is dependent on the rate of return and the dividend payout ratio. If all earnings are reinvested, meaning that the dividend payout ratio is 0, then the equity balance grows by the ROE. If equity grows by the ROE, dividends also grow by the ROE. In contrast, when the dividend payout ratio is 100 percent, none of the income is reinvested and the growth rate is 0. These two extreme situations demonstrate that the dividend payout ratio and the ROE are a function of growth. The growth rate is a function of the ROE and the payout ratio in the sustainable growth rate formula:

$$\text{Sustainable Growth} = \text{ROE} \times (1 - \text{Dividend Payout})$$

This formula can be rearranged and is much more useful when the dividend payout ratio is evaluated as a function of growth. In real companies, it is the growth rate opportunities or lack thereof that drive dividends and not the other way around. If management cannot find investments that exceed the cost of capital, it might as well distribute dividends. After rearranging the sustainable growth equation, the formula for the dividend payout ratio becomes:

$$\text{Dividend Payout} = 1 - \text{Sustainable Growth}/\text{ROE}$$

Since dividends equal the dividend payout ratio multiplied by the dividends per share, the dividends in the formula $P_0 = D_1/(k-g)$ can be expressed as:

$$D_1 = \text{EPS}_1 \times \text{Dividend Payout} = (1 - g/\text{ROE}) \times \text{EPS}_1$$

By substituting the formula for dividends into the stock price formula, the value and the P/E ratio can be expressed in terms of key value drivers—the ability to earn more than the cost of capital and the ability to grow earnings at that difference. By substituting the formula for D_1 into the formula for the current price, $D_1/(k - g)$, the price of the share becomes:

$$P_0 = \text{EPS}_1 \times (1 - g/\text{ROE})/(k - g)$$

This formula demonstrates that value is directly related to the current level of earnings, EPS_1, as well as the ROE, cost of capital, and growth. The value depends on the current level of return inherent in EPS_1 as well as the future growth rate and the rate of return. In deriving the formula, the ROE is constant and begins from the initial period. To illustrate the relationship between EPS_1 and ROE, say two companies have the same level of investment, the same cost of capital, and the same future return and growth, but they have different current levels of earnings (EPS_1). The difference in valuation between the two companies will directly depend on this difference in the current rate of return earned applied to the same level of investment. The company with the higher level of current return will have higher beginning dividends, higher cash flow and a higher value. The effect of the rate of return embedded in the current return is why the ROE in the value driver equation is often referred to as the incremental ROE. The incremental ROE applied to future investment can then be distinguished from the ROE implicit in current earnings.

If the equation is rearranged a little and the earnings are divided by the price of the share, then it can be used to define the forward P/E ratio. Here, the P/E ratio multiple is a function of the three value drivers. This equation can in theory be used to derive the cost of capital from the P/E ratio:

$$P_0/EPS_1 = (1 - g/ROE)/(k - g)$$

Deriving Implicit Assumptions about the Progression of the Incremental Return on Equity in the Equity-Based Value Driver Formula

The tricky part about the value driver formula is not the basic equation just discussed, but what happens to value when you change the growth rate and/ or the rate of return. Analysts who think they are fancy will tell you that all you need to understand is that the rate of return in the value driver formula is the incremental return on new investments and the formula can appropriately be used in valuation. They explain that the value formula does not assume that the return suddenly falls to the return input into the formula but rather it mystically moves gradually from the existing return to the new return. To see what these people mean, you can restate the formula developed earlier on an earnings basis instead of on a per-share basis:

$$\text{Equity Value}_0 = \text{Net Income}_1 \times (1 - g/ROE)/(k - g)$$

The ROE inherent in the net income$_1$ term is not necessarily the same as the ROE in the right-hand side of the equation. The $1 - g/ROE$ term drives future dividend growth where the ROE is the return on new investments. But this ROE is not the same as the ROE inherent in current income. Net income can be defined as existing ROE multiplied by existing investment, and the ROE in the value driver equation can be defined as the incremental ROE. The equation is now:

$$\text{Equity Value}_0 = \text{ROE}_1 \times \text{Current Equity}_0 \times (1 - g/\text{Incremental ROE})/(k - g)$$

To evaluate implications of the value driver formula, a theoretical analysis is created where the equity investment is divided into the existing investment and new investment. The existing investment earns the initial rate of return while the new incremental investment earns the incremental ROE. Dividends that represent cash flow to investors can then be computed from the weighted average ROE and the assumed growth as demonstrated by the following formulas.

$$\text{Total Equity Investment} = \text{Current Equity} \times (1 + \text{Growth Rate})$$

$$\text{New Equity Investment} = \text{Total Equity Investment} - \text{Current Equity}$$

$$\text{Total Income} = \text{ROE}_1 \times \text{Current Equity} + \text{Incremental ROE} \times \text{New Equity Investment}$$

$$\text{Weighted ROE} = (\text{ROE}_1 \times \text{Current Equity} + \text{Incremental ROE} \times \text{New Equity})/\text{Total Equity}$$

$$\text{Dividends} = \text{Total Return} - \text{New Equity Investment}$$

Figure 33.1 illustrates a case where the incremental return equals the existing return. In this special (and irrelevant) case, the valuation derived from the value driver formula equals the theoretical valuation as shown at the bottom of the figure.

When the incremental return is different from the current return, the value driver formula begins to produce biased and unexplainable results. A changing return means that the growth rate in dividends, which is the definition of equity cash flow, cannot be equal to the growth rate in investment that is plugged into the formula. This is because the new incremental equity investment is driven by dividends, which are in turn driven by the existing as well as the incremental rate of return. Figure 33.2 shows a case with an ROE that declines from 20 percent to 12 percent and a growth rate of 5 percent. The value driver formula overstates the value by more than 6 percent relative to the true value, where the true value is defined as a case that consists of earning 20 percent on the initial investment and earning 12 percent on new investment.

AEC	D	E	F	G	H	I	J	K	L	M	N	O	P	Q
3	**Assumptions**													
4	Current ROE	15%		Growth Rate			5%			PE - Theory		13.33		
5	Incremental ROE	15%		Cost of Equity Capital			10%			PE- Value Driver		13.33		
6	**Model**													
7	Period		0	1	2	3	4	5	6	7	8	9	10	11
8														
9	Book Value		10.00	10.50	11.03	11.58	12.16	12.76	13.40	14.07	14.77	15.51	16.29	17.10
10	Initial Investment		10.00	10.00	10.00	10.00	10.00	10.00	10.00	10.00	10.00	10.00	10.00	10.00
11	Balance of New Investment		0.00	0.50	1.03	1.58	2.16	2.76	3.40	4.07	4.77	5.51	6.29	7.10
12	Incremental Required Investment			0.50	0.53	0.55	0.58	0.61	0.64	0.67	0.70	0.74	0.78	0.81
13														
14	Return on Initial Investment	15%		1.50	1.50	1.50	1.50	1.50	1.50	1.50	1.50	1.50	1.50	1.50
15	Return on New Investment	15%		0.00	0.08	0.15	0.24	0.32	0.41	0.51	0.61	0.72	0.83	0.94
16	Total Return			1.50	1.58	1.65	1.74	1.82	1.91	2.01	2.11	2.22	2.33	2.44
17														
18	Weighted Return		15.00%	15.00%	15.00%	15.00%	15.00%	15.00%	15.00%	15.00%	15.00%	15.00%	15.00%	15.00%
19														
20	Dividends			1.00	1.05	1.10	1.16	1.22	1.28	1.34	1.41	1.48	1.55	1.63
21	Growth in Dividends				5.00%	5.00%	5.00%	5.00%	5.00%	5.00%	5.00%	5.00%	5.00%	5.00%
22	**Valuation**													
23	**Value - Theory**	**20.00**	<---- =NPV(J5,20:20)											
24	**Value - Driver Formula**	**20.00**	<---- =(1-Growth_Rate/Incremental_ROE)/(Cost_of_Equity_Capital-Growth_Rate)*initial_return											
25														
26	Percent Difference	0.00%												

FIGURE 33.1 Illustration of the Equity Value Driver Formula When Incremental Return Equals Return on Existing Equity

AEC	D	E	F	G	H	I	J	K	L	M	N	O	P	Q
3	**Assumptions**													
4	Current ROE	20%		Growth Rate			5%			PE - Theory		11.00		
5	Incremental ROE	12%		Cost of Equity Capital			10%			PE- Value Driver		11.67		
6	**Model**													
7	Period		0	1	2	3	4	5	6	7	8	9	10	11
8														
9	Book Value		10.00	10.50	11.03	11.58	12.16	12.76	13.40	14.07	14.77	15.51	16.29	17.10
10	Initial Investment		10.00	10.00	10.00	10.00	10.00	10.00	10.00	10.00	10.00	10.00	10.00	10.00
11	Balance of New Investment		0.00	0.50	1.03	1.58	2.16	2.76	3.40	4.07	4.77	5.51	6.29	7.10
12	Incremental Required Investment			0.50	0.53	0.55	0.58	0.61	0.64	0.67	0.70	0.74	0.78	0.81
13														
14	Return on Initial Investment	20%		2.00	2.00	2.00	2.00	2.00	2.00	2.00	2.00	2.00	2.00	2.00
15	Return on New Investment	12%		0.00	0.06	0.12	0.19	0.26	0.33	0.41	0.49	0.57	0.66	0.75
16	Total Return			2.00	2.06	2.12	2.19	2.26	2.33	2.41	2.49	2.57	2.66	2.75
17														
18	Weighted Return		20.00%	20.00%	19.62%	19.26%	18.91%	18.58%	18.27%	17.97%	17.69%	17.41%	17.16%	16.91%
19														
20	Dividends			1.50	1.54	1.57	1.61	1.65	1.69	1.74	1.78	1.83	1.89	1.94
21						2.33%	2.39%	2.46%	2.52%	2.58%	2.64%	2.70%	2.76%	2.82%	2.88%
22	**Valuation**													
23	**Value - Theory**	**22.00**	<---- =NPV(J5,20:20)											
24	**Value - Driver Formula**	**23.33**	<---- =(1-Growth_Rate/Incremental_ROE)/(Cost_of_Equity_Capital-Growth_Rate)*initial_return											
25														
26	Percent Difference	6.06%												

FIGURE 33.2 Value Driver Formula versus Theoretical Value When Return on Incremental Investment Is below Current Return

If the existing equity investment used as the basis for the application of the current ROE were assumed to decline rather than to stay flat, the true value of 20 shown in Figure 33.2 would be lower. The value driver formula would not change, and the bias from applying the value driver formula would be even greater. The exercise illustrated in Figure 33.2 demonstrates that the value driver formula does not produce a correct valuation even in a relatively simple case with flat growth rates and equity cash flow.

The bias from applying the value driver formula depends on the growth rate assumption as well as the difference between the current return and the future return. If the growth rate is 0 or if the difference between the current return and the incremental return is 0, there is no bias from applying the value driver formula. Figure 33.3 shows the valuation error with changing growth rates as well as different returns. When both changing growth and changing returns are simulated, the bias is not consistently positive or negative. In Figure 33.3 the cost of capital is assumed to be 12 percent and the existing ROE is assumed to be 16 percent. In cases where the incremental return equals the cost of capital of 12 percent, the bias is zero and the value driver formula becomes equivalent to the constant growth formula. However, in cases where the incremental return is below the current return and there is a positive growth, the value driver formula produces a higher number than the theoretical value. If there is no growth, the error is also 0, as is the case where the incremental return equals the existing return. In these special cases, the value driver formula produces the same results as the growth rate formula.

Assumptions: Cost of Capital   12%   Existing ROE   16%

Percent Difference Between Measured Value and Theoretical Value						
		Growth				
		-2.00%	0.00%	2.00%	4.00%	6.00%	8.00%
	24.00%	4.00%	0.00%	-4.35%	-9.09%	-14.29%	-20.00%
	22.00%	2.67%	0.00%	-3.03%	-6.49%	-10.49%	-15.15%
	20.00%	1.54%	0.00%	-1.82%	-4.00%	-6.67%	-10.00%
Incremental Return	18.00%	0.63%	0.00%	-0.78%	-1.75%	-3.03%	-4.76%
	16.00%	0.00%	0.00%	0.00%	0.00%	0.00%	0.00%
	14.00%	-0.26%	0.00%	0.35%	0.84%	1.59%	2.86%
	12.00%	0.00%	0.00%	0.00%	0.00%	0.00%	0.00%
	10.00%	1.05%	0.00%	-1.54%	-4.00%	-8.57%	-20.00%
	8.00%	3.45%	0.00%	-5.26%	-14.29%	-33.33%	-100.00%

FIGURE 33.3 Table of Bias in Value Driver Formula from Applying Different Rates of Return and Growth Rates

In simulating the cash flows using the value driver formula, a weighted average return can be established. This is computed as the ROE from existing investment weighted by the existing investment divided by the total investment plus the incremental ROE multiplied by the incremental investment divided by the total investment:

$$\text{Weighted ROE} = \text{Current ROE} \times \text{Current Investment} /$$
$$\text{Total Investment} + \text{Incremental ROE}$$
$$\times \text{Accumulated New Investment} / \text{Total Investment}$$

When applying the value driver formula using equity cash flows, if there is positive growth, the weighted average return gradually converges to the incremental return. With growth, the current level of investment is a less and less important component of the total investment. The manner in which the ROE gradually converges to the incremental ROE with different growth rates is illustrated in Figures 33.4 and 33.5. Figure 33.4 assumes 1 percent growth. Here, the ROE remains more than 200 basis points above the incremental ROE after 50 years. The second case, shown in Figure 33.5, applies 6 percent growth. This time the weighted return converges much faster to the incremental return as more of the equity consists of the new equity.

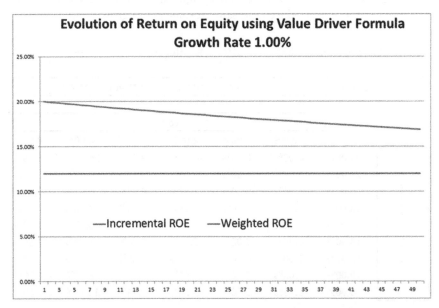

FIGURE 33.4 Weighted Average Return on Equity and Incremental Return on Equity Assuming 1 Percent Growth

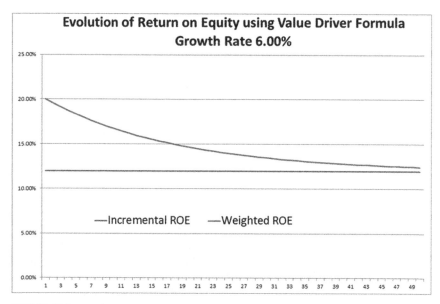

FIGURE 33.5 Weighted Average Return on Equity and Incremental Return on Equity Assuming 6 Percent Growth

Some people may be quite satisfied with the graphs shown in Figures 33.4 and 33.5 and will explain how the marginal rate of return on investments should drive value. Since the weighted average return does not suddenly decline to the incremental return, the formula seems to result in a reasonable transition period. Supporters of the value driver formula would insist that you just have to get into your head the difference between the marginal return and the existing return. In the extreme, if there is no growth, the incremental return is irrelevant. This is because the incremental return applies only to new investment and existing investment is assumed to be isolated from competitive pressures that drive the value down. The zero growth case is verified by putting a zero growth in the formula and showing that the incremental return falls out of the equation and becomes a perpuluity:

$$\text{Equity Value} = \text{ROE}_1 \times \text{Current Equity} \times (1 - 0/\text{Incremental ROE})/(k - 0)$$

$$\text{Equity Value} = \text{ROE}_1 \times \text{Current Equity}/k$$

In the zero growth case earnings are all paid as dividends, and this formula is the same as D_1/k, which is the standard growth rate formula. The existing investment of the company has no exposure to the convergence of return to the cost of capital.

The relationship between growth and convergence of total returns to the incremental return conflicts with the consumer behavior principles that underlie the formula. The general idea behind convergence of return and cost of capital is that products are supposed to have a life cycle, and competitive pressure is supposed to eventually push down returns. This is counter to the idea that if there is no growth, the return can somehow be protected and large mature companies can avoid pressures of becoming inefficient bureaucracies. The implicit assumption in the value driver formula is that the existing investment somehow is insulated from pressures to converge to incremental return forever. If you believed that existing investments can by hook or by crook continue to earn their existing rate of return in the face of competitive pressure, you are also assuming that the existing assets are some sort of thing that never dies or that these assets can be replaced and continue to earn their high return even though other new investments earn an incremental return.

In practice, more people probably care about the weighted average ROE than the incremental ROE. If you own a factory that makes portable telephones and your style of telephones falls out of favor, you would not care about some kind of theoretical incremental ROE on hypothetical new investments in new factories that you have not built yet. You would care about why your existing investment cannot make money anymore because of competitive pressure. Similarly, if you own a food business and the margins are squeezed by increasing costs of inputs, it is not the marginal return on new investments that is causing the problem. Instead, your interest is in the progression of the overall return on your equity investment. When you derive the P/E and EV/EBITDA equations from a series of different value drivers in Chapters 34 and 35, the return on overall investment and a transition period are explicit inputs into the model.

The analysis of the equity value driver formula that is driven by ROE and earnings growth demonstrates a few serious problems with trying to apply the equation as a basis for computing terminal value. First, the formula produces biased valuation if the return on new investments is different from the return on existing assets. Second, the manner in which the weighted average rate of return changes over time is not logical. If the growth rate is lower, the competitive advantage that results in a high return is probably disappearing more quickly and the convergence from current return to incremental return should probably be quicker instead of slower. There is no economic theory that suggests returns on existing investments can be maintained and that competitive pressures on existing investments can be isolated from pressures on new investments. Third, when applying the formula, the time it takes to converge is relatively long and there is no flexibility to adjust the time frame for moving the convergence of the rate of return. Finally, the length of time for the returns to converge does not account for depreciation and aging of existing assets. If the return on existing investment declines, the bias in the formula may be greater. In summary, the idea of plugging in value drivers and coming up with a result that can be plugged into the terminal value is attractive. The problem is that the value driver formula does not work.

Deriving the Value Driver Formula Using the Return on Invested Capital and the Weighted Average Cost of Capital

The value driver formula applied to prefinancing income and free cash flow to the firm (FCFF) is similar to the formula derived previously using equity returns and growth in dividends, except that NOPAT replaces earnings per share (EPS), WACC replaces the equity cost of capital, and the growth in invested capital replaces the growth in equity capital investment. When applying the value driver formula to NOPAT, the current level of return implied in the existing NOPAT generally has a different value than the incremental ROIC in the formula, just as the ROE implied in current earnings is different from the incremental ROE. To understand the logic of the formula, you can begin with the equation for free cash flow and invested capital derived from NOPAT:

$$\text{Free Cash Flow} = \text{NOPAT} + \text{Depreciation} - \text{Capital Expenditures}$$
$$- \text{Working Capital Changes} + \text{Deferred Tax}$$

$$\text{Growth in Invested Capital} = \text{Growth in Net Property, Plant, and Equipment}$$
$$+ \text{Growth in Net Working Capital}$$
$$- \text{Growth in Accumulated Deferred Tax}$$

$$\text{Growth in Invested Capital} = \text{Capital Expenditures} - \text{Depreciation Expense}$$
$$+ \text{Working Capital Changes} - \text{Deferred Tax Changes}$$

The value driver equation can be established because invested capital—net plant assets plus working capital less accumulated deferred tax—grows by capital expenditures and working capital changes, and declines by deferred tax changes and depreciation. Substituting growth for the capital expenditures, depreciation, working capital changes, and deferred tax changes, the formula for free cash flow can be rewritten as:

$$\text{Free Cash Flow} = \text{NOPAT} - \text{Growth in Invested Capital}$$

Since the NOPAT can be expressed as the current return multiplied by the invested capital, and, inversely, the invested capital = NOPAT/ROIC, the free cash formula can be further restated as:

$$\text{Free Cash Flow} = \text{ROIC} \times (\text{Invested Capital} - g \times \text{Invested Capital})$$

or, since NOPAT = Invested Capital × ROIC,

$$\text{Free Cash Flow} = \text{NOPAT} - g \times \text{NOPAT}/\text{ROIC}$$

or

$$\text{Free Cash Flow} = \text{NOPAT} \times (1 - g/\text{ROIC})$$

Given that NOPAT increases by the growth rate in invested capital, if the ROIC remains constant, the enterprise value is the FCFF/(WACC − g), or:

$$\text{Enterprise Value} = \text{NOPAT} \times (1 - g/\text{ROIC})/(\text{WACC} - g)$$

Adjusting for growth and the mathematics of using the subsequent-period cash flow, if the terminal period is time period t and the terminal growth rate is g, then:

$$\text{Enterprise Value} = \text{NOPAT}_t \times (1 + g) \times \{1 - [g/(1 + g)]/\text{ROIC}\}/(\text{WACC} - g)$$

Derivation of the value driver formula demonstrates that the growth rate applied in the formula is the growth rate in invested capital. This is not necessarily the same as the growth rate in EBITDA if the return is changing. As with the equity-based formula, the formula for enterprise value can be expressed in terms of the current return implied in the NOPAT and the return that is implied in future growth, as shown:

$$\text{Enterprise Value} = \text{Invested Capital} \times \text{ROIC}_1 \times (1 - \text{Asset Growth}/\text{ROIC}_2)/$$
$$(\text{WACC} - \text{Asset Growth})$$

The formula can be used to demonstrate that when the incremental future return equals the cost of capital, the growth rate does not matter in establishing the enterprise value. If the incremental return is the same as the cost of capital, the formula boils down to the simple perpetuity formula. The value of the company is simply the current level of invested capital multiplied by the ROIC divided by the cost of capital, which is the same as the standard perpetuity formula with no growth. To work though this formula, assume that ROIC = WACC; then:

$$\text{Enterprise Value} = \text{Invested Capital} \times \text{ROIC}_1 \times (1 - g/\text{WACC})/(\text{WACC} - g)$$

$$\text{Enterprise Value} = \text{Invested Capital} \times \text{ROIC}_1$$
$$\times [(\text{WACC} - g)/\text{WACC}]/(\text{WACC} - g)$$

The term WACC − *g* falls out of the equation, and enterprise value becomes:

$$\text{Enterprise Value} = \text{Invested Capital} \times \text{ROIC}_1/\text{WACC}$$

The last formula implies that if the cost of capital equals the return invested capital on future assets, all of the value of a company comes from the existing assets and the return on those assets relative to the cost of capital. In this situation it is not necessary to worry about future growth and the long-term prospects for the company, because each new investment adds no value. The company could grow really fast or it could decline, and it would not matter in terms of valuation. In this special case the value of the company is analogous to project finance investments, and the fact that a corporation is supposed to last indefinitely does not matter for valuation.

Biases in the Value Driver Formula in a Case with Only Working Capital

As with the formula for equity returns, a big problem with the value driver formula is that the equation is difficult and unintuitive with respect to the definition and interpretation of incremental return relative to current return. This is a big enough problem that renders the equation useless. But difficulties with the formula are even worse when one delves into the formula in more detail and applies it on an enterprise value basis rather than a simple equity basis. The value driver formula in the context of enterprise value is not only almost impossible to interpret, but it can also produce biased valuations. As with the discussion of stable ratios in Chapters 29, 30, and 31, to demonstrate how various valuation issues are applied, studying working capital is the starting point. One would think that in a hypothetical case with only working capital—meaning there are no taxes, no capital expenditures, no depreciation, and no deferred taxes—that there would not be any biases in valuation. However, when working through a case where a company has nothing other than working capital, the formula results in a biased valuation if the incremental return is not equal to the existing return.

To work through the working capital analysis, assume that you have some sort of retail or trading business in Abu Dhabi (you pay no taxes and you have virtually no plant investment, capital expenditures, or depreciation). Your primary investment is inventory. Currently you have one store that is earning a good return of 20 percent. But new retail stores will be subject to more competitive pressure, and these new stores will earn a return of only 12 percent. Further, assume the cost of capital for the business enterprise is 9 percent. The next couple of paragraphs demonstrate that the value driver formula produces biased value in this very simple case because it is impossible to construct a case where cash flow grows at the same rate as the working capital investment and at the same time the rate of return on new investment differs from the rate of return on existing plant.

To understand problems with the value driver formula in this simple example with only working capital investment, consider a couple of formulas in a case where there is no change from the existing rate of return to the incremental return. If the return on incremental investment is the same as the return on existing investment, the value driver formula produces an unbiased valuation. Without a change in the rate of return, the value driver formula produces the same result as the stable growth rate formula where you just divide the next period cash flow by the WACC minus growth. This case without changes in the rate of return provides a base for illustrating problems when the rate of return changes.

If there is no depreciation and there are no taxes, then EBITDA is the same as NOPAT. Where working capital is the only asset, then invested capital is equal to working capital. Further, if the return remains constant, then the growth rate in investment is the same as the growth rate in NOPAT. Finally, if working capital is the only asset on the balance sheet, the ratio of working capital to EBITDA contains the same information as the return on investment. WC/EBITDA that defines the level of working capital is the inverse of NOPAT/WC or EBITDA/WC, which is the return on investment. You cannot change the working capital level relative to EBITDA without also changing the return on investment.

If the only asset is working capital, the ROIC depends on the management of working capital. If you are going to increase the return on invested capital, the only thing you can do is something that will be measured by managing working capital more efficiently. By contrast, if the ROIC declines this means the working capital management is not as efficient. Nothing else affects ROIC other than the amount of EBITDA relative to working capital investment. If the growth rate in working capital investment remains constant, but the incremental ROIC declines relative to the current level of the ROIC, then the EBITDA growth must decline. There is nothing else that can happen because of the definition of return in this special case. There is nowhere else to go and no room or degrees of freedom in the equation. This all implies the EBITDA must have a different growth rate from the growth in invested capital if the return changes. It is not possible to change the ratio of working capital investment to EBITDA without changing the rate or return and vice versa:

$$\text{Working Capital Ratio} = \text{Working Capital Investment/EBITDA}$$

$$\text{Working Capital Ratio} = \text{Invested Capital/EBITDA}$$

But, since NOPAT = EBITDA,

Return on Investment = EBITDA/Invested Capital

which means:

Return on Investment = 1/Working Capital Ratio

These formulas imply that if a 20 percent return on investment is assumed, then the working capital ratio is 1 divided by the return or 1/20 percent or 500 percent. If the growth rate is 5 percent and the initial value amount of working capital is 100, then the theoretically correct enterprise value is the return of 20 percent applied to the 100 with a constant growth rate. To compute the enterprise value in the case with only working capital, your model could include: (1) working capital investment as defined by the 5 percent growth assumption, (2) EBITDA is computed through dividing the 100 working capital investment by 500 percent or multiplying the number by 20 percent, (3) free cash flow to the firm is the EBITDA that starts at 20 less the changes in working capital, and (4) the value of the firm is the present value of cash flows at 9 percent over a long-term period. Using these assumptions, the theoretical valuation using a long-term simulation model is illustrated in Figure 33.6.

When current return is the same as the incremental return, the stable growth formula results in the same value as that shown in Figure 33.6. The formula developed for stable working capital changes in Chapter 30, WC/EBITDA × EBITDA × $g/(1 + g)$, can be subtracted from EBITDA and then applied in the formula FCFF × $(1 + g)/(WACC - g)$. This yields the same value as the theoretical value from assuming that cash flow keeps growing for a couple of hundred years. Alternatively, the value can be established by employing the value driver formula with 20 percent return, 5 percent growth, and 9 percent cost of capital to NOPAT (which in this case without depreciation is the same as EBITDA):

$$\text{Enterprise Value} = \text{NOPAT}_t \times (1 + g) \times \{1 - [g/(1 + g)]/\text{ROIC}\}/(\text{WACC} - g)$$

$$536.03 = 26.8 \times 1.05 \times [1 - (0.05/1.05)/20\%]/(9\% - 5\%)$$

The problems with the value driver formula begin when the simple case is modified to reflect changing returns and/or changing growth. In the case of changing return, the working capital investment still grows at the assumed 5 percent rate, but it is segregated between one part that continues to earn 20 percent and the remainder that reflects the lower incremental return as discussed for the Abu Dhabi retail store example. The investment over and above the base working capital investment is assumed to earn a lower return

Assumptions			
WC to EBITDA - History	500%	Explicit Growth	5%
WC to EBITDA - Projected	500%	Terminal Growth	5%
Explicit Rate of Return	20%	WACC	9%
Long Term Rate of Return	20%		

Valuation with Change in Return													
Working Capital		100.00	105.00	110.25	115.76	121.55	127.63	134.01	140.71	147.75	155.13	162.89	171.03
Existing Working Capital			105.00	110.25	115.76	121.55	127.63	134.01	134.01	134.01	134.01	134.01	134.01
New Working Capital			0.00	0.00	0.00	0.00	0.00	0.00	6.70	13.74	21.12	28.88	37.02
Existing WC Ratio		500%	500%	500%	500%	500%	500%	500%	500%	500%	500%	500%	500%
New WC Ratio		500%	500%	500%	500%	500%	500%	500%	500%	500%	500%	500%	500%
EBITDA from Existing Assets			21.00	22.05	23.15	24.31	25.53	26.80	26.80	26.80	26.80	26.80	26.80
EBITDA from New Investments			0.00	0.00	0.00	0.00	0.00	0.00	1.34	2.75	4.22	5.78	7.40
EBITDA		20.00	21.00	22.05	23.15	24.31	25.53	26.80	28.14	29.55	31.03	32.58	34.21
EBITDA Growth			5.00%	5.00%	5.00%	5.00%	5.00%	0.05	5.00%	5.00%	5.00%	5.00%	5.00%
WC Change			5.00	5.25	5.51	5.79	6.08	6.38	6.70	7.04	7.39	7.76	8.14
FCFF			FALSE	FALSE	FALSE	FALSE	FALSE	FALSE	21.44	22.51	23.64	24.82	26.06
True Theoretical Value	**536.03**												
NOPAT			FALSE	FALSE	FALSE	FALSE	FALSE	28.14	FALSE	FALSE	FALSE	FALSE	FALSE
Multiplier: (1-g/(1+g)/ROIC)/(WACC-g)	20%	5%	19.05	19.05	19.05	19.05	19.05	19.05	19.05	19.05	19.05	19.05	19.05
			FALSE	FALSE	FALSE	FALSE	FALSE	536.04	FALSE	FALSE	FALSE	FALSE	FALSE
Value from Value Driver Formula	**536.04**												

FIGURE 33.6 Enterprise of Firm with Only Working Capital Investment Earning a Current and Incremental Rate of Return of 20 Percent

of 12 percent, which is still above the assumed cost of capital of 9 percent. The EBITDA earned on the incremental investment and the new investment can be summed and the change in working capital can be subtracted from the EBITDA to establish the free cash flow. This free cash flow can be valued using the 9 percent WACC to arrive at the theoretical value. An excerpt from the long-term model is illustrated in Figure 33.7. The bottom of Figure 33.7 demonstrates that when the value driver formula is applied in the case of a changing return, the computed amount from the value driver formula is substantially above the correct theoretical value.

When the working capital growth and returns are segregated as inputs in the value driver formula, it is impossible to keep the growth in free cash flow equivalent to the growth in investment. This is because the return has no degrees of freedom relative to the working capital ratio, and both have exactly the same information. The difference in effective cash flow growth relative to the input investment growth means that valuation from the value driver formula will not correspond to the true theoretical value if the growth rate changes over time or the return on investment changes. In the scenario shown earlier with 5 percent growth and 9 percent WACC, the value driver formula

Assumptions

WC to EBITDA - History	500%	Explicit Growth	5%
WC to EBITDA - Projected	833%	Terminal Growth	5%
Explicit Rate of Return	20%	WACC	9%
Long Term Rate of Return	12%		

Valuation with Change in Return

Working Capital	100.00	105.00	110.25	115.76	121.55	127.63	134.01	140.71	147.75	155.13	162.89	171.03
Existing Working Capital		105.00	110.25	115.76	121.55	127.63	134.01	134.01	134.01	134.01	134.01	134.01
New Working Capital		0.00	0.00	0.00	0.00	0.00	0.00	6.70	13.74	21.12	28.88	37.02
Existing WC Ratio	500%	500%	500%	500%	500%	500%	500%	500%	500%	500%	500%	500%
New WC Ratio	833%	833%	833%	833%	833%	833%	833%	833%	833%	833%	833%	833%
EBITDA from Existing Assets		21.00	22.05	23.15	24.31	25.53	26.80	26.80	26.80	26.80	26.80	26.80
EBITDA from New Investments		0.00	0.00	0.00	0.00	0.00	0.00	0.80	1.65	2.53	3.47	4.44
EBITDA	20.00	21.00	22.05	23.15	24.31	25.53	26.80	27.61	28.45	29.34	30.27	31.24
EBITDA Growth		5.00%	5.00%	5.00%	5.00%	5.00%	0.05	3.00%	3.06%	3.12%	3.17%	3.23%
WC Change		5.00	5.25	5.51	5.79	6.08	6.38	6.70	7.04	7.39	7.76	8.14
FCFF		FALSE	FALSE	FALSE	FALSE	FALSE	FALSE	20.91	21.41	21.95	22.51	23.10

True Theoretical Value: 373.73

NOPAT		FALSE	FALSE	FALSE	FALSE	FALSE	28.14	FALSE	FALSE	FALSE	FALSE	FALSE
Multiplier: (1-g/(1+g)/ROIC)/(WACC-g) 12%	5%	15.08	15.08	15.08	15.08	15.08	15.08	15.08	15.08	15.08	15.08	15.08
		FALSE	FALSE	FALSE	FALSE	FALSE	424.36	FALSE	FALSE	FALSE	FALSE	FALSE

Value from Value Driver Formula: 424.36

FIGURE 33.7 Excerpt from Long-Term Analysis with Changing Rate of Return

overstates the true value by 14 percent. For this simple hypothetical example with only working capital, the bias implicit in the value driver formula depends on the rate of return difference as well as the growth rate. When returns are not equivalent or growth is not zero, the mathematics of the value driver formula does not produce the correct value. Figure 33.8 illustrates errors for various

		Growth Rate				
		0%	2%	4%	6%	8%
Incremental Return	22.00%	0.00%	-1.60%	-3.41%	-5.42%	-1.12%
	20.00%	0.00%	0.00%	0.00%	0.03%	7.13%
	18.00%	0.00%	1.46%	3.31%	5.75%	16.61%
	16.00%	0.00%	2.69%	6.31%	11.47%	27.38%
	14.00%	0.00%	3.52%	8.58%	16.53%	39.09%
	12.00%	0.00%	3.67%	9.35%	19.34%	49.79%
	10.00%	0.00%	2.64%	7.06%	15.98%	50.35%
	8.00%	0.00%	-0.60%	-1.70%	-4.31%	-17.13%

FIGURE 33.8 Sensitivity Table of Value Error from Value Driver Equation in Simple Working Capital Case with Different Growth and Returns

combinations of incremental returns and growth. The general idea of coming up with a formula from value drivers in the terminal value is a good idea. The problem again is that the value driver formula does not work.

Problems of the Value Driver Formula When Invested Capital Includes Net Plant

Instead of assuming that a company's only investment is working capital, you could pretend that invested capital includes only accumulated capital expenditures associated with property and plant investment. Issues that produced valuation distortions for the case with only working capital apply in the same way to plant investment, but in the case of capital expenditures and depreciation there are some additional problems. If the plant investment somehow did not depreciate or had a one-year life, the ratio of EBIT to plant is directly analogous to the ratio of working capital to EBITDA. In the case with only plant investment, return on investment is defined as EBIT divided by net plant. This means that when the rate of return changes, the ratio of plant to EBIT must also change. If the ratio of the plant balance to EBIT changes because of different return assumptions, then the input growth rate in EBITDA cannot be the same as the resulting growth in investment. Since the growth rate in cash flow or EBITDA less capital expenditures is not the same as the growth rate in investment that is input, the value driver formula does not equal the correct value of the EBITDA. This is the same problem that caused biases when only working capital investment is included in the analysis.

The problems that arise with working capital are compounded when employing the value driver formula to depreciating assets. One additional problem is that the level of future capital expenditures depends on the growth rate of existing assets, as discussed at length in Chapter 31, where the stable ratio of capital expenditures to depreciation was derived. The analysis in that chapter demonstrates that with different historical growth rates, the true theoretical value of the firm changes. As the historical growth rate is nowhere in the value driver formula it cannot account for the age of a company's assets. If there is no input for the historical growth in the value driver formula, the equation cannot account for the way in which historical growth affects future capital expenditures. Another problem is that when depreciating assets are included in the analysis, existing investment does not remain constant, as was the case for working capital. Instead, the investment declines with accumulated depreciation. This is like the retail store in Abu Dhabi becoming less and less important as it becomes older rather than always being able to earn the 20 percent return on investment. With depreciating assets, the return on existing investment is applied to a progressively lower and lower base over time. If the return on new assets is less than the return on existing assets and if the existing balance of assets decline, the stream of income from existing assets declines. As the value driver formula overstates value even when existing assets do not decline, the problem is aggravated for depreciating assets.

To measure errors in valuation that arise from using the value driver formula, the theoretical analysis developed to evaluate stable ratios of capital expenditures to depreciation in Chapter 31 is modified. The model can be augmented to incorporate assumed changes in rates of return, which is the key element of the value driver formula. Capital expenditures and level of plant still grow at the rates that are input, but now the EBITDA generated from the net plant changes when the assumed return on investment changes. As the net plant depends on future capital expenditures and future capital expenditures depend on replacing retirements associated with historical growth, the rate of return depends in part on historical growth as well as future growth. Using the long-term simulation model augmented to include changes in return as well as growth, the value driver formula can be compared to the true theoretical enterprise value. Figures 33.9a, 33.9b, and 33.9c summarize different scenarios of growth and return changes. These figures demonstrate that the error from applying the value driver formula can become large. In a case where the existing return equals the incremental return and the growth rate is zero, the value driver formula does produce a correct valuation. In this case, with no return differences and a zero growth rate, a simple perpetuity formula could also be used. However, as soon as the growth and return assumptions are relaxed, the value driver formula results in erroneous valuations.

In Figure 33.9a, the return on existing investments implied in current NOPAT is the same as the future incremental return but the future growth rate is different from explicit period growth. This results in a 6 percent

Plant Life	15.00		
Current Return	15.00%	Historic Growth	11%
Incremental Return	15.00%	Terminal Growth	5%
	Value	Pct Difference	Multiple of NOPLAT
Theoretically Correct Value	2,859.82		32.45
Value with Driver Formula	2,687.84	-6.0%	30.50

FIGURE 33.9a Sensitivity Analysis of Value Driver Formula with Net Plant Using 11 Percent Historical Growth and 5 Percent Terminal Growth with Existing Return Equal to Incremental Return

Plant Life   15.00

Current Return   20.00%   Historic Growth   5%
Incremental Return   12.00%   Terminal Growth   5%

	Value	Pct Difference	Multiple of NOPLAT
Theoretically Correct Value	626.22		20.32
Value with Driver Formula	830.71	32.7%	26.95

FIGURE 33.9b Sensitivity Analysis of Value Driver Formula with Net Plant Using Constant Growth and Lower Incremental Return on Invested Capital Than Existing Return

Plant Life   15.00

Current Return   20.00%   Historic Growth   15%
Incremental Return   12.00%   Terminal Growth   5%

	Value	Pct Difference	Multiple of NOPLAT
Theoretically Correct Value	4,938.58		18.14
Value with Driver Formula	7,338.36	48.6%	26.95

FIGURE 33.9c Sensitivity Analysis of Value Driver Formula with Net Plant Using Change in Growth and Difference between Incremental Return and Existing Return

understatement in value. In Figure 33.9b, the growth rate is the same, but the return declines, which is the fundamental reason for applying the value driver formula. This case results in a large overstatement of value by 33 percent. In Figure 33.9c, both the growth rate and the return change resulting in an overstatement of value by 49 percent. To employ value drivers in the terminal value calculation, more work is necessary. The solution is to create a user-defined function that replicates the theoretical value as described in subsequent chapters.

CHAPTER 34

Computing Implied Price/Earnings Ratios for Use in Terminal Value Calculations

If you spend time watching financial analysts on television sounding highly intelligent in expressing their opinions about the value of a stock, they generally pontificate about both the projected earnings and the valuation. Most of the time the analysts make some kind of earnings projection (more often than not optimistic) and then employ a future price/earnings (P/E) ratio to the projected earnings to arrive at what they think the future stock price will be. What they have done is estimate equity cash flow rather than free cash flow and then apply a terminal valuation using the P/E ratio. When the analysts go on about the future earnings multiplied by the P/E, they are talking about terminal value while the dividends received during the intermediate period are like the explicit free cash flows. These valuations are analogous to all of the discounted cash flow (DCF) discussion in previous chapters except the analysis is made with equity cash flow rather than free cash flow. In computing the equity value using a future P/E ratio, the financial analysts often seem to have some kind of magical way to project the future P/E ratio that drives the valuation.

The next two chapters discuss techniques to evaluate P/E and enterprise value/earnings before interest, taxes, depreciation, and amortization (EV/EBITDA) multiples for purposes of computing terminal value, and take some mystery out of the process of evaluating multiples. Employing a multiple such as the P/E and the EV/EBITDA in terminal value involves multiplying income in the terminal year by an assumed multiple. If this approach is used, the terminal value is no longer directly sensitive to the discount rate and the growth rate, as illustrated by the simplicity of the formula for terminal value:

$$\text{Terminal Value}_t = \text{EV}/\text{EBITDA} \times \text{EBITDA}_t$$

Because there is no discount rate in this formula, one of the big advantages of using multiples in the terminal value calculation is that the sensitivity to valuation resulting from variation in the cost of capital is generally much less than ranges that result from the growth rate formula. The decline in the range of valuations that results from use of the EV/EBITDA multiple is shown in Figure 34.1. The left-hand side illustrates the wide range in value that arises from variation in the weighted average cost of capital (WACC) and terminal growth rates when the growth rate formula is used. In the first table the widest variation is from the bottom left to the top right. The right-hand side demonstrates the much smaller valuation that occurs when the EV/EBITDA ratio is used instead of the growth rate for determining the terminal value.

		Growth Formula						Terminal EV/EBITDA Ratio			
		0%	1%	2%	3%	4%			9.0x	9.5x	10.0x	10.5x	11.0x
	7%	24.9x	27.8x	32.0x	38.1x	48.4x		7%	18.6x	19.2x	19.7x	20.3x	20.9x
WACC	8%	21.4x	23.5x	26.3x	30.1x	35.9x	WACC	8%	17.5x	18.1x	18.6x	19.1x	19.6x
	9%	18.8x	20.3x	22.2x	24.8x	28.4x		9%	16.5x	17.0x	17.5x	18.0x	18.5x
	10%	16.7x	17.8x	19.2x	21.0x	23.4x		10%	15.6x	16.0x	16.5x	17.0x	17.4x
	11%	14.9x	15.8x	16.9x	18.2x	19.9x		11%	14.7x	15.1x	15.6x	16.0x	16.4x

FIGURE 34.1 EV/EBITDA Multiple Range from Applying Discounted Cash Flow Model with Growth Rate Formula and with Terminal EV/EBITDA Multiple

For companies that are already in a relatively stable phase with low growth and returns close to the cost of capital, using a multiple from comparative companies with listed stock prices is logical. If other companies in the industry have similar multiples and low growth, the multiple should be as comparable a few years from today as it is currently. However, there are a few disadvantages to applying multiples in the terminal value. First, if the growth rate, the return, or the cost of capital changes from the explicit period to the terminal period, the multiples should also change. When the company or the industry is assumed to change in terms of prospective growth, risk, or rate of return, you cannot take the numbers from some kind of comparative analysis that is dependent on current market data and use this data in the terminal period. Second, when constructing the EV/EBITDA multiples from comparative financial market data, the samples are subject to manipulation. There is subjectivity as to what companies to select and there are often wide ranges in comparative multiples. Third, the EV/EBITDA multiples should in theory be adjusted for differences in company value that occur because of tax rate differences, asset life variation, alternative operating risk, as well as different growth rate and return expectations. Academics who complain about using multiples in the DCF model insist that the multiple that is present when making comparisons using today's market conditions cannot be used in terminal value calculations. They insist that the use of multiples pollutes the whole DCF process.

Use of a multiple such as the P/E ratio or the EV/EBITDA ratio means that the valuation ultimately depends on the opinions of other people and it can be called relative valuation. To demonstrate the problem with applying comparative multiples from samples of supposedly similar companies, think about valuing homes in the United States before the financial crisis of 2008. Appraisers would play games with comparative samples where houses that sold for relatively low values would be excluded from a comparative sample, but homes with high selling prices—perhaps because of better features such as location or a new air conditioning system—would be included in the sample. As the appraiser would arrive at a higher value because of the sample selection, the loan would also be higher, and the selling price would be increased. The higher selling price of the home that was the subject of the transaction would then be used in the next appraisal, and a vicious circle would be created that pushed up appraised values because of sampling methods.

Figure 34.2 illustrates analogous problems when using multiples in the context of valuing a corporation. This figure shows how samples in deriving multiples can be very subjective and lack logic. The company being valued in Figure 34.2 is a small airfreight company with a market capitalization of

Table 3
Valuation Table

Air Freight Company Comparables

Share prices as of close: 5/30/97

Ticker	Price	52 week: High	Low	Mkt. Cap.	YTD Perf.	EPS FY96A	FY97E	FY98E	P/B	P/E FY96A	FY97E	FY98E	P/EBITDA FY96A	FY97E	FY98E	Ent.Value/EBITDA FY96A	FY97E	FY98E	P/E vs. SP500 FY96A	FY97E	FY98E
ATLS	$ 28.75	$ 59.75	$ 19.88	$ 645.4	-39.8%	$ 1.88	$ 2.10	$ 2.50	3.0x	15.3x	13.7x	11.5x	1.5x	1.1x	0.9x	8.9x	6.4x	5.0x	0.74x	0.72x	0.64x
KTTY	16.75	17.25	8.00	175.1	67.5%	0.98	$ 1.15	$ 1.45	2.9x	17.1x	14.8x	11.5x	9.5x	5.2x	4.2x	10.3x	5.7x	4.6x	0.83x	0.76x	0.64x
FDX	52.38	57.88	36.25	5,970.8	17.7%	3.32	4.24	.	2.1x	15.8x	12.4x	NA	4.4x	4.0x	3.6x	5.5x	5.0x	4.4x	0.77x	0.65x	NA
ABF	38.25	38.38	19.50	803.3	63.6%	1.28	3.40	4.00	1.9x	29.9x	11.3x	9.5x	3.3x	2.6x	2.4x	4.8x	3.8x	3.5x	1.45x	0.59x	0.53x
							Mean		2.5x	19.5x	13.0x	10.9x	4.7x	3.2x	2.6x	7.4x	5.2x	4.4x	0.9x	0.7x	0.6x
							Adj. Mean		1.3x	16.4x	13.0x	5.5x	3.9x	3.3x	3.0x	7.2x	5.3x	4.5x	0.8x	0.7x	0.3x
							High		3.0x	29.9x	14.6x	11.5x	9.5x	5.2x	4.2x	10.3x	6.4x	5.0x	1.5x	0.8x	0.6x
							Low		1.9x	15.3x	11.3x	9.5x	1.5x	1.1x	0.9x	4.8x	3.8x	3.5x	0.7x	0.6x	0.5x

Note:
Enterprise Value = Market Value + LT Debt - Cash and Equivalents
ATLS = Atlas Air
KTTY = Kitty Hawk
FDX = Federal Express
ABF = Airborne Freight

FIGURE 34.2 Example of Problems That Arise from Constructing Comparative Samples to Derive Valuation Multiples
Source: Company reports and Scott and Stringfellow estimates.

$175 million. It is compared to Federal Express with a market capitalization then of $5.971 billion. The amount of debt that affects risk is not shown in the analysis, the returns of the different companies are not known, and the price of a share of equity compared to the EBITDA is included in one column (comparing postfinancing equity value with prefinancing EBITDA).

Problems with creating a sample like the one shown in Figure 34.2 prompt the question of whether an alternative approach can be used to find implied multiples that combine returns and growth rate assumptions with market data. A solution suggested in this chapter and the next is developing equations for computing implied multiples. By calculating the P/E ratio and the EV/EBITDA ratio rather than simply plopping in numbers from the Internet, you can directly input the return on investment and the terminal growth rate while backing into the implied cost of capital.

Even though the value driver formula discussed in Chapter 33 is not useful in making valuations, the general idea of explicitly accounting for value drivers of return, growth, and cost of capital in computing terminal value and multiples is attractive. Through computing implied multiples you can create a user-defined function that accepts inputs for: (1) historical EBITDA growth, (2) projected EBITDA growth, (3) current return on invested capital, (4) prospective return on invested capital, (5) the ratio of working capital to EBITDA, (6) book life, (7) tax depreciation rate, (8) income tax rate, and (9) WACC. Once you have created a user-defined function that uses these inputs, out will pop an EV/EBITDA ratio that you can use in terminal value and other calculations. You can try out different rates of return and market growth expectations to derive the cost of capital from the current market multiple with the Goal Seek function. You also could benchmark the computed multiples to current market conditions and then adjust the EV/EBITDA multiple for incremental changes in the growth rate, the rate of return, and even the cost of capital that should decline along with more stable conditions. The user-defined function for computing multiples can also incorporate a transition period between current growth/return and long-term growth/return. To explain how such a user-defined function for computing the EV/EBITDA ratio is developed, a general review of how multiples are used and a derivation of the P/E ratio are presented in the next section.

Model for Deriving the P/E Ratio from Value Drivers

The P/E ratio and the EV/EBITDA ratio are influenced by cost of capital, growth, and return. If the P/E ratio increases because of higher expected growth, the EV/EBITDA should increase as well. Similarly, if the EV/EBITDA declines because of higher perceived risk, the P/E ratio should also decline. Differences between the P/E and EV/EBITDA multiples are driven by taxes, the lifetime of assets in computing depreciation, and debt leverage. These differences can be demonstrated by considering an extreme case of a company with no taxes, no net debt, and no depreciation. Maybe it could be our retailing company located in the United Arab Emirates that was introduced in Chapter 33. In this extreme case, the equity value is the same as the enterprise value because the company has no net debt, and the EBITDA is the same as the net income (EBITDA minus depreciation minus amortization minus interest minus taxes equals net income). Since the net income equals EBITDA and enterprise value equals the equity value, the P/E ratio also equals the EV/EBITDA ratio. This means that when factors such as growth, return, and cost of capital influence the P/E ratio, these same things will affect the EV/EBITDA ratio. The example also demonstrates that the differences between P/E and EV/EBITDA are driven by depreciation on capital expenditures, taxes, and debt, or the DA, the T, and the I in EBITDA.

Deriving the P/E ratio and the EV/EBITDA ratio from value drivers may or may not be of much value in everyday valuations. But understanding how to compute the P/E and EV/EBITDA ratios from items like growth, returns, and cost of capital forces you to see what really drives the ratios. It also allows you to benchmark the multiples and understand the effect of incremental changes to the value drivers. To demonstrate how implicit multiples can be derived, the P/E ratio is described in this chapter. The derived P/E ratio is calculated from different long-term and short-term earnings growth rates, different short-term and long-term returns on equity, and changing cost of equity capital. Through explicitly considering these three factors along with transition periods for each variable, the P/E multiple can be derived without resorting to relative valuations that are subject to sampling bias and without distortions in the value driver formula that does not produce an accurate result. If you then use the implied P/E multiples in the terminal value calculation and compute those multiples from value drivers and transition factors, your valuation is explicitly driven by things like the long-term real growth rate and the difference between the return and cost of capital.

To analyze the drivers of value and the level of the P/E ratio, growth rates can be separated into short-term and long-term growth rates. Further, the cost of capital can be broken down to its building blocks that include the real rate of interest, the inflation rate, and the risk premium. Each of these building blocks can be differentiated by time period. The rate of return earned on equity can be expressed as the cost of capital plus a premium. In setting up a model of the P/E ratio, drivers include (1) the real growth rate in earnings in the short run and the long run, (2) the rate of return earned above the cost of capital in the short run and the long run, (3) the rate of inflation in the short run and the long run, (4) the real rate of interest, and (5) the risk premium in the short run and the long run.

A model to compute the implied P/E ratio involves measuring cash flow to equity. The trick in computing equity cash flow from dividends is using the formula for the dividend payout ratio that depends on growth and return. This formula for dividend payout is explained in Chapter 33 in the context of the value driver formula:

Dividend Payout = 1 − Earnings Growth/Return on Equity

In developing the model to simulate P/E, after the implied dividend payout ratio is computed, a table of the progression in the balance of equity, the net income per share, the book value per share, and the dividends per share can be calculated. When creating this long-term simulation model, the closing balance of the equity investment is the opening balance plus the income less the dividends. The period-by-period income and dividends are then computed from the following formulas:

Net Income = Return on Equity (Short-Term, Long-term, or Transition)
× Opening Equity Balance

Dividends = Dividend Payout (Short-Term, Long-Term, or Transition)
× Net Income

Since the discount rate changes, an index of the cost of capital can be computed and the SUMPRODUCT function can be used:

Value = SUMPRODUCT (Dividends/Discount Index)

P/E Ratio = First Year Net Income/Value of Equity

Computation of the P/E ratio using a simulation model is illustrated in Figure 34.3. The model includes timing switches to define the short-term period and a long-term period. The year-by-year return, dividend payout ratio, and cost of equity are computed using the switches, and the SUMPRODUCT function. The discount rate is calculated using a compounding index because the cost of capital changes over time, as explained in Chapter 28 and illustrated in Figure 28.5. Once the equity value is computed as the present value of the dividends in the output section shown on Figure 34.3, it is divided by the next year's earnings to establish the implied P/E ratio.

To derive the P/E or the EV/EBITDA ratio that theoretically would exist with changing growth rates and returns, transition factors can be included in the analysis. When variables have time differentiation such as the short-term and long-term values shown in Figure 34.3, it is generally not reasonable to assume that the change in the variable suddenly happens in one single year.

	C	D	E	F	G	H	I	J	K	L	M	N
5	**Inputs**									**Outputs**		
6		ST	LT						Price		→	19.53
7	Inflation Rate	2.0%	1.50%		Book Val		10.00		First Year Earnings			1.42
8					ST Per		5.00		Compute P/E Ratio			13.72
9	Real ROE (no inf)	12.00%	10.00%									
10	Nominal ROE	14.24%	11.65%						Book Value			10.00
11					=SUMPRODUCT(H28:KU28/H31:KU31)				Price to Book			1.95
12	Real CoE (no inflation)	7.00%	6.00%									
13	Nominal Cost of Equity	9.14%	7.59%						Value from Value Drive			17.55
14									PE from Value Driver			24.58
15	Real Growth	5.00%	1.00%									
16	Nominal growth rate	7.10%	2.52%									
17	Dividend Payout Ratio	50%	78%		<---- =1-Nominal_growth_rate/Nominal_ROE							
18	**Period**	ROE	DPO	COE	0	1	2	3	4	5	6	7
19	Short-term Period	14.24%	50%	9.14%		TRUE	TRUE	TRUE	TRUE	TRUE	FALSE	FALSE
20	Long-term Period	11.65%	78%	7.59%		FALSE	FALSE	FALSE	FALSE	FALSE	TRUE	TRUE
21	ROE				→	14.24%	14.24%	14.24%	14.24%	14.24%	11.65%	11.65%
22	Dividend Payout					50.14%	50.14%	50.14%	50.14%	50.14%	78.41%	78.41%
23	Cost of Equity					9.14%	9.14%	9.14%	9.14%	9.14%	7.59%	7.59%
24		=SUMPRODUCT(H19:H20*$D$19:$D$20)										
25	**Book Value**											
26	Opening Equity Balance					10.00	10.71	11.47	12.28	13.16	14.09	14.45
27	Add: NI (ROE x Open Bal =H26:KU26*roe---->					1.42	1.53	1.63	1.75	1.87	1.64	1.68
28	Less: Div (DPO x NI)	=NI*dpo---->				0.71	0.76	0.82	0.88	0.94	1.29	1.32
29	Closing Balance				10.00	10.71	11.47	12.28	13.16	14.09	14.45	14.81
30												
31	Discount Rate Index	=G31*(1+H23)---->			1.00	1.09	1.19	1.30	1.42	1.55	1.67	1.79
32	*Earnings Growth*						7%	7%	7%	7%	-12%	3%

FIGURE 34.3 Illustration of Computing the Implied P/E Ratio with Value Drivers

Instead, the variable gradually moves from the short-term rate to the long-term rate. This means the transition period as well as the short-term period can be defined with timing switches. In computing values during the transition period, equations for compound growth or linear growth can be used to interpolate variables that move from a short-run value to a long-term value. The different interpolation approaches apply the following equations:

$$ROE_t = (1 + g) \times ROE_{t-1}$$

where

$$g = (ROE_{\text{long-term}} / ROE_{\text{short-term}})^{(1/(1+\text{transition period}))}$$

or

$$ROE_t = ROE_{t-1} + \text{Linear Factor}$$

where

$$\text{Linear Factor} = (ROE_{\text{long-term}} - ROE_{\text{short-term}})/(1 + \text{Transition Period})$$

Considerations about whether to use the compound growth rate equation or the linear equation depend on whether it is possible to have a negative value for one of the factors such as ROE or growth. If one of the variables can be a negative number such as negative growth rate, the formula using the compound growth does not work, but the linear factor still can be applied.

When deriving inputs for the value drivers shown in Figure 34.3, some considerations include:

- The real growth rate in the long run should not be more than the expected nominal growth rate in the economy. Without exports and imports, the growth rate in an economy is defined by population growth and productivity increases. The real growth rate is also the theoretical real rate of interest as this amount must be held back from consumption to allow future investment. The spread between the earned return on equity (ROE) and the cost of capital in the long run should narrow with increased competition and other factors as described in Chapter 32, but it should probably not be zero. Without earning a return above the cost of capital, a company has no reason to make new investments.
- Despite all of the elegant theory and many articles that are related to estimating the risk premium, a couple of simple ideas can be used to put a boundary on the number. First, when growth rates and returns are relatively low in a stable period, the risk is also probably low. Without high return and high growth, there is less room to fall. Second, if you would like a quick way to estimate the cost of capital, you can use the fact that when the cost of capital is the same as the return on equity, the market-to-book ratio should be equal to 1. You can gather data on different market-to-book ratios as well as the forward return on equity using the technique with the WORKBOOKS.OPEN statement and the INDIRECT function as described in Chapters 33 and 35. Then you can create a regression equation of the forward ROE as a function of the market-to-book ratio using the following equation:

$$M/B_i = A + B \times ROE_i$$

Using this equation, you can plug in a market-to-book ratio of 1 and compute the resulting ROE. Because of the idea that the market value equals the accumulated investment when return equals cost of capital, the point at which the market-to-book ratio is equal to 1 should be the same as the cost of equity. A graph illustrating the regression is shown in Figure 34.4.

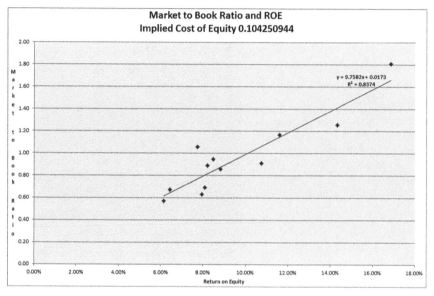

FIGURE 34.4 Use of Market-to-Book Ratio and Forward Return on Equity to Estimate the Cost of Equity Capital

CHAPTER 35

Computing an Implied EV/EBITDA Ratio in Terminal Value Calculations

C hapter 34 explains that if there were no taxes and no capital expenditures and if there was no net debt, the price/earnings (P/E) ratio and the enterprise value/earnings before interest, taxes, depreciation, and amortization (EV/EBITDA) ratio would be the same. This implies that if you want to compute the implied EV/EBITDA ratio, the fundamental factors of growth, return, and cost of capital will drive the ratio just as they do for the P/E ratio. As depreciation, taxes, and debt are the factors that cause differences between the EV/EBITDA ratio and the P/E ratio, these factors must also be accounted for when computing the implied EV/EBITDA ratio.

To establish the implied EV/EBITDA ratio rather than the implied P/E ratio from all of the factors that drive enterprise value, including return, growth, cost of capital, tax rate, plant life, working capital, and tax depreciation, must be considered. The process of making a financial model to simulate the EV/EBITDA ratio involves creating a balance of net invested capital rather than the equity balance. Chapter 24 explains that invested capital can be calculated using either the balance of net assets associated with generating EBITDA or, alternatively, a balance of financing obligations including equity and net debt devoted to financing EBITDA. The model for computing the EV/EBITDA ratio works best using the direct method that begins with the asset side of the balance sheet to establish the invested capital balance. The opening balance of invested capital is then converted to net operating profit less adjusted taxes

445

(NOPAT) and free cash flow to the firm (FCFF). Net assets grow by capital expenditures and net working capital changes, and are reduced by deferred tax changes.

To demonstrate the mechanics of computing the implied EV/EBITDA ratio from value drivers, consider a case where net plant is required to generate net operating profit after tax but without working capital and deferred taxes are not considered. This analysis uses inputs for (1) return on invested capital (ROIC), (2) weighted average cost of capital (WACC), (3) the ratio of capital expenditures to depreciation, (4) the depreciation rate on net plant, and (5) the tax rate. Using the ratio of capital expenditures to deprecation and the net depreciation rate derived from the growth rate and plant life is analogous to the way the dividend payout ratio derived from the growth rate is used in computing the P/E ratio. By working through the computation of the EV/EBITDA ratio using the ratios of capital expenditures to depreciation and the net plant depreciation rate you can, it is hoped, see the benefit of computing the stable ratios. As explained in Chapters 30 and 31, the ratio of capital expenditures to depreciation and the net depreciation rate can be calculated from user-defined functions that accept the book life of the plant and the asset growth rate. A constant growth case demonstrates the mechanics of a model to derive the EV/EBITDA ratio. This is later extended into a model that includes changing growth, returns, and cost of capital. Recall that the value driver formula falls apart when growth rate and/or return changes.

Simulation Model to Derive Implied EV/EBITDA Ratio from Invested Capital with Constant Growth

Construction of a model to derive the EV/EBITDA ratio with a constant growth assumption is derived before a more complex model that accounts for changing growth and changing returns is introduced. Figure 35.1 is an excerpt of a simulation model that calculates the EV/EBITDA ratio from the invested capital balance using an assumption of constant growth. Calculations of invested capital are analogous to computing the balance of the equity capital when deriving the P/E ratio that was illustrated in Figure 34.3. The net investment balance decreases from depreciation expense and it increases with capital expenditures. These movements in the invested capital balance from depreciation and capital expenditures shown in Figure 35.1 are computed as follows:

- The depreciation expense is computed from the opening balance multiplied by the net depreciation rate. The function explained in Chapter 30

	A / B	C	E	F	G	H	I	J	K
10	Assumptions				Outputs				
11	ROIC (Real)	12.0%		EV = NPV FCF		3,487.8 €	<---- =NPV(C17,39:39)		
12	WACC (Real)	7.0%		EBITDA		337.69	<---- =F37		
13	Growth Rate (Real)	5.0%		EV/EBITDA		10.33	<---- =H12/H13		
14	Inflation	2.0%							
15	Growth Rate Nominal	7.1%	<---- =(1+C13)*(1+C14)-1						
16	ROIC Nominal	14.2%	<---- =(1+C11)*(1+C14)-1						
17	WACC Nominal	9.1%	<---- =(1+C12)*(1+C14)-: Function						
18	Tax rate	38%							
19	Depreciation life (yrs)	15							
20	Net Plant Depr Rate	10.80%	<---- =net_depreciation_rate(C19,C15)						
21	Cap Exp to Depr	165.73%	<---- =cap_exp_depreciation_simple(C19,C15,1)						
25	Model								
26		0		1	2	3	4	5	6
27	Short-term Period	5		TRUE	TRUE	TRUE	TRUE	TRUE	FALSE
28	Long-term Period	295		FALSE	FALSE	FALSE	FALSE	FALSE	TRUE
29									
30	Opening Balance	Driver		1,000.00	1,071.00	1,147.04	1,228.48	1,315.70	1,409.12 :
31	Less: Depreciation	10.80%	=F30*$C$31 --->	108.01	115.68	123.89	132.69	142.11	152.20
32	Add: Capital Expenditure	165.73%	=$C$32*F31 --->	179.01	191.72	205.33	219.91	235.53	252.25
33	Closing Balance	1,000.00		1,071.00	1,147.04	1,228.48	1,315.70	1,409.12	1,509.17 :
34									
35	NOPLAT = ROIC x Inv	14.24%	=$C$35*F30 --->	142.40	152.51	163.34	174.94	187.36	200.66
36	EBIT = NOPLAT/(1-t)	38.0%	=F35/(1-$C$36 ->	229.68	245.98	263.45	282.15	302.19	323.64
37	EBITDA = EBIT + Depr		=F36+F31 --->	337.69	361.66	387.34	414.84	444.30	475.84
38									
39	Free Cash Flow (EBITDA - Cap Exp - EBIT x t)	=F37-F32-F36*		71.40	76.47	81.90	87.71	93.94	100.61
40									
41			10.33 <------- =EV_EBITDA_Simple(C16,C17,C15,C19,C18)						

FIGURE 35.1 Illustration of Model That Derives the EV/EBITDA Ratio from Value Drivers and User-Defined Functions

can be used to establish the net depreciation rate using inputs for plant life and growth rate using the constant growth assumption.

- Once the depreciation is established, the capital expenditures are derived through multiplying the depreciation by the ratio of capital expenditures to depreciation. For the constant growth rate case you can use a function that computes the ratio of capital expenditures to depreciation that accepts projected growth and plant life.
- After you have computed the net investment balance, the NOPAT, which is EBIT multiplied by 1, the tax rate can be computed. This is computed as the rate of return on invested capital multiplied by the opening balance of the investment.

■ Because NOPAT is equal to EBIT × (1 − tax rate), the EBIT can be derived as the NOPAT/(1 − tax rate).
■ After computing the EBIT, the depreciation expense that has already been computed as part of the invested capital balance can be added to the EBIT to derive the EBITDA.

With the EBITDA, EBIT, the tax rate, and capital expenditures computed, items for free cash flow (EBITDA, capital expenditures, and taxes) are available. You can then compile the free cash flow and compute its present value, which is the enterprise value. With the enterprise value and EBITA established, the EV/EBITDA ratio can be computed as illustrated in Figure 35.1.

Function to Derive Implied EV/EBITDA Ratio

You can make a user-defined function to compute the EV/EBITDA in a way that is similar to how capital expenditures to depreciation, deferred tax changes, asset retirements, and net plant depreciation were derived. This function allows you to compute the EV/EBITDA ratio automatically without making a whole new spreadsheet each time you would like to evaluate the EV/EBITDA ratio for purposes of computing terminal value. A function that evaluates the EV/EBITDA in net plant case (i.e., still without working capital changes, deferred taxes, and other items such as provisions) is shown in Figure 35.2. This function accepts the three drivers of growth, cost of capital, and return along with the plant life and the tax rate. The function then works through the same equations shown in Figure 35.1. Results of the function are shown in Figure 35.1 below the calculation of the EV/EBITDA ratio, demonstrating that the same result is obtained.

After writing the function for a simple case without varying growth rates, returns, and transition factors, you could create a more complex function that loops through a historical period to establish prospective retirements, as was the case for the more complex evaluation for the ratio of capital expenditures to depreciation. The more advanced function is adjusted for adding deferred taxes and working capital to the analysis using the stable working capital equation explained in Chapter 29 and the deferred tax function described in Chapter 31. The comprehensive function can also be modified to differentiate between long-term, transition, and short-term parameters using concepts of multiple FOR NEXT loops discussed in Chapter 30, where the historic period is used to establish retirements. The EV/EBITDA ratio is then finally derived from the lifetime of plant, the tax depreciation life and method, the historical growth rate in assets, and the ratio of working capital to EBITDA as well as the WACC, projected growth, tax rate, and the projected rate of return.

```
Function EV_EBITDA_Simple(ROIC, WACC, Growth, Life, Tax_Rate)

    cap_exp_ratio = cap_exp_depreciation_simple(Life, Growth, 1)
    depreciation_ratio = net_depreciation_rate(Life, Growth)
    net_investment = 1000                          ' Initialise variables
    PV_factor = 1

    For i = 1 To 300
        NOPLAT = net_investment * ROIC             ' Compute OPENING BALANCE
        EBIT = NOPLAT / (1 - Tax_Rate)
        depreciation = depreciation_ratio * net_investment
        cap_exp = cap_exp_ratio * depreciation
        EBITDA = EBIT + depreciation
        FCFF = EBITDA - cap_exp - EBIT * Tax_Rate

        If i = 1 Then EBITDA_1 = EBITDA            ' Remember the EBITDA
        PV_factor = PV_factor * (1 + WACC)         ' Accumulate the PV factor

        EV = EV + FCFF / PV_factor

        net_investment = net_investment + cap_exp - depreciation
    Next i

    EV_EBITDA_Simple = EV / EBITDA_1     ' Compute function on next period EBITDA

End Function
```

FIGURE 35.2 Function for Computing Implied EV/EBITDA Ratio without Working Capital Changes and Deferred Taxes

Comprehensive Analysis to Derive Implied EV/EBITDA Ratio with Changing Growth, Deferred Taxes, and Working Capital

An excerpt from a simulation analysis that includes deferred taxes, working capital, changing growth, and changing returns is shown in Figure 35.3. The financial model and/or function to derive the EV/EBITDA with the additional parameters are a compilation of the concepts developed from Chapters 29 through 34. Figure 35.3 illustrates how a variety of different ratios change when the growth rate changes and that the ratios do not stabilize after a single year. Instead, ratios of capital expenditure to depreciation, net plant depreciation rate, and deferred taxes take a full life cycle to change after the growth rate changes.

Results of a comprehensive analysis in terms of the EV/EBITDA ratio are shown in Figure 35.4. This figure demonstrates the inputs required for the

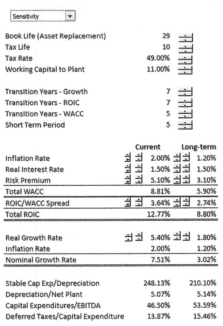
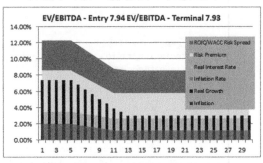
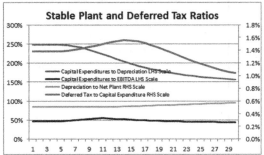

FIGURE 35.3 Excerpt from Comprehensive Model That Computes the EV/EBITDA Ratio from Value Drivers and Transition Assumptions

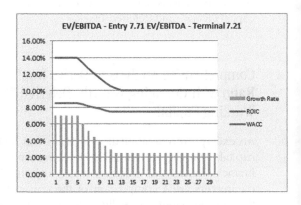

FIGURE 35.4 Illustration of Output from a Comprehensive Calculation of the Implied EV/EBITDA Ratio

analysis and compares the comprehensive analysis with the value driver formula and the growth rate method. Figure 35.4 includes periodic value drivers, transition time periods, deferred taxes, and working capital in deriving the ultimate EV/EBITDA ratio. Factors that drive the EV/EBITDA ratio include the life of the assets, tax rates, transition factors, rates of return, costs of capital, working capital ratios, and growth rates. All of the inputs that drive the ratio are either standard valuation inputs such as the growth rate and the cost of capital or should be available from elsewhere in the model. The table at the bottom left of Figure 35.4 reports the implied EV/EBITDA ratio for the current year and for the assumed terminal period. The importance of creating a comprehensive function rather than using a simple growth equation or the value driver formula is demonstrated by the difference between the model output and the value driver model or the growth model. The enterprise value computed from the alternative methods includes:

The Value Driver Equation: $EV = NOPAT \times (1 - g/ROIC)/(WACC - g)$

The Growth Rate Method: $FCFF \times (1 + g)/(WACC - g)$

Figure 35.4 illustrates that the value driver formula and the growth rate formula do not produce accurate results compared to the true value established with the function that considers historical growth and works through the investment balances. The computation of EV/EBITDA that considers historic growth, future growth, tax rates, plant life, cost of capital, and transition factors can be established in a user-defined function. This function can then be put in the left-hand columns of your financial model like the results of other functions.

CHAPTER 36

Developing Value Drivers for P/E and EV/EBITDA Ratios with Benchmarking and Regression

Creating models and functions to compute price/earnings (P/E) and enterprise value/earnings before interest, taxes, depreciation, and amortization (EV/EBITDA) multiples does not address how to come up with value driver inputs that should be put into the analysis. Let's say that you have a good idea about the current EV/EBITDA multiple, and you only want to adjust the multiple for changes in items like a lower growth rate, a different cost of capital, or a lower return on invested capital (ROIC). The problem with putting values in one of the functions to compute multiples discussed in Chapters 34 and 35 is that you do not know the biggest factor that drives any of the multiples, namely the cost of capital. When implementing the computed multiples into corporate finance models, you could attempt to focus on incremental changes from the current market multiples rather than starting from scratch in building up the multiple. To do this you can use market data for multiples and make estimates of what you think the market expectations are for growth and return as well as other inputs like the tax rate and the plant life. With current multiples observed in the market you can then apply a Goal Seek process to find the implied weighted average cost of capital (WACC) or the implied cost of equity by moving the cost of capital around until the derived multiple equals the market observed value. The idea of making incremental changes to current multiples for different growth, return, and stable cost of capital can also be accomplished by constructing a regression equation that simulates current market multiples as a function of growth, return, cost of capital, tax rate, and depreciation rate.

Benchmarking Multiples to Derive Cost of Capital

Chapters 34 and 35 demonstrate how the various factors such as growth, plant life, tax rates, returns, and most of all cost of capital should affect P/E and EV/EBITDA multiples. When evaluating the P/E ratio or the EV/EBITDA ratio, you may imagine creating a statistical test to see whether these factors actually influence the ratio that is suggested by the different equations. If projected growth for one company is higher than another and the return is above the cost of capital, the P/E ratio should be greater. Similarly, you should be able to observe P/E variances among a sample of companies from arising differences in projected future growth.

The derived EV/EBITDA ratio and the P/E ratio can be used together with the Goal Seek tool to compute implied cost of capital. This process involves inputting all of the variables necessary to calculate the multiple and then comparing the computed multiple with the actual multiple observed from market data. When you enter inputs for short-term and long-term growth in this process you should attempt to enter realistic market expectations. These expected growth rates are not the published numbers for earnings growth predicted by sell-side analysts that you can pick up on the Internet, which have been demonstrated to be optimistic and lead to overestimations of the cost of capital. When entering realistic growth rates into the derived multiples you can also input alternative estimates of the progression of return on capital to the cost of capital. After you come up with inputs and compute the implied valuation multiple you can create a Goal Seek function to derive the implied cost of capital. Using the P/E ratio, the cost of capital computed from this process is the cost of equity; if the EV/EBITDA ratio is evaluated, the weighted average cost of capital is the result.

A range in possible implied costs of capital can be simulated from different growth rates and rates of return with the Goal Seek tool and a little Visual Basic for Applications (VBA) code. To present such a range in your spreadsheet, you can first write a macro that records the Goal Seek process. This should be one line of code that includes the set cell (a formula), the target cell (a fixed input), and the changing cell (an input in the spreadsheet). One of the most common macros made in a spreadsheet is recording the Goal Seek macro and then enabling the target cell to be read from the spreadsheet rather than being input into the Goal Seek tool. The initial macro and adjustments are shown in the following statements.

Before range names:

```
Range("D8").goalseek Goal:=0, ChangingCell:=Range("D4")
```

After range names:

```
Range("EV_EBITDA").goalseek Goal:=0, ChangingCell:=Range("Cost of
Capital")
```

With target from cell in spreadsheet:

```
Range("EV_EBITDA").goalseek Goal:=Range("Target"), ChangingCell:=Range
("Cost of Capital")
```

After recording the macro you should replace the cell references with range names as shown. When creating the process you can input the actual EV/EBITDA ratio or the actual P/E ratio adjacent to the computed ratio. Next you can compute the difference and use the Goal Seek process to set the difference to zero by changing the cost of capital input. To create a table that shows the range in costs of capital given different growth rates and/or costs of capital, the data table tool does not work for two reasons. First, the output of the table is the input cell for the cost of capital rather than a formula. Second, the Goal Seek must be rerun with each new scenario. Instead of using the data table tool, the FOR NEXT process described in Chapter 16 and illustrated in Figure 16.10 can be applied to develop the sensitivity table. When creating this macro to replicate the Data Table tool you should then add the Goal Seek code just before the macro reports the results using the CELLS statement.

Downloading Data for a Sample of Companies from the Internet into a Spreadsheet

Increasing amounts of data has been published on websites in recent years. You can often (but not always) create VBA code to download data for your analysis. Once you have downloaded data on estimated growth, return, and measurable cost of capital factors for a group of companies, it can be plugged in to arrive at multiples that can be applied in the discounted cash flow model. A regression could take the form:

$$P/E = A + B \times g/ROE + C \times g + D \times Beta + E \times Debt\ to\ Capital$$

In this equation the coefficient on the g/ROE should be negative, the coefficient on the beta should be negative, and the coefficient on the growth rate should be positive. Before running the regression to establish such an equation, you can program some code to efficiently download data from the Internet and then copy new data into different spreadsheets of a workbook. In VBA there is a wonderful statement that allows you to do just this. The statement WORKBOOKS.OPEN(Range("URL")) can open all sorts of different web pages and spreadsheets that are downloadable from websites and put the data into your workbook. It can also open spreadsheet files that are downloadable once you know the URL. In the WORKBOOKS.OPEN (Range("URL")) statement, the URL should be pasted into your spreadsheet. As explained in Chapter 32, you can modify the URL to make it flexible so that it can read all sorts of data from websites of different companies. The VBA code can then be adjusted to place that data into different sheets. This technique of automatically downloading files may be one of the most useful macros for all sorts of analysis even though it is not documented in many of the thick books on VBA programming.

The process of downloading data that enables incorporation of market data into the implied P/E and EV/EBITDA analysis is illustrated in the two examples that follow. The first example that downloads data from the Slovenia stock exchange and puts information from the various companies into different sheets is illustrated in Figures 36.1 and 36.2. Figure 36.1 demonstrates how to create a URL that can be modified to accept different companies on the exchange using the INDEX function and a ticker symbol. Figure 36.2 shows

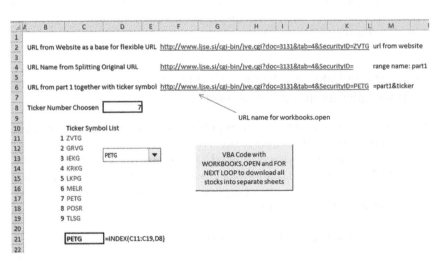

FIGURE 36.1 Illustration of How to Modify a URL to Accept Different Ticker Symbols for Reading into VBA

```
Sub get_company ()

current_book = ActiveWorkbook.Name      ' Remember the current workbook
current_sheet = ActiveSheet.Name        ' remember the current sheet

Workbooks.Open (Range("url"))           ' This is the essential function

temp_book = ActiveWorkbook.Name         ' Copy cells from workbooks.open
        Cells.Select
        Selection.Copy

Windows(current_book).Activate          ' Go back to workbook for pasting

Sheets.Add After:=Sheets(Sheets.Count)

Selection.PasteSpecial Paste:=xlPasteValues, Operation:=xlNone, _
        SkipBlanks _
        :=False, Transpose:=False       ' Paste to new sheet of current workbook

ActiveSheet.Name = Range("ticker")      ' Re-define name of sheet to be copied

Windows(temp_book).Close                ' Close the workbook from URL Read

End Sub
```

FIGURE 36.2 Illustration of How to Use the WORKBOOKS.OPEN Statement to Read Different Companies

how to use the WORKBOOKS.OPEN statement to read different companies and then pop the information into separate sheets. With the data in separate sheets you can use the data in statistical analysis from applying the INDIRECT function. Note that in the VBA code, the paste special as values is used instead of the simple Paste function. This avoids all of the irritating advertisements that are part of so many Web pages.

If you want to read from Excel or PDF files that are uploaded to websites you can use the same kind of approach. This time you press the F3 key on the website to copy the URL name to your spreadsheet. If you use the copied URL with the WORKBOOKS.OPEN statement, the macro will find and open the Excel or PDF file. After defining the URL and opening the file, you are left with putting the data into a new sheet of your current workbook. VBA code to complete this process is illustrated in Figure 36.3. When you have put all of the sheets that you read from different URLs together in a single workbook, you can use the INDIRECT function to extract data and make comparisons. The INDIRECT function was discussed in Chapters 15 and 32.

```
Sub run_stock(current_symbol)              ' Data from downloaded
                                             spreadsheets

    workbook_name = ActiveWorkbook.Name    ' Keep current workbook
    sheet_name = ActiveSheet.Name          ' keep the current sheet

    Range("Symbol").Value = current_symbol ' Ticker symbol from reading
    Workbooks.Open (qurl)                  ' Here is the main function

    Cells.Select                           ' Get all of the data
    Windows(workbook_name).Activate        ' Go back to org workbook
    Sheets.Add                             ' Add a new sheet at the end

    num = Sheets.Count
    ActiveSheet.Move After:=Sheets(num)    ' Move the sheet to end
    ActiveSheet.Name = Symbol              ' Rename the new sheet

    ActiveSheet.Paste                      ' Paste into the new sheet
    Windows("table.csv").Close             ' Close sheet from internet

End Sub
```

FIGURE 36.3 Macro for Reading Data from Excel Files Created by Website

Running Regression Analysis on Financial Data

After you have finished uploading data for comparative multiples and other statistics such as the expected growth rate as well as cost of capital indicators such as beta, stock price volatility, and debt leverage, you can make the analysis of value drivers. When using data for statistical analysis, creating a flexible range name with the OFFSET function you can add a lot of flexibility to the statistical analysis. Using the OFFSET function to create a flexible range name will allow you to change variables in the regression, select alternative companies with market data, and it will allow you to experiment with different time periods. Use of the OFFSET function to create a dynamic range name is described in detail in Chapter 15 and illustrated in Figure 15.11. If the data is arranged with companies in columns and time in rows and the data starts in range A1, then the flexible range name can be created with the OFFSET function as follows:

Range Name $= $ OFFSET(A1, 0, 0, Row Length, Column Width)

In this example the row length and the column width would be put as inputs somewhere in the sheet. By changing the number of companies in the data set and the length of the time series, the statistical results can be viewed immediately. To do this, the flexible range names can be used in statistical functions such as the LINEST, SLOPE, INTERCEPT, and RSQ functions.

With a database of financial data that is assigned to flexible range names you can see how the actual data reconciles with the simulated implied multiples and derive the implied multiples for a range of companies. Alternatively, you can run a regression on a sample of different companies. An example of such a regression that produces an *R*-squared of 61 percent is shown in the table and the graph presented in Figures 36.4 and 36.5. The table in Figure 36.4 shows that the coefficients have the expected signs. The graph in Figure 36.5 illustrates the difference between the simulated P/E ratio and the actual P/E ratio for each company in the analysis. In Figure 36.4 the selected variables that are put together with the OFFSET function and used in the regression are shaded. Outputs from the regression that are derived using the LINEST function are shown in the top right-hand side of the sheet. The flexible range name is created by changing TRUE and FALSE switches above the variable names.

Regression Results	Number in Sample					35						
	Revenue Growth	Proj G/ROE	Leverage	Equity Beta	Proj Growth	ROE	Intercept	FALSE	FALSE	FALSE	FALSE	FALSE	FALSE
	1	2	3	4	5	6	7	8	9	10	11	12	13
Coefficient	2.51	-2.53	4.16	-3.42	22.89	-5.27	15.01						
Std Error	4.78	1.54	1.66	0.81	11.52	2.90	1.17						
R-Squared	61%	1.96											
T-Statistic	0.53	-1.65	2.51	-4.20	1.99	-1.82	12.85						

Variable Selection												
Test	OK											
		1										
					Counter	1	2	3	4	5	6	7	8
R-Squared/t-Statistic	61%				12.85	-1.82	1.99	1.99	-4.20	2.51	-1.65	-1.65	0.53
Include Variable ---->	FALSE	TRUE	FALSE			TRUE	TRUE	FALSE	TRUE	TRUE	TRUE	FALSE	TRUE
Counter	1	2	3		0	1	2	2	3	4	5	5	6
					7	6	5	5	4	3	2	2	1
Variable ---->	P/E	EV/EBITDA	M/B		Intercept	ROE	:ted Growth	Hst Growth	Equity Beta	Leverage	Proj G/ROE	Hs G/ROE	Rev Grwth
Range Name -->	p_e_ratio	ev_ebitda	m_b			roe	growth	his_5_yr	beta	debt_cap			

	P/E	EV/EBITDA	M/B			ROE	Proj Growth	Hst Growth	Equity Beta	Leverage	Proj G/ROE	Hs G/ROE	Rev Grwth
General Electric	12.68	19.94	2.00		1	14.96%	9.9%	-3.3%	1.41	0.76	66%	-22%	1.3%
Apple	8.67	6.04	3.20		1	31.95%	-0.6%	71.7%	0.66	0.00	-2%	224%	15.7%
Google	14.77	13.35	3.64		1	21.91%	14.3%	20.6%	1.15	0.09	65%	94%	40.1%
JP Morgan	8.42	N/A	0.96		1	10.89%	5.6%	38.9%	1.63	0.00	51%	357%	0.5%
McDonalds	16.39	11.44	6.69		1	37.46%	7.8%	12.4%	0.34	0.47	21%	33%	4.3%
Wall Mart	13.36	8.30	3.38		1	23.48%	6.6%	9.6%	0.41	0.40	28%	41%	4.9%
Con Ed	16.08	8.77	1.52		1	9.34%	1.1%	5.8%	0.08	0.49	12%	62%	7.7%
Conagra	14.18	16.85	2.89		1	19.38%	16.8%	3.8%	0.47	0.67	87%	19%	17.8%
Coca Cola	13.17	9.62	3.93		1	26.79%	11.1%	19.5%	0.77	0.56	41%	73%	5.3%
Excelon	15.68	6.66	1.44		1	9.18%	-12.3%	-7.0%	0.56	0.48	-134%	-76%	6.0%
First Solar	11.49	4.03	0.90		1	7.51%	-12.7%	10.3%	1.35	0.14	-169%	137%	14.0%
General Mills	16.84	11.06	4.52		1	25.27%	5.1%	9.7%	1	0.49	20%	38%	6.2%
Heintz	19.03	13.32	7.66		1	36.82%	6.3%	6.6%	0.36	0.62	17%	18%	0.7%
Kellogs	15.52	14.45	9.60		1	52.75%	7.5%	3.5%	0.44	0.76	14%	7%	7.4%

FIGURE 36.4 Regression Results of P/E Equation Using Sample of Diverse Companies

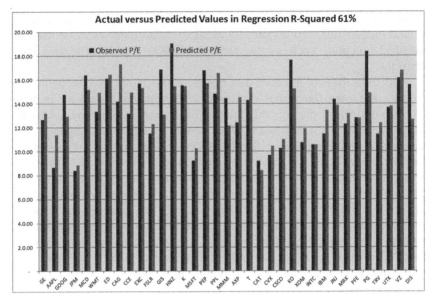

FIGURE 36.5 Expected Relative to Actual P/E Ratios from Regression Analysis

Advanced Corporate Modeling Summary

This part of the book began by emphasizing the importance of presenting the return on invested capital in your corporate models and paying particular attention to the rate of return projected for the terminal period. When discussing return on invested capital, the notion of distinguishing between financial ratios and valuation measures that use equity cash flow versus financial ratios and valuation measures that focus on free cash flow was introduced. In later chapters the value driver formula and implied multiples used to compute the equity value and enterprise value followed from this discussion and used either an equity perspective or a free cash flow perspective. To explain calculation of the return on invested capital, the balance sheet was segregated, driven by the guiding principle that net assets, which generate EBITDA should be included in invested capital. Difficult elements of the balance sheet to allocate were evaluated by creating a long-term theoretical model that mirrors the notion of corporations having an indefinite life. This sort of long-term theoretical analysis was used repeatedly in subsequent chapters.

After the background discussion of the invested capital and the ROIC, alternative terminal methods for computing value were introduced. In discussing the first method of assuming a constant growth rate applied to normalized cash flow, complex issues of normalizing the cash flow for working capital changes, capital expenditures, and deferred tax changes were addressed at length. Explanations of normalizing terminal cash flow demonstrated that in order to normalize cash flow in your models, you can create user-defined functions that compute the stable ratios of capital expenditures to depreciation and deferred tax changes to capital expenditure.

The second terminal value approach of including the ROIC versus WACC spread in terminal value was evaluated after the discussion of normalizing cash flow. While the general idea of developing a formula that can account for growth, WACC, and also return is very attractive, it was demonstrated that the value driver equation $(1 - g/\text{ROIC})/(\text{WACC} - g)$ does not yield accurate measures of value. To correct problems with the value driver formula, the final method of computing terminal value discussed was a technique that derives the P/E, market-to-book, and EV/EBITDA ratios from value drivers. These ratios can be inferred from growth rates, returns, cost of capital, plant life, tax rate, working capital ratios, and tax depreciation. Finally, techniques to combine market data with implied multiples to infer the cost of capital were discussed in this chapter.

PART IV

Complex Issues: Circular References and Other Complex Issues from Financial Structuring in Project Finance and Corporate Finance Models

CHAPTER 37

Resolving Circular References in Acquisition Models

Computing Interest Expense on the Average Balance of Debt

An issue that not too many people care about is developing an elegant way to compute the interest expense on the average of the opening and the closing debt balances in a financial model. But for a few people who spend much of their lives in front of their laptops working on financial models, this and other circular reference problems are more important than many other issues that you read about in the newspaper where politicians go around and around in a circular manner and things never seem to get resolved. The topic of interest expense on average balances and other circular reference problems in which one calculation is a function of the second, but the second depends on the first, can cause many difficulties in financial models. Complicated debt structuring issues in project finance and corporate finance models that result in circular logic and other tricky programming issues are addressed in this part of the book.

Some analysts suggest that from a philosophical standpoint, circularity should not occur in financial models. The argument is that this problem of one item depending on another and the other item depending on the first does not occur in real-life transactions and therefore it should not be part of a financial model. If circularity existed in structuring a transaction, the process would work something like what happens in the following story of a developer asking a banker for a loan. First, the developer goes to the bank and asks for a loan commitment. Then the bank uses the amount of the requested loan commitment to compute fees. After that, the developer asks for a larger loan to cover the fees. With the larger loan, more fees are charged and then the developer needs an even higher loan. With each increment, the loan amount is higher and the process keeps iterating on and on and on.

This circular reference resembles the film *Groundhog Day* in which life never moves forward and things just get stuck. Instead of such a scenario with the banker and the sponsor going around and around in increments, it is more realistic if the sponsor asks for a fixed loan commitment that will already have included the arrangement fee, the commitment fee, the debt service reserve account (DSRA), and the interest during construction. All of these fees, interest costs, and DSRA reserves can cause a circular reference problem similar to the simple fee example. When a company goes to a bank to ask for a loan in a project financing transaction, the company has already created a financial model and fixed the sizing of debt, presumably through modeling the debt service coverage or some other criterion. By fixing the amount of the debt, the circular reference goes away and there is no need to go around and around where increments of loan size influence the fees, interest, and DSRA, but these items in turn drive the loan size. Those who assert that circular references do not exist in the real world would argue that this manner of fixing variables is the way transactions really work in practice and a financial model should reflect this reality.

Notwithstanding this sort of philosophical debate about whether circular references occur in the real world, financial models are often used to derive the structure of a transaction, meaning that debt and other transaction parameters are not fixed in advance. In project finance models, various combinations of debt draws, fees, interest, and debt service reserves cannot be solved without iterating and running into a circular reference problem. The reason for this circular logic is that the fees and the loan commitment depend on the financial model, but the model itself must be computed with some kind of fee and debt commitment assumption. In analysis of the financial structure of a transaction, when the level of an item in the model depends on using the model itself, a circular logic problem simply cannot be avoided.

Circular References and Use of Opening Balances in Annual Models

Circular reference problems are not unique to project finance models. Corporate and acquisition models are often created using annual time periods, whereas interest is computed on daily cash and debt balances in real bank loans. When making calculations of interest expense in an annual model, an implicit assumption is that the cash flows occur on a continual basis throughout the year. This means that various revenue, expense, and capital expenditures can be approximated with an assumption that cash flow occurs in the middle of the year. If an implicit or explicit assumption is made that cash inflows and outflows occur on a continual basis throughout the year, it is incorrect to compute incremental interest expense or incremental interest income on the basis of the opening debt or the opening cash balance.

When you compute interest from the opening balance, over the course of the year no positive cash flow is being used to pay down debt and there is no cash buildup that increases interest income. Interest expense and/or interest income computed on the basis of opening balances means that you have made an implicit assumption that all revenues are received and all expenses and capital expenditures occur right at the very end of the year. Because cash really flows on a continual basis throughout the year, if the balance of debt does not change until the end of the period, then the interest expense and interest income calculations are not correct. Where cash flow is positive, the true interest expense is less than the interest computed on the opening debt balance, as debt is being repaid over the course of the year. The opposite occurs when cash flow is negative and the true cash flow is less than the cash flow computed in a model where opening balances are assumed.

While making the assumption that the revenues occur in the middle of the period is much more reasonable than pretending that all cash flow suddenly appears on December 31, it creates a circular logic problem. The circular reference occurs because the closing balance of the debt or cash influences the interest expense and/or interest income. But the interest expense and/or interest income is a determinant of cash flow that drives the closing debt and cash balances. The circular reference is illustrated by the diagram in Figure 37.1, which shows that the closing debt balance is driven by cash flow but cash flow is driven by interest expense and in turn the closing debt balance.

Closing Balance	→	Interest Expense
Interest Expense	→	Net Cash Flow
Net Cash Flow	→	Closing Balance

FIGURE 37.1 Circular Reference Logic Diagram of Interest Expense and Closing Debt Balance in Corporate Model

If you want your model to be precise and reflect the reduction in interest expense from positive cash flow realized over the course of the year, this circular logic problem can be tricky to resolve. While the problem of more accurately measuring interest expense is not generally a key driver in most models if the interest rate is not very high, addressing the problem does illustrate elegant ways in which user-defined functions can be used to solve problems in financial models. For many advanced financial modeling issues, including the problems of stable ratios discussed in Part 3, creating your own user-defined functions opens a whole new world of solving problems that otherwise use things like tedious copy and paste macros.

Alternative Techniques for Solving Circular Reference Logic Problems in Financial Models

There are various different ways to address the problem of circular references in financial models. Five of the possible techniques that can be used to solve circular references such as the problem of interest expense on the average debt balance in annual models and funding in project finance models are shown in Table 37.1. The table lists different techniques to resolve circular references along with comments about the problems that arise with each method. The right-hand column of the table explains that there are big problems with using the iteration button method as well as the copy and paste macro method. The remainder of this chapter illustrates problems with the iteration button and the copy and paste process and then describes how to create a flexible and transparent function using one of the last two methods shown on the table—the algebraic equation approach or the isolated function approach.

TABLE 37.1 Alternative Techniques to Address Circular Reference Problems in Financial Models

Method	Problems with Method
Use the Enable Iterative Calculation button in Excel (the iteration button).	This method can destroy models and is dangerous to use. The models become unstable, Goal Seek does not work, and errors cannot be undone. The method should virtually never be used.
Input fixed values in cells that cause the circular problem, and use a Goal Seek to find the fixed value by setting the difference to zero.	This method can avoid the dangers of the iteration button, but it means that whenever you change something in a model, you must run a Goal Seek. A second problem with this method is that it cannot be used to solve circular reference problems that occur in more than one cell.
Input fixed values in a similar manner to the Goal Seek method, but use the Solver to find multiple values at the same time.	Using the Solver resolves problems of the Goal Seek whereby circular references in multiple different cells can be computed. But it leaves the problem that you must rerun the Solver any time you change a structuring or cash flow input in the model. Another problem with this method is that the Solver can be very slow and clumsy for anything but very small models. The Solver is also problematic because all calculations used in the Solver must be in one sheet.

TABLE 37.1 (*continued*)

Method	Problems with Method
Use a copy and paste macro to find fixed values in cells that cause the circular logic with an iteration routine.	This is the most common method used these days in fancy models. You compute the item causing the circular reference and then copy and paste special the computed value to a fixed cell. The method solves the problem with Goal Seek where multiple circular references cannot be solved, and it is better than the Solver method, which can be very slow and limits the calculations to one sheet. But this method leaves the models just as clumsy as the previous Goal Seek and Solver methods, and it means the copy and paste macro must be used whenever you want to do any sensitivity analysis or optimization.
Resolve circular references using an algebraic equation.	Using algebra is an old-fashioned method that is the most elegant way to solve circular references. It requires no iteration on an indirect or a direct basis. All optimization and scenario analysis can be directly applied without any special adjustments. The problem with this method is that coming up with an algebraic solution can be tedious and sometimes almost impossible.
Resolve circular references using an isolated user-defined function that contains an iteration loop.	This method, in which calculations that cause the circular reference are repeated in a function, resolves problems with the clumsiness and the lack of transparency caused by standard copy and paste macros. All data tables, optimization, and scenario analysis can be automated, and any circular reference can be resolved. The problem with this method is that it involves a bit of old-fashioned programming and the VBA code is not understood by people used to seeing models with copy and paste macros.

In describing how to solve the circular references and some other challenging problems in financial modeling, it is helpful to simplify the problem to isolate the issue. Once the issue is isolated, complexities can be gradually added so that the process can be used in real models. The organization of this part of the book follows such an approach in describing how to resolve circular reference problems in corporate and acquisition models. An acquisition model with a cash flow sweep and a cash flow waterfall without taxes is the starting point for the analysis. This case is relatively simple to solve, because in a leveraged acquisition all of the cash flow is used to pay down debt or pay dividends rather than either building up cash balances or reducing balances of a revolving credit line. The first case of a cash sweep is also somewhat less complex because dividend payouts do not depend on net income and interest expense. Taxes, in particular net operating losses, differences between interest income and interest expense rates, and dividends are also excluded so as not to complicate the problem.

Resolution of Circular References from a Cash Flow Sweep Using the Iteration Button

To demonstrate how the problem of circular references in corporate finance and acquisition models can be solved, imagine a model with a cash flow sweep where interest expense is computed on the basis of the average debt balance rather than on the opening debt balance. In an acquisition model with a cash sweep, the cash flow available for repaying debt is the minimum of the cash flow after interest or the opening debt balance:

Debt Repayment = MIN(Cash Flow After Interest, Opening Debt Balance)

Once you have computed the cash flow after interest, you should attach the repayments in the debt schedule to the cash flow analysis as is the case for any cash flow waterfall. The debt schedule includes the usual: an opening balance, a repayment line linked to the preceding formula, a closing balance line, and an interest expense calculation. Because the interest expense is computed on the average debt balance, a component of interest depends on debt repayment, which is in turn dependent on the cash flow after interest. The circular reference can be demonstrated by splitting up the interest expense formula into two components and seeing that interest expense depends in part on the closing balance of the debt:

Interest Expense = Beginning Balance/2 × Interest Rate + Ending Balance/
2 × Interest Rate

Since the ending balance is the beginning balance less the cash sweep, the interest expense is a function of the cash sweep and debt repayment as follows:

$$\text{Interest Expense} = \text{Beginning Balance}/2 \times \text{Interest Rate}$$
$$+ (\text{Beginning Balance} - \text{Sweep})/2 \times \text{Interest Rate}$$

If you construct this cash flow sweep model with interest computed from average balances, after you calculate the interest expense a dreaded blue arrow will appear indicating you have a circular reference. The simple model that is the basis for the subsequent discussion and illustrates the circular reference is shown in Figure 37.2.

Growth	2%							
EBITDA		100.00	102.00	104.04	106.12	108.24	110.41	112.62
Debt								
Opening Balance		500.00	500.00	500.00	500.00	500.00	500.00	500.00
Less: Sweep		0.00	0.00	0.00	0.00	0.00	0.00	0.00
Closing Balance	500	500.00	500.00	500.00	500.00	500.00	500.00	500.00
Interest Rate		5%	5%	5%	5%	5%	5%	5%
Interest on Average Balance		0.00	25.00	25.00	25.00	25.00	25.00	25.00
EBITDA		100.00	102.00	104.04	106.12	108.24	110.41	112.62
Less: Interest		25.00	25.00	25.00	25.00	25.00	25.00	25.00
Less: Incremental Interest								
Sub-total		75.00	77.00	79.04	81.12	83.24	85.41	87.62
Less: Sweep		0.00	0.00	0.00	0.00	0.00	0.00	0.00
Remainder		75.00	77.00	79.04	81.12	83.24	85.41	87.62

FIGURE 37.2 Illustration of Circular Reference Arising from Cash Flow Sweep with Interest on Average Balance

Excel has a feature to resolve this kind of circular reference through making iterative calculations using a special button that you can access from the File tab. The iteration button can be accessed by going to the File tab, clicking on Formulas, and then selecting the Enable Iterative Calculation check box. The last part of this process is illustrated in Figure 37.3. After pressing the

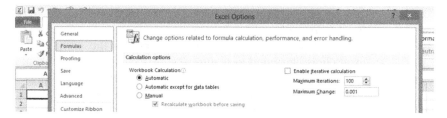

FIGURE 37.3 Finding the Iteration Button from the File Tab

button in the box shown on the excerpt in Figure 37.3, the whole circular reference issue seems to go away. This solution seems to be a nice feature of Excel that solves the circular reference problem. But using the iteration button can be a dangerous thing to do. Some of the negative consequences of using the iteration button include:

- The model can become unstable, meaning that when you make any little error that results in a bunch of #VALUEs, you cannot use the undo key. This can cause big problems, especially if you have not saved your work.
- The Goal Seek tool, which is central to a lot of analysis in a model used to structure debt and contracts in a transaction, will stop functioning and some other tools also will not work.
- If the model is large, it can become very slow if the iteration button is pressed, as the whole model will be computed over and over again.
- When the iteration button is pressed, the model equations sometimes do not even work.

The next paragraphs discuss alternative ways to resolve circular references without using the iteration button. While these methods correct the model stability problems, the various different techniques can create different problems that are even worse than those that arise from using the iteration button.

Solving Circular References from Cash Sweeps with Goal Seek and Solver

One way to resolve the circular reference problem is to compute the interest expense somewhere outside of the cash flow process in your model. After you make a second interest calculation somewhere else in the spreadsheet using the average balance of the debt, enter an arbitrary fixed value for the interest expense in the cash flow section of the model. Then you can compute the difference between the computed value that is made outside of the cash flow statement and the fixed value you entered in the cash flow statement. If the model is correct, this difference between the fixed value and the computed value should be zero. To compute the fixed value, you can use the Goal Seek tool or the Solver tool as follows:

Step 1   Link the interest expense in the cash flow statement to an arbitrary fixed value rather than the computed amount. An example of using a fixed value for interest expense in the cash sweep example is illustrated in Figure 37.4.

Step 2   Calculate the average interest expense outside of the cash flow statement above or below the fixed value that is input from step 1. Also calculate the difference between the fixed interest expense and the computed interest expense.

	D	E	F	G	H	I	J	K	L	M	N	Q	R
25													
26	Method 2: Goal Seek or Function												
27													
28	Debt Schedule												
29	Opening Balance			600.00	622.22	627.16	606.53	549.31	440.98	262.50	0.00		
30	Less: Repayment from Sweep			-22.22	-4.94	20.63	57.22	108.33	178.48	262.50	0.00	=N41	
31	Closing Balance		600	622.22	627.16	606.53	549.31	440.98	262.50	0.00	0.00		
32											=AVERAGE(N31,N29)*$F$5		
33	Computed Interest Expense			122.22	124.94	123.37	115.58	99.03	70.35	26.25	0.00		
34	Fixed Interest Expense			122.22	124.94	123.37	115.58	99.03	70.35	26.25	0.00	fixed	
35	Difference	0.00		0.00	0.00	0.00	0.00	0.00	0.00	0.00	0.00	=N33-N34	
36													
37	Cash Flow Statement												
38	Cash Flow			100.00	120.00	144.00	172.80	207.36	248.83	298.60	358.32		
39	Less: Interest Expense			122.22	124.94	123.37	115.58	99.03	70.35	26.25	0.00	=N34	
40	Cash Flow After Interest			-22.22	-4.94	20.63	57.22	108.33	178.48	272.35	358.32	=N38-N39	
41	Less: Repayments			-22.22	-4.94	20.63	57.22	108.33	178.48	262.50	0.00	=MIN(N40,N29)	
42	Equity Cash Flow			0.00	0.00	0.00	0.00	0.00	0.00	9.85	358.32	=N40-N41	
43													

FIGURE 37.4 Illustration of Model Setup for Use of the Goal Seek or Solver to Resolve Circular References with a Row for Computed Amounts, a Row for Fixed Amounts, and a Row for the Difference

Step 3   Use the Goal Seek tool to set the difference between the fixed value and the computed value to zero by finding the fixed interest expense. The set cell in the Goal Seek is the difference, the input value is zero, and the changing cell is the fixed interest expense.

Step 4   Repeat the process for each year of the model.

Instead of repeating the Goal Seek in step 4, you could use the Solver tool. To use the Solver effectively, do not put anything in the top part of the Solver screen. Then set the changing cells to the series of fixed interest expenses, and add a constraint that the difference between the computed value and the fixed value must be zero.

Both the Goal Seek method and the Solver method have many problems, including the following three:

1. If you have another circular reference somewhere else in your model, the process of using the Goal Seek or the Solver can be difficult (it may be impossible with the Goal Seek).

2. If you want to use the Goal Seek tool to do things like find debt capacity or break-even points, you cannot solve the problem because there will be two Goal Seeks. While you can find solutions to these problems with the Solver tool, the process can become very cumbersome and it does not work if Solver inputs are in different pages.

3. You cannot use most of the risk analysis tools discussed in Part 2 including the Data Table, spinner buttons, and other scenario and sensitivity tools.

Solving Basic Circular References from Cash Sweeps with a Horrible Copy and Paste Macro

An approach that is analogous to the Goal Seek method is to create a copy and paste macro that iterates until the difference between a fixed value and a computed value is equal to zero. Some people consider themselves sophisticated if they can employ this method and make a nifty-looking button that is attached to the macro and named something like model optimization. While this method is becoming more and more popular, it has all of the problems listed previously in terms of limiting risk analysis. A copy and paste macro to resolve circular references can be constructed using the following steps:

Step 1   Input a fixed value and add a row for the computed value for the item that is causing the circularity as described in the case of the Goal Seek technique (e.g., the average interest expense calculated in the debt schedule).

Step 2   Compute the year-by-year difference between the two calculations and then sum all of the differences in a separate cell. If you are really careful, you could sum the absolute value of the differences.

Step 3   Begin recording a macro. With the record button switched on, use the copy and paste special as values feature to copy from the computed interest expense to the fixed interest expense. When you make a copy and paste macro you will always copy from the computed value to the fixed value. Since you are using a macro, create range names for the computed interest expense, the fixed interest expense, and the sum of the difference.

Step 4   Use the ALT and F11 keys to go the VBA menu and modify the macro by including range names and creating a WHILE loop around the copy and paste commands. The WHILE loop repeats the copy and paste process until the sum of the differences converges to zero. First put a WHILE statement above the copy and paste statements that repeats the copy and paste process as long as the difference computed in step 2 is not zero. Then include a WEND statement below the copy and paste statements. You can be fancy with the copy and paste macro and add features to test the number of iterations and report results, but the essence of the process is simply to put a loop around the copy and paste process. Making a macro that includes a WHILE loop is illustrated in Figure 37.5.

Fancier ways to add bells and whistles to this kind of copy and paste macro by adding iteration limits, displaying the progress of iterations, and

```
Sub CopyPaste ()

While Range ("difference") <> 0 ' while statement above copy and paste
     Range ("computed") .Select

'
' Include copy and paste routing from recording the macro
'

     Selection.Copy
     Range ("fixed") .Select
     Selection.PasteSpecial Paste:=xlPasteValues, _
        Operation:=xlNone, SkipBlanks _
        :=False, Transpose:=False

Wend                ' Put the Wend at the end of copy and paste
                    routine

Application.CutCopyMode = False ' Turn of the dotted lines for copying files

End Sub
```

FIGURE 37.5 Illustration of Copy and Paste Macro to Resolve Circular References without Bells and Whistles

simplifying the copy and paste code are described in the context of project finance analysis in Chapter 40 (see Figure 40.5).

The copy and paste method for resolving circular references has many disadvantages even if you attach the macro to a fancy button and call it an optimization routine. With a copy and paste macro your financial model cannot be used together with the Goal Seek or Solver tools without a lot of other macros; data tables cannot be created for sensitivity analysis; you cannot put spinner buttons on your graphs; the iteration macro can occasionally result in an infinite loop; you have to enter a lot of range names, which is tedious; and doing any sort of optimization or sensitivity analysis with the model can become a cumbersome and ugly process. In short, most of the objectives of building the model in the first place, including risk analysis and transaction structuring, are not met.

Solving Circular References Related to a Cash Sweep Using Algebra

A more elegant solution to the problem of circular references than using macros or allowing the iteration button to be active is creating an equation that derives the interest expense from an algebraic process. The algebraic solution is complicated by taxes, dividends, and variations in interest rates between income and expense. But it is not very complicated in the cash sweep case. To demonstrate the algebraic solution, consider an acquisition model where all excess cash flow is used to pay down debt before any dividends are allowed. This is the cash sweep formula. Further, assume no taxes. In this case, the repayment of debt can be computed in the cash flow statement using the MIN function consistent with the discussion of cash flow waterfalls in Chapter 10.

When working through the circular reference functions and creating an algebraic formula, the general idea is to write down a bunch of equations that include a term for debt repayment. You can then substitute variables, rearrange things, and ultimately replace the repayment term with an equation that does not depend on interest expense. This equation for repayment of debt that does not depend on interest is then used in the cash flow section of the model rather than the normal MIN function described earlier. After creating the algebraic equation, you can convert it into a user-defined function if you choose to. In the example of a cash flow sweep with no taxes, the arguments for the function are the operating cash flow (EBITDA less working capital changes and capital expenditures), the interest rate, and the opening balance of the debt.

To solve the circular logic problem with algebra in the cash sweep case, begin by writing down a few of the equations that define interest expense and the repayment of debt from assuming that the interest is derived from the average debt balance rather than the opening debt balance, as was shown in the discussion of setting up the model:

$$\text{Interest Expense} = \text{Opening Debt Balance} \times \text{Interest Rate} - \text{Repayment} \times \text{Interest Rate}/2$$

$$\text{Repayment} = \text{MIN}(\text{Cash Flow}, \text{Opening Balance})$$

$$\text{Cash Flow} = \text{Operating Cash Flow} - \text{Interest Expense}$$

Using these equations you can create an expression for the repayment by substituting and rearranging variables. The goal of this process is to create an equation for repayment that is independent of the interest expense and the closing balance. Begin substituting variables and rearranging until the repayment does not depend on interest expense:

$$\text{Repayment} = \text{Operating Cash Flow} - (\text{Opening Debt Balance} \times \text{Interest Rate} - \text{Repayment} \times \text{Interest Rate}/2)$$

$$\text{Repayment} - \text{Repayment} \times \text{Interest Rate}/2 =$$
$$\text{Operating Cash Flow} - \text{Opening Balance} \times \text{Interest Rate}$$

$$\text{Repayment} \times (1 - \text{Interest Rate}/2) = \text{Operating Cash Flow}$$
$$- \text{Opening Balance} \times \text{Interest Rate}$$

$$\text{Repayment} = (\text{Operating Cash Flow} - \text{Opening Balance}$$
$$\times \text{Interest Rate})/(1 - \text{Interest Rate}/2)$$

After you have found an equation for debt repayment that does not depend on the interest expense, it is sometimes fairly long and burdensome to put it into a spreadsheet. As an alternative to typing out the equation, you can put the equation into a function. Then you can combine your function (named SWEEP in this example) with the MIN function as illustrated:

```
Function Sweep(EBITDA, rate, Opening_balance)
      Sweep = (EBITDA - Opening_balance * rate) / (1 - Rate/2)
End Function
```

Contents of the function and implementation of the function in the cash sweep acquisition model are illustrated in Figures 37.6 and 37.7. Developing an algebraic equation avoids all of the problems associated with the iteration button, the Goal Seek, and the copy and paste methods. The model is stable and does not require any iterative process. You can still run Goal Seeks, Solvers, and Data Tables. The model does not slow down and it is transparent. In entering the function, you can use the f_x box to guide the inputs that you are supposed to put into the formula. This is illustrated in Figure 37.7 where the inputs to the function appear in a box.

A problem with the algebraic method for solving circular references is that equations become a lot more tedious once taxes, carryforwards, and other complexities are added. But the general principle of substituting variables and rearranging equations in more complex examples is the same when you try to solve the problem in any situation. The bad news about more tedious formulas is that they can take a lot of algebra and are sometimes boring to work through. The good news is that if you create a function and use variable names that are easy to interpret, you only have to do it one time. Once you have made the function that contains the algebraic equation, you can copy it to other workbooks or even create an add-in to Excel. The formulas are generally easy to transfer from one spreadsheet to another, because by the time you get down to an income statement and a cash flow statement in a financial model, the format should be similar across models for all different types of corporations.

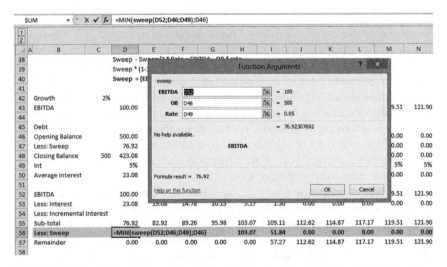

	B	C	D	E	F	G	H	I	J	K	L	M	N
31													
32	**Simple case: Sweep No Taxes**												
33			Int = (OB − sweep/2) * rate										
34			Sweep = EBITDA − Int										
35													
36			Sweep = EBITDA − (OB − Sweep/2) * Rate										
37			Sweep = EBITDA − OB * rate + Sweep/2 * Rate										
38			Sweep − Sweep/2 * Rate = EBITDA − OB * rate										
39			Sweep * (1−1/2 * Rate) = EBITDA − OB * rate										
40			Sweep = (EBITDA − OB * rate)/(1− Rate/2)										
41													
42	Growth	2%											
43	EBITDA		100.00	102.00	104.04	106.12	108.24	110.41	112.62	114.87	117.17	119.51	121.90
44													
45	Debt												
46	Opening Balance		500.00	423.08	340.16	250.89	154.92	51.84	0.00	0.00	0.00	0.00	0.00
47	Less: Sweep		76.92	82.92	89.26	95.98	103.07	51.84	0.00	0.00	0.00	0.00	0.00
48	Closing Balance	500	423.08	340.16	250.89	154.92	51.84	0.00	0.00	0.00	0.00	0.00	0.00
49	Int		5%	5%	5%	5%	5%	5%	5%	5%	5%	5%	5%
50	Average Interest		23.08	19.08	14.78	10.15	5.17	1.30	0.00	0.00	0.00	0.00	0.00
51													
52	EBITDA		100.00	102.00	104.04	106.12	108.24	110.41	112.62	114.87	117.17	119.51	121.90
53	Less: Interest		23.08	19.08	14.78	10.15	5.17	1.30	0.00	0.00	0.00	0.00	0.00
54	Less: Incremental Interest												
55	Sub-total		76.92	82.92	89.26	95.98	103.07	109.11	112.62	114.87	117.17	119.51	121.90
56	Less: Sweep		=MIN(sweep(D52;D46;D49);D46)				103.07	51.84	0.00	0.00	0.00	0.00	0.00
57	Remainder		0.00	0.00	0.00	0.00	0.00	57.27	112.62	114.87	117.17	119.51	121.90

FIGURE 37.6 Illustration of Using a Function That Incorporates the Algebraic Equation

FIGURE 37.7 Illustration of Use of the f_x Box to Enter Arguments to the SWEEP Function

Solving Circular References with Functions That Iterate around Equations That Cause the Problem

The final method for solving the circular reference problem extends the idea of creating a user-defined function method introduced in the previous section and at the same time applies some of the iteration ideas from the earlier methods. This approach solves problems in a similar manner to the algebraic method in that you need to write down equations, but you do not have to work through substituting and rearranging the equations. Creating a function with an iteration process allows you to use all of the Goal Seek and Data Table tools and keeps the model stable. Furthermore, the iterative function method often has advantages vis-à-vis the algebraic method because finding a single equation is very difficult if not impossible in many circular reference logic problems such as the case with taxes and a net operating loss.

To apply the method of creating an iterative function, the first step is to decide which equation should be fixed with the function so as to remove the circular reference. In the example that follows, the average interest expense is used. But unlike the copy and paste macro method you do not have to copy formulas and create a fixed value in the spreadsheet. Once you have decided which cell to solve for, you can write down equations for the items that are related to the equation and that are causing the circular reference. In this case you compute the average interest expense from the opening and closing debt balance, meaning you have to compute the closing balance and the cash flow sweep that constitutes the repayment. After the equations are established, all of the inputs to the equations must be included as inputs to the function because you cannot directly use cell references when writing equations in a user-defined function. Finally, an iteration process must be added to the function by which the equations are repeated until some kind of convergence test is met. The iteration process in the function could compare the interest expense from the prior iteration with the currently computed interest expense and keep going until there is no difference.

Figure 37.8 illustrates the function with an iterative process. You can begin by making a FOR NEXT loop with an arbitrary number of iterations. Next, you keep track of the prior value of the item being resolved, in this case the interest expense. Then you work through the same equations that you created in your spreadsheet. The last step in the function is testing whether the repayment computed from the prior iteration is the same as the repayment computed from the current iteration. If the values of the repayment from the last iteration and the current iteration are the same, the iteration process can be stopped and the function can be finished.

When implementing this kind of function in your financial model, it works in much the same way as the function demonstrated for the algebraic technique in Figure 37.7. The spreadsheet does not lose any functionality

```
Function average_interest (interest_rate, cash_flow,
   opening_debt_balance)

   For Iteration = 1 To 30

      last_interest = average_interest    ' maintain prior value for test

      average_interest = _
         ((opening_debt_balance + closing_debt_balance) / 2) _
            * interest_rate

      sweep = WorksheetFunction.Min (cash_flow -
            average_interest, _ opening_debt_balance)

      closing_debt_balance = opening_debt_balance - sweep

      converge = Abs (average_interest - last_interest) 'convergence

      If converge < 0.000001 Then Exit Function

   Next Iteration

End Function
```

FIGURE 37.8 Illustration of Iterative Function to Solve Circular Reference

associated with stability, sensitivity analysis, or optimization. Further, the function is fairly easy to change and adapt to more complex equations. Finally, the function does not slow down the spreadsheet calculations.

If taxes are included in the cash sweep model with a loss carryforward, developing an equation using the algebraic method becomes a lot more complex. The problem with including taxes in a financial model that contains circularity is that interest expense affects taxes, but taxes affect the cash flow available to repay debt. This adds a lot of terms to the algebraic equation. When you apply the user-defined function technique, you need to add the tax equations to the function. The example of adding taxes in the model reinforces the concept that the equations in the function must correspond to the equations in the model. In a sense you must rewrite the model in your VBA code when you use this method.

If equations for a net operating loss carryforward are included in the cash flow analysis, using the algebraic equation would not be possible because of the conditional nature of the operating loss and because of the accumulation of the carryforward. However, if the iterative function is used, then the effects of net operating loss on circularity can be included in the circular reference resolution. To incorporate the loss carryforward, the function must read in the opening carryforward balance as well as the tax rate and then work through the opening balance, increases to the carrryforward balance from negative taxable income, and uses from positive income. The carryforward can then be included in the function using the same equations that are in the model that is illustrated in Figure 37.9. For the function shown in Figure 37.9, the statements WORKSHEETFUNCTION.MIN and WORKSHEETFUNCTION.MAX demonstrate how you can use many standard functions when creating the user-defined functions.

```
Function average_interest_taxes(interest_rate, cash_flow,
opening_debt_balance, tax_rate, opening_NOL_Balance)

   For Iteration = 1 To 30
     last_sweep = sweep

     average_interest_taxes = _
         ((opening_debt_balance + closing_debt_balance) / 2) _
             * interest_rate

     taxable_income = cash_flow - average_interest_taxes

     NOL_created = WorksheetFunction.Max(0, 0 - taxable_income)

     NOL_used = WorksheetFunction.Min(opening_NOL_Balance, _
                     WorksheetFunction.Max(0, taxable_income))

     closing_NOL_Balance = opening_NOL_Balance + NOL_created -NOL_used

     adjusted_taxable_income = taxable_income + NOL_created - NOL_used

     taxes_paid = adjusted_taxable_income * tax_rate

     sweep = WorksheetFunction.Min(cash_flow - average_interest_taxes _
                             - taxes_paid, opening_debt_balance)

     closing_debt_balance = opening_debt_balance - sweep

     converge = Abs(sweep - last_sweep)

     If converge < 0.000001 Then Exit Function

   Next Iteration

End Function
```

FIGURE 37.9 Illustration of Function That Includes Tax and Net Operating Loss Calculations

Implementing the function in your model is similar to any other function in your spreadsheet like the SUM function or the AVERAGE function. With more arguments, using the f_x icon in the formula box is more important, as illustrated in Figure 37.10.

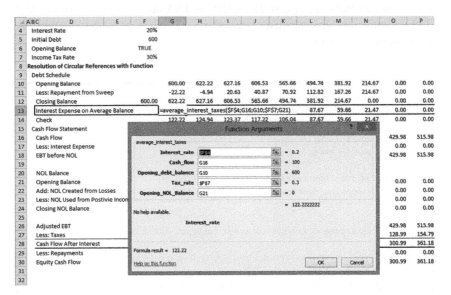

FIGURE 37.10 Illustration of Implementing a Function with Additional Arguments for the Tax Rate and the Net Operating Loss Balance

Creating a Structured Cash Flow Process in a Corporate Model to Resolve Circular References

If you thought the process of incorporating the net operating loss into an acquisition model with a cash flow sweep was not bad enough, the formulas become even more tedious and there are more complex iterative adjustments when solving the problem for a standard corporate model. Added complexities in solving circular references for a corporate model arise from differences between the interest income rate and the interest expense rate and because dividends may be deducted before computing the net cash flow. The process can also include equity issues or buybacks to meet a target capital structure. Dividends will probably have some sort of relationship with income, which in turn is driven by interest income and interest expense. The good news about this problem is that it is possible to solve the problem using an iterative user-defined function, and, after you have done it one time, you can use the same function over and over again in other models.

Structuring a Corporate Model with a Cash Flow Waterfall

Before discussing the formulas and iterative procedures for developing functions in a corporate model, a financing structure for a standard corporate model is reviewed and developed with a cash flow waterfall process. Because the interest rates for income and the interest rates for interest expense are usually assumed to be different, the surplus cash and short-term debt should not be lumped together in a single net debt and cash account as explained in Chapter 10. Instead, two accounts can be maintained with separate balances and separate inflows and outflows in the debt schedule. The account for required operating cash should be segregated from surplus cash, as should other existing debt and existing instruments that create income such as notes receivable.

When the surplus cash and the short-term debt are included as separate accounts with opening and closing balances, the end of the cash flow statement for a corporate model be structured to resemble a cash flow waterfall. As with other cash flow waterfall structures, subtotals should be set up along with using the MAX and MIN functions. Minimum cash balance can be incorporated in the analysis by comparing the required minimum balance with the opening balance. For a corporate model, the analysis of movements into the debt and cash balance accounts begins with a subtotal account for cash flow after dividends, scheduled interest, taxes, and everything else before evaluating cash and debt balances. The cash flow subtotal is the row in the model that can be used to isolate the circular reference. This line item depends on interest expense and interest income and drives the analysis of the debt and cash balance. If this cash flow subtotal line is computed from a user-defined function rather than from earlier rows in the cash flow statement, then the circular reference can be eliminated.

Potential reductions in the debt and cash account are assessed after the cash flow is established. If the first cash flow subtotal is positive, then short-term debt is reduced until it is fully paid off. If the cash flow subtotal is negative, then surplus cash is reduced until the amounts in the account are used up. After the reductions in debt and cash are evaluated first, you should create another subtotal account to evaluate additions to the accounts. This second subtotal account is used to compute the additions to surplus cash or the additional debt. If the second subtotal is positive, surplus cash is added into the cash account. If the subtotal is negative, additional debt is issued. As with the cash flow waterfall process described in Chapter 10, the MAX function is used to test whether an item is positive or negative, so you know whether the cash account or the debt account will be incremented. The MIN function is used to cap or limit an item when computing the reductions in the first step of the process where reductions in debt and cash occur. In evaluating reductions in cash and debt after the first subtotal account, both the MAX and MIN are used because the cash and debt accounts cannot decline by more than their opening balances. For the second subtotal, only the MAX function is necessary to test whether surplus cash flow is put into the cash account or negative cash flow is applied to increase debt.

The cash flow process at the bottom of a corporate model cash flow statement can be represented by the step-by-step process described next. The key to this waterfall technique is to structure the analysis such that first priority is removing items from the cash balance and debt balance accounts. At this stage, tests are made to assure that the minimum cash balance is not violated and that the debt balance does not fall below zero using the MIN function. After a second subtotal, the cash balance and the debt balance are increased.

Step 1 Compute the cash flow after dividends at the end of the cash flow statement. This remaining cash flow after dividends drives the changes in the surplus cash and the changes in the short-term debt balance. The remaining cash flow line is first divided into reductions in debt and cash using the MIN and MAX functions.

Step 2 The first priority of the cash flow waterfall is to reduce debt or reduce surplus cash balances to the maximum extent possible. If the cash flow subtotal is negative, you should remove money from the surplus cash account. Use the MAX(-cash flow,0) function to test whether the function is negative, and then compare the amount of the cash flow removed with the opening balance of the account using the MIN function:

$$\text{Reduction in Surplus Cash} = \text{MIN}(\text{MAX}(-\text{Cash Flow}, 0),$$
$$\text{Opening Surplus Cash Balance})$$

If an assumed minimum cash balance is part of the analysis, a subtotal in the debt and cash schedule establishing the maximum reduction in cash flow should be part of the test. This is the required minimum cash balance less the opening balance that is similar to other subtotal calculations discussed in Chapter 10. When the minimum cash assumption is part of the model, the potential reduction in surplus cash evaluates the negative cash flow compared to the balance of cash that is available for use. The alternative equation that includes provision for minimum cash balance is:

$$\text{Reduction in Surplus Cash} = \text{MIN}(\text{MAX}(-\text{Cash Flow},$$
$$\text{Maximum Possible Reduction in Cash}), \text{Opening Surplus Cash})$$

If the minimum cash balance is used, additional amounts that must be deposited in the cash account should also be deducted from the cash flow subtotal. If sales have increased, implying that the minimum cash balance is more, then the increase in the minimum balance must be computed before the subtotal.

Step 3 Continuing with the first subtotal that drives reductions in debt and cash balances, if the cash flow is positive, then you should remove money from the debt balance account as long as the opening balance has a positive balance. As described in Chapter 10, the MAX and MIN functions are the key to efficiently modeling a cash flow waterfall. This time the equation for reducing the debt balance when the cash balance is positive using the MAX and MIN can be written as:

$$\text{Reduction in Short-Term Debt} = \text{MIN}(\text{MAX}(\text{Cash Flow}, 0),$$
$$\text{Opening Debt Balance})$$

Step 4 After the reductions in cash and debt are computed and tested with MIN function, compute the second subtotal that is used to evaluate additions to the debt and cash account.

Step 5 The final two lines of the cash flow statement measure the increase in debt and the increase in surplus cash that will be put back into the cash and debt balances. For increases in debt and increases in cash, use the MAX(-cash,0) and the MAX(cash,0) functions. This time test for a negative cash flow to determine how much debt to add and test for positive cash flow to test for how much cash to add. When allocating the final subtotal between cash and debt do not include the MIN function:

$$\text{Increase in Cash} = \text{MAX(Cash Flow Subtotal}, 0)$$

$$\text{Increase in Debt} = \text{MAX(-Cash Flow Subtotal}, 0)$$

The format of a cash flow waterfall at the end of the corporate model using these concepts is illustrated in Figure 38.1.

Debt and Cash Balance

Debt Balance								
Opening Balance		200.00	225.94	203.59	142.64	77.24	154.70	49.18
Add: New Debt Issued		25.94	0.00	0.00	0.00	77.46	0.00	0.00
Less: Debt Repaid		0.00	22.35	60.95	65.41	0.00	105.52	49.18
Closing Balance	200.00	225.94	203.59	142.64	77.24	154.70	49.18	0.00
Interest Rate		7%	7%	7%	7%	7%	7%	7%
Interest Expense on Opening Balance		14.00	15.82	14.25	9.98	5.41	10.83	3.44
Cash Balance								
Opening Balance		20.00	0.00	0.00	0.00	0.00	0.00	0.00
Add: New Cash Generated		0.00	0.00	0.00	0.00	0.00	0.00	71.89
Less: Cash Used		20.00	0.00	0.00	0.00	0.00	0.00	0.00
Closing Balance	20.00	0.00	0.00	0.00	0.00	0.00	0.00	71.89
Interest Rate		2%	2%	2%	2%	2%	2%	2%
Interest Income on Opening Balance		0.40	0.00	0.00	0.00	0.00	0.00	0.00
Cash Flow Statement								
EBITDA		100.00	130.00	160.00	190.00	220.00	250.00	280.00
Less: Captial Expenditures		100.00	45.00	20.00	30.00	190.00	20.00	20.00
Cash From Operations		0.00	85.00	140.00	160.00	30.00	230.00	260.00
Less: Interest Expense		14.00	15.82	14.25	9.98	5.41	10.83	3.44
Add: Interest Income		0.40	0.00	0.00	0.00	0.00	0.00	0.00
Less: Dividends		32.34	46.84	64.80	84.61	102.06	113.65	135.48
Net Cash Flow		-45.94	22.35	60.95	65.41	-77.46	105.52	121.07
Add: Reduced Cash Balance when Cash is Negative		20.00	0.00	0.00	0.00	0.00	0.00	0.00
Less: Reduced Debt Balance when Cash is Postitive		0.00	22.35	60.95	65.41	0.00	105.52	49.18
Cash Flow after Reductions		-25.94	0.00	0.00	0.00	-77.46	0.00	71.89
Less: Added Cash Balance when Cash is Postive		0.00	0.00	0.00	0.00	0.00	0.00	71.89
Add: Added Debt Balance when Cash is Negative		25.94	0.00	0.00	0.00	77.46	0.00	0.00
Final Cash Flow (Should be zero)		0.00	0.00	0.00	0.00	0.00	0.00	0.00

FIGURE 38.1 Illustration of Cash Flow Process for a Corporation Modeled with a Cash Flow Waterfall

Resolving Circular References in a Corporate Model Using an Iterative User-Defined Function

When resolving circular references in the context of a corporate model that arise because of average interest expense, you could apply any of the five methods introduced in Chapter 37. If you use the iteration button, the model is unstable; if you use the Goal Seek or the copy and paste method, the model becomes nontransparent, clumsy, and unusable for sensitivity and optimization analysis; if you try the algebraic method, the equations become long and messy because of dividends, taxes, and the difference between interest income and interest expense. Given these problems, the iterative user-defined function method is described. The trick in resolving circular references in a corporate model is to fix the remaining cash flow line and compute this row with a function. This is like cutting out all of the blue arrows that appear after you enter a circular reference. The problem with breaking the circular reference with a function in this case is that cash flow is influenced by interest income, interest expense, taxes, and dividends. All of these items are affected by the debt and cash balance. To create the iterative function, you should begin by writing down the same equations that are used in the corporate model. To develop this function, you can use the following steps:

Step 1   Make a new function that will compute the subtotal for cash flow after dividends, which is the cause of the circular references.

Step 2   Write down equations for anything that is causing the circular reference in the function including interest expense, interest income, income taxes, and dividends. You can have the Visual Basic for Applications (VBA) window open next to the spreadsheet to make sure that you are mimicking all of the spreadsheet model equations in the function. If the equations in the function are not consistent with the financial model, the function will not work correctly. For example, if dividends are computed from MAX(Net Income × Payout Ratio,0) in the spreadsheet, the exact same equation must be in the function.

Step 3   Read all the variables that are necessary for computing the equations for cash flow, dividends, taxes, interest income, and interest expense into the function, including the interest income rate, the interest expense rate, the tax rate, the dividend payout ratio, and the operating cash flow before dividends, taxes, and financing. The variable names should have good descriptions in the VBA code so that you can apply the f_x method when you are entering the function into your model.

Step 4   When creating the user-defined function, you must include conditional statements that reflect the cash flow disposition

```
Function cash_flow(EBIT, cash_from_operations, interest_expense_rate, _
              interest_income_rate, opening_debt, opening_cash, _
              payout_ratio, min_cash)

For Iteration = 1 To 30

   last_cash_flow = cash_flow

   earnings = EBIT - interest_expense + interest_income
   dividends = WorksheetFunction.Max(earnings * payout_ratio, 0)

   interest_expense = (opening_debt + closing_debt) / 2 * _
           interest_expense_rate
   interest_income = ((opening_cash + closing_cash) / 2) * _
           interest_income_rate

   cash_flow = cash_from_operations - interest_expense + _
           interest_income - dividends - min_cash

   reduced_debt = _
           WorksheetFunction.Min(WorksheetFunction.Max(cash_flow,
                      0), _opening_debt)

   reduced_cash = _
           WorksheetFunction.Min(WorksheetFunction.Max(0 -
                      cash_flow,0), _opening_cash)

   cash_after_reductions = cash_flow + reduced_cash - reduced_debt

   add_debt = WorksheetFunction.Max(0 - cash_after_reductions, 0)
   add_cash = WorksheetFunction.Max(cash_after_reductions, 0)

   closing_debt = opening_debt + add_debt - reduced_debt
   closing_cash = opening_cash + add_cash - reduced_cash + min_cash

   converge = Abs(last_cash_flow - cash_flow)

   If converge < 0.000001 Then Exit Function

Next Iteration

End Function
```

FIGURE 38.2 Function for Resolving Circular Reference in Corporate Model

process as described earlier. If the cash flow is negative, compute the reduction in surplus cash and use the MIN and MAX functions to evaluate how much of the negative cash flow is applied to reduce surplus cash. The WORKSHEETFUNCTION.MIN function can be used to test how much surplus cash can be applied by comparing the opening cash balance to the amount of required cash. This implies you must read the opening debt and cash balances into the function.

Step 5   If the cash flow is positive, compute the reduction in new debt and use the MIN and MAX functions to evaluate how much of the positive cash flow is applied to the debt reduction.

Step 6   Put an iteration loop around equations in the function and make a test for when the cash flow from the prior iteration converges with the cash flow from the current iteration. The convergence can be evaluated by creating a variable that stores the prior cash flow and then compares the cash flow for the current iteration with the stored cash flow for the last iteration.

A user-defined function that can resolve circular references in a corporate model is illustrated in Figure 38.2. In creating the function, you can open the VBA window and then work through each formula. You have to isolate the area that is causing the circular reference and then make sure the inputs you read into the function such as EBITDA and interest rates are independent of the circularity. When there are formulas in the model that use functions like the MIN and MAX functions, you can use the WorksheetFunction feature of VBA.

CHAPTER **39**

Overview of Complex Project Finance Modeling Structuring Issues

S ome elements of project finance analysis and modeling are among the most difficult challenges in programming and cause continuing headaches for modelers. The worst nightmares often result from circular logic, resolution of which can sometimes make a model far less flexible for structuring analysis and can make calculations very difficult to trace. Project finance models can be very elegant, detailed, and sophisticated in terms of representing a project. They often include Visual Basic for Applications (VBA) programs to resolve circular references (for example, pressing a picture of a beautiful sculpture for operating a macro that sculpts debt). But if you are afraid to use these large and sophisticated models to evaluate the effects of different debt structures such as debt sizing from the debt service coverage ratio (DSCR) or varying the debt tenor and drawdown provisions or refinancing, then the model is all but useless. Similarly, if a model contains hundreds of lines of detail about operating expenses but it cannot be used to measure easily how a few of the key variables affect returns and ability to repay debt, then how can you call it a good model?

The remaining chapters explain how circular references and other similar problems related to sculpting debt, financing funding needs during construction, refinancing, credit enhancement provisions, and reserve accounts can be dealt with in a project finance model. The chapters work through alternative techniques that should leave your models more flexible and transparent. Project finance modeling issues addressed in this context include:

- Funding of capital expenditures, capitalized interest, and fees
- Alternative debt repayments, including sculpting debt repayment to after-tax cash flow
- Debt service reserve accounts (DSRAs)
- Maintenance reserve accounts (MRAs)
- Cash sweeps and dividend lockup covenants

- Debt refinancing and changing valuation of projects at different stages
- Incorporating portfolios of assets in real estate and other project models

Before discussing details of alternative techniques a summary of items that cannot be resolved without running into circular logic is presented in the next few paragraphs. Issues that genuinely cause circular references should be distinguished from other issues that seem to cause circularity but can be resolved in order to avoid jumping to create VBA programs as soon as some blue arrows appear in your spreadsheet.

Circular references that can limit the flexibility and transparency of a model and that seem unavoidable in a project finance model arise from debt sculpting, interest capitalization, and funding priorities. Experienced modelers may not believe this, but all project finance circular references can be resolved without copy and paste macros that arguably ruin a model. With a copy and paste macro, the model cannot be used effectively for deriving capacity pricing bids; Goal Seeks cannot be used to evaluate engineering, procurement, and construction (EPC) contracts; data tables cannot be created to demonstrate the effects of different price terms on the equity internal rate of return (IRR); spinner buttons cannot be used in graphs; and models can blow up. In short, the structuring analysis can become a cumbersome, ugly process. To solve the circular reference problem without copy and paste macros or other equally bad techniques, user-defined functions can be created that isolate the circular reference and allow all of the flexible analysis that would be present had the good old SUM function somehow been used to resolve the problem.

The general philosophy in addressing these difficult circular logic issues associated with project finance models applies this four-part approach:

1. Understand the source of the circular logic and whether some sort of resolution process is necessary. Many of the DSRA problems that seem impossible, for example, can be resolved without a circular reference and instead splitting up the construction debt from the permanent debt.
2. Program equations for the model into your spreadsheet so as to isolate the circular reference problem into a single cell if at all possible. Present the circular reference issues in a summary sources and uses table that is transparent and easy to follow.
3. Understand and isolate the portions of the model that are causing the circular reference problem and rewrite formulas from the spreadsheet into a user-defined function. This not only solves the circular reference but it creates a very good auditing tool for the model.
4. Create an iteration process around the isolated formulas in the user-defined function and use values from the function rather than the fixed cell that would otherwise be part of a copy and paste macro. For auditing

purposes, show the values computed by the model next to the values generated from the function.

Difficult Project Finance Problems: Structuring versus Risk Analysis Elements of a Model

In addressing the issues of debt sculpting, debt funding, DSRAs, and MRAs, it is essential to distinguish between the notion of using a project finance model for risk analysis and using it for contract structuring. The issue of structuring contracts in a transaction is less important in corporate finance models because you are not creating a company from scratch. Most of the challenging project finance problems discussed in the next few chapters address structuring rather than risk analysis elements of a model. One of the recurring issues in project finance structuring is that when evaluating various terms of a loan agreement, debt sizing can be derived either from the prospective cash flow available for debt service (CFADS) or, alternatively, from defined debt gearing parameters.

Structuring analysis in a project finance model refers to the process of coming up with the debt and equity commitments as well as repayments, funding amounts, and reserve accounts using a particular cash flow scenario. Issues in structuring include deriving the amount of debt in a loan agreement that may be computed from a target debt service coverage ratio; computing the bid price in a long-term contract such as a power purchase agreement derived from required return and debt parameters; developing debt repayment percentages from the debt tenor and the target debt service coverage; testing different possible structures for a debt service coverage ratio covenant; evaluating the efficacy of including different levels of credit enhancements such as DSRAs, cash sweeps, and MRAs in a transaction; and comparing the effects of different funding possibilities such as equity invested first, pro-rata funding, debt first, or an equity bridge loan.

When considering multiple transaction structuring options before a project is born, it can be difficult to evaluate different debt structuring possibilities efficiently if macros are used to resolve circular references. If a macro button must be pressed every time the debt service coverage ratio is changed, the process can be cumbersome, as you have to wait for the macro to clunk along its various iterations before determining how a certain structuring element influences returns. Further, if you would like to evaluate many different structuring options including funding and debt sculpting, the macros can become so elaborate with multiple IF statements and different tests that they can make your model almost impossible to audit. Worst of all, if the model is used to compute the required contract prices that can achieve IRR targets and DSCR objectives, changing the contract payment requires running a macro. But after you compute a new price with a Goal Seek, the copy and paste must be run again. In the end, the process of computing a Goal Seek, running the macro, recalculating the Goal Seek, and rerunning the macro can become almost impossible. This is because the macro button to size debt and/ or to sculpt the debt must be pressed each time one of the operating parameters changes. Given the difficulties in efficiently analyzing debt structuring where macros are used to resolve circular references, the next couple of chapters include explanations of how to develop algebraic equations and/or isolated iteration functions to avoid the copy and paste process.

In contrast to transaction structuring, risk analysis in a model addresses how the transaction works if certain operating assumptions are varied after the contract structure has been established. This was the entire subject of Part II. In developing risk analysis, the amount of debt, the repayment of debt, and deposits to and scheduled removals from the debt service reserve account are established and fixed. Unless covenants that look into the future are modeled, there should be no circular reference. This includes potential circularity associated with the use of prospective debt service in a debt service reserve account when cash flow sweeps are present. Aspects of the cash flow waterfall that may kick in under downside or stress scenarios such as cash flow sweeps, covenants, refinancing, backup credit facilities, and use of debt service reserves are part of the risk analysis process. Figure 39.1 illustrates a project finance structure with sculpting followed by calculation of the DSRA followed by calculation of debt funding.

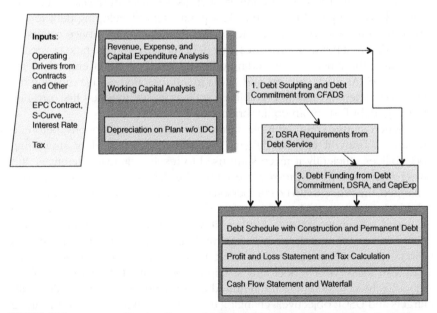

FIGURE 39.1 Structure of Project Finance Model with Debt Size Derived from Cash Flow

Items in Project Finance Models
That Cause Circularity

In resolving the problem of circular references, the first step is understanding exactly why the circular logic exists. Knowing the source of the circular reference is like being a doctor who must diagnose a problem before coming up with alternative possible cures. Once you understand precisely where the circularity comes from, you can isolate the cell or cells that cause the circularity and attempt to make the solution as transparent as possible. Three of the principal items that cause circular references in a project finance model are:

1. **Debt funding, interest during construction, and debt-related fees.** The amount of debt that is available to fund construction may be driven by a given percentage of the total defined project cost, or alternatively, the debt size may be driven by CFADS. If debt is determined from a maximum debt-to-total capital percentage, a problem arises because the total project cost includes capitalized fees during construction, capitalized interest during construction, and the balance of a debt service reserve account that is funded before operation. Since the amount of debt funding influences interest, fees, and the DSRA, but interest, fees, and the DSRA drive total project cost, a circularity problem arises. To compute the interest, fees, and the DSRA, the amount of debt borrowed that is the basis of these calculations is a required input. But this amount of debt borrowing is not known until the interest, fees, and the DSRA are computed, because the total project cost includes interest, the DSRA balance, and fees. The process can be resolved by creating a table that sums the items that cause the problem during the construction period. This summary of sources and uses of funds can be presented next to the procedure that solves the problem. These types of funding issues are addressed in Chapter 40.

2. **Sculpting, taxes, and interest during construction.** When computing debt repayments using debt sculpting, repayments are derived directly from cash flow after tax. Because the debt repayments influence tax deductible interest expense and because cash flow is defined to be after tax, a circular reference arises. Cash flow and tax drive debt and interest, but interest is a component of computing taxes. The circular reference problem is compounded because of the tax effects of depreciation that comes from interest during construction and the tax effect of amortization of fees that are compiled during construction. While this circular reference is very difficult to avoid without a copy and paste macro you can create a user-defined function that encompasses both the funding and the repayment phases of a project to solve the problem. Structuring of debt repayments and the associated tax effects are discussed in Chapter 41 and Chapter 42.

3. **Interest income, DSRAs, and taxes.** DSRAs impose a cash buffer on the project to protect lenders in the case of short-term liquidity problems. These accounts seem to create an impossible circular reference and many project finance models employ some kind of elaborate copy and paste macro associated with modeling the account. When a debt service coverage ratio is used to size debt from cash flow, the pattern of debt repayments influence the DSRA, but the interest income on the DSRA influences CFADS and the amount of debt. Despite the seemingly intractable problems created by DSRAs, many of the problems associated with the accounts can be solved through careful model structuring and thereby avoiding the need for VBA programs. However, in cases where the debt size is driven by an input gearing ratio, the total project cost is determined in part in by the DSRA but the DSRA depends on the level of debt, resulting in a funding circular problem. DSRA problems are discussed in Chapter 43.

The order of the next few chapters that cover some of the complex structuring issues in project finance models corresponds to the aforementioned three elements and includes discussion of maintenance reserves as well as refinancing, covenants, and developing a portfolio of projects:

- The first challenging item is computing the total debt commitment and the DSRA to establish the debt capacity of a project. If interest is capitalized instead of paid, part of the debt commitment is used up by interest and fees during construction meaning that not all of the debt commitment can be used to fund cash construction expenditures. To solve this funding problem, some kind of process for separately computing the transaction cost adders that come from debt to the project cost must be developed.
- The second problem is related to sizing debt and computing the amount of debt commitment from the operating cash flows. Resolution of debt sizing depends on the method of structuring repayments. If sculpting is used to size debt and structure repayments, a circularity problem associated with taxes must be resolved. If equal installment payments or annuity payments are assumed, a flexible Goal Seek process can be incorporated into a function.
- The third problem relates to DSRAs and MRAs. Once the total debt commitment and the debt repayments are established, the DSRA can be computed from prospective debt service. If the debt commitment is derived from cash flow then the debt service reserve is independent of the funding process and depends only on prospective debt service, which in turn depends on operating cash flow.

CHAPTER 40

Funding Techniques in Project Finance and the Associated Circular Reference Problems

The manner in which a project is funded with senior debt, subordinated debt, and equity during the construction phase can have important effects on the earned rate of return to equity holders. Different techniques to size debt reflect fundamental differences in philosophical approaches to lending. When funding is derived from a debt to capital ratio, the general philosophical notion is that cash flow forecasts are not required and may not even be trustworthy. Instead, the money is lent on the basis that equity holders are sensible and trustworthy people and, as they generally get paid after lenders, that the debt should be safe. In the case of lending on the basis of cash flow, a buffer of debt service relative to projected cash flow drives the process. Here a forecast of cash flow is trusted in one way or another by lenders and the debt size is backed out from analysis of the debt service coverage ratio (DSCR) and a buffer in different scenarios.

This chapter primarily uses the first philosophy of debt sizing where debt is determined from a maximum debt to capital criteria. Given the debt sizing criteria, three modeling options that may need to be addressed for the financing stage of a project finance transaction are:

1. **Funding.** In some projects with parent support from letters of credit or strong engineering, procurement, and construction contracts, the equity may not be contributed until the construction of the project is completed. In more traditionally financed projects with less parent support, the lenders may insist that equity is contributed before debt to demonstrate that the equity holders have "skin in the game" and to ensure that the investors cannot abandon the project before investing any money. In yet other cases, the equity and debt are contributed on a proportional or pro-rata basis

relative to their aggregate commitment amount. The different methods of funding pose different modeling problems and are addressed in this chapter.

2. **Capitalized interest and fees.** When financing a project, the interest accrued on a loan is sometimes paid to a lender, which increases funding needs. In other cases the interest is not paid to the lender during construction but instead is capitalized or rolled up to increase the size of the loan. As with interest costs, the fees paid to lenders can also either be currently paid or be capitalized.

3. **Bond financing.** If projects are financed with bonds instead of bank loans, the funding occurs in discrete periods and the amount of money contributed to the project from bondholders in a single construction period is often more than necessary for funding the project in that period. Since the amount of funding exceeds the uses of funds, a cash account should be modeled to account for the surplus funding.

Depending on which set of funding techniques is used, the funding section of a project finance model can be relatively simple or it can represent one of the most difficult problems in the programming of a model. Various possible combinations of funding structures are discussed in this chapter, including bond financing with draws occurring in a single period, funding on a pro-rata basis or funding equity before debt, and capitalization or current payment of fees. When some of the financing combinations are used—in particular when interest and fees are not capitalized—then circular reference can sometimes be avoided through use of algebra or through carefully structuring a model. In most other circumstances, the best solution is to write a user-defined function that solves the funding problem in a variety of different structuring possibilities.

One of the most frequent circular reference problems in funding occurs from interest and fees when the total gearing ratio is a predetermined input. To illustrate this problem, assume that the total project cost without interest and fees is $1 million and the input gearing ratio is 50 percent. The amount of borrowing actually allowed is more than 50 percent of the $1 million construction expenditures because interest and fees on the loan are capitalized to the cost of the project. If the construction period covers more than one period in the model, then there is no easy algebraic formula that can be developed to find the amount of debt issued associated with the cost, including interest and fees. Instead, calculation of the amount of the loan requires some kind of Goal Seek function, copy and paste macro, or user-defined function that depends on the interest rate.

To analyze the circularity problem associated with funding, the next section begins with cases where no circularity exists. After that, subsequent sections address various structural features that cause circularity and are added one item at a time to illustrate why the circularity arises and how to resolve the particular circularity problem. A fundamental idea in working through these circular logic issues is that it is good to first find, and then to fully understand the ultimate source of the circular reference and to solve the problem at the source rather than treating a symptom of the problems after you see a lot of blue arrows. Through understanding the original source of the circularity, redundant circular references should not be included in the macros or functions. Solving redundant circular references can cause big problems in a model in terms of flexibility and transparency.

Case 1: No Circular Reference—Pro-Rata Funding, Interest Paid during Construction, and Debt Size from Cash Flow

Circular references can arise from the manner in which debt and equity fund construction and from the way in which interest and fees during construction are paid or capitalized. The case described in this section is a situation where circular logic does not exist. This case is important as a base because you can use it to see how relaxed assumptions from this base scenario result in circular logic. Assume the amount of debt funding is determined in advance from applying a DSCR to the cash flow available for debt service (CFADS). This means the debt size does not depend on the project cost and that the debt size is not a function of interest during construction because it only depends on future cash flow. Further assume that debt is borrowed on a pro-rata basis as a function of the amount of money that is spent on physical construction. The drawdown percentages are computed from a schedule where the construction expenditure for the current period is divided by the total construction cost. This means that the drawdown percentage is independent of the equity or debt financing. For example, if one-fifth of the total expenditures is made in the first period, one-fifth of the total debt is drawn.

In this case where debt is sized on the basis of a target DSCR and funding is pro-rata, the amount of equity funding can be computed on a residual basis from the total funding needs less the debt funding. The debt funding comes from multiplying the aggregate debt size by the pro-rata percentage. If the interest during construction is paid and not capitalized, it does not affect the size of the debt and there is no circular reference. The reason there is no circular reference in this special case is that the total debt and equity funding can be determined from the construction expenditures without making any adjustments for interest expense and fees that are paid on the debt. The step-by-step approach for computing funding in this introductory

case of pro-rata draws and debt sizing determined from cash flows is as
follows:

Step 1   Compute cash funding requirements for each period from con-
             struction expenditures plus the interest paid.
Step 2   Calculate the debt draw percentages for each period where draw
             percentage = Construction$_t$/Σ Construction.
Step 3   Derive the amount of debt funding per construction period from
             the draw percentage using the formula:

$$\text{Debt Funding} = \text{Fixed Debt Commitment}$$
$$\times \text{Draw Percentage(i.e., Independent of Funding)}$$

Step 4   Compute the equity funding as the residual amount of funding
             requirements from step 1 minus debt funding computed in step 3,
             just as equity cash flow or dividends is the residual amount in the
             cash flow waterfall for a project finance model:

$$\text{Equity Funding} = \text{Funding Requirements} - \text{Debt Funding}$$

The set-up of this modeling process shown in Figure 40.1 is the basis for
evaluating subsequent cases. The first step is computing the debt draws for the
three-year construction period that, in this case, is independent of later steps in
the model. Calculation of the total uses of funds and the funding requirements
shown on the bottom left-hand side drives the equity financing requirements.
Accumulated equity and debt balances are presented on the right-hand side.
Note that the debt commitment is independent of the funding process as it is
assumed to come from cash flow and DSCR analysis.

Assumptions				Debt Schedule			
Construction Period	3			Opening Balance	-	26,666.67	53,333.33
EPC Cost	100,000			Add: Debt Draws	26,666.67	26,666.67	26,666.67
Debt Commitment from CFADS	80,000			Add: Interest Capitalised	-	-	-
Interest Rate	10%			Closing Balance	26,666.67	53,333.33	80,000.00
Debt Funded	80,000						
Equity Commitment	28,000			Interest Rate	10%	10%	10%
Interest Paid	TRUE			Interest Recorded	-	2,666.67	5,333.33
Funding Ratio	1			Interest Paid	-	2,666.67	5,333.33
				Interest Capitalised	-	-	-
Debt Funded							
Funding Percent	33.33%	33.33%	33.33%	**Equity Balance**			
Debt Funded	26,666.67	26,666.67	26,666.67	Total Commitment	28,000.00	28,000.00	28,000.00
				Equity Commited	-	6,666.67	16,000.00
Period	-2	-1	0	Remaining	28,000.00	21,333.33	12,000.00
Uses of Funds							
Construction	33,333.33	33,333.33	33,333.33	Opening Balance	-	6,666.67	16,000.00
Add: Interest Paid	-	2,666.67	5,333.33	Add: Equity Commited	6,666.67	9,333.33	12,000.00
Total Funding Needs	33,333.33	36,000.00	38,666.67	Closing Balance	6,666.67	16,000.00	28,000.00
Sources of Funds							
Debt	26,666.67	26,666.67	26,666.67	**Checks**			
Equity (Residual after Debt)	6,666.67	9,333.33	12,000.00	Computed Debt	80,000.00		
Total	33,333.33	36,000.00	38,666.67	Fixed Debt	80,000.00		

FIGURE 40.1 Sources and Uses of Funds and Debt Schedule for Pro-Rata Case Where
Debt Is Given from Cash Flow and No Circular Logic Is Present

Case 2: Circular Reference from Pro-Rata Funding with Capitalized Interest or Debt Ratio Input

If the total debt commitment is defined by a given debt-to-capital ratio rather than from prospective cash flow and the DSCR, or if debt is determined by a given DSCR and interest is capitalized, then the headaches begin. In the second case the funding is still assumed to be derived from pro-rata funding. When interest is capitalized rather than paid to lenders during the construction period, the total amount of debt that can be used to pay for the cash expenditures of the project is not known until the interest cost is computed. If an input debt ratio is applied, the interest during construction affects the project cost, which in turn affects the total debt commitment. Both of these situations cause a circular reference as illustrated in Figures 40.2 and 40.3. The diagram in Figure 40.2 demonstrates that periodic debt draws to fund cash construction drive the capitalized interest, but capitalized interest drives the accumulated amount of debt that can be used to fund construction. This amount of debt funding in turn determines the interest during construction.

FIGURE 40.2 Circular Logic Diagram for Capitalized Interest in the Funding Phase of a Project

A circular reference problem similar to the capitalized interest issue arises when the debt commitment is determined from a given or input debt-to-capital ratio, as shown in Figure 40.3. This causes a circular reference because debt is driven by total project cost, including interest and fees, which are labeled adders in Figure 40.3. But the adders are in turn driven by the amount of debt.

FIGURE 40.3 Circular Logic Diagram in the Case of a Given Debt-to-Capital Ratio Used for Debt Sizing

The circular reference from a scenario where the debt-to-capital ratio is fixed in advance is shown in Figure 40.4. The arrows in Figure 40.4 illustrate how the interest during construction drives the total project cost, but the total cost in turn drives the debt and the interest. In this diagram, a summary of the sources and uses of funds during the construction period is presented so that you can see the total project cost. If you could make the interest during construction or the total debt commitment a fixed cell in the summary sources and uses of funds analysis, you could remove the arrows that signify the circular reference.

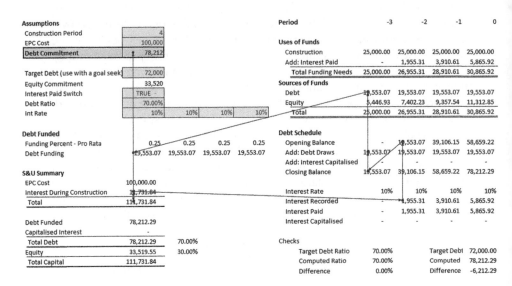

FIGURE 40.4 Illustration of Circular References in Model with Input Debt-to-Capital Ratio

As discussed in Chapter 37, there are five general approaches that can be used to resolve this type of circular reference problem:

- The first approach is to use the iteration option in Excel, which seems very simple but can lead to big problems when you are using the model in structuring analysis. The target debt in Figure 40.4 is included to illustrate problems with the iteration button. If the Goal Seek is used to find the debt ratio that equates committed debt with the target debt amount, the process does not work.
- The second option to solve the circular reference is to replace the cell for accumulated interest during construction in the summary sources and uses summary with a fixed amount. Then you can recompute the interest during construction and other debt-related adders somewhere else in the sheet. With the fixed and computed cells you can use a Goal Seek to set the difference between the fixed level and the computed level to zero. This option is problematic because multiple Goal Seeks may be necessary if you want to find the debt-to-capital ratio the matches the target input. After one Goal Seek is used, it cannot be used again to solve things like bid prices, break-even points, or other optimization analyses.

- The third option is to set-up a fixed and computed cell as in the Goal Seek method. Then you could create a macro that copies and pastes computed values of the accumulated interest during construction and other adders into the fixed cell that is used to compute total project cost. Once you have copied the computed cell to the fixed cells, you can write a macro with an iteration loop. A copy and paste macro such as this is common in project finance models but it has the same problems in terms of limiting the flexibility of the model that is associated with the Goal Seek method.
- The fourth option is to develop an algebraic solution that accumulates the interest during construction and is independent of the debt commitment. This takes a lot of work because the interest during construction is computed over multiple periods.
- The fifth option is to create a structured user-defined function that re-creates the accumulated interest during construction in the summary sources and uses of funds statement. This process requires two FOR NEXT loops. The first FOR NEXT loop computes period-by-period interest during construction across the construction periods. The second FOR NEXT loop is an iteration process that recomputes the accumulated interest during construction from the first loop until the interest during construction stabilizes.

In a sense, the first three options are tantamount to giving up on keeping a model flexible and transparent, whereas the fourth option of developing a set of algebraic functions can be a big challenge requiring a lot of creativity and perseverance. The fifth option of creating a user-defined function can be used to solve the circular reference, but it is more complex than the functions introduced for corporate models because the accumulated interest during construction must be evaluated over the entire construction period. The main problem in creating a user-defined function is to be careful with spelling variable names and to make sure the function has the same equations that are in your spreadsheet. The iteration check box option, the copy and paste macro, and the user-defined function in the context of the funding circularity problem are addressed in the subsequent paragraphs.

As discussed in Chapter 37, Excel has an option to resolve circular references through making iterative calculations. Recall that to use this option you press the iteration button from the File tab. In a large project finance model with the type of funding circular logic discussed for this funding case, leaving a circular reference in a file using the iteration option is dangerous. With the iteration button switched on, the large models become unstable and almost impossible to work with in terms of risk analysis and financial structuring. Furthermore, the Goal Seek function, which may be one of the most useful tools in deriving a contractual structure that meets various conflicting objectives of different stakeholders, no longer works.

To resolve the funding problem with a copy and paste macro you can use the following step-by-step process:

1. Replace the accumulated interest during construction that is part of the summary sources and uses table, showing the project cost with a fixed cell. This summary sources and uses of funds statement that accumulates funds over the pre-operation period can comprise the area of the model where the circular references related to funding will be resolved. Making the summary sources and uses of funds statement is useful no matter what circular method resolution is applied.
2. Link the accumulated interest during construction in the summary sources and uses statement that is causing the circular reference to a fixed number. If multiple items such as fees, accumulated interest during construction, and the debt service reserve account (DSRA) cause the funding circularity, then you can add these numbers into a subtotal and use the fixed value of this subtotal in computing the total project cost.
3. Create a cell for the calculated total debt adders that is linked to the total project cost calculation. The computed adders are the sum of interest during construction and fees from the debt schedule.
4. Evaluate the difference between the computed debt adders and the fixed debt adders in a separate cell. The macro will work by copying and pasting the computed subtotal in step 3 to the fixed cells in step 1 over and over again until this difference cell becomes 0.
5. To create the macro, start recording the macro and then repeat step 4. Copy the computed subtotal in step 3 to the fixed cells in step 1. After doing the copy and paste, stop recording the macro. You then need to modify it in order to copy over and over until the difference goes to zero.
6. To modify the macro so that it repeats the copy and paste routine until the difference goes to zero, you can add two lines to the macro and make a WHILE loop. (There are many other ways to accomplish this with FOR NEXT loops and other code that can do the same thing.) Using the WHILE loop, a line above the copy and paste code begins the loop with the WHILE statement. The second line associated with the loop below the copy and paste code ends the WHILE loop. The WHILE function can be written something like WHILE RANGE("Difference") <> 0, meaning that the process will continue as long as the cell containing the difference is not zero. The WEND statement simply tells what commands should be repeated until the difference becomes zero.
7. As with any other macro, you should name the ranges so the macro will be flexible when you insert or delete rows or columns in your sheet.

A copy and paste macro that performs these steps and contains some extra bells and whistles is demonstrated in Figure 40.5. The variable named Iteration

```
Sub copy_and_paste()

    Iteration = 1                          ' create a counter
                                           for the iteration

    While Round(Range("difference"), 4) <> 0  ' round the difference

        Iteration = Iteration + 1
        If Iteration > 100 Then Exit Sub   ' limit the
                                           iterations to 100

        Range("fixed_amount") = Range("computed_amount")

        Application.StatusBar = "Iteration " & Iteration
    Wend

    Application.StatusBar = False          ' re-set the status bar

End Sub
```

FIGURE 40.5 Copy and Paste Macro with Iteration Count and Display

keeps track of how many times the copy and paste macro is looping around. It is good practice to create an IF statement in the macro to limit the number of iterations so that the loop does not continue indefinitely. It is also useful to round the difference range in case an exact value is not computed. The macro shown in Figure 40.5 uses the APPLICATION.STATUSBAR function to document how many times the computed cells are copied to the fixed cell. When you set up the copy and paste macro, if there is only one cell such as the debt adders that is fixed rather than an entire row of cells being copied, then all of the copy and paste coding created when you copy the macro can be replaced with a simple statement such as RANGE("Fixed_Amount") = RANGE("Computed_Amount").

The problem with the copy and paste macros is that they can make the models far less transparent and flexible, because each time an input such as the debt-to-capital ratio is changed it is necessary to run the macro. Eventually, when macros are added for the sculpting with tax problem and the DSRA, remembering where all of the fixed cells are, and replicating the process can be messy.

To make a user-defined function for resolving the circular reference problem associated with funding and interest during construction, you could create a function that computes the total debt commitment or, alternatively, the total debt adders. In either case it is necessary to loop through the construction period. Figure 40.6 shows a function for computing the debt commitment. This function is somewhat more complex then the circular

functions in Chapters 37 and 38 because you have to compute the interest over
the whole construction period before you can recalculate the total debt
commitment and test for convergence. Since the debt commitment amount
depends on the total interest during construction aggregated over the construction period, the total project cost should be computed outside of the
construction phase FOR NEXT loop. The iteration loop is a second FOR NEXT
loop around the construction loop. Computing a function with these two loops
to resolve this circular reference is shown in Figure 40.6. The figure illustrates
the spreadsheet with formulas next to the function. This demonstrates that
when you write the function you are just repeating the same equations that
you wrote in your financial model.

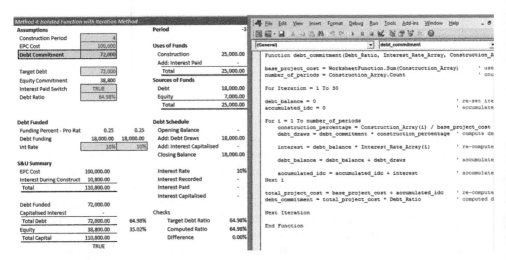

FIGURE 40.6 Illustration of Function with Excel Sheet to See Formulas

Case 3: Pro-Rata Funding with Capitalized Fees

If the total debt commitment is determined from the cash flow rather than a
debt-to-capital ratio and up-front and commitment fees are capitalized or paid,
another circular reference problem arises. In the case of capitalized fees, part
of the debt commitment is taken up by the fees, meaning that less funding is
available to finance cash construction. In the case of paid fees, the fees cannot
be determined until the debt commitment is known. The fee problem differs a
bit from the interest during construction because while the interest is computed from the debt balance that is accumulated in increments over the
construction period, the calculation of up-front or commitment fees requires
the total debt commitment.

To demonstrate the process of computing fees, begin by assuming a simple one construction period model, which is later extended to multiple construction periods. The one construction period example with capitalized fees is represented by the following formulas:

$$\text{Total Debt Commitment} = \text{Debt Funding} + \text{Capitalized Fees}$$

$$\text{Up-Front Capitalized Fees} = \text{Total Debt Commitment} \times \text{Fee Percent}$$

$$\text{Total Debt Commitment} = \text{Debt Funding} + \text{Total Debt Commitment} \\ \times \text{Fee Percent}$$

Once these equations that include debt funding are established, the function shown in Figure 40.6 that included only capitalized interest can be modified to include the fee equations. That's all. After you understand the general approach of making a function that mirrors the financial model equations, you can include more and more items.

In addition to up-front fees, commitment fees are generally charged by the lender during the construction period for debt that is committed but not funded. From the perspective of the lender, the commitment that is not funded represents a risky asset and must receive compensation with some kind of fee. As with the up-front fee, a problem arises if the commitment fee is capitalized rather than paid because the commitment fees change the debt commitment relative to the amount of money that must be borrowed. In the commitment fee case, the total amount of debt that can be used to fund the cash expenditures of the project is not known until the fees are computed. But the fees are a function of the total amount of the debt commitment, which is not known until the debt funding is computed. And the debt commitment depends on the fees themselves. As with the prior example for capitalized interest, a circular diagram can be drawn for capitalized fees, shown in Figure 40.7.

Total Debt Commitment   Capitalized Fees
Capitalized Fees   Debt Funding
Debt Funding   Total Debt Commitment

FIGURE 40.7 Circular Logic Diagram of Debt Commitment and Commitment Fees

To solve the circular reference problem of commitment fees, an equation for the debt that has not been borrowed can be added to the user-defined function and the commitment fees can be computed as the commitment fee percent multiplied by the undrawn balance. To add this commitment fee calculation into the function shown in Figure 40.6, the process of defining the equations from the financial model is the same as for the other circular reference problems. The first step is making the calculations on your spread-sheet. The second step is reprogramming the equations into a function that contains an iterative loop.

Case 4: Cascade with Equity Funded before Debt That Can Be Solved with Backward Induction

If the owner of a project does not provide any credit support to the lenders during the construction phase or, alternatively, if the sponsor of the project has weak credit, then lenders often require the equity contribution to be funded before any debt is borrowed. When equity is contributed before debt, the equity internal rate of return on a project is reduced relative to the pro-rata funding method because the negative equity cash flow occurs earlier, and equity owners must still wait until commercial operation before receiving positive cash flow.

Before addressing circular reference problems caused by the timing of equity funding, this section presents the general mechanics of modeling an ordered cascade of debt and equity draws with alternative funding priority. When priorities of funding are modeled such as the equity going in first assumption, the programming technique is similar to the cash flow waterfall mechanics. The difference is that this time the cash flow is all negative. As with modeling any cash flow waterfall, the programming process is expedited by: (1) using a lot of subtotals, (2) setting up criteria for the maximum amount of debt or equity that is still available for funding deficit cash flow, (3) making all of the calculations in the cash flow analysis and not in the debt or equity schedules, and (4) using the MIN function with opening balances or criteria derived from opening balances. This time the waterfall process begins with cash funding requirements rather than earnings before interest, taxes, depreciation, and amortization and works through the priority order of the funding rather than the priority order of cash flow distributions.

The following layout demonstrates how you can set up a funding cascade to compute the equity and debt funding. The key to implementing these equations is using the MIN function to compute the amount of equity funding before any debt funding is used.

> Funding Needs (Construction Plus Debt Service Reserve Funding Plus Interest and Fees Paid)
> Total Equity Commitment (Project Cost × Equity Percent, or Project Cost − Debt Commitment)
> Less: Equity Already Funded (Opening Balance of Equity Below)
> **Remaining Equity Available for Funding**
> Opening Equity Balance

Add: Equity Issued from Funding Analysis Using MIN Function of Funding Needs and Remaining Equity Balance
Closing Equity Balance
Subtotal 1: Cash Flow after Equity Funding
Equals: Debt Funding Required

One of the keys to making the preceding calculation is to compute the remaining equity balance available for funding the project, which increases as new equity is issued in each period. This process can be demonstrated by writing down a few formulas that distinguish between debt funded and debt commitment. The equations for debt funding and debt commitment apply whether the total debt commitment is computed from the total project cost multiplied by the given debt-to-capital ratio or it is computed from a sizing analysis of the DSCR and the prospective cash flow. The following calculations are onetime accumulated amounts that should be made by adding amounts over the entire construction period:

$$\text{Accumulated Total Funding Needs} = \text{Sum(Construction, DSRA, Interest, and Fees Paid)}$$
$$\text{Accumulated Debt Funding} = \text{Total Debt Commitment} - \text{Capitalized Interest and Fees}$$
$$\text{Total Equity Commitment} = \text{Accumulated Funding Needs} - \text{Debt Funding}$$

Calculations on a period-by-period basis during the construction period include:

$$\text{Remaining Equity Commitment}_t = \text{Total Equity Commitment} - \text{Opening Equity Balance}_t$$
$$\text{Closing Equity Balance}_t = \text{Opening Equity Balance}_t + \text{Equity Funded}_t$$
$$\text{Equity Funded}_t = \text{MIN(Remaining Funding}_t, \text{Current Funding Needs}_t)$$
$$\text{Opening Equity Balance}_t = \text{Closing Equity Balance}_{t-1}$$

Funding a project using the equity first priority causes circular reference problems because the equity commitment that starts the process depends on the amount of debt funding. But the debt funding requirement is driven by the amount of interest during construction and the fees, which depends on timing of the debt and in turn on the equity funding itself. Further, the fees are driven by the equity funding because the greater the equity funding, the less time the debt is outstanding over the construction period and the higher the commitment fee. A circular reference problem also occurs when the interest is paid rather than capitalized during construction. If interest is paid, then interest is included in funding requirements. This interest included in funding requirement drives the amount of debt funding and thus also the equity commitment, which starts the process. Figure 40.8 illustrates how the circular problem arises when there is an equity first priority for the funding order and when interest is capitalized (funding needs include construction expenditures and debt service reserve funding).

Equity Funding ← Funding Needs minus Debt Funding
Debt Funding → Interest Charged, Fees Charged
Interest and Fees → Equity Funding

FIGURE 40.8 Circular Logic Diagram of Equity Funding, Debt Funding, and Interest during Construction

The circular reference problem resulting from the equations for computing the funding cascade using the equity first funding technique is illustrated in Figure 40.9. As with the second case involving interest during construction, a summary sources and uses of funds accumulated for the construction period is included as part of the process to define the total equity funded and the total debt commitment. Figure 40.9 demonstrates that the accumulated interest during construction at the top left of the diagram creates the circular problem. This implies that if you can fix the interest during construction, you can resolve the circular reference.

S&U Summary									
EPC Cost	100,000.00				Uses of Funds				
Interest During Construction	8,821.05				Construction	25,000.00	25,000.00	25,000.00	25,000.00
Total	108,821.05				Add: Interest Paid	-	323.58	2,855.94	5,641.53
					Total Funding Needs	25,000.00	25,323.58	27,855.94	30,641.53
Debt Funded	87,056.84	80.00%			Sources of Funds				
Equity	21,764.21	20.00%			Debt	3,235.79	25,323.58	27,855.94	30,641.53
Total Capital	108,821.05	100.00%			Equity	21,764.21	(0.00)	(0.00)	(0.00)
					Total	25,000.00	25,323.58	27,855.94	30,641.53
Funding Cascade									
Equity Commitment	21,764.21	21,764.21	21,764.21	21,764.21	Debt Schedule				
Equity Funded (Opening Balan	0.00	21,764.21	21,764.21	21,764.21	Opening Balance	-	3,235.79	28,559.37	56,415.31
Remaining Equity	21,764.21	0.00	0.00	0.00	Add: Debt Draws	3,235.79	25,323.58	27,855.94	30,641.53
					Closing Balance	3,235.79	28,559.37	56,415.31	87,056.84
Opeing Equity Balance	0.00	21,764.21	21,764.21	21,764.21					
Add: Equity Funding	21,764.21	0.00	0.00	0.00	Interest Rate	10%	10%	10%	10%
Closing Equity Balance	21,764.21	21,764.21	21,764.21	21,764.21	Interest Recorded	-	323.58	2,855.94	5,641.53
Construction Funding	25,000.00	25,000.00	25,000.00	25,000.00	Debt Ratio	80.00%			
Interest Paid	0.00	323.58	2,855.94	5,641.53					
Total Funding	25,000.00	25,323.58	27,855.94	30,641.53	Function IDC	8,821.05 <---- =debt_adders(O22,O19:R19,O6:R6)			
					Computed	8,821.05			
Equity Funding	21,764.21	0.00	0.00	0.00	Difference	0.00			
Debt Funding	3,235.79	25,323.58	27,855.94	30,641.53					

FIGURE 40.9 Illustration of Circular Reference in Model Where Equity Is Issued before Debt in a Funding Cascade

If the debt commitment is known from prospective cash flow along with a given DSCR, the circular reference problem can be solved using a backward induction approach. Using the backward induction technique, the closing balance of debt equals the next year opening balance rather than the normal situation where opening balance equals the prior year closing balance. With backward induction, the last period closing debt balance is established and then the opening balance is reduced for each period until it reaches zero. When the opening debt balance is pushed down to zero in earlier and earlier periods of the construction phase, then the equity funding must start and continue for the remaining earlier periods of the construction phase. As the closing balance is the next period opening balance except in the last period of construction, the opening balance must be calculated. For debt during the construction period computed with backward induction, the opening balance is the closing balance of the debt less the draws and less the interest capitalized. This implies that the opening balance declines. Eventually the opening balance reaches zero. To prevent the debt balance falling below zero, the debt draws must be constrained using a MIN function. The MIN function compares the closing balance with the debt draws and assures that the debt draws cannot be more than the closing balance. After the debt draws fall to zero because of the MIN function, the equity funding kicks in.

If backward induction is applied and if the total debt commitment is derived from prospective cash flow and the DSCR, a circular reference can be avoided. The circular reference does not exist because the debt commitment driven by cash flow is independent of the equity balance. To set up a backward-moving debt balance table in the context of the funding cascade, you can begin with the closing debt balance at the end of the construction period using a TRUE/FALSE switch. At this point the closing balance is equal to the amount of the total debt commitment, including all capitalized interest and fees. When beginning with the closing balance at the end of the construction period, the opening balance is computed as: opening balance = closing balance − debt draws − interest and fees capitalized. The prior period closing balance is the next period opening balance in a process that works backward. This contrasts with the normal case where the closing balance is computed from the opening balance plus the draws and the capitalized interest and fees, and the opening balance is the prior closing balance. Once the opening balance is derived, the amount of debt draws is computed from the funding requirements and is limited with a MIN function so that the opening balance cannot be negative. The MIN function has the form MIN(funding requirements, closing balance).

If the debt-to-capital ratio drives financing or if you do not want to use backward induction, you can write a user-defined function to compute the debt adders (the interest during construction, DSRA, and fees). As with the other functions, you should type the same equations in the function that are in the financial model. The aggregate sources and uses are computed outside a FOR NEXT loop that works through the construction period. For this function the order of equations makes a difference and interest should be computed before closing balances are derived. A completed function where the interest is paid and the debt funding is driven by an input ratio is shown in Figure 40.10. For functions that require a loop over the construction period, some inputs are read as array variables such as the interest rate and the construction expenditure. Other equations for interest during construction are similar to those shown in Figure 40.6. If you want to create a cascade with debt rather than equity being issued first, you could develop a similar function but begin by deriving the remaining equity rather than the remaining equity.

```
Function debt_adders(Debt_Ratio, Interest_Rate_Array, Construction_
    Array)

base_project_cost = WorksheetFunction.Sum(Construction_Array)
number_of_periods = Construction_Array.Count        ' Construction periods

For Iteration = 1 To 30                              ' Iter to find adders
    Total_cost = base_project_cost + accum_idc
    Debt_funded = Total_cost * Debt_Ratio           ' Work through S&U
    Equity_Funded = Total_cost - Debt_funded         ' Eq Funding is start
    Opening_Equity_Balance = 0                       ' Initialise variables

    last_idc = accum_idc
    Debt_Balance = 0
    accum_idc = 0
    interest = 0

    For i = 1 To number_of_periods
        Remaining_equity = Equity_Funded - Opening_Equity_Balance
        interest = Debt_Balance * Interest_Rate_Array(i)
        funding_needs = Construction_Array(i) + interest
        Equity_funding = _
            WorksheetFunction.Min(Remaining_equity, funding_needs)
        debt_draws = funding_needs - Equity_funding
        accum_idc = accum_idc + interest
        Debt_Balance = Debt_Balance + debt_draws
        Opening_Equity_Balance = Opening_Equity_Balance + Equity_funding
    Next i

    If Abs(accum_idc - last_idc) < 0.001 Then
        debt_adders = accum_idc
        Exit Function
    End If
Next Iteration

End Function
```

FIGURE 40.10 Function for Deriving Total Debt Adders with Equity Priority Funding

Case 5: Bond Financing in a Single Period

If bonds are used to finance a project, the total debt draws occur in a single date at some point during the construction phase. As proceeds from the bonds normally exceed the funding needs, a bond fund account can be established in the model that holds the extra cash. A model with bond financing is shown in Figure 40.11. Draws in the sources of funds providing cash that meets funding needs are linked to the bond account using a MIN function. The MIN function compares the funding requirements with the opening balance of the funding account. This is analogous to the manner in which the cascade works where the remaining balance is used to test the amount that can be funded with equity. You can keep taking money out of the account until the opening balance is less than the required funding needs, as shown in this equation:

$$\text{Debt Draws in Funding} = \text{MIN}(\text{Opening Balance of Bond Fund,} \\ \text{Funding Needs})$$

		01-août-11	01-sept-11	01-oct-11	01-nov-11	01-déc-11	01-janv-12
Start Date							
End Date	31-juil-11	31-août-11	30-sept-11	31-oct-11	30-nov-11	31-déc-11	31-janv-12
Bond Financing							
Total Financing Requirements Less Interest Income		5,338,504	13,835,790	22,827,546	14,031,490	4,711,866	-
Bond Financing Date	30-sept-11						
Bond Financing Amount	30,000,000						
Bond Financing Switch		FALSE	TRUE	FALSE	FALSE	FALSE	FALSE
Bond Cash Account							
Opening Balance		-	-	30,000,000	7,172,454	-	-
Add: Draws from Financing		-	30,000,000	-	-	-	-
Less: Amounts Used for Funding		-	-	22,827,546	7,172,454	-	-
Closing Balance		-	30,000,000	7,172,454	-	-	-
Annual Interest Income Rate		2.00%	2.00%	2.00%	2.00%	2.00%	2.00%
Periodic Interest Income Rate		0.17%	0.17%	0.17%	0.17%	0.17%	0.17%
Interest Income Amount		-	-	49,547	11,846	-	-
Remaining Funding Needs		5,338,504	13,835,790	-	6,859,036	4,711,866	-
Sub Debt Percent		93.33%	93.33%	93.33%	93.33%	93.33%	93.33%
Equity Percent		6.67%	6.67%	6.67%	6.67%	6.67%	6.67%
Sub Debt Financing	7,000,000	4,982,603	12,913,404	-	6,401,767	4,397,742	-
Equity Financing	500,000	355,900	922,386	-	457,269	314,124	-
Total	7,500,000						

FIGURE 40.11 Illustration of Funding Section of Model with Bond Financing

The modeling process for bond funding begins with the period-by-period funding requirements as in the previous cases. One exception is that the interest income from the bond account is used as an element to reduce the amount of funding needs. Adjustments to increase or decrease the bond cash balance account include the initial amount of the bond financing and the use of cash to meet funding requirements, which is the smaller of the use of the opening balance of the cash account or the funding requirements. The bond funding account has the following form:

Opening Balance
Add: Bond Funding in Single Period from Date Input
Less: Use of Bond Funding from MIN function
Closing Balance

After the bond account is used up, the remaining funding process is the same as in the other funding techniques. The example shown in Figure 40.11 assumes the remaining funding needs come from equity and subdebt funding.

Setting up the funding process for discrete bond issues funded at particular dates can be accomplished by the following step-by-step process:

Step 1   Compute period-by-period total funding requirements that includes a row for deduction of interest income earned on the bond fund.

Step 2   Create a TRUE/FALSE switch variable in the timeline that is TRUE at the date of the bond issuance.

Step 3   Construct a table for the bond fund including the opening balance, additions, and withdrawals for a bond cash account. Additions are the bond financing amount multiplied by the switch established in step 2. Subtractions from the bond fund depend on the funding requirements.

Step 4   Compute subtractions from the bond fund account using the MIN function:

$$\text{Subtractions} = \text{MIN(Total Funding Requirements,}$$
$$\text{Opening Balance of Cash Account)}$$

Step 5   Compute interest income on the bond cash account from the opening balance and link it to the funding requirements analysis discussed in step 1. If the opening balance is used, then no circular reference occurs.

Step 6   After the bond funding account is extinguished, compute the remaining funding requirements and use one of the aforementioned techniques to compute the funding from other sources.

CHAPTER 41

Debt Sculpting in a Project Finance Model

D etermining the debt size and establishing the structure of debt repayments are often the most time-consuming and important structuring
elements of a project finance transaction. When structuring debt, lenders can
start with the prospective cash flow and the target level of the debt service
coverage. The size of the debt commitment that will make the computed debt
service coverage ratio (DSCR) equal the target amount is then determined. For
example, the target minimum DSCR to obtain a BBB–rating could be 1.4 using
base case cash flow. Alternatively, the debt may be sized by evaluating cash
flows in the downside case, and the target DSCR may have a lower value such
as 1.2. A financial institution may then choose the lower debt size resulting
from the two different debt-sizing techniques. Project finance transactions
often also have a debt leverage constraint. If the debt size results in a level of
debt leverage above some number like 80 percent, then the debt size is also
constrained by the financing ratio.

Debt repayments computed on the basis of annuity payments imply that
the debt service is constant over the life of the loan. Alternatively, repayments
can be computed on the basis of equal installments where the debt repayments are level over time. In these two situations a Goal Seek process and/or
Visual Basic Applications (VBA) can be used to establish the debt size, as
discussed in Chapter 42. In the cases of equal installments or annuity
payments, the DSCR is not constant over the life of the loan unless by chance
the cash flow happens to have the same pattern as the debt service over time.
Instead of targeting the minimum DSCR for one period and allowing the
remaining coverage ratios in periods other than the minimum period to have
higher DSCRs, the debt repayments can be varied over time so that the DSCR is
the same in each period. The notion of deriving the debt repayments together
with the debt size in order to meet a single target or multiple target DSCR ratios

is known as sculpting. The manner in which debt sculpting results in debt service tied to the cash flow is illustrated in Figure 41.1.

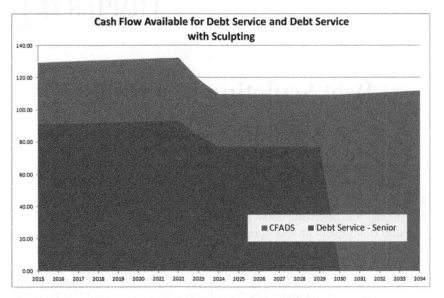

FIGURE 41.1 Cash Flow Available for Debt Service and Debt Service in Project Finance Model for Structuring Analysis

There are a variety of different ways to compute debt repayments and make the sculpting process seem relatively simple. This chapter reviews four different techniques that demonstrate sizing the debt at the same time as computing repayments. Unfortunately, the simple methods become a whole lot more difficult when taxes and the debt service reserve account (DSRA) interest income are included in the calculation of cash flow available for debt service (CFADS). The discussion of sculpting begins with an artificial case with no taxes and no DSRA. After different sculpting methods in the simple no-tax case are reviewed, sculpting techniques in more complex situations that include a DSRA and taxes are addressed.

Four methods that can be used to compute sculpting provide a survey of various spreadsheet tools and alternative mathematical formulations. The first method uses the Solver tool to find both the size of the debt and each debt repayment given the pattern of expected cash flow. The second approach uses algebra along with the Goal Seek tool to size the debt and at the same time find the debt repayments. The third method uses the fact that the present value of cash flow at the debt interest rate equals the amount of debt initially issued in computing debt size. This present value calculation that derives debt size along with algebra from the second method can establish the repayment amount and the debt size. The fourth method sizes the debt using a backward induction method through setting the closing debt balance at the end of the debt tenor to zero. Once the closing balance is established, the opening balance of the debt is computed for periods earlier than the debt tenor. The opening balance gradually builds up period by period to the commercial operation date. The debt level at the commercial operation date defines the debt size using this backward induction approach.

Sculpting Method 1: Use of Solver

The general objective of sculpting is to derive debt repayments so that the DSCR will be equal to a target value in each period given the varying operating cash flow. To illustrate the alternative sculpting approaches, a case is used where the operating cash flow varies over time and where earnings before interest, taxes, depreciation, and amortization equals the CFADS. After setting up a debt schedule with an arbitrary amount of initial debt you could imagine using multiple Goal Seeks to solve for the periodic repayment in each period such that the computed DSCR equals the target DSCR. Whenever multiple Goal Seeks are required, you can switch to the Solver tool, which allows you to find values for multiple target cells instead of only one cell. When running the Solver to find debt repayments by changing each repayment such that the target DSCR equals the computed DSCR, the process works nicely to find the debt repayment. But the closing balance of the debt does not reach a value of zero unless you happened to enter an amount of initial debt that by chance is at just the right amount to repay all of the debt.

Making sure that the debt is fully repaid, meaning that the closing balance at the debt tenor is zero, is a central part of the process for all of the sculpting approaches. The way in which you can set the closing debt balance to zero is to change the initial amount of debt issued at commercial operation. The fact that you have to set the debt size and the debt repayments together highlights the notion that in any of the sculpting techniques, the task is to find each periodic debt repayment and at the same time derive the initial debt capacity. Using the Solver tool, the closing debt can be set to zero by adding an additional constraint on top of the DSCR constraints. This added constraint sets the closing balance of the debt to zero. In implementing the Solver, when you add another constraint, an additional target (by changing) variable should be added that allows the size of the debt issued to change.

The mechanical process for using the Solver to sculpt debt as illustrated in Figure 41.2 includes the following steps.

- Access the Solver from the Data ribbon in Excel. If the Solver option is not present, then go to the File tab, find the add-ins, and press the GO button to install the Solver.
- When entering items in the Solver tool, it is not necessary to put anything into the top section named SET OBJECTIVE (except when you are recording a macro around the Solver). For the sculpting problem, leave

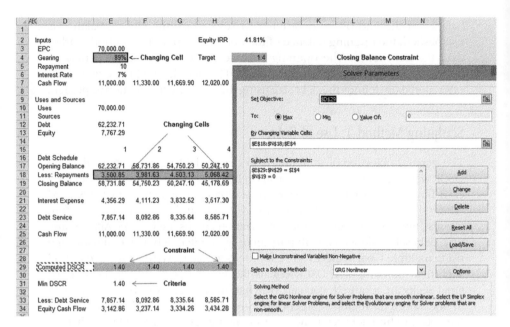

FIGURE 41.2 Illustration of Using the Solver to Perform Debt Sculpting Analysis in the Structuring Process of Project Finance

the SET OBJECTIVE blank. The top section replicates the Goal Seek tool, meaning that you can generally use the Solver instead of the Goal Seek.

- Put the debt amount or the debt leverage percentage along with the repayment amount for each period in the CHANGING CELLS or target section of the Solver. You can put ranges of multiple cells and/or individual cell references in the CHANGING CELLS part of the Solver.
- Add a constraint to the Solver. Define the constraint to be that the entire row for the computed DSCR to be equal to the entire row for the target DSCR. Alternatively, you can make the constraint that the difference between the target DSCR and the computed DSCR in each period is equal to zero.
- Add a second constraint that the final debt balance is equal to zero.

If you are running the Solver multiple times it may be helpful to set up a macro to rerun the Solver. Then you can just press a button and the Solver can be repeated without continually going to the Data tab and sometimes having to reenter all of the arguments. Unfortunately, adding a macro to run the Solver is a bit complex because the VBA code must be adjusted to allow the Solver to work. This process for enabling the Solver to run with a macro involves:

Step 1   Press the Alt-F11 key to get the VBA menu.
Step 2   Go to the TOOLS, REFERENCE tab, and then click on the Solver option from the VBA screen.

Step 3   After beginning to record a macro, reset the Solver.
Step 4   Make sure the first part of the Solver with the SET OBJECTIVE is
            not blank. To do this, you could set the ending debt to zero.
Step 5   Reenter the arguments into the Solver.
Step 6   Edit the VBA code and add the statement UserFinish = FALSE after
            the SolverSolve.

An example of the Solver code with the adjusted finish is illustrated next. All of the lines of code except the last line come from simply recording the macro after running the Solver.

```
SolverReset
SolverOk SetCell:="$I$5", MaxMinVal:=3, ValueOf:="0",
ByChange:="$G$32,$G$46"
SolverAdd CellRef:="$L$2", Relation:=2, FormulaText:="0"
SolverSolve UserFinish = False
```

The disadvantage of the Solver method is that it is clumsy and it performs very slowly in a large model. If you change the tenor of the debt, then you would have to go back to the Solver tool and reenter all of the repayments and the target DSCR arrays. You could enter a series of flexible range names using the OFFSET function as described in Chapter 15, but this is time-consuming and not very transparent. Because of these problems, it is not likely that you would use the Solver method in your real models. However, it is useful to begin the discussion with this method because it illustrates the various considerations that must be made in establishing the repayments and at the same time sizing the debt. In particular, the notion that the debt is sized by setting the ending debt to zero is important for all of the methods.

Sculpting Method 2: Goal Seek and Algebra

A more elegant solution for sculpting debt is to compute debt repayments using an algebraic formula tied to cash flow and then size the debt with the Goal Seek tool by setting the ending debt to zero. The process used in this second method involves rearranging the basic equation for DSCR, which is defined as the cash flow available for debt service divided by the debt service, together with the formula that debt service is defined as interest expense plus the debt repayments. Using the Goal Seek tool, repayments can be derived as a function of the DSCR combined with the operating cash flow and then the ending debt balance can be set to zero. The fundamental formulas used for applying the method are shown next. This formula can be applied only if the interest expense is computed from the opening balance of the debt, implying the cash flows occur at the end of the period:

$$DSCR = Cash\ Flow/(Interest + Repayment)$$

$$(Repayment + Interest) \times DSCR = Cash\ Flow$$

$$Repayment = Cash\ Flow/DSCR - Interest$$

When using this equation for repayment derived from cash flow and DSCR, the repayment produces the target DSCR, namely the DSCR that you input. The bad news is that the formula does not mean the ending balance of debt at the final repayment date is zero as was the case with the Solver. To deal with the problem of a nonzero ending debt, the Goal Seek tool can be used to determine the leverage percent or the total debt commitment in order to set the ending debt balance to zero:

Set Closing Balance to Zero by Changing Initial Debt Issued

You can add a macro to the Goal Seek so that any time you change an input into the model you can resize the debt. One difficulty with writing a macro around the Goal Seek is that the location in the spreadsheet of the ending debt cell may vary depending on the term of the debt. To fix this problem, you can use the SUMPRODUCT function along with a TRUE/FALSE test that puts the ending debt in the same cell no matter what the tenor of the debt is, as illustrated:

$$Goal\ Seek\ Debt = SUMPRODUCT(Closing\ Debt\ Balance\ Row$$
$$\times (Period = Term\ of\ Debt))$$

The result of this SUMPRODUCT function can then be used as the BY CHANGING item in the Goal Seek. You could also use the SUMIF function with a debt tenor switch for the range, TRUE for the criteria and the closing debt balance. Using the SUMPRODUCT or the SUMIF formula, the macro can be made in a flexible manner to establish the debt level that works with the sculpting. While this method is more flexible than the Solver method, the approach still requires a Goal Seek function. The Goal Seek must be run after changing any input for operating cash flow, the interest rate on debt, the tenor of the debt, or the target DSCR. If you are structuring the model to find a price that will realize an equity internal rate of return target, this means two Goal Seek functions must be run. Whenever two Goal Seeks that depend on each other are included in the model, after you run one Goal Seek it changes the way the second Goal Seek works. After you run the second Goal Seek, it changes the way the first one operates.

Sculpting Method 3: Net Present Value of Target Debt Service

An elegant way to solve the sculpting problem is to use the repayment formula (repayment = cash flow/DSCR − interest) discussed in the previous approach for computing debt repayments and then also to use the fact that the net present value (NPV) of debt service equals the nominal remaining value of the debt. When implementing this net present value method in your financial model, the Goal Seek can be avoided, and then you can compute both the debt size and debt repayments without running any Goal Seek, Solver, or macro at all. The trick in this calculation is to use the fact that the present value of the debt service equals the debt size and also to make the debt service be independent of the interest expense or repayment calculations in the debt schedule. If the debt service from interest expense and repayments in the debt schedule is used to compute the present value of the debt, then the debt service depends on the initial balance of the debt, but the debt balance is the present value of the debt. This makes you end up with a hopeless circular reference. The whole problem can be solved by using the notion that the target debt service can be defined as the CFADS/target DSCR. If you use the target debt service rather than components of the debt schedule in the present value formula, then the present value of the series of debt service numbers does not depend on the balances of debt in the debt schedule. With this formula the present value is independent of the debt, and net present value of debt service is used as the initial closing balance in the debt balance table. Using this technique, the whole sculpting process can be boiled down to the following three formulas:

$$\text{Required Debt Service} = \text{CFADS}/\text{Target DSCR}$$

and

$$\text{Total Debt Issued} = \text{NPV}(\text{Interest Rate}, \text{Required Debt Service})$$

$$\text{Repayment} = \text{Required Debt Service} - \text{Interest Expense}$$

The big advantage of this method is that the DSCR can be entered as an input and the size of the debt is immediately established. There is no Solver, no Goal Seek, no macro. This is the kind of thing you want to make a financial model really flexible. All of the risk analysis tools such as data tables can be applied, and you can use the Goal Seek and Solver tools to optimize the contract structure.

When applying the NPV formula as the basis for debt sculpting, the repayment and the target debt service must occur only in the debt repayment periods. To implement the NPV method a switch variable can be created for the debt repayment phase of the project. Then the target debt service as well as the repayment shown in the preceding formulas should be multiplied by the debt repayment switch.

An issue that arises when applying this formula is that the NPV function cannot be used if the interest rate varies over time. In project finance transactions, the credit spread often increases over the term of the debt to encourage refinancing, meaning the initial debt will probably only be out-standing in the downside case. Further, when computing the present value of the loan with changing interest rates, the normal formula for the discount factor—$1/(1 + $ interest rate$)^\wedge$period—does not work. This is because the compounding effects of earlier changes in interest rates are ignored in the formula. To illustrate the problem with sculpting when interest rates change, assume an extreme case where the interest rate is 50 percent in the first year and then for some reason it falls to zero in the second year. Also assume that the target debt service from CFADS divided by the DSCR is 100 in each of the two years. In this case the present value of the cash flow using the traditional discounting formula $1/(1 + r)^\wedge t$ is 166.7. There is no discounting of the second target debt service flow but the first cash flow is substantially discounted:

$$PV \text{ of Cash Flow} = 100/(1.5) + 100/1.0 = 66.67 + 100 = 166.67$$

If the present value amount of 166.7 is substituted for the initial debt balance in a debt schedule, then the balance of the closing balance of debt does not fall to zero at the end of the debt term, but incorrectly remains 50, as illustrated in Figure 41.3.

Year		1	2
Target Debt Service		100.00	100.00
Interest Rate		50%	0%
PV Factor		1.50	1.00
Present Value		66.67	100.00
Accumulated PV	166.67		
Opening Balance		166.67	150.00
Less: Repayment		16.67	100.00
Closing Balance	166.67	150.00	50.00
Interest		83.33	0.00
Debt Service		100.00	100.00

FIGURE 41.3 Illustration of the Problem from Using $1/(1 + $ Rate$)^\wedge$year to Discount Cash Flows in Sculpting When the Interest Rate Changes

The discounting problem in Figure 41.3 occurs because the value of the second 100 cash flow should be reduced by the 50 percent interest rate that occurred in the first period. In this extreme example you have to pay the 50 percent interest rate in the first year on the amount you have not paid back if you want to borrow the 100 in the second year. As with other circumstances when discount rates change (see, for example, Chapter 28), you cannot ignore the discounting effects related to the cost of money in the prior years. When adjusting for prior period discounting, the present value in the second year should be 100/1.5 or 66.67, which is the same as the value from the first year. With this adjustment, the total debt is 133.33. The correct discount factor can be computed by first calculating an index of the interest rate in the same manner as you would compute the index for the inflation rate. After the interest rate index is computed, the discount factor is 1 divided by the index, as illustrated:

$$\text{Index}_t = \text{Index}_{t-1} \times (1 + \text{Rate}_t)$$

$$\text{Discount Factor} = 1/\text{Index}_t$$

In the little example when the compound discount factor is used, then the discount factor is 1.5 for both years. In the second year when the interest rate is zero, the index remains at the same level as the first year. With the corrected discounting process, the total present value of the debt is 133.3 and closing balance of the debt falls appropriately to zero as shown in Figure 41.4. The idea of computing a compound interest index is useful for other problems in

Year		1	2
Target Debt Service		100.00	100.00
Interest Rate		50%	0%
Interest Rate Index	1.00	1.50	1.50
PV Factor		0.67	0.67
Present Value		66.67	66.67
Accumulated PV	133.33		
Opening Balance		133.33	100.00
Less: Repayment		33.33	100.00
Closing Balance	133.33	100.00	0.00
Interest		66.67	0.00
Debt Service		100.00	100.00

FIGURE 41.4 Illustration of Using a Compound Interest Rate Index to Compute the Present Value of Debt for Sculpting

project finance models in addition to calculating the size of debt from sculpting. In particular, the same approach can be used to compute the present value of cash flow over the loan life for the loan life coverage ratio and the present value of cash flow over the project life for the project life coverage ratio.

Sculpting Method 4: Backward Induction

The process of sculpting starts with prospective cash flow generated from a project after commercial operation and then works backward from the prospective cash flow to find debt service. With periodic debt service established, the backward process continues in order to arrive at the amount of debt that a project can support to cover the debt service and just repay all of the debt by the final period. A fourth method for computing sculpting works backward conforming to these ideas and can be used to compute the sculpted debt repayments as well as the amount of debt issued. To apply this approach you begin with the closing balance of debt at the end of the debt term rather than the normal balance of the debt at the beginning of commercial operation. If you begin with the closing balance at the end of the loan tenor instead of the opening balance, you can work backward and make the closing balance equal to the prior opening balance rather than the typical opening balance equal to the prior closing balance. The backward induction method can sometimes eliminate circular reference problems in complex cases and solve sculpting issues without macros, Goal Seeks, or Solvers. Through beginning with the zero closing balance at the end of the debt term and working backward, no present value formula is necessary. Even if you will not use this backward induction, it is instructive to work through ideas in the repayment formula for other aspects of a financial model such as the DSRA.

In setting the closing debt balance to zero at the end of the debt term, it is convenient to create a TRUE/FALSE switch for the final period in which the loan will be outstanding.

Closing Debt Balance = IF(Debt Tenor, 0, Next Period Opening Balance)

For periods except this end of the debt term period, the closing balance is equal to the next period opening balance. This contrasts with the normal case in which the opening balance is equal to the prior period closing balance. Once the closing balance is set from the preceding equation, the opening balance is equal to the closing balance plus the repayments. This contrasts with the normal case in which the closing balance is equal to the opening balance minus the repayments.

$$\text{Closing Debt Balance} = \text{Next Period Opening Debt Balance}$$

$$\text{Opening Debt Balance} = \text{Closing Debt Balance} + \text{Debt Repayment}$$

The debt repayments cannot be computed using the formula CFADS/DSCR – interest expense as in the prior example without creating a circular reference. The circular reference occurs because the interest expense depends on the opening debt balance and not the closing balance. But the opening balance of the debt is now a function of the debt repayment itself, which in turn is a function of the interest expense. With algebra you can compute the debt repayment that does not depend on the interest expense. To avoid circularity, the current interest expense can be computed as a function of the closing balance of the debt instead of the opening balance. Through substituting the opening balance with the closing balance plus repayment, interest expense can be expressed as a function of the repayment and the next period interest expense as shown:

$$\text{Interest Expense} = \text{Opening Balance} \times \text{Interest Rate}$$

$$\text{Interest Expense} = \text{Closing Balance} \times \text{Interest Rate} + \text{Repayment} \times \text{Interest Rate}$$

$$\text{Interest Expense} = \text{Repayment} \times \text{Interest Rate} + \text{Next Period Interest Expense}$$

With the definition of interest expense in the last equation, the repayment can be derived from the debt service so as to remain independent of the interest. Since the debt service can be defined as the CFADS divided by the target DSCR, no circular reference problem should be present. The repayment computed independently of the interest expense is illustrated in the subsequent set of equations. All elements that include repayment are moved to the left-hand side of the equation. The third equation substitutes the interest expense from the earlier formulas and the fourth and fifth equations rearrange things to come up with an equation for repayment that is independent of interest expense:

$$\text{Required Debt Service} = \text{Interest Expense} + \text{Repayment}$$

$$\text{Repayment} = \text{Required Debt Service} - \text{Interest Expense}$$

$$\text{Repayment} = \text{Required Debt Service} - \text{Repayment} \times \text{Interest Rate} - \text{Closing Balance} \times \text{Interest Rate}$$

$$\text{Repayment} + \text{Repayment} \times \text{Interest Rate} = \text{Required Debt Service} - \text{Closing Balance} \times \text{Interest Rate}$$

$$\text{Repayment} = (\text{Required Debt Service}$$
$$- \text{Closing Balance} \times \text{Interest Rate})/$$
$$(1 + \text{Interest Rate})$$

In applying the backward induction method, the above repayment equation is used, the closing balance at the debt tenor is set to zero, and the opening balance is computed as the closing balance plus the debt repayment. Starting from the end, the closing and opening balances grow when you go backward because you are adding the debt repayments to arrive at progressive increases in the opening balance. Finally, the opening debt balance at the start of commercial operation defines the total debt commitment.

Sculpting Approaches in Complex Cases with Taxes, Debt Service Reserve Accounts, and Interest Income

The CFADS defined in a loan agreement is intended to represent cash flow that is available to pay debt service. CFADS should measure all net cash flows that are available to pay debt service. Revenues that are collected after accounting for working capital changes are available for paying debt service, but only after operating expenses are paid and after provisions for reserves are input into a maintenance reserve account. In most circumstances, taxes paid are deducted from the revenues, and interest income earned on reserve accounts is also included in the CFADS. A final item that may or may not be included in the definition of CFADS is the changes in the DSRA that may provide cash or require cash. Inclusion of taxes, interest income, and changes in the DSRA complicate the debt sculpting process because the level of these items depends on debt, which in turn is a function of the items themselves and creates circular logic. Problems associated with taxes and the DSRA in the context of sculpting are discussed in the remainder of the chapter.

Problem 1: Interest Income in Cash Flow Available for Debt Service

The first potential circular reference problem associated with sculpting involves interest income computed on DSRAs. CFADS is used to compute sculpted repayments, but the CFADS depends on interest income from the DSRA. The DSRA in turn depends on debt. The problem of circularity from income associated with DSRAs is illustrated in Figure 41.5.

If your model is computed on a semiannual basis with a six-month DSRA, the DSRA represents the next debt service payment. In this relatively common situation, an algebraic formula can be used to resolve the sculpting problem without a circular reference. This technique uses the third NPV method

FIGURE 41.5 Circular Logic Diagram of DSRA, Interest Income, CFADS, and Sculpting

discussed earlier. To avoid a circular reference, the trick is to recognize that the opening balance of the DSRA is equal to the debt service, as illustrated by the following equations:

$$\text{Interest Income} = \text{Opening DSRA Balance} \times \text{Interest Income Rate}$$

$$\text{Closing Debt Service Reserve Balance} = \text{Next Period Debt Service}$$

$$\text{Opening Debt Service Reserve Balance} = \text{Current Debt Service}$$

Once you recognize that current debt service is the same as the opening debt service reserve balance, a series of other formulas fall into place. The following list of equations demonstrates that you can just adjust the formula for the target debt service to incorporate the interest income (in the formulas DS stands for debt service). If you compute target debt service with this formula, then the target debt service and the associated NPV does not depend on the interest income:

$$DS = (\text{Operating Cash Flow} + \text{Interest Income})/\text{Target DSCR}$$

$$DS = \text{Operating Cash Flow}/\text{DSCR} + DS \times \text{Income Rate}/\text{DSCR}$$

$$DS - DS \times \text{Income Rate}/\text{DSCR} = \text{Operating Cash Flow}/\text{DSCR}$$

$$DS = (\text{Operating Cash Flow}/\text{DSCR})/(1 - \text{Income Rate}/\text{DSCR})$$

If you put this formula in a financial model, the debt service can be made independent of the interest income, and the present value of the debt service can still be used to compute the balance of the debt. The present value function can be applied to the fourth debt service equation in the previous set. Other problems caused by the DSRA are discussed in Chapter 43, including cases where the debt service is not computed for one six-month model period.

Problem 2: Sculpting and the Interest Expense Deduction for Income Taxes

When you include income taxes in your model and taxes are part of the definition of CFADS, the problem of sculpting becomes much more difficult. The challenging problem arises because the amount of debt drives the interest expense, which in turn drives taxes. But the taxes influence CFADS, which drives the debt calculation. Unfortunately, a simple equation like the one shown in the previous section for interest income on the DSRA cannot be used to conveniently solve the problem. The circular reference problem with taxes and debt sculpting is illustrated in Figure 41.6.

Debt and Sculpting	→	Interest Expense
Interest Expense	→	Taxes
Taxes	→	CFADS
CFADS	→	Debt and Sculpting

FIGURE 41.6 Circular Logic Diagram of Debt Sizing, Interest Expense, Taxes, and CFADS Arising from Sculpting

The circular reference problem from sculpting and tax is illustrated in Figure 41.7. The example includes a construction phase and an operating phase. It demonstrates that as soon as taxes come into play the feared arrows show up. The complexity of the arrows suggests that this circular reference is challenging. This example does not include depreciation on interest during construction that further complicates the issue.

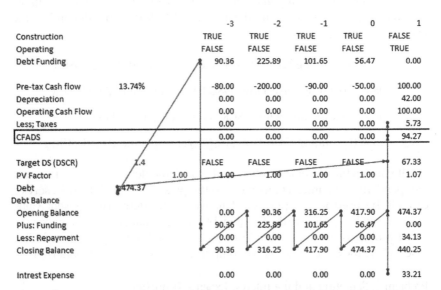

		-3	-2	-1	0	1
Construction		TRUE	TRUE	TRUE	TRUE	FALSE
Operating		FALSE	FALSE	FALSE	FALSE	TRUE
Debt Funding		90.36	225.89	101.65	56.47	0.00
Pre-tax Cash flow	13.74%	-80.00	-200.00	-90.00	-50.00	100.00
Depreciation		0.00	0.00	0.00	0.00	42.00
Operating Cash Flow		0.00	0.00	0.00	0.00	100.00
Less; Taxes		0.00	0.00	0.00	0.00	5.73
CFADS		0.00	0.00	0.00	0.00	94.27
Target DS (DSCR)	1.4	FALSE	FALSE	FALSE	FALSE	67.33
PV Factor	1.00	1.00	1.00	1.00	1.00	1.07
Debt	474.37					
Debt Balance						
Opening Balance		0.00	90.36	316.25	417.90	474.37
Plus: Funding		90.36	225.89	101.65	56.47	0.00
Less: Repayment		0.00	0.00	0.00	0.00	34.13
Closing Balance		90.36	316.25	417.90	474.37	440.25
Intrest Expense		0.00	0.00	0.00	0.00	33.21

FIGURE 41.7 Illustration of Circular Reference from Sculpting and Income Taxes in Project Finance Model

The circular reference problem illustrated in Figure 41.7 can be just about avoided if the backward method introduced earlier is modified for incorporation of taxes. If this method is used, some tedious equations can be developed to find the debt balance. However, even this backward induction method falls apart when you incorporate the tax effects of depreciation on interest during construction.

When employing the backward induction technique, an equation can be developed to compute debt repayments where the repayments are a function of interest rates as well as tax rates but not of interest expense. The process of creating an equation for the debt repayment with taxes is demonstrated next. To begin, the required debt service is defined as a function of CFADS less taxes.

$$CFADS = Operating\ Cash\ Flow - Taxes$$

$$DS = (Operating\ Cash\ Flow - Taxes)/Target\ DSCR$$

With these equations you can create a separate equation for taxes that is substituted into the required debt service calculation. In the equations shown next, T is the tax rate, and the tax equation is substituted into the previous debt service equation, yielding a modified equation for target debt service:

$$Taxes = (Operating\ Cash\ Flow - Depreciation - Interest) \times T$$

$$DS = (Operating\ Cash\ Flow - Operating\ Cash\ Flow \times T + Depreciation \\ \times T + Interest \times T)/DSCR$$

$$DS = [Operating\ Cash\ Flow \times (1 - T) + (Depreciation + Interest) \times T]/DSCR$$

The last equation cannot be used to compute the present value of debt service, because it still includes interest expense. To come up with a formula that does not include interest you can rearrange the equation by collecting the debt repayment terms and putting them on the left-hand side of the equation. As the backward induction method will be applied with an equation for debt repayment, the closing balance can be computed without creating a circularity problem.

To create an equation that is independent of interest, begin with the equation for the interest expense that was the first step in the simple no-tax case. To make the equation manageable, various abbreviations are used as follows: CB, closing balance; IR, interest rate; RP, repayment; DS, debt service; OCF, operating cash flow; T, tax rate; and DP, depreciation expense. With these abbreviations, the formula for debt service is:

$$Interest = CB \times IR + RP \times IR$$

$$DS = Interest + RP$$

$$Interest + RP = [OCF \times (1 - T) + (DP + Interest) \times T]/DSCR$$

Substituting the first formula for interest expense into the last equation yields a longer equation that includes interest rate and the repayment:

$$CB \times IR + RP \times IR + RP = [OCF \times (1 - T) + (DP + CB \times IR + RP \times IR) \times T]/DSCR$$

Finally, collect any terms that contain repayment and move them to the left-hand side of the equation. You then end up with an equation for repayment that is independent of the debt service or the interest expense:

$$RP \times IR + RP - RP \times IR \times T/DSCR = [OCF \times (1 - T) + (DP + CB \times IR) \\ \times T]/DSCR - CB \times IR$$

$$RP \times (1 + IR - IR \times T/DSCR) = [OCF \times (1 - T) + (DP + CB \times IR) \\ \times T]/DSCR - CB \times IR$$

$$RP = \{[OCF \times (1 - T) + (DP + CB \times IR) \times T]/DSCR - CB \times IR\}/ \\ (1 + IR - IR \times T/DSCR)$$

The last equation in the previous set can be used to define debt repayments when applying the backward induction approach where the debt balance is set to zero period of the debt maturity. Since the closing debt balance is the next period opening balance and the repayment is added to find the opening balance, the debt gradually builds up. As for the backward induction case without taxes, the debt at commercial operation defines the debt commitment. This equation is long and certainly not transparent, but the difficult problem of sculpting seems to be solved with no circular reference. It is just too bad that this seemingly elegant is the solution does not quite work. The remaining problem is the depreciation expense on interest during construction, which is introduced at the end of the next section.

Problem 3: Debt Service Reserve Account with Taxes and the Tax Effect of Depreciation on Interest during Construction

If there is a debt service reserve account (DSRA) and no depreciation on interest during construction, then sculpting can be resolved without a circular reference as discussed in problem 1. The size of the DSRA is determined independently of the sculpting calculation, and the initial size of the debt service reserve does not directly affect the debt sizing. However, if interest income from the DSRA is included with taxes, the sculpting problem becomes complex.

The following equation shows how the previous tax equation can be modified to include the effect of interest income on the DSRA, as well as the tax effect of that interest income. In this equation additional abbreviations are used as follows: R, interest income rate; I, interest expense rate; OI, other interest deductions; OP, other principal payments; and SI, subordinated interest expense. The derivation process for arriving at the equation is similar to the process for establishing the equation in the previous section. Needless to say, implementing this equation in a backward induction process would be painful because of the length of the equation.

$$RP = [(OCF \times (1 - T)/DSCR + CB \times (R \times T/DSCR + R \times DP \times I$$
$$\times (1 - T)/DSCR - R) + (OI + OM) \times DP \times I \times (1 - T)/DSCR - OI$$
$$- OP + (OI + SI) \times T/DSCR]/[1 + R - R \times T/DSCR - R \times DP \times I$$
$$\times (1 - T)/DSCR - DP \times I \times (1 - T)/DSCR]$$

Even if you put this very long formula into your model with backward induction, there is a remaining issue with the method that continues to produce circularity. The term DP used in the equation to represent depreciation is not independent of the repayment because it includes depreciation on interest during construction and amortization of fees booked during construction. Because the debt sculpting process affects a component of the depreciation expense related to interest during construction, when you define depreciation expense as the total depreciation including depreciation on capitalized interest and amortization of up-front and commitment fees in this formula, all of the work will still result in a circular reference. A diagram demonstrating why the tax effect of interest during construction causes problems with circular logic is in Figure 41.8.

Debt
Interest during Construction
Depreciation Expense
Taxes
CFADS

Interest during Construction
Depreciation Expense
Taxes
CFADS
Debt

FIGURE 41.8 Circular Logic Diagram of Depreciation on Interest during Construction, Taxes, CFADS, and Debt Size

Attempting to make the depreciation on interest during construction and the amortization of fees independent of the debt commitment is a lot more difficult than deriving the long equation in the earlier paragraph. To derive the depreciation on interest during construction you need to work through the period-by-period construction phase. The equation also does not work in cases when there is a tax loss carryforward because the tax carryforward is accumulated and then tested with a MIN function from the opening balance. In these cases a user-defined function or copy and paste macro must be used.

Solving Difficult Sculpting Problems with User-Defined Functions

Instead of working through the backward induction and the tedious algebra, you can solve the sculpting circular reference problem with a user-defined function that has an iteration loop. This is the fourth time a user-defined function has been discussed to resolve circular reference logic, and it has more complexities than the previous cash flow sweep, corporate model funding, and project finance model funding examples. After demonstrating how you can write a user-defined function to solve this problem, you should be convinced that you can resolve just about any circular reference problem with this user-defined function method. In the case of sculpting and taxes, the additional complications arise from the depreciation on interest during construction. The circular logic comes because sculpting drives debt commitment, but debt commitment drives interest during construction, and depreciation on interest during construction drives taxes and CFADS, which is the determinant of debt sizing with sculpting. Because interest during construction is affected by timing of expenditures during the construction period, but resolution of the circular reference for the associated depreciation depends on the pattern of operating cash flow during the operation phase, the function must have a loop around both the prospective cash flows in the operation period and another loop around capital expenditures in the construction period. Because the debt commitment must be fixed to solve the sculpting problem from interest deductions associated with taxes, the debt-related adders must account for the effects of the interest during construction and the fees.

You can divide the user-defined function into two parts corresponding to the construction phase and the operation phase. The first part establishes the debt commitment using a sculpting process during the operating phase given an assumed value for interest during construction. The second part derives the interest during construction from simulating cash flow during the construction period assuming the debt commitment is given. Once you have created these two parts of the function with two different FOR NEXT loops, you can create a third function that calls the other two functions and includes the iteration loop.

To demonstrate the process, three different functions that correspond to the three tasks are shown in Figures 41.9, 41.10, and 41.11. Figure 41.9 illustrates the master iteration loop that calls the other functions that compute

```
Function scuplt(DSCR, cash_flow, construction, interest_rate, tax_rate, _
            depreciation, construction_period, operation_period) As Variant

'
' Read in all of the variables that will be used by all functions
' Define as variant because array is output
'

Dim output(2)              ' Define an array for output of the function

For Iteration = 1 To 30    ' Put iteration around both functions

    last_debt = debt       ' Record the prior value for convergence test

    debt = debt_capacity(DSCR, cash_flow, interest_rate, tax_rate, _
                    depreciation, accum_idc, _
                    operation_period, last_debt)

    accum_idc = funding(debt, construction, _
                    interest_rate, construction_period)

    output(1) = debt       ' For array function, put outputs into an array
    output(2) = accum_idc

Next Iteration

If Abs(last_debt - debt) < 0.0001 Then
    scuplt = output        ' Define the output of the function
    Exit Function
End If

End Function
```

FIGURE 41.9 Primary Function for Computing Debt Sculpting That Calls Debt Size Function and Interest during Construction Functions

```
Function debt_capacity_DSRA(DSCR, cash_flow, interest_rate, tax_rate, _
                            depreciation, accum_idc, operation_period, _
                            prior_debt, inc_rate)
Dim Target_DebtS(100) As Single

total_periods = cash_flow.Count        ' Get total periods for the loop
Total_Plant = WorksheetFunction.Sum(depreciation)
For Iteration = 1 To 10

Debt_Balance = prior_debt   ' Starting level of debt from prior iteration
PV_factor = 1
debt = 0                    ' This is the debt that is computed from NPV

For i = 1 To total_periods
    If operation_period(i) = True Then      ' Operation period switch
        Interest = Debt_Balance * interest_rate(i)
        Dep_rate = depreciation(i) / Total_Plant
        IDC_dep = Dep_rate * accum_idc

        If i > 1 Then int_income = Target_DebtS(i) * inc_rate(i)
        taxes = (cash_flow(i) - depreciation(i) - Interest - _
                IDC_dep + int_income) * tax_rate(i)

        CFADS = cash_flow(i) - taxes + int_income
        Target_DS = CFADS / DSCR
        PV_factor = PV_factor * (1 + interest_rate(i))
        debt = debt + Target_DS / PV_factor
        repayment = Target_DS - Interest
        Debt_Balance = Debt_Balance - repayment
        Target_DebtS(i) = Target_DS
    End If
Next i
prior_debt = debt
Next Iteration
debt_capacity_DSRA = debt
End Function
```

FIGURE 41.10 Secondary Function for Debt Sculpting That Computes Debt Capacity of the Project over the Debt Repayment Phase

the interest during construction and the amount of debt sculpting. This is the function that is used in your financial model. The function shown in Figure 41.9 must also read all of the variables that will be used by the other functions. Debt is first computed from the target DSCR, cash flow, taxes, and the interest rate and the internally calculated accumulated interest during construction, which is zero in the first pass. Unlike the other iterative functions discussed in previous chapters, this function produces two outputs that are

```
Function funding(debt, construction, interest_rate, construction_period)

total_periods = construction.Count              ' Get total periods
total_cost = WorksheetFunction.Sum(construction) ' Total cost
Debt_Balance = 0
accum_idc = 0                                   ' Be careful to re-set items
that accumulate

For i = 1 To total_periods
    If construction_period(i) = True Then    ' Loop over the const period

        If total_cost > 0 Then funding_ratio = construction(i) / total_cost

        debt_funding = funding_ratio * debt
        Interest = Debt_Balance * interest_rate(i)

        Debt_Balance = Debt_Balance + debt_funding  ' Accumulate Items
        accum_idc = accum_idc + Interest

    End If
Next i

funding = accum_idc

End Function
```

FIGURE 41.11 Secondary Function for Computing Sculpting That Computes Interest during Construction over the Construction Phase

required in the project finance model. The first output is the total debt, and the second is the amount of accumulated interest during construction that can be called the debt adders if fees are included in the analysis. Since two outputs are produced by the function, the function can be defined as a VARIANT and an array should be defined to produce the output. This primary function that calls the other two functions, reads in all of the variables, performs the iterations, and produces an array output is shown in Figure 41.9.

The function that derives the debt commitment is made with a FOR NEXT loop over the debt repayment period. This function, which is illustrated in Figure 41.10, derives the present value of the debt from the after tax CFADS. In writing equations you have to be a little careful about defining the beginning debt balance, because you want to retain the last iteration of the debt balance. A debt balance is defined by the present value of the target debt service and it is recomputed for multiple iterations. When you read in an array into a function like that shown in Figure 41.10, you also should be careful about remembering to put the array indexes in your code. Finally, note that the function shown in Figure 41.10 requires the accumulated interest during construction depreciation as an input, which has not even been calculated in the first iteration and is the cause of one of the circular reference problems.

The second function called by the master sculpting function shown in Figure 41.9 is the calculation of interest during construction computed over the construction phase. This function is similar to the funding functions discussed in Chapter 40 that resolved circular references related to debt adders. In the example of the interest during construction function shown in Figure 41.11, the function assumes pro-rata funding, no fees, and interest paid rather than being capitalized. The function in Figure 41.11 that works over the construction phase could be modified to incorporate alternative assumptions.

Figure 41.12 illustrates how to implement the sculpting function and how to verify that the function produces the correct results. You can use the f_x item on the menu to find the names of all of the inputs. Unfortunately, when there are more than a few inputs you cannot look at them all at the same time on the pop-up menu and you must scroll down. When using the user-defined function there is no requirement to mess up your model with range names. In Figure 41.12 the debt is computed in a separate cell from the function to make sure that your function is correct. To check that you have made the same calculations in the function as in your financial model, you can test whether

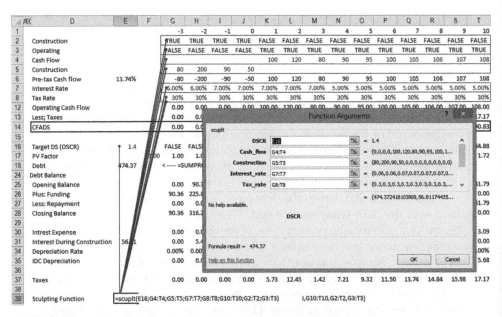

FIGURE 41.12 Implementing the Sculpting Function in a Financial Model

the result of the function is the same as the model by calculating the present value of CFADS. Since that cell to compute the PV of CFADS is not used in the debt balance calculation, there is no circular reference. The debt calculation from the user-defined function is like a fixed cell when you use a copy and paste macro. A by-product of creating this type of user-defined function is that you are repeating and documenting the model equations and thereby checking your models.

CHAPTER 42

Automating the Goal Seek Process for Annuity and Equal Installment Repayments

Some project finance loans are structured with repayments that are not sculpted to cash flow, but rather are repaid in either equal installments or with annuity repayments. These styles of repayment are illustrated in Figures 42.1 and 42.2. Figure 42.1 shows a project financing transaction with equal installment payments resulting in total debt service that declines over the loan life as the interest expense is reduced from a declining debt balance. Figure 42.2 demonstrates an annuity repayment structure where the debt service is the same over the loan life. This annuity repayment structure implies that the declines in interest expense are offset by increased repayments over the loan life. If the debt commitment is an input to the model and repayments are computed on the basis of either equal installment payments or annuity payments, then the amount of the total debt capacity can be computed using the Goal Seek or the Solver to conform to the debt service coverage ratio (DSCR) constraint. Applying the Goal Seek or the Solver to resolve circular references creates many of the same problems as applying the copy and paste macros. The Goal Seek must be rerun every time you want to put in any new terms for a pricing contract or any other aspect of the transaction structure. A more elegant approach is to make the model flexible and more transparent is by writing a user-defined function to replicate the Goal Seek process in a dynamic manner. This chapter first explains how to size debt using the equal installment and the annuity methods with the Goal Seek and then describes the more flexible user-defined functions.

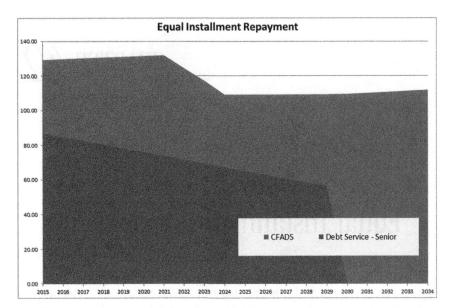

FIGURE 42.1 Illustration of Cash Flow and Debt Service Graph with Level Repayment Structure

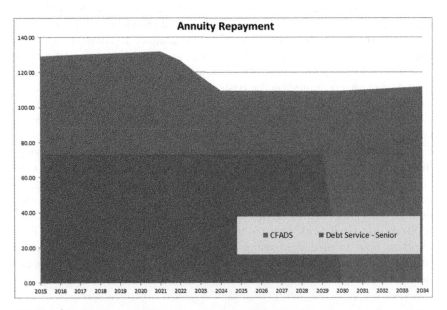

FIGURE 42.2 Illustration of Cash Flow and Debt Service Graph with Annuity Repayment Structure

Debt Sizing with Level Repayments or Annuity Repayments Using a Goal Seek Macro

When the target minimum DSCR is input, the level of debt commitment can be derived to yield the minimum DSCR given alternative equations for the debt repayment. Since the repayments are not sculpted, the DSCR in the period of when the minimum is reached will not be the same as the DSCRs for other periods. If an equal installment repayment structure is used, the debt repayment is the total debt commitment divided by the term of the debt. When the annuity repayment method is employed, the PPMT function can be applied to compute repayments from the periodic interest rate, the period of the model, the total debt term, and the initial amount of the debt at commercial operation. For either method you can use the Goal Seek to find the debt size that results in a minimum DSCR that is equal to the target DSCR. You can also create a macro around the Goal Seek using the following four steps:

1. Enter the target debt service coverage in your model and name the range for the target DSCR using the SHIFT, CNTL, F3 key.
2. Switch on the record macro button and use the Goal Seek tool to set the minimum debt service coverage ratio computed in the model to the target DSCR by changing the debt commitment.
3. Turn off the macro and modify the recorded macro by using the macro edit button or the ALT, F11 shortcut.
4. When editing the macro, you will see code that defines the Goal Seek process. Replace the fixed number in the middle of the statement with the range name for the cell reference representing the target input DSCR.

```
Before: Range ("F14") .GoalSeek Goal:=1.5, ChangingCell:=Range
   ("F4")
After: Range ("F14") .GoalSeek Goal:=Range ("F20"),
   ChangingCell:=Range ("F4")
```

After replacing the fixed cell with the range reference, replace all of the cell references with range names. This is something you should always do because otherwise the macro will not work when you insert or delete rows and/or columns in your spreadsheet.

```
Range ("C_DSCR") .GoalSeek Goal:=Range ("Target"),
   ChangingCell:=Range ("Debt")
```

Create a spinner button linked to the target debt service coverage ratio. Since the debt service coverage is expressed as a decimal, you should use an intermediate cell and divide that cell by 100 as explained in Chapter 14. Once you have made the spinner button, attach the goal seek macro to it by right-clicking on the spinner button.

Computing Debt Size for Equal Installment Structuring with a User-Defined Function

Instead of using a macro and attaching it to spinner buttons you can compute the debt size in the equal installment case with a function. You could do this in two different ways. One way is to make a dynamic Goal Seek function with a FOR NEXT loop that reduces the size of steps of debt size as explained in Chapter 9. Alternatively, you can create a two-step process that first finds the period of the minimum DSCR and then uses a formula starting with the cash flow available for debt service (CFADS) to back into the debt size. As the minimum DSCR period could change when the debt size changes, an iterative loop should be put around the process that is similar to the iterative process used in resolving circular functions. The process of finding the minimum DSCR involves computing taxes and making adjustments for the depreciation on interest during construction as discussed in Chapter 42.

The first part of the process is creating a loop to work around operating periods and compute the DSCR in each period. This loop must include the tax effects that the interest expense and the interest during construction depreciation have on the CFADS. Once inputs for the CFADS are established, you can compute the minimum DSCR by comparing the current period DSCR to the minimum DSCR. After finding the minimum DSCR, save the cash flow and the period number of the minimum DSCR. This first part of the process involving finding the minimum DSCR in a comprehensive example is illustrated in Figure 42.3.

Once the minimum DSCR and the cash flow in the minimum period have been established, you can use a formula to derive the implied debt size. This can be accomplished by recognizing that the debt balance declines by a constant amount each period. If you multiply the number of periods by the repayment, you can find the accumulated repayment that defines the debt balance. Repayment is derived from the debt service that is computed from the CFADS. The formula for deriving the repayment is found using the following process:

In the first period: Repayment = Total Debt Balance/Debt Tenor

In later periods: Repayment = Remaining Debt Balance/Remaining Tenor

Remaining Balance = (Total Balance − Year of Debt × Repayment)

Repayment = (Total Balance − Year of Debt × Repayment)/
(Tenor Year of Debt)

```
Function Level_Debt (Opening_Debt_Balance, Interest_Rate_Array, start_repay, _
         end_repay, EBITDA_Array, amort_rate, _
         Tax_Rate, Depreciation_Expense_Array, Accumulated_IDC, _
         Accumulated_Fees, DSCR, plant_cost, _
         debug1, MRA_Funding_Array, Added_Dep_Array)

Base_Debt_Balance = Opening_Debt_Balance
term = end_repay - start_repay + 1          ' Find the implied term of the
                                              debt
min_DSCR = 100000000                        ' Set the DSCR very high for
                                              computing the minimum
NOL_Balance = 0
Period = 0

For i = start_repay To end_repay Step 1     ' loop through each repayment
                                              period
    Period = Period + 1
    EBITDA = EBITDA_Array(i)                 ' Define EBITDA for period
    Int_Rate = Interest_Rate_Array(i)        ' Define Interest Rate

    Interest_Expense = Opening_Debt_Balance * Int_Rate
    EBT = EBITDA - Current_depreciation_Expense - Interest_Expense + _
        interest_income

    Adjusted_EBT = EBT + Tax_loss - NOL_Used
    Taxes_Paid = Adjusted_EBT * Tax_Rate

    cfads = EBITDA - Taxes_Paid + interest_income - MRA_Funding_Array(i)

    Level_Repay = Base_Debt_Balance / term
    Debt_Service = Interest_Expense + Level_Repay

    If (Debt_Service > 0) Then
        If Debt_Service > 0 Then DSCR_Period = cfads / Debt_Service
    Else: DSCR_Period = 100
    End If

    If DSCR_Period < min_DSCR Then           ' Find the minimum DSCR
        min_DSCR = DSCR_Period
        min_yr = Period
        min_CFADS = cfads
        int_rate_min = Int_Rate  ' Find the interest rate at min period
    End If
End Function
```

FIGURE 42.3 Illustration of the Portion of a Function for Debt Sizing from Equal Installments That Finds Minimum DSCR

```
Function Level_Debt (Opening_Debt_Balance, Interest_Rate_Array,
          start_repay, _end_repay, EBITDA_Array, amort_rate, _
          Tax_Rate, Depreciation_Expense_Array, Accumulated_IDC, _
          Accumulated_Fees, DSCR, plant_cost, _
          debug1, MRA_Funding_Array, Added_Dep_Array)

Base_Debt_Balance = Opening_Debt_Balance

term = end_repay - start_repay + 1   ' Find the implied term of the debt

min_DSCR = 100000000        ' Set the DSCR very high for the minimum

For i = start_repay To end_repay Step 1   ' loop through each repayment period

    If DSCR_Period < min_DSCR Then      ' Find the minimum DSCR
      min_DSCR = DSCR_Period
      min_yr = Period
      min_CFADS = cfads
      int_rate_min = Int_Rate
    End If

    Opening_Debt_Balance = Opening_Debt_Balance - Level_Repay

Next i   ' Finish of loop around the years

' Re-compute the debt balance from the minimum DSCR

    factor1 = min_CFADS / DSCR
    factor2 = (int_rate_min * (term - min_yr + 1) + 1) / term

    debt_balance = factor1 / factor2

    Level_Debt = debt_balance
End Sub
```

FIGURE 42.4 Illustration of the Portion of a Function for Debt Sizing from Equal Installments That Computes the Debt Balance

$$\text{Repayment} + \text{Year} \times \text{Repayment}/(\text{Tenor} - \text{Year}) = \text{Total Balance}/ (\text{Tenor} - \text{Year})$$

$$\text{Repayment} \times (1 + \text{Year}/(\text{Tenor} - \text{Year}) = \text{Total Balance}/(\text{Tenor} - \text{Year})$$

$$\text{Repayment} = [\text{Total Balance}/(\text{Tenor} - \text{Year})]/[1 + \text{Year}/(\text{Tenor} - \text{Year})]$$

Once you have computed the repayment in the minimum DSCR period from the last formula, you can derive the total balance that yields the DSCR in the minimum DSCR period. With the balance of debt established you can create an iteration loop and rerun the year-by-year loop. The iteration process is necessary because the year of the minimum DSCR may change when the debt commitment changes. If the year of the minimum DSCR does not change then convergence has been achieved.

The portion of a function with these calculations is shown in Figure 42.4. The factor1 term finds the total debt service. When the first factor is divided by the second factor, the debt balance is derived.

Computing Debt Size for Annuity Structure with User-Defined Function

Calculating the debt size with annuity payments is somewhat easier than the equal installment case because the debt service does not change over the life of the loan. This means the year of the minimum debt service that is defined by the operating cash flow does not depend on the debt size. Once you have computed the period of the minimum cash flow after tax, you can use a few formulas to derive the level of the debt. The only reason you may need an iteration loop is because taxes drive the CFADS. Debt influences taxes and taxes change the cash flow available for debt service. This may affect the period of the minimum DSCR.

Once the minimum DSCR period is established, the debt balance can be derived. Begin by establishing debt service that can be used to find the debt balance because the payment as a percent of the original debt remains constant. The debt payment percent is in turn defined by the PMT function using a value of -1.0 for the present value.

$$DSCR = \text{Minimum CFADS/Debt Service or}$$
$$\text{Debt Service} = \text{Minimum CFADS/DSCR}$$

$$\text{Debt Service} = \text{Debt Commitment} \times \text{Payment Percent}$$

Therefore,

$$\text{Debt Commitment} \times \text{Payment Percent} = \text{Minimum CFADS/DSCR}$$

implying

$$\text{Debt Commitment} = (\text{Minimum CFADS/DSCR})/\text{Payment Percent}$$

where

$$\text{Payment Percent} = \text{PMT(Rate, Debt Tenor, } -1.0)$$

CHAPTER 43

Modeling Debt Service
Reserve Accounts

P roject finance loans and some leveraged acquisition loans include requirements to put cash aside in a restricted bank account. The idea is to ensure
that a liquidity buffer is available to meet prospective debt service requirements. A typical requirement in project finance is that six months of prospective debt service must be held in a cash account. Such an account ensures that
temporary declines in cash flow will not cause a default because of insufficient
liquidity. It also ensures that if something bad happens and the debt needs to
be restructured, there will be sufficient time to make alternative arrangements.
For owners of the project, the problem with locking up cash in this manner
is that holding cash on the balance sheet and earning a return much lower than
the overall equity return can be very expensive in terms of internal rate of
return (IRR) on equity. The reason that a funded debt service reserve account
(DSRA) has such negative effects on returns is that the interest income rate is
generally much lower than the overall return on the project. If a project
borrows money at a rate of 7 percent to fund the debt service reserve
account (DSRA) and then puts the borrowed money right back into the
same bank, it may receive interest income at a much lower rate, say 1.5
percent. This interest rate differential can have a significant negative effect on
the equity IRR in the case of projects with tight coverage where the equity
contribution may be so small that it is similar to the size of the DSRA. An
alternative to holding cash in a DSRA that is sometimes permitted by lenders
is to use a letter of credit. In this case a commitment fee must be paid so that
cash is available when necessary, but the project does not experience the cost
of borrowing money at a high rate and earning a much lower rate.

Modeling of DSRAs is often associated with some kind of long macro that
copies and pastes an entire row in a model because of seemingly impossible to

resolve circular references. Circular references seem to arise because of the manner in which the DSRA is funded and also because of the way the DSRA is computed from prospective debt service. While programming the DSRA can be complex, some issues associated with the DSRA do not necessarily have to cause major headaches if the structure of the DSRA equations is formulated in a careful and structured manner in the model. This chapter demonstrates that circular references are not necessarily inherent in modeling the DSRA if the debt size is established from prospective cash flow combined with the target debt service coverage ratio. A couple of tricks, including separating construction debt from permanent debt and structuring cash sweeps before DSRA movements in a cash flow waterfall can reduce circularity problems.

Two of the reasons DSRAs seem to present tricky modeling issues are because (1) the DSRA is computed from the debt service on a prospective basis and (2) the size of the debt service reserve is tied to the amount of debt issued. Since the debt service reserve balances depend on the next period debt service and the next period cash, the debt service may depend in part on movements into and out of the debt service reserve, implying a difficult circularity problem. Other programming issues with the DSRA include: (1) computing changes in the DSRA on a period-by-period basis that arise from changes in debt service, (2) calculating subtractions from the DSRA in a cash flow waterfall when there is deficit cash flow, (3) building up the DSRA from cash flow in a project, (4) adjusting amounts of the required debt service reserve to account for interest expense changes that arise from a cash flow sweep, and (5) transferring amounts from a cash reserve built up during the construction period into a DSRA at the commercial operation.

Structuring the Debt Service Reserve Account in a Project Finance Model

The DSRA can be considered negative debt in an analogous manner to the way surplus cash is subtracted from gross debt to arrive at net debt in a corporate analysis. Following this logic, cash in a DSRA should be modeled in a similar manner to senior and subordinated debt facilities like surplus cash in a corporate model. An account with an opening balance, additions and subtractions, a closing balance, and interest income (instead of interest expense) should be structured. Before setting up the reserve account, you should establish the required amount that should be in the debt service reserve. As the DSRA balance should equal this required balance when it has not been used to make up for deficit cash flow, the net required inflows to the account can be computed as the required balance less the opening balance of the account. Specific steps to structure the DSRA include:

Step 1   Compute the amount of the required balance of the DSRA from prospective debt service. The required balance can include a few rows—the first for the current scheduled debt service, another for the prospective debt service, and still another for the accumulated interest on a cash flow sweep. If you are working with a monthly model, the OFFSET function can be used together with the SUM function to look ahead when computing the future debt service. The prospective debt service should be independent of interest expense reductions that arise from the current period cash sweep as discussed later in this chapter.

Step 2   Set up the opening balance, deposits, and removals from the DSRA account. Include a line item for withdrawals from the account that are used to fund deficit cash flow and will be calculated in the cash flow waterfall.

Step 3   Subtract the opening balance of the DSRA balance in step 2 to determine positive or negative amounts that that are required to be deposited or can be withdrawn from the account. This can be defined as the required DSRA funding. In the period before construction ends, the required debt service amount is the debt service from the prospective first operating period. For this period, just before construction finishes, the opening balance of the DSRA is zero, implying that the required funding in the period just before construction is the first period debt service.

Step 4   In structuring the funding needs and sources and uses of funds analysis, include the amount required to be funded in the DSRA in the last period of construction. This can be computed by multiplying the required DSRA funding in step 3 by a TRUE/FALSE switch that is TRUE only in the last period of construction.

Step 5   When laying out the cash flow waterfall, include a line item for top-ups of the DSRA before any analysis of cash flow sweeps. To make sure there is enough cash flow to top up the account, create a subtotal line in the cash flow statement named something like the cash flow before DSRA flows. If this amount is positive, then the DSRA can be funded up to the amount that is required as illustrated:

$$\text{DSRA Top Up} = \text{MIN}(\text{MAX}(\text{cash flow for DSRA}, 0),$$
$$\text{Required DSRA Funding})$$

Step 6   When you set up the cash flow waterfall, include a subtotal line to reflect the potential for negative cash flows. If negative cash flows are present, evaluate whether the deficit amount can be met from the reserve balance. The ability to meet the negative cash flow from the reserve account depends on the amount of money in the

DSRA at the beginning of the period. The formula for withdrawals from the DSRA to meet deficit funding is:

$$\text{DSRA Withdrawls} = \text{MIN(Opening Balance of DSRA,}$$
$$\text{MAX(-Subtotal Cash Flow, 0))}$$

The setup of a DSRA with required balances and required top-ups is illustrated in Figure 43.1.

Start of period	01-mars-13	01-avr-13	01-mai-13	01-nov-13	01-mai-14	01-nov-14	01-mai-15	01-nov-15 (
End of period Base Case ▼	31-mars-13	30-avr-13	31-oct-13	30-avr-14	31-oct-14	30-avr-15	31-oct-15	30-avr-16
Year	2013	2013	2013	2014	2014	2015	2015	2016
Reserve Balances								
Debt Service Reserve Account								
Debt for Interest	0.00	64,566.58	62,083.25	59,599.92	57,116.59	54,633.26	52,149.93	49,666.60
Interest on Opening Balance	0.00	0.00	1,452.75	1,396.87	1,341.00	1,285.12	1,297.54	1,238.56
Scheduled Repayment	0.00	0.00	2,483.33	2,483.33	2,483.33	2,483.33	2,483.33	2,483.33
Total Debt Service for DSRA	0.00	0.00	3,936.08	3,880.20	3,824.33	3,768.45	3,780.87	3,721.89
Required Balance	0.00	3,936.08	3,880.20	3,824.33	3,768.45	3,780.87	3,721.89	3,662.91
Required topup	0.00	3,936.08	-55.87	-55.87	-55.87	12.42	-58.98	-58.98
Opening Balance	0.00	0.00	3,936.08	3,880.20	3,824.33	3,768.45	3,780.87	3,721.89
Less withdrawals	0.00	0.00	0.00	0.00	0.00	0.00	0.00	0.00
Add: Net Top-ups	0.00	3,936.08	-55.87	-55.87	-55.87	12.42	-58.98	-58.98
Closing Balance	0.00	3,936.08	3,880.20	3,824.33	3,768.45	3,780.87	3,721.89	3,662.91
DSRA Funded at Construction	0.00	3,936.08	0.00	0.00	0.00	0.00	0.00	0.00
Required Net Top-up Operation	0.00	0.00	-55.87	-55.87	-55.87	12.42	-58.98	-58.98
Cash lock-up account								
Opening Balance	0.00	0.00	0.00	0.00	0.00	0.00	0.00	0.00
Add Cash trapped	0.00	0.00	0.00	0.00	0.00	0.00	0.00	0.00
Less Cash released								
Closing Balance	0.00	0.00	0.00	0.00	0.00	0.00	0.00	0.00

FIGURE 43.1 Illustration of Debt Service Reserve Account Setup

Avoiding Circular References in Funding Debt Service Reserve Accounts through Separating Construction Debt from Permanent Debt

The level of the DSRA is driven by the debt commitment, which in turn depends on either the project cost or the cash flow. If the debt service coverage ratio (DSCR) is used to size debt and if there is no interest income on the DSRA, then the size of the debt commitment depends on after-tax operating cash flow and it is not dependent by the size of the DSRA. The diagram in Figure 43.2 shows that if the DSCR and operating cash flow drive debt capacity, then the DSRA does not affect the cash flow available for debt service (CFADS) and therefore the DSRA does not cause circularity unless

Debt Service Reserve	→	Debt Sculpting
Debt Sculpting	→	Operating Cash Flow (CFADS)
CFADS	<>	Debt Service Reserve

FIGURE 43.2 Diagram That Illustrates Lack of Circular Logic from DSRA If Debt Is Sized from Prospective Cash Flow

there is interest income. In terms of funding during construction, the DSRA simply reallocates the funding between construction and other funding uses. Despite this theoretical lack of circular logic, the DSRA often seems to generate elaborate copy and paste macros. The messy copy and paste macros are often worse than other macros because they copy and paste entire rows of formulas. These macros can make the model a whole lot less flexible.

If the debt is sized from prospective cash flow, many of the DSRA problems that seem to result in circular logic can be avoided by separating the construction financing in the debt schedule from the term or permanent financing. The trick is to make the permanent financing a function of the fixed amount of debt (from the user-defined functions discussed in Chapters 41 and 42 or from a copy and paste macro) rather than from the accumulated construction debt. The debt service is driven by the debt balance after the construction period and can be determined independently of the debt in the funding analysis, which includes a component for funding the DSRA. The trick to avoiding circularity associated with the DSRA (without interest income) where debt is driven by prospective cash flow and the DSCR is important enough to warrant the following step-by-step description:

Step 1   Separate the construction debt from the permanent term debt during the operating period through creating two different loan schedules in the debt section of the model. The construction loan is paid off at the period before the commercial operation date through creating a final construction period TRUE/FALSE switch. Repayment at the end of the construction period is, for the construction loan, modeled by summing the opening balance plus draws as well as capitalized interest and fees for the period just before commercial operation.

Construction Debt Repayment = (Opening Balance + Draws + Capitalized Interest and Fees) × Switch

Step 2   Create a separate account for permanent term debt where the amount of the loan that is drawn or issued comes not from the payoff of the construction debt, but instead arises from the loan commitment defined by the sculpting process. When you make the debt issuance for the term debt independent of the construction debt, many of the circularity problems are reduced or eliminated.

Term Debt Issued = Commitment from Sculpting Function

× Switch for End of Construction

Step 3   Include the DSRA in the funding requirements and source and use analysis that drive the amount of debt and equity financing. When the DSRA is part of the funding requirements, a circular reference does not arise because the DSRA comes from the debt commitment and does not have anything to do with amounts that make up the financing calculations.

Funding = Construction + DSRA Funding Needs

× Funding Switch

Avoiding Circular References Due to Cash Flow Sweeps and the Debt Service Reserve Account

A cash flow sweep seems to create an impossible circular reference when modeling the DSRA because the prospective interest expense that drives the debt service reserve requirement depends on DSRA movements. The problem comes about because cash flow for the sweep depends on the DSRA itself. If there is a cash flow sweep, the ending debt balance is reduced from cash flow that influences the next period interest expense. While the model logic seems to produce circular logic, the cash flow sweep should not create a circular reference problem from a conceptual standpoint. DSRA provisions in the loan agreement that define prospective required balances should not require a forecast of uncertain prospective cash flow from the cash flow sweep in order to project the interest expense. Instead, the real information available for sizing the DSRA is the interest expense computed from the opening balance of the loan before consideration of the cash flow sweep.

By carefully constructing the formula for the next period required debt service, you should be able to eliminate the circular reference problem arising from a cash flow sweep. Interest expense for the current period is the beginning balance of the debt multiplied by the interest rate. In the subsequent period, the interest expense declines as the debt is repaid. This means that the prospective period interest expense can be defined as the opening balance of the debt less the next period repayments multiplied by the next period interest rate, all of which do not depend on the debt service reserve flows.

Current Period Interest = Opening Debt Balance × Interest Rate

Next Year Interest = Closing Debt Balance × Interest Rate (Next Period)

Next Year Interest = (Opening Debt Balance − Repayment) × Interest Rate

The last equation and, most important, putting the DSRA flows for deficit cash flow below the cash flow sweep in the cash flow waterfall are the keys to avoiding the circular reference. Using this equation as the interest component of future debt service requirement assures that the debt repayment does not depend on the future cash flow. Now the debt service reserve calculation is not a function of estimating the cash flow, which should be the case in a real loan agreement.

CHAPTER 44

Modeling Maintenance Reserve Accounts

In project financing and some other transactions, lenders require cash reserves to be set aside to accumulate money for the prospective payment of major maintenance expenditures. Examples of such maintenance expenditures include the overhaul of a wind turbine or the periodic resurfacing of a toll road. Holding cash reserves in a separate account generally causes the rate of return on equity for the overall project to be lower, as the earnings on the cash account will almost always be much less than either the equity return or the borrowing interest rate. The cash in a maintenance reserve or a debt service reserve account is in a sense sleeping. The developers of a project can complain that they must pay an interest rate of 7 percent to borrow money for the reserve account that is put right back into the bank and earns an interest rate of only 1 percent.

At first blush it seems that the modeling of these maintenance reserve accounts (MRAs) does not seem to pose too many programming issues. If major maintenance occurs in discrete similar time periods such as every five years, you can just add a switch for the maintenance period and then ensure that enough money is accumulated in the reserve accounts so that funds will be available to pay for the major maintenance activities. However, there are pesky programming issues with testing for the maintenance period, computing the contributions to the reserve by looking forward to the prospective maintenance expenditure, and adjusting the reserve calculations in the latter portion of the loan tenor after which putting money aside in an MRA will not be necessary. Programming techniques that are useful for calculating the reserves include establishing a switch for the maintenance period, creating a counter variable to track the remaining periods until the next expenditure, using the OFFSET function to find the prospective amount of money required for the reserves, and computing a debt repayment phase TRUE/FALSE switch to make sure that contributions do not occur for expenditures after the debt is repaid. These modeling issues are discussed for different cases of increasing complexity in the rest of this chapter.

MRA Case 1: Constant Maintenance Time Period Increments and Level Expenditures

To address programming issues associated with MRAs, a simplified case is used to introduce the issue. This case does not include complications of (1) changing levels of major maintenance expenditures in different periods, (2) major maintenance expenditures occurring in a later period than the final debt payment, and (3) nonconstant time periods between expenditures. In this first case, the OFFSET function is not necessary and the principal issue involves establishing a TRUE/FALSE switch to define the period of the expenditure. The inputs that define this case are the amount of the maintenance expenditure and the time period between expenditures expressed in periods or years. For this situation where maintenance occurs on a regular basis and the level of expenditure does not change, the step-by-step process to incorporate the MRA in a financial model involves:

Step 1   Calculate a switch variable for the maintenance period. To do this you can create a TRUE/FALSE switch that uses the MOD function. This function computes the remainder between two numbers. The MOD function can be used with the time period counter of the model and the maintenance period as illustrated in the following equation. When the MOD function is zero, meaning there is no remainder, then the switch is TRUE, such as if the maintenance period is 5 and the model period is 5, 10, or 15. This switch is referred to as the MOD switch in the discussion that follows.

$$MOD(Period, Maintenance\ Period) = 0$$

The MOD switch can be adjusted to be turned on only during the operating period or the debt repayment period. This can be done through multiplying the first switch by the operating period:

Maintenance Switch = MOD Switch × Operating Period Switch

Step 2   Compute the spend amount and the contribution to the MRA. Using the maintenance switch, the total amount spent as well as the contributions to the MRA can be established. The total amount spent for maintenance is the input for constant expenditure multiplied by the maintenance switch. Periodic contributions to the maintenance reserve are the total amount spent divided by the time periods between the expenditures. This amount should also be multiplied by a debt repayment switch, as contributions are not generally required for expenditures that occur after debt repayment.

Step 3   Construct an MRA schedule with an opening and closing balance. Contributions to the reserve account increase the balance and expenditures during the maintenance period reduce the balance. At the end of the debt repayment period, the reserve balance should be zero.

Step 4   Reduce the operating cash flow in the expenditure period either by classifying the major maintenance expenditure as a capital expenditure or an operating expense. If the expenditure is classified as a capital expenditure, the depreciation function discussed in Chapter 9 can be used. These adjustments for maintenance expenditure and depreciation should be reflected in the project IRR calculation.

Step 5   Adjust the cash flow waterfall to include MRA contributions, MRA reductions, and income on the MRA balance as well as the expenditures. The profit and loss statement should incorporate the expenses and/or depreciation expense and the interest income. It should not include the contributions or withdrawls from the MRA.

MRA Case 2: Constant Time Period Increments and Changing Expenditures

If the maintenance expenditures are not the same in each period because, for example, they increase with inflation, then the problem of determining MRA contributions becomes more complex. The difficulty comes about because of the necessity to look into forward periods and see what future expenditures will be, so you can determine current contributions to the reserve account. Beginning at the commercial operation date when cash flow is first generated, the contributions to the MRA should reflect the next expenditure, which may occur five or more years into the future. When you must look forward or backward from a cell, the OFFSET function should come into mind. In order to apply the OFFSET function you can create a counter for the number of periods until the next expenditure. If the number of periods between expenditures is 10, then a counter beginning with 1 and ending with 10 can be established by using the switch variable. Once the counter is put into the model, this number should be subtracted from the input total time periods between the expenditures. This difference between the total time periods and the counter yields the remaining periods until the next expenditure. The remaining periods until the next expenditure should be 0 for the period of the expenditure. With the remaining time periods until the next expenditure computed, you can apply the OFFSET function.

The MRA contribution should also be adjusted so that no funding is made for expenditures that occur after the final debt repayment. The purpose of the MRA is to protect the lenders, so for expenditures that will occur after the loan matures no MRA is necessary. To make this adjustment, the amount of the maintenance expenditure can be multiplied by the debt repayment switch before it is looked up with the OFFSET function. Through adjusting the basis for the OFFSET function using the debt repayment switch, prospective expenditures after the debt repayment period do not generate contributions and the last expenditure does not have to be in the final debt repayment period. To verify the calculations, a test variable can be created to make sure the MRA balance is 0 at the end of each spend period and is 0 at the end of the debt term.

Steps to accomplish the MRA contributions and withdrawals with varying expenditures include:

Step 1   Use the MOD function as in the first case to determine the spend periods.

Step 2   Enter the time periods between expenditures as a row in the spreadsheet. If the periods between expenditures are 5, then this row will contain 5 for each period.

Step 3   Use the spend period switch as the basis for computing the counter variable until the next spend date. Reset the counter variable to 0 at the period when an expenditure occurs. For the counter to accumulate to the time period between expenditures, a variable can be created from the TRUE/FALSE switch.

Counter = IF(OR(Spend Switch, Precommercial Switch), 0,

Last Counter + 1)

Step 4   Compute the periods until the next spend as the total periods between expenditure minus the period counter. This variable is necessary for the OFFSET function to look forward and pull the future expenditure back to the current column.

Remaining Periods = Total Periods between Spend − Counter

Step 5   Calculate the total inflated expenditure for MRA through multiplying the base expenditure by the inflation index. A separate line should also be computed where this inflated expenditure is multiplied by the debt repayment switch so that no reserve is accumulated for expenditures after the debt is repaid.

Spend Subject to MRA = Expenditure × Debt Repayment Switch

Step 6   Create a separate line for the prospective expenditure that contains the OFFSET function. The OFFSET function uses the inflated expenditure adjusted by the repayment switch as the cell reference, no movement in rows and the periods as the column to move to the right.

$$\text{Prospective Expenditure} = \text{OFFSET(Spend Subject to MRA, 0,}$$
$$\text{Remaining Periods)}$$

Step 7   Divide the prospective future required expenditure computed using the OFFSET function by the total number of periods between the expenditures. Use an IF test to make sure that a divide by 0 does not occur.

$$\text{MRA Contribution} = \text{Prospective Expenditure}/$$
$$\text{Periods between Spend}$$

Step 8   Compute the MRA balance and then make a test variable to ensure that the account goes to 0 in the spend period. The formula for this test could be something like the following equation:

$$\text{Test} = \text{IF(Spend Switch, Closing MRA} = 0, \text{TRUE)}$$

MRA Case 3: Varying Time Period Increments and Changing Expenditures Using the MATCH Function

The preceding example assumed maintenance expenditures were made in identical time increments. If the expenditures are input with varying time periods as illustrated in Figure 44.1, a different method using the MATCH and INDEX functions can solve the problem. To apply this method, specific dates beginning with the commercial operation date should be input to define the maintenance periods. In Figure 44.1, the number of periods is input in one of the right-hand columns, and these period increments derive the dates shown in the left-hand column. The table includes a switch defining whether the expenditure occurs during the repayment period. This switch can be evaluated with the LOOKUP function as shown in the figure.

With varying time periods between expenditures, the MOD function cannot be applied. Instead, to find the expenditure period, a MATCH function can be used with the FALSE switch. The MATCH function compares the dates in the input table with dates in the time line. When the result of the MATCH function is a number rather than the #N/A symbol, the period is a maintenance spend period. When the result of the MATCH is #N/A, the result signifies that there is no major maintenance expenditure. To make a TRUE/FALSE switch for the maintenance

AE(	H	I	J	K	L	M	N	O
61								
62		Expenditure	Adjusted	Period to		Debt Repay		
63	Date	MM USD/year	Expenditure	Next Exp	Year Inc.	Switch		
64	01-mars-16							
65	01-mars-21	20	20	10	5	TRUE	=LOOKUP(H65,$8:$8,$15:$15)	
66	01-mars-28	100	100	14	7	TRUE	=LOOKUP(H66,$8:$8,$15:$15)	
67	01-mars-35	60	60	14	7	TRUE	=LOOKUP(H67,$8:$8,$15:$15)	
68	01-mars-36	80	80	2	1	TRUE	=LOOKUP(H68,$8:$8,$15:$15)	
69	01-mars-38	20	20	4	2	TRUE	=LOOKUP(H69,$8:$8,$15:$15)	
70	01-mars-40	65	0	4	2	FALSE	=LOOKUP(H70,$8:$8,$15:$15)	

FIGURE 44.1 Example of Inputs for Maintenance Expenditures with Varying Time Periods

period, you can add another row using the ISNUMBER function. The ISNUMBER function produces a value of TRUE when there is a maintenance period, and for the #N/A values the ISNUMBER produces a value of FALSE.

Solving the MRA problem with varying periods and varying expenditures can be accomplished without the OFFSET function. Alternatively, you can also use the MATCH and INDEX functions. Steps of the process are summarized as follows and illustrated in Figure 44.2:

AE(	D		E	CM	CN	CO	CP	CQ	CR
7	Start of Period	Sensitivity Case ▼		01-sept-35	01-mars-36	01-sept-36	01-mars-37	01-sept-37	01-mars-38
8	End of Period			29-févr-36	31-août-36	28-févr-37	31-août-37	28-févr-38	31-août-38
231	**Reserve Balance**								
232									
233	Reserve Account (Index and Match Method)								
234	Match of Date (Step 1)		=MATCH(N7,$H$63:$H$69,0)	#N/A	5	#N/A	#N/A	#N/A	6
235	Resurfacing Switch (Step 2 - ISNUMBER)		=ISNUMBER(N234)	FALSE	TRUE	FALSE	FALSE	FALSE	TRUE
236	Resurfacing Expenditure (Step 3 with Index)		=IFERROR(INDEX($I$63:$I$69,N234),0)	-	80.00	-	-	-	20.00
237	Match of Row (Match with 1)		=MATCH(N7,$H$63:$H$69,1)	4.00	5.00	5.00	5.00	5.00	6.00
238	Future Maintenance (Index)		=IFERROR(INDEX($J$64:$J$69,N237),FALSE)	80.00	20.00	20.00	20.00	20.00	-
239	Prospective Periods (Index)		=IFERROR(INDEX($K$64:$K$69,N237),FALSE)	2.00	4.00	4.00	4.00	4.00	4.00
240	Funding of Reserve (Prospective Exp/Periods)		=IF(N238,N239/N238)	40.00	5.00	5.00	5.00	5.00	-
241									
242	Reserve Account (Offset and Countif)								
243	Opening Balance		=M246	40.00	80.00	5.00	10.00	15.00	20.00 ·
244	Add: Contributions		=N240*1	40.00	5.00	5.00	5.00	5.00	-
245	Less: Withdrawls		=N236*N15	-	80.00	-	-	-	20.00
246	Closing Balance		=N243+N244-N245	80.00	5.00	10.00	15.00	20.00 ·	0.00 ·
247									

FIGURE 44.2 Example of Implementing Maintenance Reserve Account with Varying Maintenance Periods and Amounts

Step 1   Use the MATCH function with the FALSE or 0 switch combined with the start of period date in the time line to find the expenditure for the period. In periods other than the spend period the result is #N/A.

MATCH of Expenditure Date = MATCH(Start Period Date in
Model, Series of Dates in Table, FALSE)

Step 2   Create a SWITCH variable for the maintenance spend period (TRUE if a spend period) by using the ISNUMBER function from the result of the MATCH function in step 1.

Maintenance Switch = ISNUMBER(Match of Expenditure Date)

Step 3   Compute the maintenance expenditure by using the INDEX function together with the match of the maintenance date. To avoid #N/A, an IF statement that tests whether the maintenance switch is TRUE can be used rather than multiplying the result by the maintenance switch. As with the previous OFFSET method, the actual expenditure should be distinguished from the expenditure subject to an MRA that depends on the debt repayment switch by including two separate rows.

Maintenance Expenditure = IF(Maintenance Switch,

INDEX(Expenditure Series Input from Input Table,

Match of Expenditure Date))

Step 4   Compute the maintenance expenditure subject to requirements that contributions are made to the MRA. After the debt is repaid, there is no need to put money aside in the MRA for prospective expenditures. The MRA is necessary only to ensure that the project will not have to borrow money to pay expenditures while a loan is outstanding. To make this adjustment, the input section should be adjusted by the debt repayment switch as shown in Figure 44.1.

Maintenance Expenditure Subject to MRA = Maintenance

Expenditure × Debt Repayment Switch

Step 5   Compute the number of periods until the next expenditure. This is necessary so that you can compute contributions to the MRA from the prospective expenditure in step 4. To do this, use the MATCH function again, but this time with the TRUE or 1 switch instead of the FALSE switch. This will produce a number that corresponds to the row of the input table.

Maintenance Row Number = MATCH(Start Period in Model,

Series of Dates in Table, TRUE)

Step 6   Compute the number of periods until the next maintenance expenditure through using the INDEX function that looks into the input table shown in Figure 44.1. When you use the INDEX function for finding the number of prospective periods, the array for the INDEX function should begin with the second row date in the input table rather than the first row. The prior periods are used as the base of the INDEX function because the periods from the prior expenditure should change in the period after the spend switch.

Periods to Next Maintenance Spend = INDEX(Prior Period Array, Maintenance Row from MATCH in Step 5)

Step 7   Compute the next period expenditure amount that will be subject to the MRA contributions using the maintenance expenditure row and the debt repayment switch. This requires a two-step process that uses the INDEX function and the debt repayment switch.

Next Maintenance Spend = INDEX(Next Expenditure Array × Debt Repayment, Maintenance Row)

Step 8   Compute the contributions to the MRA through dividing the next period maintenance expenditure by the number of periods until the next period expenditure. Both of these numbers are computed from the INDEX function.

Step 9   Compute a balance schedule of the MRA with an opening balance, contributions, withdrawals, and a closing balance. Finally, make a test to ensure that the closing balance does not decline below 0.

An illustration of the process for computing the maintenance reserve using these steps is shown in Figure 44.2. The figure shows the end of a project where one of the expenditures is not subject to the MRA. MRA contributions are determined from the prospective expenditures and prospective periods between expenditures.

CHAPTER 45

Refinancing and Valuing a Project Given Risk Changes over the Life of a Project

As a project goes through different stages of its life, its risk can change dramatically because of elimination of construction risks, building up an historical track record, resolution of permitting risks, and many other factors. When the risk of anything changes, its value also changes. Any project finance analysis should in theory account for risk changes across phases when assessing a variety of valuation metrics from both a debt and an equity perspective. This idea of risk changing during different phases may be most relevant for project financing but it can also apply to corporate finance. If a corporation somehow reaches the stable state where growth slows and return is close to the cost of capital, the risk is surely also different. Accounting for changes in risk during the life of a project is an essential part of the valuation analysis that is very often ignored. Risk changes over the life of a project should be incorporated in a project finance model in a number of different ways. The project should be valued at different discount rates that reflect the changing risk of the project. Measured rates of return on the project should be adjusted so as to reflect the changes in risk, meaning the internal rate of return (IRR) does not really work. Financing assumptions for a project should incorporate the ability to refinance a project after the risk profile has changed. The political risk of a project can also change dramatically, and the use of a country risk premium usually undervalues a project dramatically.

Computed Internal Rate of Return with Changes in Discount Rate over Project Life

When a project is being developed there is often a large chance that the project will not proceed. This is particularly true in the case of geothermal projects and oil projects where large and speculative exploration expenditures are made to find resources. Expenditures during the exploration phase or the development phase that have a high probability of producing nothing should have a different IRR requirement than other expenditures. At the other end of the spectrum, after a project has a history and established resource potential, traffic volumes, operating costs, and political acceptability, the risk may be only slightly higher than the risk-free rate. Between the speculative development stage and the stable stage, many risks, including political risks, are reduced. After the construction period and the technical risks have been resolved the projected cash flow of the project still comes from the consulting studies. A few years later, once real data exists on production, demand, prices, cost structure, and political acceptance, the risks are reduced even more.

A big problem with using the IRR as an indicator of value is that it does not reflect the changes in risk and gives equal weight to exploration expenditures as revenues received during the stable stage. If there is a 40 percent chance that an exploration expenditure of 200 will be successful and the required return on subsequent construction expenditures of 1000 is 10 percent, then the required IRR after including the development expenditure is 15.8 percent. Similar changes in the discount rate as the change from 15.8 to 10 percent can be gauged with other phases in the project life. Problems with using a country risk premium can be demonstrated by converting the usually overstated premium into the probability of political expropriation. Taking country risk premiums from, say, the New York University Stern School of Business website and adjusting the IRR is like extracting money from a developing country.

When valuing a project you can assume the project is sold after a given period and that the buyer will gradually demand a lower and lower IRR until the stable phase is reached. If the project is sold rather than held over its life, the realized IRR will be higher with an assumed sale as long as the IRR over the entire life of the project is higher than the IRR required by the new buyer. The IRR computed with the sale can be established by calculating the net present value of future cash flows and then using this number as an assumed exit value. You can make the sale date a variable, include a sale date TRUE/FALSE switch, and then compute the optimal date of sale using a data table. Increased IRR in cases where the project is sold rather than held for its life reflects the reduced risk regardless of whether the project is actually sold. If a project was held by a publicly listed company, its stock price would theoretically increase after the risk declines. This is not measured by the IRR. Thus, the argument that the IRR with an assumed sale should not be evaluated when the project will be held until its life is finished is not valid because this simply reflects the declining risk of the project that cannot be measured with the normal IRR.

Effects of Refinancing on the Value of a Project

After a project has begun operations and has demonstrated stable cash flow for a few years, it may be able to pay off existing debt and issue new debt with more advantageous terms because of reduced risk. If the amount of the debt from refinanced debt exceeds the balance of the existing debt, then equity investors can pay themselves a super dividend with the surplus cash. The timing of this super dividend relative to the increased debt service that is paid later in the life of the project for the refinanced debt has a positive effect on the equity IRR. As part of the refinancing, the project may achieve a lower interest rate, have a longer tenor, or it may be able to increase the size of the debt. Refinancing debt that was originally used to finance the project can have significant positive effects on the economics of a project in terms of the realized equity IRR. If the project meets or exceeds its expected cash flow after a few years, the risk may have diminished a lot compared to risks during the construction phase and periods just after commercial operation, when all information is still from consulting studies. When lenders perform their due diligence, for them to have some real history is generally much more valuable than the cash flow projections made by a consultant. Once actual financial statements can be reviewed, the lenders may accept a lower debt service coverage ratio (DSCR), a longer tenor, less burdensome debt service reserve account (DSRA) provisions, and narrower credit spreads. If you make a model of a project-financed investment and ignore potential benefits from refinancing, one could argue that you have not made a complete analysis of the returns on the project.

The problem with modeling refinancing is that you do not know (1) when the refinancing will occur, (2) what sort of metrics lenders will use such as the DSCR to determine the size of the new loan, (3) what the terms of the new debt will be such as the tenor of the new debt and the DSRA provisions, (4) what kind of fees will be charged for the new loan, and (5) whether there will be multiple refinancing after the first financing. All of these uncertainties imply that if you include refinancing in your model, you should make sure the techniques are very flexible so that all sorts of refinancing terms and timing can be incorporated.

Refinancing can be a particularly important assumption in situations where the original loan is repaid relatively early and/or the terms of the first loan are not very attractive. By contrast, if the DSCR on the original loan is low and/or the tenor of the loan is long and/or sculpting is applied in structuring repayments, then there is not much upside from the refinancing. You can get an idea of the potential for refinancing by looking at a graph of cash flow and debt service over the life of a project. If there is a lot of area in the graph that is not shaded with debt service, then there is more potential for gaining benefits from refinancing. Instances where refinancing can be attractive may occur with relatively new technology or in countries that do not have much history in project financing. In these situations the terms of the original loan may not be beneficial from the standpoint of levering the equity IRR.

To illustrate the effects of refinancing, Figures 45.1, 45.2, 45.3, and 45.4 show different scenarios of initial financing and refinancing using the same operating cash flow. In the scenario shown on Figure 45.1, the original financing was assumed to be aggressive with a 1.2 DSCR used to size the debt, a debt tenor of 19 years, sculpted repayments, and DSRA structured with a letter of credit. In this case, the project IRR of 5.36 percent is increased to a 20.33 percent equity IRR because the all-in cost of debt is less than the after-tax project IRR. Figure 45.1 shows that unless interest rates can change by virtue of the refinancing, the potential upside is limited because there is very little area between the debt service and the cash flow on the graph to work with. By including the user-defined functions for sculpting and funding

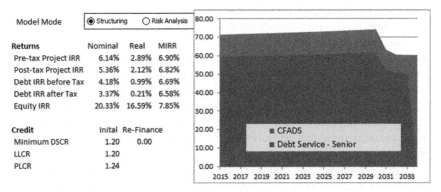

FIGURE 45.1 Illustration of Cash Flow and Debt Service Diagram with Little Potential for Benefits from Refinancing

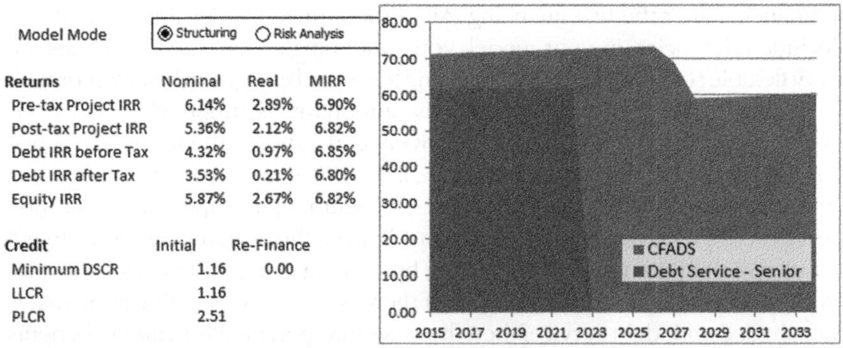

FIGURE 45.2 Illustration of Cash Flow and Debt Service in Case with Conservative Financing and Short Debt Tenor

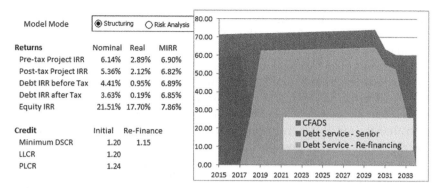

FIGURE 45.3 Illustration of Cash Flow and Debt Service in Aggressive Initial Financing Case with Aggressive Refinancing

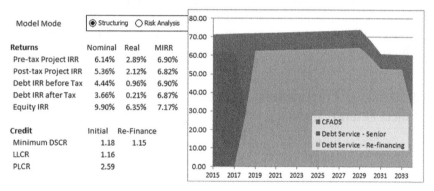

FIGURE 45.4 Illustration of Cash Flow and Debt Service in Conservative Initial Financing Case with Aggressive Refinancing

discussed in Chapter 40 and Chapter 41, you can change the debt structuring and examine the type of contract price that is acceptable given the financing structure.

In the second case, shown in Figure 45.2, the same operating cash flows are assumed, yielding the 5.36 percent project IRR. But this time a less aggressive initial financing structure is assumed. The debt tenor is eight years, the gearing level is 50 percent, and annuity repayments are applied. With this financing structure, the equity IRR falls all the way down to 5.87 percent. When refinancing is added to the two scenarios presented in Figures 45.1 and 45.2, the financial implications are very different. If a new refinancing sized from a 1.15 DSCR with sculpting and a tenor that allows a one-year buffer or tail before the end of the project life is assumed, the equity IRR increases by a small amount from 20.65 percent to 21 percent in the aggressive financing case. Results of this case with refinancing are illustrated in Figure 45.3. On the other hand, if the same refinancing is assumed in the conservative financing case, the equity IRR increases from 5.87 percent up to 9.90 percent. This refinancing case with the much larger positive effect on the equity IRR is shown on Figure 45.4. The main reason that refinancing has such a positive effect on the equity IRR in the second case is that the new debt sized from a 1.15 DSCR produces a higher level of debt than the initial 50 percent gearing amount. This difference in debt size is distributed as a super dividend.

Some argue that including refinancing in a model is speculative because you do not know what the financial markets will be like in the future and you do not know what kind of terms would be offered for a mature project in the future. However, you could just as well argue that to assume no refinancing would be an extreme assumption, as very many projects seem to be refinanced on a continual basis. Just because an assumption is difficult to predict does not mean it should be arbitrarily assigned a value of zero. You would not make this kind of zero assumption for the price of oil just because it is difficult to predict.

Mechanics of Implementing Refinancing into a Project Finance Model

To implement flexible refinancing in a project finance model, some of the essential things to include are: (1) time switches for the refinancing date and the refinanced debt repayment period, (2) a separate sources and uses of funds analysis in the refinancing period or periods, (3) a new debt schedule for the refinanced debt, (4) a user-defined function to compute the size of the debt given the new DSCR, and (5) provisions in the existing debt schedule to repay the debt early with proceeds from the refinanced debt. Once you are comfortable with creating switches from the period codes, creating the added sources and uses of funds analysis, and structuring debt schedules, which are all fundamental elements in structuring a model without refinancing, programming the refinancing is nothing new.

Inputs for refinancing are demonstrated in Figure 45.5. Other than the date of refinancing and a TRUE/FALSE switch that allows you to turn the refinancing on or off, the inputs should be similar to inputs for the initial debt. As with any debt facility, you need to define (1) the size of the debt, (2) the way it is borrowed with drawdowns, (3) the manner in which the debt is repaid in terms of debt tenor and repayment type, (4) the interest and fees paid to the lender while the debt is outstanding, and (5) credit enhancements such as the DSRA and covenants. Figure 45.5 includes a function that sizes the refinanced debt from the DSCR and the prospective cash flow.

	D	E	F	G	H
162	**Re-Financing Assumptions**				
163	Re-Financing Switch	Switch	TRUE	☑	
164	Year of Re-Financing	Year	4		
165	Date of Re-financing	Date	01-mai-17		
166					
167	Re-financing Target DSCR	Times	1.14		
168	Re-financing Debt Term	Year	13		
169					
170	Start of Re-financing	Date	01-nov-17		
171	End of Refinanced Debt	Date	01-nov-30		
172					
173	Re-financing Amount		149,850.05		
174					
175	Starting NOL in Re-finance Period	EUR 000	29,586.55		
176	Credit Spread on Re-financing	Percent	2.00%		
177	Fees on Re-financing	Percent	1.50%		
178					
179	=sculpt_debt_refinance(N19:FN19,N450:FN450,N487:FN487,F89,Working!N482:FN482,F167,0,F175)*F163				

FIGURE 45.5 Illustration of Inputs for Refinanced Debt in a Project Finance Model

Figure 45.6 illustrates how refinancing can be incorporated into a project finance model. The first step is setting up the switches for refinancing. Switches and refinancing inputs are inputs to a user-defined function that sizes debt. The debt sizing function is much like the function illustrated in

			01-nov-16	01-mai-17	01-nov-17	01-mai-18	01-nov-18	01-mai-19	01-nov-19	01-mai-20
Start of period	Base Case ▼		01-nov-16	01-mai-17	01-nov-17	01-mai-18	01-nov-18	01-mai-19	01-nov-19	01-mai-20
End of period			30-avr-17	31-oct-17	30-avr-18	31-oct-18	30-avr-19	31-oct-19	30-avr-20	31-oct-20
Debt Repayment Period	01-mai-13		TRUE	TRUE	TRUE	TRUE	TRUE	TRUE	TRUE	TRUE
Debt Retirement Period	01-mai-26		FALSE	FALSE	FALSE	FALSE	FALSE	FALSE	FALSE	FALSE
Re-financing Date	01-mai-17		FALSE	TRUE	FALSE	FALSE	FALSE	FALSE	FALSE	FALSE
Re-financing Repayment Period	01-nov-17		FALSE	FALSE	TRUE	TRUE	TRUE	TRUE	TRUE	TRUE
Re-Financing										
Sources and Uses for Re-financing										
Sources										
New Debt	Refin Amt	150,004.68	0.00	150,004.68	0.00	0.00	0.00	0.00	0.00	0.00
Proceeds from DSRA										
Total Sources			0.00	150,004.68	0.00	0.00	0.00	0.00	0.00	0.00
Uses										
Payment of Fees	Fee Percent	1.50%	0.00	2,250.07	0.00	0.00	0.00	0.00	0.00	0.00
Repayment of Debt			0.00	45,071.26	0.00	0.00	0.00	0.00	0.00	0.00
New DSRA										
Dividends to Equity			0.00	102,683.34	0.00	0.00	0.00	0.00	0.00	0.00
Total Uses			0.00	150,004.68	0.00	0.00	0.00	0.00	0.00	0.00
Debt Balance for Re-financing										
Opening Balance			0.00	0.00	150,004.68	146,545.57	142,368.18	138,119.03	133,559.86	128,881.27
Add: Draws from Re-financing			0.00	150,004.68	0.00	0.00	0.00	0.00	0.00	0.00
Less: Repayments after Re-financing			0.00	0.00	3,459.11	4,177.39	4,249.15	4,559.17	4,678.59	4,963.57
Closing Balance			0.00	150,004.68	146,545.57	142,368.18	138,119.03	133,559.86	128,881.27	123,917.70
Base Annual Interest Rate			2.00%	2.00%	2.00%	2.00%	2.00%	2.00%	2.00%	2.00%
Credit Spread on Re-financing	Refi CS	2.00%	2.00%	2.00%	2.00%	2.00%	2.00%	2.00%	2.00%	2.00%
Total Annual Interest Rate			4.00%	4.00%	4.00%	4.00%	4.00%	4.00%	4.00%	4.00%
Periodic Interest Rate			2.00%	2.00%	2.00%	2.00%	2.00%	2.00%	2.00%	2.00%
Interest Expense on Re-financing			0.00	0.00	3,000.09	2,930.91	2,847.36	2,762.38	2,671.20	2,577.63

FIGURE 45.6 Illustration of Incorporating Refinancing into a Project Finance Model with Timing Switches, Sources and Uses of Funds Analysis, and a New Debt Schedule

Figure 41.10 and discussed in Chapter 41 to size the debt from the DSCR with income taxes using sculpting. Sources and uses of funds analysis in the refinancing period begins with the funds realized from refinancing and ends up at the bottom with equity (in this case, dividends) as usual. Other tricks in putting refinancing into your model involve creating a line on the sources and uses of funds statement during refinancing that accounts for the remaining balance of the original debt using the refinancing switch. Payoff of existing debt must be calculated on the basis of the opening balance less any scheduled repayments and repayments from the cash flow sweep that occurred in the year of the refinancing. The closing balance of existing debt cannot be used in the sources and uses of funds analysis, because the closing balance already includes reduction in the debt balance from the refinancing itself. The cash flow analysis should be modified to include lines for new debt financing, debt service on the refinancing, and repayment of existing debt. The profit and loss statement and the cash flow statement must include the interest on the current debt as well as the refinanced debt as well as fees or fee amortization from the refinanced debt.

CHAPTER 46

Covenants and Cash Flow Sweeps in Project Finance Models

When negotiating loan agreements, one of the issues that may be analyzed with a financial model are the credit enhancements, including the level of covenants and cash flow sweeps. Along with the debt service reserve account (DSRA), these provisions could be called credit enhancements because they improve the safety of loans from the lender perspective. Loan covenants can range from mandating that the equipment is in good working order and providing financial statements to lenders, to strict limitations on payment of dividends. Covenants that limit dividends change the cash flow distribution pattern over time between lenders and equity shareholders and/or subordinated debt investors. For modeling purposes, it is the latter type of negative financial covenant that limits dividends that are generally evaluated. These covenants can influence returns to equity investors because they affect the timing of cash flows that are paid out as dividends. The effect of equity cash flow timing resulting from covenants is analogous to the way that refinancing influences the equity internal rate of return (IRR) because of the acceleration of dividends. Covenants should be analyzed in the context of a fundamental aspect of project finance loans that some dividends must be allowed before all of the debt is paid off. If equity investors had to wait decades for any cash return at all they probably would not make investments.

Covenants that limit dividend payments can take the form of cash flow traps that prevent dividends when times are bad and there is not much cash flow available for dividends anyway. Cash trap or dividend lockup covenants often require that the prior period, current period, and next period debt service coverage ratios (DSCRs) must be above some minimum criteria. For example, if the covenant is 1.15, then approximately 15 percent of the cash flow (or less in a really bad period) can be captured to protect lenders and be put away in a lockup cash reserve account. Alternatively, the credit enhancement can be in the form of cash flow sweeps, which limit the cash flow that can be distributed when times may be either good or bad. A cash flow sweep may be linked to the ratio of debt to earnings before interest, taxes, depreciation, and amortization (EBITDA). Here, the sweep may mandate that if the debt-to-EBITDA ratio is above some level, a predetermined percentage of the cash flow must be used to pay down debt rather than being allowed to be distributed as a dividend. Lenders can be creative in defining cash flow sweeps and can limit the dividends if all sorts of specific criteria are not met, such as the wake effect on a wind farm.

Covenants and cash sweeps do not change the operating cash flow of a project and they cannot transform a bad project into a good project. If the present value of cash flow is less than the debt, there is nothing a banker can do with debt structure to protect lenders. Instead, the covenants can only change the timing of who receives the money and in what order. With more restrictive covenants, the equity holders must wait longer to get their dividend payments. Without covenants, the equity holders can receive all of the cash flows that are left over after paying scheduled debt service.

Credit enhancements, including the DSRAs, sweeps, and traps, involve a trade-off between risk for lenders and return for shareholders. This trade-off could be assessed with a financial model using the various risk analysis techniques discussed in Part II. The benefit of a cash flow sweep in terms of lender protection depends on the volatility of the cash flow. If cash flow is increasing over time and not volatile, such as for a toll road or an airport, the covenant will not be effective in reducing risk because in downside cases when cash flow is low at the beginning of the project, there are no dividends to trap. However, in other situations, if the cash flow can suddenly fall off a cliff after a few years in the event of a financial or other crisis, the sweep and covenants can be effective in protecting lenders from situations where a lot of dividends are paid only to have the loan subsequently default. Figure 46.1 illustrates a hypothetical case where cash flow suddenly declines. With a cash flow sweep covenant, dividends are limited as shown in the right-hand panel. The left-hand panel shows the same operating cash flow where dividends are allowed. Without reductions in the level of debt that result from the cash flow sweep, the dividends can aggravate or even cause a default later on in the life of the loan.

Mechanics of Modeling Covenants and Cash Flow Sweeps

The mechanics of implementing covenants in a project finance model involve the oft-repeated cash flow waterfall techniques. In the case of cash flow sweeps, subtotals are included in the cash flow waterfall, line items in the debt schedule are linked directly to the cash flow statement, and the MIN and MAX functions are used to compute sweep amounts after the subtotals in the cash flow statement. In modeling cash trap covenants, the cash that is not allowed

Effect of Cash Sweep with Declining Cash Flows

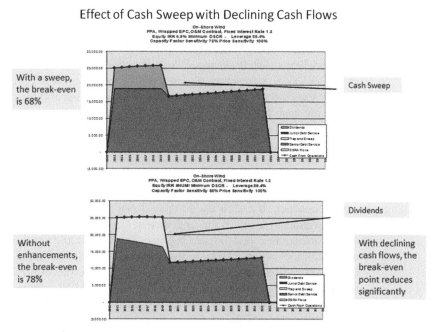

FIGURE 46.1 Illustration of the Effect of a Cash Flow Sweep When Cash Flows Suddenly Decline

to be paid in dividends can be used to pay off debt earlier than scheduled, or, more typically, it can be placed in a cash reserve account. If trapped cash is used to prepay debt, the trapped cash should be linked to a line item in the debt schedule, as is the case for a cash flow sweep. If the cash is applied to a lock-up reserve account, a separate account should be set up somewhere near the debt service reserve account in the model.

The following step-by-step process explains how you can incorporate a cash trap or a cash sweep covenant into the cash flow waterfall part of a project finance model:

Step 1   Add subtotal rows to the cash flow statement below the scheduled debt service that tabluates the cash flow that is available for a cash sweep and/or the cash flow before the cash trap covenant.

Step 2   To model a cash trap covenant, include a TRUE/FALSE switch variable below the cash flow waterfall that tests whether the covenant has or has not been violated. This test could be measured from the debt service coverage ratio or, in the case of a leveraged buyout, from the debt-to-EBITDA ratio.

Step 3   Multiply the dividend lock-up covenant TRUE/FALSE switch variable by the cash flow before cash traps subtotal to compute the amount of cash trapped. You could also include a MAX function when making the multiplication to make sure that you are not trapping negative cash flow.

Step 4   For modeling a cash flow sweep, include a line item that lists the cash flow sweep percentage as a function of the debt-to-EBITDA ratio or some other criterion. Put the sweep percentage above or below the cash flow statement. This sweep percentage may be tied to the debt-to-EBITDA ratio or some other criterion.

Step 5   Multiply the cash sweep percentage by the cash flow before sweep subtotal in the cash flow waterfall.

Step 6   The cash flow that is trapped or swept and cannot pay dividends must go somewhere. It is generally used to prepay debt in the case of a sweep. If cash is used to pay down debt, then the MIN function must be used in the cash sweep line to assure that the sweep does not exceed the debt balance. The MIN should test the amount of the sweep relative to the opening debt balance minus the scheduled debt repayments that have already been accounted for above the cash sweep in the cash flow waterfall MIN(opening balance less repayments, subtotal × cash sweep percent). With a cash sweep, the scheduled debt repayment must also include a

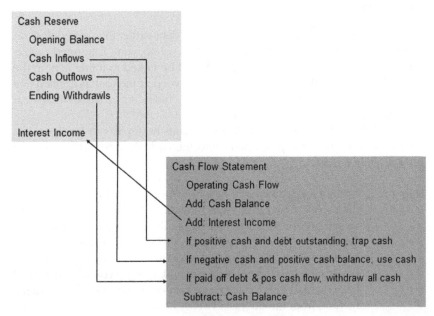

FIGURE 46.2 Illustration of Connecting Reserve Account to Cash Flow Waterfall in Modeling a Cash Trap Covenant

MIN statement relative to the opening balance, because the debt balance is reduced from the cash flow sweep. To make sure negative cash is not swept, the MAX function should also be used in the cash sweep equation. Figure 46.2 illustrates how the process for covenants or cash flow sweeps links the cash flow statement to a reserve balance or the debt schedule.

Step 7   In the case of a dividend trap covenant, the cash that is deposited in the lock-up reserve can be released and paid as dividends if the debt service coverage ratio is above the covenant level. To release the cash you can multiply the opening balance of the lock-up reserve by the opposite of the lock-up test, meaning that when the test is FALSE the dividends can be released. The released cash computed as the opening balance multiplied by the switch should then be included in the cash flow statement. This cash released amount can then be linked to the lock-up reserve account.

CHAPTER 47

Asset Portfolios, Progress Payments, and Lease Rolls in Real Estate Models

R eal estate analysis and modeling encompass a combination of aspects from both corporate finance and project finance. The financial model of a hotel project or a commercial building has many similar characteristics to project finance analysis. These investments move through different stages, revenue contracts are important in risk analysis, and the financial analysis is driven by cash flows and internal rates of return (IRRs) rather than reported profits on the income statement. However, hotels and commercial buildings do not have a precise defined life, prospective cash flow analysis relies on rental market history, and the projects are often valued using a flexible terminal date driven by market multiples—characteristics that resemble corporate analysis. Other real estate investments such as residential and commercial mixed development projects have more elements in common with corporate analysis. These mixed developments consist of portfolios that contain several individual projects with different cash flow patterns and different risks. Financing is driven by loan-to-value leverage ratios rather than cash flow coverage ratios such as the debt service coverage ratio and the residual values at some terminal date are central to the valuation. Yet the individual developments that comprise these mixed-use investments do have similarities to project finance analysis. Their value is defined by stages, IRRs are used rather than net present value of free cash flow, they have no historic financial statements, and risks can potentially be mitigated by a series of contracts.

Even though real estate analysis applies modeling concepts from both corporate and project finance analysis, there are some unique modeling issues associated with real estate models. A few of the issues are the following:

- Putting together portfolios of real estate projects in which each individual project has a different start date, holding period, and construction profile.
- Incorporating dates for components of projects that do not begin at the start of a quarter or a month as is commonly assumed in project finance modeling.
- Computing progress payment revenues that may be received from residential properties earlier than the dates at which the projects are completed and that may depend on alternative marketing strategies.
- Calculating different spending patterns for capital expenditures known as S-curves that are flexible enough to reflect different construction period tenors as well as sensitivity analysis with respect to delay.
- Reflecting a portfolio of revenue lease contracts for commercial buildings that have different lease terms, potential idle time periods between new leases, and renewal probabilities.
- Evaluating the financing of a portfolio of different projects where there is no single defined commercial operation date for the overall bundle of projects and where some projects are producing cash flow while other projects continue to require financing of capital expenditures.

In explaining how to deal with these complex issues this chapter builds upon earlier chapters that address project finance models issues related to setting up project phases and establishing time period switches. The focus here is on features of a real estate model that are different from a project finance model. Unique aspects in the structure of real estate models include:

- In modeling a single project such as a multifamily development or a hotel, the sale of a project after a given holding period is often assumed using a market multiple and a cap rate.
- In modeling developments that include a portfolio of different projects, cash flow is normally generated from some projects before construction of all of the projects is completed. This means that a separate sources and uses of funds analysis or a separate funding cascade analysis is not a good way to structure models, as it is with project finance analysis.
- In modeling real estate projects, there are often multiple units and buildings that are started and completed at different dates. To consolidate projects with different start and end dates, separate project-by-project time lines should generally be established and coordinated with a common master time line for all projects.

- In modeling commercial real estate investments, the analysis should incorporate the effects of different lease terms with alternative expiry dates. Modeling idle time and lease renewals can result in long and nontransparent formulas because revenues are computed on a different basis for the initial lease term, subsequent idle periods, prospective fixed leases, and spot market rentals.
- To model portfolios of investments with start dates and end dates that do not occur at the beginning of the period in the model, a user-defined function can be created that yields the percentage of the period the project is under construction and/or the percentage of the period in which it is being operated.
- In modeling some real estate projects, you may have to incorporate multiple participating tranches of debt and equity with different return targets and sharing mechanisms in the cash flow waterfall.

Modeling a Single Real Estate Project

Discussion of real estate financial models in this chapter begins with a single project and later puts projects together into a portfolio. Modeling a single project is similar to modeling a normal project finance investment, with the exception that a holding period is defined after which the project is sold. Operating inputs that drive the value of the project include the occupancy rate that varies over the life of the project, potentially volatile market rental rates, occupancy rates that are probably correlated with the rental rates, and fixed and variable operating expenses. Instead of using the total project life to measure the operating period as in a typical project finance model, a holding period before which the project is sold applies. Then, as with acquisition models, the project is sold at an assumed exit date. The exit proceeds may be computed through dividing the terminal cash flow by a statistic called the capitalization rate (cap rate).

A cap rate measures the pretax cash flow generated from rental payments divided by the current market value as measured by purchase and sales transactions. It is approximately the same as the inverse of the ratio of enterprise value to earnings before interest, taxes, depreciation, and amortization (EV/EBITDA). In applying the cap rate in a model, you can create a terminal value TRUE/FALSE switch similar to the switch created for acquisition and corporate models. The theory behind the cap rate is very similar to the ideas underlying computing the terminal value that were discussed in Part 3 using the final year cash flow divided by the cost of capital minus the growth rate. Say you believe the growth rate in rents is 2.5 percent and the cap rate is 5 percent, then the implied weighted average cost of capital (WACC) is 7.5 percent, as shown in the following formula. With a higher growth rate in rental payments, the cap rate should be lower, and if the cash flows are less risky, then the cap rate is also reduced.

$$\text{Cap Rate} = \text{WACC} - g \text{ or } \text{WACC} = \text{Cap Rate} + g$$

The cap rate and the proceeds from selling a real estate asset can be affected by some accounting and tax issues. Many purchase and sales transactions occur for real estate investment trusts where there are no tax consequences. Here, the cap rate and the calculation of WACC are simple. In other circumstances, when an asset is sold, a capital gain tax can be computed as the sales proceeds less the net book value of the fixed assets. The tax treatment may have to be accounted for in exit proceeds of a financial model and the implied WACC from the cap rate formula. If capital allowance or tax depreciation can be used after the sale of a project, the seller requires higher proceeds and the buyer is willing to pay more for the asset.

Modeling Multiple Projects That Are Part of a Combined Portfolio with Percent of Time Function

One of the challenging aspects of real estate modeling can be to account for multiple projects that are part of a combined portfolio with different construction start dates, construction completion dates and holding periods as well as alternative cash flow generation formulas. When creating such a model, the occupancy rates, the construction periods, the S-curves, the timing of proceeds from selling residential projects, and other items should be flexible. The remainder of this chapter addresses various tricky aspects of modeling such a real estate portfolio. An effective way to structure a model with different projects in a portfolio is to create a user-defined function that computes the percentage of a particular period that a project is being constructed and the percentage of the period that the project is occupied by tenants. This percentage of time user-defined function largely replaces the timing switches in a model. An alternative method discussed at the end of the chapter is to use a combination of the INDEX function and the Data Table tool without the user-defined function. This second approach is analogous to creating scenarios, which is discussed in Chapter 17. No matter what method is used to consolidate a portfolio of projects, the first essential step is to establish a common time line that will be used for all projects. This time line should be placed at the top of the spreadsheet page and it does not depend on any individual project. The model is structured so that each column of the spreadsheet has the same date and the projects are placed in different columns to conform to those dates. You can then add up all of the items for separate projects in one column to obtain the aggregate capital expenditure, operating cash flow, and terminal proceeds for the calendar period defined by the column. This contrasts with many project finance models where the start date of the model and the start date of the construction or development are the same, and the spreadsheet page is separated between the precommercial phase and the postcommercial stage.

To model a portfolio of projects you should generally define the key time periods for different individual projects. A portion of the input page is shown in Figure 47.1 with various dates. The temporary occupation permit (TOP) date shown for each project is analogous to the commercial operation date in project finance. In Figure 47.1 the construction start date and the TOP date is not at the beginning of the period.

Start Date	01-janv-13
Periods per Year	12
Months per Period	1
Days per 360 Period	30
Holding Period	5

Rental Growth	1.00	Base Rental Rate
Inflation Rate Cde	1.00	Base Inflation
Cap Rate	4%	
Growth for Cap Rate	2%	

		1	2	3		4	5	6	7		8	9	10	11
Operating Assumptions			Timing Assumptions				General Assumptions				Construction Cost Assumptions			
							Gross	NLA per			Constr			
			Code		Cnstr		Area	Unit (Sq	# of		Cost		S-Curve	S-Curve
	Project IRR	Number	Cnstr Start	Months	TOP Date	Sq Foot	Foot	Units	$S/Gross	Sens %	Code	Name
Land		1	01-janv-13	11	01-déc-13	1		1	500,000	90%	1.00	Land
Infrastructure		2	01-oct-13	11	01-sept-14	1		1	100,000	90%	1.00	Land
Residential 1	25.46%	3	01-oct-16	19	01-mai-18	1,000	950.00	250	50	90%	10.00	Res Fast
Residential 2	18.74%	4	01-janv-18	19	01-août-19	1,000	950.00	140	70	90%	10.00	Res Fast
Residential 3	24.48%	5	01-janv-15	19	01-août-16	1,000	800.00	200	55	90%	10.00	Res Fast
Retail	29.68%	6	13-juin-16	19	13-janv-18	150,000	90,000.00	1	160	90%	4.00	Coml Fast
Office	25.37%	7	30-mars-16	19	30-oct-17	100,000	60,000.00	1	170	90%	7.00	Office Fast
Shopping Centre	20.21%	8	14-juil-16	19	14-févr-18	80,000	48,000.00	1	180	90%	4.00	Coml Fast

FIGURE 47.1 Excerpt from Input Real Estate Model with Portfolio of Projects

The method that can just about be classified as a magic trick to make the portfolio modeling much easier is to create a user-defined function that accepts the project start and end dates and then uses the master time line on the top of the page to determine what percentage of each period a project is operating or under construction. Excel does not have a function that automatically does this, and if you tried to make a formula to compute the percent of time a project is in service and is in its last year, it would be horribly long and messy. Instead you can make a user-defined function that measures what percentage of the period a project is in service or under construction that accepts four different arguments. Two of the arguments are the start date and the end date of the master time line with no locked cells (via the F4 key) for the column. The other two inputs are the start and end of the project that should have fixed references for the column. Figure 47.2 shows how this function works for three different projects where the percent of the period for the start of operation and end of operation are not 100 percent. Once you have developed this function, you can use these percentages for a lot of other calculations. In Figure 47.2, the start and end dates are included in the special left-hand side columns of the model to make the process more transparent.

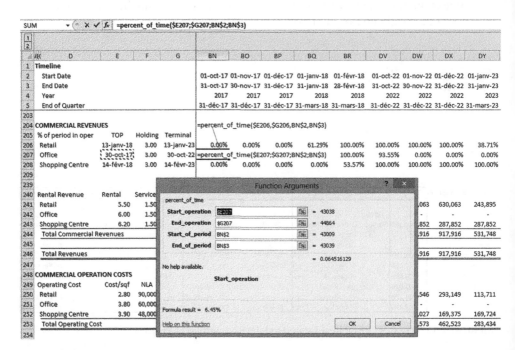

FIGURE 47.2 Use of Percent of Time Function

The VBA code for the percent of time function involves setting up different techniques to calculate the ratio of time depending on whether a project has not yet been born, is in the period of birth, is operating, or is in the period of its end. The ratio can be computed by using the integer numbers that define the various dates. For periods after the birth period and before the death period, the ratio is defined as 100 percent. The percent of a period function is programmed through comparing the beginning and end dates of a project with master time line start and end dates. The tricky aspect of this function is to compute the portion of the period for the first birth period and the last death period. This function can be useful for many modeling applications other than real estate models when key dates do not occur at the exact beginning or end of a period. Construction of the percent of time function is demonstrated in Figure 47.3.

```
Function percent_of_time(start_operation, end_operation, _
                    start_of_period, end_of_period)

If start_operation > start_of_period Then
     ratio = 0
End If
'
' Partial period at birth of the project
'
If start_operation >= start_of_period _
        And start_operation < end_of_period Then

     ratio = (end_of_period - start_operation) / (end_of_period - _
                          start_of_period + 1)
End If
'
' Full period when the ratio is 1.0
'
If start_operation <= start_of_period And end_operation > end_of_period Then
     ratio = 1
End If
'
' Partial period at end
'
If end_operation >= start_of_period And end_operation <= end_of_period Then
     ratio = (end_operation - start_of_period) / (end_of_period - _
                          start_of_period + 1)

End If
'
' After the death of the project
'
If end_operation < start_of_period Then
     ratio = 0
End If

percent_of_time = ratio   ' definition of the function

End Function
```

FIGURE 47.3 Code for Percent of Time Function

In addition to the percent of time function, a couple of other user-defined functions can be helpful in creating a project portfolio. Two functions that can make the modeling process much easier include:

1. A function that computes the TOP date of a project given the S-curve. This allows you to enter different S-curve arrays, and then automatically derive different TOP dates. If you use a different S-curve and keep the construction start date the same, the TOP date changes, which in turn is used to determine the operational revenues. This function adds the number of periods defined in the S-curve to the start of construction date so that you can use the percent of time user-defined function.
2. A function that computes the revenue received for a residential project given a combined progress payment schedule and a sales or marketing schedule. This problem involves working with two different series of dates, one for the progress payment and another for the marketing schedule. Some projects may receive the whole series of progress payments, and other residential projects that are sold later receive the revenues during subsequent periods and must accumulate the payments that were scheduled. The function should allow you to enter different marketing and progress payment scenarios and see how the revenue changes.

Modeling a Portfolio with the INDEX Function and Data Table Tools

The second method that can be used to create a portfolio is to combine the INDEX function with the Data Table tool. This method involves developing a template model for one project that is flexible enough to compute the operating cash flow, capital expenditures, and depreciation expense for each separate project. The template should be designed to accept any one of the projects, much like a regular financial model can accept different scenarios. To implement the technique, each project is assigned a code number, much like the way a master scenario page works.

To use this second method, you should set up a project assumption table where inputs to all of the projects are structured in a consistent manner. When making a template that can accept inputs for each individual project, you can use the INDEX function along with a code number that defines the individual project in the portfolio. In the example shown in Figure 47.4, the INDEX function is used to define the construction cost, the sale price, the construction profile, and the time periods from the project code number. If the inputs are set up in a structured manner, the amounts can be extracted for each separate project through defining a row and column number with the INDEX function.

SECTION 1: Assumptions

Dates		IRR for Porfolio
General Start Date	01-avr-10	Equity IRR 16.77%
Periods in Modčterly		Pre-tax IRR 15.42%
Periods per Year	4	IRR for Project 24.03%
Months per Period	3	Residential 2 ▼
Days per 360 Period	90	

Operating Assumptions

	Cde #	TOP Date	Constr Cost	Gross Area Sq Foot	Units	S-Curve Code	Net Floor Area	Rental Rate	Service Charge	Occup Rate	Hold Per	Cap Rate	Op Cost	Rental Code	Sales Price	Prog Code
Land	1	01-juil-10	50,000	1	1	1.00						5%				1
Infrastructure	2	01-oct-10	1,000	1	1	2.00						5%				1
Residential 1	3	01-juil-13	50	1,000	100	3.00	800					5%			110	4
Residential 2	4	01-janv-15	70	1,000	80	3.00	800					5%			120	3
Residential 3	5	01-janv-16	55	1,000	120	4.00	800					5%			130	4
Commercial 1	6	01-avr-15	85	150,000	1	4.00	90,000	6.00	2.00	1.00	5.00	5%	5.00	1.00		1
Commercial 2	7	01-janv-16	95	100,000	1	4.00	60,000	6.00	2.00	2.00	5.00	5%	5.00	4.00		1
Commercial 3	8	01-oct-17	90	80,000	1	4.00	48,000	6.00	2.00	3.00	5.00	5%	5.00	5.00		1

FIGURE 47.4 Illustration of Setup for Project Portfolio Using the INDEX and Data Table Method for Consolidation

Using the master time line you can compute a period code in the template model. This is accomplished through comparing the commercial operation date with the common start date in the master time line. If the inputs in the example in Figure 47.4 are used, the period codes are different for the first project and the second project—there would be a larger negative number for the project with the further-out date.

The manner in which the template model for individual components of the portfolio can be set up is illustrated in Figure 47.5. The top part of the figure lists the code number for the project that is an input like the master scenario number discussed in Chapter 17. With the project code number entered, a series of INDEX functions is used to establish inputs for the template model. In Figure 47.4, another code number is used to define the S-curve table that in turn is used to compute construction expenditures as a function of the time period counter. After the S-curve code number extracted, the S-curve can be established by using a LOOKUP function.

Once the cash flow model for a single project is developed, various series from the individual projects should be aggregated for creating a financial model. As usual, the EBITDA, capital expenditures, working capital changes, and depreciation are the items needed to establish free cash flow and begin the financing aspects of the model. The aggregation can be automated by creating a one-way data table with the Data Table tool using the code number as the column input. To see how the process of using the INDEX and Data Table works in construction a portfolio of projects, assume that the common start date of the master time line is January 1, 2014, and that there are two

/EG	D	E	F	G	H	Z	AA	AB	AC	AD
70	Code Number	7								
71	Name	Commercial 2	=INDEX($D$13:$D$20,E70)							
72	S-Curve Code	4.00	=INDEX(J13:J20,E70)							
73	TOP Date	01-janv-16	=INDEX(F13:F20,E70)							
74	Periods before TOP Date	23.00	=DAYS360(E4,E73)/E9							
75	Periods of Construction	463.97	=DAYS360(E72,E73)/E9							
76	Holding Period in Years	5	=INDEX($O$13:$O$20,E70)							
77	Holding Period - Periods	20	=E76*E6							
78	Construction Cost	95	=INDEX(G13:G20,E70)							
79	Gross Area	100000	=INDEX(H13:H20,E70)							
80	Net Area	60000	=INDEX(K13:K20,E70)							
94										
95	Start Date	4/1/2010	7/1/2010	10/1/2010	1/1/2011	7/1/2015	10/1/2015	1/1/2016	4/1/2016	7/1/2016
96	End Date	6/30/2010	9/30/2010	12/31/2010	3/31/2011	9/30/2015	12/31/2015	3/31/2016	6/30/2016	9/30/2016
97	Year	2010	2010	2010	2011	2015	2015	2016	2016	2016
101	Period	-22.00	-21.00	-20.00	-19.00	-1.00	0.00	1.00	2.00	3.00
102	Construction Switch	FALSE	FALSE	FALSE	FALSE	TRUE	TRUE	FALSE	FALSE	FALSE
103	Holding Switch	FALSE	FALSE	FALSE	FALSE	FALSE	FALSE	TRUE	TRUE	TRUE
104	Terminal Switch	FALSE	FALSE	FALSE	FALSE	FALSE	FALSE	FALSE	FALSE	FALSE
110	Total Cost	9,500,000	9,500,000	9,500,000	9,500,000	9,500,000	9,500,000	9,500,000	9,500,000	9,500,000
111	Match	#N/A	#N/A	#N/A	1.00	19.00	20.00	#N/A	#N/A	#N/A
112	S-Curve	FALSE	FALSE	FALSE	0	0.0625	0.0625	FALSE	FALSE	FALSE
114	Construction Expenditures - Int	0.00	0.00	0.00	0.00	671,758.59	675,092.48	0.00	0.00	0.00
115										
116	Revenues									
117	Net Floor Area	60,000	60,000	60,000	60,000	60,000	60,000	60,000	60,000	60,000
118	Occupancy Rate	FALSE	FALSE	FALSE	FALSE	FALSE	FALSE	60%	60%	60%
119	Revenue per Sq Foot	24.00	24.00	24.00	24.00	24.00	24.00	24.00	24.00	24.00
120	Rental Growth Rate - Annual	FALSE	FALSE	FALSE	FALSE	FALSE	FALSE	0.03	0.03	0.03
122	Rental Growth Index	1.00	1.00	1.00	1.00	1.00	1.00	1.01	1.01	1.02
124	Total Revenues	-	-	-	-	-	-	870,408	876,864	883,368

FIGURE 47.5 Inputs and Time Line Setup in Template Single Project Model

operating projects in the portfolio. The first project has an operating start date in 2016 and a two-year construction period while the second project has a later operating start date of 2017. In this example, the master year 2014 column for the initial project is −1, and the year 2014 column for the second project is −2. The master time line year 2015 column is in the second construction period for the first project and it is the first construction period for the second project. Because of this, the construction expenditures are placed in different columns for the two projects.

When aggregating the data, the code for the individual project is entered as the column sensitivity, and the column input is the project code number used in defining the INDEX function inputs. Once you have created the data table that is illustrated in Figure 47.6, you can simply add up the cash flows for different projects.

After cash flows are aggregated, the financial module of a real estate model can be developed. Since there are multiple pieces of the portfolio with different periods of construction and operating cash flow, the model should not begin with a sources and uses of funds analysis. Instead you can begin by building a debt schedule with a working capital facility and a permanent debt facility. A set of financing equations can also be developed to issue equity

AB C	D	E	F	G	H	I	J	K	IW
5 Period			1/1/2014	1/1/2015	1/1/2016	1/1/2017	1/1/2018	1/1/2019	
25 Code Number		1							
29 Total Periods prior to operation		3							
30 First Period in Counter		-2	=1-E29						
31 Profile Index+1		1	=INDEX(I11:I13,E25)						
32 Cost		1,000.00							
34 Period Code		-2	-1	0	1	2	3	4	
35 Construction Switch		TRUE	TRUE	TRUE	FALSE	FALSE	FALSE	FALSE	
36 Construction Profile		0	0.5	0.5	FALSE	FALSE	FALSE	FALSE	
37 Cost		1,000.00	1,000.00	1,000.00	1,000.00	1,000.00	1,000.00	1,000.00	
38 Construction		0	500	500	0	0	0	0	
39 Cash Proceeds from Sales Price		0	0	0	1500	0	0	0	
40 Revenue Recognized		0	750	750	0	0	0	0	
41 Cash Flow Analysis									
42 Total Proceeds from Sales									
43 Residential Type 1		-	-	-	1,500.0	-	-	-	=F39
44 1 Residential Type 1		-	-	-	1,500.0	-	-	-	=TABLE(,E25)
45 2 Residential Type 2		-	-	-	-	2,500.0	-	-	=TABLE(,E25)
46 3 Commecial		-	-	-	-	-	-	3,200.0	=TABLE(,E25)
47 Construction Expenditures									
48 Residential Type 1		-	500.0	500.0	-	-	-	-	=F38
49 1 Residential Type 1		-	500.0	500.0	-	-	-	-	=TABLE(,E25)
50 2 Residential Type 2		-	-	1,000.0	1,000.0	-	-	-	=TABLE(,E25)
51 3 Commecial		-	-	-	-	1,500.0	1,500.0	-	=TABLE(,E25)
52 Net Cash Flow									
53 1 Residential Type 1		(500.0)	(500.0)	1,500.0	-	-	-	=F44-F49	
54 2 Residential Type 2		-	(1,000.0)	(1,000.0)	2,500.0	-	-	=F45-F50	
55 3 Commecial		-	-	-	(1,500.0)	(1,500.0)	3,200.0	=F46-F51	
56 Total		(500.0)	(1,500.0)	500.0	1,000.0	(1,500.0)	3,200.0	=SUM(F53:F55)	

FIGURE 47.6 Illustration of Using the Data Table Tool to Aggregate Individual Projects in a Portfolio

before or after the issuance of debt, as discussed in the context of project finance funding in Chapter 40. As usual, methods to develop the debt schedule and a cash flow statement with a waterfall involve structuring the cash flow statement and using the MIN and MAX functions and making a lot of subtotals. It is hoped that you can see that even if these waterfall techniques may look a bit different in different models, they all have a similar skeleton.

In some real estate projects cash flow is generated from receiving progress payments before construction is complete. This cash that is generated from selling a project reduces the need for additional debt. If the proceeds are more than the total amount of debt required, the cash can be deposited into a reserve account. If there is money in this cash reserve account and future financing needs occur, then the reserve account is used for those future cash needs. If there is no debt left, then dividends can be distributed in an analogous manner to a cash flow sweep. This cash process can be modeled in a similar manner to the cash build-up technique that is described in a standard corporate model in Chapter 38, where deficit cash flow is funded by raising new debt, and surplus cash goes to retiring cash and/or reducing debt.

About the Author

Edward **Bodmer** provides financial and economic consulting services to a variety of clients, and he teaches professional development courses in an assortment of modeling topics (project finance, mergers and acquisitions, renewable energy, and electric power). He is passionate about teaching in Africa, South America, Asia, and Europe, and much of the unique modeling he has developed has arisen from discussions with participants in his courses. Mr. Bodmer's consulting activities include developing complex project finance, corporate finance, and simulation models; providing expert testimony and analysis on financial and economic issues before regulatory agencies; and advisory services to support merger and acquisition projects. In addition, he has been involved in formulating significant government policy related to electricity deregulation and energy efficiency; he has prepared models and analyses for the Asian Development Bank, Argonne National Laboratory, and the city of Chicago; he has evaluated energy purchasing decisions for many corporations; and he has provided advice on corporate strategy. Mr. Bodmer has taught customized courses for MIT's Sloan Business School, Shell Oil, Gasprom Bank, Capitaland, DBS, Society General, General Electric, HSBC, Citibank, CIMB, Lindlakers, HSBC, Saudi Aramco, and many other financial, energy, and industrial clients.

Mr. Bodmer was formerly vice president at the First National Bank of Chicago and president of the Energy Exchange of Chicago. He received a BSc in finance from the University of Illinois and an MBA in econometrics from the University of Chicago. He has authored many articles and is in the process of completing a second text on valuation theory. Mr. Bodmer was born in Manchester, England, and has lived in Switzerland, the United Kingdom, and the United States. Further information about his work and unique analytical approaches to different issues are described on the website, www.wiley.com/go/internationalvaluation.

About the Website

This book includes a companion website, which can be found at www .wiley.com/go/internationalvaluation (password: bodmer123). This site includes hundreds of exercises, model examples, and case studies and is integral to the book. It contains hundreds of customized exercises; many template project finance, corporate finance, and acquisition models; and a number of featured completed models of business enterprises in a wide variety of industries. In addition, you can download special utilities to read PDF files into Excel, to make automated waterfall charts, to automatically color cells linked to different sheets, to create a table of contents with hyperlinks, and much more.

Exercises and complete models are arranged by chapter, meaning that you can follow along the discussion in each chapter with different Excel files. You can also see how the principles are applied in actual situations. Upon opening each file, you will find a link to a video that explains the modeling process.

Index

Printed and bound by CPI Group (UK) Ltd, Croydon, CR0 4YY

16/04/2025

14658508-0005